Perspectives on World Politics

Third edition

Perspectives on World Politics has been essential reading for students of international relations since the beginning of the 1980s and this new edition fully updates this key text for the twenty-first century.

Focusing on three competing analytical perspectives, the first and second editions provided a clear and coherent organization of the divergent conceptual tools used to study world politics, as well as reflecting key debates and responses to changes in the world arena. This third edition builds on the success of its predecessors by presenting a substantially revised set of readings within essentially the same perspectives:

- Power and Security
- Interdependence and Globalization
- Dominance and Resistance

This book also includes a much-expanded fourth section, Perspectives and World Politics, which reflects the methodological and normative debates that have emerged or intensified during the period since publication of the previous edition.

Perspectives on World Politics includes forty-three contributions from leading international experts and is essential reading for students and academics with interests in politics and international relations.

Richard Little is Professor of International Politics at the University of Bristol. He is a previous editor of the *Review of International Studies* and chair of the British International Studies Association. He is co-author with Barry Buzan of *International Systems in World History* (2000) which has been translated into Chinese.

Michael Smith is Professor of European Politics and Jean Monnet Chair in the Department of Politics, International Relations and European Studies at Loughborough University. He has published widely in the area of international relations and foreign policy analysis. He is co-author with Mark Webber of *Foreign Policy in a Transformed World* (2002) and co-editor with Christopher Hill of *International Relations and the European Union* (2005).

Perspectives on World Politics
Third edition

Edited by Richard Little and Michael Smith

Routledge
Taylor & Francis Group

LONDON AND NEW YORK

Third edition published 2006
by Routledge
2 Park Square, Milton Park, Abingdon, Oxon OX14 4RN

Simultaneously published in the USA and Canada
by Routledge
270 Madison Avenue, New York NY 10016

First published 1980 by Routledge
Second edition published 1991 by Routledge

Routledge is an imprint of the Taylor and Francis Group

© 1980, 1991, 2006 Richard Little and Michael Smith for selection and
editorial matter; the publishers and contributors for individual chapters

Typeset in Baskerville by RefineCatch Ltd
Printed and bound in Great Britain by
TJ International Ltd, Padstow, Cornwall

All rights reserved. No part of this book may be reprinted or
reproduced or utilised in any form or by any electronic, mechanical or
other means, now known or hereafter invented, including photocopying
and recording, or in any information storage or retrieval system,
without permission in writing from the publishers.

British Library Cataloguing in Publication Data
A catalogue record for this book is available from the British Library

Library of Congress Cataloging in Publication Data
A catalog record for this book has been requested

ISBN10: 0–415–32275–8 (hbk)
ISBN10: 0–415–32276–6 (pbk)

ISBN13: 9–78–0–415–32275–1 (hbk)
ISBN13: 9–78–0–415–32276–8 (pbk)

Contents

Acknowledgements   ix

Introduction   1

PART I
The politics of power and security   13

1.1   **States and statehood**   17
        K.J. HOLSTI

1.2   **The idea of the state and national security**   29
        BARRY BUZAN

1.3   **Continuity and change in the states system**   36
        ROBERT H. JACKSON

1.4   **The nation-state in the global economy**   45
        ROBERT GILPIN

1.5   **The spiral of international insecurity**   54
        ROBERT JERVIS

1.6   **Strategies for survival**   62
        JOHN J. MEARSHEIMER

1.7   **State power and the structure of international trade**   72
        STEPHEN D. KRASNER

1.8   **Cooperation and international regimes**   81
        ROBERT O. KEOHANE

1.9   **Structural realism after the Cold War**   90
        KENNETH N. WALTZ

1.10   **The stability of a unipolar world**   99
        WILLIAM C. WOHLFORTH

1.11   **Law, strategy and history**   111
        PHILIP BOBBITT

PART II
The politics of interdependence and globalization   121

2.1   **The state of globalization: towards a theory of state
        transformation**   125
        MARTIN SHAW

2.2   **Institutions, strategic restraint, and the persistence of
        American postwar order**   133
        G. JOHN IKENBERRY

2.3   **Inter-state cooperation and institutional choice**   142
        ANDREW MORAVCSIK

2.4   **European integration from the 1980s: state-centric v. multi-
        level governance**   151
        GARY MARKS, LIESBET HOOGHE AND KERMIT BLANK

2.5   **The power of international organizations**   164
        MICHAEL N. BARNETT AND MARTHA FINNEMORE

2.6   **Transnational advocacy networks in international politics**   171
        MARGARET E. KECK AND KATHRYN SIKKINK

2.7   **Power, interdependence and the information age**   186
        ROBERT O. KEOHANE AND JOSEPH S. NYE, JR

2.8   **Globalization and the evolution of rules**   195
        WAYNE SANDHOLTZ

2.9   **A framework for the study of security communities**   204
        EMANUEL ADLER AND MICHAEL BARNETT

2.10   **Global civil society**   213
        JAN AART SCHOLTE

2.11   **Cosmopolitanism: globalization tamed?**   222
        DAVID HELD

PART III
The politics of dominance and resistance   229

3.1   **A structural theory of imperialism**   233
        JOHAN GALTUNG

3.2   **The rise and future demise of the world capitalist system: concepts for comparative analysis**   242
IMMANUEL WALLERSTEIN

3.3   **The multinational corporation and the law of uneven development**   251
STEPHEN HYMER

3.4   **Capitalist globalization and the transformation of the state**   260
WILLIAM I. ROBINSON

3.5   **Neoliberal cosmopolitanism**   270
PETER GOWAN

3.6   **Globalizing capitalism and the rise of identity politics**   278
FRANCES FOX PIVEN

3.7   **The globalized war economy**   286
MARY KALDOR

3.8   **The new development-security terrain**   295
MARK DUFFIELD

3.9   **The imagined economies of globalization**   302
ANGUS CAMERON AND RONEN PALAN

3.10 **Conceptualizing resistance to globalization**   311
CHRISTINE B.N. CHIN AND JAMES H. MITTELMAN

3.11 **The dynamics of anti-globalization**   321
JAMES PETRAS AND HENRY VELTMEYER

PART IV
Perspectives and world politics   331

4.1   **On the costs of realism**   335
ROBERT L. ROTHSTEIN

4.2   **Three ideologies of political economy**   342
ROBERT GILPIN

4.3   **The future of the American empire**   352
SUSAN STRANGE

4.4   **Social forces, states and world orders: beyond international relations theory**   359
ROBERT W. COX

4.5   **Reflections on war and political discourse: realism, just war, and feminism in a nuclear age**   **368**
JEAN BETHKE ELSHTAIN

4.6   **Masculinities, IR and the 'gender variable'**   **376**
CHARLOTTE HOOPER

4.7   **International relations: one world, many theories**   **386**
STEPHEN M. WALT

4.8   **The rise and fall of the inter-paradigm debate**   **395**
OLE WÆVER

4.9   **Four sociologies of international politics**   **405**
ALEXANDER WENDT

4.10   **Realist constructivism**   **415**
SAMUEL BARKIN

Index   423

Acknowledgements

The publishers would like to thank the following for permission to reprint their material: Cambridge University Press for K.J. Holsti, 'States and Statehood' in K.J. Holsti, *Taming the Sovereigns: Institutional Change in International Politics* (2004); Pearson Education Ltd for Barry Buzan, 'The Idea of the State and National Security', in Barry Buzan, *People, States and Fear: The National Security Problem in International Relations* (1983); Oxford University Press for Robert H. Jackson, 'Continuity and Change in the States System', in Robert H. Jackson and Alan James (eds), *States in a Changing World* (1993); Princeton University Press for Robert Gilpin, 'The Nation-State in the Global Economy', in Robert Gilpin, *Global Political Economy: Understanding the International Economic Order* (2001); Princeton University Press for Robert Jervis, 'The Spiral of International Insecurity', in Robert Jervis, *Perception and Misperception in International Politics* (1976); W. W. Norton & Company for John J. Mearsheimer, 'Strategies for Survival', in John J. Mearsheimer, *The Tragedy of Great Power Politics* (2001); Johns Hopkins University Press for Stephen D. Krasner, 'State Power and the Structure of International Trade', *World Politics*, 28: 3 (1976); Princeton University Press for Robert O. Keohane, 'Cooperation and International Regimes', in Robert O. Keohane, *After Hegemony: Cooperation and Discord in the World Political Economy* (1984); MIT Press Journals for Kenneth N. Waltz, 'Structural Realism after the Cold War', *International Security*, 25: 1 (2000); MIT Press Journals for William C. Wohlforth, 'The Stability of a Unipolar World', *International Security*, 24: 1 (1999); Penguin Group (UK) for Philip Bobbitt, 'Law, Strategy and History', in Philip Bobbit, *The Shield of Achilles: War, Peace, and the Course of History* (2002); Routledge/ Taylor & Francis Ltd for Martin Shaw, 'The State of Globalization: Towards a Theory of State Transformation', *Review of International Political Economy*, 4: 3 (1997), http:// www.tandf.co.uk; MIT Press Journals for G. John Ikenberry, 'Institutions, Strategic Restraint, and the Persistence of American Postwar Order', *International Security*, 23: 3 (1998–1999); Cornell University Press for Andrew Moravcsik, 'Inter-State Cooperation and Institutional Choice', in Andrew Moravcsik, *The Choice for Europe: Social Purpose and State Power from Messina to Maastricht* (1998); Blackwell Publishing for Gary Marks, Liesbet Hooghe and Kermit Blank, 'European Integration from the 1980s: State-Centric v. Multi-Level Governance', *Journal of Common Market Studies*, 4: 3 (1996); MIT Press Journals for Michael N. Barnett and Martha Finnemore, 'The Politics, Power, and Pathologies of International Organizations', *International Organization*, 53: 4 (1999); Cornell University Press for Margaret E. Keck and Kathryn Sikkink, 'Transnational Advocacy Networks in International Politics', in Margaret E. Keck and Kathryn Sikkink, *Activists beyond Borders: Transnational Advocacy Networks in International Politics* (1998); Pearson Education for Robert O. Keohane and Joseph S. Nye, Jr., 'Power, Interdependence and the Information Age', in Robert O. Keohane and Joseph S, Nye, Jr., *Power and Interdependence* (2001); Routledge/Taylor & Francis for Wayne Sandholtz, 'Globalization and the Evolution of Rules', in Aseem Prakash and Jeffrey A. Hart (eds), *Globalization and Governance* (1999); Cambridge University Press for Emanuel Adler and Michael Barnett, 'A Framework for the Study of Security Communities', in Emanuel Adler and Michael Barnett (eds), *Security Communities* (1998); Palgrave Macmillan Publishers for Jan Aart Scholte, 'Global Civil Society', in Ngaire Woods (ed.), *The Political Economy of Globalization* (2000); Cambridge University Press for David Held, 'Cosmopolitanism: Globalization Tamed?', *Review of International Studies*, 29 (2003), © British International Studies Association, published by Cambridge University Press, reprinted with permission; Sage Publications (and Johan Galtung) for Johan Galtung, 'A Structural Theory of Imperialism', *Journal of Peace Research*, 13: 2 (1971); Cambridge University Press for Immanuel Wallerstein, 'The Rise and Future Demise of the World Capitalist System: Concepts for Comparative Analysis', *Comparative Studies in Society and History*, 14: 4 (1974); © Society for the Comparative Study of Society and History, published by Cambridge University Press, reproduced with permission; Simon & Schuster for permission to reprint Stephen Hymer, 'The Multinational Corporation and the Law of Uneven Development', in J.N. Bhagwati (ed.), *Economics and World Order* (1972), originally published by Collier-Macmillan; Routledge/Taylor & Francis for William I. Robertson, 'Capitalist Globalization and the Transformation of the State', in M. Rupert and H. Smith (eds), *Historical Materialism and Globalization* (2002); *New Left Review* for permission to reprint Peter Gowan, 'Neoliberal Cosmopolitanism', *New Left Review*, 11 (2001); The Merlin Press Ltd for Frances Fox Piven, 'Globalizing Capitalism and the Rise of Identity Politics', *Socialist Register* (1995); Polity Press for permission to reprint Mary Kaldor, 'The Globalized War Economy', in Mary Kaldor, *New and Old Wars: Organized Violence in a Global Era* (2001); Zed Books for Mark Duffield, 'The New Development-Security Terrain', in Mark Duffield, *Global Governance and the New Wars: The Merging of Development and Security* (2001); Sage Publications for Angus Cameron and Ronen Palan, 'Introduction', in Angus Cameron and Ronen Palan, *The Imagined Economies of Globalization* (2004); Palgrave Macmillan for Christine B.N. Chin and James H. Mittleman, 'Conceptualizing Resistance to Globalization', in Barry K. Gills (ed.), *Globalization and the Politics of Resistance* (2000); Zed Books for James Petras and Henry Veltmeyer, 'The Dynamics of Anti-Globalization', in James Petras and Henry Veltmeyer, *System in Crisis: The Dynamics of Free Market Capitalism* (2003); The Academy of Political Science for Robert L. Rothstein, 'On the Costs of Realism', *Political Science Quarterly*, LXXXVII: 3 (1972); Princeton University Press for Robert Gilpin, 'Three Ideologies of Political Economy', in *The Political Economy of International Relations* (1987); *Journal of International Affairs* for Susan Strange, 'The Future of the American Empire', *Journal of International Affairs*, 42: 1 (1988); *Millennium* for Robert W. Cox, 'Social Forces, States and World Orders: Beyond International Relations Theory', *Millennium: Journal of International Studies*, 10: 2 (1981); Sage Publications for Jean Bethke Elshtain, 'Reflections on War and Political Discourse: Realism, Just War, and Feminism in a Nuclear Age', *Political Theory*, 13: 1 (1985); Cambridge University Press for Charlotte Hooper, 'Masculinities, IR and the "Gender Variable" ', *Review of International Studies*, 25 (1999); *Foreign Policy* for Stephen M. Walt, 'International Relations: One World, Many Theories', *Foreign Policy*, 110 (1998); Cambridge University Press for Ole Wæver, 'The Rise and Fall of the Inter-Paradigm Debate', in Steve Smith, Ken Booth and Marysia Zalewski (eds), *International Theory: Positivism and Beyond* (1996); Cambridge University Press for Alexander Wendt, 'Four Sociologies of International Politics', in Alexander Wendt, *Social Theory of International Politics* (1999); Blackwell Publishing for Samuel Barkin, 'Realist Constructivism', *International Studies Review*, 5: 4 (2003).

Every effort has been made to contact copyright holders for their permission to reprint material in this book. The publishers would be grateful to hear from any copyright holder who is not here acknowledged and will undertake to rectify any errors or omissions in future editions of this book.

Introduction

Richard Little and Michael Smith

The study of world politics

World politics as an area of academic inquiry and practical activity holds at one and the same time immense promise and immense potential difficulty. Its promise – and a major reason for its attractiveness to students at all levels as well as to politicians and practitioners – lies in its focus on phenomena which are heavy with implications for the continued existence and flourishing of humankind. Questions of security and prosperity, order and justice, war and peace, and ultimately life and death, have always formed a major preoccupation of those engaged in the field. Although these questions have always been important, the attempt to establish the study of world politics as an academic discipline was largely a product of the twentieth century: indeed, the emergence of an identifiable area of study, known widely as International Relations, was one of the less apocalyptic consequences of the First World War. The growing awareness throughout the last century that international events have important implications for political life at all levels was also accompanied by a persistent expansion and diversification of the subject. As we move into the twenty-first century, the analysis of world politics has become one of the most rapidly expanding fields of study in higher education, with an increasing number of people wanting to develop some understanding of what is happening in world politics.

The difficulties and problems that have attended the study of world politics are in many ways the mirror image of its appeal. A focus on global problems at a time when the ramifications of political activity have extended almost daily, inevitably raises questions about complexity and change. Scholars in the field, no less than the practitioners who have to wrestle with the problems thrown up by world politics, have become resigned to the fact that the subject and its subject matter are in a constant state of flux. We will come back later in this introduction to the difficulties thrown up by the task of constantly trying to deal with the ubiquity of complex change in world politics, but it is clear at this stage that specialists have no alternative but to fire at a moving target.

A further difficulty associated with the task of studying world politics is raised, first, by the recognition that a comprehensive description of the world political scene ought logically to include the whole of human knowledge and, second, by the fact that some of the most important aspects of the subject are precisely those that are likely to be least accessible. All these difficulties should sound a warning to those who enter the field. A warning, maybe, but not by any means a discouragement: the problems and difficulties inherent in the study of world politics make it one of the most challenging fields of inquiry or action available to scholars or practitioners.

There are several major dimensions to the challenge of investigating world politics, which can briefly be noted here. First, there is a challenge of *organization* and *ordering*: how are the phenomena of such a complex field to be moulded into some kind of coherent ordered description? One expression of this problem can be found in the so-called 'level-of-analysis' problem that has beset international studies and aroused periodic debate. At its simplest, this dilemma reduces to a choice of the unit to be studied in any inquiry: is it to be the whole system of world politics, or a particular geographic area, or a set of specific problems, or a particular social or political grouping, or the individual? Such difficulties of choice and discrimination relate closely to the second challenge that can be noted here: the challenge of *theory*. How is it possible to formulate viable and testable theories about an area of such complexity and diversity as world politics? Traditionally, the subject was studied by diplomatic historians who were unconcerned about questions of theory, with the result that their analysis was built on important but often unexamined assumptions that were effectively hidden from view. But since the middle of the twentieth century, especially in the United States, there have been serious and systematic attempts to transform the study of world politics into a social science.

From the start, however, there has been a deep division about how this can be done and it profoundly affects how to fulfil a third challenge – the promotion of either *explanation* or *understanding* of world politics. On one side of the divide in the social sciences it is envisaged that there will be gradual accumulation of theory and evidence rather akin to the approach of the natural sciences. However, the social sciences as a whole have encountered difficulty in attempts to formulate explanatory laws of human behaviour, and world politics confronts them with a singularly intractable field. As a consequence, the challenge of *explanation* has proved extremely resistant to the assaults of scholarship and analysis: in an area where there is little tried and tested theory, and in which it is a considerable achievement to produce an ordered and coherent description of events, the relationship of cause and effect, of motivation and action, presents a daunting obstacle. On the other side of the divide, however, it is argued that it is a mistake to use the natural sciences as a model because human behaviour is utterly different from the phenomena studied in the natural sciences. The challenge on this side of the divide is to develop an *understanding* of human behaviour. To do this it is necessary to penetrate the language, rules, and culture of any group that is being studied. When this is done, it can be seen, for example, that the ancient Greek understanding of war was very different from the understanding that prevails today. It follows that it is meaningless to try to develop general or universal laws of behaviour. Unsurprisingly. both camps have tended to argue that those on the other side of the divide are employing an approach that is methodologically incoherent. But there is a case to be made in favour of methodological pluralism that assumes these are not mutually exclusive approaches. Although these methodological debates are not the central focus of this reader, the general orientation is unquestionably one that favours a pluralistic approach to the study of world politics.

These predominantly academic problems also spill over into a final area of difficulty: the gap between scholarly investigation and practical politics. Because of the complexity and changing nature of the subject, it is all too easy to conclude that the challenges of the field are likely to render useless all but the most basic exercises of description, and that attempts at theory are likely to have no practical relevance in the day-to-day conduct of affairs. Yet most in the field are firmly of the view that good theory must have some implications for policy making.

Given the complexities and difficulties of investigating world politics, it is unsurprising to find that there are also substantial disagreements about how best to introduce students to the subject. We do not think that there is only one way to teach world politics, but we do think that there is considerable merit in demonstrating that the study of world politics can be approached from a number of very different perspectives and this is the approach adopted in this reader. It is assumed that there is no single way of coming to terms with the complex and changing nature of world politics. There is thus an inherent need for a pluralistic approach to the subject matter. The readings in this book are intended to address the questions that arise as soon as the validity of this position is accepted. In one way, the approach taken has a good deal in common with that implied by a study of the 'level-of-analysis' problem, which alerts students to the fact than an initial orientation or preconception can colour the questions they ask, the methods they employ, and the answers they arrive at. So, for example, it makes a big difference whether we approach world politics at the level of the individual or the state. Here, however, the focus is not simply on different facets of an agreed 'world' but rather on different versions of the 'world' as a whole, which colour and at the same time reflect issues of method, values and action. It makes a big difference, for instance, whether you think that hostility between great powers is an inevitable feature of world politics or a feature that can be managed and, potentially, eliminated.

The approach here is based on the conviction that there exist in the study of world politics certain definable perspectives, which shape the forms of academic activity and practical politics where they are implicitly or explicitly adopted. Three such perspectives form the core of the material here: there may be others which could be identified, and it is not always clear where the boundaries of each perspective lie, but this does not affect the basic premise outlined above. To illustrate the approach in more detail, the next section of this introduction assesses each in turn, in relation to some central concerns of world politics. We will then return and look in a little more detail at the status of these perspectives.

Three perspectives on world politics

The three perspectives on world politics that provide the framework for the selection of material in this reader stem from widely differing temporal and political contexts. After what E.H. Carr has described as the initial 'utopian' phase of the study of world politics, there developed during the late 1930s and 1940s a definable focus on *the politics of power and security*. In this first perspective, the stress is laid on the quasi-anarchical nature of the world political system and the consequent concern of states with national security. During the 1960s and 1970s, it became evident that a second perspective had emerged – not to supplant the first in its entirety, but to offer a radically different view based on *the politics of interdependence and globalization*. Here there is a much more pluralist approach to world politics, one that takes account of the vast numbers of deterritorialized or globalized actors that have created interdependent networks across state boundaries. At the same time, and from fundamentally different historical and philosophical roots, there has emerged a third perspective based on *the politics of dominance and resistance*. In many ways, this radical perspective predated the others, since it drew on the work of Marx, Lenin and others in the nineteenth and early twentieth centuries; but it experienced a resurgence with the process of decolonization in the 1950s and 1960s and with the associated problem of economic and social development in new states. How could the poor and weak of the world orient themselves towards and operate within a global system that seemed to place them at a perpetual disadvantage?

From this discussion, it should be apparent that the problems raised by these perspectives have concrete historical roots, and that they concern not only academic theory but political action. Some of the implications of these relationships are brought out by the selections in the final section of the reader, which have been chosen to provide a 'perspective on perspectives'. A good way of exploring these problems further here, and of highlighting the distinctive concerns of each perspective, is by comparing their approaches to three questions of substance in world politics. First, what appear as the significant *actors* in world politics in each case? Second, what view of the global political *process* is implied by each perspective? Finally, what kinds of *outcomes* are emphasized by each approach, and what kind of world do they see as emerging from the actors and processes dealt with?

The politics of power and security

Since this perspective could also be described in terms of 'state-centric politics', there can be no confusion over its assumption of state dominance. This is not to deny that other groups can operate in world politics; rather, it is to assert that the state is dominant to such an extent that other groups gain influence only in so far as they can affect the politics of states. International organizations, economic groupings and other bodies are part of the context within which states operate, but they play an essentially subordinate or contingent role. Perhaps the central attribute that marks the state off from other bodies is its assumed monopoly of the legitimate use of force: as a result of this, states are enabled to pursue their other claims in the international system. Among these claims are those to control over a defined territory, to external sovereignty, and to recognition through exchange of diplomatic missions and admission to international organizations such as the United Nations. The problem is that, although states to this extent form an exclusive 'club', there is also intense competition between the members of the 'club' for scarce resources. In this context, the idea of 'resources' denotes not simply raw materials for the generation of wealth, nor simply the territory that may furnish raw materials, but also things which are much less tangible such as security. Security – based on territory or other assets – is seen as a limited resource that is central to the concerns of all states but which none can enjoy completely. Nor can all enjoy it in equal measure: at the core of the 'power and security' approach is the assumption that there is an international hierarchy in which military might and economic capacity define the rank of any given state, and in which international power distribution is a major factor in the making of national policies.

The actors in a 'power and security' approach are thus defined as states, commonly seeking to assure their own security and prosperity within the limits of scarce resources. Such a definition is important to a view of the significant processes in world politics, since their importance is clearly derived from the involvement of states. At the level of the state itself, foreign policy can be seen clearly as the process by which national (state) interests are pursued within an insecure world. The assumption is made that states act: in other words, the state moves as a single unit in pursuit of unified objectives. These objectives – and the exertion of power in pursuit of them – constitute the product of a process of rational choice in which the interests and resources of the state in question and of other states are assessed, the implications of particular choices are weighed and action is taken. Foreign politics is a matter of high secrecy and involves only a very restricted elite working on behalf of the state. This follows logically from the assumption that foreign policy is overwhelmingly concerned with matters of national security (both military and economic); in an insecure world could it be otherwise? Such being the case, it is clear that success or failure in foreign policy is a matter of the appropriate application of power. In any given relationship the state that most effectively and appropriately wields its power will prevail, with almost mathematical certainty.

A view of foreign policy as being concerned with national security and defence of national interests virtually dictates that the international political system (that is to say, the interstate system) will be characterized by competition and conflict. This is especially likely given the inevitable absence of any institutions accepted by and binding of all members of the system. The interstate system is an 'insecurity community' in which war is an ever present 'contingent liability', and in which the axiom 'might is right' applies. That it does not apply universally is due to the existence of a core of practices which produce a minimum of international order: international law, the balance of power, the fear of war itself, the exercise of responsible leadership by hegemonic powers. On the whole, however, the outcome of the 'politics of power and security' is an international system which operates according to a power hierarchy and in which there is a continuing tension between the concerns and activities of individual states and the demands of the system as a whole. States cannot escape the demands of the system, although it is possible to deflect or balance them in advantageous ways.

The politics of interdependence and globalization

Although the state remains a significant – if not the most significant – actor in the second perspective, its role undergoes a transformation. There is a central paradox here – between the growing concern of most states, especially those in industrialized countries with what goes on in other societies, and the limited abilities of many states to achieve their objectives in their ever-broadening area of concerns. The state itself – partly as a consequence – becomes penetrated by other states or by a variety of other actors, and can no longer lay claim in many cases to the control of territory and the external sovereignty which are the building blocks of the 'politics of power and security'. Notions of power and of power hierarchy are undermined since it becomes clear that a state that is 'powerful' or well-endowed in one area can be extraordinarily weak in others and vulnerable to its apparent inferiors. Alongside the state emerges a whole range of new, non-state actors that have distinctive areas of concern and arenas of activity. 'Subnational' actors with a base in one state can develop activities which significantly affect the policies of that state in other states or which bypass the state machinery completely. 'Supranational' actors – of which the European Union is the most highly developed example – can in limited areas achieve the ability to over-ride the authority of the state and produce policies which entail a diminution of state sovereignty. 'Transnational' actors headed by the multinational corporations (MNCs) can establish operations with a multinational base giving them in theory at least the ability to transfer activities and resources across state boundaries on a large scale. Within this perspective, there are variations in the extent to which the 'death of the state' is predicted or diagnosed: what is clear, however, is that it is no longer taken for granted as the dominant actor in the international sphere, nor is it seen as the uniform building block of a privileged 'club'. How could it be, when the financial resources of the largest MNCs exceed those of all but a handful of states, and when a host of transnational non-governmental actors have a voice in international fora?

Although the state is no longer, in the 'politics of interdependence and globalization' perspective, seen as the sole gatekeeper for international political processes, foreign policy does still matter. In this perspective, however, foreign policy is difficult to separate from wider political processes at home and abroad since its subject matter is of much more immediate impact. The foreign policy system itself thus becomes penetrated, with action emerging not as the result of rational calculation by a unitary decision-making body, but rather as the outcome of complex political and organizational processes. We become aware that not only the public and special-interest groups are involved in foreign policy questions but also that the foreign policy machinery itself is an arena for political competition and dissent. The state becomes disaggregated, and so does the foreign policy process. Externally, the proliferation of channels for action and interaction accompanies the proliferation of issues and their increasing politicization to make foreign policy a matter of delicate management and coalition building rather than the comparatively simple safeguarding of national positions. New actors can intervene to complicate processes, and it is no longer the case that the hierarchy conditions outcomes. Indeed, there is no clear and uncontested hierarchy in newly politicized issue areas, and much activity has to be devoted to the building of rules and institutions to regulate the new agenda.

The international system in these conditions 'explodes'. A system of 'mixed actors' creates the potential for a multitude of coalitions and balances, corresponding to the intersection of novel and existing issues and the absence of a clear or unified global hierarchy. Although it could be said that a global military hierarchy, based especially on nuclear weapons or on other weapons of mass destruction (WMD), still exists, such an assertion becomes debateable in conditions where first, WMD do not constitute a rational policy instrument and, second, the proliferation of WMD capacity threatens to complicate the picture and create new instabilities. World politics become simultaneously more diffuse, penetrating new regions and activities, and more interconnected with linkages between a variety of actors. The resulting conditions of interdependence – between actors and states – increase both the mutual sensitivity of those engaged in world politics and, in many cases, their mutual vulnerability to new forces. For many analysts this means that interdependence between national societies has been supplanted by processes of globalization, in which activities are increasingly de-linked from territory of national authorities, and in which there are new forms of unpredictability and potential instability. The response of those who espouse the second perspective is to call for enhanced mechanisms of management; in a way, they are calling for the construction of systems of behaviour of rules and standards (often termed regimes or forms of global governance) to constrain the actors and support the pursuit of the common good, whereas in the 'politics of power and security' the hierarchy and the imperatives of national security form a perpetual constraint. For the rather primitive imperatives of the first perspective are substituted a set of beliefs in managerial procedures, in the fruits of multilateral negotiation and in the need for cosmopolitan values; these have to be established and maintained in conditions of polyarchy, where the sources of power are widely dispersed.

The politics of dominance and resistance

An analysis of world politics based on the examination of dominance and resistance structures implies yet a third view of the role of the actors and of the processes which take place in the global system. Although the state still acts as a focus of activity and coercive power, it stands in a particular structural relationship to dominant economic and political interests, which use it as a channel or a support for the pursuit of their aims. The state achieves less autonomy as an actor in world politics since in many ways it is merely the recruit or the representative of other, more fundamental interests. Where the state is adequate to the task of supporting dominant interests – chiefly those of big capital – then it will be used, but where it fails to match up to the increasingly global needs and activities characteristic of large corporations, then it will be discarded or ignored.

Such a view implies that the real actors in world politics are dominant class or economic interests. It also implies that those in dependent positions within the global structure are systematically prevented from achieving any kind of capacity for autonomous action. A critical stage in the analysis of any actor within this perspective is therefore an assessment of its location within the global structure. In terms of classical imperialist theories, such a location is largely determined by relations between metropolitan powers and colonial areas – relations which are formalized by territorial occupation and administrative dominance. Where formal territorial imperialism does not exist, as it has not to any marked degree since the collapse of the Soviet Empire at the start of the 1990s, new concepts become important in the study of relations between dominant and dependent groups. One of the most fruitful of these concepts has been that of centre–periphery relationships, in which the major determinant of international action has been seen as the confrontation between the dominant 'centre' of developed capitalism and the dependent 'periphery' of the less developed areas. The ideas of 'centre' and 'periphery' are not identical with particular groups of states, since it is part of this perspectives' argument that relations between centre and periphery exist within, as well as between, nations. From this situation emerge a host of cross-cutting relationships, in which the common interests of those at the 'centre of the centre' and 'centre of the periphery' form a major source of exploitation for peripheral groups. The processes of globalization, in this perspective, are a further development and deepening of this tendency to global imperialism and subordination, giving new power and pervasiveness to the forces of global capital.

It is apparent from this discussion that the systematic and structural patterns of dominance and dependence within the international system define the 'actorness' of groups within the system. The processes whereby the structure is sustained and developed are equally a reflection of the fundamental imbalance between elements of the system. In the days of the great colonial empires, the mechanisms were formal and institutional as well as social and political in nature: the very rules of international life sanctioned armed intervention and division of territory between the metropolitan European powers. The decline of the nineteenth-century empires during the first two-thirds of the twentieth century was dramatic but it did not imply that the processes of dominance and dependence had disappeared. In fact, it was possible to discern a distinctive process of 'underdevelopment' that consolidated the continuing dominance of the centre at the expense of the periphery. Such a process in specific cases is sustained by a number of mechanisms: by exploitation, in which the balance of benefits from international processes of exchange is biased towards the centre; by penetration, in which the forms and standards of the centre are pursued by 'recruits' among the elite of peripheral nations at the expense of the mass; and by fragmentation, through which a policy of 'divide and rule' dilutes the potential influence of dependent areas in their struggle to resist dominant forces. Although there may seem to be changes, and a process of development may seem to take place in dependent areas, this does not alter the brutal basic fact of systematic disadvantage that gives 'structural power' to certain groups at the expense of others.

The outcome of these processes can only be described as a vicious circle, made more vicious still in the twenty-first century by the intensification of globalization and by the emergence of such phenomena as the globalized economy of warfare and militarism. The rich get richer and the poor, in relative terms, can only get poorer as the structures of dominance and dependence are consolidated; not only this, but the poor are subjected to interventions in both the military and the economic realms that emphasize their subordination. In contrast to the view implied by the 'politics of interdependence and globalization', attempts at management and reform within the existing structure are seen here as ultimately futile; indeed, they are themselves the weapons of those whose central interest is in the continuation of the existing system and the benefits it confers upon the privileged. Similarly, the second perspective's focus on cosmopolitan ideas is seen by third perspective analysts as one of the means by which the dominance of 'Western' values is perpetuated and extended. In the final analysis, the contradictions and conflicts of interest produced by the prevailing structure can only be resolved by its collapse and its replacement by a more equitable global system. Given that the privileged cannot be expected to connive at their own destruction, such an outcome can only be the result of a traumatic upheaval, possibly induced by the growing internal contradictions of the advanced societies or by the upsurge of revolutionary discontent in the periphery. This gives rise to ideas and practices of resistance that can emerge in many forms, and often from the 'bottom up' in the form of transnational anti-globalization movements as well as through national governments.

An overall view

The preceding discussion has uncovered at least some of the central features of the three perspectives examined. More particularly, it appears that it is possible to distinguish between them according to their approaches to the three questions posed earlier: who are the *actors* in world politics, what are the characteristics of the global political *process*, and what kinds of *outcomes* express the nature of the world system? Although it is wise to be cautious and to be aware of the dangers inherent in the drawing of boundaries between approaches, the kinds of contrasts that have emerged can be crudely summarized as in Table 1.

It should be clear that the three perspectives examined express broad differences of philosophy and of emphasis in the study of world politics. They may intersect or overlap at particular points, but it would be difficult to argue that they are simply special cases of one broader 'reality'. Three major areas of divergence can be mentioned here in support of such a judgement. First, it is apparent that each perspective embodies a distinctive view of the relationship between the whole and the parts in the world political arena. A view based on the 'politics of power and security' postulates a constant tension between the interests of states and the dynamics of the state system that creates an atmosphere of insecurity and the possibility of violence. An approach in terms of 'interdependence and globalization', on the other hand, enshrines a view of the world as a pluralist political system within which there is a constant process of mutual and multilateral adaption to events. The 'politics of dominance and resistance', finally, centre upon a world in which the existing structure conditions all political action, and in which the actions and interests of the parts are reflections of the

Table 1 The three perspectives on world politics

Perspective	Power and security	Interdependence and globalization	Dominance and resistance
Actors	States	State and non-state organizations	Economic classes and their representatives
Processes	Competitive pursuit of national interest	Management of global problems	Exploitation and resistance
Outcomes	Limited order within an anarchical society	Rule-governed behaviour in a polyarchical society	Resistance within a centre–periphery structure; conflict between bottom–up and top–down processes

relationships built into the system as a whole. Resistance itself reflects the desire to transform these relationships and to create a new form of inclusive global structure.

A second area of divergence, linked to the first, concerns the possibilities for change or reform in the world system. Whereas the 'politics of power and security' is in many ways a conservative approach to world politics basing its analysis on the existing distribution of global power it does admit the possibility of macro-political change as the potential of particular states grows or declines. It does not, however, contemplate a change in the dominant role of the state in general, of the type that is almost a precondition for the 'politics of interdependence and globalization'; in this second perspective the state becomes capable of reform or transformation, and the global system itself is seen as demanding effective management. Such a reformist view, implying that political actions can enable the existing system more effectively to meet the demands of its members is denied by the 'politics of dominance and resistance'. Since the system embodies structural dominance and dependence, reform is out of the question and the only way of achieving fundamental change is through the resistance needed to bring about fundamental transformation.

As a consequence of divergences over the relationship between whole and parts, and over the possibility of reform and change the three perspectives finally diverge in terms of their relationship to values and political action. The watchword of those who espouse the 'politics of power and security' is 'political realism', in which the sober and rational calculation of interests and capabilities is a central activity and the means of action should be carefully matched to the demands of particular circumstances. Whilst the need for appropriateness and calculation is by no means denied by the 'politics of interdependence and globalization', a major place is accorded to other values based on the possibility of progress and the development of new norms and conventions of behaviour. The 'politics of dominance and resistance' focus far less on the capacity for progress by adaptation and far more on the need for radical political action to exacerbate the contradictions of a system that systematically oppresses some of its members.

With these contrasts, the argument comes almost full circle. At the beginning of this Introduction it was remarked that the study of world politics poses particular challenges for the scholar, student, and practitioner alike, in terms of description, theory and explanation, and in terms of the links between academic endeavour and political actions. None of the three perspectives presented here and in the remainder of this reader can be seen in isolation from each other or the world in which they have emerged. They offer, to at least a modest degree, an illustration of the ways in which perspectives can shape the form of academic activity and practical politics in a complex world.

A perspective on perspectives

The aim of this section is to discuss why we think that it is still appropriate to use the idea of competing perspectives to introduce students to the analysis of world politics. The first edition of this reader was published in 1981 and a second edition was published a decade later. This third edition appears after an even longer interval. The world looks very different in the twenty-first century than it did at the end of the 1970s when the ideas underlying this reader were first developed. At that time, the strategy of containment that had guided the 'West' during the Cold War was looking very fragile. Far from being contained, the Soviet Union seemed to be intent on extending its sphere of influence into Africa, Asia and Latin America, while the 'West' was often seen to be curtailing its overseas interests, especially with the ending of European colonialism. Sending troops into Afghanistan in 1979, therefore, was seen to be an extremely provocative act by the Soviet Union and the United States, in particular, considered the move to be very alarming. In contrast to the Soviet Union, the United States was extremely reluctant to engage in any future military interventions after they withdrew in 1973 from the war in Vietnam. As a consequence, it began to look as if the balance of power was tipping in the Soviets' favour.

Yet within a decade, by 1990, when the second edition of the reader was being put together, it was being argued that the Cold War had been 'won' by the West and that liberalism represented the permanent wave of the future. Despite these triumphalist assertions, it was very unclear what the future would bring. After all, the Soviet Union was still in existence, and even though it had lost control in Eastern Europe, still no one was predicting its demise. On the contrary, there was a major debate at that time about whether the power of the United States was on the wane. By contrast, at the start of the twenty-first century, the United States was being compared to the Roman Empire and it was widely accepted, not only that the international system had become unipolar, but that there was no reason to suppose, notwithstanding the 11 September 2001 attacks, that this situation was going to change in the near future. Even so, by 2005, as this third edition of the reader was going to press, the United States found itself bogged down in Iraq with no signs that it had any chance of achieving its objective of turning Iraq into a stable democracy.

How relevant are the perspectives that we identified more than quarter of a century ago, given this fundamental transformation at the end of the twentieth century, with the Soviet Union no longer part of the political landscape and the United States left as 'the lonely superpower'? The first and most obvious point to make is that it is still very easy to identify these perspectives within the current literature on world politics. It follows that it remains as important as ever to recognize that everything that we read is coming from a particular perspective. So, for example, the analysis in the previous two paragraphs does not represent a neutral or unmediated account of the end of the twentieth century, but is rooted in the 'power and security' perspective. Consequently, it is useful to know that not everyone working within this perspective would accept the prognosis that unipolarity will persist, because some analysts assume that there is a powerful incentive for other great powers in the system to counteract or balance the power of the United States (compare extracts 1.10 and 1.11).

It also seems important and relevant to us to recognize and acknowledge that analysts working from the 'interdependence and globalization' perspective and the 'dominance and resistance' perspective present very different accounts of what happened at the end of the twentieth century. Those working within the 'interdependence and globalization' perspective have been impressed by the steady growth and extension of actors and processes that are either helping to constrain the power of the state or are actively aiming to change the behaviour of states. There is generally no suggestion that states are about to become extinct, but there is an almost universal assumption within this perspective that it is simply anachronistic to view the state as an impermeable container. From this perspective, therefore, there has been steady but persistent change over a very long period of time and it is certainly too early to say yet whether the end of the Cold War accelerated the processes of change. By contrast, advocates of the 'dominance and resistance' perspective are much more pessimistic about the reputed benefits that were reaped at the end of the Cold War. At the same time, they are also highly sceptical about the claim made by the 'power and security' perspective that there has been a major transformation in world politics. The 'dominance and resistance' perspective, throughout the Cold War, viewed the Soviet Union as a state that was locked into a subordinate position within the world capitalist system. The end of the Cold War, therefore, has had very little impact on the way that this perspective structures world politics.

Of course, this perspective acknowledges that the changes identified by the other two perspectives have taken place, but its proponents continue to insist that there is very little evidence that the structures that maintain relations of dominance and exploitation have weakened in any significant way or are likely to do so in the near future; hence the need for mobilization and resistance itself.

It was relatively unusual at the beginning of the 1980s to organize a textbook about world politics on the basis of competing perspectives. By the start of the 1990s, however, the strategy was much more widely employed. There was also a widespread tendency to label the perspectives as realism, liberalism and Marxism. These labels, of course, highlight the essentially ideological dimension of the perspectives. As discussed in the previous section, this element was certainly present in the way our conception of perspectives is related to change, with the power and security perspective being related to a conservative or realist perspective, the interdependence and globalization perspective related to a reformist perspective, and the dominance and resistance perspective related to a radical perspective. But it is also apparent that the three perspectives cannot simply be distinguished on ideological grounds. As Table 1 makes clear, the analytical foci of the three perspectives are very different, and it can also be suggested that the perspectives operate on different levels of analysis. Because of the complex, multifaceted character of the perspectives, therefore, the use of restricting and primarily ideological labels is formally eschewed here, although we make frequent reference, nevertheless, to the labels.

Despite the widespread use of a perspectival approach by the time the second edition of this reader was published, there was also, perhaps inevitably, criticism. Susan Strange, who was one of the leading British academics in the field of world politics, argued that by identifying divergent perspectives, students were being encouraged to think that there are incompatible views of the world. She likened the perspectives to 'three toy trains on separate tracks, travelling from different starting-points and ending at different (predetermined) destinations.'[1] On the basis of this criticism, Strange went on to insist that it is necessary to break down the ideological barriers that separate the advocates of the three perspectives. Once this is done, she argues, then it bcomes possible to develop a much more pragmatic approach to both analysis and policy making, drawing on the insights provided by each perspective.

Strange's position, however, fails to acknowledge that there is no agreement about the direction we are heading in. The ideological differences cannot be completely eliminated. She also fails to acknowledge that the perspectives are not simply divided on ideological grounds. There are important analytical differences. Finally, she is incorrect when she assumes that there is no communication between the different perspectives. While the tracks may never cross – to continue the metaphor – the drivers, if not necessarily all the passengers, are constantly monitoring the progress of the other trains.

Although we continue to think that it is important to expose students to the different perspectives, it is nevertheless true that there are other ways of approaching world politics. We acknowledged this in the first edition by establishing a fourth section to discuss the nature and significance of perspectives. This section was expanded in the second edition and it has been further expanded in this edition.

A note on the selection and arrangement of material

A number of criteria have influenced the selection of material for this reader. First, in line with the framework outlined in this introduction, each section is intended to represent as fairly as possible the assumptions shared by authors writing within the perspective: in the case of the final section the aim was to include material which explicitly assessed the implications of perspectives for the study and practice of world politics. Second, and as a consequence of these initial aims, it has been the concern of the editors to ensure that each individual selection reflects as fully as possible within the inevitable constraints of space the chief arguments of its author. Third, wherever possible, the editors have made selections that illustrate the application of ideas within a perspective to particular examples, although no case studies as such have been included. Finally, although it has not been possible, for obvious reasons, to adhere rigidly to an approach based on 'actors', 'processes' and 'outcomes' within each perspective, such an orientation was implicit in the collection of material.

Each section is preceded by a general introduction to the selections it contains, and each selection by a short introductory summary of content. Since in some cases the original material was accompanied by extensive footnotes and references, the editors decided to edit these in accordance with a uniform set of criteria. Thus notes are included where either there is a quotation in the text or an author is referred to by name or direct reference is made to a particular body of literature. It is hoped that this approach combines the maximum of economy in notes with as accurate a reflection as possible of the original author's intentions.

Although almost 25 per cent longer than the second edition, producing this new edition has involved a series of difficult decisions about what to excise and what to include. In the end, although we still saw considerable merit in all the items in the second edition, the vast majority of the items in this edition are new.

Note

1   Susan Strange, *States and Markets: An Introduction to Political Economy* (Pinter Publishers, London, 1988), p. 16.

Part I

The politics of power and security

The extracts in this section have all been written in recent years. This reflects a bias in selection because this 'power and security' perspective is very closely associated with the realist tradition that claims to have very long antecedents. As a consequence, contemporary realists frequently make reference to Thucydides' *The Peloponnesian War*, Machiavelli's *The Prince*, and Hobbes' *Leviathan* in an attempt to demonstrate the longevity and universality of their perspective on world politics. Although these authors were writing in very different historical contexts – Thucydides in the Greek city states, Machiavelli in the city states of Renaissance Italy, and Hobbes in the early modern European states – according to contemporary realists, they all share remarkably similar precepts about politics. In particular, they focus on the centrality of the state and the importance of power for maintaining the security of the state. We have not included extracts from these historical texts, however, because the focus in this book is on how contemporary writers analyse world politics. Nevertheless, whereas the other two perspectives are primarily concerned with exploring the forces of change in world politics, most of the extracts in this section are concerned with the continuing centrality of the state and some of the enduring features of world politics.

There is obviously a conservative element to this perspective and it is often noted when the study of world politics was established as an academic field of study, after the First World War, but more especially, after the Second World War, that those working within this perspective chose to identify themselves as realists and to contrast their own willingness to look at the unyielding features of world politics with the work of their critics, whom they identified as idealists. From the realist perspective, their opponents were overly optimistic about the potential for change in world politics. Throughout the Cold War, with the United States and the Soviet Union operating on the basis of mutual assured destruction, MAD when abbreviated, realists had little difficulty finding evidence to justify and reinforce their point of view. But the willingness of the Soviet Union, under Gorbachev, to call an end to the Cold War and to move out of Eastern Europe, followed soon after by the collapse of the Soviet Union, was seen by many critics of realism to sound the death knell of the perspective. This prophecy, however, has proved to be premature. Realists have continued to hold their own in the post-Cold War era. They point to the fact that the end of the Cold War has not led to general disarmament, and that states remain as concerned about power and security as they always have in the past. But given this position, the failure of major states to balance against the United States poses something of a puzzle for some realists. They have responded in a variety of different ways, indicating that the perspective is more diverse than is sometimes presupposed.

The items in this section of the book have been chosen to demonstrate that realist thinkers have a sophisticated assessment of world politics and that the approach is more complex and diverse than is sometimes acknowledged by its critics. The first four items focus on the continued centrality of the state in world politics and they reject the view that the state is becoming an obsolete institution. At the same time, however, it is also acknowledged that the state can take a wide variety of forms in contemporary world politics. Holsti (1.1) distinguishes states from earlier polities, such as the Greek and Italian city states, and he also argues that the ideas and norms that define states have developed across more than three centuries, and the state has simultaneously become increasingly mutifunctional across time. In the contemporary era he acknowledges that there are many weak and failed states but he dismisses the argument about the obsolesence of the state in favour of the argument that states are continuing to become more complex. Buzan (1.2) focuses in more detail than Holsti on the idea of the state, which he views as a more ambiguous component in world politics than is usual from the realist perspective. He focuses specifically on the contribution of national security to the idea of the state and explores the complex relationship that exists between the ideas of nation and state. Because the relationship between state and nation varies, however, he argues that the conception of national security will take different forms. He concludes that if the idea of the state is contested or not widely and firmly adhered to, then it is vulnerable to revolution, civil war, or disintegration.

This point is picked up by Jackson (1.3) who views the state from the perspective of the states system. Jackson defines the system in terms of a society of states that is regulated by rules of the game. The central rule relates to sovereignty or statehood which is firmly established and reinforced by the norm of non-intervention. The major consequence of these inter-related rules is that although there was an enormous proliferation of small and weak states in the twentieth century that would not have survived in earlier periods, almost all have persisted. The norms that establish territorial legitimacy are now worldwide, with the result that even states that have collapsed internally, because of ethnic conflict or the like, persist as juridical entities. Jackson acknowledges the growth of regionalism and focuses, in particular, on the development of the European Union, but he insists that the idea of statehood is so firmly entrenched that it is unlikely that the states system will give way to an alternative form of world organization in the near future. Gilpin (1.4) develops the same line of argument in the context of economics and globalization. He argues that many of the developments associated with globalization have, in practice, been implemented by states. He accepts that these developments have made macroeconomic decision making more difficult for the state, but that most states still maintain a good deal of control over their own economies. Too often, according to Holsti, advocates of the globalization thesis fail to appreciate that states have never had unfettered control over their own economies.

The next five items focus on factors and processes that relate to the interaction between states. From a realist perspective, one of the primary concerns for states is the need to achieve security. But realists have always acknowledged that the existence of a security dilemma lies at the heart of world politics. The nature of this dilemma is examined by Jervis (1.5). He argues that because states operate in an anarchy, they tend to assume the worst of each other and rely on armaments to increase their sense of security. Such a strategy, however, inevitably increases the insecurity of their neighbours, who respond in a similar fashion, thereby generating a spiral of insecurity. The next item is an extract by Mearsheimer (1.6) from his theory of great power behaviour. Like Jervis, he also assumes that world politics have always been characterized by chronic insecurity. He argues that uncertainty about the intentions of other states pushes great powers to expand their power base in an attempt to achieve regional hegemony, maximum wealth, pre-eminent land power and, in recent times, nuclear superiority. No European state ever achieved regional hegemony because of the balance of power, although in the contemporary world it is accepted that the United States has achieved the status of a regional, although not a global hegemon. Mearsheimer then goes on to explore the strategies that Great Powers have used across history to increase their power capabilities. Although he identifies war as a key Great Power strategy, the other strategies that he puts forward suggest that Great Powers will avoid war whenever possible.

Although the tendency in this perespective is to focus on the relationship between power and security, there is a recognition that the international distribution of power also has a significant impact on international economic structures. Krasner (1.7) draws on empirical evidence from the nineteenth and twentieth centuries to demonstrate that the degree of 'openness' in the international economy is related to the concentration of international power. There is a link between the maintenance of free trade that necessarily requires mutual cooperation among states and the emergence of Britain and the United States as hegemons. In other words, a hegemon can help to overcome the inhibitions to cooperation that anarchy sets up. Krasner, however, is forced to shift his level of analysis from the system to the state in order to explain why Britain's commitment to free trade lasted after its power had started to decline and it was some time after the United States became a hegemonic power that it began to promote an open international economy. Keohane (1.8) extends this argument and insists that a hegemon is not, in theory or practice, necessary for cooperation to take place in an anarchic arena. Keohane argues that mutual interests can be sufficient to allow states to overcome the mutual suspicions that realists insist are an inevitable product of anarchy.

The final three items in this section provide very different responses to what is happening in world politics in the aftermath of the Cold War. Waltz (1.9) directly confronts the argument that critical developments that have taken place in world politics since the end of the Cold War have completely undermined realist thinking. He looks specifically at the growth of democracy, interdependence, and international institutions. All three developments have been closely associated with the establishment of a more peaceful and stable world. Waltz endeavours to show that the arguments supporting this conclusion are fundamentally flawed and that realist concepts and assumptions remain as relevant as they ever were. He illustrates this position through an exploration of the balance of power theory. According to the theory, a unipolar world is highly unstable and any dominant power will quickly come to be challenged by rivals. From Waltz's perspective, these rivals are already on the horizon. Wohlforth (1.10), by contrast, argues that the twenty-first century is very different from the previous two centuries, when the balance of power theory did apply. He insists that we are operating in a system where there is no rival state to the United States and that if this country pursues wise strategies, then there is no reason why the future should not be both stable and peaceful.

Bobbitt (1.11) offers a much more radical thesis than is presented by Waltz or Wohlforth and it is developed at length in the book from which this extract is taken. In essence, he argues that if we examine the history of Europe, what we observe is a cycle of system-wide wars; during each cycle, the nature of the state is transformed and at the end of the cycle there is a system wide peace treaty where the Great Powers establish a new constitutional order for the international society of states. During the 'long war' of the twentieth century – 1914 to 1990 – the nation state has been transformed into a market state. But what we are still waiting for is a new constitutional order. His concern is that there is insufficient awareness that the nature of world politics has been transformed. In the extract, he argues that the strategic calculus that operated during the long war is now redundant because the world no longer faces the kind of state-centred threats that have undermined their security in the past.

The book was written before 11 September 2001, but the attack by Al Qaeda certainly gave Bobbitt's book additional resonance.

The extracts in this section provide an overview of a realist perspective that is often associated with a conservative, state-centric and essentially pessimistic view of world politics. Although Mearsheimer does unquestionably paint a very bleak view of how great powers behave, and Bobbitt opens up the possibility of a distopian future, he, like most of the other authors, still assumes that some kind of world order is possible. The other two perspectives, however, although coming from very different positions, are much more open to the potential for reform or even radical change.

1.1 States and statehood

K.J. Holsti

Source: *Taming the Sovereigns: Institutional Change in International Politics* (Cambridge University Press, Cambridge, 2004), pp. 28–72.

Holsti identifies the sovereign state as the foundational actor of international relations. Having outlined its essential features, he traces how the practices, ideas, and norms that help to define the state have evolved from the seventeenth century through to the present day. Although now the prevailing form of political authority, Holsti accepts that not all states are successful. But he challenges the widely accepted view that states are becoming obsolete and argues instead that states are becoming more complex.

Societies and smaller groups throughout history have formed organizations that provide and sustain them with security, access to resources, social rules, and means of continuity. Frequently they also devised, embodied, or sought more ephemeral objectives or qualities such as identity, glory, renown, and reputation. The institutional forms they have taken have varied greatly. Even terms we commonly use to designate polities – tribes, clans, empires, principalities, city-states, protectorates, sultanates, or duchies – would not begin to cover the actual diversity of political forms. [. . .]

Our concern, however, is with states, the only contemporary political organizations that enjoy a unique legal status – sovereignty – and that, unlike other types of polities, have created and modified enduring public international institutions. They are thereby the foundational actors of international relations. Other types of polities may ultimately become states but until they have transformed themselves into public bodies – moral agents representing some sort of community – they do not have the legal standing of states. [. . .]

Polities that had many but not all the features of states include the Han Empire, the Greek city-states, the Roman state, the Aztec and Inca empires, the Byzantine Empire, and the Italian city-states. We would not include in this list thousands of polities that once may have been politically and militarily formidable but otherwise lacked most of the critical attributes of statehood. The Visigoths, Lombards, Franks, Vandals, and Huns, for example, are better known for their depredations than for political continuity and the creation of international institutions. Others such as the Cimbri, Knights Templars, Samnites, Taurisci, Tigurini, Carbo, or Frisians, have disappeared into the mists of history. They lacked the essential qualities of statehood that provide polities with both legitimacy and longevity. What are these? A non-inclusive list would contain at least the following: (1) fixed position in space (territoriality); (2) the politics of a public realm (differentiation between private and public realms); (3) institutionalized political organizations (continuity independent from specific leaders or other individuals); (4) and a multiplicity of governmental tasks and activities (multifunctionalism), based on (5) legitimizing authority structures. [. . .]

The late seventeenth-century Westphalian state

At the beginning of the fifteenth century, Europe remained dotted with hundreds of different polities, overlapping jurisdictions, a low degree of differentiation between private and public realms, and divided loyalties. No prince could predictably prevail over his feudal barons, independent towns, or even church authorities. To muster military strength he had to rely on purchasing armies or making alliances with subordinates who had their own – though seasonal – military capacities. By 1700, in contrast, most princes could effectively suppress most challenges to their authority, although the costs of doing so were often ruinous. [. . .]

Practices: the great power grab

The struggle to establish central authority – to bring to life the various assertions of internal sovereignty – could not be conducted unilaterally by the royal figures. They faced resistance and opposition from a variety of sources, including towns and cities, the landed aristocracy, the church, and the peasantry. In order to prevail they had to make alliances, concede charters and grants of autonomy, buy off the aristocracy, purchase loyalty through the sale of offices, put down rebellions and resistance with force, and, as in the case of Peter's Russia, physically annihilate the opposition. Power and authority during the medieval era had resided in many centers, including the church, local assemblies and councils, and in the various landed estates, towns, duchies, and principalities. In the construction of the Absolutist State, those claiming sovereignty had to curtail the ancient rights and privileges of these bodies. [. . .]

The issue of taxation was thus critical. Until the fifteenth century, approximately, princes could pay for most of the very limited functions of government from income deriving from their own estates. By the seventeenth century, the costs of administration and war had grown dramatically and no royal household had the means to sustain them.

The strategies for obtaining the necessary funds and support varied. In France, Richelieu ordered the destruction of all town fortifications, thus rendering them defenseless against royal troops. Louis XIV initiated the "court" at Versailles, an institution widely copied in other centralizing monarchies. [. . .]

By the end of the seventeenth century the centralizing authorities prevailed throughout much of Europe. The polity increasingly had those characteristics we listed as essential for statehood. It was fixed in space and time; the idea of patrimony – the state as a private realm – was in decline everywhere but in France and Spain; governance was becoming increasingly institutionalized as a vehicle distinct from the dynast or dynasty; and the state was well along the way to becoming multifunctional. [. . .]

No account of the growing multifunctionality of the state would be complete without mention of two intertwined "services" that became fully concentrated under central authority. Taxation and the military, each of which fed upon the other in a closed symbiotic relationship, were perhaps the most important characteristics of the seventeenth-century state. [. . .]

Most experts now agree that the geopolitical competition and war were the main motors driving the development of bureaucracy and public finance in the seventeenth-century state.

Braun notes that almost every major taxation change in Europe during this epoch was occasioned by the preparation and commissioning of wars.[1] There were four main sources of revenues for these expanding requirements: (1) the personal possessions of the crown, (2) sale of offices, (3) public taxation, and (4) income from colonies. The first was inadequate in relation to the vastly increasing expenditures required to create and sustain permanent bureaucracies and armies. The second, perfected in France and Spain, generated only about 15 percent of the state's needs. The third was the predominant source, but it was never adequate to meet growing needs. Colonies were available only for some countries (particularly Spain). To meet the shortfalls, crowns often mortgaged their kingdoms to private financiers. Most seventeenth-century states were thus fundamentally weak: they had to extort, tax, and borrow to pay for their growing armies and bureaucracies, all with the result that loyalty (except among those with sinecures), legitimacy, and credit-ratings were compromised. They thus had to have myths, ideas, and ideologies to prop up their legitimacy.

Ideas

The extension of state activities in the seventeenth century was accompanied by a number of ideas that explained and justified them. We cannot say that ideas caused the practices or vice versa. Both were closely intertwined. In some cases ideas seemed to precede practices; in others, the reverse was the case. We have to see both ideas and practices as reinforcing each other.

The most important ideas associated with the seventeenth-century state reflected declining patrimonialism. Already in the fifteenth-century Italian city-states the concept of *raison d'état* – the differentiation between the private interests of the ruler and the welfare of the state – developed. Although Machiavelli's great *problematique* in *The Prince* was how leaders can retain power, the text is filled with references to the notion of public responsibility. In seventeenth-century thinking, the prince was not free to do as he pleased. He was constrained by law, by God's intentions, and by the welfare of the body politic. All his or her actions had to be undertaken within the context of an obligation to the state.

To legitimize the great power grabs and taxation for supporting armies and bureaucracies, the monarchs required ideological justifications. Theories of the divine origins of royal rule provided the main ideas. Robert Filmer (1588–1653) developed the most exhaustive treatment of the issue, although his ideas were mainly expansions of notions appearing already in the sixteenth century. [. . .]

But it may be a paradox that while publicists and ideologues of the royal houses were busy developing theories of absolutism against the claims of local authorities and bodies, another theory of rights was also becoming established. This was the right to private property, another revolutionary concept and one that placed serious constraints on the royal prerogative to tax. It also distinguished the European form of absolutism from its parallels in the Ottoman Empire, Shogun Japan, or Imperial China. The age of absolutist public authority in Europe was, as Perry Anderson suggests, also the age in which 'absolute' private property was progressively consolidated. To the extent that this was the case, absolute rule was inherently limited.[2]

In addition to the basis of their rule, European dynasts also needed ideas to justify and explain the significant increases in seventeenth-century state extraction. The Cameralists and Mercantilists provided them. Reason of state – the long-term welfare of the community – requires public finances and economic leadership. Only the state can provide it, and thus it must become the main productive force. Everything within an organic society requires its own proportionate place in a complex economic and social structure. [. . .]

We see here a notion of a contract: the government can extract, but it can do so only to redistribute what it takes in terms of government functions to provide security from external threats and to protect the life and property of royal subjects. This is a distinctly public view of finances and implies constraints on frivolous spending. The state is an agent of redistribution, not an agent for the personal gain of the monarch. So, despite terms such as absolutism and the venal practices of the Spanish and French kings of the period, the political vocabulary and discourses of the seventeenth century abound with notions of constraint, obligations, and responsibilities. The distinction between the public and dynastic interests in government was becoming more common, although in France it did not become firmly established until the 1789 revolution. [. . .]

But perhaps the most influential ideas surrounding statehood in the early modern period derived from the logic and political demands of the Reformation. The Lutheran claims against the Roman church constituted a major assault on the bases of Catholic influence (and even authority) throughout Europe. The idea that the princes should have the authority to determine the religion of their subjects (the Peace of Augsburg, 1555), and thus that religion is essentially a *local* affair, undermined the medieval cosmology of a united and organic Christian community. And in order to make claims to freedom of religious choice stick, the Lutheran and Calvinist rulers in the Holy Roman Empire and elsewhere had to mobilize all resources available to turn themselves into powerful states. [. . .]

Norms

The main moral and legal canon surrounding the seventeenth-century state was sovereignty, or supreme rule within the realm. It was at once an aspiration, a fragile fact, and a norm in the sense that it provided a standard against which royal behavior and status could be measured and judged. Europe's rulers had been making assertions of sovereignty for several centuries, often without much effect either internally or externally. By the seventeenth century, however, sets of ideas had defined in considerable detail that which was sought, for example, by fourteenth-century kings in their long efforts to free themselves from the competition and control of the church. Henry VIII's final takeover of the church and its properties, his establishment of the Church of England, and the extension of his authority over numerous ecclesiastical matters was a major watershed, one that others sought to emulate later. By the sixteenth century, writers and publicists had begun to enunciate what was appearing in practice: the increased concentration of power and authority around the royal figure. Jean Bodin (1530–96) was among the first to offer a conceptual solution to the wars, revolutions, and general chaos of the times: a clear-cut statement that order must rely upon some continuous and legitimate authority that transcends a particular ruler. Sovereignty, he suggested in his *Six Books on the Commonwealth* (1576), is an "absolute and perpetual power vested in the commonwealth" but exercised by one center, whether a monarch, an assembly, or an aristocracy. Sovereignty does not lie with an individual or group, but is an attribute of the commonwealth. Bodin rejected medieval notions of shared sovereignty – as between landed estates, town assemblies, and territorial princes – and insisted it is indivisible. The essential idea is that there can be no competing authority (as distinct from power) either within or exterior to the realm. The facts may differ, but sovereignty is the norm. Anything that deviates from the norm is thus a violation, an injustice, a wrong, or an error that must be remedied. Sovereignty is not a status or condition that fluctuates (a variable) with the rising and falling fortunes of individual leaders. It is an attribute of a continuous and distinct political community inhabiting a defined realm. It cannot wax and wane, be shared, or diluted. States may be big or small, weak or strong, peaceful or chaotic, but so long as there is exclusive legal authority – the *right* to make and apply laws for the community – there is sovereignty. By the end of the seventeenth century, town assemblies might draft or alter local laws but such initiatives required implicit or explicit royal consent. And, finally, only sovereigns could send diplomatic delegations abroad, establish embassies, and make treaties with other sovereigns.

The Peace of Westphalia

Ideas, practices, and norms of stateness and sovereignty were intermingled in the two treaties negotiated at Osnabrück and Münster that comprised the 1648 Peace of Westphalia. The lengthy document includes a long list of territorial revisions, exchanges of towns, castles, and fortifications, compensation for some of the noble victims of war, a nascent scheme for conflict resolution, the elevation of France and Sweden as guarantors of the treaty, and many other matters. It does not, however, mention the word sovereignty. Yet the 1648 settlement was a watershed because it engraved in Europe's first great multilateral treaty the essential ideas of sovereignty. [. . .]

The late seventeenth-century state in many parts of Europe now contained most of the ingredients of our definition of a state: territoriality, at least the beginning of a distinction between private and public realms (the distinction between dynastic and state interests), the institutionalization of political bodies guaranteeing continuity through time, multifunctional tasks, and legitimate authority. It lacked, nevertheless, a sound basis in a sense of community or loyalty. Individuals may or may not have felt loyalty to the royal figure – most were probably indifferent – but there was little sense of a national community. Hobbes' "commonweal" was made up of atomistic individuals, not of a society as we understand the term today. Indeed, most political thought of the era was highly individualistic, whether discussing political and property rights, or the duties of obedience to the absolute ruler. The nation part of the state, the idea of group solidarity and identity, did not appear widely until the nineteenth century.

Nation and state in nineteenth-century Europe: growing complexity

The English and French revolutions of 1688 and 1789 largely destroyed the normative bases of royal rule and substituted for them the novel idea that authority derives ultimately from the people. The ideas of popular sovereignty and rule by consent were truly revolutionary and helped pave the way for the concept of citizenship (resurrected by the French from Roman usage) which in turn was linked to the rights of individuals.

The concept of the citizen, while still individualistic, nevertheless suggests a larger body, a community of citizens. At the time of the French Revolution, those who had been royal subjects automatically became French citizens. Theorists and politicians of the age now portrayed France as a community of citizens transcending the diversity of languages, dialects, religions, and races that existed within the traditional boundaries of the French kingdom.

This community was not, however, a spontaneous emanation from revolutionary citizens. Throughout Europe, the state itself took the lead in creating a sense of national community.

It did this through its control of education, through the promotion and/or suppression of local languages and dialects, and through military conscription. It also employed the traditional means of military displays and pomp to inculcate feelings of loyalty. The development of a sense of nationhood took many different forms and occurred in different places at different times. [. . .]

Among the other innovations of the nineteenth century, we can add the following:

- a single currency and fiscal system
- a national language(s) that superseded or supplemented local languages
- national armies based on conscription from among the entire male population
- national police organizations to enforce a disarmed public and to engage in various forms of social surveillance and coercion against criminal (and sometimes political) activity
- the greatly expanded social and commercial services provided by the state, to include education and some elementary welfare services, all of which in the seventeenth century had been provided through private means such as extended families and the church
- state leadership in organizing, funding, and regulating industrialization
- the direct involvement of citizens in local, regional, and national governance through legislative and other types of deliberative bodies.

Two other characteristics of the nineteenth-century state were particularly important. Governance became increasingly based on legal means and deliberative processes, and less on royal whims, prejudices, and status considerations that were so prominent in seventeenth- and eighteenth-century rule. [. . .]

The second extraordinary characteristic of the late nineteenth-century state was its militarization. Between 1880 and 1914 most European states built massive military machines costing an ever-increasing proportion of national wealth. Finer cites a few figures that are symbolic of the trend. British military expenditures in the last decade of the nineteenth century amounted to about £36 million.[3] In the next decade they increased to £876 million, that is, more than a twenty-fold expansion within less than twenty years. [. . .]

The contemporary state

The critical importance of states as the main agents of international relations and the essential format for protecting, promoting, and sustaining the national community is revealed in part by their numbers. In the medieval era, there were about five hundred polities with some state-like characteristics. Through the processes of aggregation, integration, marriages, and conquests these units eventually emerged as twenty-one states, principalities, and independent cities in Europe in 1875. [. . .]

In the twentieth century there were three major explosions of state-making: the first in 1919, the second in the three decades after World War II, and the third in the early 1990s. In all cases, war was the main engine of historical change. In 1918–19 a number of constituent nationalities within the great empires of central Europe and the Balkans revolted and achieved independence. The new states ran from Finland in the north to Yugoslavia in the south. Now Europe suddenly had eight more states, actually nine since Norway had peacefully seceded from Sweden in 1905. The second great wave of state-making followed World War II. It started in 1947 with India's independence and was essentially completed by 1975 with the withdrawal of Portugal from Angola and Mozambique. Fifty-one governments signed the Charter of the United Nations in 1945. By 1970 the organization had 150 members. During this same period Cyprus, Malta, East Germany, Greenland, and Iceland joined the roster of European states, which, however, had lost Estonia, Latvia, and Lithuania through Soviet conquests in 1940.

After the end of the Cold War, a raft of new states appeared, including thirteen former republics of the Soviet Union. They achieved independence primarily through peaceful means. Yugoslavia, however, broke up into its constituent republics through violence and massive orgies of killing and ethnic cleansing. If we include Russia, Ukraine, Belarus, and the rest of the former Soviet republics, today Europe is composed of fifty-one countries compared with twenty-one in 1875. Worldwide, candidates for future statehood include Montenegro, Palestine, the Faroe Islands, Turkish Cyprus, and Somaliland. Any number of armed secessionist movements in what used to be known as the Third World could push the number higher. United Nations membership will probably reach 200 within the next decade. [. . .]

The practices of contemporary statehood

Among the many new and growing functions of the state, moral and ethical leadership, regulation, and instruction are significant. In the European context at the time of the early Westphalian state, religious institutions sustained these tasks. Today, in states where religious and government institutions are separate, they share these functions, but with one big difference: religious institutions do not have enforcement capacity. Most contemporary states set limits, regulate, or otherwise define policies relating to population growth and sexual relations, and to the sale and/or possession of alcohol, tobacco, and drugs. They propagate norms relating to behaviors of citizenship, and define a host of regulations governing other private activities. In states where religious and state institutions are not separated (e.g., Iran) the state may establish regulations that guide the full range of public and private behavior, from codes of dress, through appropriate relationships between the sexes, to what individuals may read or watch on television. As the name implies, in states with totalitarian regimes (e.g., North Korea) there is no realm of "private" behavior; the state regulates every facet of individuals' lives, including what, where, and how much they eat! The state is much more than an administrative or justice-providing institution. It has become the great moral teacher and regulator.

The multifunctional tasks of governments have to be paid for. State practices in the twentieth century included massive intervention in the market economy and dramatic growth of taxation. The standardized universal income tax is an invention of the twentieth century – imposed in most countries as a temporary measure to finance participation in World War I – and has grown to extract prodigious proportions of personal wealth. In a typical OECD country today, government receipts, mostly through taxes, constitute more than 40 percent of the Gross Domestic Product (GDP). [. . .]

Ideas

The ways we look at the world, perceive events, and conduct our daily activities – our mental frames of reference – are highly conditioned by statehood and our ideas about states. So are our identities. Nationality and occupation are among the main forms of identity today as anyone learns quickly when traveling abroad. They were not several centuries ago, when religion and family lineage were of greater importance. Our statistics, our political systems, and our plethora of political symbols all derive from "stateness." Most people are roughly familiar with the geography and history of their own country. The further one moves away, however, the more public knowledge dissipates. Even among political elites, knowledge of other countries and cultures is often rudimentary, highly stereotyped, and often just plain wrong. Large numbers of people throughout the world maintain suspicious attitudes toward anything that is "foreign." [. . .]

Norms

The predominant norm of statehood today is self-rule. We no longer tolerate one "people" ruling over others, even if it is not in a colonial-type relationship. In the seventeenth and eighteenth centuries there was nothing peculiar about a German from Hanover becoming the king of England, or a Swedish king exercising sovereignty over Lübeck, a German city, or of the Spanish king as sovereign over Naples. This was normal practice. In contrast, the norms of statehood in the Versailles Treaty and the League of Nations Covenant sustain a view of the state as a contiguous entity based on distinct peoples who have self-rule, that is, government by "one's own". Under contemporary international law, a polity that does not have self-rule cannot become a state. It is some sort of dependency, and thus does not have a crucial element of statehood. [. . .]

The norms of self-determination and self-rule have helped to create more than 140 new states since 1945, and to de-legitimize all forms of imperial or suzerain-type relationships. The self-ruling state is now universally recognized and assumed to be the "natural" form of political organization. But in some cases the realities of statehood are not consistent with the norms. Some states have collapsed, others, like some of their seventeenth-century predecessors, cannot establish effective authority over their territories, and still others remain states primarily by virtue of outside support. While the state is the predominant form of legitimate authority over distinct societies, it is by no means universally successful.

The problem of weak states

[. . .] Unlike their European predecessors, however, most post-1945 states began with democratic constitutions, and with an international set of norms that promoted and sustained self-determination, self-government, and independence. Many of these paraphernalia of popular sovereignty were "delivered" as part of the de-colonization process. But the problem was that many of the colonies-turned-states were in fact fictions. They had the appurtenances of states – flags, armies, capital cities, legislatures, and ambassadors – but they did not have the other requisites of statehood, such as a clear distinction between public and private realms, government institutionalization, and effective multifunctionality. Most had only weak civil societies. Many were polities, but not functioning states as we have defined them. Few populations had deeply ingrained senses of national identity; most, in fact, remained primordial, fixed around clans, tribes, religious groups, or limited geographic regions. The fiat of the "national" government often extended no further than the suburbs of the capital city, beyond which local leaders, based on a variety of claims to legitimacy, ruled. The modern symbol of sovereignty, a monopoly over the legitimate use of force, plus the effective disarmament of society, existed more in rhetoric than in fact.

These and other characteristics of some new states constitute a syndrome that Barry Buzan has called the *weak state* and Robert Jackson has termed *quasi-states*.[4] The terms may differ, but the phenomena to which they direct attention are similar. Weak states have all the attributes of sovereignty for external purposes – they are full members of the international community and have exactly the same legal standing as the oldest or most powerful states in the system – but they severely lack the internal attributes of sovereignty. [. . .]

Weak and failed (or collapsed) states became the object of considerable attention during the 1990s. With the end of the Cold War, analysts began to acknowledge that rebellions, civil wars, and massacres taking place in the Third World and elsewhere were not just the manifestations of great power competition or ideological incompatibilities. Suddenly, observers discovered the phenomenon of "ethnic wars," overlooking the fact that wars within states having nothing to do with Cold War competition had been part of the Third World landscape for many years. Civil wars and wars of secession in Burma, Sudan, Eritrea, Nigeria, and elsewhere long preceded the collapse of the Berlin Wall.

Some states have moved from original weakness to collapse. They are the ultimate failures of contemporary statehood. In 1991, Somalia became the symbol of the *collapsed state*, ostensibly a new phenomenon in international politics. Lebanon in 1976, Angola and Mozambique (perhaps more aborted than collapsed states because they began to fall apart immediately upon independence) and Chad between 1980 and 1982 all had the symptoms of the state moving toward collapse. [. . .]

On the other hand, many originally weak states have avoided or overcome the syndrome and today function much as their European forebears. Singapore, Malaysia, Mauritius, Tanzania, Barbados, and Trinidad are prominent examples. But a fair number of former colonies cannot yet sustain the qualities of statehood outlined earlier, including effective control over a defined territory, a clear distinction between public and private realms, political institutionalization, and effective multifunctionality.

One final characteristic of weak states needs emphasis because it is largely an artifact of the twentieth century and finds no predecessors in the state-building enterprise in Europe during the early modern period. Unlike Hobbes' Leviathan, which had the main purpose of maintaining order and providing security for members of the commonwealth, many weak states have been a major threat to their populations. The state, instead of being a vessel of security and national community, has become a menace to parts of its population. Since World War II, more people have been killed by the agents of their own state than by foreign invaders. Where the state is captured by one individual or a political clique that has no foundation in popular legitimacy, opposition to arbitrary rule is often met by widespread oppression and killing. The citizens of Kampuchea, Equatorial Guinea, China, or Uganda in the 1970s, of South Africa at the height of apartheid in the 1980s, or of Rwanda in 1994 and Sudan today faced murderous regimes that in some cases have counted their victims in the hundreds of thousands, and even in millions. Such are the sources of secessionism. The seventeenth century did not have precedents for the many politicides of the past one hundred years.

The state and change: the case for transformation

[. . .] The literature on this question is notable more for its volume and scope of assertions than for systematic empirical inquiry. Much is claimed, but not much has been verified according to the methodological canons of the social sciences. Yet, the case has become so prominent that it has almost become conventional wisdom. The state is in the process of transformation toward weakness. If present trends continue, the transformation will be toward obsolescence.

Transformationalists approach the problem from two perspectives. The first suggests that the *authority* of the state is "leaking," "moving up," or "evaporating" toward forces, agents, and entities beyond it, including international organizations, transnational associations, the global market, or the global civil society. The second suggests that *individuals within* states are increasingly questioning the authority of the state, withholding loyalty to it, and developing new loyalties toward more accommodating or psychologically satisfying identity groups such as ethnic associations, churches, and regional groupings. [. . .]

The late Susan Strange, a noted international political economist, presents an exemplary and robust case for the first type of state transformation in her study *The Retreat of the State*.[5] Her main thesis is that state power and authority are "leaking" to globalized markets and their main agents, transnational corporations (TNCs), to international criminals, and to international organizations. [. . .]

Strange examines recent trends in the three sectors to support this basic position. There are numerous interesting and compelling illustrations as, for example, the multi-billion-dollar international drug trade that not only escapes government efforts to curtail it, but actually involves collusion because governments have been unwilling to regulate the banks through which the profits of the trade are "laundered." [. . .]

In addition to the cases Strange discusses, we might add the role of the World Bank (IBRD) and International Monetary Fund (IMF), both international organizations that help sustain the globalizing world economy. A weak developing country seeking outside support has little choice but to accept the "conditionality" attached to loans. [. . .] Can we then speak of states as critical agents in the international political realm when the real locus of authority and power today resides outside the country? Overall, in Strange's estimation, the authority of the state is "retreating," a trend that in the long run portends obsolescence.

James Rosenau has made one of the most interesting arguments regarding the erosion of state authority through shifting loyalties and the appearance of various particularisms – the second approach to state obsolescence or regression.[6] He emphasizes phenomena such as declining loyalties to the state as seen, for example, in resistance to conscription, in tax cheating and evasion, migration, and declining voter participation. Increasingly people judge states not on the basis of presumed authority, but by performance. When states fail to perform according to expectations, people resist, withdraw, or shift their loyalties in other ways. The explanation lies in the increased analytical skills of people gained through universal education, increased literacy, and the availability of new information technologies. If many people no longer submit automatically to state authority, then either loyalty will be directed elsewhere to polities that can effectively challenge the state, or in the extreme, the state may become obsolete or in some other way become transformed. The trend is already well on the way, for authority is escaping both to the outside and within the state. [. . .]

Critique of the state transformation/ obsolescence argument

The arguments for transformation and/or obsolescence are partly persuasive, even if based on highly selected indicators and cases. Five major theoretical difficulties come to mind, however: (1) confusion of influence and power with authority; (2) conceptions of power based on zero-sum assumptions; (3) lack of benchmarks; (4) confusion of the legitimacy of the state with the performance of governments; and (5) setting the bar of state authority too high. There are also a number of empirical difficulties. [. . .]

To claim that TNCs, financial markets, drug cartels, and international organizations all have power in international political relationships and over states is undeniable. But that is not the same as having authority over states and it does not mean that state authority is retreating. It may mean, however, that states are increasingly constrained in their freedom to make policy choices. States may be losing autonomy (although this is also arguable), but this is not the same as losing authority.

A second problem is that Strange assumes a zero-sum quality to power and influence. If TNCs have political influence today, she implies, it must mean that someone has lost it, and that someone is the state. In her view, it does not seem conceivable that both states and transnational actors and agents of various kinds may be increasing their power simultaneously, or that states voluntarily and purposefully increase the stature and possible influence of transnational or international bodies so as to promote their own purposes. [. . .]

Another problem with the state transformation or obsolescence argument is that it offers no benchmarks. What is the standard against which states are supposedly "eroding?" [. . .] If we use 1960 as our standard, then in some states there has been some retrenchment of state activities. But in most states the figures indicate a *slowing down of the rate of growth of state functions but no decline.* Indeed, for most industrial countries, social security transfers as a percentage of GDP actually increased through the 1970s and 1980s. This hardly comprises evidence of the transformation or obsolescence of the state. [. . .]

Rosenau's suggestion that shifting loyalties within the state are evidence of its erosion requires similar interrogation. There is, first, confusion between loyalty to a state and support of a government. Increased political participation, a widespread sense of public confidence, and increasing intellectual skills that enable citizens to judge government performance and sometimes to oust them indicates little about loyalty to the state. In virtually every polity organized as a state, there are opponents of government. In parliamentary systems, they are organized as "the loyal opposition." Millions join political parties that seek to replace incumbents. This is normal. Only in cases of secession do we see the withdrawal of loyalty to the state. Here, separatists and secessionists deny legitimacy to the state and seek to create a state of their own. But this is the key point. They are not denying the legitimacy of statehood as such, but only of a particular state.

Does the illicit drug trade, estimated to involve purchases and profits close to one trillion dollars annually and directly costing taxpayers hundreds of million dollars to control (not very successfully), indicate the loss of state authority? [. . .] Only if we assume that states have been, are, and should be omnipotent – a standard against which we can measure – could we successfully argue that the inability to control the trade in *stupefiants* represents a retreat of the state.[7] If the state did for smoking or alcohol what it has done for *stupefiants*, we would have exactly the same problem but on a more massive scale. That a state cannot effectively enforce such bans hardly warrants the conclusion that it is declining, disappearing, or transforming. *The argument sets the bar of state capacity far too high.* The failure to control effectively all trafficking in drugs may be more indicative of impossible goals than of a "retreat" of state authority.

The case for complexity

The types of changes we have seen in the contemporary state have been primarily related to the extension and proliferation of government activities, that is, to growing complexity rather than to transformation. The odds are pretty good that states as we know them will be around for a lot longer than most TNCs, transnational criminal groups, and even international organizations. The state remains the primary agent of international relationships and is the only one that has the quality and status of sovereignty. It is primarily states that create and sustain international institutions such as diplomacy, trade, international law, and the like. It is primarily states, through their practices and the ideas, beliefs, and norms that underlie them, that sustain and change those institutions. Other types of entities (e.g., banks) may create private international institutions of various kinds, but they seek to regulate only a single domain. In many cases, these sets of regulations do not *replace* the activities of states, but supplement them, or are entirely new. Collapsed or failed states show us what life would be like without states. In the absence of other more attractive alternatives, none of which seems to be on the horizon, we remain the inhabitants of an international society of states. [. . .]

Notes

1   R. Braun, "Taxation, Sociopolitical Structure, and State-Building: Great Britain and Branden-burg-Prussia" in C. Tilly (ed.), *The Formation of National States in Western Europe* (Princeton University Press, Princeton, 1975), p. 311.
2   P. Anderson, *Lineages of the Absolute State* (Verso, London, 1979), p. 429.
3   S. Finer, "State- and Nation-Building in Europe: The Role of the Military" in C. Tilly (ed.), *The Formation of National States in Western Europe* (Princeton University Press, Princeton, 1975), p. 162.
4   B. Buzan, *People, States and Fear: The National Security Problem in International Relations*, 2nd edition (Harvester-Wheatsheaf, London, 1991) and R. Jackson, *Quasi States: Sovereignty, International Relations and the Third World* (Cambridge University Press, Cambridge, 1990).
5   S. Strange, *The Retreat of the State: The Diffusion of Power in the World Economy* (Cambridge University Press, Cambridge, 1996).
6   J. Rosenau, *Turbulence in World Politics: A Theory of Change and Continuity* (Princeton University Press, Princeton, 1990).
7   I prefer the French term for mind-altering drugs because it more clearly indicates the consequences of their use and does not confuse them with legitimate medicines.

1.2 The idea of the state and national security

Barry Buzan

Source: *People, States and Fear: The National Security Problem in International Relations* (Harvester-Wheatsheaf, Brighton, 1983), pp. 44–53.

Buzan argues that the state is an ambiguous component in world politics, reflecting a variety of forces and processes. In this extract, his central concern is with the purposes expressed by states, and in particular with the ways in which ideas and values provide a 'cement' for states and their identity. A specific manifestation of state purposes is the notion of national security, and much of Buzan's argument refers to this.

The idea of the state

The notion of purpose is what distinguishes the idea of the state from its physical base and its institutions. The physical base simply exists, and has to be dealt with because of that fact. The institutions are created to govern, and to make the state work, but their functional logic falls a long way short of defining the totality of the state. Although institutions are, as we shall see, closely tied to aspects of the idea of the state, it is, as Kenneth Dyson points out, a 'category error' to conflate the idea of the state with its apparatus.[1] The European Community, for example, has institutions, but to the dismay of Mitrany-style functionalist theorists and others, these have failed by themselves to act as a gravitational core for the accretion of a European super-state. The missing element is a sense of purpose. No consensus exists about what the Community should be doing, how it should be doing it, or what it should, as an evolving political entity, be striving to become. With states, we should expect to find a clearer sense of both purpose and form, a distinctive idea of some sort which lies at the heart of the state's political identity. What does the state exist to do? Why is it there? What is its relation to the society which it contains? Why some particular size and form of state, when a glance at any historical atlas will reveal a variety of possible alternatives? In defining the idea of the state, reference to basic functions of providing civil order, collective goods and external defence does not take us very far. Although these functional considerations inevitably form part of the idea of the state, they indicate little about what binds the people into an entity which requires such services. Something more than a simple desire to escape the state of nature is at work in the creation and maintenance of states. Otherwise there would be no barrier to the founding of a universal state which would solve the state of nature problem without causing the troublesome intermediary of a fragmented international system of sovereign states.

A broad hint as to one direction worth exploring in search of the idea of the state is given by the term national security itself. Why *national* security? National security implies strongly that the object of security is the nation, and this raises questions about the links between nation and state. A nation is defined as a large group of people sharing the same cultural, and possibly the same racial, heritage, and normally living in one area. If the nation and the state coincide, then we can look for the purpose of the state in the protection and expression of an independently existing cultural entity: nation would define much of the relationship between state and society. This fact would give us some handles on what values might be at stake, and what priorities they might have, in the definition of national security. If the purpose of the state is to protect and express a cultural group, then life and culture must come high on the list of national security priorities. A pure modal of the nation-state would require that the nation precede the state, and in a sense give rise to it, as in the case of Japan, China, Germany and others. But it is obvious from a quick survey of the company of states that very few of them fit this model. Some nations have no state, like the Kurds, the Palestinians, the Armenians, and, before 1947, the Jews. Many nations are divided into more than one state, like the Koreans, the Germans, the Irish and the Chinese. And some states contain several nations, like India, the Soviet Union, Nigeria and the United Kingdom.

Given this evidence, either national security in a strict sense is a concept with only limited application to the state, or else the relationship between state and nation is more complex than that suggested by the primal model. The definition of nation imposes no condition of permanence, and since both culture and race are malleable qualities, there is no reason why states cannot create nations as well as be created by them. The United States provides an outstanding example of this process by which diverse territories and peoples can be forged into a self-regarding nation by the conscious action of the state. The possibility of state institutions being used to create nations, as well as just expressing them, considerably complicates and enriches the idea of nation. Since nations represent a pattern which covers the whole fabric of humanity, new nations cannot be created without destroying, or at least overlaying, old ones. The only exception to this rule is where new nations can be created on previously uninhabited territory, since mere emigration need not destroy the contributing nation(s). The United States benefited from this factor, though it destroyed the Indian nations in the process, but contemporary efforts at nation-building must take place in the more difficult context of *in situ* populations, there being no more large, habitable areas outside state control.

One obvious implication of this expanded view of the nation is that extensive grounds for conflict exist between natural nations and the attempts of states to create nations which coincide with their boundaries. The civil war in Nigeria, and the struggles of the Kurds, illustrate this problem, which provides an ironic level of contradiction in the meaning of national security. Clearly, from the point of view of efficient government, having state and nation coincide provides tremendous advantages in terms of unifying forces, ease of communication, definition of purpose, and such-like. The nation-state is therefore a powerful ideal, if not a widespread reality.

From this discussion we can conclude that the link between state and nation is not simple, and that the nation as the idea of the state, particularly in national security terms, will not be simple either. Several models of possible nation-state links suggest themselves. First is the primal *nation-state*, of which Japan is probably the strongest example. Here the nation precedes the state, and plays a major role in giving rise to it. The state's purpose is to protect and express the nation, and the bond between the two is deep and profound. The nation provides the state with both a strong identity in the international arena, and a solid base of domestic legitimacy – solid enough to withstand revolutionary upheavals, as in the case of France at the end of the eighteenth century, or defeat and occupation by foreign powers, as in the case of France and Japan during the 1940s.

The second model has been called the *state-nation*, since the state plays an instrumental role in creating the nation, rather than the other way around. The model is top-down rather than bottom-up. As suggested above, this process is easiest to perform when populations have been largely transplanted from elsewhere to fill an empty, or weakly held, territory. Thus the United States, Australia and many Latin American countries provide the best models. The state generates and propagates uniform cultural elements like language, arts, custom and law, so that over time these take root and produce a distinctive, nation-like, cultural entity which identifies with the state. Citizens begin to attach their primary social loyalties to the state-nation, referring to themselves as Americans, Chileans, Australians, and such-like, and eventually, if all works well, an entity is produced which is similar in all respects except history to a primal nation-state. The state-nation model can also be tried in places where the state incorporates a multitude of nationalities, though here it requires the subordination of the indigenous nations on their own territory, a much tougher task than the incorporation of uprooted immigrants. Many African states, faced with complex tribal divisions, seem to look to the state-nation process as their salvation, and even a multination state like India sometimes appears to lean in this direction.

While a mature state-nation like the United States will differ little from a nation-state in respect of the security implications of the state–nation link, immature state-nations like Nigeria will be highly vulnerable and insecure in this regard. The idea of the state as represented by the nation will be weakly developed and poorly established, and thus vulnerable to challenge and interference from within and without. Separatists may try to opt out, as the Ibos did in Nigeria. Or one domestic group may try to capture the nation-building process for its own advantage, as the whites tried to do in Rhodesia. Or the whole fragile process may be penetrated by stronger external cultures, as symbolised by the 'Coca-colaisation' of many Third World states, and the general complaint about western cultural imperialism. So long as such states fail to solve their nationality problem, they remain vulnerable to dismemberment, intervention, instability and internal conflict in ways not normally experienced by states in harmony with their nations.

The third model is the *part-nation-state*. This is where a nation is divided up among two or more states, and where the population of each state consists largely of people from that nation. Thus, the Korean, Chinese, and until 1973 the Vietnamese nations were divided into two states, while the German nation is split among three, though here some might argue that Austria, like Denmark and the Netherlands, is sufficiently distinctive to count as a nation in its own right. This model does not include nations split up among several states, but not dominant in any, like the Kurds. A variant of this model is where a nation-state exists, but a minority of its members fall outside its boundaries, living as minority groups in neighbouring states. Germany during the 1920s and 1930s, and Somalia today, illustrate this case. The mystique of the unified nation-state frequently exercises a strong hold on part-nation-states, and can easily become an obsessive and overriding security issue. Rival part-nation-states like East and West Germany, and North and South Korea, almost automatically undermine each other's legitimacy, and the imperative for reunification is widely assumed to be an immutable factor that will re-emerge whenever opportunity beckons. Germany's reunification drive during the 1930s, and Vietnam's epic struggle of nearly three decades, illustrate the force of this drive, and explain the intractable nature of what is still referred to as 'the German problem' in Europe. Part-nation-states frequently commit themselves to an intense version of the state-nation process in an attempt to build up their legitimacy by differentiating their part of the nation from the other parts. The frenzied competition between the two systems in North and South Korea provides perhaps the best contemporary illustration of this strategy, which, given time, has some prospects of success. Part-nation-states, then, can represent a severe source of insecurity both to themselves and to others. Their case offers the maximum level of contradiction in the idea of national security as applied to states, for it is precisely the nation that makes the idea of the state insecure.

The fourth model can be called the *multination-state*, and comprises those states which contain two or more substantially complete nations within their boundaries. Two sub-types exist within this model which are sufficiently distinct almost to count as models in their own right, and we can label these the *federative state* and the *imperial state*. Federative states, at least in theory, reject the nation-state as the ideal type of state. By federative, we do not simply mean any state with a federal political structure, but rather states which contain two or more nations without trying to impose an artificial state-nation over them. Separate nations are allowed, even encouraged, to pursue their own identities, and attempts are made to structure the state in such a way that no one nationality comes to dominate the whole state structure. Canada and Jugoslavia offer clear examples of this model, and countries like Czechoslovakia, the United Kingdom, New Zealand and India can be interpreted at least partly along these lines. Obviously, the idea of a federative state cannot be rooted in nationalism, and this fact leaves a dangerous political void at the heart of the state. The federative state has to justify itself by appeal to less emotive ideas like economies of scale – the argument that the component nations are too small by themselves to generate effective nation-states under the geopolitical circumstances in which they are located. Such states have no natural unifying principle, and consequently are more vulnerable to dismemberment, separatism and political interference than are nation-states. Nationality issues pose a constant source of insecurity for the state, as illustrated by Jugoslavia, and national security can be easily threatened by purely political action, as in the case of General de Gaulle's famous 1967 'Vive le Québec libre' speech in Canada.

Imperial states are those in which one of the nations within the state dominates the state structures to its own advantage. The hegemony of the Great Russians within the Tsarist and Soviet states provides one example, the dominance of the Punjabis in Pakistan another. Several kinds of emphasis are possible within an imperial state. The dominant nation may seek to suppress the other nationalities by means ranging from massacre to cultural and racial absorption, with a view to transforming itself into something like a nation-state. It may seek simply to retain its dominance, using the machinery of the state to enforce its position without trying to absorb or eliminate other groups, or it may adopt the more subtle approach of cultivating a non-nationalist ideology which appears to transcend the national issue while in fact perpetuating the status quo. Imperial states contain possibilities of transformation into all the other types, and, like federative states, are vulnerable to threats aimed at their national divisions. Such states may be threatened by separatism, as in Ethiopia, by shifts in the demographic balance of the nations, as often mooted about the Soviet Union, or by dismemberment, as in the case of Pakistan. The stability of the imperial state depends on the ability of the dominant nation to retain its control. If its ability is weakened either by internal developments or external intervention, the state structure stands at risk of complete collapse, as in the case of Austria-Hungary after the First World War. Political threats are thus a key element in the national security problem of imperial states.

These models represent ideal types, and as with any such classification, not all real world cases fit smoothly into them. Numerous ambiguities occur on the boundaries of the models, and some minor 'special case' categories can be found. Switzerland, for example, contains fragments of three nations organised along federative lines, but has no distinctive or dominant national group of its own. France fits most closely into the nation-state mould, but

Breton nationalists might claim with some justice that, from their minority viewpoint, the French state appears more imperial in nature. Similarly, French-Canadians might claim that Canada is more imperial than federative, just as smaller and weaker groups in Jugoslavia complain about Serbian dominance. Conversely, imperial states like the Soviet Union may try to disguise themselves as federative ones. Appearances may also be deceptive in that periods of strength and prosperity may hide domestic rifts and give the appearance of a nation-state, only to give way to separatism when prosperity or central authority diminishes. The rise of regional nationalism in declining Britain illustrates this case.

Despite these difficulties, the models give us a useful framework within which to consider the links between state and nation. They make it clear that national security with regard to the nation can be read in several different ways, and that consequently different states will experience very different kinds of insecurity and security in relation to the nationality question. Some states may derive great strength from their link to the nation, whereas for others the links between state and nation might define their weakest and most vulnerable point. The importance of the nation as a vital component in the idea of the state has to be measured externally as well as internally. Unless the idea of the state is firmly planted in the minds of the population, the state as a whole has no secure foundation. Equally, unless the idea of the state is firmly planted in the 'minds' of other states, the state has no secure environment. Because the idea of national self-rule has a high legitimacy in the international system, a firmly established link between state and nation acts as a powerful moderator on the unconstrained operation of the international anarchy, and is therefore a vital element of national security. We shall explore this point in more detail when we come to look at international security. On that level, the confluence between the nation as a legitimising idea underpinning the state, and sovereignty, as the principal idea underpinning the anarchical society of the international system as a whole, becomes centrally important to developing a concept of international security.

While the concept of nation provides us with considerable insight into the idea of the state, it falls short of exhausting the subject. Nationalism adds a fundamental and ubiquitous demographic factor to the basic functions of the state, but it still leaves plenty of room for additional notions of purpose. There is great scope for variety in the way in which the state fulfils its responsibility to the nation, and there is even scope for higher ideological purposes aimed at transcending nationalism. These additional notions, however, differ from nationalism in that they tend to be less deeply-rooted, and therefore more vulnerable to disruption. A firmly established nation reproduces itself automatically by the transfer of culture to the young, and once established is extremely difficult to remove by measures short of obliteration. The well-founded nation is, in this sense, more stable and more secure than the state. What might be called the 'higher' ideas of the state, such as its principles of political organisation, are fragile by comparison, and thus more sensitive as objects of security. For example, fascism as an idea of the state was largely purged out of Germany, Japan and Italy by relatively brief and mild periods of foreign occupation. Similar measures would scarcely have dented the sense of nation in those countries.

The idea of the state can take many forms at this higher level, and our purposes here do not require us to explore these definitively. An indication of the types and range will suffice to give us an adequate sense of their security implication. Organising ideologies are perhaps the most obvious type of higher idea of the state. These can take the form of identification with some fairly general principle, like Islam or democracy, or some more specific doctrine, like republicanism. Many varieties of political, economic, religious and social ideology can serve as an idea of the state, and will be closely connected to the state's institutional structures. In some cases, an organising ideology will be so deeply ingrained into the state that change would have transformational, or perhaps fatal, implications. Democracy and capitalism, for example, are so basic to the construction of the United States that it is hard to imagine the American state without them. In other cases, organising ideologies have only shallow roots, and large changes in official orientation occur frequently. Many Third World states display this tendency, as organising ideologies come and go with different leaderships, never having time to strike deeper roots among the population. Since these ideologies address the bases of relations between state and society they define the conditions for both harmony and conflict in domestic politics. If the ideas themselves are weak; or if they are weakly held within society; or if strongly held, but opposed, ideas compete within society; then the state stands on fragile foundations.

Different organising ideologies may represent different ends, as in the case of the Islamic state which emerged in Iran after the fall of the Shah, in comparison with the monarchist and materialist values which preceded it. But they may also represent different convictions about means, as in the liberal democratic versus the communist approaches to achieving material prosperity. They can also come in both positive and negative forms. The United States, for instance, pursues democracy and capitalism as positive values, but at the same time gives anti-communism almost equal weight as a negative organising principle. Since organising ideologies are so closely tied to state institutions, we can deal with much of their security side when we discuss the institutional component of the state.

Other concepts can also serve as, or contribute to, the idea of the state. A sense of national purpose can spring from ideas about racial preservation, as in South Africa, or from ideas relating to a larger civilisation, as in pre-1917 Russian images of the Tsarist empire as a third Rome. Even simple fear or hatred of some external group might provide a substantial part of the idea of the state. One would expect to find this in a state occupying a highly exposed position, as, for example, in the Austrian empire at the height of the Ottoman expansions. Power [. . .] can also be seen as a purpose of the state. In a pure Realist view, states seek power not only as a means to protect or pursue other values, but also as a means of advancing themselves in the Social-Darwinistic universe of the international system. Power is thus the end, as well as the means, of survival, each state struggling to prove its superiority in the context of a ceaseless general competition. Each state will have its own unique idea, which in reality will be a compilation of many elements. In Japan, for example, the nation, and the values associated with national culture, would constitute a large slice of the idea of the state, but democratic and capitalist ideas would also weigh significantly. In the Soviet Union, nationalism would perhaps count for less, with pride of place going to the ideological foundations of the Soviet state.

The problem is how to apply a concept like security to something as ephemeral as an idea, or a set of ideas. Where the idea is firmly established, like that of an ancient nation, the problem of security is mitigated by the inherent difficulty of instigating change. But for higher ideas, even defining criteria for security is not easy, let alone formulating policies. Most organising ideologies are themselves essentially contested concepts, and therefore impossible to define with precision, and probably in a constant process of evolution by nature. Given this amorphous character, how is one to determine that the idea has been attacked or endangered? The classic illustration here is the old conundrum about democracy and free speech. If free speech is a necessary condition of democracy, but also a licence for anti-democratic propaganda, how does one devise a security policy for democracy? The component ideas which go to make up a concept like democracy change over time, as any history of Britain over the last two centuries will reveal. Even the cultural ideas which bind the nation do not remain constant, as illustrated by the 'generation gap' phenomena, in which older generations clash with younger ones about a wide range of cultural norms and interpretations. The natural ambiguity and flexibility of these ideas mean that security cannot be applied to them unless some criteria exist for distinguishing between acceptable and unacceptable sources and forms of change, a task beyond reasonable hope of complete fulfilment given, among other things, the weakness of our understanding of many of the cause–effect relationships involved. Ideas are, by their very nature, vulnerable to interplay with other ideas, which makes it extraordinarily difficult to apply a concept like security to them.

In part because of this indeterminate character of the ideas, it is possible to see them as potentially threatened from many quarters. Organising ideologies can be penetrated, distorted, corrupted, and eventually undermined by contact with other ideas. They can be attacked through their supporting institutions, and they can be suppressed by force. Even national cultures are vulnerable in this way, as illustrated on a small scale by French sensitivity to the penetration of the national language by English words and usages. Because of this broad spectrum vulnerability, an attempt to apply the concept of security to the idea of the state can lead to exceedingly sweeping criteria being set for attaining acceptable levels of security, a fact that can give rise to a dangerous streak of absolutism in national security policy. Making the idea of the state secure might logically be seen to require either a heavily fortified isolationism aimed at keeping out corrupting influences, or an expansionist imperial policy aimed at eliminating or suppressing threats at their source. Thus, one reading of German and Japanese expansionism up to the Second World War is that neither nation could make itself secure without dominating the countries around it. The Wilsonian idea of making the world safe for democracy by eliminating other forms of government has overtones of this theme about it, as does the idea common to many new revolutionary governments that they can only make their own revolution secure by spreading similar revolutions beyond their borders.

[. . .] it is worth considering who holds the idea of the state. An important undercurrent of the above discussion has been that a strong idea of some sort is a necessary component of a viable state, and the clear implication has been that the idea of the state must not only be coherent in its own right, but also widely held. Unless an idea is widely held, it cannot count as part of the idea of the state, but only as one of the ideas contained within the state, as in the distinction between a nation-state and a federative multi-nation state. From this perspective, it does not matter if ideas like nationalism and democracy stem from, and serve the interests of, particular groups or classes, so long as they command general support. Indeed, one of the advantages of an ambiguous idea like democracy is that its very looseness and flexibility allow it to attract a broad social consensus. Narrower ideas almost by definition imply greater difficulty in generating a popular base, and thus point to a larger role for institutions in underpinning the structure of the state. If the idea of the state is strong and widely held, then the state can endure periods of weak institutions, as France has done, without serious threat to its overall integrity. If the idea of the state is weakly held, or strongly contested, however, then a lapse in institutional strength might well bring the whole structure crashing down in revolution, civil war, or the disintegration of the state as a physical unit.

Note

1   K. Dyson, *The State Tradition in Western Europe* (Martin Robertson, Oxford, 1980), p. 3.

1.3 Continuity and change in the states system

Robert H. Jackson

Source: Robert H. Jackson and Alan James (eds), *States in a Changing World* (Clarendon, Oxford, 1993), pp. 346–7.

Jackson examines the overall dynamics and direction of the contemporary global states system in the light of a world where regions remain a significant focal point for states. He identifies four sources of change. First, an extraordinary expansion in the membership of the states system in the twentieth century that has produced a system where members possess equal statehood but very unequal power. Although many states are disintegrating, the rules of the game prevent them from going out of existence. This has helped to fuel a second dynamic, with a diminution of international war being offset by an expansion of enduring civil wars. Third, there is growing inequality between states and regions that is unlikely to diminish in the near future. Finally, despite growing regional integration, there are no signs of a new system emerging to replace the states system.

The purpose of this chapter is to identify important points of difference and similarity in the regional States systems with a view to discerning some intimations of the overall dynamics and directions of our contemporary global society of States. Are the changes which are so evident in the contemporary world, particularly economic changes but also demographic, technological, ideological, and similar changes, fostering new varieties of international and transnational organization which undermine the foundations of sovereign statehood? Is the independent State becoming obsolete at least in some respects? Or is the existing States system based on the principle of sovereignty likely to adapt without fundamental alteration to all such changes? In short, what are the prospects for sovereign statehood?

Before considering these questions it is important to emphasize that the huge diversity which exists internationally is accompanied by, or – rather – is based upon, an identity and equality of status. All the territorial units (States) which collectively make up the international society enjoy the same formal condition: they are all equally sovereign. That means, given the way in which the term is used by States to refer to their international aspect, that their Constitutions are independent of any other Constitution. It is this international autonomy, and this alone, which makes them eligible to participate in international relations in their own right. [. . .]

It is the conjunction between equal status and unequal power which gives the relations of States so much of their intellectual and political interest, especially in this democratic age. The conjunction between equality of status and inequality of stature is not in itself at all an unusual political condition: citizenship, after all, is an equal legal status shared by individuals who may be very unequal in wealth, influence, intelligence, talent, and other respects. Status and stature rarely coincide. But the substantial inequalities and disparities between the formally equal States of the world are usually far greater than those between citizens within countries, and they take effect in a democratic context which now frowns on the projection of force across international boundaries to achieve national purposes – except in very restricted circumstances, such as responses to unambiguous acts of aggression as in the case of Iraq's invasion of Kuwait or desperate humanitarian crises as in the case of political anarchy and famine in Somalia. The weakness or smallness of sovereign States was a greater international disability in the past than it is today. [. . .]

State survival

What general observations can be made concerning the relationship between equal state-hood and unequal power in the post-1945 States system? [. . .]

In the twentieth century we witnessed a remarkable proliferation of independent States due to the breakup of empires, just as the nineteenth century witnessed a corresponding reduction owing primarily to political unification in Europe and colonization in Asia and Africa.

The global society of States has settled into a conservative middle-aged pattern in which death may be postponed indefinitely despite the continuing enormous variations of power between both regions and States. States do not expire naturally and existing States would either have to be killed off or willed out of existence. Almost everywhere today, however, it is unthinkable that State jurisdictions as represented on political maps could be changed by force without the consent of the sovereign governments involved – which was the historical practice well into the present century. [. . .] Because statesmen usually will not freely choose to go out of business, most contemporary States consequently seem destined to survive indefinitely. Even the momentous transformations which resulted in the demise of East and West Germany and the birth (or rebirth) of many territorial entities which previously were subordinate parts of the former Soviet Union ultimately depended on the consent of Moscow. The Berlin wall was knocked down only after Gorbachev signalled he would do nothing to stop it from happening. [. . .]

[The] post-1945 doctrine of non-intervention (and non-colonization) is making it possible for weak and disunified States to survive which in the not very distant past might have been conquered, partitioned, or in other ways eliminated by stronger internal or external powers. This poses a novel international problem which the States system has been wrestling with since the end of colonialism: accommodating and supporting independent States (which in other eras or circumstances might not have survived or even acquired independence in the first place) while at the same time responding to humanitarian crises (which are increasingly difficult for world opinion to ignore).

Since 1945 the world has witnessed the emergence of a large number of weak States of which many are extremely disorganized and divided internally. [. . .] [T]his high birth-rate was until recently due entirely to Western decolonization in Asia, Africa, the Caribbean, and Oceania. Decolonization was one of the twentieth century's watershed changes which resulted in widespread and wholesale transfers of sovereignty from a few Western imperial States to a large number of ex-colonial Third World governments. Until recently this pro-liferation of new States seemed to be at an end. But the breakup of the Soviet and Yugoslav federations – which is strongly reminiscent of decolonization – has resulted in yet another wave of States which are either newly sovereign (e.g. Slovenia and Croatia) or have been born again (e.g. Estonia, Latvia, and Lithuania). [. . .]

The possibility of it happening elsewhere is different from one region to the next and difficult to gauge, of course, but in general it is not great. This is owing in no small part to the fact that there are no more empires or quasi-empires to decolonize – unless one conceives as quasi-empires existing multi-ethnic States which are not democracies – of which there are many in Asia and Africa. Perhaps ironically, the egalitarian ethos which has spread from domestic to international politics underwrites the legitimacy of existing territorial jurisdictions whatever their internal conditions happen to be. Power differentials between States are today as great as at any time in the centuries-long history of the modern States system – probably they are greater – but they cannot have a lawful effect in the acquisition of territory by force against the will of an existing sovereign government. The doctrine of non-intervention enshrined in Article 2 of the UN Charter forbids it and a general inclination of major powers against intervention (except where a definite national interest is at stake) reinforces it. Otherwise there is a heavy reluctance to become involved in the problems of somebody else's sovereign jurisdiction – even where there are documented massive violations of human rights, as in Bosnia-Herzegovina and Somalia in 1992.

This egalitarian doctrine represents a fundamental change in international orthodoxy. It is underestimated by many students of contemporary international relations, who have perhaps not yet adjusted theories which are still based very considerably on historical power politics. The implications are profound: for if international boundaries can no longer be redrawn as a result of force they are (for reasons stated below) probably not going to change at all – unless some exceptional event occurs in which consent to such change is given, as happened in the former Soviet Union. [. . .]

The long-term declining birth-rate of sovereign States is certainly not owing to any lack of candidates which aspire to self-determination. Sub-Saharan Africa and Latin America contain numerous ethno-linguistic groups which might opt for independence if the opportunity presented itself. There are countries in South East Asia, South Asia, and the Middle East which frustrate the desire of certain segments of their populations to become independent countries themselves or to join independent neighbours. Even a few States in Western Europe (Spain and Britain) and in North America (Canada) – which are among the most integrated countries anywhere – also have their secessionists. The fact is that the political map could be very different if groups with a desire for independent statehood were accommodated by the States system.

[. . .] The probably numerous 'ethnonations' today which do not possess sovereign statehood but harbour a desire for it are frustrated by the existing pattern of territorial jurisdiction which derives in most places from a process of colonial map-making that was often ignorant of indigenous boundaries or indifferent to them. It is interesting to speculate about the future of this sometimes violent friction between sovereign jurisdiction and ethnic identity. Fred Parkinson argues that it is likely to be a cause of disruption and disorder in years to come as the doctrine of *uti possidetis* comes under extreme pressure from ethnic groups asserting a right of self-determination.[1] It is most certainly a major source of the civil wars which have plagued ex-colonial regions in the post-1945 period.

However, in a States system in which fundamental rules of the game are the recognition of existing international boundaries and the doctrine of non-intervention, a crucial (and sometimes overlooked) requirement in the formation of new States is (as indicated) the willingness of sovereigns to allow it to happen – as Gorbachev and Yeltsin allowed the birth or rebirth of (some of) the nationalities of the former USSR. It is noteworthy that the only acceptable and workable basis in this case was the former internal borders of the USSR which were simply internationalized. This fits conveniently with the doctrine of *uti possidetis*. Where sovereigns refuse it usually does not happen unless exceptional circumstances favour it – as in the case of Slovenian and Croatian independence against the will of (Serbian-dominated) Yugoslavia but with the blessing of Germany, Austria, and (more reluctantly and belatedly) other members of the EC as well as the USA. Again, the only legitimate basis was internationalization of the internal borders of former Yugoslavia. [. . .]

Statesmen are strongly disinclined to entertain any claims for self-determination which would involve loss of territory. Herein lies the tragedy of the Kurds, for example, who straddle the borders of Iraq, Iran, and Turkey, none of which is prepared to give up Kurdish-occupied territory and at least the first two of which are prepared to silence the Kurds – if necessary by State violence and terror. Even the 1990–1 Gulf War which resulted in the defeat of Iraq did not result in Kurdish independence – the UN and the coalition powers (especially Turkey) were at pains not to dismember Iraq. Most statesmen are prepared to collaborate to prevent the independence of ethnonationalities. [. . .] In this respect, the doctrine of *uti possidetis* continues to have strong backing in a world of numerous multi-ethnic States.

[. . .] Even if governmental force is not sufficient to put down rebellions, and separatists become in effect a State within a State, the international community can thwart the inner State's international emergence by refusing to recognize it or enter into overt relations with it. In short, international recognition and participation can 'trump' sociological determination or armed force in the game of sovereign statehood. At least this was the predominant tendency from 1945 until the time of writing.

The chances of jurisdictional death are also slight in every region surveyed in this book and for similar reasons. Indeed, death if anything is even less likely because births by separation are possible without a corresponding termination of sovereign statehood, as the cases of Bangladesh and Pakistan, Singapore and Malaysia, Slovenia and Yugoslavia, the Baltic States and the Soviet Union cum Russia have indicated. The death-rate of States fell almost to zero during the Cold War: before 1989 the last significant international jurisdictional disappearances in Europe – apart from Germany which was divided in 1945 – were registered by Soviet absorption of the Baltic States of Estonia, Latvia, and Lithuania in 1940. It is interesting how memories of independence were kept alive and how rebirth of these sovereign jurisdictions was swift once it finally was clear that Moscow would no longer thwart it. [. . .]

Until as recently as the end of the First World War the birth and death of sovereign entities and the transfer of territorial jurisdictions from one State to another was a predictable and legitimate consequence of war and peace. Today, however, it is increasingly unimaginable owing not least to the norm of territorial legitimacy which has spread around the world and has preserved thoroughly disintegrated States, such as Chad, Sudan, Uganda, Ethiopia, and even totally anarchic Lebanon and Somalia. Most deaths in the future may have to depend on voluntary acts of political euthanasia. [. . .]

As indicated, most sovereign governments are extremely reluctant either to give up territory or to combine their jurisdictions voluntarily. On the contrary, the existing territorial pattern of sovereign statehood in all of the major regions of the world seems to have acquired a sanctity which few if any powers are prepared to violate or even dispute, presumably because they desire to avoid not only the universal condemnation but also the threat to international order which such an action would provoke. Since 1945 there have been very few significant territory grabs anywhere in the world. Israel is one State that has attempted territorial conquest but this can be explained by her national insecurity and her siege mentality. The Israeli military occupations of the West Bank, the Golan Heights, and the Gaza strip have never been internationally recognized.

War and civil war

One of the more promising developments of international relations since 1945 has been the declining incidence of war – that is, international warfare. Although Europe and America experienced the Cold War they have not faced unambiguous international war since 1945: the superpowers were poised for war for four decades but managed to avoid going to war. The Cold War of course involved several hot wars outside the West, most notably the Korean and Vietnam Wars and also various wars between Israel and some of its Arab enemies in the Middle East. The most devastating and long-lasting was the Vietnam War which involved major intervention by outside powers – but this was in many respects a civil war and not an international war.

Perhaps the most serious regional conflict (measured by death and injury, destruction and damage) was the first Gulf War between Iraq and Iran (1980–8) which inflicted heavy casualties on both sides but primarily on very young, poorly trained, and ill-equipped Iranian conscripts mobilized by the Mullah disciples of Khomeni to carry out fanatical and what proved to be useless bloodletting assaults against well-dug-in Iraqi soldiers. The second Gulf War between Iraq and a coalition of Western and Arab powers led by the USA (1990–1) was internationalized and also far sharper and shorter. [. . .]

[Jackson gives other examples of international wars.]

But if the following points are considered it seems surprising that there have not been more international wars in recent decades: the number of sovereign States has multiplied more than threefold since 1945; local sovereigns are now located in every quarter of the globe; Third World governments are far more heavily armed than their colonial predecessors ever were; and very few are democratic or even constitutional governments and many are controlled by military regimes. Consequently there are many more national interests and military powers than there used to be with a corresponding potential for international armed conflict. But wars have not increased in proportion to the number of States and their potentially conflicting national interests.

On the other hand, however, violent discord within States between governments and armed opposition groups is almost a common occurrence – particularly in the former colonial regions of Asia and Africa and also in Latin America. In the late 1980s serious civil wars were being waged in Angola, Ethiopia, Sri Lanka, Sudan, Mozambique, Cambodia, Burma, Afghanistan, Nicaragua, and El Salvador. Foreign intervention by one or both superpowers in some of these wars profoundly increased their production of casualties and refugees: for example the Afghanistan War. When the Cold War came to an end in 1989–91 and the superpowers withdrew many of these wars began to be wound down: Angola, Ethiopia, Cambodia, Nicaragua, El Salvador, and (perhaps) Mozambique. But civil wars occurred without major foreign intervention (Sudan) and continued in spite of foreign withdrawal (Afghanistan). The various internal factions at war in Afghanistan were well able to wage war after Soviet withdrawal and declining American interest and support. Some civil wars may even be caused by foreign withdrawal: the conflict in Somalia broke out in 1991 following the end of the Cold War and the withdrawal of the superpowers from the Horn of Africa. The quasi-civil wars in parts of the former Yugoslavia and USSR were provoked by the breakdown of communist States at the end of the Cold War.

Some anti-government rebels persist in their warfare against State authorities for extended periods: a civil war in Ethiopia began in 1962 and lasted almost thirty years. The on-again, off-again civil war in Sudan has lasted for almost as long. This is surprising in light of the fact that very few post-1945 civil wars have resulted in the dismemberment of existing States or formation of new States: the partition of Pakistan which led to the independence of Bangladesh is one exception; perhaps a dismemberment of Bosnia-Herzegovina will prove to be another exception. Secessionists seem not to realize that their chances of gaining sovereign statehood in the contemporary international society are slim without consent of the sovereign government they are fighting against and recognition by the international community. Perhaps they believe they can use force to coerce such consent, but this has rarely happened and usually requires the total defeat of a sovereign government – as in Ethiopia in 1991. Consequently, civil wars – with or without foreign intervention – drag on endlessly with neither winners nor losers – just prolonged and seemingly useless bloodletting – as in Sudan. [. . .]

This, too, may be owing – at least in part – to the conservative inclination and practice of contemporary States and the States system to recognize the international legitimacy and territorial integrity of all existing States, including even countries which lack internally legitimate governments and contain profoundly alienated ethnonational regions.

Sovereignty, inequality, and dependency

'Sovereignty' has been aptly characterized by Anthony Payne as 'the ideology which legitimizes the post-war international system.' As J. D. B. Miller puts it: 'a sovereign State, however small, is a formidable adversary in terms of publicity.' These remarks point to the normative means by which the survival of even the tiniest countries is internationally guaranteed today. State survival nowadays is seen as a matter of right rather than power.

The smallness or weakness of many States draws them into external relationships of quasi-trusteeship with international organizations and important States. The Caribbean and Pacific countries and also many Sub-Saharan States are for all intents and purposes wards of the United Nations system, the European Economic Community, the Commonwealth, Francophonie, and other international organizations. Many Third World States are heavily dependent on the IMF and the World Bank. They rely on the international community not only for their liberty but also for their welfare. This dependency system is in many important respects the successor to Western colonialism. It is difficult to imagine how such countries would manage to get on without some such supporting and sustaining external framework.

Of course, many weaker States have also entered into bilateral relations with more significant powers located either within their region or outside. Such relations often have earmarks not of classical suzerainty in which sovereignty becomes 'an empty shell' but rather of international clientelism and dependency. The historical role of the former Soviet Union in Eastern Europe and that of the USA in Central America is illustrative. The superpowers during the Cold War supported faithful clients across great distances, as in the case of the USA and Israel and the Soviet Union and Cuba. [. . .]

In addition to these more conventional patron–client relations there have also been instances of what could be termed 'reverse suzerainty' in which richer powers actively solicit requests for support, for example in votes at the UN, from countries which in most respects are poor and insignificant. The USA, France, and various other wealthy States have cultivated clienteles from among Third World States mainly through the allocation of foreign aid. Japan has been moving in this direction in North East and South East Asia. Canada has sought to play the role of benefactor to numerous minor States of the Commonwealth and Francophonie presumably for the purpose of increasing her stature in these organizations as a rival to Britain and France. Australia plays a similar role in the Commonwealth particularly in relation to Oceanic members.

These relations are bound to continue indefinitely because they are driven by the sharp and indeed profound material inequalities between States both within regions and in the world at large. Following the end of the Cold War the impoverished States of Sub-Saharan Africa became noticeably worried that Western-funded international aid would be redirected from the Third World to Eastern Europe and the former Soviet Union. Their fears have not been groundless: the West's interest in Africa has declined and its corresponding interest in Russia and other East European or ex-Soviet States has undoubtedly increased since the remarkable international changes of 1989–91. The finances and other economic resources available for international aid are definitely limited and will no doubt be distributed where the political and economic returns are greatest. Sub-Saharan Africa is not likely to be a very high priority. On the other hand, the existing international framework for distributing aid is well entrenched and the many aid agencies, public and private, can be expected to demand that there be no substantial reductions of financial and technical assistance to Sub-Saharan Africa and other poorest parts of the Third World. This framework prevents international aid from being directed wholly by the individual and collective interests of the developed donor countries, somewhat in the same way that institutions of the Welfare State constrain the allocation of resources by markets within States.

However, there is little sign that gross existing inequalities between States and regions (such as are recorded in annual reports of the World Bank) will begin to be substantially reduced in the foreseeable future. It would require very substantial foreign investment to begin to roll back the vast ocean of poverty and underdevelopment. The poorest countries are often far from the most attractive investment opportunities in a world in which private capital is highly mobile and can be invested where the returns are greatest and safest. It would require determined international collaboration between States deliberately to transfer wealth from rich countries to poor ones to counter market dictates. The public funds required would also be very great and could only be mobilized either from taxation or borrowing in the developed countries – both of which were unpopular in most of these countries in the early 1990s. [. . .]

Change or continuity?

States and regions and the global States system as a whole seem destined to persist indefinitely more or less in their existing shape. [. . .] There is no definite intimation of any alternative arrangement and certainly not a world government of some kind. The current pattern of sovereign-state jurisdiction is not expected to change either. International boundaries are of course changing in what formerly was the Soviet Union and Yugoslavia as these areas experience a postponed process of national self-determination reminiscent of decolonization. These changes could create demonstration effects elsewhere especially where mobilized and politicized ethnicity runs counter to the doctrine of *uti possidetis*. But it seems more likely that the existing pattern of sovereign-State jurisdiction will hold if only because it is almost impossible to contemplate change without a corresponding threat of instability. [. . .]

What should probably be expected, therefore, is continuing shifts in the broadly defined balance of power, as States, and increasingly also regions, compete in the great race for economic, technological, and scientific supremacy. Some will gain while others will lose ground and still others will stay more or less in the same position. Perhaps Mexico (and even some other countries of Latin America) will develop more rapidly with new opportunities for investment and markets provided under the terms of the 1992 North American Free Trade Agreement (NAFTA) with the USA and Canada. Perhaps North East and possibly even South East Asia will advance significantly under Japanese commercial leadership. Perhaps parts of Eastern Europe (the Czech Republic predecessor to Czechoslovakia, Hungary, Poland, possibly Slovenia, and perhaps Croatia and the Baltic States) will progress more speedily as a result of their geographical proximity to the new Germany – the dynamic heartland of the European economy. [. . .]

If Russia and America are not yet merely the equals of other major powers owing to their still awesome military might, they are no longer the paramount powers they once were. The USSR was never an economic power and Russia will remain in the position of its predecessor until economic reforms have an effect which could be years if not decades away. The US share of world economic production has declined significantly from its artificially high levels at the end of the Second World War. At the same time Japan (the hub of North East Asia) and Germany (the engine of the EC) are economic powers which together with associated countries are beginning to rival the USA. But Japan is extremely cautious and even inhibited in its outward projection of non-commercial and particularly military influence, and the EC has proven more often than not to be seriously deficient in any capacity to articulate and project a co-ordinated foreign and military policy – as the (second) Gulf War and the wars in the Balkans clearly indicate. This may leave the USA as the solitary superpower possessing both unrivalled military clout and still consequential economic strength.

However, neither the USA nor the EC nor Japan is a hegemonic power in the classical imperial sense. There is today less economic reason to expand one's national territory than there was in the past. Economic interests of States can be pursued through international trade and other transactions and agreements without going to the enormous trouble of acquiring and governing foreign territory. [. . .]

Human capital and the institutional arrangements that can best generate it and take advantage of it are the *sine qua non* of State prosperity and status in the contemporary world.

And to the extent that States today are eager to enter into international economic relations in order to develop, they also must be willing not only to trade with other States but do whatever else may be necessary to compete internationally – including making themselves available to foreign investment. Such an 'open' international economy makes territory (and the economic resources contained within it) accessible and exploitable without resort to sovereign control. [. . .]

However, an open international economy does not require the abandonment or even any substantial loss of State sovereignty properly understood as constitutional independence. Canada and Mexico may be willing to trade more freely with the USA but they certainly are not about to surrender to America's manifest destiny to enclose the entire North American continent within its domestic jurisdiction. [. . .]

When a future different from the present is foreseen it usually involves the expectation of increased regionalism in the form of trading blocs. The most elaborate example is of course the EC which other regions cannot ignore and must to some extent imitate. But far from reducing the significance of member States, the European community has in fact strengthened them. What has evidently changed is not the location of sovereignty or the legal standing of member States *vis-à-vis* the community: Brussels is still the servant and not the master of the EC States. Europe is still far from being a federal State under a government responsible to an elected European parliament: it remains a conventional international organization under a Council of Ministers representing the member States of the Community. [. . .]

But the most significant prospects for regional ascendancy in the longer term lie, perhaps paradoxically, in the old heartland of the international system: Europe. The division in this book between Eastern and Western Europe which is entirely faithful to a reality that lasted for more than forty years has been undermined by dramatic and almost entirely unforeseen political changes in the East. For consider what could be in the offing if Gorbachev's rhetoric about a 'European home' were to turn eventually into some kind of reality.

What would happen if Eastern Europe and European parts of the former Soviet Union became reintegrated with Western Europe after a fifty – or in some cases a seventy-five–year absence? In other words, what would be the result of an expansion and intensification of trade, commerce, investment, communications, travel, and migration in a land mass stretching from the Atlantic to the Urals (not to mention the Pacific in the case of Russia) with a highly educated population of half a billion and a concentration of wealth that is unrivalled anywhere? The potential for economic development of the whole of Europe assisted by the EC is greater than in any other major region, including the Americas and North East Asia – not to mention the Pacific Rim as a whole – where intra-regional differences of geography, culture, ideology, education, living standards, and the rest are far greater. The European continent could once again become the global centre: a 'super-Europe'. [. . .]

But even this grandiose scenario need not entail any decline of sovereign statehood. Whereas Western Europe already discloses a process of regional integration based on economics which is remarkable in the annals of the States system, at the same time there is to date no firm indication that constitutional independence is clearly on the wane for its component States. The EC still has a long way to go before it resembles the USA. In short, the emergence of organized regional blocs is entirely consistent with a States system and only discloses a change in the ways in which sovereign governments choose to relate to each other: regionalism only means that they relate far more intimately and intensively to their geographical neighbours than to other States or regions. This is in sharp contrast to the age of imperialism, when Britain, France, and other colonial powers had intensive commercial as well as political relations with geographically distant dependencies.

If these speculations are consistent with present realities and possibilities it suggests that sovereign States and the States system formed by them will be around at least for the time being and probably for much longer than that. The development of regionalism is not undermining the sovereign State as the foundation upon which the political organization of the world is erected; it is not an alternative framework of political life. Instead, it is a new adaptation of a long-standing method of organizing and conducting relations among peoples. [. . .]

Granted the States system can be exploited by abusive or corrupt élites, often encourages national parochialism and prejudice, and has periodically – some would say regularly – led to devastating wars and other kinds of human suffering. But no human institution is fail-safe or foolproof. The States system still remains a remarkably flexible political arrangement that has accommodated if it has not actually facilitated arguably the greatest freedom and certainly the highest living standards ever recorded in human history. The affluent and democratic countries of the West are proof of what can be achieved within the framework of independent statehood. Why should anyone expect such a system to be abandoned at the very moment of its greatest success?

Note

1   *uti possidetis* – according to this norm, existing international boundaries are the pre-emptive basis for determining territorial jurisdictions in the absence of mutual agreement to do otherwise.

1.4 The nation-state in the global economy

Robert Gilpin *

Source: *Global Political Economy: Understanding the International Economic Order* (Princeton University Press, Princeton, 2001), pp. 362–76.

Gilpin contests the view that globalization is eroding national economies and rendering the state obsolete as an economic actor. He argues first that many of the reputed effects of globalization are the result of national policies. He then shows that although globalization has made macroeconomic policy formation more complex and risky for states, they still retain considerable control over their own economies. He concludes by showing that a broader historical perspective reveals that states have never had unfettered control of their economies.

The idea that the nation-state has been undermined by the transnational forces of economic globalization has appeared in writings on the international system and on the international economy. Many writings have argued that international organizations (IOs) and non-governmental actors are replacing nation-states as the dominant actors in the international system. [. . .] This chapter disagrees with such views and argues that the nation-state continues to be the major actor in both domestic and international affairs.

At the beginning of the twenty-first century, the nation-state is clearly under serious attack from both above and below, and there is no doubt that there have been very important changes. [. . .] economic globalization and transnational economic forces are eroding economic sovereignty in important ways. Nevertheless, both the extent of globalization and the consequences of economic globalization for the nation-state have been considerably exaggerated. For better or for worse, this is still a state-dominated world.

As Vincent Cable of the Royal Institute of International Affairs (London) has noted, it is not easy to assess globalization's implications for the nation-state.[1] Although the economic role of the state has declined in certain significant ways, it has expanded in others and, therefore, it is inaccurate to conclude that the nation-state has become redundant or anachronistic. As Cable says, the situation is "much messier" than that. The impact of the global economy on individual nations is highly uneven, and its impact varies from issue to issue; finance is much more globalized than are services and industrial production. While globalization has reduced some policy options, the degree of reduction is highly dependent on national size and economic power; the United States and Western Europe, for example, are much less vulnerable to destabilizing financial flows than are small economies. Indeed, the importance of the state has even actually increased in some areas, certainly with respect to promoting international competitiveness through support for R & D, for technology policy, and for other assistance to domestic firms.

Economic globalization is much more limited than many realize, and consequently, its overall impact on the economic role of the state is similarly limited. Moreover, although economic globalization has been a factor in whatever diminishment of the state may have occurred, ideological, technological, and international political changes have had an even more powerful influence. Furthermore, many and perhaps most of the social, economic, and other problems ascribed to globalization are actually due to technological and other developments that have little or nothing to do with globalization. Even though its role may have diminished somewhat, the nation-state remains preeminent in both domestic and international economic affairs. To borrow a phrase from the American humorist Mark Twain, I would like to report that the rumors of the death of the state "have been greatly exaggerated."

The limited nature of economic globalization

In one sense, globalization has been taking place for centuries whenever improvements in transportation and communications have brought formerly separated peoples into contact with one another. The domestication of the horse and camel, the invention of the sailing ship, and the development of the telegraph all proved powerful instruments for uniting people, although not always to their liking. For thousands of years, ideas, artistic styles, and other artifacts have diffused from one society to another and have given rise to fears similar to those associated with economic globalization today. Nevertheless, it is important to discuss the economic globalization that has resulted from the rapid economic and technological integration of national societies that took place in the final decades of the twentieth century, especially after the end of the Cold War. This recent global economic integration has been the result of major changes in trade flows, of the activities of multinational corporations and of developments in international finance.

Despite the increasing significance of economic globalization, the integration of the world economy has been highly uneven, restricted to particular economic sectors, and not nearly as extensive as many believe. As a number of commentators have pointed out, there are many ways in which the world is less integrated today than it was in the late nineteenth century. This should remind us that although the technology leading to increased globalization may be irreversible, national policies that have been responsible for the process of economic globalization have been reversed in the past and could be reversed again in the future.

As the twenty-first century opens, the world is not as well integrated as it was in a number of respects prior to World War I. Under the gold standard and the influential doctrine of laissez-faire, for example, the decades prior to World War I were an era when markets were truly supreme and governments had little power over economic affairs. Trade, investment, and financial flows were actually greater in the late 1800s, at least relative to the size of national economic and the international economy, than are today. Twentieth-century changes appear primarily in the form of the greatly increased speed and absolute magnitude of economic flows across national borders and in the inclusion of more and more countries in the global economy. Yet, economic globalization is largely confined to North America, Western Europe, and Pacific Asia. And even though these industrial economies have become much more open, imports and investments from abroad are still small compared to the size of the domestic economies. For example, American imports rose from 5 percent of the total U.S. production in 1970 to just 13 percent in 1995, even though the United States was the most globalized economy.

Although trade has grown enormously during the past half century, trade still accounts for a relatively small portion of most economies; moreover, even though the number of "tradables" has been increasing, trade is still confined to a limited number of economic sectors. The principal competitors for most firms (with important exceptions in such areas as motor vehicles and electronics) are other national firms. The largest portions of foreign direct investment flows are invested in the United States, Western Europe, and China; a very small portion of the investment in sectors other than raw materials and resources has been invested in most less developed countries. International finance alone can be accurately described as a global phenomenon. Yet, even the globalization of finance must be qualified, as much of international finance is confined to short-term and speculative investment.

The most important measure of the economic integration and interdependence of distinct economies is what economists call the "law of one price." If identical goods and services in different economies have the same or nearly equal prices, then economists consider these economies to be closely integrated with one another. However, evidence indicates that the prices of identical goods around the world differ considerably whether measured by *The Economist* magazine's Big Mac index or by more formal economic measures. When the law of one price is applied to the United States, it is clear that American prices differ greatly from those of other countries, especially Japan's. Price differentials in the cost of labor around the world are particularly notable, and there are large disparities in wages. All of this clearly suggests that the world is not as integrated as many proclaim.

The significant and sizable decline in migration is one of the major differences between late-nineteenth-century globalization and globalization of the early twenty-first century. During the past half century, the United States has been the only country to welcome large numbers of new citizens. Although Western Europe has accepted a flood of refugees and "guest workers," the situation in those countries has been and remains tenuous; few have been or will be offered citizenship. The globalization of labor was considerably more advanced prior to World War I than afterward. In the late nineteenth century, millions of Europeans crossed the Atlantic to settle as permanent residents in North America; West Europeans also migrated in significant numbers to such "lands of recent settlement" as Australia, Argentina, and other temperate-zone regions. There were large migrations of Indians and Chinese to Southeast Asia, Africa, and other tropical regions. All these streams of migration became powerful determinants of the structure of the world economy. In the early twenty-first century, labor migration is no longer a major feature of the world economy, and even within the European Union, migration from one member nation to another is relatively low.

Barriers to labor migration are built by policies intended to protect the real wages and social welfare of the nation's citizens, and the modern welfare state is based on the assumption that its benefits will be available only to its own citizens. Some reformers in industrialized countries have constructed an ethical case that national wealth should be shared with the destitute around the world, but to my knowledge, even they have not advocated elimination of the barriers to international migration in order to enable the poor to move to more wealthy countries and thus decrease international income disparities. I find it remarkable that in the debate over globalization, little attention has been given to the most important factor of production; namely, labor and labor migration. For the billions of people in poor countries, national borders certainly remain an important feature of the global economy.

Alleged consequences of economic globalization

The conjuncture of globalization with a number of other political, economic, and techno-logical developments transforming the world makes it very difficult to understand economic globalization and its consequences. Among far-reaching economic changes at the end of the twentieth century have been a shift in industrialized countries from manufacturing to services and several revolutionary technological developments associated with the computer, including emergence of the internet and information economy. The skills and education required by jobs in the computer age place unskilled labor in the industrialized countries at a severe disadvantage in their wages and job security.

Although some economic and technological developments associated with the computer, including the rapid advances in telecommunications, have certainly contributed to the pro-cess of globalization, and globalization in some cases has accentuated these economic and technological changes, the two developments are not synonymous. In fact, the contemporary technological "revolution" has been a far more pervasive and, in many ways, a much more profound development than is globalization, at least thus far. [. . .]

Many of the problems alleged to be the result of economic globalization are really the consequence of unfortunate national policies and government decisions. Environmentalists rage against globalization and its evils; yet, most environmental damage is the result of the policies and behaviors of national governments. Air, water, and soil pollution result primarily from the lax policies of individual nations and/or from their poor enforcement procedures. The destruction of the Amazon forest has been caused principally by the Brazilian govern-ment's national development policies; in the United States, forest clear-cutting is actually promoted by generous government subsidies to logging companies.

In Western Europe, globalization is frequently blamed for many of the problems that have emerged from the economic and political integration of the region. Both globalization and regionalism are characterized by lowered economic barriers, restructuring of business, and other economic/social changes; it is easy, therefore, to see why some have conflated the two developments into one. Yet, globalization and regionalism are different, especially in the goals that each is seeking to achieve.

Effectiveness of macroeconomic policy

Since the end of World War II, and especially since governments accepted Keynesian economics in the early postwar era, national governments in the advanced industrialized economies have been held responsible for national economic performance. States were assigned the tasks of promoting national economic stability and steering their economies between the undesirable conditions of recession and inflation. Through macroeconomic policies, the state has been able to control, at least to some extent, the troubling vicissitudes of the market. However, the argument that the power of the state over economic affairs has significantly declined implies that national governments can no longer manage their econ-omies. While it is true that macroeconomic policy has become more complicated in the highly integrated world economy of the twenty-first century, these policies do still work and can achieve their goals at least as well as in the past. What better example than the Federal Reserve's very successful management of the American economy in the mid-to-late 1990s! Moreover, today as in the past, the principal constraints on macroeconomic policy are to be found at the domestic rather than at the international level.

Macroeconomic policy consists of two basic tools for managing a national economy: fiscal policies and monetary policies. The principal instruments of fiscal policy are taxation and government expenditures. Through lowering or raising taxes and/or increasing or decreasing national expenditures, the federal government (Congress and the Executive) can affect the national level of economic activities. Whereas a federal budget deficit (spending more than tax receipts) will stimulate the economy, a budget surplus (spending less than tax receipts) will decrease economic activities. Monetary policy works through its determination of the size and velocity of a nation's money supply. The Federal Reserve can stimulate or depress the level of economic activities by increasing or restricting the supply of dollars available to consumers and producers. The principal method employed by the Federal Reserve to achieve this goal is to determine the national level of interest rates; whereas a low interest rate stimulates economic growth, a high rate depresses it.

Many commentators argue that the effectiveness of monetary policy has been significantly reduced by increased international financial flows. If, for example, a central bank lowers interest rates to stimulate the economy, investors will transfer their capital to other economies with higher interest rates and thus counter the intended stimulus of lower rates. Similarly, if a central bank increases interest rates in order to slow the economy, investment capital will flow into the economy, counter the intended deflationary effects of higher rates, and stimulate economic activities. In all these ways, economic globalization is believed to have undermined the efficacy of fiscal and monetary policy. Therefore, some consider national governments no longer able to manage their economies.

To examine this contention, it is helpful to apply the logic of the "trilemma" or "irreconcilable trinity". Every nation is confronted by an inevitable trade-off among the following three desirable goals of economic policy: fixed exchange rates, national autonomy in macroeconomic policy, and international capital mobility. A nation might want a stable exchange rate in order to reduce economic uncertainty and stabilize the economy. Or it might desire discretionary monetary policy to avoid high unemployment and steer the economy between recession and inflation. Or a government might want freedom of capital movements to facilitate the conduct of trade, foreign investment, and other international business activities. Unfortunately, a government cannot achieve all three of these goals simultaneously. It can obtain at most two. For example, choosing a fixed and stable exchange rate along with some latitude for independent monetary policies would mean forgoing freedom of capital movements, because international capital flows could undermine both exchange rate stability and independent monetary policies. On the other hand, a country might choose to pursue macroeconomic policies to promote full employment, but it then would have to sacrifice either a fixed exchange rate or freedom of capital movement.

Such an analysis tells us that although economic globalization does constrain government policy options, it does not impose a financial straitjacket on national macroeconomic policies. Whether an individual nation does or does not have the capacity for an independent macroeconomic policy is itself a policy choice. If a nation wants the capability to pursue an independent macroeconomic policy, it can achieve that goal by abandoning either fixed exchange rates or capital mobility. Different countries do, in fact, make different choices. The United States, for example, prefers independent monetary policy and freedom of capital movements and therefore sacrifices exchange rate stability; members of the European Economic Monetary Union (EMU), on the other hand, prefer fixed exchange rates and have created a common currency to achieve this goal. Some other countries that place a high value on macroeconomic independence – China, for example – have imposed controls on capital movements.

Different domestic economic interests also have differing preferences. Whereas export businesses have a strong interest in the exchange rate, domestic-oriented businesses place a higher priority on national policy autonomy. Investors prefer freedom of capital movement, whereas labor tends to be opposed to such movement, unless the movement should mean increased investment in their own nation. Economic globalization in itself does not prevent a nation from using macroeconomic policies for managing its economy.

The mechanisms employed to conduct monetary policy have not been seriously affected by globalization. Although various central banks operate differently from one another, an examination of the ways in which the American Federal Reserve (the Fed) steers the American economy is instructive and reveals that, at least in the American case, globalization has had only minimal effects.

Through its power to increase or decrease the number of dollars available to consumers and producers (liquidity), the Fed is able to steer the overall economy. The level of national economic activity is strongly influenced by the size of the nation's money supply; an increase in the money supply stimulates economic activities and a decrease slows down economic activity. The Fed has three basic instruments to influence the nation's supply of money. The first directly affects the money supply; the other tools work indirectly through the banking system.

The Fed's primary means for management of the economy is "open market operations," conducted through the Open Market Desk of the Federal Reserve Bank of New York. Through sale or purchase of U.S. government bonds directly to the public, the Fed can influence the overall level of national economic activity. If, for example, the Fed wants to slow the economy, it sells U.S. Government bonds. This takes money or liquidity out of the economy. If, on the other hand, the Fed wants to stimulate the economy, it uses dollars to purchase U.S. Government bonds and thus increases the money or liquidity in the economy.

The Fed can also change the discount rate, which is the interest rate on loans that the Fed makes directly to the nation's commercial banks. The Fed, for example, loans money to banks whose reserves fall below the Fed's reserve requirements (see below); this may happen if a bank has made too many loans or is experiencing too many withdrawals. By lending to private banks and increasing the reserves of those banks, the Fed enables banks to make more loans and thus to increase the nation's money supply. Whereas raising the discount rate decreases loans and money creation, lowering of the discount rate increases loans and money creation. These changes in turn have a powerful influence on the overall level of economic activity.

Another tool that the Fed has available is its authority to determine the reserve require-ments of the nation's banks. Reserve requirements specify the minimal size of the monetary reserves that a bank must hold against deposits subject to withdrawal. Reserve requirements thus determine the amount of money that a bank is permitted to lend and, thereby, how much money the bank can place in circulation. Through raising or lowering reserve requirements, the Fed sets a limit on how much money the nation's banks can inject into the economy. However, this method of changing the money supply is used infrequently because changed reserve requirements can be very disruptive to the banking system.

Globalization and a more open world economy have had only minimal impact on the Fed's ability to manage the economy. Yet the effectiveness of open market operations has probably been somewhat reduced by growth of the international financial market, and the purchase or sale of U.S. securities by foreigners certainly affects the national money supply. In the late 1990s, it was estimated that approximately $150 billion was held overseas. How-ever, the effect of that large amount is minimized by the size of the more than $8 trillion domestic economy. Also, the American financial system (like that of other industrialized countries) exhibits a "home bias"; that is to say, most individuals keep their financial assets in their own currency. It is possible, however, that central banks in smaller and weaker economies find that their ability to manage their own money supply has been decreased, as was exemplified by the 1997 Asian financial crisis.

One should note that the continuing power of the Fed over the banks and the money supply through control of the interest rate has been challenged by the development of the credit card and other new forms of money. These credit instruments have decreased, at least somewhat, the effectiveness of the Fed's use of this instrument to control the economy. Still more problematic for the Fed is the increasing use of e-money in Internet commerce. In effect, these developments mean that the monopoly of money creation once held by the Fed and the banking system is being diluted. Through use of a credit card and/or participation in e-commerce, an individual or business can create money. Yet, at some point e-money and other novel forms of money must be converted into "real" or legal tender, and, at that point the Fed retains control of the creation of real money. Thus, although the monetary system has become much more complex, the Fed still has ultimate control over that system and through it, the overall economy.

Although the power of central banks over interest rates and the money supply has been somewhat diminished, as long as cash and bank reserves remain the ultimate means of exchange and of settlement of accounts, central banks can still retain control over the money supply and hence of the economy. In fact, even if everyone switched to electronic means of payment but credit issuers still settled their balances with merchants through the banking system (as happens with credit cards now), central banks would still retain overall control. However, one day, e-money could displace other forms of money. If and when this develops, financial settlements could be carried out without going through commercial banks, and central banks would lose their ability to control the economy through interest rates. Such a development could lead to the "denationalization" of money. However, it seems reasonable to believe that some public authority would still be needed to control inflation and monitor the integrity of the computer system used for payments settlements.

With respect to *reserve requirements*, intense competition among international banks has induced some central banks to reduce reserve requirements in order to make the domestic banking industry more competitive internationally. Japanese banks, for example, have long been permitted by the government to keep much smaller reserves than American banks. One of the major purposes of the Basle Agreement (1988), was to make reserve requirements more uniform throughout the world. Rumor has it that this agreement was engineered by the Fed to decrease the international competitiveness of Japanese and other foreign banks vis-à-vis American international banks. Whatever the underlying motive, the agreement has been described as a response to financial globalization, and the establishment of uniform international reserve requirements has largely reestablished their effectiveness as instruments of policy.

The most important constraints on macroeconomic policy are found at the domestic level. If an economy were isolated from the international economy, fiscal policy would be constrained by the cost of borrowing. If a national government were to use deficit spending to stimulate its economy, the resulting budget deficit would have to be financed by domestic lenders. In that situation, an upper limit would be placed on government borrowing, because as the budget deficit and the costs of servicing that deficit rose, bond purchasers would become more and more fearful that the government might default on its debt and/or use monetary policy to inflate the money supply and thus reduce the real value of the debt. Increased risk as debt rises causes lenders to stop lending and/or to charge higher and higher interest rates; this then discourages further borrowing by the government. Also, another important constraint on monetary policy in a domestic economy is the threat of inflation; this threat places an upper limit on the ability of a central bank to stimulate the economy by increasing the money supply and/or lowering the interest rate. At some point, the threat of inflation will discourage economic activity. In short, there are limits on macroeconomic policy that have nothing whatsoever to do with the international economy – and these domestic constraints existed long before anyone had heard the term "globalization."

Economic globalization has made the task of managing an economy easier in some ways and more difficult in others. On the one hand, globalization has enabled governments to borrow more freely; the United States in the 1980s and 1990s borrowed heavily from Japanese and other foreign investors in order to finance a federal budget deficit and a high rate of economic growth. However, this debt-financed growth strategy, as Susan Strange pointed out first in *Casino Capitalism* and again in *Mad Money*, is extraordinarily risky and can not continue forever.[2] Fearing collapse of the dollar, investors could one day flee dollar-denominated assets for safer assets denominated in other currencies. The consequences of such flight could be devastating for the United States and for the rest of the world economy. Thus, although economic globalization has increased the latitude of governments to pursue expansionary economic policies through borrowing excessively abroad, such serious financial crises of the postwar era as the Mexican crisis in 1994–1995, the 1997 East Asian financial crisis, and the disturbing collapse of the Russian ruble in August 1998 demonstrate the huge and widespread risks associated with such a practice.

Economic globalization and the greater openness of domestic economies have also modified the rules of economic policy. Certainly, the increasing openness of national economies has made the exercise of macroeconomic policy more complex and difficult. This does not mean that a national government can no longer guide the economy around the dangerous shoals of inflation and recession, but it does mean that the risk of shipwreck has grown.

The need for a historical perspective

The globalization thesis lacks a historical perspective. Those individuals who argue that globalization has severely limited economic sovereignty appear to believe that governments once possessed unlimited national autonomy and freedom in economic matters. Their argument assumes that nation-states have enjoyed unrestricted ability to determine economic policy and manage their economies and that governments were free because they were not subordinate to or encumbered by transnational market forces. As proponents of the globalization thesis contrast economic policy in the twenty-first century to this imagined past, they conclude that nation-states, for the first time ever, have become constrained by the increased integration of national economies through trade, financial flows, and the activities of multinational firms. In effect, having assumed that states once had complete economic freedom, these individuals misperceive the reality of the fundamental relationship between the state and the economy. When viewed from a more accurate historical perspective, the relationship of state and market in the contemporary era is neither particularly startling nor revolutionary.

In the decades prior to World War I, national governments had little effective control over their economies. Under the classical gold standard of fixed exchange rates, governments were more tightly bound by what Barry Eichengreen has called "golden fetters" than they are in the early-twenty-first century world of flexible rates.[3] Moreover, as Nobel Laureate Arthur Lewis has noted, prior to World War I the economic agenda of governments everywhere was limited to the efforts of central banks to maintain the value of their curren-cies.[4] As Keynes pointed out in *The Economic Consequences of the Peace* (1919), national eco-nomic policy did not concern itself with the welfare of the "lower orders" of society. This minor and highly constrained role of the state in the economy changed dramatically with World War I and subsequent economic and political developments.

Throughout the twentieth century, the relationship of state and market indeed changed significantly as governments harnessed their economies for total war and to meet their citizens' rising economic expectations. The world wars of the twentieth century, the Great Depression of the 1930s, and the immense economic demands of the Cold War elevated the state's role in the economy. During periods of intense concern about security, national governments used new tools to manage their economies and began to exercise unprecedented control over their economies. The Great Depression, the rise of organized labor, and the sacrifices imposed on societies by World War II led Western governments to expand their activities to guarantee the welfare of their citizens. For some years, the per-ceived success of the communist experiment also encouraged governments to help Keynes's "lower orders," and after World War II, governments in every advanced economy assumed responsibility for promotion of full employment and provision of a generous and high level of economic welfare.

Conclusion

The argument that the nation-state is in retreat is most applicable to the United States, Western Europe, and perhaps Japan. The end of the Cold War represented the end of a century and a half of rapid economic development and political/military conflict. Since the American Civil War (1861–1865), the Franco-Prussian War (1870–1871), and the Russo-Japanese War (1904–1905), the forces of nationalism, industrialization, and state-creation had driven the industrialized powers of Europe, the United States, and Japan. World War I, World War II, and the Cold War forged the modern nation-state as an economic and war-making machine. During these decades of interstate rivalry, the economy was often harnessed to the needs of the national war machine. This bellicose epoch appears to have ended, and the industrialized countries may be retreating to their more modest late-nineteenth-century status. Yet, one must ask whether the forces of nationalism, industializa-tion, and state-creation might not be causing a repeat of the tragic Western experience in the developing economies of Asia, Africa, and elsewhere! Thus far, there is little evidence to suggest that these countries will avoid repeating the mistakes made by the industrialized world.

Notes

* Written with the assistance of Jean M. Gilpin.
1 Vincent Cable, "The Diminished Nation-State: A Study in the Loss of Economic Power" in *What Does the Future Hold For Us?*, *Daedalus* 124(2), 1995, pp. 23–53.
2 Susan Strange, *Casino Capitalism* (Blackwell, Oxford, 1986); and *Mad Money: From the Author of Casino Capitalism* (Manchester University Press, Manchester, 1998).
3 Barry Eichengreen, *Golden Fetters: The Gold Standard and the Great Depression* (Oxford University Press, New York, 1992).
4 W. Arthur Lewis, *Growth and Fluctuations 1870–1913* (Allen and Unwin, London, 1978).

1.5 The spiral of international insecurity

Robert Jervis

Source: *Perception and Misperception in International Politics* (Princeton University Press, Princeton, 1976), pp. 63–76.

Jervis argues that the attempts of one state to achieve security precipitate a feeling of insecurity in other states. All states tend to assume the worst of others and respond accordingly. Their collective actions unintentionally generate a spiral of insecurity and, in a situation of anarchy, there can be no solution to this security dilemma. The dilemma is further exacerbated, according to Jervis, by the inflexible images that it generates in the minds of decision makers both of their own intentions and of those of their opposite numbers.

The lack of a sovereign in international politics permits wars to occur and makes security expensive. More far-reaching complications are created by the fact that most means of self-protection simultaneously menace others. Rousseau made the basic point well:

> It is quite true that it would be much better for all men to remain always at peace. But so long as there is no security for this, everyone, having no guarantee that he can avoid war, is anxious to begin it at the moment which suits his own interest and so forestall a neighbour, who would not fail to forestall the attack in his turn at any moment favourable to himself, so that many wars, even offensive wars, are rather in the nature of unjust precautions for the protection of the assailant's own possessions than a device for seizing those of others. However salutary it may be in theory to obey the dictates of public spirit, it is certain that, politically and even morally, those dictates are liable to prove fatal to the man who persists in observing them with all the world when no one thinks of observing them towards him.[1]

In extreme cases, states that seek security may believe that the best, if not the only, route to that goal is to attack and expand. Thus the tsars believed that 'that which stops growing begins to rot', the Japanese decision-makers before World War II concluded that the alternative to increasing their dominance in Asia was to sacrifice their 'very existence', and some scholars have argued that German expansionism before World War I was rooted in a desire to cope with the insecurity produced by being surrounded by powerful neighbors.[2] After World War I France held a somewhat milder version of this belief. Although she knew that the war had left her the strongest state on the Continent, she felt that she had to increase her power still further to provide protection against Germany, whose recovery from wartime destruction might some day lead her to try to reverse the verdict of 1918. This view is especially likely to develop if the state believes that others have also concluded that both the desire for protection and the desire for increased values point to the same policy of expansionism.

The drive for security will also produce aggressive actions if the state either requires a very high sense of security or feels menaced by the very presence of other strong states. Thus Leites argues that 'the Politburo [. . .] believes that its very life [. . .] remains acutely threatened as long as major enemies exist. Their utter defeat is a sheer necessity of survival.' This view can be rooted in experience as well as ideology. In May 1944 Kennan wrote: 'Behind Russia's stubborn expansion lies only the age-old sense of insecurity of a sedentary people reared on an exposed plain in the neighborhood of fierce nomadic peoples.'[3]

Even in less extreme situations, arms procured to defend can usually be used to attack. Economic and political preparedness designed to hold what one has is apt to create the potential for taking territory from others. What one state regards as insurance, the adversary will see as encirclement. This is especially true of the great powers. Any state that has interests throughout the world cannot avoid possessing the power to menace others. For example, as Admiral Mahan noted before World War I, if Britain was to have a navy sufficient to safeguard her trading routes, she inevitably would also have the ability to cut Germany off from the sea. Thus even in the absence of any specific conflicts of interest between Britain and Germany, the former's security required that the latter be denied a significant aspect of great power status.

When states seek the ability to defend themselves, they get too much and too little – too much because they gain the ability to carry out aggression; too little because others, being menaced, will increase their own arms and so reduce the first state's security. Unless the requirements for offense and defense differ in kind or amount, a status quo power will desire a military posture that resembles that of an aggressor. For this reason others cannot infer from its military forces and preparations whether the state is aggressive. States therefore tend to assume the worst. The other's intentions must be considered to be co-extensive with his capabilities. What he can do to harm the state, he will do (or will do if he gets the chance). So to be safe, the state should buy as many weapons as it can afford.

But since both sides obey the same imperatives, attempts to increase one's security by standing firm and accumulating more arms will be self-defeating. [. . .]

These unintended and undesired consequences of actions meant to be defensive constitute the 'security dilemma' that Herbert Butterfield sees as that 'absolute predicament' that 'lies in the very geometry of human conflict. [. . .] [H]ere is the basic pattern for all narratives of human conflict, whatever other patterns may be superimposed upon it later.' From this perspective, the central theme of international relations is not evil but tragedy. States often share a common interest, but the structure of the situation prevents them from bringing about the mutually desired situation. This view contrasts with the school of realism represented by Hans Morgenthau and Reinhold Niebuhr, which sees the drive for power as a product of man's instinctive will to dominate others. As John Herz puts it, 'It is a mistake to draw from the universal phenomenon of competition for power the conclusion that there is actually such a thing as an innate "power instinct". Basically it is the mere instinct of self-preservation which, in the vicious circle [of the security dilemma], leads to competition for ever more power.'[4]

Arms races are only the most obvious manifestation of this spiral. The competition for colonies at the end of the nineteenth century was fueled by the security dilemma. Even if all states preferred the status quo to a division of the unclaimed areas, each also preferred expansion to running the risk of being excluded. The desire for security may also lead states to weaken potential rivals, a move that can create the menace it was designed to ward off. For example, because French statesmen feared what they thought to be the inevitable German attempt to regain the position she lost in World War I, they concluded that Germany had to be kept weak. The effect of such an unyielding policy, however, was to make the Germans less willing to accept their new position and therefore to decrease France's long-run security. Finally, the security dilemma can not only create conflicts and tensions but also provide the dynamics triggering war. If technology and strategy are such that each side believes that the state that strikes first will have a decisive advantage, even a state that is fully satisfied with the status quo may start a war out of fear that the alternative to doing so is not peace, but an attack by its adversary. And, of course, if each side knows that the other side is aware of the advantages of striking first, even mild crises are likely to end in war. This was one of the immediate causes of World War I, and contemporary military experts have devoted much thought and money to avoiding the recurrence of such destabilizing incentives. [. . .]

Psychological dynamics

The argument sketched so far rests on the implications of anarchy, not on the limitations of rationality imposed by the way people reach decisions in a complex world. Lewis Richardson's path-breaking treatment of arms races describes 'what people would do if they did not stop to think'. Richardson argues that this is not an unrealistic perspective. The common analogy between international politics and chess is misleading because 'the acts of a leader are in part controlled by the great instinctive and traditional tendencies which are formulated in my description. It is somewhat as if the chessmen were connected by horizontal springs to heavy weights beyond the chess-board.'[5]

Contemporary spiral theorists argue that psychological pressures explain why arms and tensions cycles proceed as if people were not thinking. Once a person develops an image of the other – especially a hostile image of the other – ambiguous and even discrepant information will be assimilated to that image. [. . .] If they think that a state is hostile, behavior that others might see as neutral or friendly will be ignored, distorted, or seen as attempted duplicity. This cognitive rigidity reinforces the consequences of international anarchy.

Although we noted earlier that it is usually hard to draw inferences about a state's intentions from its military posture, decision-makers in fact often draw such inferences when they are unwarranted. They frequently assume, partly for reasons to be discussed shortly, that the arms of others indicate aggressive intentions. So an increase in the other's military forces makes the state doubly insecure – first, because the other has an increased capability to do harm, and, second, because this behavior is taken to show that the other is not only a potential threat but is actively contemplating hostile actions.

But the state does not apply this reasoning to its own behavior. A peaceful state knows that it will use its arms only to protect itself, not to harm others. It further assumes that others are not fully aware of this. As John Foster Dulles put it: 'Khrushchev does not need to be convinced of our good intentions. He knows we are not aggressors and do not threaten the security of the Soviet Union.' Similarly, in arguing that 'England seeks no quarrels, and will never give Germany cause for legitimate offence', Crowe assumed not only that Britain was benevolent but that this was readily apparent to others.[6] To take an earlier case, skirmishing between France and England in North America developed into the Seven Years' War partly because each side incorrectly thought the other knew that its aims were sharply limited. Because the state believes that its adversary understands that the state is arming because it sees the adversary as aggressive, the state does not think that strengthening its arms can be harmful. If the other is aggressive, it will be disappointed because the state's strengthened position means that it is less vulnerable. Provided that the state is already fairly strong, however, there is no danger that the other will be provoked into attacking. If the other is not aggressive, it will not react to the state's effort to protect itself. This means that the state need not exercise restraint in policies designed to increase its security. To procure weapons in excess of the minimum required for defense may be wasteful, but will not cause unwarranted alarm by convincing the other that the state is planning aggression.

In fact, others are not so easily reassured. As Lord Grey realized – after he was out of power:

> The distinction between preparations made with the intention of going to war and precautions against attack is a true distinction, clear and definite in the minds of those who build up armaments. But it is a distinction that is not obvious or certain to others [. . .] Each Government, therefore, while resenting any suggestion that its own measures are anything more than for defense, regards similar measures of another Government as preparation to attack.

Herbert Butterfield catches the way these beliefs drive the spiral of arms and hostility:

> It is the peculiar characteristic of the [. . .] Hobbesian fear [. . .] that you yourself may vividly feel the terrible fear that you have of the other party, but you cannot enter into the other man's counter-fear, or even understand why he should be particularly nervous. For you know that you yourself mean him no harm, and that you want nothing from him save guarantees for your own safety; and it is never possible for you to realize or remember properly that since he cannot see the inside of your mind, he can never have the same assurance of your intentions that you have. As this operates on both sides the Chinese puzzle is complete in all its interlockings and neither party can see the nature of the predicament he is in, for each only imagines that the other party is being hostile and unreasonable.[7]

Because statesmen believe that others will interpret their behavior as they intend it and will share their view of their own state's policy, they are led astray in two reinforcing ways. First, their understanding of the impact of their own state's policy is often inadequate – i.e. differs from the views of disinterested observers – and, second, they fail to realize that other states' perceptions are also skewed. Although actors are aware of the difficulty of making their threats and warnings credible, they rarely believe that others will misinterpret behavior that is meant to be more compatible with the other's interests. Because we cannot easily establish an objective analysis of the state's policy, these two effects are difficult to dis-entangle. But for many purposes this does not matter because both pressures push in the same direction and increase the differences between the way the state views its behavior and the perceptions of others.

The degree to which a state can fail to see that its own policy is harming others is illustrated by the note that the British foreign secretary sent to the Soviet government in March 1918 trying to persuade it to welcome a Japanese army that would fight the Germans: 'The British Government have clearly and constantly repeated that they have no wish to take any part in Russia's domestic affairs, but that the prosecution of the war is the only point with which they are concerned.' When reading Bruce Lockhart's reply that the Bolsheviks did not accept this view, Balfour noted in the margin of the dispatch: 'I have constantly impressed on Mr. Lockhart that it is *not* our desire to interfere in Russian affairs.

He appears to be very unsuccessful in conveying this view to the Bolshevik Government.'[8] The start of World War I witnessed a manifestation of the same phenomenon when the tsar ordered mobilization of the Baltic fleet without any consideration of the threat this would pose even to a Germany that wanted to remain at peace. [. . .]

The same inability to see the implications of its specific actions limits the state's appreciation of the degree to which its position and general power make it a potential menace. As Klaus Epstein points out in describing the background to World War I, 'Wilhelmine Germany – because of its size, population, geographical location, economic dynamism, cocky militarism, and autocracy under a neurotic Kaiser – was feared by all other Powers as a threat to the European equilibrium; this was an objective fact which Germans should have recognized.'[9] Indeed even had Germany changed her behavior, she still would have been the object of constant suspicion and apprehension by virtue of being the strongest power in Europe. And before we attribute this insensitivity to the German national character, we should note that United States statesmen in the postwar era have displayed a similar inability to see that their country's huge power, even if used for others' good, represents a standing threat to much of the rest of the world. Instead the United States, like most other nations, has believed that others will see that the desire for security underlies its actions.

The psychological dynamics do not, however, stop here. If the state believes that others know that it is not a threat, it will conclude that they will arm or pursue hostile policies only if they are aggressive. For if they sought only security they would welcome, or at least not object to, the state's policy. Thus an American senator who advocated intervening in Russia in the summer of 1918 declared that if the Russians resisted this move it would prove that 'Russia is already Germanized'. This inference structure is revealed in an exchange about NATO between Tom Connally, the chairman of the Senate Foreign Relations Committee, and Secretary of State Acheson:

> Now, Mr. Secretary, you brought out rather clearly [. . .] that this treaty is not aimed at any nation particularly. It is aimed only at any nation or any country that contemplates or undertakes armed aggression against the members of the signatory powers. Is that true?
>
> Secretary Acheson. That is correct, Senator Connally. It is not aimed at any country; it is aimed solely at armed aggression.
>
> The Chairman. In other words, unless a nation other than the signatories contemplates, meditates or makes plans looking toward, aggression or armed attack on another nation, it has no cause to fear this treaty.
>
> Secretary Acheson. That is correct, Senator Connally, and it seems to me that any nation which claims that this treaty is directed against it should be reminded of the Biblical admonition that 'The guilty flee when no man pursueth.'
>
> The Chairman. That is a very apt illustration.
>
> What I had in mind was, when a State or Nation passes a criminal act, for instance, against burglary, nobody but those who are burglars or getting ready to be burglars need have any fear of the Burglary Act. Is that not true?
>
> Secretary Acheson. Very true.
>
> The Chairman. And so it is with one who might meditate and get ready and arm himself to commit a murder. If he is not going to indulge in that kind of enterprise, the law on murder would not have any effect on him, would it?
>
> Secretary Acheson. The only effect it would have would be for his protection, perhaps, by deterring someone else. He wouldn't worry about the imposition of the penalties on himself, but he might feel that the statute added to his protection.[10]

[. . .] When the state believes that the other knows that it is not threatening the other's legitimate interests, disputes are likely to produce antagonism out of all proportion to the intrinsic importance of the issue at stake. Because the state does not think that there is any obvious reason why the other should oppose it, it will draw inferences of unprovoked hostility from even minor conflicts. [. . .] If, on the other hand, each side recognizes that its policies threaten some of the other's values, it will not interpret the other's reaction as indicating aggressive intent or total hostility and so will be better able to keep their conflict limited.

The perceptions and reactions of the other side are apt to deepen the misunderstanding and the conflict. For the other, like the state, will assume that its adversary knows that it is not a threat. So, like the state, it will do more than increase its arms – it will regard the state's explanation of its behavior as making no sense and will see the state as dangerous and hostile. When the Soviets consolidated their hold over Czechoslovakia in 1948, they knew this harmed Western values and expected some reaction. But the formation of NATO and the explanation given for this move were very alarming. Since the Russians assumed that the United States saw the situation the same way they did, the only conclusion they could draw was that the United States was even more dangerous than they had thought. As George Kennan put the Soviet analysis in a cable to Washington:

> It seemed implausible to the Soviet leaders, knowing as they did the nature of their own approach to the military problem, and assuming that the Western powers must have known it too, that defensive considerations alone could have impelled the Western governments to give the relative emphasis they actually gave to a program irrelevant in many respects to the outcome of the political struggle in Western Europe (on which Moscow was staking everything) and only partially justified, as Moscow saw it, as a response to actual Soviet intentions. [. . .] The Kremlin leaders were attempting in every possible way to weaken and destroy the structure of the non-Communist world. In the course of this endeavor they were up to many things which gave plenty of cause for complaint on the part of Western statesmen. They would not have been surprised if these things had been made the touchstone of Western reaction. But why, they might ask, were they being accused precisely of the one thing they had *not* done, which was to plan, as yet, to conduct an overt and unprovoked invasion of Western Europe? Why was the imputation to them of this intention being put forward as the rationale for Western rearmament? Did this not imply some ulterior purpose [. . .]?[11]

The Russians may have been even more alarmed if, as Nathan Leites has argued, they thought that we behaved according to the sensible proverb of 'whoever says A, says Z' and had knowingly assigned Czechoslovakia to the Russian sphere of influence during the wartime negotiations. 'How could, they must ask themselves, the elevation of an already dominant Czechoslovak Communist Party to full power in 1948 change the policies of Washington which had agreed to the presence of the Soviet Army in Czechoslovakia in 1945? Washington, after all, could hardly imagine that Moscow would indefinitely tolerate the presence of enemies [. . .] within its domain!' The American protests over the takeover must then be hypocrisy, and the claim that this event was alarming and called for Western rearmament could only be a cover for plans of aggression.[12] [. . .]

The explication of these psychological dynamics adds to our understanding of international conflict, but incurs a cost. The benefit is in seeing how the basic security dilemma becomes overlaid by reinforcing misunderstandings as each side comes to believe that not only is the other a potential menace, as it must be in a setting of anarchy, but that the other's behavior has shown that it is an active enemy. The inability to recognize that one's own actions could be seen as menacing and the concomitant belief that the other's hostility can only be explained by its aggressiveness help explain how conflicts can easily expand beyond that which an analysis of the objective situation would indicate is necessary. But the cost of these insights is the slighting of the role of the system in inducing conflict and a tendency to assume that the desire for security, rather than expansion, is the prime goal of most states. [. . .]

Both the advantages and pitfalls of this elaboration of the security dilemma are revealed in Kenneth Boulding's distinction between

> two very different kinds of incompatibility. [. . .] The first might be called 'real' incompatibility, where we have two images of the future in which realization of one would prevent the realization of the other. [. . .] The other form of incompatibility might be called 'illusory' incompatibility, in which there exists a condition of compatibility which would satisfy the 'real' interests of the two parties but in which the dynamics of the situation or illusions of the parties create a situation of perverse dynamics and misunderstandings, with increasing hostility simply as a result of the reactions of the parties to each other, not as a result of any basic differences of interest.[13]

This distinction can be very useful but it takes attention away from the vital kind of system-induced incompatibility that cannot be easily classified as either real or illusory. If both sides primarily desire security, then the two images of the future do not clash, and any incompatibility must, according to one reading of the definition, be illusory. But the heart of the security dilemma argument is that an increase in one state's security can make others less secure not because of misperception or imagined hostility, but because of the anarchic context of international relations.

Under some circumstances, several states can simultaneously increase their security. But often this is not the case. For a variety of reasons, many of which have been discussed earlier, nations' security requirements can clash. While an understanding of the security dilemma and psychological dynamics will dampen some arms-hostility spirals, it will not change the fact that some policies aimed at security will threaten others. To call the incompatibility that results from such policies 'illusory' is to misunderstand the nature of the problem and to encourage the illusion that if the states only saw themselves and others more objectively they could attain their common interest.

Notes

1 Rousseau, *A Lasting Peace through the Federation of Europe*, translated by C.E. Vaughan (Constable, London, 1917), pp. 78–9.
2 Quoted in Adam Ulam, *Expansion and Coexistence* (Praeger, New York, 1968), p. 5; quoted in Butow, *Tojo and the Coming of the War* (Princeton University Press, NJ, 1961), p. 203; Klaus Epstein, 'Gerhard Ritter and the First World War', in H.W. Koch (ed.), *The Origins of the First World War* (Macmillan, London, 1972), p. 290.
3 Nathan Leites, *A Study of Bolshevism* (Free Press, Glencoe, Illinois, 1953), p. 31; quoted in Arthur Schlesinger Jr, 'The Origins of the Cold War', *Foreign Affairs*, 46 (October 1967), p. 30.
4 Herbert Butterfield, *History and Human Relations* (Collins, London, 1951), pp. 19–20; John Herz, *Political Realism and Political Idealism* (University of Chicago Press, Chicago, 1959), p. 4.
5 Lewis Richardson, *Statistics of Deadly Quarrels* (Boxwood Press, Pittsburgh; Quadrangle, Chicago, 1960), p. xxiv; Lewis Richardson, *Arms and Insecurity* (Boxwood Press, Pittsburgh; Quadrangle, Chicago, 1960), p. 227.

6 Quoted in Richard Nixon, *Six Crises* (Doubleday, Garden City, NY, 1962), p. 62; Eyre Crowe, 'Memorandum on the Present State of Relations with France and Germany, January 1907' in G.P. Gooch and H. Temperley (eds), *British Documents on the Origins of the War, 1898–1914*, vol. 3 (HMSO, London, 1928).
7 Edward Grey, *Twenty-five Years*, vol. 1 (Hodder and Stoughton, London, 1925), p. 91; Butterfield, *History and Human Relations*, pp. 19–20.
8 Quoted in John Wheeler-Bennett, *Brest-Litovsk* (Norton, New York, 1971), pp. 295–6.
9 Epstein, 'Gerhard Ritter and the First World War', p. 293.
10 Quoted in Peter Filene, *Americans and the Soviet Experiment 1917–1933* (Harvard University Press, Cambridge, Mass., 1967), p. 43; Senate Committee on Foreign Relations, *Hearings, North Atlantic Treaty*, 81st Congress, 1st Session, p. 17.
11 George Kennan, *Memoirs*, vol. 2, *1950–1963* (Little, Brown, Boston, 1972), pp. 335–6.
12 Leites, *A Study of Bolshevism*, pp. 42, 34.
13 Kenneth Boulding, 'National Images and International Systems', *Journal of Conflict Resolution*, 3 (June 1959), p. 130.

1.6 Strategies for survival

John J. Mearsheimer

Source: *The Tragedy of Great Power Politics* (W. W. Norton & Co., New York, 2001), pp. 29–31; 138–67.

Mearsheimer's theory, building on five bedrock assumptions, postulates that the structure of the international system causes great powers to think and act offensively and to seek hegemony. As a consequence, all great powers aim for regional hegemony, maximum wealth, pre-eminent land power and nuclear superiority. It is then argued that great powers have followed six strategies (war, blackmail, bait and bleed, bloodletting, balancing and buck-passing) to achieve these goals. Bandwagoning and appeasement are depicted as strategies to avoid.

Why states pursue power

My explanation for why great powers vie with each other for power and strive for hegemony is derived from five assumptions about the international system. None of these assumptions alone mandates that states behave competitively. Taken together, however, they depict a world in which states have considerable reason to think and sometimes behave aggressively. In particular, the system encourages states to look for opportunities to maximize their power vis-à-vis other states.

Bedrock assumptions

The first assumption is that the international system is anarchic, which does not mean that it is chaotic or riven by disorder. It is easy to draw that conclusion, since realism depicts a world characterized by security competition and war. By itself, however, the realist notion of anarchy has nothing to do with conflict; it is an ordering principle, which says that the system comprises independent states that have no central authority above them. "Sovereignty, in other words, inheres in states because there is no higher ruling body in the international system." There is no "government over governments."

The second assumption is that great powers inherently possess some offensive military capability, which gives them the wherewithal to hurt and possibly destroy each other. States are potentially dangerous to each other, although some states have more military might than others and are therefore more dangerous. A state's military power is usually identified with the particular weaponry at its disposal, although even if there were no weapons, the individuals in those states could still use their feet and hands to attack the population of another state. After all, for every neck, there are two hands to choke it.

The third assumption is that states can never be certain about other states' intentions. Specifically, no state can be sure that another state will not use its offensive military capability to attack the first state. This is not to say that states necessarily have hostile intentions. Indeed, all of the states in the system may be reliably benign, but it is impossible to be sure of that judgment because intentions are impossible to divine with 100 percent certainty. There are many possible causes of aggression, and no state can be sure that another state is not motivated by one of them. Furthermore, intentions can change quickly, so a state's intentions can be benign one day and hostile the next. Uncertainty about intentions is unavoidable, which means that states can never be sure that other states do not have offensive intentions to go along with their offensive capabilities.

The fourth assumption is that survival is the primary goal of great powers. Specifically, states seek to maintain their territorial integrity and the autonomy of their domestic political order. Survival dominates other motives because, once a state is conquered, it is unlikely to be in a position to pursue other aims. [. . .] States can and do pursue other goals, of course, but security is their most important objective.

The fifth assumption is that great powers are rational actors. They are aware of their external environment and they think strategically about how to survive in it. In particular, they consider the preferences of other states and how their own behavior is likely to affect the behavior of those other states, and how the behavior of those other states is likely to affect their own strategy for survival. Moreover, states pay attention to the long term as well as the immediate consequences of their actions.

Operational state goals

Although I have emphasized that great powers seek to maximize their share of world power, more needs to be said about what that behavior entails. This section will therefore examine the different goals that states pursue and the strategies they employ in their hunt for more relative power.

Regional hegemony

Great powers concentrate on achieving four basic objectives. First, they seek regional hegemony. Although a state would maximize its security if it dominated the entire world, global hegemony is not feasible, except in the unlikely event that a state achieves nuclear superiority over its rivals (see below). The key limiting factor is the difficulty of projecting power across large bodies of water, which makes it impossible for any great power to conquer and dominate regions separated from it by oceans. Regional hegemons certainly pack a powerful military punch, but launching amphibious assaults across oceans against territory controlled and defended by another great power would be a suicidal undertaking. Not surprisingly, the United States, which is the only regional hegemon in modern history, has never seriously considered conquering either Europe or Northeast Asia. A great power could still conquer a neighboring region that it could reach by land, but it would still fall far short of achieving global hegemony.

Not only do great powers aim to dominate their own region, they also strive to prevent rivals in other areas from gaining hegemony. Regional hegemons fear that a peer competitor might jeopardize their hegemony by upsetting the balance of power in their backyard. Thus, regional hegemons prefer that there be two or more great powers in the other key regions of the world, because those neighbors are likely to spend most of their time competing with each other, leaving them few opportunities to threaten a distant hegemon. [. . .]

Although every great power would like to be a regional hegemon, few are likely to reach that pinnacle. As mentioned already, the United States is the only great power that has dominated its region in modern history. There are two reasons why regional hegemons tend to be a rare species. Few states have the necessary endowments to make a run at hegemony. To qualify as a potential hegemon, a state must be considerably wealthier than its local rivals and must possess the mightiest army in the region. During the past two centuries, only a handful of states have met those criteria: Napoleonic France, Wilhelmine Germany, Nazi Germany, the Soviet Union during the Cold War, and the United States. Furthermore, even if a state has the wherewithal to be a potential hegemon, the other great powers in the system will seek to prevent it from actually becoming a regional hegemon.

Maximum wealth

Second, great powers aim to maximize the amount of the world's wealth that they control. States care about relative wealth, because economic might is the foundation of military might. In practical terms, this means that great powers place a high premium on having a powerful and dynamic economy, not only because it enhances the general welfare, but also because it is a reliable way to gain a military advantage over rivals. [. . .]

Parenthetically, great powers are likely to view especially wealthy states, or states moving in that direction, as serious threats, regardless of whether or not they have a formidable military capability. After all, wealth can rather easily be translated into military might. [. . .]

Great powers also seek to prevent rival great powers from dominating the wealth-generating areas of the world. In the modern era, those areas are usually populated by the leading industrial states, although they might be occupied by less-developed states that possess critically important raw materials. Great powers sometimes attempt to dominate those regions themselves, but at the very least, they try to ensure that none falls under the control of a rival great power. Areas that contain little intrinsic wealth are of less concern to great powers. [. . .]

Preeminent land power

Third, great powers aim to dominate the balance of land power, because that is the best way to maximize their share of military might. In practice, this means that states build powerful armies as well as air and naval forces to support those ground forces. But great powers do not spend all of their defense funds on land power. As discussed below, they devote considerable resources to acquiring nuclear weapons; sometimes they also buy independent sea power and strategic airpower. But because land power is the dominant form of military power, states aspire to have the most formidable army in their region of the world.

Nuclear superiority

Fourth, great powers seek nuclear superiority over their rivals. In an ideal world, a state would have the world's only nuclear arsenal, which would give it the capability to devastate its rivals without fear of retaliation. That huge military advantage would make that nuclear-armed state a global hegemon, in which case my previous discussion of regional hegemony would be irrelevant. Also, the balance of land power would be of minor importance in a world dominated by a nuclear hegemon. It is difficult, however, to achieve and maintain nuclear superiority, because rival states will go to great lengths to develop a nuclear retaliatory force of their own. Great powers are likely to find themselves operating in a world of nuclear powers with the assured capacity to destroy their enemies – a world of mutual assured destruction, or MAD.

Some scholars, especially defensive realists, argue that it makes no sense for nuclear-armed states in a MAD world to pursue nuclear superiority. In particular, they should not build counterforce weapons – i.e., those that could strike the other side's nuclear arsenal – and they should not build defensive systems that could shoot down the adversary's incoming nuclear warheads, because the essence of a MAD world is that no state can be assured that it has destroyed *all* of its rival's nuclear weapons, and thus would remain vulnerable to nuclear devastation. It makes more sense, so the argument goes, for each state to *be* vulnerable to the other side's nuclear weapons. Two reasons underpin the assertion that nuclear-armed states should not pursue nuclear superiority. MAD is a powerful force for stability, so it makes no sense to undermine it. Furthermore, it is almost impossible to gain meaningful military advantage by building counterforce weapons and defenses. No matter how sophisticated those systems might be, it is almost impossible to fight and win a nuclear war, because nuclear weapons are so destructive that both sides will be annihilated in the conflict. Thus, it makes little sense to think in terms of gaining military advantage at the nuclear level.

Great powers, however, are unlikely to be content with living in a MAD world, and they are likely to search for ways to gain superiority over their nuclear-armed opponents. Although there is no question that MAD makes war among the great powers less likely, a state is likely to be more secure if it has nuclear superiority. Specifically, a great power operating under MAD still has great-power rivals that it must worry about, and it still is vulnerable to nuclear attack, which although unlikely, is still possible. A great power that gains nuclear superiority, on the other hand, is a hegemon and thus has no major rivals to fear. Most important, it would not face the threat of a nuclear attack. Therefore, states have a powerful incentive to be nuclear hegemons. This logic does not deny that meaningful nuclear superiority is an especially difficult goal to achieve. Nevertheless, states will pursue nuclear advantage because of the great benefits it promises. In particular, states will build lots of counterforce capability and push hard to develop effective defenses in the hope that they might gain nuclear superiority. [. . .]

Strategies for gaining power

War

War is the most controversial strategy that great powers can employ to increase their share of world power. Not only does it involve death and destruction, sometimes on a vast scale, but it became fashionable in the twentieth century to argue that conquest does not pay and that war is therefore a futile enterprise. [. . .]

The claim that war is a losing proposition takes four basic forms. Some suggest that aggressors almost always lose. In the past, states that initiated war, however, won roughly 60 percent of the time. Others maintain that nuclear weapons make it virtually impossible for great powers to fight each other, because of the danger of mutual annihilation. Nuclear weapons make great-power war less likely, but they do not render it obsolete. Certainly none of the great powers in the nuclear age has behaved as if war with another major power has been ruled out.

The other two perspectives assume that wars are winnable, but that successful conquest leads to Pyrrhic victories. The two focus, respectively, on the costs and on the benefits of war. These concepts are actually linked, since states contemplating aggression invariably weigh its expected costs and benefits.

The costs argument, which attracted a lot of attention in the 1980s, is that conquest does not pay because it leads to the creation of empires, and the price of maintaining an empire eventually becomes so great that economic growth at home is sharply slowed. [. . .]

According to the benefits argument, military victory does not pay because conquerors cannot exploit modern industrial economies for gain, especially those that are built around information technologies. The root of the conqueror's problem is that nationalism makes it hard to subdue and manipulate the people in defeated states. [. . .]

There is no question that great powers sometimes confront circumstances in which the likely costs of conquest are high and the expected benefits are small. In those cases, it makes no sense to start a war. But the general claim that conquest almost always bankrupts the aggressor and provides no tangible benefits does not stand up to close scrutiny.

There are many examples of states expanding via the sword and yet not damaging their economies in the process. [. . .]

Regarding the benefits argument, conquerors can exploit a vanquished state's economy for gain, even in the information age. Wealth can be extracted from an occupied state by levying taxes, confiscating industrial output, or even confiscating industrial plants.

But even if one rejects the notion that conquest pays economic dividends, there are three other ways that a victorious aggressor can shift the balance of power in its favor. The conqueror might employ some portion of the vanquished state's population in its army or as forced labor in its homeland. Napoleon's military machine, for example, made use of manpower raised in defeated states. In fact, when France attacked Russia in the summer of 1812, roughly half of the main invasion force – which totalled 674,000 soldiers – was not French. [. . .]

Furthermore, conquest sometimes pays because the victor gains strategically important territory. In particular, states can gain a buffer zone that helps protect them from attack by another state, or that can be used to launch an attack on a rival state. For example, France gave serious consideration to annexing the Rhineland before and after Germany was defeated in World War I. [. . .]

Finally, war can shift the balance of power in the victor's favor by eliminating the vanquished state from the ranks of the great powers. Conquering states can achieve this goal in different ways. They might destroy a defeated rival by killing most of its people, thereby eliminating it altogether from the international system. States rarely pursue this drastic option, but evidence of this kind of behavior exists to make states think about it. The Romans, for example, annihilated Carthage, and there is reason to think that Hitler planned to eliminate Poland and the Soviet Union from the map of Europe.

Blackmail

A state can gain power at a rival's expense without going to war by threatening to use military force against its opponent. Coercive threats and intimidation, not the actual use of force, produce the desired outcome. If this blackmail works, it is clearly preferable to war, because blackmail achieves its goals without bloody costs. However, blackmail is unlikely to produce marked shifts in the balance of power, mainly because threats alone are usually not enough to compel a great power to make significant concessions to a rival great power. Great powers, by definition, have formidable military strength relative to each other, and therefore they are not likely to give in to threats without a fight. Blackmail is more likely to work against minor powers that have no great-power ally. Nevertheless, there are cases of successful blackmail against great powers. [. . .]

Bait and bleed

Bait and bleed is a third strategy that states might employ to increase their relative power. This strategy involves causing two rivals to engage in a protracted war, so that they bleed each other white, while the baiter remains on the sideline, its military strength intact. There was concern in the United States during the Cold War, for example, that a third party might surreptitiously provoke a nuclear war between the superpowers. Also, one of the super-powers might have considered provoking its rival to start a losing war in the Third World. For example, the United States could have encouraged the Soviet Union to get entrapped in conflicts like the one in Afghanistan. But that was not American policy. In fact, there are few examples in modern history of states pursuing a bait-and-bleed strategy. [. . .]

The fundamental problem with a bait-and-bleed strategy is that it is difficult to trick rival states into starting a war that they would otherwise not fight. There are hardly any good ways of causing trouble between other states without getting exposed, or at least raising suspicions in the target states. Moreover, the states being baited are likely to recognize the danger of engaging each other in a protracted war while the baiter sits untouched on the sidelines, gaining relative power on the cheap. States are likely to avoid such a trap. Finally there is always the danger for the baiter that one of the states being baited might win a quick and decisive victory and end up gaining power rather than losing it.

Bloodletting

Bloodletting is a more promising variant of this strategy. Here, the aim is to make sure that any war between one's rivals turns into a long and costly conflict that saps their strength. There is no baiting in this version; the rivals have gone to war independently, and the bloodletter is mainly concerned with causing its rivals to bleed each other white, while it stays out of the fighting. As a senator, Harry Truman had this strategy in mind in June 1941 when he reacted to the Nazi invasion of the Soviet Union by saying, "If we see that Germany is winning we ought to help Russia, and if Russia is winning we ought to help Germany, and that way let them kill as many as possible." [. . .]

Strategies for checking aggressors

Great powers not only seek to gain power over their rivals, they also aim to prevent those foes from gaining power at their expense. Keeping potential aggressors at bay is sometimes a rather simple task. Since great powers maximize their share of world power, they invest heavily in defense and typically build formidable fighting forces. That impressive military capability is usually sufficient to deter rival states from challenging the balance of power. But occasionally, highly aggressive great powers that are more difficult to contain come on the scene. Especially powerful states, like potential hegemons, invariably fall into this category. To deal with these aggressors, threatened great powers can choose between two strategies: balancing and buck-passing. They invariably prefer buck-passing, although sometimes they have no choice but to balance against the threat.

Balancing

With balancing, a great power assumes direct responsibility for preventing an aggressor from upsetting the balance of power. The initial goal is to deter the aggressor, but if that fails, the balancing state will fight the ensuing war. Threatened states can take three measures to make balancing work. First, they can send clear signals to the aggressor through diplomatic channels (and through the actions described below) that they are firmly committed to maintaining the balance of power, even if it means going to war. The emphasis in the balancer's message is on confrontation, not conciliation. In effect, the balancer draws a line in the sand and warns the aggressor not to cross it. The United States pursued this type of policy with the Soviet Union throughout the Cold War; France and Russia did the same with Germany before World War I.

Second, threatened states can work to create a defensive alliance to help them contain their dangerous opponent. This diplomatic maneuver, which is often called "external balancing," is limited in a bipolar world, because there are no potential great-power alliance partners, although it is still possible to ally with minor powers. During the Cold War, for example, both the United States and the Soviet Union had no choice but to ally with minor powers, because they were the only great powers in the system. Threatened states place a high premium on finding alliance partners, because the costs of checking an aggressor are shared in an alliance – an especially important consideration if war breaks out. Furthermore, recruiting allies increases the amount of firepower confronting the aggressor, which in turn increases the likelihood that deterrence will work.

These benefits notwithstanding, external balancing has a downside: it is often slow and inefficient. [. . .] Putting together balancing coalitions quickly and making them function smoothly is often difficult, because it takes time to coordinate the efforts to prospective allies or member states, even when there is wide agreement on what needs to be done. Threatened states usually disagree over how the burdens should be distributed among alliance members. After all, states are self-interested actors with powerful incentives to minimize the costs they pay to contain an aggressor. This problem is compounded by the fact that alliance members have an impulse to buck-pass among themselves, as discussed below. Finally, there is likely to be friction among coalition members over which state leads the alliance, especially when it comes to formulating strategy.

Third, threatened states can balance against an aggressor by mobilizing additional resources of their own. For example, defense spending might be increased or conscription might be implemented. This action, which is commonly referred to as "internal balancing," is self-help in the purest sense of the term. But there are usually significant limits on how many additional resources a threatened state can muster against an aggressor, because great powers normally already devote a large percentage of their resources to defense. Because they seek to maximize their share of world power, states are effectively engaged in internal balancing all the time. Nevertheless, when faced with a particularly aggressive adversary, great powers will eliminate any slack in the system and search for clever ways to boost defense spending.

There is, however, one exceptional circumstance in which a great power will increase defense spending to help deter an aggressor. Offshore balancers like the United Kingdom and the United States tend to maintain relatively small military forces when they are not needed to contain a potential hegemon in a strategically important area. Usually, they can afford to have a small army because their distant rivals tend to focus their attention on each other, and because the stopping power of water provides them with abundant security.

Therefore, when it is necessary for an offshore balancer to check a potential hegemon, it is likely to sharply expand the size and strength of its fighting forces, as the United States did in 1917, when it entered World War I, and in 1940, the year before it entered World War II.

Buck-passing

Buck-passing is a threatened great power's main alternative to balancing. A buck-passer attempts to get another state to bear the burden of deterring or possibly fighting an aggressor, while it remains on the sidelines. The buck-passer fully recognizes the need to prevent the aggressor from increasing its share of world power but looks for some other state that is threatened by the aggressor to perform that onerous task.

Threatened states can take four measures to facilitate buck-passing. First, they can seek good diplomatic relations with the aggressor, or at least not do anything to provoke it, in the hope that it will concentrate its attention on the intended "buck-catcher." [. . .]

Second, buck-passers usually maintain cool relations with the intended buck-catcher, not just because this diplomatic distancing might help foster good relations with the aggressor, but also because the buck-passer does not want to get dragged into a war on the side of the buck-catcher. The aim of the buck-passer, after all, is to avoid having to fight the aggressor. [. . .]

Third, great powers can mobilize additional resources of their own to make buck-passing work. It might seem that the buck-passer should be able to take a somewhat relaxed approach to defense spending, since the strategy's objective is to get someone else to contain the aggressor. But save for the exceptional case of the offshore balancer discussed earlier, that conclusion would be wrong. Leaving aside the fact that states maximize relative power, buck-passers have two other good reasons to look for opportunities to increase defense spending. By building up its own defenses, a buck-passer makes itself an imposing target, thus giving the aggressor incentive to focus its attention on the intended buck-catcher. The logic here is simple: the more powerful a threatened state is, the less likely it is that an aggressor will attack it. Of course, the buck-catcher must still have the wherewithal to contain the aggressor without the buck-passer's help. [. . .]

Fourth, it sometimes makes sense for a buck-passer to allow or even facilitate the growth in power of the intended buck-catcher. That burden-bearer would then have a better chance of containing the aggressor state, which would increase the buck-passer's prospects of remaining on the sidelines. [. . .]

The allure of buck-passing

Buck-passing and putting together a balancing coalition obviously represent contrasting ways of dealing with an aggressor. Nevertheless, there is a strong tendency to buck-pass or "free-ride" inside balancing coalitions, although the danger that buck-passing will wreck the alliance is a powerful countervailing force. [Nevertheless] great powers seem clearly to prefer buck-passing to balancing. One reason for this preference is that buck-passing usually provides defense "on the cheap." After all, the state that catches the buck pays the substantial costs of fighting the aggressor if deterrence fails and war breaks out. Of course, buck-passers sometimes spend considerable sums of money on their own military to facilitate buck-passing and to protect against the possibility that buck-passing might fail.

Buck-passing can also have an offensive dimension to it, which can make it even more attractive. Specifically, if the aggressor and the buck-catcher become involved in a long and costly war, the balance of power is likely to shift in the buck-passer's favor; it would then be in a good position to dominate the postwar world. [. . .]

Passing the buck is also an attractive option when a state faces more than one dangerous rival but does not have the military might to confront them all at once. Buck-passing might help reduce the number of threats. [. . .]

Buck-passing is not a foolproof strategy, however. Its chief drawback is that the buck-catcher might fail to check the aggressor, leaving the buck-passer in a precarious strategic position. [. . .]

Furthermore, in cases where the buck-passer allows the military might of the buck-catcher to increase, there is the danger that the buck-catcher might eventually become so powerful that it threatens to upset the balance of power, as happened with Germany after it was unified in 1870. [. . .]

Strategies to avoid

Some argue that balancing and buck-passing are not the only strategies that threatened states might employ against a dangerous opponent. Appeasement and bandwagoning, so the argument goes, are also viable alternatives. But that is wrong. Both of those strategies call for conceding power to an aggressor, which violates balance-of-power logic and increases the danger to the state that employs them. Great powers that care about their survival should neither appease nor bandwagon with their adversaries.

Bandwagoning happens when a state joins forces with a more powerful opponent, conceding that its formidable new partner will gain a disproportionate share of the spoils they conquer together. The distribution of power, in other words, will shift further against the bandwagoner and in the stronger state's favor. Bandwagoning is a strategy for the weak. Its underlying assumption is that if a state is badly outgunned by a rival, it makes no sense to resist its demands, because that adversary will take what it wants by force anyway and inflict considerable punishment in the process. The bandwagoner must just hope that the trouble-maker is merciful. Thucydides' famous dictum that "the strong do what they can and the weak suffer what they must" captures the essence of bandwagoning.

This strategy, which violates the basic canon of offensive realism – that states maximize relative power – is rarely employed by great powers, because they have, by definition, the wherewithal to put up a decent fight against other great powers, and because they certainly have the incentive to stand up and fight. Bandwagoning is employed mainly by minor powers that stand alone against hostile great powers. They have no choice but to give in to the enemy, because they are weak and isolated. [. . .]

With appeasement, a threatened state makes concessions to an aggressor that shift the balance of power in the recipient's favor. The appeaser usually agrees to surrender all or part of the territory of a third state to its powerful foe. The purpose of this allowance is behavior modification: to push the aggressor in a more pacific direction and possibly turn it into a status quo power. The strategy rests on the assumption that the adversary's aggressive behavior is largely the result of an acute sense of strategic vulnerability. Therefore, any steps taken to reduce that insecurity will dampen, and possibly eliminate, the underlying motive for war. Appeasement accomplishes this end, so the argument goes, by allowing the appeaser to demonstrate its good intentions and by shifting the military balance in the appeased state's favor, thus making it less vulnerable and more secure, and ultimately less aggressive.

Unlike the bandwagoner, who makes no effort to contain the aggressor, the appeaser remains committed to checking the threat. But like band-wagoning, appeasement contradicts the dictates of offensive realism and therefore it is a fanciful and dangerous strategy. It is unlikely to transform a dangerous foe into a kinder, gentler opponent, much less a peace-loving state. Indeed, appeasement is likely to whet, not shrink, an aggressor state's appetite for conquest. There is little doubt that if a state concedes a substantial amount of power to an acutely insecure rival, that foe would presumably feel better about its prospects for survival. That reduced level of fear would, in turn, lessen that rival's incentive to shift the balance of power in its favor. But that good news is only part of the story. In fact, two other considerations trump that peace-promoting logic. International anarchy, as emphasized, causes states to look for opportunities to gain additional increments of power at each other's expense. Because great powers are programmed for offense, an appeased state is likely to interpret any power concession by another state as a sign of weakness – as evidence that the appeaser is unwilling to defend the balance of power. The appeased state is then likely to continue pushing for more concessions. It would be foolish for a state not to gain as much power as possible, because a state's prospects for survival increase as it accumulates additional increments of power. Furthermore, the appeased state's capability to gain even more power would be enhanced probably substantially by the additional power it was granted by the appeaser. In short, appeasement is likely to make a dangerous rival more, not less, dangerous.

1.7 State power and the structure of international trade

Stephen D. Krasner

Source: *World Politics*, vol. XXVIII, no. 3 (1976), pp. 317–47.

Krasner sets out to reassert the power of states to determine the character of the international system. He takes the structure of international trade in the nineteenth and twentieth centuries as an example and demonstrates that the degree of 'openness' in that structure can be partially explained by the distribution of economic power among states. In particular, he argues that the existence of a hegemonic state leads to a higher level of free trade than that found when the distribution of power is more equal.

Introduction

In recent years, students of international relations have multinationalized, transnationalized, bureaucratized, and transgovernmentalized the state until it has virtually ceased to exist as an analytic construct. Nowhere is that trend more apparent than in the study of the politics of international economic relations. The basic conventional assumptions have been undermined by assertions that the state is trapped by a transnational society created not by sovereigns, but by nonstate actors. Interdependence is not seen as a reflection of state policies and state choices (the perspective of balance-of-power theory), but as the result of elements beyond the control of any state or a system created by states.

This perspective is at best profoundly misleading. It may explain developments within a particular international economic structure, but it cannot explain the structure itself. That structure has many institutional and behavioral manifestations. The central continuum along which it can be described is openness. International economic structures may range from complete autarky (if all states prevent movements across their borders), to complete openness (if no restrictions exist). In this paper I will present an analysis of one aspect of the international economy – the structure of international trade: that is, the degree of openness for the movement of goods as opposed to capital, labor, technology, or other factors of production.

Since the beginning of the nineteenth century, this structure has gone through several changes. These can be explained, albeit imperfectly, by a state-power theory: an approach that begins with the assumption that the structure of international trade is determined by the interests and power of states acting to maximize national goals. [. . .]

The causal argument: state interests, state power, and international trading structures

Neoclassical trade theory is based upon the assumption that states act to maximize their aggregate economic utility. This leads to the conclusion that maximum global welfare and Pareto optimality are achieved under free trade. While particular countries might better their situations through protectionism, economic theory has generally looked askance at such policies. [. . .]

State preferences

Historical experience suggests that policy makers are dense, or that the assumptions of the conventional argument are wrong. Free trade has hardly been the norm. Stupidity is not a very interesting analytic category. An alternative approach to explaining international trading structures is to assume that states seek a broad range of goals. At least four major state interests affected by the structure of international trade can be identified. They are: political power, aggregate national income, economic growth, and social stability. The way in which each of these goals is affected by the degree of openness depends upon the potential economic power of the state as defined by its relative size and level of development.

Let us begin with aggregate national income because it is most straightforward. Given the exceptions noted above, conventional neoclassical theory demonstrates that the greater the degree of openness in the international trading system, the greater the level of aggregate economic income. This conclusion applies to all states regardless of their size or relative level of development. The static economic benefits of openness are, however, generally inversely related to size. Trade gives small states relatively more welfare benefits than it gives large ones. Empirically, small states have higher ratios of trade to national product. They do not have the generous factor endowments or potential for national economies of scale that are enjoyed by larger – particularly continental – states.

The impact of openness on social stability runs in the opposite direction. Greater open-ness exposes the domestic economy to the exigencies of the world market. That implies a higher level of factor movements than in a closed economy, because domestic production patterns must adjust to changes in international prices. Social instability is thereby increased, since there is friction in moving factors, particularly labor, from one sector to another. The impact will be stronger in small states than in large, and in relatively less developed than in more developed ones. Large states are less involved in the international economy: a smaller percentage of their total factor endowment is affected by the international market at any given level of openness. More developed states are better able to adjust factors: skilled workers can more easily be moved from one kind of production to another than can unskilled laborers or peasants. Hence social stability is, *ceteris paribus*, inversely related to openness, but the deleterious consequences of exposure to the international trading system are mitigated by larger size and greater economic development.

The relationship between political power and the international trading structure can be analyzed in terms of the relative opportunity costs of closure for trading partners. The higher the relative cost of closure, the weaker the political position of the state. Hirschman has argued that this cost can be measured in terms of direct income losses and the adjustment costs of reallocating factors.[1] These will be smaller for large states and for relatively more developed states. Other things being equal, utility costs will be less for large states because they generally have a smaller proportion of their economy engaged in the international economic system. Reallocation costs will be less for more advanced states because their factors are more mobile. Hence a state that is relatively large and more developed will find its political power enhanced by an open system because its opportunity costs of closure are less. The large state can use the threat to alter the system to secure economic or noneconomic objectives. Historically, there is one important exception to this generalization – the oil-exporting states. The level of reserves for some of these states, particularly Saudi Arabia, has reduced the economic opportunity costs of closure to a very low level despite their lack of development.

The relationship between international economic structure and economic growth is elusive. For small states, economic growth has generally been empirically associated with openness.[2] Exposure to the international system makes possible a much more efficient allocation of resources. Openness also probably furthers the rate of growth of large countries with relatively advanced technologies because they do not need to protect infant industries and can take advantage of expanded world markets. In the long term, however, openness for capital and technology, as well as goods, may hamper the growth of large, developed countries by diverting resources from the domestic economy, and by providing potential competitors with the knowledge needed to develop their own industries. Only by maintaining its technological lead and continually developing new industries can even a very large state escape the undesired consequences of an entirely open economic system. [. . .]

From state preferences to international trading structures

The next step in this argument is to relate particular distributions of potential economic power, defined by the size and level of development of individual states, to the structure of the international trading system, defined in terms of openness.

Let us consider a system composed of a large number of small, highly developed states. Such a system is likely to lead to an open international trading structure. The aggregate income and economic growth of each state are increased by an open system. The social instability produced by exposure to international competition is mitigated by the factor mobility made possible by higher levels of development. There is no loss of political power from openness because the costs of closure are symmetrical for all members of the system.

Now let us consider a system composed of a few very large, but unequally developed states. Such a distribution of potential economic power is likely to lead to a closed structure. Each state could increase its income through a more open system, but the gains would be modest. Openness would create more social instability in the less developed countries. The rate of growth for more backward areas might be frustrated, while that of the more advanced ones would be enhanced. A more open structure would leave the less developed states in a politically more vulnerable position, because their greater factor rigidity would mean a higher relative cost of closure. Because of these disadvantages, large but relatively less developed states are unlikely to accept an open trading structure. More advanced states cannot, unless they are militarily much more powerful, force large backward countries to accept openness.

Finally, let us consider a hegemonic system – one in which there is a single state that is much larger and relatively more advanced than its trading partners. The costs and benefits of openness are not symmetrical for all members of the system. The hegemonic state will have a preference for an open structure. Such a structure increases its aggregate national income. It also increases its rate of growth during its ascendency – that is, when its relative size and technological lead are increasing. Further, an open structure increases its political power, since the opportunity costs of closure are least for a large and developed state. The social instability resulting from exposure to the international system is mitigated by the hegemonic power's relatively low level of involvement in the international economy, and the mobility of its factors.

What of the other members of a hegemonic system? Small states are likely to opt for openness because the advantages in terms of aggregate income and growth are so great, and their political power is bound to be restricted regardless of what they do. [. . .] The potentially dominant state has symbolic, economic, and military capabilities that can be used to entice or compel others to accept an open trading structure.

At the symbolic level, the hegemonic state stands as an example of how economic development can be achieved. Its policies may be emulated, even if they are inappropriate for other states. Where there are very dramatic asymmetries, military power can be used to coerce weaker states into an open structure. [. . .]

Most importantly, the hegemonic state can use its economic resources to create an open structure. In terms of positive incentives, it can offer access to its large domestic market and to its relatively cheap exports. In terms of negative ones, it can withhold foreign grants and engage in competition, potentially ruinous for the weaker state, in third-country markets. The size and economic robustness of the hegemonic state also enable it to provide the confidence necessary for a stable international monetary system, and its currency can offer the liquidity needed for an increasingly open system.

In sum, openness is most likely to occur during periods when a hegemonic state is in its ascendancy. Such a state has the interest and the resources to create a structure characterized by lower tariffs, rising trade proportions, and less regionalism. There are other distributions of potential power where openness is likely, such as a system composed of many small, highly developed states. But even here, that potential might not be realized because of the problems of creating confidence in a monetary system where adequate liquidity would have to be provided by a negotiated international reserve asset or a group of national currencies. Finally, it is unlikely that very large states, particularly at unequal levels of development, would accept open trading relations.

These arguments, and the implications of other ideal typical configurations of potential economic power for the openness of trading structures, are summarized in Figure 1.

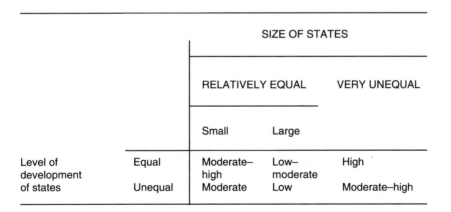

Figure 1 Probability of an open trading structure with different distributions of potential economic power

The dependent variable: describing the structure of the international trading system

The structure of international trade has both behavioral and institutional attributes. The degree of openness can be described both by the *flow* of goods and by the *policies* that are followed by states with respect to trade barriers and international payments. The two are not unrelated, but they do not coincide perfectly.

In common usage, the focus of attention has been upon institutions. Openness is associated with those historical periods in which tariffs were substantially lowered: the third quarter of the nineteenth century and the period since the Second World War.

Tariffs alone, however, are not an adequate indicator of structure. They are hard to operationalize quantitatively. Tariffs do not have to be high to be effective. If cost functions are nearly identical, even low tariffs can prevent trade. Effective tariff rates may be much higher than nominal ones. Non-tariff barriers to trade, which are not easily compared across states, can substitute for duties. An undervalued exchange rate can protect domestic markets from foreign competition. Tariff levels alone cannot describe the structure of international trade.

A second indicator, and one which is behavioral rather than institutional, is trade proportions – the ratios of trade to national income for different states. Like tariff levels, these involve describing the system in terms of an agglomeration of national tendencies. A period in which these ratios are increasing across time for most states can be described as one of increasing openness.

A third indicator is the concentration of trade within regions composed of states at different levels of development. The degree of such regional encapsulation is determined not so much by comparative advantage (because relative factor endowments would allow almost any backward area to trade with almost any developed one), but by political choices or dictates. Large states, attempting to protect themselves from the vagaries of a global system, seek to maximize their interests by creating regional blocs. Openness in the global economic system has in effect meant greater trade among the leading industrial states. Periods of closure are associated with the encapsulation of certain advanced states within regional systems shared with certain less developed areas.

A description of the international trading system involves, then, an exercise that is comparative rather than absolute. A period when tariffs are falling, trade proportions are rising, and regional trading patterns are becoming less extreme will be defined as one in which the structure is becoming more open.

[Krasner goes on to investigate the evidence available for the period 1820–1970, using these three indicators, and comes to the following conclusions.]

If we put all three indicators – tariff levels, trade proportions, and trade patterns – together, they suggest the following periodization:

> Period I (1820–79): Increasing openness – tariffs are generally lowered; trade proportions increase. Data are not available for trade patterns. However, it is important to note that this is not a universal pattern. The United States is largely unaffected: its tariff levels remain high (and are in fact increased during the early 1860s) and American trade proportions remain almost constant.
>
> Period II (1879–1900): Modest closure – tariffs are increased; trade proportions decline modestly for most states. Data are not available for trade patterns.

Period III (1900–13): Greater openness – tariff levels remain generally unchanged; trade proportions increase for all major trading states except the United States. Trading patterns become less regional in three out of the four cases for which data are available.

Period IV (1918–39): Closure – tariff levels are increased in the 1920s and again in the 1930s; trade proportions decline. Trade becomes more regionally encapsulated.

Period V (1945–c.1970): Great openness – tariffs are lowered; trade proportions increase, particularly after 1960. Regional concentration decreases after 1960. However, these developments are limited to non-communist areas of the world.

The independent variable: describing the distribution of potential economic power among states

Analysts of international relations have an almost *pro forma* set of variables designed to show the distribution of potential power in the international *political* system. It includes such factors as gross national product, per capita income, geographical position, and size of armed forces. A similar set of indicators can be presented for the international *economic* system.

Statistics are available over a long period of time for per capita income, aggregate size, share of world trade, and share of world investment. They demonstrate that, since the beginning of the nineteenth century, there have been two first-rank economic powers in the world economy – Britain and the United States. The United States passed Britain in aggregate size sometime in the middle of the nineteenth century and, in the 1880s, became the largest producer of manufactures. America's lead was particularly marked in technologically advanced industries turning out sewing machines, harvesters, cash registers, locomotives, steam pumps, telephones, and petroleum. Until the First World War, however, Great Britain had a higher per capita income, a greater share of world trade, and a greater share of world investment than any other state. The peak of British ascendance occurred around 1880, when Britain's relative per capita income, share of world trade, and share of investment flows reached their highest levels. Britain's potential dominance in 1880 and 1900 was particularly striking in the international economic system, where her share of trade and foreign investment was about twice as large as that of any other state.

It was only after the First World War that the United States became relatively larger and more developed in terms of all four indicators. This potential dominance reached new and dramatic heights between 1945 and 1960. Since then, the relative position of the United States has declined, bringing it quite close to West Germany, its nearest rival, in terms of per capita income and share of world trade. The devaluations of the dollar that have taken place since 1972 are reflected in a continuation of this downward trend for income and aggregate size.

The relative potential economic power of Britain and the United States is shown in Tables 1 and 2.

In sum, Britain was the world's most important trading state from the period after the Napoleonic Wars until 1913. Her relative position rose until about 1880 and fell thereafter. The United States became the largest and most advanced state in economic terms after the First World War, but did not equal the relative share of world trade and investment achieved by Britain in the 1880s until after the Second World War.

Table 1 Indicators of British potential power (ratio of British value to next highest)

	Per capita income	Aggregate size	Share of world trade	Share of world investment[a]
1860	.91 (US)	.74 (US)	2.01 (FR)	n.a.
1880	1.30 (US)	.79 (1874–83 US)	2.22 (FR)	1.93 (FR)
1900	1.05 (1899 US)	.58 (1899 US)	2.17 (1890 GERM)	2.08 (FR)
1913	.92 (US)	.43 (US)	1.20 (US)	2.18 (1914 FR)
1928	.66 (US)	.25 (1929 US)	.79 (US)	.64 (1921–29 US)
1937	.79 (US)	.29 (US)	.88 (US)	.18 (1930–38 US)
1950	.56 (US)	.19 (US)	.69 (US)	.13 (1951–55 US)
1960	.49 (US)	.14 (US)	.46 (1958 US)	.15 (1956–61 US)
1972	.46 (US)	.13 (US)	.47 (1973 US)	n.a.

[a]Stock 1870–1913; Flow 1928–50.
Years are in parentheses when different from those in first column.
Countries in parentheses are those with the largest values for the particular indicator other than Great Britain.

Table 2 Indicators of US potential power (ratio of US value to next highest)

	Per capita income	Aggregate size	Share of world trade	Share of world investment flows
1860	1.10 (GB)	1.41 (GB)	.36 (GB)	Net debtor
1880	.77 (GB)	1.23 (1883 GB)	.37 (GB)	Net debtor
1900	.95 (1899 GB)	1.73 (1899 GB)	.43 (1890 GB)	n.a.
1913	1.09 (GB)	2.15 (RUS)	.83 (GB)	Net debtor
1928	1.51 (GB)	3.22 (USSR)	1.26 (GB)	1.55 (1921–30 UK)
1937	1.26 (GB)	2.67 (USSR)	1.13 (GB)	5.53 (1930–38 UK)
1950	1.78 (GB)	3.15 (USSR)	1.44 (GB)	7.42 (1951–55 UK)
1960	2.05 (GB)	2.81 (USSR)	2.15 (1958 GB)	6.60 (1956–61 UK)
1972	1.31 (GERM)	n.a.	1.18 (1973 GERM)	n.a.

Years are in parentheses when different from those in first column.
Countries in parentheses are those with the largest values for the particular indicator other than the United States.

Testing the argument

The contention that hegemony leads to a more open trading structure is fairly well, but not perfectly, confirmed by the empirical evidence presented in the preceding sections. The argument explains the periods 1820 to 1879, 1880 to 1900, and 1945 to 1960. It does not fully explain those from 1900 to 1913, 1919 to 1939, or 1960 to the present.

[Krasner goes on to examine evidence for the fluctuations in British and American influence, and especially for the fact that there appear to be 'time-lags' in adaptations to a changed power distribution. He concludes thus:]

In sum, although the general pattern of the structure of international trade conforms with the predictions of a state-power argument – two periods of openness separated by one of closure – corresponding to periods of rising British and American hegemony and an inter-regnum, the whole pattern is out of phase. British commitment to openness continued long after Britain's position had declined. American commitment to openness did not begin until well after the United States had become the world's leading economic power and has continued during a period of relative American decline. The state-power argument needs to be amended to take these delayed reactions into account.

Amending the argument

The structure of the international trading system does not move in lockstep with changes in the distribution of potential power among states. Systems are initiated and ended, not as a state-power theory would predict, by close assessments of the interests of the state at every given moment, but by external events – usually cataclysmic ones. The closure that began in 1879 coincided with the Great Depression of the last part of the nineteenth century. The final dismantling of the nineteenth-century international economic system was not precipitated by a change in British trade or monetary policy, but by the First World War and the Depression. The potato famine of the 1840s prompted abolition of the Corn Laws; and the United States did not assume the mantle of world leadership until the world had been laid bare by six years of total war. Some catalytic external event seems necessary to move states to dramatic policy initiatives in line with state interests.

Once policies have been adopted, they are pursued until a new crisis demonstrates that they are no longer feasible. States become locked in by the impact of prior choices on their domestic political structures. The British decision to opt for openness in 1846 corresponded with state interests. It also strengthened the position of industrial and financial groups over time, because they had the opportunity to operate in an international system that furthered their objectives. That system eventually undermined the position of British farmers, a group that would have supported protectionism if it had survived. Once entrenched, Britain's export industries, and more importantly the City of London, resisted policies of closure. In the interwar years, the British rentier class insisted on restoring the prewar parity of the pound – a decision that placed enormous deflationary pressures on the domestic economy – because they wanted to protect the value of their investments.

Institutions created during periods of rising ascendancy remained in operation when they were no longer appropriate. For instance, the organization of British banking in the nineteenth century separated domestic and foreign operations. The Court of Directors of the Bank of England was dominated by international banking houses. Their decisions about British monetary policy were geared toward the international economy. Under a different institutional arrangement more attention might have been given after 1900 to the need to revitalize the domestic economy. The British state was unable to free itself from the domestic structures that its earlier policy decisions had created, and continued to follow policies appropriate for a rising hegemony long after Britain's star had begun to fall.

Similarly, earlier policies in the United States begat social structures and institutional arrangements that trammeled state policy. After protecting import-competing industries for a century, the United States was unable in the 1920s to opt for more open policies, even though state interests would have been furthered thereby. Institutionally, decisions about tariff reductions were taken primarily in congressional committees, giving virtually any group seeking protection easy access to the decision-making process. When there were conflicts among groups, they were resolved by raising the levels of protection for everyone. It was only after the cataclysm of the Depression that the decision-making processes for trade policy were changed. The Presidency, far more insulated from the entreaties of particular societal groups than congressional committees, was then given more power. Furthermore, the American commercial banking system was unable to assume the burden of regulating the international economy during the 1920s. American institutions were geared toward the domestic economy. Only after the Second World War, and in fact not until the late 1950s, did American banks fully develop the complex institutional structures commensurate with the dollar's role in the international monetary system.

Having taken the critical decisions that created an open system after 1945, the American Government is unlikely to change its policy until it confronts some external event that it cannot control, such as a worldwide deflation, drought in the great plains, or the malicious use of petro-dollars. In America perhaps more than in any other country 'new policies', as E.E. Schattschneider wrote in his brilliant study of the Smoot-Hawley Tariff in 1935, 'create new politics',[3] for in America the state is weak and the society strong. State decisions taken because of state interests reinforce private societal groups that the state is unable to resist in later periods. Multinational corporations have grown and prospered since 1950. International economic policy making has passed from the Congress to the Executive. Groups favoring closure, such as organized labor, are unlikely to carry the day until some external event demonstrates that existing policies can no longer be implemented.

The structure of international trade changes in fits and starts; it does not flow smoothly with the redistribution of potential state power. Nevertheless, it is the power and the policies of states that create order where there would otherwise be chaos or at best a Lockian state of nature. The existence of various transnational, multinational, transgovernmental, and other nonstate actors that have riveted scholarly attention in recent years can only be understood within the context of a broader structure that ultimately rests upon the power and interests of states, shackled though they may be by the societal consequences of their own past decisions.

Notes

1   Albert O. Hirschman, *National Power and the Structure of Foreign Trade* (University of California Press, Berkeley, 1945), pp. 13–34.
2   Simon Kuznets, *Modern Economic Growth: Rate, Structure and Spread* (Yale University Press, New Haven, 1966), p. 302.
3   E.E. Schattschneider, *Politics, Pressure and the Tariff: A Study of Free Enterprise in Pressure Politics as Shown in the 1929–1930 Revision of the Tariff* (Prentice-Hall, New York, 1935).

1.8 Cooperation and international regimes

Robert O. Keohane

Source: *After Hegemony: Cooperation and Discord in the World Political Economy* (Princeton University Press, Princeton, 1984), pp. 51–63.

Keohane's aim is to identify ways in which states will cooperate in the absence of a hegemonial power able to impose its will on others. In this extract, he focuses on two central aspects of the problem: first, the nature of cooperation, which arises out of the need to manage conflicting or discordant interests, and second, the role played by international regimes in conditioning cooperation. In all of this, Keohane argues, 'sovereignty remains a constitutive principle' and state authorities play a crucial role.

Cooperation must be distinguished from harmony. Harmony refers to a situation in which actors' policies (pursued in their own self-interest without regard for others) *automatically* facilitate the attainment of others' goals. The classic example of harmony is the hypothetical competitive-market world of the classical economists, in which the Invisible Hand ensures that the pursuit of self-interest by each contributes to the interest of all. In this idealized, unreal world, no one's actions damage anyone else; there are no 'negative externalities', in the economists' jargon. Where harmony reigns, cooperation is unnecessary. It may even be injurious, if it means that certain individuals conspire to exploit others. Adam Smith, for one, was very critical of guilds and other conspiracies against freedom of trade. Cooperation and harmony are by no means identical and ought not to be confused with one another.

Cooperation requires that the actions of separate individuals or organizations – which are not in pre-existent harmony – be brought into conformity with one another through a process of negotiation, which is often referred to as 'policy coordination'. Charles E. Lindblom has defined policy coordination as follows:[1]

> A set of decisions is coordinated if adjustments have been made in them, such that the adverse consequences of any one decision for other decisions are to a degree and in some frequency avoided, reduced, or counterbalanced or overweighed.

Cooperation occurs when actors adjust their behavior to the actual or anticipated preferences of others, through a process of policy coordination. To summarize more formally, *intergovernmental cooperation takes place when the policies actually followed by one government are regarded by its partners as facilitating realization of their own objectives, as the result of a process of policy coordination.*

With this definition in mind, we can differentiate among cooperation, harmony, and discord, as illustrated by Figure 1. First, we ask whether actors' policies automatically

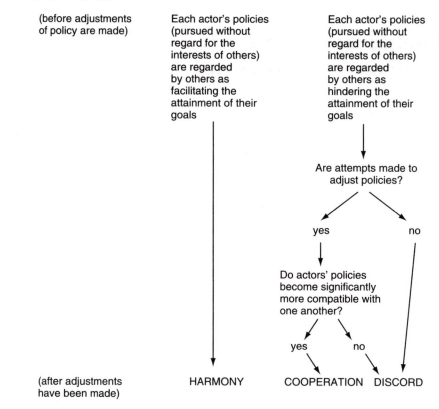

Figure 1 Harmony, cooperation, and discord

facilitate the attainment of others' goals. If so, there is harmony: no adjustments need to take place. Yet harmony is rare in world politics. Rousseau sought to account for this rarity when he declared that even two countries guided by the General Will in their internal affairs would come into conflict if they had extensive contact with one another, since the General Will of each would not be general for both. Each would have a partial, self-interested perspective on their mutual interactions. Even for Adam Smith, efforts to ensure state security took precedence over measures to increase national prosperity. In defending the Navigation Acts, Smith declared: 'As defence is of much more importance than opulence, the act of navigation is perhaps, the wisest of all the commercial regulations of England.'[2] Waltz summarizes the point by saying that 'in anarchy there is no automatic harmony'.[3]

Yet this insight tells us nothing definitive about the prospects for cooperation. For this we need to ask a further question about situations in which harmony does not exist. Are attempts made by actors (governmental or nongovernmental) to adjust their policies to each others' objectives? If no such attempts are made, the result is discord: a situation in which governments regard each others' policies as hindering the attainment of their goals, and hold each other responsible for these constraints.

Discord often leads to efforts to induce others to change their policies; when these attempts meet resistance, policy conflict results. Insofar as these attempts at policy adjustment succeed in making policies more compatible, however, cooperation ensues. The policy coordination that leads to cooperation need not involve bargaining or negotiation at all. What Lindblom calls 'adaptive' as opposed to 'manipulative' adjustment can take place: one country may shift its policy in the direction of another's preferences without regard for the effect of its action on the other state, defer to the other country, or partially shift its policy in order to avoid adverse consequences for its partner. Or nonbargained manipulation – such as one actor confronting another with a *fait accompli* – may occur.[4] Frequently, of course, negotiation and bargaining indeed take place, often accompanied by other actions that are designed to induce others to adjust their policies to one's own. Each government pursues what it perceives as its self-interest, but looks for bargains that can benefit all parties to the deal, though not necessarily equally.

Harmony and cooperation are not usually distinguished from one another so clearly. Yet, in the study of world politics, they should be. Harmony is apolitical. No communication is necessary, and no influence need be exercised. Cooperation, by contrast, is highly political: somehow, patterns of behavior must be altered. This change may be accomplished through negative as well as positive inducements. Indeed, studies of international crises, as well as game-theoretic experiments and simulations, have shown that under a variety of conditions strategies that involve threats and punishments as well as promises and rewards are more effective in attaining cooperative outcomes than those that rely entirely on persuasion and the force of good example.

Cooperation therefore does not imply an absence of conflict. On the contrary, it is typically mixed with conflict and reflects partially successful efforts to overcome conflict, real or potential. Cooperation takes place only in situations in which actors perceive that their policies are actually or potentially in conflict, not where there is harmony. Cooperation should not be viewed as the absence of conflict, but rather as a reaction to conflict or potential conflict. Without the specter of conflict, there is no need to cooperate.

The example of trade relations among friendly countries in a liberal international political economy may help to illustrate this crucial point. A naive observer, trained only to appreciate the overall welfare benefits of trade, might assume that trade relations would be harmonious: consumers in importing countries benefit from cheap foreign goods and increased competition, and producers can increasingly take advantage of the division of labor as their export markets expand. But harmony does not normally ensue. Discord on trade issues may prevail because governments do not even seek to reduce the adverse consequences of their own policies for others, but rather strive in certain respects to increase the severity of those effects. Mercantilist governments have sought in the twentieth century as well as the seventeenth to manipulate foreign trade, in conjunction with warfare, to damage each other economically and to gain productive resources themselves. Governments may desire 'positional goods', such as high status, and may therefore resist even mutually beneficial cooperation if it helps others more than themselves. Yet even when neither power nor positional motivations are present, and when all participants would benefit in the aggregate from liberal trade, discord tends to predominate over harmony as the initial result of independent governmental action.

This occurs even under otherwise benign conditions because some groups or industries are forced to incur adjustment costs as changes in comparative advantage take place. Governments often respond to the ensuing demands for protection by attempting, more or less effectively, to cushion the burdens of adjustment for groups and industries that are politically influential at home. Yet unilateral measures to this effect almost always impose adjustment costs abroad, and discord continually threatens. Governments enter into international negotiations in order to reduce the conflict that would otherwise result. Even substantial potential common benefits do not create harmony when state power can be exercised on behalf of certain interests and against others. In world politics, harmony tends to vanish: attainment of the gains from pursuing complementary policies depends on cooperation.

Observers of world politics who take power and conflict seriously should be attracted to this way of defining cooperation, since my definition does not relegate cooperation to the mythological world of relations among equals in power. Hegemonic cooperation is not a contradiction in terms. Defining cooperation in contrast to harmony should, I hope, lead readers with a Realist orientation to take cooperation in world politics seriously rather than to dismiss it out of hand. To Marxists who also believe in hegemonic power theories, however, even this definition of cooperation may not seem to make it relevant to the contemporary world political economy. From this perspective, mutual policy adjustments cannot possibly resolve the contradictions besetting the system because they are attributable to capitalism rather than to problems of coordination among egoistic actors lacking common government. Attempts to resolve these contradictions through international cooperation will merely transfer issues to a deeper and even more intractable level. Thus it is not surprising that Marxian analyses of the international political economy have, with few exceptions, avoided sustained examinations of the conditions under which cooperation among major capitalist countries can take place. Marxists see it as more important to expose relationships of exploitation and conflict between major capitalist powers on the one hand and the masses of people in the periphery of world capitalism on the other. And, from a Leninist standpoint, to examine the conditions for international cooperation without first analyzing the contradictions of capitalism, and recognizing the irreconcilability of conflicts among capitalist countries, is a bourgeois error.

This is less an argument than a statement of faith. Since sustained international coordination of macroeconomic policies has never been tried, the statement that it would merely worsen the contradictions facing the system is speculative. In view of the lack of evidence for it, such a claim could even be considered rash. Indeed, one of the most perceptive Marxian writers of recent years, Stephen Hymer, recognized explicitly that capitalists face problems of collective action and argued that they were seeking, with at least temporary prospects of success, to overcome them. As he recognized, any success in internationalizing capital could pose grave threats to socialist aspirations and, at the very least, would shift contradictions to new points of tension.[5] Thus even were we to agree that the fundamental issue is posed by the contradictions of capitalism rather than the tensions inherent in a state system, it would be worthwhile to study the conditions under which cooperation is likely to occur.

International regimes and cooperation

One way to study cooperation and discord would be to focus on particular actions as the units of analysis. This would require the systematic compilation of a data set composed of acts that could be regarded as comparable and coded according to the degree of cooperation that they reflect. Such a strategy has some attractive features. The problem with it, however, is that instances of cooperation and discord could all too easily be isolated from the context of beliefs and behavior within which they are embedded. This book does not view cooperation atomistically as a set of discrete, isolated acts, but rather seeks to understand patterns of cooperation in the world political economy. Accordingly, we need to examine actors' expectations about future patterns of interaction, their assumptions about the proper nature of economic arrangements, and the kinds of political activities they regard as legitimate. That is, we need to analyze cooperation within the context of international institutions, broadly defined, [. . .] in terms of practices and expectations. Each act of cooperation or discord affects the beliefs, rules, and practices that form the context for future actions. Each act must therefore be interpreted as embedded within a chain of such acts and their successive cognitive and institutional residues.

This argument parallels Clifford Geertz's discussion of how anthropologists should use the concept of culture to interpret the societies they investigate. Geertz sees culture as the 'webs of significance' that people have created for themselves. On their surface, they are enigmatical; the observer has to interpret them so that they make sense. Culture, for Geertz, 'is a context, something within which [social events] can be intelligibly described'.[6] It makes little sense to describe naturalistically what goes on at a Balinese cock-fight unless one understands the meaning of the event for Balinese culture. There is not a world culture in the fullest sense, but even in world politics, human beings spin webs of significance. They develop implicit standards for behavior, some of which emphasize the principle of sovereignty and legitimize the pursuit of self-interest, while others rely on quite different principles. Any act of cooperation or apparent cooperation needs to be interpreted within the context of related actions, and of prevailing expectations and shared beliefs, before its meaning can be properly understood. Fragments of political behavior become comprehensible when viewed as part of a larger mosaic.

The concept of international regime not only enables us to describe patterns of cooperation; it also helps to account for both cooperation and discord. Although regimes themselves depend on conditions that are conducive to interstate agreements, they may also facilitate further efforts to coordinate policies. To understand international cooperation, it is necessary to comprehend how institutions and rules not only reflect, but also affect, the facts of world politics.

Defining and identifying regimes

When John Ruggie introduced the concept of international regimes into the international politics literature in 1975, he defined a regime as 'a set of mutual expectations, rules and regulations, plans, organizational energies and financial commitments, which have been accepted by a group of states'.[7] More recently, a collective definition, worked out at a conference on the subject, defined international regimes as 'sets of implicit or explicit principles, norms, rules and decision-making procedures around which actors' expectations converge in a given area of international relations. Principles are beliefs of fact, causation, and rectitude. Norms are standards of behavior defined in terms of rights and obligations. Rules are specific prescriptions or proscriptions for action. Decision-making procedures are prevailing practices for making and implementing collective choice.'[8]

This definition provides a useful starting-point for analysis, since it begins with the general conception of regimes as social institutions and explicates it further. The concept of norms, however, is ambiguous. It is important that we understand norms in this definition simply as standards of behavior defined in terms of rights and obligations. Another usage would distinguish norms from rules and principles by stipulating that participants in a social system regard norms, but not rules and principles, as morally binding regardless of considerations of narrowly defined self-interest. But to include norms, thus defined, in a definition of necessary regime characteristics would be to make the conception of regimes based strictly on self-interest a contradiction in terms. [. . .] I will maintain a definition of norms simply as standards of behavior, whether adopted on grounds of self-interest or otherwise. [. . .]

The principles of regimes define, in general, the purposes that their members are expected to pursue. For instance, the principles of the postwar trade and monetary regimes have emphasized the value of open, nondiscriminatory patterns of international economic transactions; the fundamental principle of the nonproliferation regime is that the spread of nuclear weapons is dangerous. Norms contain somewhat clearer injunctions to members about legitimate and illegitimate behavior, still defining responsibilities and obligations in relatively general terms. For instance, the norms of the General Agreement on Tariffs and Trade (GATT) do not require that members resort to free trade immediately, but incorporate injunctions to members to practise nondiscrimination and reciprocity and to move toward increased liberalization. Fundamental to the nonproliferation regime is the norm that members of the regime should not act in ways that facilitate nuclear proliferation.

The rules of a regime are difficult to distinguish from its norms; at the margin, they merge into one another. Rules are, however, more specific: they indicate in more detail the specific rights and obligations of members. Rules can be altered more easily than principles or norms, since there may be more than one set of rules that can attain a given set of purposes. Finally, at the same level of specificity as rules, but referring to procedures rather than substances, the decisionmaking procedures of regimes provide ways of implementing their principles and altering their rules.

An example from the field of international monetary relations may be helpful. The most important principle of the international balance-of-payments regime since the end of World War II has been that of liberalization of trade and payments. A key norm of the regime has been the injunction to states not to manipulate their exchange rates unilaterally for national advantage. Between 1958 and 1971 this norm was realized through pegged exchange rates and procedures for consultation in the event of change, supplemented with a variety of devices to help governments avoid exchange-rate changes through a combination of borrowing and internal adjustment. After 1973 governments have subscribed to the same norm, although it has been implemented more informally and probably less effectively under a system of floating exchange rates. Ruggie has argued that the abstract principle of liberalization, subject to constraints imposed by the acceptance of the welfare state, has been maintained throughout the postwar period: 'embedded liberalism' continues, reflecting a fundamental element of continuity in the international balance-of-payments regime. The norm of nonmanipulation has also been maintained, even though the specific rules of the 1958–71 system having to do with adjustment have been swept away.[9]

The concept of international regime is complex because it is defined in terms of four distinct components: principles, norms, rules, and decisionmaking procedures. It is tempting to select one of these levels of specificity – particularly, principles and norms or rules and procedures – as *the* defining characteristic of regimes. Such an approach, however, creates a false dichotomy between principles on the one hand and rules and procedures on the other. As we have noted, at the margin norms and rules cannot be sharply distinguished from each other. It is difficult if not impossible to tell the difference between an 'implicit rule' of broad significance and a well-understood, relatively specific operating principle. Both rules and principles may affect expectations and even values. In a strong international regime, the linkages between principles and rules are likely to be tight. Indeed, it is precisely the linkages among principles, norms, and rules that give regimes their legitimacy. Since rules, norms, and principles are so closely interwined, judgements about whether changes in rules constitute changes *of* regime or merely changes *within* regimes necessarily contain arbitrary elements.

Principles, norms, rules, and procedures all contain injunctions about behavior: they prescribe certain actions and proscribe others. They imply obligations, even though these obligations are not enforceable through a hierarchical legal system. It clarifies the definition of regime, therefore, to think of it in terms of injunctions of greater or lesser specificity.

Some are far-reaching and extremely important. They may change only rarely. At the other extreme, injunctions may be merely technical, matters of convenience that can be altered without great political or economic impact. In-between are injunctions that are both specific enough that violations of them are in principle identifiable and that changes in them can be observed, and sufficiently significant that changes in them make a difference for the behavior of actors and the nature of the international political economy. It is these intermediate injunctions – politically consequential but specific enough that violations and changes can be identified – that I take as the essence of international regimes.

A brief examination of international oil regimes, and their injunctions, may help us clarify this point. The pre-1939 international oil regime was dominated by a small number of international firms and contained explicit injunctions about where and under what conditions companies could produce oil, and where and how they should market it. The rules of the Red Line and Achnacarry or 'As-Is' agreements of 1928 reflected an 'anti-competitive ethos': that is, the basic principle that competition was destructive to the system and the norm that firms should not engage in it.[10] This principle and this norm both persisted after World War II, although an intergovernmental regime with explicit rules was not established, owing to the failure of the Anglo-American Petroleum Agreement. Injunctions against price-cutting were reflected more in the practices of companies than in formal rules. Yet expectations and practices of major actors were strongly affected by these injunctions, and in this sense the criteria for a regime – albeit a weak one – were met. As governments of producing countries became more assertive, however, and as formerly domestic independent companies entered international markets, these arrangements collapsed; after the mid-to-late 1960s, there was no regime for the issue-area as a whole, since no injunctions could be said to be accepted as obligatory by all influential actors. Rather, there was a 'tug of war' in which all sides resorted to self-help. The Organization of Petroleum Exporting Countries (OPEC) sought to create a producers' regime based on rules for prorationing oil production, and consumers established an emergency oil-sharing system in the new International Energy Agency to counteract the threat of selective embargoes.

If we were to have paid attention only to the principle of avoiding competition, we would have seen continuity: whatever the dominant actors, they have always sought to cartelize the industry one way or another. But to do so would be to miss the main point, which is that momentous changes have occurred. At the other extreme, we could have fixed our attention on very specific particular arrangements, such as the various joint ventures of the 1950s and 1960s or the specific provisions for controlling output tried by OPEC after 1973, in which case we would have observed a pattern of continual flux. The significance of the most important events – the demise of old cartel arrangements, the undermining of the international majors' positions in the 1960s, and the rise of producing governments to a position of influence in the 1970s – could have been missed. Only by focusing on the intermediate level of relatively specific but politically consequential injunctions, whether we call them rules, norms, or principles, does the concept of regime help us identify major changes that require explanation.

As our examples of money and oil suggest, we regard the scope of international regimes as corresponding, in general, to the boundaries of issue-areas, since governments establish regimes to deal with problems that they regard as so closely linked that they should be dealt with together. Issue-areas are best defined as sets of issues that are in fact dealt with in common negotiations and by the same, or closely coordinated, bureaucracies, as opposed to issues that are dealt with separately and in uncoordinated fashion. Since issue-areas depend on actors' perceptions and behavior rather than on inherent qualities of the subject-matters, their boundaries change gradually over time. Fifty years ago, for instance, there was no oceans issue-area, since particular questions now grouped under that heading were dealt with separately; but there was an international monetary issue-area even then. Twenty years ago trade in cotton textiles had an international regime of its own – the Long-Term Agreement on Cotton Textiles – and was treated separately from trade in synthetic fibers. Issue-areas are defined and redefined by changing patterns of human intervention; so are international regimes.

Self-help and international regimes

The injunctions of international regimes rarely affect economic transactions directly: state institutions, rather than international organizations, impose tariffs and quotas, intervene in foreign exchange markets, and manipulate oil prices through taxes and subsidies. If we think about the impact of the principles, norms, rules, and decisionmaking procedures of regimes, it becomes clear that insofar as they have any effect at all, it must be exerted on national controls, and especially on the specific interstate agreements that affect the exercise of national controls. International regimes must be distinguished from these specific agreements; [. . .] a major function of regimes is to facilitate the making of specific cooperative agreements among governments.

Superficially, it could seem that since international regimes affect national controls, the regimes are of superior importance – just as federal laws in the United States frequently override state and local legislation. Yet this would be a fundamentally misleading conclusion. In a well-ordered society, the units of action – individuals in classic liberal thought – live together within a framework of constitutional principles that define property rights, establish who may control the state, and specify the conditions under which subjects must obey governmental regulations. In the United States, these principles establish the supremacy of the federal government in a number of policy areas, though not in all. But world politics is decentralized rather than hierarchic: the prevailing principle of sovereignty means that states are subject to no superior government. The resulting system is sometimes referred to as one of 'self-help'.

Sovereignty and self-help mean that the principles and rules of international regimes will necessarily be weaker than in domestic society. In a civil society, these rules 'specify terms of exchange' within the framework of constitutional principles. In world politics, the principles, norms, and rules of regimes are necessarily fragile because they risk coming into conflict with the principle of sovereignty and the associated norm of self-help. They may promote cooperation, but the fundamental basis of order on which they would rest in a well-ordered society does not exist. They drift around without being tied to the solid anchor of the state.

Yet even if the principles of sovereignty and self-help limit the degree of confidence to be placed in international agreements, they do not render cooperation impossible. Orthodox theory itself relies on mutual interests to explain forms of cooperation that are used by states as instruments of competition. According to balance-of-power theory, cooperative endeavors such as political-military alliances necessarily form in self-help systems. Acts of cooperation are accounted for on the grounds that mutual interests are sufficient to enable states to overcome their suspicions of one another. But since even orthodox theory relies on mutual interests, its advocates are on weak ground in objecting to interpretations of system-wide cooperation along these lines. There is no logical or empirical reason why mutual interests in world politics should be limited to interests in combining forces against adversaries. As economists emphasize, there can also be mutual interests in securing efficiency gains from voluntary exchange or oligopolistic rewards from the creation and division of rents resulting from the control and manipulation of markets.

International regimes should not be interpreted as elements of a new international order 'beyond the nation-state'. They should be comprehended chiefly as arrangements motivated by self-interest: as components of systems in which sovereignty remains a constitutive principle. This means that, as Realists emphasize, they will be shaped largely by their most powerful members, pursuing their own interests. But regimes can also affect state interests, for the notion of self-interest is itself elastic and largely subjective. Perceptions of self-interest depend both on actors' expectations of the likely consequences that will follow from particular actions and on their fundamental values. Regimes can certainly affect expectations and may affect values as well. Far from being contradicted by the view that international behavior is shaped largely by power and interests, the concept of international regime is consistent both with the importance of differential power and with a sophisticated view of self-interest. Theories of regimes can incorporate Realist insights about the role of power and interest, while also indicating the inadequacy of theories that define interests so narrowly that they fail to take the role of institutions into account.

Regimes not only are consistent with self-interest but may under some conditions even be necessary to its effective pursuit. They facilitate the smooth operation of decentralized international political systems and therefore perform an important function for states. In a world political economy characterized by growing interdependence, they may become increasingly useful for governments that wish to solve common problems and pursue complementary purposes without subordinating themselves to hierarchical systems of control.

Notes

1 C. Lindblom, *The Intelligence of Democracy* (Free Press, New York, 1965), p. 227.
2 A. Smith, *The Wealth of Nations* (Chicago University Press, Chicago, 1976 edn), p. 487.
3 K. Waltz, *Man, The State and War* (Columbia University Press, 1959), p. 182.
4 Lindblom, *The Intelligence of Democracy*, pp. 33–4 and ch. 4.
5 S. Hymer, 'The Internationalization of Capital', *Journal of Economic Issues*, 6: 1 (March 1972).
6 C. Geertz, *The Interpretation of Cultures* (Basic Books, New York, 1973), p. 14.
7 J. Ruggie, 'International Responses to Technology: concepts and trends', *International Organization*, 29: 3 (Summer 1975), pp. 557–84, at p. 570.
8 S. Krasner (ed.), *International Regimes* (Cornell University Press, Ithaca, 1983), p. 2.
9 J. Ruggie, 'International Regimes, Transactions and Change', in Krasner (ed.), *International Regimes*, pp. 195–232.
10 L. Turner, *Oil Companies in the International System* (George Allen and Unwin, London, 1978), p. 30.

1.9 Structural realism after the Cold War

Kenneth N. Waltz

Source: *International Security*, vol. 25, no. 1 (2000), pp. 5–41.

Waltz examines three developments that are seen to be transforming the post-Cold War world: the expansion of democracy, the growth of interdependence and the rise of international institutions. He challenges the assumption that these three developments are necessarily promoting peaceful international relations and are thereby rendering realism obsolete. Waltz insists that realism retains its explanatory power in the contemporary world and argues that the evidence is already beginning to show that, as the balance of power theory predicts, unipolarity is giving way to multipolarity.

Some students of international politics believe that realism is obsolete. They argue that, although realism's concepts of anarchy, self-help, and power balancing may have been appropriate to a bygone era, they have been displaced by changed conditions and eclipsed by better ideas. New times call for new thinking. Changing conditions require revised theories or entirely different ones [. . .]

Democracy and peace

The end of the Cold War coincided with what many took to be a new democratic wave. The trend toward democracy combined with Michael Doyle's rediscovery of the peaceful behavior of liberal democratic states *inter se* contributes strongly to the belief that war is obsolescent, if not obsolete, among the advanced industrial states of the world.[1] [. . .]

Proponents of the democratic peace thesis write as though the spread of democracy will negate the effects of anarchy. No causes of conflict and war will any longer be found at the structural level. Francis Fukuyama finds it "perfectly possible to imagine anarchic state systems that are nonetheless peaceful."[2] He sees no reason to associate anarchy with war. Bruce Russett believes that, with enough democracies in the world, it "may be possible in part to supersede the 'realist' principles (anarchy, the security dilemma of states) that have dominated practice [. . .] since at least the seventeenth century."[3] Thus the structure is removed from structural theory. Democratic states would be so confident of the peace-preserving effects of democracy that they would no longer fear that another state, so long as it remained democratic, would do it wrong. The guarantee of the state's proper external behavior would derive from its admirable internal qualities.

Every student of international politics is aware of the statistical data supporting the democratic peace thesis. Everyone has also known at least since David Hume that we have no reason to believe that the association of events provides a basis for inferring the presence of a causal relation. John Mueller properly speculates that it is not democracy that causes peace but that other conditions cause both democracy and peace.[4] Some of the major democracies – Britain in the nineteenth century and the United States in the twentieth century – have been among the most powerful states of their eras. Powerful states often gain their ends by peaceful means where weaker states either fail or have to resort to war. Thus, the American government deemed the democratically elected Juan Bosch of the Dominican Republic too weak to bring order to his country. The United States toppled his government by sending 23,000 troops within a week, troops whose mere presence made fighting a war unnecessary. Salvador Allende, democratically elected ruler of Chile, was systematically and effectively undermined by the United States, without the open use of force, because its leaders thought that his government was taking a wrong turn. [. . .]

One can of course say, yes, but the Dominican Republic and Chile were not liberal democracies nor perceived as such by the United States. Once one begins to go down that road, there is no place to stop. [. . .] I am tempted to say that the democratic peace thesis in the form in which its proponents cast it is irrefutable. A liberal democracy at war with another country is unlikely to call it a liberal democracy.

Democracies may live at peace with democracies, but even if all states became democratic, the structure of international politics would remain anarchic. The structure of international politics is not transformed by changes internal to states, however widespread the changes may be. In the absence of an external authority, a state cannot be sure that today's friend will not be tomorrow's enemy. Indeed, democracies have at times behaved as though today's democracy is today's enemy and a present threat to them. [. . .]

In the latter half of the nineteenth century, as the United States and Britain became more democratic, bitterness grew between them, and the possibility of war was at times seriously entertained on both sides of the Atlantic. France and Britain were among the principal adversaries in the great power politics of the nineteenth century, as they were earlier. Their becoming democracies did not change their behavior toward each other. In 1914, democratic England and France fought democratic Germany, and doubts about the latter's democratic standing merely illustrate the problem of definition. Indeed, the democratic pluralism of Germany was an underlying cause of the war. In response to domestic interests, Germany followed policies bound to frighten both Britain and Russia. And today if a war that a few have feared were fought by the United States and Japan, many Americans would say that Japan was not a democracy after all, but merely a one-party state.

What can we conclude? Democracies rarely fight democracies, we might say, and then add as a word of essential caution that the internal excellence of states is a brittle basis of peace.

Democratic wars

Democracies coexist with undemocratic states. Although democracies seldom fight democracies, they do, as Michael Doyle has noted, fight at least their share of wars against others. Citizens of democratic states tend to think of their countries as good, aside from what they do, simply because they are democratic. Thus former Secretary of State Warren Christopher claimed that "democratic nations rarely start wars or threaten their neighbors." One might suggest that he try his proposition out in Central or South America. Citizens of democratic states also tend to think of undemocratic states as bad, aside from what they do, simply because they are undemocratic. Democracies promote war because they at times decide that the way to preserve peace is to defeat nondemocratic states and make them democratic. [. . .]

Crusades are frightening because crusaders go to war for righteous causes, which they define for themselves and try to impose on others. One might have hoped that Americans would have learned that they are not very good at causing democracy abroad. But, alas, if the world can be made safe for democracy only by making it democratic, then all means are permitted and to use them becomes a duty. The war fervor of people and their representatives is at times hard to contain.

That peace may prevail among democratic states is a comforting thought. The obverse of the proposition – that democracy may promote war against undemocratic states – is disturbing. If the latter holds, we cannot even say for sure that the spread of democracy will bring a net decrease in the amount of war in the world. [. . .]

If the world is now safe for democracy, one has to wonder whether democracy is safe for the world. When democracy is ascendant, a condition that in the twentieth century attended the winning of hot wars and cold ones, the interventionist spirit flourishes. The effect is heightened when one democratic state becomes dominant, as the United States is now. Peace is the noblest cause of war. If the conditions of peace are lacking, then the country with a capability of creating them may be tempted to do so, whether or not by force. The end is noble, but as a matter of *right*, Kant insists, no state can intervene in the internal arrangements of another. As a matter of *fact*, one may notice that intervention, even for worthy ends, often brings more harm than good. The vice to which great powers easily succumb in a multipolar world is inattention; in a bipolar world, overreaction; in a unipolar world, overextention.

Peace is maintained by a delicate balance of internal and external restraints. States having a surplus of power are tempted to use it, and weaker states fear their doing so. The laws of voluntary federations, to use Kant's language, are disregarded at the whim of the stronger, as the United States demonstrated a decade ago by mining Nicaraguan waters and by invading Panama. In both cases, the United States blatantly violated international law. In the first, it denied the jurisdiction of the International Court of Justice, which it had previously accepted. In the second, it flaunted the law embodied in the Charter of the Organization of American States, of which it was a principal sponsor.

If the democratic peace thesis is right, structural realist theory is wrong. One may believe, with Kant, that republics are by and large good states *and* that unbalanced power is a danger no matter who wields it. Inside of, as well as outside of, the circle of democratic states, peace depends on a precarious balance of forces. The causes of war lie not simply in states or in the state system; they are found in both. Kant understood this. Devotees of the democratic peace thesis overlook it.

The weak effects of interdependence

[. . .] That interdependence promotes war as well as peace has been said often enough. What requires emphasis is that, either way, among the forces that shape international politics, interdependence is a weak one. Interdependence within modern states is much closer than it is across states. The Soviet economy was planned so that its far-flung parts would be not just interdependent but integrated. Huge factories depended for their output on products exchanged with others. Despite the tight integration of the Soviet economy, the state fell apart. Yugoslavia provides another stark illustration. Once external political pressure lessened, internal economic interests were too weak to hold the country together. One must wonder whether economic interdependence is more effect than cause. Internally, interdependence becomes so close that integration is the proper word to describe it. Interdependence becomes integration because internally the expectation that peace will prevail and order will be preserved is high. Externally, goods and capital flow freely where peace among countries appears to be reliably established. Interdependence, like integration, depends on other conditions. It is more a dependent than an independent variable. States, if they can afford to, shy away from becoming excessively dependent on goods and resources that may be denied them in crises and wars. States take measures, such as Japan's managed trade, to avoid excessive dependence on others.

The impulse to protect one's identity – cultural and political as well as economic – from encroachment by others is strong. When it seems that "we will sink or swim together," swimming separately looks attractive to those able to do it. From Plato onward, utopias were set in isolation from neighbors so that people could construct their collective life uncontaminated by contact with others. With zero interdependence, neither conflict nor war is possible. With integration, international becomes national politics. The zone in between is a gray one with the effects of interdependence sometimes good, providing the benefits of divided labor, mutual understanding, and cultural enrichment, and sometimes bad, leading to protectionism, mutual resentment, conflict, and war.

The uneven effects of interdependence, with some parties to it gaining more, others gaining less, are obscured by the substitution of Robert Keohane's and Joseph Nye's term "asymmetric interdependence" for relations of dependence and independence among states.[5] Relatively independent states are in a stronger position than relatively dependent ones. If I depend more on you than you depend on me, you have more ways of influencing me and affecting my fate than I have of affecting yours. Interdependence suggests a condition of roughly equal dependence of parties on one another. Omitting the word "dependence" blunts the inequalities that mark the relations of states and makes them all seem to be on the same footing. Much of international, as of national, politics is about inequalities. Separating one "issue area" from others and emphasizing that weak states have advantages in some of them reduces the sense of inequality. Emphasizing the low fungibility of power furthers the effect. If power is not very fungible, weak states may have decisive advantages on some issues. Again, the effects of inequality are blunted. But power, not very fungible for weak states, is very fungible for strong ones. The history of American foreign policy since World War II is replete with examples of how the United States used its superior economic capability to promote its political and security interests.

In a 1970 essay, I described interdependence as an ideology used by Americans to camouflage the great leverage the United States enjoys in international politics by making it seem that strong and weak, rich and poor nations are similarly entangled in a thick web of interdependence.[6] In her recent book, *The Retreat of the State*, Susan Strange reached the same conclusion, but by an odd route. Her argument is that "the progressive integration of the world economy, through international production, has shifted the balance of power away from states and toward world markets." She advances three propositions in support of her argument: (1) power has "shifted upward from weak states to stronger ones" having global or regional reach; (2) power has "shifted sideways from states to markets and thus to non-state authorities deriving power from their market shares"; and (3) some power has "evaporated" with no one exercising it.[7] In international politics, with no central authority, power does sometimes slip away and sometimes move sideways to markets. When serious slippage occurs, however, stronger states step in to reverse it, and firms of the stronger states control the largest market shares anyway. One may doubt whether markets any more escape the control of major states now than they did in the nineteenth century or earlier – perhaps less so since the competence of states has increased at least in proportion to increases in the size and complications of markets. [. . .]

Under the Pax Britannica, the interdependence of states became unusually close, which to many portended a peaceful and prosperous future. Instead, a prolonged period of war, autarky, and more war followed. The international economic system, constructed under American auspices after World War II and later amended to suit its purposes, may last longer, but then again it may not. The character of international politics changes as national interdependence tightens or loosens. Yet even as relations vary, states have to take care of themselves as best they can in an anarchic environment. Internationally, the twentieth century for the most part was an unhappy one. In its last quarter, the clouds lifted a little, but twenty-five years is a slight base on which to ground optimistic conclusions. Not only are the effects of close interdependence problematic, but so also is its durability.

The limited role of international institutions

One of the charges hurled at realist theory is that it depreciates the importance of institutions. The charge is justified, and the strange case of NATO's (the North Atlantic Treaty Organization's) outliving its purpose shows why realists believe that international institutions are shaped and limited by the states that found and sustain them and have little independent effect. Liberal institutionalists paid scant attention to organizations designed to buttress the security of states until, contrary to expectations inferred from realist theories, NATO not only survived the end of the Cold War but went on to add new members and to promise to embrace still more. Far from invalidating realist theory or casting doubt on it, however, the recent history of NATO illustrates the subordination of international institutions to national purposes.

Explaining international institutions

The nature and purposes of institutions change as structures vary. In the old multipolar world, the core of an alliance consisted of a small number of states of comparable capability. Their contributions to one another's security were of crucial importance because they were of similar size. Because major allies were closely interdependent militarily, the defection of one would have made its partners vulnerable to a competing alliance. The members of opposing alliances before World War I were tightly knit because of their mutual dependence. In the new bipolar world, the word "alliance" took on a different meaning. One country, the United States or the Soviet Union, provided most of the security for its bloc. The withdrawal of France from NATO's command structure and the defection of China from the Soviet bloc failed even to tilt the central balance. Early in the Cold War, Americans spoke with alarm about the threat of monolithic communism arising from the combined strength of the Soviet Union and China, yet the bloc's disintegration caused scarcely a ripple. American officials did not proclaim that with China's defection, America's defense budget could safely be reduced by 20 or 10 percent or even be reduced at all. Similarly, when France stopped playing its part in NATO's military plans, American officials did not proclaim that defense spending had to be increased for that reason. Properly speaking, NATO and the WTO (Warsaw Treaty Organization) were treaties of guarantee rather than old-style military alliances.

Glenn Snyder has remarked that "alliances have no meaning apart from the adversary threat to which they are a response."[8] I expected NATO to dwindle at the Cold War's end and ultimately to disappear. In a basic sense, the expectation has been borne out. NATO is no longer even a treaty of guarantee because one cannot answer the question, guarantee against whom? Functions vary as structures change, as does the behavior of units. Thus the end of the Cold War quickly changed the behavior of allied countries. In early July of 1990, NATO announced that the alliance would "elaborate new force plans consistent with the revolutionary changes in Europe." By the end of July, without waiting for any such plans, the major European members of NATO unilaterally announced large reductions in their force levels. Even the pretense of continuing to act as an alliance in setting military policy disappeared.

With its old purpose dead, and the individual and collective behavior of its members altered accordingly, how does one explain NATO's survival and expansion? Institutions are hard to create and set in motion, but once created, institutionalists claim, they may take on something of a life of their own; they may begin to act with a measure of autonomy, becoming less dependent on the wills of their sponsors and members. NATO supposedly validates these thoughts. [. . .]

The institutionalist interpretation misses the point. NATO is first of all a treaty made by states. A deeply entrenched international bureaucracy can help to sustain the organization, but states determine its fate. Liberal institutionalists take NATO's seeming vigor as confirmation of the importance of international institutions and as evidence of their resilience. Realists, noticing that as an alliance NATO has lost its major function, see it mainly as a means of maintaining and lengthening America's grip on the foreign and military policies of European states [. . .]

Using the example of NATO to reflect on the relevance of realism after the Cold War leads to some important conclusions. The winner of the Cold War and the sole remaining great power has behaved as unchecked powers have usually done. In the absence of counterweights, a country's internal impulses prevail, whether fueled by liberal or by other urges. The error of realist predictions that the end of the Cold War would mean the end of NATO arose not from a failure of realist theory to comprehend international politics, but from an underestimation of America's folly. The survival and expansion of NATO illustrate not the defects but the limitations of structural explanations. Structures shape and shove; they do not determine the actions of states. A state that is stronger than any other can decide for itself whether to conform its policies to structural pressures and whether to avail itself of the opportunities that structural change offers, with little fear of adverse affects in the short run.

Do liberal institutionalists provide better leverage for explaining NATO's survival and expansion? According to Keohane and Martin, realists insist "that institutions have only marginal effects."[9] On the contrary, realists have noticed that whether institutions have strong or weak effects depends on what states intend. Strong states use institutions, as they interpret laws, in ways that suit them. [. . .]

What is true of NATO holds for international institutions generally. The effects that international institutions may have on national decisions are but one step removed from the capabilities and intentions of the major state or states that gave them birth and sustain them. The Bretton Woods system strongly affected individual states and the conduct of international affairs. But when the United States found that the system no longer served its interests, the Nixon shocks of 1971 were administered. International institutions are created by the more powerful states, and the institutions survive in their original form as long as they serve the major interests of their creators, or are thought to do so.

Balancing power: not today but tomorrow

With so many of the expectations that realist theory gives rise to confirmed by what happened at and after the end of the Cold War, one may wonder why realism is in bad repute. A key proposition derived from realist theory is that international politics reflects the distribution of national capabilities, a proposition daily borne out. Another key proposition is that the balancing of power by some states against others recurs. Realist theory predicts that balances disrupted will one day be restored. A limitation of the theory, a limitation common to social science theories, is that it cannot say when. William Wohlforth argues that though restoration will take place, it will be a long time coming. Of necessity, realist theory is better at saying what will happen than in saying when it will happen. Theory cannot say when "tomorrow" will come because international political theory deals with the pressures of structure on states and not with how states will respond to the pressures. The latter is a task for theories about how national governments respond to pressures on them and take advantage of opportunities that may be present. One does, however, observe balancing tendencies already taking place.

Upon the demise of the Soviet Union, the international political system became unipolar. In the light of structural theory, unipolarity appears as the least durable of international configurations. This is so for two main reasons. One is that dominant powers take on too many tasks beyond their own borders, thus weakening themselves in the long run. [. . .] The other reason for the short duration of unipolarity is that even if a dominant power behaves with moderation, restraint, and forbearance, weaker states will worry about its future behavior. America's founding fathers warned against the perils of power in the absence of checks and balances. Is unbalanced power less of a danger in international than in national politics? Throughout the Cold War, what the United States and the Soviet Union did, and how they interacted, were dominant factors in international politics. The two countries, however, constrained each other. Now the United States is alone in the world. As nature abhors a vacuum, so international politics abhors unbalanced power. Faced with unbalanced power, some states try to increase their own strength or they ally with others to bring the international distribution of power into balance. The reactions of other states to the drive for dominance of Charles V, Hapsburg ruler of Spain, of Louis XIV and Napoleon I of France, of Wilhelm II and Adolph Hitler of Germany, illustrate the point. Will the preponderant power of the United States elicit similar reactions? Unbalanced power, whoever wields it, is a potential danger to others. The powerful state may, and the United States does, think of itself as acting for the sake of peace, justice, and well-being in the world. These terms, however, are defined to the liking of the powerful, which may conflict with the preferences and interests of others. In international politics, overwhelming power repels and leads others to try to balance against it. With benign intent, the United States has behaved and, until its power is brought into balance, will continue to behave in ways that sometimes frighten others. [. . .]

The absence of serious threats to American security gives the United States wide latitude in making foreign policy choices. A dominant power acts internationally only when the spirit moves it. One example is enough to show this. When Yugoslavia's collapse was followed by genocidal war in successor states, the United States failed to respond until Senator Robert Dole moved to make Bosnia's peril an issue in the forthcoming presidential election; and it acted not for the sake of its own security but to maintain its leadership position in Europe. American policy was generated not by external security interests, but by internal political pressure and national ambition.

Aside from specific threats it may pose, unbalanced power leaves weaker states feeling uneasy and gives them reason to strengthen their positions. The United States has a long history of intervening in weak states, often with the intention of bringing democracy to them. American behavior over the past century in Central America provides little evidence of self-restraint in the absence of countervailing power. Contemplating the history of the United States and measuring its capabilities, other countries may well wish for ways to fend off its benign ministrations. Concentrated power invites distrust because it is so easily misused. To understand why some states want to bring power into a semblance of balance is easy, but with power so sharply skewed, what country or group of countries has the material capability and the political will to bring the "unipolar moment" to an end? [. . .]

The candidates for becoming the next great powers, and thus restoring a balance, are the European Union or Germany leading a coalition, China, Japan, and in a more distant future, Russia. [. . .]

[Waltz goes on to discuss the likelihood of these states developing policies that will constrain future US action.]

American leaders seem to believe that America's preeminent position will last indefinitely. The United States would then remain the dominant power without rivals rising to challenge it – a position without precedent in modern history. Balancing, of course, is not universal and omnipresent. A dominant power may suppress balancing as the United States has done in Europe. Whether or not balancing takes place also depends on the decisions of governments. Stephanie Neuman's book, *International Relations Theory and the Third World*, abounds in examples of states that failed to mind their own security interests through internal efforts or external arrangements, and as one would expect, suffered invasion, loss of autonomy, and dismemberment. States are free to disregard the imperatives of power, but they must expect to pay a price for doing so. Moreover, relatively weak and divided states may find it impossible to concert their efforts to counter a hegemonic state despite ample provocation. This has long been the condition of the Western Hemisphere.

In the Cold War, the United States won a telling victory. Victory in war, however, often brings lasting enmities. Magnanimity in victory is rare. Winners of wars, facing few impediments to the exercise of their wills, often act in ways that create future enemies. Thus Germany, by taking Alsace and most of Lorraine from France in 1871, earned its lasting enmity; and the Allies' harsh treatment of Germany after World War I produced a similar effect. In contrast, Bismarck persuaded the kaiser not to march his armies along the road to Vienna after the great victory at Königgrätz in 1866. In the Treaty of Prague, Prussia took no Austrian territory. Thus Austria, having become Austria-Hungary, was available as an alliance partner for Germany in 1879. Rather than learning from history, the United States is repeating past errors by extending its influence over what used to be the province of the vanquished. This alienates Russia and nudges it toward China instead of drawing it toward Europe and the United States. Despite much talk about the "globalization" of international politics, American political leaders to a dismaying extent think of East *or* West rather than of their interaction. With a history of conflict along a 2,600 mile border, with ethnic minorities sprawling across it, with a mineral-rich and sparsely populated Siberia facing China's teeming millions, Russia and China will find it difficult to cooperate effectively, but the United States is doing its best to help them do so. Indeed, the United States has provided the key to Russian-Chinese relations over the past half century. Feeling American antagonism and fearing American power, China drew close to Russia after World War II and remained so until the United States seemed less, and the Soviet Union more, of a threat to China. The relatively harmonious relations the United States and China enjoyed during the 1970s began to sour in the late 1980s when Russian power visibly declined and American hegemony became imminent. To alienate Russia by expanding NATO, and to alienate China by lecturing its leaders on how to rule their country, are policies that only an overwhelmingly powerful country could afford, and only a foolish one be tempted, to follow. The United States cannot prevent a new balance of power from forming. It can hasten its coming as it has been earnestly doing.

In this section, the discussion of balancing has been more empirical and speculative than theoretical. I therefore end with some reflections on balancing theory. Structural theory, and the theory of balance of power that follows from it, do not lead one to expect that states will always or even usually engage in balancing behavior. Balancing is a strategy for survival, a way of attempting to maintain a state's autonomous way of life. To argue that bandwagoning represents a behavior more common to states than balancing has become a bit of a fad. Whether states bandwagon more often than they balance is an interesting question. To believe that an affirmative answer would refute balance-of-power theory is, however, to misinterpret the theory and to commit what one might call "the numerical fallacy" – to draw a qualitative conclusion from a quantitative result. States try various strategies for survival. Balancing is one of them; bandwagoning is another. The latter may sometimes seem a less demanding and a more rewarding strategy than balancing, requiring less effort and extracting lower costs while promising concrete rewards. Amid the uncertainties of international politics and the shifting pressures of domestic politics, states have to make perilous choices. They may hope to avoid war by appeasing adversaries, a weak form of bandwagoning, rather than by rearming and realigning to thwart them. Moreover, many states have insufficient resources for balancing and little room for maneuver. They have to jump on the wagon only later to wish they could fall off.

Balancing theory does not predict uniformity of behavior but rather the strong tendency of major states in the system, or in regional subsystems, to resort to balancing when they have to. That states try different strategies of survival is hardly surprising. The recurrent emergence of balancing behavior, and the appearance of the patterns the behavior produces, should all the more be seen as impressive evidence supporting the theory.

Notes

1   Michael W. Doyle, "Kant, Liberalism and World Politics," *American Political Science Review*, 80, 1986, pp. 1151–69.
2   Francis Fukuyama, *The End of History and the Last Man* (Free Press, New York, 1992), pp. 245–6.
3   Bruce Russett, *Grasping the Democratic Peace: Principles for a Post Cold-War Peace* (Princeton University Press, Princeton, 1993).
4   John Mueller, *Quiet Cataclysm: Reflections on the Recent Transformations of World Politics* (Harper Collins, New York, 1995).
5   Robert O. Keohane and Joseph S. Nye, *Power and Interdependence*, 2nd ed. (Harper Collins, New York, 1989).
6   Kenneth N. Waltz, 'The Myth of Interdependence' in Charles P. Kindleberger, ed., *The International Corporation* (MIT Press, Cambridge, Mass, 1970).
7   Susan Strange, *Retreat of the State: The Diffusion of Power in the World Economy* (Cambridge University Press, New York, 1996) pp. 46–189.
8   Glenn H. Snyder, *Alliance Politics* (Cornell University Press, Ithaca, 1997) p. 192.
9   Robert O. Keohane and Lisa L. Martin, "The Promise of Institutionalist Theory," *International Security* 20, 1995, pp. 42–46.

1.10 The stability of a unipolar world

William C. Wohlforth

Source: *International Security*, vol. 24, no. 1 (1999), pp. 5–41.

Wohlforth challenges the assumption of the balance of power theory that unipolarity is inherently unstable and that US dominance will soon be challenged and unipolarity will give way to a multipolar world. He argues, first, that in contrast to the hegemonic powers that emerged in the nineteenth and twentieth centuries, there are no states that can challenge the existing preeminence of the United States; second, that this unipolar system will be more stable and peaceful than previous systems; and third, that if the United States pursues wise policies, then unipolarity will last as long as the bipolar Cold War era.

Lonely at the top: the system is unipolar

Unipolarity is a structure in which one state's capabilities are too great to be counterbalanced. Once capabilities are so concentrated, a structure arises that is fundamentally distinct from either multipolarity (a structure comprising three or more especially powerful states) or bipolarity (a structure produced when two states are substantially more powerful than all others). At the same time, capabilities are not so concentrated as to produce a global empire. Unipolarity should not be confused with a multi- or bipolar system containing one especially strong polar state or with an imperial system containing only one major power.

Is the current structure unipolar? The crucial first step in answering this question is to compare the current distribution of power with its structural predecessors. The more the current concentration of power in the United States differs from past distributions, the less we should expect post-Cold War world politics to resemble that of earlier epochs. I select two cases that allow me to compare concentrations of power in both multipolar and bipolar settings: the Pax Britannica and the Cold War. Within these two cases, I highlight two specific periods – 1860–70 and 1945–55 – because they reflect the greatest concentrations of power in the system leader, and so have the greatest potential to weaken the case for the extraordinary nature of the current unipolarity. I also include a second Cold War period in the mid-1980s to capture the distribution of power just before the dramatic changes of the 1990s.

Quantitative comparison

To qualify as polar powers, states must score well on *all* the components of power: size of population and territory; resource endowment; economic capabilities; military strength; and "competence," according to Kenneth Waltz.[1] Two states measured up in 1990. One is gone. No new pole has appeared: 2 - 1 = 1. The system is unipolar.

The reality, however, is much more dramatic than this arithmetic implies. [. . .]

Table 1 shows how U.S. relative power in the late 1990s compares with that of Britain near its peak, as well as the United States itself during the Cold War. The United States' economic dominance is surpassed only by its own position at the dawn of the Cold War – when every other major power's economy was either exhausted or physically destroyed by the recent world war – and its military superiority dwarfs that of any leading state in modern international history. [. . .]

The United States not only has the largest high-technology economy in the world by far, it also has the greatest concentration in high-technology manufacturing among the major powers. (See Table 2). Total U.S. expenditures on research and development (R&D) nearly equal the combined total of the rest of the Group of Seven richest countries (and the G-7 accounts for 90 percent of world spending on R&D). Numerous studies of U.S. technological leadership confirm the country's dominant position in all the key "leading sectors" that are most likely to dominate the world economy into the twenty-first century.

The U.S. combination of quantitative and qualitative material advantages is unprecedented, and it translates into a unique geopolitical position. Thanks to a decades-old policy of harnessing technology to the generation of military power, the U.S. comparative advantage in this area mirrors Britain's naval preeminence in the nineteenth century. At the same time, Washington's current brute share of great power capabilities – its aggregate potential compared with that of the next largest power or all other great powers combined – dwarfs Britain's share in its day. The United States is the only state with global power projection capabilities; it is probably capable, if challenged, of producing defensive land-power dominance in the key theaters; it retains the world's only truly blue-water navy; it dominates the air; it has retained a nuclear posture that may give it first-strike advantages against other nuclear powers; and it has continued to nurture decades-old investments in military logistics and command, control, communications, and intelligence. By devoting only 3 percent of its gross domestic product (GDP) to defense, it outspends all other great powers combined – and most of those great powers are its close allies. Its defense R&D expenditures are probably greater than those of the rest of the world combined (Table 2). None of the

Table 1 Comparing hegemonies

a *Gross domestic product as percentage of "hegemon"*

Year	United States	Britain	Russia	Japan	Austria	Germany	France	China
1870	108	100	90	n.a.	29	46	75	n.a.
1950	100	24	35	11	n.a.	15	15	n.a.
1985	100	17	39	38	n.a.	21	18	46
1997 (PPP)	100	15	9	38	n.a.	22	16	53
1997 (exchange rate)	100	16	5	50	n.a.	25	17	10

b *Military expenditures as percentage of "hegemon"*

Year	United States	Britain	Russia	Japan	Austria	Germany	France	China
1872	68	100	120	n.a.	44	65	113	n.a.
1950	100	16	107	n.a.	n.a.	n.a.	10	n.a.
1985	100	10	109	5	n.a.	8	8	10
1996	100	13	26	17	n.a.	14	17	13

Table 2 Information-age indicators for the major powers, 1995–97

	High-technology manufacturing (1995, percentage)	Total R&D expenditures (1995, percentage)	Defense R&D expenditures (1995–96, percentage)	Utility invention patents granted in the United States (1997, thousands)	PCs per 1,000 people (1997)	Internet hosts per 10,000 people (July 1998)	Scientists and engineers in R&D per million people (1985–95)
United States	41	53	80	61	407	976	3,732
Britain	6	6	7	2	242	201	2,417
Japan	30	22	2	23	202	107	5,677
France	5	8	8	n.a.	174	73	2,537
Germany	10	11	3	6.8	255	141	3,016
China	8	n.a.	n.a.	n.a.	6	.16	537
Russia	n.a.	n.a.	n.a.	n.a.	32	9	4,358

major powers is balancing; most have scaled back military expenditures faster than the United States has. One reason may be that democracy and globalization have changed the nature of world politics. Another possibility, however, is that any effort to compete directly with the United States is futile, so no one tries.

Qualitative comparison

Bringing historical detail to bear on the comparison of today's distribution of power to past systems only strengthens the initial conclusions that emerge from quantitative comparisons. [. . .] These (quantitative) indicators miss two crucial factors that only historical research can reveal: the clarity of the balance as determined by the events that help decisionmakers define and measure power, and the comprehensiveness of the leader's overall power advantage in each period. Together these factors help to produce a U.S. preponderance that is far less ambiguous, and therefore less subject to challenge, than that of previous leading states.

The end of the Cold War and the collapse of the Soviet Union were much more effective tests of material power relationships than any of the systemic wars of the past two centuries. One reason is simple arithmetic. The greater the number of players, the more difficult it is for any single war or event to clarify relations of power throughout the system. Even very large wars in multipolar systems do not provide unambiguous tests of the relative power of the states belonging to the victorious coalition. And wars often end before the complete defeat of major powers. The systemic wars of the past left several great states standing and ready to argue over their relative power. By contrast, bipolarity was built on two states, and one collapsed with more decisiveness than most wars can generate. The gap between the capabilities of the super-powers, on the one hand, and all other major powers, on the other hand, was already greater in the Cold War than any analogous gap in the history of the European states system. Given that the United States and the Soviet Union were so clearly in a class by themselves, the fall of one from superpower status leaves the other much more unambiguously "number one" than at any other time since 1815.

Moreover, the power gap in the United States' favor is wider than any single measure can capture because the unipolar concentration of resources is *symmetrical*. Unlike previous system leaders, the United States has commanding leads in all the elements of material power: economic, military, technological, and geographical. All the naval and commercial powers that most scholars identify as the hegemonic leaders of the past lacked military (especially land-power) capabilities commensurate with their global influence. Asymmetrical power portfolios generate ambiguity. When the leading state excels in the production of economic and naval capabilities but not conventional land power, it may seem simultaneously powerful and vulnerable. Such asymmetrical power portfolios create resentment among second-tier states that are powerful militarily but lack the great prestige the leading state's commercial and naval advantages bring. At the same time, they make the leader seem vulnerable to pressure from the one element of power in which it does not excel: military capabilities. The result is ambiguity about which state is more powerful, which is more secure, which is threatening which, and which might make a bid for hegemony.

Britain's huge empire, globe-girdling navy, and vibrant economy left strong imprints on nineteenth-century world politics, but because its capabilities were always skewed in favor of naval and commercial power, it never had the aggregate advantage implied by its early industrialization. Indeed, it was not even the international system's unambiguous leader until Russia's defeat in Crimea in 1856. The Napoleonic Wars yielded *three* potential hegemons: Britain, the decisive naval and financial power; Russia, the preeminent military power on the continent; and France, the state whose military prowess had called forth coalitions involving all the other great states. From 1815 to 1856, Britain had to share leadership of the system with Russia, while the power gap between these two empires and France remained perilously small. Russia's defeat in Crimea punctured its aura of power and established Britain's uncontested primacy. But even after 1856, the gap between London and continental powerhouses such as France, Russia, and Prussia remained small because Britain never translated its early-industrial potential into continental-scale military capabilities. The Crimean victory that ushered in the era of British preeminence was based mainly on *French* land power. And Britain's industrial advantage peaked before industrial capabilities came to be seen as the sine qua non of military power.

The Cold War power gap between the United States and the Soviet Union was much smaller. World War II yielded ambiguous lessons concerning the relative importance of U.S. sea, air, and economic capabilities versus the Soviet Union's proven conventional military superiority in Eurasia. The conflict clearly showed that the United States possessed the greatest military potential in the world – if it could harness its massive economy to the production of military power and deploy that power to the theater in time. Despite its economic weaknesses, however, Stalin's empire retained precisely those advantages that Czar Nicholas I's had had: the ability to take and hold key Eurasian territory with land forces. The fact that Moscow's share of world power was already in Eurasia (and already in the form of an armed fighting force) was decisive in explaining the Cold War. It was chiefly because of its location (and its militarized nature) that the Soviet Union's economy was capable of generating bipolarity. At the dawn of the Cold War, when the United States' economy was as big as those of all other great powers combined, the balance of power was still seen as precarious.

In both the Pax Britannica and the early Cold War, different measures show power to have been concentrated in the leading state to an unusual degree. Yet in both periods, the perceived power gaps were closer than the measures imply. Asymmetrical power portfolios and small power gaps are the norm in modern international history. They are absent from the distribution of power of the late 1990s. Previous postwar hegemonic moments therefore cannot compare with post-Cold War unipolarity. Given the dramatically different power distribution alone, we should expect world politics to work much differently now than in the past.

Unipolarity is peaceful

Unipolarity favors the absence of war among the great powers and comparatively low levels of competition for prestige or security for two reasons: the leading state's power advantage removes the problem of hegemonic rivalry from world politics, and it reduces the salience and stakes of balance-of-power politics among the major states. This argument is based on two well-known realist theories: hegemonic theory and balance-of-power theory. Each is controversial, and the relationship between the two is complex. For the purposes of this analysis, however, the key point is that both theories predict that a unipolar system will be peaceful.

How to think about unipolarity

Hegemonic theory has received short shrift in the debate over the nature of the post-Cold War international system. This omission is unwarranted, for the theory has simple and profound implications for the peacefulness of the post-Cold War international order that are backed up by a formidable body of scholarship. The theory stipulates that especially powerful states ("hegemons") foster international orders that are stable until differential growth in power produces a dissatisfied state with the capability to challenge the dominant state for leadership. The clearer and larger the concentration of power in the leading state, the more peaceful the international order associated with it will be.

The key is that conflict occurs only if the leader and the challenger disagree about their relative power. That is, the leader must think itself capable of defending the status quo at the same time that the number two state believes it has the power to challenge it. The set of perceptions and expectations necessary to produce such conflict is most likely under two circumstances: when the overall gap between the leader and the challenger is small and/or when the challenger overtakes the leader in *some* elements of national power but not others, and the two parties disagree over the relative importance of these elements. Hence both the overall size and the comprehensiveness of the leader's power advantage are crucial to peacefulness. If the system is unipolar, the great power hierarchy should be much more stable than any hierarchy lodged within a system of more than one pole. Because unipolarity is based on a historically unprecedented concentration of power in the United States, a potentially important source of great power conflict – hegemonic rivalry – will be missing.

Balance-of-power theory has been at the center of the debate, but absent so far is a clear distinction between peacefulness and durability. The theory predicts that any system comprised of states in anarchy will evince a tendency toward equilibrium. As Waltz puts it, "Unbalanced power, whoever wields it, is a potential danger to others."[2] This central proposition lies behind the widespread belief that unipolarity will not be durable (a contention I address below). Less often noted is the fact that as long as the system remains unipolar, balance-of-power theory predicts peace. When balance-of-power theorists argue that the post-Cold War world is headed toward conflict, they are not claiming that unipolarity causes conflict. Rather, they are claiming that unipolarity leads quickly to bi- or multipolarity. It is not unipolarity's peacefulness but its durability that is in dispute.

Waltz argued that bipolarity is less war prone than multipolarity because it reduces uncertainty. By the same logic, unipolarity is the least war prone of all structures. For as long as unipolarity obtains, there is little uncertainty regarding alliance choices or the calculation of power. The only options available to second-tier states are to bandwagon with the polar power (either explicitly or implicitly) or, at least, to take no action that could incur its focused enmity. As long as their security policies are oriented around the power and preferences of the sole pole, second-tier states are less likely to engage in conflict prone rivalries for security or prestige. Once the sole pole takes sides, there can be little doubt about which party will prevail. Moreover, the unipolar leader has the capability to be far more interventionist than earlier system leaders. Exploiting the other states' security dependence as well as its unilateral power advantages, the sole pole can maintain a system of alliances that keeps second-tier states out of trouble.

Until the underlying distribution of power changes, second-tier states face structural incentives similar to those of lesser states in a region dominated by one power, such as North America. The low incidence of wars in those systems is consistent with the expectations of standard, balance-of-power thinking. Otto von Bismarck earned a reputation for strategic genius by creating and managing a complex alliance system that staved off war while working disproportionately to his advantage in a multipolar setting. It does not take a Bismarck to run a Bismarckian alliance system under unipolarity. No one credits the United States with strategic genius for managing security dilemmas among American states. Such an alliance system is a structurally favored and hence less remarkable and more durable outcome in a unipolar system.

The missing systemic sources of conflict

To appreciate the sources of conflict that unipolarity avoids, consider the two periods already discussed in which leading states scored very highly on aggregate measures of power: the Pax Britannica and the Cold War. Because those concentrations of power were not unipolar, both periods witnessed security competition and hegemonic rivalry. The Crimean War is a case in point. The war unfolded in a system in which two states shared leadership and *three* states were plausibly capable of bidding for hegemony. Partly as a result, neither the statesmen of the time nor historians over the last century and a half have been able to settle the debate over the origins of the conflict. The problem is that even those who agree that the war arose from a threat to the European balance of power cannot agree on whether the threat emanated from France, Russia, or Britain. Determining which state really did threaten the equilibrium – or indeed whether any of them did – is less important than the fact that the power gap among them was small enough to make all three threats seem plausible at the time and in retrospect. No such uncertainty – and hence no such conflict – is remotely possible in a unipolar system.

Similar sources of conflict emerged in the Cold War. The most recent and exhaustively researched accounts of Cold War diplomacy reveal in detail what the numerical indicators only hint at: the complex interplay between U.S. overall economic superiority, on the one hand, and the Soviet Union's massive conventional military capabilities, on the other. This asymmetrical distribution of power meant that the gap between the two top states could be seen as lopsided or perilously close depending on one's vantage. The fact that the United States was preeminent only in nonmilitary elements of power was a critical factor underlying the Cold War competition for power and security. To produce a military balance, Washington set about creating a preponderance of other capabilities, which constituted a latent threat to Moscow's war planners and a major constraint on its diplomatic strategy. Hence both Moscow and Washington could simultaneously see their rivalry as a consequence of the other's drive for hegemony – sustaining a historical debate that shows every sign of being as inconclusive as that over the origins of the Crimean War. Again, no such ambiguity, and no such conflict, is likely in a unipolar system.

Both hegemonic rivalry and security competition among great powers are unlikely under unipolarity. Because the current leading state is by far the world's most formidable military power, the chances of leadership conflict are more remote than at any time over the last two centuries. Unlike past international systems, efforts by any second-tier state to enhance its relative position can be managed in a unipolar system without raising the specter of a power transition and a struggle for primacy. And because the major powers face incentives to shape their policies with a view toward the power and preferences of the system leader, the likelihood of security competition among them is lower than in previous systems.

Unipolarity is durable

Unipolarity rests on two pillars. I have already established the first: the sheer size and comprehensiveness of the power gap separating the United States from other states. This massive power gap implies that any countervailing change must be strong and sustained to produce structural effects. The second pillar – geography – is just as important. In addition to all the other advantages the United States possesses, we must also consider its four truest allies: Canada, Mexico, the Atlantic, and the Pacific. Location matters. The fact that Soviet power happened to be situated in the heart of Eurasia was a key condition of bipolarity.

Similarly, the U.S. position as an offshore power determines the nature and likely longevity of unipolarity. Just as the raw numbers could not capture the real dynamics of bipolarity, power indexes alone cannot capture the importance of the fact that the United States is in North America while all the other potential poles are in or around Eurasia. The balance of power between the sole pole and the second-tier states is not the only one that matters, and it may not even be the most important one for many states. Local balances of power may loom larger in the calculations of other states than the background unipolar structure. Efforts to produce a counterbalance globally will generate powerful countervailing action locally. As a result, the threshold concentration of power necessary to sustain unipolarity is lower than most scholars assume.

Because they fail to appreciate the sheer size and comprehensiveness of the power gap and the advantages conveyed by geography, many scholars expect bi- or multipolarity to reappear quickly. They propose three ways in which unipolarity will end: counterbalancing by other states, regional integration, or the differential growth in power. None of these is likely to generate structural change in the policy-relevant future.

Alliances are not structural

Many scholars portray unipolarity as precarious by ignoring all the impediments to balancing in the real world. If balancing were the frictionless, costless activity assumed in some balance-of-power theories, then the unipolar power would need more than 50 percent of the capabilities in the great power system to stave off a counterpoise. Even though the United States meets this threshold today, in a hypothetical world of frictionless balancing its edge might be eroded quickly. But such expectations miss the fact that alliance politics always impose costs, and that the impediments to balancing are especially great in the unipolar system that emerged in the wake of the Cold War.

Alliances are not structural. Because alliances are far less effective than states in producing and deploying power internationally, most scholars follow Waltz in making a distinction between the distribution of capabilities among states and the alliances states may form. A unipolar system is one in which a counterbalance is impossible. When a counterbalance becomes possible, the system is not unipolar. The point at which this structural shift can happen is determined in part by how efficiently alliances can aggregate the power of individual states. Alliances aggregate power only to the extent that they are reliably binding and permit the merging of armed forces, defense industries, R&D infrastructures, and strategic decisionmaking. A glance at international history shows how difficult it is to coordinate counterhegemonic alliances. States are tempted to free ride, pass the buck, or bandwagon in search of favors from the aspiring hegemon. States have to worry about being abandoned by alliance partners when the chips are down or being dragged into conflicts of others' making. The aspiring hegemon, meanwhile, has only to make sure its domestic house is in order. In short, a single state gets more bang for the buck than several states in an alliance. To the extent that alliances are inefficient at pooling power, the sole pole obtains greater power per unit of aggregate capabilities than any alliance that might take shape against it. Right away, the odds are skewed in favor of the unipolar power.

The key, however, is that the countercoalitions of the past – on which most of our empirical knowledge of alliance politics is based – formed against centrally located land powers (France, Germany, and the Soviet Union) that constituted relatively unambiguous security threats to their neighbors. Coordinating a counterbalance against an *offshore* state that has *already* achieved unipolar status will be much more difficult. Even a declining offshore unipolar state will have unusually wide opportunities to play divide and rule. Any second-tier state seeking to counterbalance has to contend with the existing pro-U.S. bandwagon. If things go poorly, the aspiring counterbalancer will have to confront not just the capabilities of the unipolar state, but also those of its other great power allies. All of the aspiring poles face a problem the United States does not: great power neighbors that could become crucial U.S. allies the moment an unambiguous challenge to Washington's preeminence emerges. In addition, in each region there are smaller "pivotal states" that make natural U.S. allies against an aspiring regional power. Indeed, the United States' first move in any counterbalancing game of this sort could be to try to promote such pivotal states to great power status, as it did with China against the Soviet Union in the latter days of the Cold War.

New regional unipolarities: a game not worth the candle

To bring an end to unipolarity, it is not enough for regional powers to coordinate policies in traditional alliances. They must translate their aggregate economic potential into the concrete capabilities necessary to be a pole: a defense industry and power projection capabilities that can play in the same league as those of the United States. Thus all scenarios for the rapid return of multipolarity involve regional unification or the emergence of strong regional unipolarities. For the European, Central Eurasian, or East Asian poles to measure up to the United States in the near future, each region's resources need to fall under the de facto control of one state or decisionmaking authority. In the near term, either true unification in Europe and Central Eurasia (the European Union [EU] becomes a de facto state, or Russia recreates an empire) or unipolar dominance in each region by Germany, Russia, and China or Japan, respectively, is a necessary condition of bi- or multipolarity.

The problem with these scenarios is that regional balancing dynamics are likely to kick in against the local great power much more reliably than the global counterbalance works against the United States. Given the neighborhoods they live in, an aspiring Chinese, Japanese, Russian, or German pole would face more effective counterbalancing than the United States itself.

If the EU were a state, the world would be bipolar. To create a balance of power globally, Europe would have to suspend the balance of power locally. Which balance matters more to Europeans is not a question that will be resolved quickly. A world with a European pole would be one in which the French and the British had merged their conventional and nuclear capabilities and do not mind if the Germans control them. The EU may move in this direction, but in the absence of a major shock the movement will be very slow and ambiguous. Global leadership requires coherent and quick decisionmaking in response to crises. Even on international monetary matters, Europe will lack this capability for some time. Creating the institutional and political requisites for a single European foreign and security policy and defense industry goes to the heart of state sovereignty and thus is a much more challenging task for the much longer term.

The diffusion of power

In the final analysis, alliances cannot change the system's structure. Only the uneven growth of power (or, in the case of the EU, the creation of a new state) will bring the unipolar era to an end. Europe will take many decades to become a de facto state – if it ever does. Unless and until that happens, the fate of unipolarity depends on the relative rates of growth and innovation of the main powers.

I have established that the gap in favor of the United States is unprecedented and that the threshold level of capabilities it needs to sustain unipolarity is much less than the 50 percent that analysts often assume. Social science lacks a theory that can predict the rate of the rise and fall of great powers. It is possible that the United States will decline suddenly and dramatically while some other great power rises. If rates of growth tend to converge as economies approach U.S. levels of per capita GDP, then the speed at which other rich states can close the gap will be limited. Germany may be out of the running entirely. Japan may take a decade to regain the relative position it occupied in 1990. After that, if all goes well, sustained higher growth could place it in polar position in another decade or two. This leaves China as the focus of current expectations for the demise of unipolarity. The fact that the two main contenders to polar status are close Asian neighbors and face tight regional constraints further reinforces unipolarity. The threshold at which Japan or China will possess the capabilities to face the other *and* the United States is very high. Until then, they are better off in a unipolar order.

As a poor country, China has a much greater chance of maintaining sustained high growth rates. With its large population making for large gross economic output, projections based on extrapolating 8 percent yearly growth in GDP have China passing the United States early in the twenty-first century. But these numbers must be used with care. After all, China's huge population probably gave it a larger economy than Britain in the nineteenth century. The current belief in a looming power transition between the United States and China resembles pre-World War I beliefs about rising Russian power. It assumes that population and rapid growth compensate for technological backwardness. China's economic and military modernization has a much longer road to travel than its gross economic output suggests. And managing the political and social challenges presented by rapid growth in an overpopulated country governed by an authoritarian regime is a formidable task. By any measure, the political challenges that lie athwart Beijing's path to polar status are much more substantial than those that may block Washington's efforts to maintain its position. Three decades is probably a better bet than one.

The balance of power is not what states make of it

For some analysts, multipolarity seems just around the corner because intellectuals and politicians in some other states want it to be. Samuel Huntington notes that "political and intellectual leaders in most countries strongly resist the prospect of a unipolar world and favor the emergence of true multipolarity."[3] No article on contemporary world affairs is complete without obligatory citations from diplomats and scholars complaining of U.S. arrogance. The problem is that policymakers (and scholars) cannot always have the balance of power they want. If they could, neither bipolarity nor unipolarity would have occurred in the first place. Washington, Moscow, London, and Paris wanted a swift return to multipolarity after World War II. And policymakers in all four capitals appeared to prefer bipolarity to unipolarity in 1990–91. Like its structural predecessor, unipolarity might persist despite policymakers' wishes.

Most of the counterbalancing that has occurred since 1991 has been rhetorical. Notably absent is any willingness on the part of the other great powers to accept any significant political or economic costs in countering U.S. power. Most of the world's powers are busy trying to climb aboard the American bandwagon even as they curtail their military outlays. Military spending by all the other great powers is either declining or holding steady in real terms. While Washington prepares for increased defense outlays, current planning in

Europe, Japan, and China does not suggest real increases in the offing, and Russia's spending will inevitably decline further. This response on the part of the other major powers is understandable, because the raw distribution of power leaves them with no realistic hope of counterbalancing the United States, while U.S.-managed security systems in Europe and Asia moderate the demand for more military capabilities.

Neither the Beijing–Moscow "strategic partnership" nor the "European troika" of Russia, Germany, and France entailed any costly commitments or serious risks of confrontation with Washington. For many states, the optimal policy is ambiguity: to work closely with the United States on the issues most important to Washington while talking about creating a counterpoise. Such policies generate a paper trail suggesting strong dissatisfaction with the U.S.-led world order and a legacy of actual behavior that amounts to bandwagoning. These states are seeking the best bargains for themselves given the distribution of power. That process necessitates a degree of politicking that may remind people faintly of the power politics of bygone eras. But until the distribution of power changes substantially, this bargaining will resemble real-politik in form but not content.

Conclusion: challenges for scholarship and strategy

If unipolarity is so robust, why do so many writers hasten to declare its demise? The answer may lie in the common human tendency to conflate power *trends* with existing relationships. The rush to proclaim the return of multipolarity in the 1960s and 1970s, to pronounce the United States' decline in the 1980s, to herald the rise of Japan or China as superpowers in the 1980s and 1990s, and finally to bid unipolarity adieu after the Cold War are all examples. In each case, analysts changed reference points to minimize U.S. power. In the bipolarity debate, the reference point became the extremely tight alliance of the 1950s, so any disagreement between the United States and Europe was seen as a harbinger of multipolarity. [. . .]

Todays's distribution of power is unprecedented, however, and power-centric theories naturally expect politics among nations to be different than in past systems. In contrast to the past, the existing distribution of capabilities generates incentives for cooperation. The absence of hegemonic rivalry, security competition, and balancing is not necessarily the result of ideational or institutional change. This is not to assert that realism provides the best explanation for the absence of security and prestige competition. Rather, the conclusion is that it offers an explanation that may compete with or compliment those of other theoretical traditions. As a result, evaluating the merits of contending theories for understanding the international politics of unipolarity presents greater empirical challenges than mant scholars have acknowledged.

Because the baseline expectations of all power-centric theories are novel, so are their implications for grand strategy. Scholars' main message to policymakers has been to prepare for multipolarity. Certainly, we should think about how to manage the transition to a new structure. Yet time and energy are limited. Constant preparation for the return of multipolarity means not gearing up intellectually and materially for unipolarity. Given that unipolarity is prone to peace and the probability that it will last several more decades at least, we should focus on it and get it right.

The first step is to stop calling this the 'post-Cold War record.' [. . .] Calling the current period the true Pax Americana may offend some, but it reflects reality and focuses attention on the stakes involved in U.S. grand strategy.

[. . .] Because the current concentration of power in the United States is unprecedentedly clear and comprehensive, states are likely to share the expectation that counterbalancing would be a costly and probably doomed venture. As a result, they face incentives to keep their military budgets under control until they observe fundamental changes in the capability of the United States to fulfill its role. The whole system can thus be run at comparatively low costs to both the sole pole and the other major powers. Unipolarity can be made to seem expensive and dangerous if it is equated with a global empire demanding U.S. involvement in all issues everywhere. In reality, unipolarity is a distribution of capabilities among the world's great powers. It does not solve all the world's problems. Rather, it minimizes two major problems – security and prestige competition – that confronted the great powers of the past. Maintaining unipolarity does not require limitless commitments. It involves managing the central security regimes in Europe and Asia, and maintaining the expectation on the part of other states that any geopolitical challenge to the United States is futile. As long as that is the expectation, states will likely refrain from trying, and the system can be maintained at little extra cost.

The main criticism of the Pax Americana, however, is not that Washington is too interventionist. A state cannot be blamed for responding to systemic incentives. The problem is U.S. reluctance to *pay up*. Constrained by a domestic welfare role and consumer culture that the weaker British hegemon never faced, Washington tends to shrink from accepting the financial, military, and especially the domestic political burdens of sole pole status. At the same time, it cannot escape the demand for involvement. The result is cruise missile hegemony, the search for polar status on the cheap, and a grand global broker of deals for which others pay. The United States has responded to structural incentives by assuming the role of global security manager and "indispensable nation" in all matters of importance. But too often the solutions Washington engineers are weakened by American reluctance to take any domestic political risks.

The problem is that structural pressures on the United States are weak. Powerful states may not respond to the international environment because their power makes them immune to its threat. The smaller the number of actors, the greater the potential impact of internal processes on international politics. The sole pole is strong and secure enough that paying up-front costs for system maintenance is hard to sell to a parsimonious public. As Kenneth Waltz argued, "Strong states [. . .] can afford not to learn."[4] If that was true of the great powers in multi- or bipolar systems, it is even truer of today's unipolar power. The implication is that instead of dwelling on the dangers of overinvolvement and the need to prepare for an impending multipolarity, scholars and policymakers should do more to advertise the attractions of unipolarity.

Notes

1   Kenneth N. Waltz, *Theory of International Politics* (Addison-Wesley, Reading, Mass, 1979), p. 131.
2   Kenneth N. Waltz, "Evaluating Theories," *American Political Science Review* vol. 91, no. 4, December 1997, 915–916, p. 915.
3   Samuel P. Huntington, "The Lonely Superpower," *Foreign Affairs*, vol. 78, no. 2 (March/April), 1999, p. 42.
4   Kenneth N. Waltz, *Theory of International Politics* (Addison-Wesley, Reading, Mass, 1979), p. 195.

1.11 Law, strategy and history

Philip Bobbitt

Source: *The Shield of Achilles: War, Peace and the Course of History* (Penguin Books, London, 2002), pp. 5–17.

Bobbitt argues that the strategic calculus that operated during what he calls the 'long war' that lasted from 1914 to 1989 is now redundant because states no longer face identifiable state-centred threats that have undermined their security in the past. The basic objectives of the strategic calculus used in the past – deterrence, compellance, and reassurance – need to be reconfigured. In the contemporary world, states must include in the calculus of force the need to maintain world order.

The State exists by virtue of its purposes, and among these are a drive for survival and freedom of action, which is strategy; for authority and legitimacy, which is law; for identity, which is history. To put it differently, there is no state without strategy, law, and history, and, to complicate matters, these three are not merely interrelated elements, they are elements each composed at least partly of the others. The precise nature of this composition defines a particular state and is the result of many choices. States may be militaristic, legalistic, and traditional to varying degrees, but every state is some combination of these elements and can be contrasted with every other state – and with its own predecessors – in these ways.

The legal and strategic choices a society confronts are often only recombinations of choices confronted and resolved in the past, now remade in a present condition of necessity and uncertainty. Law cannot come into being until the state achieves a monopoly on the legitimate use of violence. Similarly, a society must have a single legitimate government for its strategic designs to be laid; otherwise, the distinction between war and civil war collapses, and strategy degenerates into banditry. Until the governing institutions of a society can claim for themselves the sole right to determine the legitimate use of force at home and abroad, there can be no state. Without law, strategy cannot claim to be a legitimate act of state. Only if law prevails can it confer legitimacy on strategic choices and give them a purpose. Yet the legitimacy necessary for law and for strategy derives from history, the understanding of past practices that characterizes a particular society.

Today, all major states confront the apparently bewildering task of determining a new set of rules for the use of military force. Commentators in many parts of the world have observed a curious vacillation and fecklessness on the part of the great powers at the very time those powers ought to be most united in their goals, for the Long War that divided them has now ended. Or perhaps it is the end of the Long War that accounts for such widespread confusion. Because the ideological confrontation that once clearly identified the threats to the states of either camp has evaporated, it has left these states uncertain as to how to configure, much less deploy, their armed forces. What seems to characterize the present period is a confusion about how to count the costs and benefits of intervention, prepared-ness, and alliance. What does the calculus for the use of force yield us when we have done our sums? Only an unconvincing result that cannot silence the insistent question: "What are our forces for?" Because no calculus can tell us that. We are at a moment when our under-standing of the very purposes of the State is undergoing historic change. Neither strategy nor law will be unaffected. Until this change is appreciated, we will continue the dithering and the ad hockery, the affectations of cynicism and the placid deceit that so typifies the international behavior of the great powers in this period, a period that ought to be the hour of our greatest coherence and conviction. It is not that the United States did or did not decide to go into Somalia or Bosnia; it's that the United States has made numerous decisions, one after the other, in both directions. And the same thing may be said of the pronouncements of the other great powers regarding North Korea, Iraq, and Rwanda. "Ad hoc strategies" is almost a contradiction in terms, because the more states respond to the variations of the hour, the less they benefit from strategic planning.

The reason the traditional strategic calculus no longer functions is that it depends on certain assumptions about the relationship between the State and its objectives that the end of this long conflict has cast in doubt. That calculus was never intended to enable a state to choose between competing objectives: rather, that calculus depends upon the axiomatic requirement of the State to survive by putting its security objectives first. We are now entering a period, however, in which the survival of the State is paradoxically imperiled by such threat-based assumptions because the most powerful states do not face identifiable state-centered threats that in fact imperil their security. Having vanquished its ideological competitors, the democratic, capitalist, parliamentary state no longer faces great-power threats, threats that would enable it to configure its forces by providing a template inferred from the capabilities of the adversary state. Instead, the parliamentary state manifests vul-nerabilities that arise from a weakening of its own legitimacy. This constitutional doubt is only exacerbated by the strategic confusion abroad for which it is chiefly responsible. So the alliance of parliamentary great powers,[1] having won their historic triumph, find themselves weaker than ever, constantly undermining their own authority at home by their inability to use their influence effectively abroad. With a loosening grip on their domestic orders, these powers are ever less inclined to devote themselves to maintaining a world order. The stra-tegic thinking of states accustomed to war does not fit them for peace, which requires harmony and trust, nor can such thinking yet be abandoned without risking a collapse of legitimacy altogether because the State's role in guaranteeing security is the one responsibil-ity that is not being challenged domestically and thus the one to which it clings. We have entered a period in which, however, states must include in the calculus of force the need to maintain world order. This is not the first such period; indeed, the last epoch of this kind was ended by the eruption of the conflict that has just closed, leaving us so disoriented. Accord-ingly, there is much to learn from the study of that conflict, and also from earlier eras that were marked by changes in the constitutional form and strategic practices of the State.

Preliminarily, there are a few widespread preconceptions that must be put to one side. In contrast to the prevalent view that war is the result of a decision made by an aggressor, I will assume that, as a general matter, it takes two states to go to war. The common picture many Americans and Europeans have of states at war is that they came into hostilities as a result of the aggression of one party. It is like a class bully in a schoolyard who provokes a fistfight in order to terrorize his classmates. But the move to war is an act of the State and not of boys. States that wish to aggrandize themselves, or to depredate others, may employ aggression, but they do not seek war. Rather it is the state against whom the aggression has been mounted, typically, that makes the move to war, which is a legal and strategic act, when that state determines it cannot acquiesce in the legal and strategic demands of the aggressor. So it was with Germany, Britain, and France in 1939. So it was with Athens and Sparta in 431 B.C. A corollary to this idea is the perhaps counterintuitive notion that sometimes a state will make the move to war even when it judges it will lose the war that ensues. A state that decides it can no longer acquiesce in a deteriorating position must ask itself whether, if it chooses to resist, it will nevertheless be better off, even if it cannot ultimately prevail in the eventual conflict.

Many persons in the West believe that war occurs only because of miscalculation; sometimes this opinion is combined with the view that only aggressors make war. Persons holding these two views would have a hard time justifying the wisdom of Alliance resistance to Communism the last fifty years because it was usually the U.S. and her allies and not the Soviets who resolutely and studiedly escalated matters to crises threatening war. Besides the obvious cases involving Berlin in 1952, or Cuba in 1962, we might add the decisions to make the move to war in South Korea and in South Viet Nam, the nature and motivations of which decisions are underscored by the persistent refusals of the Americans and their allies to bomb China or invade North Viet Nam. That is, in both cases the allied forces fought to stop aggression by going to war and declined to employ decisive counteraggression.

Those persons who concede these facts and conclude that these decisions were wrong, and yet who applaud the victory of the democracies in the Cold War, are perhaps obliged to reconsider their views. For it was this peculiar combination of a willingness to make the move to war coupled with a benign nonaggression, even protectiveness, toward the other great powers that ultimately gave the Alliance victory. Sometimes this matter is confused in the debate over precisely how this victory was achieved. Was the Cold War won because U.S.-led forces militarily denied Communist forces those strategic successes that would have sustained a world revolution? Or was it won because northern-tier markets were able to build an international capitalist system that vastly outperformed the socialist system (and an international communications network that informed the world of this achievement)? Such a debate misses the point, perhaps because it is suffused with the assumptions about war and miscalculation to which I have referred. Neither military nor economic success alone could have ended the Cold War, because neither alone could deliver legitimacy to the winning state, or deny it to the loser. Moreover, neither military nor economic success was possible without the other: can one imagine a European Union having developed without Germany, or with a Germany strategically detached from the West? Even the ill-fated American mission in Viet Nam contributed to the ultimate Alliance victory: a collapse of military resistance in Indochina in 1964 would have had political effects on the very states of the region whose economies have since become so dynamic (analogous to those effects that would have been felt in Japan following a collapse of resistance in Korea in 1950). The political and economic, far from being decisive causal factors on their own, are really two faces of the same phenomenon. Only the coherent union of a constitutional order and a strategic vision could achieve the kind of results that ended, rather than merely interrupted, such an epochal war. We shall have to bear this in mind with regard to maintaining either success, political or economic, in the future.

Contemporary imagination, however, like so many aspects of contemporary life, is suffused with presentism. This is often commented on by those who lament the current lack of interest in the past, but it is equally manifest, ironically, in our projections about the future. This leads us to the third preconception that must be dismissed: namely, that future states of affairs must be evaluated in comparison with the present, rather than with the unknowable future. One encounters this often in daily life, in the adolescent's decision to quit school so "I can make more money" (because going to school pays less than working in a fast-food shop) or the columnist's claim that "if we balanced the budget, interest rates would drop and growth would increase" (because the government would not be adding to the demand for borrowed money). In those cases the speaker is making the mistake of comparing a future state of affairs with the present, and omitting to imagine what an alternative future state of affairs might be like (if he stayed in school and qualified for a better job; if the government steeply increased taxes in order to balance the budget), which would provide the proper comparison. [. . .]

The calculus employed by a state in order to determine when it is appropriate to make the move to war is, similarly, future-oriented. It asks: will the state be better or worse off, in the future, if in the present the state resorts to force to get its way? For half a millennium, the State has been an attractive institution for making political decisions precisely because it is potentially imperishable. The State, being highly future-oriented, can channel resources into the future and harness present energy for deferred gains. But this quality of futurism is also its vulnerability: the State is a clumsy instrument for persuading people to make sacrifices when objectives are in doubt, or to parry subtle long-term threats, because the interests of the people can easily be severed from those of the State when long-term objectives and goals are at issue. In the long term, as Keynes remarked, we are all dead. In periods in which the objectives to be pursued by the State are unclear, its very habits of orientation toward the future do not help to marshal the popular will, and thus the State is apt to be disabled from carrying out commitments that may be necessary for its ultimate security and the welfare of future generations to which it is, *faute de mieux*, committed. Threats such as the destruction of the ecology, the erosion of the capital base, potential threats to its critical infrastructure, and especially demographic developments all play on this vulnerability, for each such threat can call on a vocal domestic constituency that, out of reasonable motives but a present-minded orientation, can paralyze rational action. And, it should be noted, military power can quickly erode if a state does not accurately conceptualize the threats it actually faces, and thus neglects to adopt a strategy that meets those threats.

It is interesting to ask just what the United States, for example, at the end of the twentieth century took to be the objectives of its strategic calculus. According to a Pentagon White Paper at the time, there were three such objectives: deterrence, compellance, and reassurance.[2] It can be easily shown, however, that these three objectives were hangovers from the era just past, indeed that they were borrowed from theories about the objectives of nuclear strategy. What is less obvious is that, at the end of the war the Alliance had just won, objectives such as these were worse than useless because they tended to obscure the tasks that the United States had to undertake in order to redefine the goals of its national security policy. Let us look at each of the three purported objectives.

Deterrence is an extraordinarily limited theory that relies on a reasonable but extraordinarily broad assumption. That assumption is that the State will make decisions as a result of balancing the benefits to be achieved by a course of action against the costs incurred in pursuing those benefits by the particular means proposed. This assumption, in turn, depends on the commonsense observation that human beings can imagine pain greater than that they now endure, that they can imagine happiness greater than that in which they now delight, and that they will evaluate possible futures in terms of their mixtures of these two imaginary states. For instance, deterrence is a common means in criminal law, in the classroom, even in the family. "Don't even think of parking here" reads a familiar sign that reflects this approach.

As a strategy, deterrence makes most sense in the extreme case of nuclear deterrence, where the interest of the state in simple survival intersects the clarity of the danger of annihilation. Deterrence is more problematic, however, when the calculations on which it relies become more complex, or when these calculations are clouded by cultural differences and varying attitudes toward risk, or when the facts on which such calculations depend are uncertain or colored by wishful thinking. In other words, the idea of deterrence is itself so much a part of human nature that it can be applied only as it is affected by the various fallacies and shortcomings to which human nature is prey. Moreover, the strategic theory of deterrence is of a very limited application. It is scarcely deterrence, much less nuclear deterrence, that prevents the United States from invading Canada (or the other way around). Our political relations with Canada – an amalgam of our mutual history (including past wars against each other), our shared institutions, our intertwined economies, our alliances – are what render the idea of an attack by one on the other absurd enough to have been the basis for a popular satiric comedy. Rather, military deterrence is a concept that is useful *within* war or the approach to war, once political relations have become so strained that hostilities only await opportunity. It is only because we have lived for so long at war that we are inclined to miss this point, and that we have come to think of deterrence as a prominent feature of the international relations of a peacetime regime.

Drawing on work by the economist Jacob Viner, Bernard Brodie introduced into American strategic thinking the remarkable idea of nuclear deterrence. To see how revolutionary an innovation this was, we need only recall Brodie's famous conclusion. He wrote, "Thus far the chief purpose of our military establishment has been to win wars. From now on its chief purpose must be to avert them. *It can have almost no other useful purpose.*"[3] This makes a great deal of sense when dealing with nuclear weapons. The destructiveness of such weapons and their possession by our adversaries required a revolution in thinking about the purposes of our military forces. The military managers and politicians of the 1950s who were inclined to treat nuclear weapons as though they were simply bigger bombs had to learn a new, eerie form of strategic calculation. Deterrence, as a general matter, however, is a poor mission statement for a state's armed forces. No state, even one as wealthy as the United States, can afford to maintain the forces that would successfully deter all other states acting independently or in combination. One can see from the Pentagon White Paper that this idea of Brodie's in the nuclear context – the use of armed forces to avert war – has now infiltrated the conventional, that is, the non-nuclear mission statement. Not only is it unrealistic to assert that the United States must maintain forces so vast as to be a matter of general, conventional deterrence. It also begs the one important question at the end of the Cold War: whom are we supposed to deter? Only when this question is answered can we so configure our forces as to realize such a policy. Deterrence does not come with its own specifications. If it takes two to war, then the idea of deterring wars without a specified adversary or threat is nonsense. The simple intuitive appeal of being so strong militarily that no one dares threaten you is an absurd idea for a state. Indeed, such an idea, however appealing, can actually weaken the state because the diversion of its resources into an undirected defense establishment undermines the economic and political strength the state will require should it find itself in a dangerous confrontation.

Advances in weapons technology make it possible for the leading states of the developed world to produce weapons of mass destruction that are so deadly relative to their size and cost that they can bypass even the most sophisticated attempts at defense by attrition. A corollary to this fact is that these weapons can be deployed clandestinely, so that the possibility of retaliation can be defied, and thus the strategy of deterrence rendered inoperable.

Compellance, too, is an idea that originated in the strategy of nuclear weapons and has been imported by the White Paper into the world of conventional forces. There is some considerable irony in this. Thomas Schelling introduced the neologism "compellance" as a complement to "deterrence" because this ancient concept of the use of force had become lost in the bizarre new world of nuclear strategy.[4] Schelling used "compellance" to describe the coercive use of nuclear weapons. This occurs when the threat of the use of such weapons seeks to compel an adversary state to actually do something it would otherwise not do, rather than merely refrain from doing something it would like to do (which is the purpose of deterrence). Compellance has been a purpose for armed force or, indeed, violence generally throughout the life of mankind. Yet it too is inappropriate as a mission statement for American forces. Only if we have a clear political objective can we determine what form of compellance is appropriate strategically. To say the mission of our forces is "compellance" is very like saying the mission of our minds is "thought." It is both a true and an empty sentence.

Compellance has had a good run lately. It was compellance that forced Saddam Hussein to evacuate Kuwait, once he had occupied and annexed it. It was compellance that forced Slobodan Milosevic to abandon Kosovo, a province he hitherto controlled utterly. These were worthy objectives, even if our execution of our war plans was not faultless. It would be good to have had a Bush Doctrine or a Clinton Doctrine, spelling out precisely for what reason and in what contexts the United States will compel other states by force, not only because the public in a democracy has a right to such an articulation of purpose, but also because without such limiting guidelines, compellance has a way of bringing forth countervailing force. When he was asked what the lesson of the Gulf War was, the Indian chief of staff is reported to have said, "Never fight the United States without nuclear weapons."

Interestingly, the third idea said to make up the mission of U.S. forces today is an idea also drawn from nuclear strategy. Sir Michael Howard is the father of the notion of "reassurance" in nuclear strategy.[5] In a series of essays and lectures he stressed reassurance as the key element in American nuclear strategy – an element not directed at our adversaries, but toward our allies. Much stronger forces are required, he concluded, to reassure a nervous ally who is dependent on U.S. nuclear protection than are actually required to deter a targeted enemy from attack. Like the contributions of Brodie and Schelling, this insight has been of crucial importance in the development and understanding of nuclear strategy. I doubt, however, that it can be of much use in the absence of a threat to the Atlantic Alliance, or to any of the states who have relied upon the American nuclear umbrella. Of what exactly are we to reassure our allies?

Reassurance as an idea in nuclear strategy depends on the crucial distinction between *extended* and *central* deterrence. The former term applies to the extension of American nuclear protection to Europe and Japan; the latter term refers to the threat of nuclear retaliation to deter attack on the American homeland. I have argued elsewhere that extended deterrence has driven U.S. nuclear strategy, not central deterrence. Reflecting on the evolution of nuclear strategy in *Democracy and Deterrence*, I concluded in 1983 that:

> The fate of the world does not hang on whether the U.S. or the USSR reduce their weapons or on whether they freeze their technologies. Indeed it should be easy to see that were either goal pursued too single-mindedly, there would result a much more dangerous world as other powers entered the nuclear field, approaching parity with the superpowers. Rather, our situation will be determined by whether Euro-Japanese

security is enhanced, from their perspective, by our strategies, military and diplomatic; whether the public can be made to understand and support such steps as do enhance the extended environment when it has been told more or less constantly that it is the number of weapons and the advance of technology that causes (or cures) the problem [. . .][6]

I still endorse this view, but such reassurance is now far less easy to achieve because it has largely ceased to be defined. Reassurance played a crucial role during the final phase of the Long War, from 1949 to 1990, because it prevented multipolarity – the proliferation of nuclear weapons to states such as Germany and Japan – and thereby made possible the quite stable deterrence relationship between the United States and the Soviet Union. Reassurance, I will argue, has an equally vital role to play in the twenty-first century as our strategies move toward a greater emphasis on defense and deception. This will not be possible, however, if we continue to think and plan as though the stable relations that attended the possessors of weapons of mass destruction in the Cold War are somehow intrinsic to such weapons. Indeed, in my view the use of nuclear weapons is likelier in the first fifty years of the twenty-first century than at any time in the last fifty years of the twentieth century, but we are lulled into complacency about this because of the nuclear stability we experienced in that period. As one commentator has put it,

> our current strategic thought tends to project this peculiar experience into the future. It assumes that the use of mass destruction weapons will either be deterred or be confined to localized disasters caused by strategically incompetent terrorists. Competent adversaries, this thinking implicitly assumes, will have to emulate the "revolutionary" military technology that we now possess, but at the same time adhere to our old, counter-revolutionary strategy, as worked out in our superpower rivalry with the former Soviet Union. But, unfortunately, our old strategy is not an immutable law of nature. A highly competent enemy might well emerge who will seek to destroy the United States by using mass destruction weapons in a truly revolutionary kind of warfare.[7]

Thus we won't be able to reassure our peer competitors because we will fail to appreciate the true threats they face. Instead, mesmerized by "rogue states" whose hostility to the United States is essentially a by-product of our global reach that frustrates their regional ambitions, we will find ourselves increasingly at odds with the other great powers. Until we know what will serve the function of maintaining the Alliance that has become a proto-world order, we know not what to assure our allies of (or insure them against). The problem for the United States has become to identify its interests and future threats so that it can use its power to strengthen the world order that it has fought, successfully, to achieve, and that can, if properly structured and maintained, re-enforce American security to a far greater degree than the United States could possibly do alone. This is essentially an intellectual problem, just as the solution devised by the United States and its allies to the universal vulnerability that attended the development of nuclear weapons was an intellectual solution. But faced with the immense difficulties of anticipating a new strategic environment – both at the state level, where peer competitors may emerge as threats, and at the technological level, where weapons of mass destruction make nonsense out of our defense preparations – who is eager to take the bureaucratic and political risks inherent in accepting this challenge? How much more likely it is that we will extrapolate from the world we know, with incompetent villains and heroic (and recent!) success stories.

Our present world, this "Indian summer"[8] as one writer puts it, not only presents a beguiling invitation to complacency reinforced by new technological possibilities. It also offers an opportunity to undertake some fundamental reassessments without the terrible pressure of war. Recent American successes in the Gulf War and in Yugoslavia, however, may tend to discourage any too-radical revisions.

Paul Bracken correctly concludes,

> The focus on the immediate means that a larger, more important question is not being asked: should planners redesign the U.S. military for an entirely new operational environment, taking account of revolutionary changes in military technology and the possible appearance of entirely new kinds of competitors?[9]

And Fred Iklé adds that

> military planners, as well as most scholars, would shrug off these cosmic questions and instead nibble at the edges of the problem – worrying, say, about whether a tactical nuclear weapon could be stolen in Russia and sold to Iran, or whether Iraq might still be hiding some Second World War-type biological or chemical agents.[10]

A failure to take seriously the new strategic environment can have costly consequences in the domestic theatre as well. Should the use of a weapon of mass destruction occur, the state in which this happens will undergo a crisis in its constitutional order. How it prepares for this crisis will determine the fate of its society, not only its sheer survival, but the conditions of that survival. Some societies may become police states in an effort to protect themselves; some may disintegrate because they cannot agree on how to protect themselves.

The constitutional order of a state and its strategic posture toward other states together form the inner and outer membrane of a state. That membrane is secured by violence; without that security, a state ceases to exist. What is distinctive about the State is the requirement that the violence it deploys on its behalf must be legitimate; that is, it must be accepted within as a matter of law, and accepted without as an appropriate act of state sovereignty. Legitimacy must cloak the violence of the State, or the State ceases to be. Legitimacy, however, is a matter of history and thus is subject to change as new events emerge from the future and new understandings reinterpret the past. The standards against which state legitimacy is measured have undergone profound change, animated by innovations in the strategic environment and transformations of the constitutional order of states.

It is often said today that the nation-state is defunct.[11] Recently, in a single year, two books were published with almost identical titles, *The End of the Nation-State* and *The End of the Nation-State: The Rise of Regional Economies.*[12] To these can now be added Martin van Creveld's distinguished *The Rise and Decline of the State.*[13] There are skeptics, however, who point out that both nationalism and the State are thriving enterprises. Moreover, for all the transfer of functions to the private sector, we don't really want the State to fade away altogether. There are many things we want the State and not the private sector to do because we want our politics rather than the market to resolve certain kinds of difficult choices. And, it must be conceded, the market itself has need of the State to set the legal framework that permits the market to function.

What is wrong in this debate over the demise of the nation-state is the identification of the nation-state with the State itself. We usually date the origin of the nation-state to the Peace of Westphalia in 1648 that ended the Thirty Years' War and recognized a constitutional system of states. In fact, however, the nation-state is relatively new – being little more than a century old – and has been preceded by other forms of the State, including forms that long antedated the Thirty Years' War. The nation-state is dying, but this only means that, as in the past, a new form is being born. This new form, the *market-state*, will ultimately be defined by its response to the strategic threats that have made the nation-state no longer viable. Different models of this form will contend. It is our task to devise means by which this competition can be maintained without its becoming fatal to the competitors.

Notes

1 A great power is a state capable of initiating an epochal war, that is, a conflict that threatens the constitutional survival of the leaders of the society of states.
2 U.S. Department of the Army, *Decisive Victory: America's Power Projection Army* (Department of the Army, Washington, D.C., 1994).
3 Bernard Brodie, "Implications for Military Policy" in *The Absolute Weapon: Atomic Power and World Order*, ed. Bernard Brodie (Harcourt, Brace, 1946) p. 76.
4 Thomas C. Schelling, *Arms and Influence* (Yale University Press, New Haven, 1966).
5 Michael Howard, "Lessons of the Cold War," *Survival* 36 (1994–5) p. 165.
6 Philip Bobbitt, *Democracy and Deterrence* (St Martin's Press, New York, 1988) p. 286.
7 Fred Iklé, "The Next Lenin: On the Cusp of Truly Revolutionary Warfare," *The National Interest* 47, (1997) p. 9.
8 Written before September 11, 2001.
9 Paul Bracken, "The Military After Next," *The Washington Quarterly* 16 (1993) p. 157.
10 Iklé (fn7) p. 9.
11 Jean-Marie Guehenno, *The End of the Nation-State* (University of Minnesota Press, 1995).
12 Kenichi Ohmae, *The End of the Nation-State: The Rise of Regional Economies* (Free Press, New York, 1995).
13 Martin van Creveld, *The Rise and Decline of the State* (Cambridge University Press, 1999).

Part II

The politics of interdependence and globalization

Introduction

The extracts in this part reflect and evaluate a set of changes and transformations that have created a new form of pluralism in contemporary world politics. As early as the 1970s, dissatisfaction with the precepts of realism and the traditional state-centric approach to world politics had emerged. The critique of realism that emerged at that stage was based on three central challenges: to the claim that the state was necessarily the dominant actor in world politics and acted on behalf of all of its citizens; to the claim that national security and 'high politics' dominated the arena of world politics; and to the notion that competition, insecurity and political violence were the central components of the political process in the world arena. As a result of this critique, the study of world politics became more a study of differentiation between a variety of groups acting for a variety of ends through a variety of channels than of the 'society of states'. States did not lose their importance, however: rather, they had to be seen in the context of this more diverse and fluid world arena. In the 1970s and 1980s, therefore, studies of interdependence, transnational relations and international integration appeared in increasing numbers, reflecting the ever more apparent pluralism of world politics and the challenges to state dominance.

During the 1990s, these established trends developed further. Indeed, some would say that since the end of the Cold War in the early 1990s, and with the increasing fluidity and diversity of economic, social and political processes, both the world arena and the study of world politics have been transformed. There continues to be a strong focus on the ways in which states have to cope with the impact of global change, drawing on the major changes in the state system during the 1990s and emphasizing the new institutional and negotiating contexts confronting state authorities. Alongside this, however, there has been a further significant development of interest in transnational processes and the influence of non-state actors such as international organizations or cross-national networks of political activists. Accompanying this there has also been a surge of attention to the processes and problems generally described as those of 'globalization', in which intensification of transnational linkages in politics, political economy and various forms of communications and information technologies have produced a transformation not only of institutions but also of ideas and cultural interactions.

The pieces gathered in this part of the book are selected in order to address some of the key issues that have emerged from these processes of changes and tranformation, and to underline the fact that in many cases 'old' institutions and problems have persisted into a transformed political world. The first four selections thus all address the problems of the state as an actor in this changing world, and some of the changed contexts into which state authorities have to project their influence. Shaw (2.1) focuses on the ways in which processes of globalization have transformed the nature and activities of states, but he does this within a historical context which emphasizes the role of the 'Western state' centred in the North Atlantic, Japan and Australasia. He goes on to suggest that in this way the 'Western state' has the potential to become a 'global state', in the sense that it is the predominant model for institutions and ideas relating to statehood. But at the same time, he shows that one of the key features of statehood in the age of globalization is the increasing variety of statehood and state authorities, which makes simple prognostications about the models for future forms of statehood a dangerous exercise. Ikenberry (2.2) develops further one of the key themes in Shaw's argument, by focusing on the ways in which the 'Western state' in the form of the United States and its allies, has continued to dominate the post-Cold War order. This is not, however, a simple state-centric or power-based argument, since Ikenberry is concerned to show how this Western dominated order is sustained by the moderation of state power, by the building of cooperative processes and institutions and by shared ideas about the 'logic of order'. Ikenberry thus argues that the 'Western' order has 'constitutional characteristics' that profoundly modify the realist vision of competitive and hierarchical relations between states. This general argument is illustrated more specifically by Moravcsik (2.3), who explores the rationality of international cooperation with specific reference to the European Union. According to Moravcsik, cooperation between states in the European Union has reflected key processes of national preference formation, interstate bargaining and institutional choice, in which the 'choice for Europe' has led to pooling or delegation of sovereignty in key areas of state activity. The final selection in this group, by Gary Marks, Elisabeth Hooghe and Kermit Blank (2.4), goes further down this track, by suggesting that although interstate bargaining can account for significant parts of what has happened in European integration, it is increasingly accompanied if not supplanted by a very different process, that of 'multi-level governance'. In this growing set of processes, decision-making power is shared across several levels of authority and between many different types of political actor. As a result, state executives lose significant amounts of control over key policy areas, and the separation between 'domestic' and 'international' politics is increasingly challenged. Although this type of 'new politics' is most apparent in Western Europe, it is also increasingly discernible in other regions of the world, with the growth of new institutions for cooperation and regulation.

The second group of extracts in this part move on to explore the diversity of institutions, groups and processes that characterize a world of transnational relations and exchanges. As before, they do not claim that the influence of states and national executives has disappeared; but they take as a central part of their arguments that there are new processes and phenomena over which states have comparatively little control. They also give an increasingly prominent role not only to new institutions but to the role of ideas in conferring power and leverage on new types of international actors. Barnett and Phinnemore (2.5) focus on the ways in which international organizations can develop power independent of the states that created them, and they do so in large part by stressing the ways in which international agencies can generate new norms and 'social knowledge'. This social constructivist approach to world politics has become increasingly prominent since the end of the Cold War, arguably as the result of the new fluidity of identities and allegiances noticeable in the 'new world disorder'. Barnett and Phinnemore use it to argue that the definition of shared tasks and the promotion of models of political organization is a key function of international organizations, and that this gives new meaning to the concept of power in world politics. Keck and Sikkink (2.6) pursue another aspect of this 'new world politics' by exploring the ways in which transnational groups, especially what they call 'advocacy networks' focused on particular causes, can gain access to the political process, These networks can provide resources both in international and in domestic political processes, by exploiting the gaps in control of communications and ideas, and by being able to cross the increasingly blurred boundaries between 'home' and 'abroad'. Their activities challenge the established practices of sovereignty, and although they can often operate alongside state authorities, their very existence erodes the centrality of such national authorities in world politics. Keohane and Nye (2.7) focus strongly on one of the themes identified by both Barnett and Phinnemore and Keck and Sikkink: that of information and communication. The impact of new information and communication technologies, adding up to what they describe as the 'information revolution', has given new dimensions to what they describe as 'complex interdependence', in which the role of states is less central and there are multiple channels of communication and exchange between societies. Keohane and Nye argue that as a result it is possible to identify a new 'politics of credibility' in world politics, in which political effectiveness depends on the capacity to convey credible information on specific issues and problems, rather than on established mechanisms of state authority.

The final group of extracts takes up a number of the themes already raised, but relates them directly to processes of 'order' and 'governance' in the world arena. The growth of diversity and of the interconnectedness that is basic to all ideas of globalization automatically creates questions about who is in control and how that control might be exercised. Wayne Sandholtz (2.8) approaches this issue from a belief that world politics constitutes a social system, defined by rules and institutions, and that globalization creates the demand for new rules and institutions to govern new relationships of communication and exchange. Not all rules are completely new: often they are modifications of existing principles and applied through existing institutions; they also exist not only in terms of material exchanges, but also in terms of norms and normative discourses about the nature of world order. Adler and Barnett (2.9) take a rather different approach, since they focus on the demand for security in a fluid and unpredictable world, which is often taken to be a key problem of globalization. They identify the central qualities of 'security communities' and the ways in which they reflect 'stable expectations of peaceful change' among groups of states and societies. Their argument generates a number of important questions about the nature of 'community' and identity in the world arena, and about processes of governance and institution building in world politics. In the final two extracts, Jan-Aart Scholte and David Held shift the emphasis to the overall nature of 'global civil society' and the ways in which new forms of international solidarity might shape the globalization process. Scholte (2.10) explores the key features of 'global civil society': that is to say, the growing range of groups and institutions that set out to influence policies, norms and social structures in the world arena. As with other extracts in this part, he emphasizes the fact that alongside the burgeoning array of groups and networks in a globalizing world, there are persistent and influential national authorities. Held (2.11) focuses on the problems of governance created by globalization, and argues explicitly that national and state authorities do not possess the resources to meet these challenges. He proposes 'cosmopolitanism' as a way in which politics can be re-framed in the global age to reflect the needs of individuals as well as state or other institutions. By doing so, he reflects the central fact that many of the debates covered in this part of the book are about norms and values as well as about practical problems of political organization and institutions.

It should be clear on the basis of this summary that the politics of interdependence, globalization and cosmopolitanism centre on diversity, change and global pluralism. It should also be clear that the authors represented here take different views of (for example) the centrality of the state, of international organizations and of transnational networks. Some of the authors would be close in many ways to a realist, state-centric perspective; others would reject this as either misleading or dangerous, but would not reject the importance of states and national authorities as such. Finally, it is apparent that the authors selected here focus predominantly on the politics of the 'developed' or 'industrial' world, although many are sensitive to the differences between this world and that of less developed societies. Their approach is predominantly reformist, admitting diversity and uncertainty but asserting the possibility of cooperative solutions to central issues. This has some echoes of the 'top-down' politics characteristic of a realist perspective, whilst it moves beyond that by taking a liberal view on the importance of non-state actors and the individual. Such a position is challenged strongly by the final perspective (Part III) with its view of world politics 'from the bottom up' and a very different position on the meaning of globalization.

2.1 The state of globalization: towards a theory of state transformation

Martin Shaw

Source: *Review of International Political Economy*, vol. 4, no. 3 (1997), pp. 497–513.

Shaw focuses on the ways in which processes of globalization have transformed the nature and activities of states. He identifies the 'Western state' centred on the North Atlantic, Japan and Australasia as the dominant form of state in the late twentieth and early twenty-first centuries, and goes on to show how this might be an emergent form of 'world state'. The argument demonstrates that the idea of a 'global state' remains problematic because of the persistent variety and unevenness of state forms.

[Shaw starts by arguing that out of a complex historical process there has emerged a dominant 'Western' form of state.]

Theorizing the emergent global state

How do we understand the emerging global state forms centred on the western state conglomerate? So far, theory has tended to see the global context of state power in one of two limiting ways, both of which tacitly assume the old identity of state as nation-state. On the one hand, global forms of state power are subsumed under the 'international', which itself assumes the national as the fundamental unit of analysis. The study of international organizations and regimes, for example, sees these as extensions of the nation-state.

On the other hand, there are new, generally more radical, discourses which move beyond the international to global politics, but assume that globalization diminishes the state element of 'governance'. A literature on 'governance without government',[1] in a 'post-statist world order',[2] focuses on how regulation takes place through international organizations and civil society as well as through nation-states. While this literature correctly sees that governance now involves more than the nation-state, it mistakenly implies that this should lead us to replace a 'state' perspective with the perspective of governance. To conclude from the relative decline or bypassing of the nation-state that state as such has become less important is to miss the central contexts of globalization. [. . .]

[. . .] we need to understand the globally dominant contemporary form of the state as the western state conglomerate, which is developing increasing global reach and legitimacy in the post-Cold War would. Provocatively perhaps, I would take this further and argue that we should understand this state form as an emergent *global state*. This state is fragmentary, undoubtedly, and possibly unstable. It constitutes, however, a more or less coherent raft of state institutions which possess, to some degree, global reach and legitimacy, and which function as a state in regulating economy, society and politics on a global scale.

A large body of literature now recognizes globalization in economic, social and cultural senses, and with it 'global society'.[3] Why then is it so unthinkable to look at the globalization of political and military power, and with it the global state? The concept is unfamiliar, certainly, but much of its difficulty is to do with the culture of the social sciences which is saturated with a concept of state as centralized nation-state. In this context, a global state can only be understood in terms of a 'world government' which obviously does not and is not likely to exist. I use the term in a rather different way, and in the remainder of this article I provide an elaboration and justification.

One reason for our difficulty in recognizing global state developments is that they are manifested in complex, rapidly changing and often highly contrasting forms. Different theoretical approaches tend to latch on to different sides of these developments. For marxists and 'Third World' theorists, for example, the Gulf War represented a manifestation of 'imperialism', centred on strategic control of oil. In contrast, western military action to protect Kurdish refugees, following the war, represented for many International Relations analysts a new form of 'humanitarian intervention'.

These and other paradigms compete to offer simple characterizations of global state power. In reality, however, global state power crystallizes as both 'imperialist' and 'humanitarian', and indeed in other forms. Mann's argument that states involve 'polymorphous crystallization', and that different crystallizations dominate different institutions, is particularly important here.[4] He gives as an example the American state, crystallizing.

> as conservative-patriarchal one week when restricting abortion rights, as capitalist the next when regulating the savings and loans banking scandal, as a superpower the next when sending troops abroad for other than national economic interests. These varied crystallizations are rarely in harmony or in dialectical opposition to one another; usually they just differ. They mobilize differing, if overlapping and intersecting, power networks.[5]

We need to extend this analysis in understanding the emergent global state. In the Iraqi wars of 1991, Western and global state power crystallized as both 'imperialist' and 'humanitarian' as well as in other forms, at quickly succeeding stages of the crisis.[6] Within this kind of global crisis, the American state crystallizes sometimes as a nation-state, at other times as centre of the western state, at others still as the centre of global state power. Without understanding this diversity, we will lapse into one-sidedness or downright confusion and fail to grasp global political change.

In order to understand the global state which crystallizes in these diverse forms, we must first define the state. In particular, the continuing significance of military-political power as the primary criterion for the existence of 'a state' needs to be explained. Most discussion of states in the social sciences has implied a slippage from a military-centred definition towards a juridical or economic management-based definition. It is because of this slippage that many have concluded that the state is weakened by globalization. I am assuming that the classic military-political definition is still relevant: that military relations still define the relations between distinct states and hence the parameters of global relations of power.

To understand what is a state – and conversely, when a state is not a state – I return to Weber's definition [. . .], which centres on the monopoly of legitimate violence in a given territory. Before 1945, state leaders (and others) often acted as if Weber's definition was true and they did in fact hold a monopoly of legitimate violence. In a world of nation-states, the demarcation of one state from another was the potential for violence between them. Our discussion has raised the issue of what then happens to states, and to our understanding of state, when this potential has been removed, as it has since 1945 between western states – and more problematically since 1989 between western states and Russia.

The most important change is that the control of violence is ceasing to be divided vertically between different nation-states and empires. Instead, it is being divided horizontally between different levels of power, each of which claims some legitimacy and thus fragments the nature of 'state'. On the one hand, there is the internationalization of legitimate force. On the other there are the processes of 'privatization' (or 'reprivatization') of force, which have been increasingly discussed in the 1990s, in which individuals, social groups and non-state actors are more widely using force and claiming legitimacy for their usage. At the same time, some nation-states, at least, retain some of their classic control of violence.

This situation calls for a revision of Weber's definition. Fortunately Mann, in his study of nineteenth-century states, has already provided a looser version. For him,

1   The state is a differentiated set of institutions and personnel
2   embodying centrality, in the sense that political relations radiate to and from a centre, to cover a
3   territorially demarcated area over which it exercises
4   some degree of authoritative, binding rule making, backed up by some organized political force.[7]

As Mann points out, this is an institutional rather than a functional definition and crucially for our purposes it abandons the idea of a monopoly of legitimate force. A state involves, Mann suggests, merely 'some degree of authoritative rule making' and 'some organized political force'.

This definition is particularly suited to the complex, overlapping forms of state power which exist in the late twentieth century in conditions of globalization. Taking Mann's criteria in turn, I argue that the emergent global state can be considered a state, and that an additional fifth criterion needs to be added if we are to make sense of the situation of overlapping levels of state power.

States, according to Mann's first point, involve 'a differentiated set of institutions and personnel': differentiated, he means, in relation to society. The important word here is actually 'set'. Mann makes it clear that states are not necessarily homogenized and closely integrated institutions, but they consist of more or less discrete and often disjointed apparatuses. 'Under the microscope, states "Balkanize" ', he argues, quoting Abrams's neat formulation that 'The state is the unified symbol of an actual disunity.'[8] Mann avers that 'Like cock-up-foul-up theorists I believe that states are messier and less systematic and unitary than each single theory suggests.'[9] The idea that states are institutional 'messes' rather than the homogenous structures of ideal type is of central importance to my understanding of the global state.

Just as the emergent global society is highly distinctive in 'including' a large number of national societies, the global state is unusual in 'including' a large number of nation-states. Nevertheless, this is not an entirely unprecedented situation. Multinational states do not always take the relatively neat centralized forms of the UK or (in a different sense) the former Soviet Union. Mann himself analyses the highly complex (and from an ideal-typical point of view, idiosyncratic) forms of the Austro-Hungarian empire. The western-centred global state is, however, an aggregation of institutions of an unprecedented kind and on an unprecedented scale. If we examine it in action, for example in Bosnia-Herzegovina, we see an amazing plethora of global, western and national state institutions – political, military and welfare – complemented by an equally dazzling and complex array of civil society organizations. As this example underlines, the global state is truly the biggest 'institutional mess' of all.

The second question is in what sense the global state meets Mann's second criterion of 'embodying centrality, in the sense that political relations radiate to and from a centre'. To put the issue another way, when is an institutional mess so messy that it cannot be seen as a single set of institutions at all? In what sense do the UN, NATO and various other international organizations, together with the USA and the various western nation-states, constitute a single set of institutions?

Clearly there is no straightforward constitutional order in the global state, but there is an order and it does have elements of a constitution. The centre – Washington rather than New York – seems clear, and the fact that political relations rediate to and from it has now been confirmed in all serious global crises of the post-1989 period, from Kuwait to Dayton. The continuing centrality of the USA to war management worldwide, and to all the major attempts at 'peace settlements' from the Middle East and Yugoslavia to South Africa and even Northern Ireland, underlines this point.

There are two apparent anomalies in this situation which lead probably to much of the theoretical confusion. First, the centre of the western and emergent global state is constituted primarily by the centre of a nation-state, the USA. Second, political relations radiate to and from this centre through diverse sets of institutions. There is the UN itself, which confers global legitimacy on the US state (and in which that state does have a constitutional role as a permanent member of the Security Council, and a de facto role which goes beyond that). There is NATO, which is increasingly confirmed as the effective organization of western military power on a global as well as a regional scale. There are the numerous western-led world economic organizations, from the exclusive G7 to the wider OECD and the increasingly global WTO. And last but not least, there are the bilateral relations of the American state with virtually all other nation-states.

All these networks overlap, however, and the critical point is that the role of the US administration in each of them is determined not only by its 'national' interests but by the exigencies of global leadership. Of course, other nation-states, especially the UK and France but in different ways Germany and Japan and also Russia and China, as well as regional organizations, notably the EU, also have very important roles in the developing global state. The internal structure of the global state is uncertain and evolving. The roles of the various states and power networks are all contested, problematic and changing, and in the Russian and Chinese cases especially unstable. Nevertheless their development is governed not just by the interplay of national interests but by the demands of world political and economic management.

Mann's third criterion, that a state possesses a 'territorially demarcated area' over which it exercises some degree of authoritative, binding rule making, backed up by some organized political force, is obviously also problematic, but does not in my view negate the concept of a global state. The territorially demarcated area of the interlocking global power networks is, in principle, the world. The fact that other state organizations claim lesser territorial jurisdictions, regional in the case of the EU, national in the case of nation-states, subnational in the case of local state authorities, does not contradict this. The idea of overlapping territorial jurisdictions is not new but it has a particular contemporary salience. There is a systematic sharing of sovereignty which is relativizing the previously unique sovereignty of the nation-state.

This leaves us with Mann's fourth point, the existence of 'some degree of authoritative, binding rule making', backed up by 'some organized political force'. Authoritative global rule making actually takes several different forms. There are the institutional arrangements which bind states together in the various inter-state organizations, so that they regulate the internal structure of the global state and the roles of nation-states within it. There is the body of international law which binds individuals and institutions in civil society as well as state institutions. There are the wide range of international conventions and agreements which regulate global economy and society. Rule making is undoubtedly patchy and in some areas incoherent, but it is proceeding apace. Mann's 'some degree' seems particularly apposite.

Rule making in the global state clearly has the backing of 'some organized political force': the armed forces of the USA, UK, France, in some circumstances Russia, and many other states, have been deployed in the names of NATO and the UN. Increasingly, too, international law is acquiring a machinery of courts, tribunals and police, even if it remains heavily dependent on nation-states, and has selective application and limited real enforcement capacity.

The global state appears to meet Mann's definition of a state. However, although this definition clearly permits a conceptualization of overlapping levels of state power, it says nothing specifically about the situation of overlapping and the ways in which different 'states' in this sense will articulate. We need therefore to add a new criterion: that a state (particular) must be.

5   to a significant degree *inclusive* and *constitutive* of other forms or levels of state power (i.e. of state power in general in a particular time and space).

This criterion is essential. Clearly nation-states, in the present period, are still generally inclusive and constitutive of subnational forms, although perhaps less so that in the recent past (in the European Union, for example, regions are starting to be constituted by EU as well as national state power). To a considerable extent, too, nation-states also constitute regional and global forms of state, as well as (by definition) the international. In contrast, local and regional state forms within nation-states are generally only weakly inclusive or constitutive.

The inclusiveness and constitutiveness of the various transnational forms of state is not easy to determine. Clearly the global state institutions of the UN system have been, in principle, inclusive of the entire range of nation-states, even if in practice important states have been excluded or have excluded themselves from all or parts of the system. To date, however, the UN system has been only weakly constitutive of its component nation-states. The western state, on the other hand, became highly constitutive of its component nation-states during the Cold War, and largely remains so. The European state (European Union) has gradually strengthened both its inclusiveness and its constitutiveness of member nation-states – although this is very much a matter of contention – but its articulation with the transatlantic western state is problematic.

Once we examine this criterion, the global state is evidently a problematic level of state power. In many ways its western core remains stronger than the global form itself. It is evident, however, that the western state is operating globally, in response to global imperatives and the need for global legitimation. The western state has begun to be constituted within broader global rather than narrowly western parameters. The global level rather than the narrowly western is *becoming* constitutive, too, of the component nation-states. Still, it seems best to define the global state, even more than global society or culture, as an emergent, still contingent and problematic reality.

The fact that the western state acts as a global state is due to the manifold pressures and contradictions of global governance. These include not merely threats to western interests (as with Kuwaiti oil or the danger of a wider Balkan war), but also the imperatives of globally legitimate principles, the claims of insurgent and victimized groups (such as the Kurds and Bosnians), the contradictions of global media coverage and the demands of an emergent global civil society. The fact that the west has largely continued to cohere, despite the end of the Cold War, and has assumed global roles despite the manifest reluctance of the main western states to pursue a global leadership role, testifies to the structural significance of these trends in global society.

At rare moments, such as the Gulf mobilization, the Somalian and Haitian interventions and the Dayton settlement, western governments appear to have chosen leadership. The scarcity of these moments, compared to the occasions on which they have seemed to want to turn their backs, suggests, however, that in the end they have had leadership thrust upon them. In the end it is the logic of the new global political-military situation, including the articulation of domestic politics with global issues, which has compelled the west and especially the USA to act as the centre of an emergent global state.

These pressures function to hold together, more or less, a western-centred global state, just as the pressures of world war and Cold War formed the context of earlier stages in the development of a coherent western state. The fact that these pressures are more diffuse does not necessarily mean that they are ineffectual, although it does raise a question mark over the process. While global crises push the process of global state formation forward and make it visible, they also bare its weak coherence and contradictions, including the internal conflicts of the western core. Although the western state proved itself relatively stable during the Cold War, it may be that the challenges involved in its new global role may ultimately threaten that stability. It is therefore theoretically possible that the global state could simply fragment, and the world could revert in the medium term at least to an anarchy of national and regional state institutions fundamentally at odds with the globalization of economy, society and culture. Such a development is, however, unlikely, but to acknowledge its possibility under-lines the uncertainty and incoherence of the current forms of global state. It may also imply the need for constructive thinking about their development.

So far on balance the trends discussed above have worked to maintain the general cohesion of the western-global state. Despite important temporary disagreements, it appears that the common interests of the component national and regional forms of state within the west favour its long-term stability. The major contradictions of the western-centred global state are its relatively weak effectiveness in controlling violence and its relatively poor legitimacy with state elites and societies in the non-western world. The nexus of the western state with the UN as a legitimating institution is manifestly fragile. In the long term, it will only survive if it manages to achieve greater effectiveness and legitimacy, which will require substantial social change as well as institution building.

There are, moreover, important issues in the articulation of the global state with the regional and national states which it partly includes and constitutes. These relationships are plural and variable. A full analysis of the contemporary state needs to examine these forms alongside the globalized western state power.

To explicate the nature of contemporary 'nation-states' and their relations with global state power, it is necessary to grasp the huge variation which exists in the 'states' described by this term. Robert Cooper has proposed a three-fold categorization of contemporary 'nation-states' as 'postmodern', 'modern' and 'pre-modern'.[10] While the terminology carries questionable theoretical overtones, it catches a division of states which is useful for this analysis.

First, within the west, 'nation-states' are no longer classic nation-states. They are 'post-modern' in the sense that they are very fully articulated with transnational western and global power networks. Of course, states vary enormously in the extent to which they mimic the characteristics of traditional nation-states. The USA and post-imperial Britain and France each retain a clear capacity for significant independent military action in some circumstances – although even in the American case, dependence on the wider framework of western and global power networks has increased. At the other extreme, the Canadian, Benelux and Scandinavian states have largely surrendered their capacity for independent initiative to NATO and the UN. Western states are also variably embedded in more or less dominant positions in the wide range of global economic institutions. These institutions powerfully reinforce the political-military integration of western states.

Within the west, it is important to note the special significance of the European state. This is a unique state form as well as a key component of the western state in general. It too meets all but one of Mann's criteria, in some cases better than the western-global state as a whole. The key qualification is that the forms of force available to the EU are very limited and its capacity for mobilizing military power, or even political power to deal with military issues, is still very weak. The European situation is the extreme case of the general feature of modern state organization which we have discussed. For the foreseeable future, there are likely to exist in Europe several distinctive levels of state organization, at the national, European, western (transatlantic) and global levels (not to mention sub-national regional state forms).[11]

Beyond the western state lies a never-never land of minor states, like the central and eastern Europeans, smaller East Asian and many Latin American and African states, which also have weak autonomous power. Although some states – especially those which have only recently claimed independence – pride themselves on their 'nation-state' status, these are also not really nation-states in the classic sense. They shelter under western power: although they are currently more weakly integrated into it than western states, they have no serious strategic options apart from closer relationships with the western-centred global state. In the European context, this reality is reflected in the aspirations of the smaller central and eastern states to join the EU, NATO, etc.

The relations of western and these allied 'nation-states' to regional, western and global state forms are increasingly institutionalized. Mann dubs the period after 1945 'the age of institutionalized nation-states', partly because states were based on institutionalized compromises between classes, but also – more relevant to our purposes – because relations between states were highly institutionalized.[12] The role of each nation-state corresponds to a complex set of understandings and systems of regulation within the west as a whole.

The second major group of states consists of major independent centres of state power, which correspond best to the classic model of the 'modern' nation-states. Beyond the west and its periphery lie the great non-western states including India and Brazil as well as Russia and China, and lesser powers such as Iraq, Iran and Serbia. These states mostly acknowledge the reality of western global dominance by partial incorporation into western-led global institutions and by avoiding potential military confrontations with the west. On the other hand, many of them mobilize substantial military power which they may well use in confrontations with each other and with minor states or insurgent movements, and which may then bring them into conflict with the western-UN centre. The most critical long-term issues for the western and emergent global state are their relations with the states in this group. The latter's fuller incorporation into global state institutions would largely neutralize any danger of serious inter-state war.

The third category consists of territories where the state does not even reach the level of a stable nation-state, let alone full participation in global institutions. Here the conditions for stable state forms of any kind are weak. Instead, state power is fragmentary, often based crudely on violence with threadbare legitimacy. In some cases state power has degenerated into warlordism and gangsterism. This has been an increasingly common pattern in parts of Africa and the former Soviet Union (not to mention Yugoslavia). Cooper labels this case 'pre-modern' although this highlights the problem of his terminology. Although 'ancient' ethnic or tribal hatreds may be mobilized, the technologies of communication and armament used in mobilizing are often state-of-the-art, and diaspora-based global power networks are exploited. During the 1990s, managing the violent disintegration of states in this group has been a major challenge generating pressures for continuing global state development.

This account of the articulation of different categories of 'nation-state' with global state developments shows the continuing interdependence and mutual constitutiveness of these two major forms. This is the problem which the state theory of the twenty-first century will need to address, and which globalization theory will need to understand if it is to escape from the sterile counterposition of state and globalization.

Notes

1   James N. Rosenau and Otto Czempiel, *Governance without Government: Order and Change in World Politics* (Cambridge University Press, Cambridge, 1992).
2   Richard N. Falk, 'State of Siege: Will Globalisation Win Out?', *International Affairs* 73(1), January 1997: 125.
3   See Martin Shaw, *Global Society and International Relations* (Polity, Cambridge, 1994).
4   Michael Mann, *The Sources of Social Power*, vol. II (Cambridge University Press, Cambridge, 1986), pp. 75–88. Mann identifies six 'higher-level' crystallizations in his analysis of nineteenth-century western states, as capitalist, ideological-moral, militarist, patriarchal and at points on continua of representativeness and morality. This categorization needs expansion to deal with the greater complexities of late twentieth-century state crystallizations.
5   ibid., p. 736.
6   I have analysed this phenomenon in *Civil Society and Media in Global Crises* (Pinter, London, 1996).
7   Mann, *The Sources of Social Power*, vol. II, p. 55.
8   ibid., p. 53.
9   ibid., p. 88.
10 Robert Cooper, *The Post-Modern State and the World Order* (Demos, London, 1996).
11 The argument about a nation-state versus a federal concept of European integration is therefore misnamed on both sides, since neither mere linkages of nation-states nor a classic federation is on offer, but rather this independent plurality of forms of state power.
12 Michael Mann, 'As the Twentieth Century Ages', *New Left Review* 214 (November–December 1995): 116.

2.2 Institutions, strategic restraint, and the persistence of American postwar order

G. John Ikenberry

Source: *International Security*, vol. 23, no. 3 (1998–1999), pp. 43–78.

Ikenberry wishes to explain the persistence of cooperative, stable and interdependent relations between the United States and its major allies, particularly after the end of the Cold War, and does so by looking back to the Western order created after 1945. In contrast to neo-realist explanations based on the distribution of power, he emphasizes the ways in which the institutional foundations of Western political order create a 'logic of order' and a set of 'constitutional characteristics' surrounding stable relations between the dominant state and its allies. By doing so, he provides an important modification to ideas of competitive inter-state relations in world politics.

[Ikenberry starts by discussing the foundations of the post-1945 Western order, and then moves on to discuss the nature of order more generally.]

The debate about order

The debate over American grand strategy after the Cold War hinges on assumptions about the sources and character of Western order. Neorealism advances two clearly defined answers to the basic question of how order is created among states: balance of power and hegemony. Both are ultimately pessimistic about the future stability and coherence of economic and security relations between the United States, Europe, and Japan.

Balance-of-power theory explains order – and the rules and institutions that emerge – as the result of balancing to counter external or hegemonic power. Order is the product of the unending process of balancing and adjustment among states under conditions of anarchy. Balancing can be pursued both internally and externally – through domestic mobilization and through the formation of temporary alliances among threatened states to resist and counterbalance a looming or threatening concentration of power. Under conditions of anarchy, alliances will come and go as temporary expedients, states will guard their autonomy, and entangling institutions will be resisted.

A second neorealist theory, hegemonic stability theory, holds that order is created and maintained by a hegemonic state, which uses power capabilities to organize relations among states. The preponderance of power held by a state allows it to offer incentives, both positive and negative, to the other states to agree to participation within the hegemonic order. According to Robert Gilpin, an international order is, at any particular moment in history, the reflection of the underlying distribution of power of states within the system.[1] Over time, that distribution of power shifts, leading to conflicts and ruptures in the system, hegemonic war, and the eventual reorganization of order so as to reflect the new distribution of power capabilities. It is the rising hegemonic state or group of states, whose power position has been ratified by war, that defines the terms of the postwar settlement – and the character of the new order.

The continuity and stability of the Western postwar order is a puzzle for both varieties of neorealism. With the end of the Cold War, balance-of-power theory expects the West, and particularly the security organizations such as the North Atlantic Treaty Organization (NATO) and the U.S.–Japan alliance, to weaken and eventually return to a pattern of strategic rivalry. The "semi-sovereign" security posture of Germany and Japan will end, and these countries will eventually revert back to traditional great powers. The Soviet threat also served to dampen and contain economic conflict within the West – and after the Cold War, economic competition and conflict among the advanced industrial societies is expected to rise. Neorealist theories of hegemony also expect that the gradual decline of American power – magnified by the Cold War – should also lead to rising conflict and institutional disarray. More recently, some realists have argued that it is actually the extreme preponderance of American power, and not its decline, that will trigger counterbalancing reactions by Asian and European allies.

The basic thrust of these neorealist theories is that relations among the Western states will return to the problems of anarchy after the Cold War: economy rivalry, security dilemmas, institutional decay, and balancing alliances. The fact that post-Cold War relations among the Western industrial countries have remained stable and open, and economic interdependence and institutionalized cooperation have actually expanded in some areas, is a puzzle that neorealism is hard-pressed to explain. Despite sharp shifts in the distribution of power within the West, the political order among the industrial democracies has remained quite stable. Highly asymmetrical relations between the United States and the other advanced industrial countries – in the 1940s and again today – or declines in those asymmetries – in the 1980s – have not altered the basic stability and cohesion in relations among these countries.

Liberal theories provide some promising leads in explaining features of the postwar Western order, but they too are incomplete. Many of these theories would also predict order and stability in the West – but their causal arguments are too narrow. The key focus of liberal institutional theory is the way in which institutions provide information to states and reduce the incentives for cheating. But this misses the fundamental feature of order among the advanced industrial countries: the structures of relations are now so deep and pervasive that the kind of cheating that these theories worry about either cannot happen, or if it does it will not really matter because cooperation and the institutions are not fragile but profoundly robust. The basic problem is that these institutionalist arguments have not incorporated the structural features of Western order in their explanations. In particular, they miss the problems of order associated with the great asymmetries of power between Western states, the path-dependent character of postwar institutions, and the importance of the open and accessible character of American hegemony.

In general terms, liberal theories see institutions as having a variety of international functions and impacts – serving in various ways to facilitate co-operation and alter the ways in which states identify and pursue their interests. Liberal theories have also identified and stressed the importance of institutions among states that serve as foundational agreements or constitutional contracts – what Oran Young describes as "sets of rights and rules that are expected to govern their subsequent interactions."[2] Liberal institutional theories are helpful in explaining why specific institutions in the West may persist – even after the power and interests that established them have changed. But there has been less attention to the ways that institutions can be used as strategies to mitigate the security dilemma and overcome incentives to balance. Liberal theories grasp the ways in which institutions can channel and constrain state actions, but they have not explored a more far-reaching view in which leading states use intergovernmental institutions to restrain the arbitrary exercise of power and dampen the fears of domination and abandonment.

The approach to institutions I am proposing can be contrasted with two alternative theories – the rationalist (or "unsticky") theory of institutions, and the constructivist (or "disembodied") theory of institutions. Rationalist theory sees institutions as agreements or contracts between actors that function to reduce uncertainty, lower transactions costs, and solve collective action problems. Institutions provide information, enforcement mechanisms, and other devices that allow states to realize joint gains. Institutions are explained in terms of the problems they solve – they are constructs that can be traced to the actions of self-interested individuals or groups. Constructivist theory sees institutions as diffuse and socially constructed worldviews that bound and shape the strategic behavior of individuals and states. Institutions are overarching patterns of relations that define and reproduce the interests and actions of individuals and groups. Institutions provide normative and cognitive maps for interpretation and action, and they ultimately affect the identities and social purposes of the actors. A third position advanced here sees institutions as both constructs and constraints. Institutions are the formal and informal organizations, rules, routines, and practices that are embedded in the wider political order and define the "landscape" in which actors operate. As such, institutional structures influence the way power is distributed across individuals and groups within a political system – providing advantages and resources to some and constraining the options of others.

This approach to institutions gives attention to the ways in which institutions alter or fix into place the distribution of power within a political order. It offers a more "sticky" theory of institutions than the rationalist account, but unlike constructivism, institutional stickiness is manifest in the practical interaction between actors and formal and informal organizations, rules, and routines. Because of the complex causal interaction between actors and institutions, attention to historical timing and sequencing is necessary to appreciate the way in which agency and structure matter.

Debates over post-Cold War order hinge on claims about the character of relations among the major industrial democracies. Neorealist theories trace order to the operation of the balance of power or hegemony, and they anticipate rising conflict and strategy rivalry within the West. Liberal theories are more inclined to see continuity and inertia in the institutions and relations of postwar order, even if threats disappear and power balances shift sharply. It is the sharply contrasting view of institutional "stickiness," as Robert Powell argues, that differentiates realist and liberal institutional theories.[3] The argument advanced here is that institutions are potentially even more "sticky" than liberal theories allow, capable under specific circumstances of locking states into stable and continuous relations that place some limits on the exercise of state power, thereby mitigating the insecurities that neorealism traces to anarchy and shifting power balances.

[Ikenberry goes on to explore the nature of the 'constitutional bargain' reached among Western powers after 1945 and to stress the importance of 'strategic restraint' by the USA in creating and maintaining it. He then proceeds to investigate why such processes might occur.]

Strategic restraint and power conservation

Why would a newly hegemonic state want to restrict itself by agreeing to limits on the use of hegemonic power? The basic answer is that a constitutional settlement conserves hegemonic power, for two reasons. First, if the hegemonic state calculates that its overwhelming postwar power advantages are only momentary, an institutionalized order might "lock in" favorable arrangements that continue beyond the zenith of its power. In effect, the creation of basic ordering institutions are a form of hegemonic investment in the future. The hegemonic state gives up some freedom on the use of its power in exchange for a durable and predictable order that safeguards its interests in the future.

This investment motive rests on several assumptions. The hegemonic state must be convinced that its power position will ultimately decline – that it is currently experiencing a momentary windfall in relative power capabilities. If this is the state's strategic situation, it should want to use its momentary position to get what it wants. On the other hand, if the new hegemon calculates that its power position will remain preponderant into the foreseeable future, the incentive to conserve its power will disappear. Also, the hegemon must be convinced that the institutions it creates will persist beyond its own power capabilities – that is, it must calculate that these institutions have some independent ordering capacity. If institutions simply are reflections of the distribution of power, the appeal of an institutional settlement will obviously decline. But if institutions are potentially "sticky," powerful states that are farsighted enough to anticipate their relative decline can attempt to institutionalize favorable patterns of cooperation with other states that persist even as power balances shift.

The second reason why a hegemon might want to reach agreement on basic institutions, even if it means giving up some autonomy and short-term advantage, is that it can reduce the "enforcement costs" of maintaining order. The constant use of power capabilities to punish and reward secondary states and resolve conflicts is costly. It is far more effective over the long term to shape the interests and orientations of other states rather than directly shape their actions through coercion and inducements. A constitutional settlement reduces the necessity of the costly expenditure of resources by the leading state on bargaining, monitoring, and enforcement.

It remains a question why weaker states might not just resist any institutional settlement after the war and wait until they are stronger and can negotiate a more favorable settlement. Several factors might make this a less attractive option. First, without an institutional agreement, the weaker states will lose more than they would under a settlement, where the hegemonic state agrees to forgo some immediate gains in exchange for willing participation of secondary states. Without an institutional settlement, bargaining will be based simply on power capacities, and the hegemonic state will have the clear advantage. The option of losing more now to gain more later is not attractive for a weak state that is struggling to rebuild after war. Its choices will be biased in favor of gains today rather than gains tomorrow. The hegemon, on the other hand, will be more willing to trade off gains today for gains tomorrow. The difference in the two time horizons is crucial to understanding why a constitutional settlement is possible.

A second reason why weaker states might opt for the institutional agreement is that – if the hegemon is able to credibly demonstrate strategic restraint – it does buy them some protection against the threat of domination or abandonment. As realist theory would note, a central concern of weak or secondary states is whether they will be dominated by the more powerful state. In an international order that has credible restraints on power, the possibility of indiscriminate and ruthless domination is mitigated. Just as important, the possibility of abandonment is also lessened. If the hegemonic state is rendered more predictable, the secondary states do not need to spend as many resources on "risk premiums," which would otherwise be needed to prepare for either domination or abandonment. In such a situation, the asymmetries in power are rendered more tolerable for weaker states.

Importantly, institutional agreement is possible because of the different time horizons that the hegemonic and secondary states are using to calculate their interests. The leading state agrees to forgo some of the gains that it could achieve if it took full advantage of its superior power position, doing so to conserve power resources and invest in future returns. The weaker states get more returns on their power in the early periods, but in agreeing to be locked into a set of postwar institutions, they give up the opportunity to take full potential advantage of rising relative power capacities in later periods. These alternative calculations are summarized in Figures 1 and 2. The leading state trades short-term gains for long-term gains, taking advantage of the opportunity to lay down a set of institutions that will ensure a favorable order well into the future. Gains in the later periods are greater than what that state's power capacities alone, without the institutional agreement, would otherwise yield. Weaker and secondary states give up some later opportunities to gain a more favorable return on their rising relative power, but in return they get a better postwar deal in the early postwar period. The option of losing more now so as to gain more later is not an attractive option for a weak state that is struggling to rebuild after war. But beyond this, the weaker states also get an institutional agreement that provides some protections against the threat of domination or abandonment – if the leading state is able to credibly demonstrate strategic restraint.

Taken together, the Western postwar order involves a bargain: the leading state gets a predictable and durable order based on agreed-upon rules and institutions – it secures the acquiescence in this order of weaker states, which in turn allows it to conserve its power. In return, the leading state agrees to limits on its own actions – to operate according to the same rules and institutions as lesser states – and to open itself up to a political process in which the weaker states can actively press their interests upon the more powerful state. The hegemonic or leading state agrees to forgo some gains in the early postwar period in exchange for rules

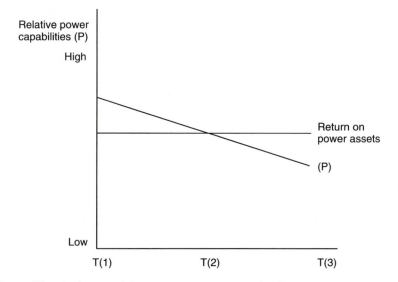

Figure 1 Time horizons and the return on power assets: leading state

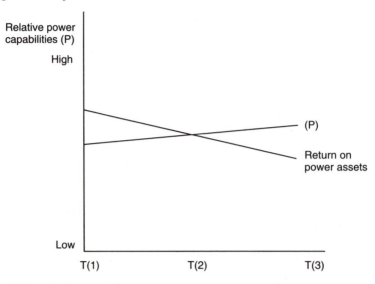

Figure 2 Time horizons and the return on power assets: secondary state

and institutions that allow it to have stable returns later, while weaker states are given favorable returns up front and limits on the exercise of power.

Strategies of restraint: bonding, binding, and voice opportunities

The American postwar hegemonic order could take on constitutional characteristics because of the way institutions, created by and operated between democratic states, could be wielded to facilitate strategic restraint. Institutions can shape and limit the way power can be used in the system, thereby rendering asymmetric postwar power relations less potentially exploitive and commitment more certain. The returns to power are reduced. Where institutions create restraints on power, weaker and secondary states have less fear of abandonment, or domination is lessened. Institutions can also dampen the effects of the security dilemma and reduce the incentives for weaker and secondary states to balance against the newly powerful state. By creating a mutually constraining environment, institutions allow states to convey assurances to each other and mitigate the dynamics of anarchy.

The hegemonic state has a disproportionate role in creating confidence in postwar order: it has the most capacity to break out of its commitments and take advantage of its position to dominate or abandon the weaker and secondary states. As a result, in its efforts to draw other states into the postwar order, the leading state will have strong incentives to find ways to reassure these other states, to demonstrate that it is a responsible and predictable wielder of power and that the exercise of power is, at least to some acceptable degree, circumscribed. To achieve this goal, the leading state can pursue strategies that involve bonding, binding, and institutionalized voice opportunities.

Bonding means to certify state power: to make it open and predictable. A powerful leading state with a governmental decisionmaking process – and wider political system – that is open and transparent, and that operates according to predictable institutional rules and procedures, can reassure weaker and secondary states that the exercise of power will not be arbitrary or exploitive.

[. . .] when a state is open and transparent to outside states, it reduces the surprises and allows other states to monitor the domestic decisionmaking that attends the exercise of power. The implication of this argument is that democratic states have an advantage in the process of bonding. Democratic states have a more ready capacity to incur the costs of bonding because those costs will be relatively low. Democratic states already have the decentralized and permeable institutions that provide secondary states with information, access, and ultimately reassurance.

The leading state can go beyond internal openness to establish formal institutional links with other states, limiting state autonomy and allowing other states to have institutionalized "voice opportunities" in the decisionmaking of the leading state.

[. . .] the institutionalization of relations between weak and strong states, when it creates voice opportunities for the weaker states, can be a solution for these weaker states that want to work with but not be dominated by stronger states.

Deudney [. . .] describes the dynamic of binding, but emphasizes its other feature: it is a practice of establishing institutional links between the units that reduce their autonomy vis-à-vis one another.[4] In agreeing to be institutionally connected, states mutually constrain each other and thereby mitigate the problems of anarchy that lead to security dilemmas and power balancing. According to Deudney, binding practices are particularly available to and desired by democratic polities that want to resist the state-strengthening and centralizing consequences of balance-of-power orders. Binding restricts the range of freedom of states – whether weak or strong – and when states bind to each other, they jointly reduce the role and consequences of power in their relationship.

Each of these strategies involves the institutionalization of state power. Asymmetries of power do not disappear, but institutions – democratic institutions and intergovernmental institutions – channel and circumscribe the way that state power is exercised. Institutions make the exercise of power more predictable and less arbitrary and indiscriminate, up to some point. When a newly hegemonic state seeks to create a mutually acceptable order, doing so to preserve and extend the returns to its power into the future, institutions can be an attractive tool: they lock other states into the order, and they allow the leading state to reassure and co-opt other states by limiting the returns to power.

[Ikenberry goes on to explore in detail the creation and maintenance of Western institutions after 1945, and the ways in which these institutions limited the 'returns to power' in the Western system. He concludes as follows.]

Conclusion

The twentieth century may be ending, but the American century is in full swing. The character of American power is as interesting and remarkable as the fact of its existence. American domination or hegemony is very unusual, and the larger Western political order that surrounds it is unique as well. Fundamentally, American hegemony is reluctant, open, and highly institutionalized – or in a word, liberal. This is what makes it acceptable to other countries that might otherwise be expected to balance against hegemonic power, and it is also what makes it so stable and expansive.

Even with the end of the Cold War and the shifting global distribution of power, the relations between the United States and the other industrial countries of Europe and Asia remain remarkably stable and cooperative. This article offers two major reasons why American hegemony has endured and facilitated cooperation and integration among the major industrial countries rather than triggered balancing and estrangement. Both reasons underscore the importance of the liberal features of American hegemony and the institutional foundations of Western political order.

First, the United States moved very quickly after World War II to ensure that relations among the liberal democracies would take place within an institutionalized political process. In effect, the United States offered the other countries a bargain: if the United States would agree to operate within mutually acceptable institutions, thereby muting the implications of power asymmetries, the other countries would agree to be willing participants as well. The United States got the acquiescence of the other Western states, and they in turn got the reassurance that the United States would neither dominate nor abandon them.

The stability of this bargain comes from its underlying logic: the postwar hegemonic order is infused with institutions and practices that reduce the returns to power. This means that the implications of winning and losing are minimized and contained. A state could "lose" in intra-Western relations and yet not worry that the winner would be able to use those winnings to permanently dominate. This is a central characteristic of domestic liberal constitutional orders. Parties that win elections must operate within well-defined limits. They cannot use their powers of incumbency to undermine or destroy the opposition party or parties. They can press the advantage of office to the limits of the law, but there are limits and laws. This reassures the losing party; it can accept its loss and prepare for the next election. The features of the postwar order – and, importantly, the open and penetrated character of the American polity itself – has mechanisms to provide the same sort of assurances to America's European and Asian partners.

Second, the institutions of American hegemony also have a durability that comes from the phenomenon of increasing returns. The overall system – organized around principles of openness, reciprocity, and multilateralism – has become increasingly connected to the wider and deeper institutions of politics and society within the advanced industrial world. As the embeddedness of these institutions has grown, it has become increasingly difficult for potential rival states to introduce a competing set of principles and institutions. American hegemony has become highly institutionalized and path dependent. Short of large-scale war or a global economic crisis, the American hegemonic order appears to be immune to would-be hegemonic challengers. Even if a large coalition of states had interests that favored an alternative type of order, the benefits of change would have to be radically higher than those that flow from the present system to justify change. But there is no potential hegemonic state (or coalition of states) and no set of rival principles and organizations even on the horizon. The world of the 1940s contained far more rival systems, ideologies, and interests than the world of the 1990s. The phenomenon of increasing returns is really a type of positive feedback loop. If initial institutions are established successfully, where the United States and its partners have confidence in their credibility and functioning, this allows these states to make choices that serve to strengthen the binding character of these institutions.

The postwar Western order fits this basic logic. Its open and decentralized character invites participation and creates assurances of steady commitment. Its institutionalized character also provides mechanisms for the resolution of conflicts and creates assurances of continuity. Moreover, like a marriage, the interconnections and institutions of the partnership have spread and deepened. Within this open and institutionalized order, the fortune of particular states will continue to rise and fall. The United States itself, while remaining at the center of the order, also continues to experience gains and losses. But the mix of winning and losing across the system is distributed widely enough to mitigate the interest that particular states might have in replacing it. In an order where the returns to power are low and the returns to institutions are high, stability will be an inevitable feature.

Notes

1   R. Gilpin, *War and Change in World Politics* (Cambridge University Press, Cambridge, 1981).
2   O. Young, "Political Leadership and Regime Formation: On the Development of Institutions in International Society," *International Organization* 45(3), 1991, p. 282.
3   R. Powell, "Anarchy in International Relations Theory: The Neorealist and Neoliberal Debate," *International Organization* 48(2), 1994, pp. 313–44.
4   Daniel Deudney, "The Philadelphian System: Sovereignty, Arms Control, and Balance of Power in the American States-Union," *International Organization*, 49(2), 1995, pp. 191–228; and Deudney, "Binding Sovereigns: Authorities, Structures, and Geopolitics in Philadelphian Systems" in Thomas Biersteker and Cynthia Weber (eds.) *State Sovereignty as Social Construct* (Cambridge University Press, Cambridge, 1996), esp. pp. 213–16.

2.3 Inter-state cooperation and institutional choice

Andrew Moravcsik

Source: *The Choice for Europe: Social Purpose and State Power from Messina to Maastricht* (Cornell University Press, Ithaca, NY, 1998), pp. 67–77.

Moravcsik puts forward a 'rationalist' framework of international cooperation, in which states act rationally in pursuit of their preferences. According to this model, cooperation (in this case within the European Communities between the 1950s and 1990s) reflects three stages: national preference formation, inter-state bargaining, and the choice of international institutions. The extract here focuses particularly on the latter process, that of institutional choice, especially in relation to the pooling or delegation of sovereignty within the European Communities.

Institutional choice: pooling and delegation of sovereignty

We now turn to the third analytical stage in the rationalist framework of international cooperation: institutional choice. Given substantive agreement, when and why do EC governments delegate or pool decision-making power in authoritative international institutions? Why do they not always retain the prerogative to make future unilateral decisions?

This question, central to modern theories of international cooperation, takes on particular significance in the case of the EC because of the uniquely rich set of institutions it has evolved. The EC comprises four major branches: the Council of Ministers, an intergovernmental decision-making body that routinely legislates by qualified majority vote; the Commission, a powerful technocratic secretariat with formal agenda-setting powers in many areas; the Parliament, a directly elected assembly with more limited powers than any national equivalent but greater influence than any international counterpart; and the Court of Justice, a constitutional court in some ways more powerful than those of many national systems. These institutions transcend the coordinating rules and administrative secretariats found in most international organizations; they manifestly impinge on national sovereignty.

Constraints on sovereignty can be imposed in two ways: pooling or delegation of authoritative decision-making. Sovereignty is *pooled* when governments agree to decide future matters by voting procedures other than unanimity. In the EC legislative process, such decisions occur primarily through qualified majority voting (QMV) in the Council of Ministers, where a supermajority of weighted votes is required for passage. Sovereignty is *delegated* when supranational actors are permitted to take certain autonomous decisions, without an intervening interstate vote or unilateral veto. The Commission enjoys such autonomy in some matters of antitrust enforcement, daily implementation of regulations, and, to a more limited extent, external trade and accession negotiations. Perhaps most important, the

Commission has been granted in most areas of economic legislation a unique right to propose legislation and can amend proposals at any time. The Parliament possesses a different sort of pooled sovereignty, in which national representatives, generally organized in political parties, can influence the legislative process. For its part, the European Court also enjoys independent powers of judicial scrutiny and enforcement, at least insofar as domestic courts are prepared to implement its decisions. The Maastricht Treaty foresees, in addition, the creation of an autonomous European central bank.

These novel institutional practices, Perry Anderson observes, emerged for the most part not through inattention, emulation, or revolution, as one can argue was the case with national state-building, but through deliberate design "without historical precedent."[1] While this is slightly overstated – the powers of the Court appear to constitute a partial exception – the deliberate quality of the provisions for pooling through QMV is evident from "their selective application to EC policy areas" and the way in which they have been "changed quite differently and discriminately [. . .] within policy areas" over time.[2] Similar observations apply to pooled sovereignty in the Parliament and delegation to the Commission. A central task of any comprehensive account of major European decisions is thus to understand conditions under which member-states choose to forego ad hoc decision-making under the unanimity rule in order to pool or delegate sovereignty. Why would sovereign governments in an anarchic international system choose to delegate decision-making power rather than make decisions themselves? This question lies at the heart of the modern study of international regimes and of political delegation more generally.

There are three plausible explanations for the delegation and pooling of sovereignty in the context of the EC. These stress, respectively, belief in federalist ideology, the need for centralized technocratic coordination and planning, and the desire for more credible commitments. Each explanation generates a distinctive set of predictions concerning variation along three dimensions of institutional choice: delegation and pooling across issues and countries, domestic cleavages and discourse, and the nature of institutional controls over those to whom power is delegated. The resulting hypotheses are summarized in Table 1.

Ideology: federalism vs. nationalism?

The willingness of governments to pool or delegate control over policy, one explanation suggests, stems from prevailing ideological beliefs about national sovereignty. Some national publics, elites, and parties are more federalist; others are more nationalist. National positions concerning institutional form reflect these beliefs rather than the substantive consequences of transferring sovereignty – a view linked to ideological variants of the geopolitical explanation of national preferences explored earlier in this chapter. Such ideas and ideologies may reflect distinctive historical memories of World War II, partisan positions, preferred styles of domestic governance, or broad geopolitical calculations. Whatever the source, we have seen, Germany (along with Benelux and Italy) has traditionally been the most federalist of the three major EC members. France has been less so, balancing nationalism and federalism, with centrist parties generally favoring a more federalist position. Britain is least federalist. The indigenous pro-European movement is weaker than on the Continent, while there is a strong tradition of nationalist appeals at the extremes of both major parties. Three hypotheses follow.

On the first dimension, *delegation and pooling across issues and countries*, the ideological explanation predicts systematic variation across countries rather than across issues. Governments of "federalist" countries and parties should favor consistently delegation and pooling,

Table 1 Institutional choice: theories and hypotheses

Dimensions	Federalist ideology	Technocratic management	Credible commitments
Cross-issue and cross-national variation	Support for delegation and pooling varies across countries, not issues. The most important split divides federalist and nationalist governments. The pressures are stronger where issues are ideologically salient – e.g., increases in EC Parliamentary power.	Support for delegation and pooling varies across issues, not across countries. Delegation and perhaps pooling are particularly likely when distributional conflict is low and issues are technically, legally, or politically complex.	Support for delegation and pooling varies across both countries and issues, paralleling national support for substantive cooperation. Institutional delegation and pooling emerge when joint gains, an incentive to defect, and future uncertainty call intertemporal bargains into question. Governments with extreme preferences, at greater risk of being outvoted or overruled, tend to be cautious. Concern about compliance induces delegation: concern about obstruction or log-rolling induces pooling.
Domestic cleavages and discourse	Domestic cleavages pit European federalists against nationalist opponents. Support tends to center in national parliaments, federalist parties and movements, or public opinion Domestic discourse, even behind the scenes, stresses ideology.	Pressure for delegation and pooling comes from experts and officials, with a secondary role for societal elite supporters of a given policy. Domestic discourse stresses optimal technocratic solutions to problems through central planning.	Domestic groups that favor or oppose policy goals take the same view on transfers of sovereignty. Domestic discourse focuses on securing commitments to implementation and compliance. More populist groups remain skeptical.
Institutional form	Institutions empower democratic or otherwise ideologically legitimate decision-makers, spearheaded by domestic and European Parliamentary federalists. Oversight provision reinforce democratic legitimacy and control.	Institutions empower technocratic experts. Minimal democratic, legal, or political oversight required, because there are few conflicting interests in areas of technocratic consensus.	Institutions establish actors and procedures that assure predictable, usually fair, compliance or implementation. National governments carefully limit the scope of mandates, generating an inverse relation between the scope and extent of mandates. To bolster credibility, democratic involvement is limited.

whereas governments of "nationalist" countries and parties should oppose them – independently of substantive consequences of cooperation.

On the second dimension, *domestic cleavages and discourse*, we should observe domestic divisions along the lines of general public or partisan views about state sovereignty, rather than concrete economic or regulatory interests. "Pro-European" groups will favor delegation and pooling independently of substantive concerns, whereas "nationalist" groups will oppose them. Ideologically motivated leaders, governments, or societal groups, whether favourable or opposed, will focus their attention and rhetoric primarily on the most salient symbolic issues connected with sovereignty transfers, such as the powers of the Parliament *vis-à-vis* national parliaments, majority voting and national vetoes, and the general scope of EC competences *vis-à-vis* those powers reserved to subsidiary levels of national and subnational government. In this regard the ideological approach remains resolutely nonfunctional. Perry Anderson's observation is typical: "A customs union, even equipped with an agricultural fund, did not require a supranational Commission armed with powers of executive direction, a High Court [and] a Parliament. [. . .] The actual machinery of the Community is inexplicable without [. . .] the federalist vision of Europe developed above all by Monnet and his circle."[3]

On the third dimension, *the identity of and institutional controls on those holding delegated or pooled powers*, the ideological explanation predicts that EC institutions will be designed to enhance legitimacy by empowering democratically elected officials and neutral judges. Policy processes are therefore transparent and salient and subject to direct democratic oversight. This is the position consistently supported over the years by the "European federalist" movement. Not by chance has this movement been based traditionally in the European Parliament, whence it voiced strong criticisms of the "democratic deficit" and the centralization of EC policy-making in the Commission and the Council of Ministers.

Technocratic governance: the need for centralized expertise and information?

A second explanation for patterns in the delegation and pooling of sovereignty focuses on the need for centralized experts to manage complex, modern, transnational economies. In this view, modern economic planning is a highly complex activity requiring considerable technical and legal information. Such information is most efficiently provided by a single centralized authority. This explanation – closely related to elements of the supranational explanation of interstate bargaining considered earlier – assumes that the collective-action problem facing governments is one of coordinating the production of information. Centralized authorities are best placed to exploit informational economies of scale and overcome coordination problems or national mistrust, thereby generating and disseminating sufficient information required for more efficient decision-making. Around expert proposals – technocratic "focal points" – governments coordinate their activities.

Like the supranational explanation of substantive bargains, the technocratic explanation of institutional choice is associated with Monnet and Haas, both of whom justified a need for centralized expertise by arguing that modern economies require extensive state intervention and planning by knowledgeable, neutral experts. Rational investment decisions, they argued, are best made by centralized technocrats; transfers of sovereignty establish planning capacity. Hence Monnet sought to promote integration in those areas, such as atomic energy, with high levels of technical complexity and state intervention; Haas predicted the success of such efforts. Since a "post-industrial" economy can easily produce enough to satisfy citizens,

Haas wrote in 1964, there need be relatively little ideological or distributive conflict over economic policy; the central problem is instead "upgrading the common interest" through the application of proper technocratic expertise.[4] The Commission's influence is thus often attributed to its technical competence, which, according to Lindberg, "ensures that its proposals command the serious attention of the member governments."[5] Interpretations of the Commission's influence that rely heavily on focal points, technical expertise, and epistemic communities have recently reemerged among scholars who stress the Commission's role.[6]

Whence the advantage of the Commission, Parliament, and Court in providing expert information and analysis? One alternative is to delegate authority to national experts who meet regularly: Why is this not done? Even Council of Ministers committees, Haas argued, were essentially nonideological and non-partisan, consisting of "high civil servants meeting [. . .] and working out common policies on the basis of their perception of the technical policies inherent in whatever is being discussed."[7] It is hardly obvious that delegated or highly structured decision-making is more efficient than looser arrangements. In a study of "multi-organizational systems" – of which the EC is surely a prime international example – Donald Chisholm has observed, "Where formal organizational arrangements are absent, insufficient or inappropriate for providing the requisite coordination, informal adaptations develop [which] may be quite stable and effective, more so perhaps than formal hierarchical arrangement. Furthermore, because informal organization permits the continued existence of formally autonomous organizations in the face of mutual interdependence, it can achieve other values, such as reliability, flexibility and representativeness, that would otherwise be precluded or substantially diminished under formal arrangements."[8] It is thus unclear, in the technocratic view, why delegation or pooling is required.

One common explanation is that expert information and analysis may require considerable time, money, and expertise to generate yet can be disseminated easily – in short, they are public or club goods within an international organization. They are therefore likely to be underprovided by individual governments, since the costs of provision are relatively high relative to the benefits accruing to any single state. (Governments may also withhold expert information for fear of exploitation if they reveal it.) Yet it is unlikely that the Commission, with a few thousand officials, let alone the Parliament or Court, has more time, money, or expertise at its disposal than a major European government. A more plausible explanation is that Commission officials occupy a privileged position "at the center of an [institutionalized] network of knowledge" – an epistemic community of technical experts committed to political goals and linked through networks of national and international bureaucracies. Scientific and technical elites, it has been argued, are constituted in self-conscious networks within which information, expertise, and shared values are easily disseminated. By manipulating information through such networks, national and supranational officials construct "domestic and international coalitions in support of their policies" and "legitimate package deals." Such actions may generate policies that go beyond the initial intentions of governments – a phenomenon said to be common in international organizations. The EC Court, Parliament, and Commission might also, by virtue of proximity and expertise, be relatively expert in EC legal and administrative procedures, which may give them a comparative advantage in designing original solutions and inventing institutional options – said to be a key skill of successful international entrepreneurs.

If the technocratic explanation of pooling and delegation is correct, hypotheses follow along the three dimensions introduced above. On the first, *variation across issues and countries*, the technocratic theory predicts that institutional choices vary more by issue than by country. Delegation is likely where issues are technically complex (e.g., environmental, agricultural, and finance policy). Governments should be largely in agreement concerning the need for such delegation. We should expect delegation where conflict of interest is low and governments are concerned more with the efficiency of policy-making than with the distribution of gains. Given the low level of conflict assumed by the technocratic explanation, however, it is unclear why governments should ever pool, as opposed to delegate, sovereignty. On the second dimension, *domestic cleavages and discourse*, technocratic elites should play a prominent role in domestic debates. Domestic discussions should be concerned more with the efficiency of policy-making than with the distributional outcomes. On the third dimension, *the identity of and institutional controls on those holding delegated or pooled powers*, we should see institutions designed to empower technocratic elites. Little democratic, legal, or political oversight should be required, because of the lack of conflicting interests in areas of expert consensus.

Credible commitments: locking in policy coordination?

If the federalist explanation for institutional choice is in essence ideological and the technocratic explanation informational, an explanation based on the need for credible commitments is quintessentially political. Pooling and delegation are, in this view, "two-level" strategies designed to precommit governments to a stream of future decisions by removing them from the unilateral control of individual governments. By pooling or delegating the right to propose, legislate, implement, interpret, and enforce agreements, governments restructure future domestic incentives, encouraging future cooperation by raising the cost of nondecision or noncompliance. Governments are likely to accept pooling or delegation as a means to assure that other governments will accept agreed legislation and enforcement, to signal their own credibility, or to lock in future decisions against domestic opposition.

If governments seek credible commitments, why do they pool and delegate sovereignty instead of promulgating precise rules in advance? The answer lies in uncertainty about the future. Pooling and delegation can be viewed as solutions to the problem of "incomplete contracting," which arises when member governments share broad goals but find it too costly or technically impossible to specify all future contingencies involved in legislating or enforcing those goals. Governments therefore require efficient means of precommitting to a series of smaller, uncertain decisions staggered at a series of times in the future, some of which are likely to be inconvenient but which taken as a whole benefit each of them. The alternative to delegation and pooling, namely a series of "package deals" linking together various issues explicitly, makes it more difficult to structure intertemporal trade-offs. Issues must be negotiated in large unwieldy bundles. Pooling and delegation may also be used to precommit governments to decisions before the costs and benefits become clear enough to generate opposition – a technique commonly employed in trade negotiations; the equivalent in the United States are "fast track" provisions and GATT norms of reciprocity and nondiscrimination. The lack of precise *ex ante* knowledge about the form, details, and outcome of future decisions precludes more explicit contracts but also helps defuse potential opposition from disadvantaged groups. Majority voting, Commission initiative, or third-party enforcement in the Treaty (like most domestic constitutions) serve as "relational contracts" among member-states – binding agreements that do not specify detailed plans but precommit governments or delegated authorities to common sets of principles, norms, and decision-making and dispute-resolution procedures. Bargaining continues among national governments but under new institutional circumstances designed to assure a particular level of agreement.

In what ways do pooling and delegation bolster the credibility of international commitments? This question hardly arises in domestic settings, where constitutional rules are straightforwardly enforceable, but in the international realm, where there is no state with a monopoly of legitimate force, more subtle mechanisms must suffice. Pooling and delegation may raise the visibility of noncooperation, creating a focal point for mobilization by domestic groups not involved in a particular decision but supportive of subsequent or related decisions. Once sovereignty has been pooled or delegated, any attempt to reestablish unilateral control poses a challenge to the legitimacy of the institution as a whole and may require governments to launch costly and risky renegotiation of the institutions, perhaps involving a suspension of cooperation. International institutions may often enjoy broad ideological support, automatically mobilizing still more groups in favor of any single decision. Such ideological support may also permit national politicians to reduce the political costs of unpopular policies by "scapegoating" international institutions or foreign governments. Finally, international institutions may help establish reputations for member governments, reputations easily damaged by noncompliance in a few areas.

International institutions are particularly likely to be useful for this purpose where no domestic equivalents exist. For example, it is difficult to imagine, absent institutional centralization, Germany credibly committing not to subsidize its farmers or Italy credibly committing to subordinate its monetary policy to those of its neighbors. In monetary policy, the centralization of institutional control over monetary policy in an international institution may increase the credibility of domestic reform. If domestic workers and legislators or international investors and speculators consider targets more credible, it has been argued, they will not challenge them and the output cost of disinflation will be lower. There is considerable evidence, [. . .] that governments believed that institutions had precisely these consequences. EC institutions are linked in the public mind to normatively desirable policy outcomes, such as successful trade liberalization and postwar peace. Exclusion from any policy is viewed in some countries with great suspicion. Such ideological linkages permit the EC to be employed as a "scapegoat" in countries where it is a popular organization. Finally, the centralization of future decisions concerning a single currency in a European central bank raises the costs of unilateral behavior, which would require the time-consuming and difficult reconstitution of unilateral decision-making procedures – during which time diplomatic opposition or economic reactions may discourage noncompliance.

The decision to precommit through pooling or delegation marks a willingness to accept an increased political risk of being outvoted or overruled on any individual decision. The specific level of pooling or delegation reflects a reciprocal cost-benefit analysis: governments renounce unilateral options in order to assure that all governments will coordinate their behavior in particular ways. In agreeing to negotiate together in GATT, for example, France and Germany each surrendered unilateral control over tariff negotiations in exchange for greater assurances that they would combine forces, accept common decision-making, and be represented internationally by the Commission. From this perspective, we can think of unanimity voting, pooling, and delegation as striking different balances between the efficiency of common decisions and the desire of individual countries to reduce political risks by retaining a veto. As compared to unanimity voting, which permits recalcitrant governments to demand side-payments, thus encouraging log-rolling, lowest common denominator bargains, or outright obstruction, QMV and to an even greater extent delegation reduce the bargaining power of potential opponents, encouraging a higher level of compromise.

Three hypotheses follow. On the first dimension, *variation across issues and countries*, the credibility explanation predicts that delegation and pooling will vary by issue and country.

Delegation and pooling are most likely to arise in issue-areas where joint gains are high and distributional conflicts are moderate, and where there is uncertainty about future decisions. If there were high conflict, some governments would be likely to reserve their powers. Where decisions are lumpy and risky, with little consensus on desired outcomes or very intense preferences involved, governments are likely to reserve unanimity rights. Where there is little uncertainty and prescribed future behavior involves a clearly defined set of actions aimed at a single goal – for example, the orderly elimination of tariffs – states gain little domestically or internationally from pooling and delegation and tend to opt instead for specific binding rules. Pooling and delegation are therefore most likely to be found in limited domains, such as specific issue-areas, implementation, enforcement, and secondary legislation, where a large number of smaller decisions over an extended period, each uncertain, take place within the broader context of a previous decision. Examples include the setting of commodity prices, the steering of monetary policy, and the conduct of competition (antitrust) policy – each of which requires constant adaptation to new economic or political circumstances. The credible commitments explanation predicts no consistent variation by country; national positions vary instead by country and by issue. In those areas where governments favor integration and expect to join a qualified majority coalition (or gain support from supranational actors), they support pooling and delegation. Those that do not favor integration or are not likely to muster a majority oppose grants of sovereignty.

On the second dimension, *domestic cleavages and discourse*, the credibility explanation predicts that the positions taken by domestic groups will mirror their substantive interests. The most intense supporters of delegation will be those that benefit most from future compliance with the common rules. Governments transfer sovereignty to commit other governments to accept policies favored by key domestic constituencies and perhaps also to precommit the government to policies opposed by domestic groups unsupportive of the government. Domestic discourse stresses concern with future compliance.

On the third dimension, *the identity of and institutional controls on those holding delegated or pooled powers*, the credibility explanation predicts an inverse correlation between the scope and the extent of delegation. The idea is to assure future promulgation or implementation of rules despite national opposition, which requires a measure of autonomy and neutrality. We should observe governments limiting political risk by nesting specific decisions inside a set of larger decisions reached by unanimity. To enhance credibility yet maintain control, moreover, arrangements tend to be insulated from direct democratic control but are strictly limited by governmental oversight, resulting in a "democratic deficit."

Unlike the ideological and technocratic explanations, the credibility explanation generates precise predictions concerning the nature of support for pooling and delegation. Where the major institutional objective of those who support cooperation is to facilitate future legislation, pooling is more likely; where the concern is to assure the implementation of and compliance with laws, delegation is more likely. The reason is clear. Legislation is, at least potentially, a more open-ended function, so tighter control is maintained. Adjudication, implementation, and enforcement are narrower functions, so governments can afford looser control and greater efficiency.

Notes

1   Perry Anderson, "Under the Sign of the Interim," *London Review of Books*, 4 January 1996, p. 17.

2   Thomas Koenig and Thomas Braeuninger, "The Constitutional Choice of Rules: An Application of the Absolute and Relative Power Concepts to European Legislation," Mannheimer Zentrum für Europäische Sozialforschung AB II/17 (Mannheim, 1997), p. 14.
3   Anderson, "Under the Sign of the Interim," p. 14.
4   Ernst B. Haas, "Technocracy, Pluralism and the New Europe" in Stephen R. Graubard (ed.) *A New Europe?* (Boston, 1964), pp. 62–68.
5   Leon Lindberg, *The Political Dynamics of European Economic Integration* (Stanford University Press, Standford, 1963).
6   E.g., Laura Cram, *Policy-Making in the EU: Conceptual Lenses and the Integration Process* (London, 1997).
7   Haas, "Technocracy, Pluralism and the New Europe," pp. 65ff.
8   Donald Chisholm, *Coordination Without Hierarchy: Informal Structures in Multiorganizational Systems* (Berkeley, 1989), pp. 17–18.

2.4 European integration from the 1980s: state-centric v. multi-level governance

Gary Marks, Liesbet Hooghe and Kermit Blank

Source: *Journal of Common Market Studies*, vol. 4, no. 3 (1996), pp. 341–78.

Marks and his co-authors present two models of the European integration process: a 'state-centric' model in which European integration does not challenge the autonomy of nation states, and in which the process is driven by inter-state bargains (compare Moravcsik, selection 2.3); and a 'multi-level governance' model where decision-making power is shared across several levels and types of actors. In this second model, state executives lose significant amounts of control over decision making, and the separation between domestic and international politics is eroded. This extract explores the significance of the two models for policy-making in the European Union.

[Marks and his colleagues explore the features of the two models, and continue as follows.]

Policy-making in the European Union

The questions we are asking have to do with who decides what in European Union policy-making. If the state-centric model is valid, we would find a systematic pattern of state executive dominance. That entails three conditions. National governments, by virtue of the European Council and the Council of Ministers, should be able to impose their preferences collectively upon other European institutions, i.e. the European Commission, the European Parliament and the European Court of Justice. In other words, the latter three European institutions should be agents effectively controlled by state-dominated European institutions. Second, national governments should be able to maintain individual sovereignty *vis-à-vis* other national governments. And thirdly, national governments should be able to control the mobilization of subnational interests in the European arena. If, however, the multi-level governance model is valid, we should find, first, that the European Council and Council of Ministers share decisional authority with supranational institutions; second, that individual state executives cannot deliver the outcomes they wish through collective state executive decisions; and, finally, that subnational interests mobilize directly in the European arena or use the EU as a public space to pressure state executives into particular actions.

We divide the policy-making process into four sequential phases: policy initiation, decision-making, implementation and adjudication. We focus on informal practices in addition to formal rules, for it is vital to understand how institutions actually shape the behaviour of political actors in the European arena.

Policy initiation: commission as agenda-setter with a price – listen, make sense, and time aptly

In political systems that involve many actors, complex procedures and multiple veto points, the power to set the agenda is extremely important. The European Commission alone has the formal power to initiate and draft legislation, which includes the right to amend or withdraw its proposal at any stage in the process, and it is the think-tank for new policies (Article 155, EC). From a multi-level governance perspective, the European Commission has significant autonomous influence over the agenda. According to the state-centric model, this formal power is largely decorative: in reality the European Commission draws up legislation primarily to meet the demands of state executives.

At first sight, the practice of policy initiation is consistent with a state-centric interpretation. Analysis of 500 recent directives and regulations by the French Conseil d'Etat found that only a minority of EU proposals were spontaneous initiatives of the Commission. Regulatory initiative at the European level is demand driven rather than the product of autonomous supranational action, but the demands come not only from government leaders. A significant number of initiatives originate in the European Parliament, the Economic and Social Committee, regional governments, and various private and public-interest groups.

Such data should be evaluated carefully. For one thing, regulatory initiative at national and European levels is increasingly intermeshed. In its report, the Conseil d'Etat estimated that the European Commission is consulted beforehand on 75–80 per cent of French national legislation. Jacques Delors' prediction that by the year 2000 about 80 per cent of national economic and social legislation would be of Community origin has a solid base in reality. Moreover, it is one thing to be the first to articulate an issue, and quite another to influence how that issue will be taken up, with whom, and under what set of rules. And in each of these respects the influence of the Commission extends beyond its formal role, partly because of its unique political and administrative resources, discussed below, and partly because the Council is stymied by intergovernmental competition.

An organization that may serve as a powerful principal with respect to the Commission is the European Council, the summit of the political leaders of the Member States (plus the President of the Commission) held every six months. The European Council has immense prestige and legitimacy and a quasi-legal status as the body which defines 'general political guidelines' (Title 1, Art. D, Treaty of the European Union). However, its control of the European agenda is limited because it meets rarely and has only a skeleton permanent staff. The European Council provides the Commission with general policy mandates rather than specific policy proposals, and such mandates have proved to be a flexible basis for the Commission to build legislative programmes.

More direct constraints on the Commission originate from the Council of Ministers and the European Parliament. Indeed, the power of initiative has increasingly become a shared competence, permanently subject to contestation, among the three institutions. The Council (Article 152, EC) and, since the Maastricht Treaty, the European Parliament (Article 138b, EC) can request the Commission to produce proposals, although they cannot draft proposals themselves. Council Presidencies began to exploit this window in the legal texts from the mid-1980s, when state executives began to attach higher priority to the Council Presidency. Several governments bring detailed proposals with them to Brussels when they take over the Council Presidency. Another way for the Council to circumvent the Commission's formal monopoly of legislative proposal is to make soft law, i.e. by ratifying common opinions, resolutions, agreements, and recommendations.

The effect of this on the Commission's agenda-setting role is double edged. On the one hand, the Commission finds it politically difficult to ignore detailed Council initiatives or soft law, even though their legal status is vague. On the other hand, state executives are intent on using the European arena to attain a variety of policy goals, and this gives the Commission allies for integrationist initiatives.

The European Parliament has made use of its newly gained competence in Article 138b. In return for the approval of the Santer Commission in January 1995, it extracted from the Commission President a pledge to renegotiate the code of conduct (dating from 1990) between the two institutions in an effort to gain greater influence on the Commission's pen, its right of initiative.

The European Council, the Council, and the European Parliament have each succeeded in circumscribing the Commission's formal monopoly of initiative more narrowly, though none can claim that it has reduced the position of the Commission to that of an agent. Agenda-setting is now a shared and contested competence among the four European institutions, rather than monopolized by one actor.

But the diffusion of control over the EU's agenda does not stop here. Interest groups have mobilized intensively in the European arena and, while their power is difficult to pinpoint, it is clear that the Commission takes their input seriously. The passage of the Single European Act precipitated a rapid growth of European legislation and a corresponding increase in interest group representation in Europe. An outpouring of case study research suggests that the number and variety of groups involved is as great, and perhaps greater, than in any national capital. National and regional organizations of every kind have mobilized in Brussels, and these are flanked by a large and growing number of European peak organizations and individual companies from across Europe. [. . .]

Subnational authorities now mobilize intensively in Brussels. Apart from the Committee of the Regions, established by the Maastricht Treaty, individual subnational authorities have set up almost 100 regional offices in Brussels and a wide variety of interregional associations.

Agenda-setting is therefore increasingly a shared and contested competence, with European institutions competing for control, and interest groups and subnational actors vying to influence the process. This is not much different from the situation in some national polities, particularly those organized federally.

As a consequence, it is often difficult to apportion responsibility for particular initiatives. This is true for the most intensively studied initiative of all – the internal market programme – which was pressed forward by business interests, the Commission, and the European Parliament, as well as by state executives. Because the Commission plays a subtle initiating role, its influence is not captured by analysis of which institution formally announces a new policy. For example, the White Paper on *Growth, Competitiveness and Employment* was publicly mandated by the European Council in June 1993, but it did so in response to detailed guidelines for economic renewal tabled by the Commission President.

The Commission has considerable leverage, but it is conditional, not absolute. It depends on its capacity to nurture and use diverse contacts, its ability to anticipate and mediate demands, its decisional efficiency, and the unique expertise it derives from its role as think-tank of the European Union.

The Commission is always on the look-out for information and political support. It has developed an extensive informal machinery of advisory committees and working groups for consultation and pre-negotiation, some of which are made up of Member State nominees, but others of interest group representatives and experts who give the Commission access to independent information and legitimacy. The Commission has virtually a free hand in creating new networks, and in this way it is able to reach out to new constituencies, including a variety of subnational groups. [. . .]

The extent to which the Commission initiates policy (Article 155) depends also on its alacrity. A striking example of this is the European Energy Charter, a formal agreement between Russia and west European states guaranteeing Russian energy supply after the collapse of the Soviet Union. An EU policy came into being because the Commission pre-empted an alternative intergovernmental approach preferred by the Dutch, German, and British governments. Acting on a vague mandate of the European Council in June 1990, the Commission negotiated a preliminary agreement with the Russian government in 1991. Member State executives, presented with a *fait accompli*, accepted the European Community as the appropriate forum for the Charter and gave the Commission a toe-hold in inter-national energy policy, a note-worthy incursion in a policy area which had been dominated by national governments.

The Commission's capacity to move quickly is a function of its internal cohesion. An example from industrial policy illustrates the limits of the Commission's agenda-setting power when it is internally divided. In Spring 1990, Europe's largest electronics firms pres-sured the Commission for a European strategy in the semi-conductors' sector as a means of securing EU financial support and market protection. The Commission was paralysed for months as a result of internal disagreements. When it eventually produced a policy recom-mendation for a European industrial policy in the beginning of 1991, most firms had shifted their strategy to other arenas. The French firms, Bull and Thomson, had obtained guaran-tees from the French government for financial support, while others like Siemens and Olivetti were exploring strategic alliances with American or Japanese firms.

As the think-tank of the European Union, the Commission has responsibility for investi-gating the feasibility of new EU policies, a role that requires the Commission to solicit expertise. In this capacity it produces annually 200–300 reports, White Papers, Green Papers, and other studies and communications. Some are highly technical studies about, say, the administration of milk surpluses. Others are influential policy programmes such as the 1985 White Paper on the Internal Market, the 1990 reform proposals for Common Agri-cultural Policy which laid the basis for the European position in the GATT negotiations, or the 1993 White Paper on *Growth, Competitiveness and Employment* which argued for more labour market flexibility.

As a small and thinly staffed organization, the Commission has only a fraction of the resources available to central state executives, but its position as interlocutor with national governments, subnational authorities and a large variety of interest groups gives it unparal-leled access to information. The Commission has superior in-house knowledge and expertise in agriculture, where one-quarter of its staff is concentrated. It has formidable expertise in external trade and competition, the two other areas where Commission competence is firmly established. In other areas, the Commission relies on Member State submissions, its exten-sive advisory system of public and private actors, and paid consultants.

The European Commission is a critical actor in the policy initiation phase, whether one looks at formal rules or practice. If one surveys the evidence one cannot conclude that the Commission serves merely as an agent of state executives. The point is not that the Commission is the only decisive actor. We discern instead a system of multi-level governance involving competition and interdependence among the Commission, Council, and European Parliament, each of which commands impressive resources in the intricate game of policy initiation.

Decision-making: state sovereignty in retreat

According to the Treaties, the main legislative body in the EU is not the European Parliament, but the Council of Ministers, an assembly of Member State executives. Until the Single European Act, the Council was the sole legislative authority. The thrust of the state-centric argument is to give great weight to the legislative powers of state executives in the decision-making stage. At this stage, state executives may be said to be in complete control. They adjust policies to their collective preferences, define the limits of European collaboration, determine the role of the European Commission and the ECJ and, if need be, curtail their activities. If previous decisions have unintended consequences, these can be corrected by the Council.

There is some plausibility to this argument, but it is one-dimensional. In the first place, one must take into account the serious constraints under which individual governments have operated since the Single European Act. Second, one should recognize that even collectively, state executives exert conditional, not absolute, control. State executive dominance is eroded in the decision-making process by the legislative power of the European Parliament, the role of the European Commission in overcoming transaction problems, and the efforts of interest groups to influence outcomes in the European arena.

The most transparent blow to state sovereignty has come from the successive extension of qualified majority voting under the Single European Act and the Maastricht Treaty. Qualified majority voting is now the rule for most policy areas covered by the original Treaty of Rome, including agriculture, trade, competition policy, transport, and policy areas concerned with the realization of the internal market, though there are important exceptions which include the EU budget, taxation, capital flows, self-employed persons and professions, visa policy (qualified majority from 1 January 1996), free movement of persons, and rights of employed persons. The decision-making rules are complex, but the bottom line is clear: over broad areas of EU competence individual state executives may be outvoted.

The practice of qualified majority voting is complicated by the Luxembourg Compromise and by a 'veto culture' which is said to have predominated in the Council of Ministers. Under the Luxembourg Compromise state executives can veto decisions subject to majority rule if they claim that their national vital interests are at stake. The Luxembourg Compromise features far more strongly in academic debates about the EU than in the practice of European politics. It was invoked less than a dozen times between 1966 and 1981, and it has been used even less frequently since that time. [. . .]

In this context, second order rules about the adoption of alternative voting procedures are extremely important. Amendments to the Council's Rules of Procedure in July 1987 have made it much easier to initiate a qualified majority vote. While previously only the Council President could call a vote, it now suffices that one representative – and that could be the Commission – demands a ballot and is supported by a simple majority of the Council.

One of the most remarkable developments in the 1980s has been the transformation of the notion of 'vital national interest'. State executives wishing to exercise a Luxembourg veto have become dependent on the acquiescence of *other* state executives. They can no longer independently determine whether their vital national interest is at stake. As the British (1982), German (1985), Greek (1988) and French (1992–93) cases suggest, the conditions are restrictive. The Luxembourg Compromise has come to operate effectively only for decisions which involve some combination of the following characteristics: the perception of an unambiguous link to vital national interests; the prospect of serious domestic political damage to the government concerned; a national government which can credibly threaten to damage the general working of the European Union. While it originally legitimized unconditional defence of state sovereignty (de Gaulle vetoed the budgetary reform of 1965 on the grounds that it was too supranational), the notion of vital national interest has evolved to justify only defence of substantive interests, not defence of national sovereignty itself.

Even if a Member State executive is able to invoke the Luxembourg Compromise, the veto remains a dull weapon. It cannot block alternative courses of action, as the German Federal government experienced in 1985 after it had stopped a Council regulation on lower prices for cereal and colza. The Commission simply invoked its emergency powers and achieved virtually the same reductions unilaterally. Moreover, a veto rarely settles an issue, unless the status quo is the preferred outcome for the vetoing government. But even in the two cases where the status quo was more desirable than the proposed change (the German and French cases), neither government was able to sustain the status quo. The German government was bypassed by the Commission; the French government was unable to block the GATT accord and, moreover, received only modest financial compensations in return for its acquiescence.

All in all, since the mid-1980s, the Luxembourg Compromise has been a weak instrument for the defence of state sovereignty. The British, German, Greek and French governments did not gain much by invoking or threatening to invoke it. Each came to accept that its options were severely constrained by European decisions. [. . .]

State executives have built a variety of specific safeguards into the Treaties. There are numerous derogations for particular states, especially on matters of taxation, state aids, monetary policy and energy policy. The Single European Act and the Maastricht Treaty preserve unanimity for the most sensitive or contested policy areas.

These qualifications soften the blow to national sovereignty. But a sensible discussion of the overall situation turns on the *extent* to which national sovereinty has been compromised, rather than on whether this has happened. Even under the doubtful premise that the Council is the sole decision-maker, it is now the case that state sovereignty has been pooled among a group of states in most EU policy areas.

Collective state control exercised through the Council has diminished. That is first of all due to the growing role of the European Parliament in decision-making. The SEA and the Maastricht Treaty established co-operation and co-decision procedures which have transformed the legislative process from a simple Council-dominated process into an complex balancing act between Council, Parliament and Commission. Since the Maastricht Treaty, the two procedures apply to the bulk of EU legislation. The procedures are designed to encourage consensual decision-making between the three institutions. It is impossible for the Council to take legislative decisions without the support of at least one of the two other institutions unless it is unanimous. Moreover, the procedures enhance the agenda-setting power of the European Parliament.

The co-operation procedure gives the Commission significant agenda-setting capacity. It may decide to take up or drop amendments from either the Council or Parliament, a power that makes it a broker – a consensus crafter – between the two institutions.

The intermeshing of institutions is particularly intricate under the co-decision procedure, under which the Parliament obtains an absolute veto, although it loses some agenda-setting power to the Council. If the Parliament or Council rejects the other's positions, a concili-ation committee tries to hammer out a compromise. The committee consists of representa-tives from both institutions, with the Commission sitting in as broker. A compromise needs the approval of an absolute majority in the Parliament and a qualified majority in the Council. If there is no agreement, the initiative returns to the Council, which can then make a take-it-or-leave-it offer, which the Parliament can reject by absolute majority. So the Parliament has the final word.

Even though the outcome of the co-decision procedure is likely to be closer to the preferences of the Council than those of the Commission of Parliament, it does not simply reflect Council preferences. Under both procedures the Council is locked in a complex relationship of co-operation and contestation with the two other institutions. This is multi-level governance in action, and is distinctly different from what would be expected in a state-centric system.

The erosion of collective state control goes further than this. It is difficult for state executives to resolve transaction costs in the egalitarian setting of the Council, particularly now, given that there are 15 such actors. The Council usually lacks information, expertise, and the co-ordination to act quickly and effectively, and this induces it to rely on the European Commission for leadership.

The Commission, as a hierarchical organization, is usually able to present a more coherent position than the Council. Furthermore, Commission officials bring unusual skills to the negotiation table. As administrators, they have often been working on a particular policy issue for years; career mobility tends to be lower than for top echelons of most national administrations (Bellier, 1994). In addition, they have access to information and expertise from a variety of sources in the European Union. They tend to be exceptionally skilled political negotiators acclimatized to the diverse political styles of national representatives and the need to seek consensual solutions. Formal decision rules in the Council help the Commission to focus discussion or broker compromise. While Member State representatives preside at Council of Ministers' meetings and Council working groups, the Commission sits in to clarify, redraft, and finalize the proposal – in short, it holds the pen. [. . .]

Cohesion policy offers an example of how the Commission may step beyond its role of umpire to become a negotiator. In establishing the framework for structural funds for 1994–99 in the summer of 1993, Commission officials negotiated bilaterally with officials from the relevant states. It was the Belgian presidency which acted as umpire. In such cases, the Commission becomes effectively a 13th (or, since 1995, a 16th) partner around the bargaining table. This can even be true for the most intergovernmental aspect of European Union politics: treaty bargaining, as an example from Maastricht illustrates. When the British government refused the watered down social provisions in the Maastricht Treaty, Jacques Delors put on the table his original, more radical, social policy programme of 1989 and proposed to attach it as a special protocol to the Treaty, leaving Britain out. Faced with the prospect that the whole negotiation might break down, the other 11 state executives hastily signed up to a more substantial document than they had originally anticipated.

In sum, the Council is the senior actor in the decision-making stage, but the European Parliament and the Commission are indispensable partners. The Commission's power is predominantly soft in that it is exercised by subtle influence rather than sanction. Except for agriculture, external trade and competition policy, where it has substantial executive autonomy, it can gain little by confrontation. Its influence depends on its ability to craft consensus among institutions and among Member State executives. However, extensive reliance on qualified majority voting has enabled the Commission to be bolder, as it does not have to court all state executives at once.

The European Parliament's position is based more on formal rules. Its track record under co-operation and co-decision shows that it does not eschew confrontations with the Council. In return for its assent to enlargement and the GATT-agreement in 1994, it extracted from the Council a formal seat in the preparatory negotiations for the intergovernmental conference of 1996–97. In the meantime, it is intent on making the most of its power, even if it treads on the toes of its long-standing ally, the European Commission. During its hearings on the Santer Commission in January 1995, the European Parliament demanded that the Commission accept parliamentary amendments 'as a matter of course', and withdraw proposals that it rejects. Commission officials have described these proposals as 'outrageous' on the grounds that the Commission 'would more or less lose its ability to operate'.[1]

As a whole, EU decision-making can be characterized as one of multiple, intermeshing competencies, complementary policy functions, and variable lines of authority – features that are elements of multi-level governance.

Implementation: opening the European arena – breaking the state mould

Multi-level governance is prominent in the implementation stage. Although the Commission has formal executive powers and national governments are in principle responsible for implementation, in practice these competencies are shared. On the one hand, national governments monitor the executive powers of the Commission closely, though they do so in conjunction with subnational governments and societal actors. On the other hand, the Commission has become involved in day-to-day implementation in a number of policy areas, and this brings it into close contact with subnational authorities and interest groups. As in the initiation and decision-making stage, mutual intrusion is contested.

The Commission's formal mandate gives it discretion to interpret legislation and issue administrative regulations bearing on specific cases. It issues 6–7,000 administrative regulations annually. However, only a tiny proportion of the Commission's decisions are unilateral. Since the 1980s, the Council and the individual national governments have become intimately involved. Many regulations have their own committee attached to them. Balancing Commission autonomy and state involvement is an open-ended and conflictual process in the European Union, and this is also apparent in comitology. Rules of operation vary across policy areas and are a source of contention between the Commission, usually supported by the Parliament, and the Council. Some committees are only advisory; others can prevent the Commission from carrying out a certain action by qualified majority vote; and a third category must approve Commission actions by qualified majority. In each case the Commission presides.

At first sight, comitology seems to give state executives control over the Commission's actions in genuine principal-agent fashion. But the relationship between state actors and European institutions is more complex. Comitology is weakest in precisely those areas where the Commission has extensive executive powers, e.g. in competition policy, state aids, agriculture, commercial policy and the internal market. Here, the Commission has significant space for autonomous action.

State-centrists may argue that state executives prefer to delegate these powers to achieve state-oriented collective goods, such as control over potential distortion of competition or a stronger bargaining position in international trade. But one result is that state executives have lost exclusive control in a range of policy areas. To mention just three examples among the many discussed in this chapter: they no longer control competition within their borders; they cannot aid national firms as they deem fit; they cannot autonomously conduct trade negotiations. [. . .]

Although comitology involves state actors in the European Commission's activities, this intermeshing is not necessarily limited to *central* state actors. Because the issues on the table are often technical in nature, Member State governments tend to send those people who are directly responsible or who are best informed about the issue at home. These are regularly subnational officials, or representatives of interest groups or other non-governmental bodies. Subnational participation in comitology is prevalent for Member States organized along federal or semi-federal lines. But, in recent years, subnational actors have been drawn into the European arena from more centralized Member States.

To the extent that EU regulations affect policy areas where authority is shared among central and subnational levels of government, effective implementation requires contacts between multiple levels of government. Environmental policy is an example of this, for in several European countries competencies in this area are shared across different territorial levels. To speed up implementation of environmental law, the Commission began in 1990 to arrange so-called 'package' meetings to bring together central, regional and local government representatives of a Member State. Such meetings are voluntary, but in the first year of its operation seven countries made use of them. The Spanish central government, for example, was keen to use the Commission's presence to pressure its autonomous provinces into compliance with EU environmental law, but to do so it conceded them access to the European arena.

The majority of participants in comitology are not national civil servants, but interest group representatives (particularly from farming, union, and employer organizations) alongside technical experts, scientists and academics. These people are mostly selected, or at least approved of, by their national government. One can plausibly assume that national governments find it more difficult to persuade technical experts, interest group representatives, and private actors than their own officials to defend the national interest. In practice therefore, comitology, which was originally a mechanism for central state oversight over Commission activities, has had the intended consequence of deepening the participation of subnational authorities and private actors in the European arena.

A second development [. . .] is the direct involvement of Commission officials in day-to-day policy implementation. The Commission was never expected to perform ground-level implementation, except in unusual circumstances (such as competition policy, fraud, etc.). Yet, in some areas this has changed. The most prominent example is cohesion policy, which now absorbs about one-third of the EU budget. The bulk of the money goes to multi-annual regional development programmes in the less developed regions of the EU. The 1989 reform prescribes the involvement of Commission, national, regional, local and social actors on a continuing basis in all stages of the policy process: selection of priorities, choice of programmes, allocation of funding, monitoring of operations, evaluation and adjustment of programmes. To this end, each recipient region or country is required to set up an elaborate system of monitoring committees, with a general committee on top, and a cascade of subcommittees focused on particular programmes. Commission officials can and do participate at each level of this tree-like structure. Partnership is implemented unevenly across the EU, but just about everywhere it institutionalizes some form of direct contact between the Commission and non-central government actors including, particularly, regional and local authorities, local action groups and local businesses. Such links break open the mould of the state, so that multi-level governance encompasses actors within as well as beyond existing states.

Adjudication: an activist court in a supranational legal order

State-centrists have argued that a European legal order and effective European Court of Justice (ECJ) are essential to state co-operation. Unilateral defection is difficult to detect, and thus it is in the interest of states to delegate authority to a European Court to monitor compliance. The ECJ also mitigates incomplete contracting problems by applying general interstate bargains to future contingencies. In this vein, the ECJ may be conceptualized as an agent of constituent Member States. However, a number of scholars have argued convincingly that the ECJ has become more than an instrument of Member States. The Court has been active in transforming the legal order in a supranational direction. But the Court could not have done this without a political ally at the European level: the European Commission. Nor could it have established the supremacy of European law without the collaboration of national courts, and this collaboration has altered the balance of power between national courts and national political authorities.

Through its activist stance, the ECJ has laid the legal foundation for an integrated European polity. By means of an impressive body of case law, the Court has established the Treaty of Rome as a document creating legal obligations directly binding on national governments and individual citizens alike. Moreover, these obligations have legal priority over laws made by the Member States. Directly binding legal authority and supremacy are attributes of sovereignty, and their application by the ECJ indicates that the EU is becoming a constitutional regime.

The Court was originally expected to act as an impartial monitor 'to ensure that in the interpretation and application of the treaties the law is observed' (Article 164 EEC, Article 136 Euratom, Article 31 ECSC) but, from the beginning, the Court viewed these interstate treaties as more than narrow agreements. The Court's expansive role is founded on the failure of the treaties to specify the competencies of major EU institutions. Instead, the treaties set out 'tasks' or 'purposes' for European co-operation, such as the customs union (Treaty of Rome), the completion of the internal market (Single European Act) or economic and monetary union (Maastricht Treaty). The Court has constitutionalized European law and expanded European authority in other policy areas by stating that these were necessary to achieve these functional goals.

Court rulings have been pivotal in shaping European integration. However, the ECJ depends on other actors to force issues on the European political agenda and condone its interpretations. Legislators (the European Council, Council of Ministers, Commission and Parliament) may always reverse the course set by the Court by changing the law or by altering the Treaties. In other words, the ECJ is no different from the Council, Commission or European Parliament in that it is locked in mutual dependence with other actors.

One outcome of this interlocking is the principle of 'mutual recognition', which became the core principle of the internal market programme in the landmark case of *Cassis de Dijon* (1979) in which the Court stated that a product lawfully produced in one Member State must be accepted in another. Some have argued that the ruling was based on the ECJ's reading of the interests of the most influential state executives, France and Germany, but detailed analysis of the evidence suggests that the Court made the decision autonomously, notwithstanding the opposition of the French and German governments. It was the Commission that projected the principle of mutual recognition onto a wider agenda, the single market initiative, and it did this as early as July 1980 when it announced to the European Parliament and the Council that the *Cassis* case was the foundation for a new approach to market harmonization.

National courts have proved willing to apply the doctrine of direct effect by invoking Article 177 of the Treaty of Rome which stipulates that national courts may seek 'authoritative guidance' from the ECJ in cases involving Community law. In such instances, the ECJ provides a preliminary ruling, specifying the proper application of Community law to the issue at hand. While this preliminary ruling does not formally decide the case, in practice the Court is rendering a judgment of the 'constitutionality' of a particular statute or administrative action in the light of its interpretation of Community law. The court that made the referral cannot be forced to acknowledge the interpretations by the ECJ, but if it does, other national courts usually accept these decisions as a precedent. Preliminary rulings expand ECJ influence, and judges at the lowest level gain a *de facto* power of judicial review, which had been reserved to the highest court in the state. Article 177 gives lower national courts strong incentives to circumvent their own national judicial hierarchy. With their support, much of the business of interpreting Community law has been transferred from national high courts to the ECJ and lower courts.

ECJ decisions have become accepted as part of the legal order in the Member States, shifting expectation about decision-making authority from a purely national-based system to one that is more multi-level. The doctrines of direct effect and supremacy were constructed over the strong objections of several Member State executives. Yet, its influence lies not in its scope for unilateral action, but in the fact that its rulings and inclusive mode of operation create opportunities for other European institutions, particularly the Commission, for private interests, and national institutions (lower national courts), to influence the European agenda or enhance their power.

Conclusion

Multi-level governance does not confront the sovereignty of states directly. Instead of being explicitly challenged, states in the European Union are being melded gently into a multi-level polity by their leaders and the actions of numerous subnational and supranational actors. State-centric theorists are right when they argue that states are extremely powerful institutions that are capable of crushing direct threats to their existence. The institutional form of the state emerged because it proved a particularly effective means of systematically wielding violence, and it is difficult to imagine any generalized challenge along these lines. But this is not the only, nor even the most important, issue facing the state. One does not have to argue that states are on the verge of political extinction to believe that their control of those living in their territories has significantly weakened.

It is not necessary to look far beyond the state itself to find reasons that might explain how such an outcome is possible. When we disaggregate the state into the actors that shape its diverse institutions, it is clear that key decision-makers, above all those directing the state executive, may have goals that do not coincide with that of projecting state sovereignty into the future. As well as being a goal in itself, the state may sensibly be regarded as a means to a variety of ends that are structured by party competition and interest group politics in a liberal democratic setting. A state executive may wish to shift decision-making to the supranational level because the political benefits outweigh the cost of losing control. Or a state executive may have intrinsic grounds to shift control, for example to shed responsibility for unpopular decisions.

Even if state executives want to maintain sovereignty, they are often not able to do so. A state executive can easily be outvoted because most decisions in the Council are now taken under the decision rule of qualified majority, and moreover, even the national veto, the ultimate instrument of sovereignty, is constrained by the willingness of other state executives to tolerate its use. But the limits on state sovereignty are deeper. Even collectively, state executives do not determine the European agenda because they are unable to control the supranational institutions they have created at the European level. The growing diversity of issues on the Council's agenda, the sheer number of state executive principals and the mistrust that exists among them, and the increased specialization of policy-making have made the Council of Ministers reliant upon the Commission to set the agenda, forge compromises, and supervise compliance. The Commission and the Council are not on a par, but neither can their relationship be understood in principal-agent terms. Policy-making in the EU is characterized by mutual dependence, complementary functions and overlapping competencies.

The Council also shares decision-making competencies with the European Parliament, which has gained significant legislative power under the Single European Act and the Maastricht Treaty. Indeed, the Parliament might be conceived of as a principal in its own right in the European arena. The Council, Commission and Parliament interact within a legal order which has been transformed into a supranational one through the innovative jurisprudence of the European Court of Justice. The complex interplay among these contending institutions in a polity where political control is diffuse often leads to outcomes that are second choice for all participants.

The character of the Euro-polity at any particular point in time is the outcome of a tension between supranational and intergovernmental pressures. We have argued that, since the 1980s, it has crystallized into a multi-level polity. States no longer serve as the exclusive nexus between domestic politics and international relations.

Direct connections are being forged among political actors in diverse political arenas. Traditional and formerly exclusive channels of communication and influence are being sidestepped. With its dispersed competencies, contending but interlocked institutions, shifting agendas, multi-level governance opens multiple points of access for interests, while it privileges those interests with technical expertise that match the dominant style of EU policy-making. In this turbulent process of mobilization and counter-mobilization it is patently clear that states no longer serve as the exclusive nexus between domestic politics and international relations. Direct connections are being forged among political actors in diverse political arenas.

However, there is nothing inherent in the current system. Multi-level governance is unlikely to be a stable equilibrium. There is no widely legitimized constitutional framework. There is little consensus on the goals of integration. As a result, the allocation of competencies between national and supranational actors is ambiguous and contested. It is worth noting that the European polity has made two U-turns in its short history. Overt supranationalist features of the original structure were overshadowed by the imposition of intergovernmental institutions in the 1960s and 1970s. From the 1980s, a system of multi-level governance arose, in which national governmental control became diluted by the activities of supranational and subnational actors.

These developments have engendered strong negative reactions on the part of declining social groups represented in nationalist political movements. Ironically, much of the discontent with European integration has been directed towards state executives themselves and the pragmatic and elitist style in which they have bargained institutional change in the EU.

The EU-wide series of debates unleashed by the Treaty of Maastricht have forced the issue of sovereignty onto the agenda. Where governing parties themselves shy away from the issue, it is raised in stark terms by opposition parties, particularly those of the extreme right. Several Member State governments are, themselves, deeply riven on the issues of integration and sovereignty. States and state sovereignty have become objects of popular contention – the outcome of which is as yet uncertain.

Note

1 *Financial Times*, 14–15.1.1995.

2.5 The power of international organizations

Michael N. Barnett and Martha Finnemore

Source: 'The politics, power and pathologies of international organizations', *International Organization*, vol. 53, no. 4 (1999), pp. 695–732. The extract is from pp. 707–15.

Barnett and Finnemore take a constructivist approach, in contrast to the rationalist methodology of (for example) Moravcsik (selection 2.3). This means that they emphasize the ways in which international organizations can exploit their status as constitutive bodies in the world arena to create 'social knowledge' and define norms. In this enquiry, it is important to explore the extent to which international organizations can develop power independent of the states that created them. Central to this process is the way in which bureaucracies create rules and 'social knowledge' by defining shared tasks and transferring models of political organization around the world. The authors in this extract develop their conception of power and the ways in which international organizations can wield it.

[Barnett and Finnemore begin with a critique of rationalist approaches, and then move on to the question of power.]

The power of IOs

IOs can become autonomous sites of authority, independent from the state "principals" who may have created them, because of power flowing from at least two sources: (1) the legitimacy of the rational-legal authority they embody, and (2) control over technical expertise and information. The first of these is almost entirely neglected by the political science literature, and the second, we argue, has been conceived of very narrowly, leading scholars to overlook some of the most basic and consequential forms of IO influence. Taken together, these two features provide a theoretical basis for treating IOs as autonomous actors in contemporary world politics by identifying sources of support for them, independent of states, in the larger social environment. Since rational-legal authority and control over expertise are part of what defines and constitutes any bureaucracy (a bureaucracy would not be a bureaucracy without them), the autonomy that flows from them is best understood as a constitutive effect, an effect of the way bureaucracy is constituted, which, in turn, makes possible (and in that sense causes) other processes and effects in global politics.

Sources of IO autonomy and authority

To understand how IOs can become autonomous sites of authority we turn to Weber and his classic study of bureaucratization. Weber was deeply ambivalent about the increasingly bureaucratic world in which he lived and was well-attuned to the vices as well as the virtues of this new social form of authority. Bureaucracies are rightly considered a grand achievement, he thought. They provide a framework for social interaction that can respond to the increasingly technical demands of modern life in a stable, predictable, and nonviolent way; they exemplify rationality and are technically superior to previous forms of rule because they bring precision, knowledge, and continuity to increasingly complex social tasks. But such technical and rational achievements, according to Weber, come at a steep price. Bureaucracies are political creatures that can be autonomous from their creators and can come to dominate the societies they were created to serve, because of both the normative appeal of rational-legal authority in modern life and the bureaucracy's control over technical expertise and information. We consider each in turn.

Bureaucracies embody a form of authority, rational-legal authority, that modernity views as particularly legitimate and good. In contrast to earlier forms of authority that were invested in a leader, legitimate modern authority is invested in legalities, procedures, and rules and thus rendered impersonal. This authority is "rational" in that it deploys socially recognized relevant knowledge to create rules that determine how goals will be pursued. The very fact that they embody rationality is what makes bureaucracies powerful and makes people willing to submit to this kind of authority. According to Weber,

> in legal authority, submission does not rest upon the belief and devotion to charismatically gifted persons [. . .] or upon piety toward a personal lord and master who is defined by an ordered tradition. [. . .] Rather submission under legal authority is based upon an *impersonal* bond to the generally defined and functional "duty of office." The official duty – like the corresponding right to exercise authority: the "jurisdictional competency" – is fixed by *rationally established* norms, by enactments, decrees, and regulations in such a manner that the legitimacy of the authority becomes the legality of the general rule, which is purposely thought out, enacted, and announced with formal correctness.[1]

When bureaucrats do something contrary to your interests or that you do not like, they defend themselves by saying "Sorry, those are the rules" or "just doing my job." "The rules" and "the job" are the source of great power in modern society. It is because bureaucrats in IOs are performing "duties of office" and implementing "rationally established norms" that they are powerful.

A second basis of autonomy and authority, intimately connected to the first, is bureaucratic control over information and expertise. A bureaucracy's autonomy derives from specialized technical knowledge, training, and experience that is not immediately available to other actors. While such knowledge might help the bureaucracy carry out the directives of politicians more efficiently, Weber stressed that it also gives bureaucracies power over politicians (and other actors). It invites and at times requires bureaucracies to shape policy, not just implement it.

The irony in both of these features of authority is that they make bureaucracies powerful precisely by creating the appearance of depoliticization. The power of IOs, and bureaucracies generally, is that they present themselves as impersonal, technocratic, and neutral – as not exercising power but instead as serving others; the presentation and acceptance of these claims is critical to their legitimacy and authority. Weber, however, saw through these claims. According to him, the depoliticized character of bureaucracy that legitimates it could be a myth: "Behind the functional purposes [of bureaucracy], of course, 'ideas of culture-values' usually stand."[2] Bureaucracies always serve some social purpose or set of cultural values.

That purpose may be normatively "good," as Weber believed the Prussian nationalism around him was, but there was no a priori reason to assume this.

In addition to embodying cultural values from the larger environment that might be desirable or not, bureaucracies also carry with them behavioral dispositions and values flowing from the rationality that legitimates them as a cultural form. Some of these, like the celebration of knowledge and expertise, Weber admired. Others concerned him greatly, and his descriptions of bureaucracy as an "iron cage" and bureaucrats as "specialists without spirit" are hardly an endorsement of the bureaucratic form. Bureaucracy can undermine personal freedom in important ways. The very impersonal, rule-bound character that empowers bureaucracy also dehumanizes it. Bureaucracies often exercise their power in repressive ways, in the name of general rules because rules are their raison d'être. This tendency is exacerbated by the way bureaucracies select and reward narrowed professionals seeking secure careers internally – people who are "lacking in heroism, human spontaneity, and inventiveness."[3] Following Weber, we investigate rather than assume the "goodness" of bureaucracy.

Weber's insights provide a powerful critique of the ways in which international relations scholars have treated IOs. The legitimacy of rational-legal authority suggests that IOs may have an authority independent of the policies and interests of states that create them, a possibility obscured by the technical and apolitical treatment of IOs by both realists and neoliberals. Nor have realists and neoliberals considered how control over information hands IOs a basis of autonomy. Susan Strange, at the forefront among realists in claiming that information is power, has emphatically stated that IOs are simply the agents of states. Neoliberals have tended to treat information in a highly technocratic and depoliticized way, failing to see how information is power. As IOs create transparencies and level information asymmetries among states (a common policy prescription of neoliberals) they create new information asymmetries between IOs and states. Given the neoliberal assumption that IOs have no goals independent of states, such asymmetries are unimportant; but if IOs have autonomous values and behavioral predispositions, then such asymmetries may be highly consequential.

Examples of the ways in which IOs have become autonomous because of their embodiment of technical rationality and control over information are not hard to find. The UN's peacekeepers derive part of their authority from the claim that they are independent, objective, neutral actors who simply implement Security Council resolutions. UN officials routinely use this language to describe their role and are explicit that they understand this to be the basis of their influence. As a consequence, UN officials spend considerable time and energy attempting to maintain the image that they are not the instrument of any great power and must be seen as representatives of "the international community" as embodied in the rules and resolutions of the UN. The World Bank is widely recognized to have exercised power over development policies far greater than its budget, as a percentage of North/South aid flows, would suggest because of the expertise it houses. While competing sites of expertise in development have proliferated in recent years, for decades after its founding the World Bank was a magnet for the "best and brightest" among "development experts." Its staff had and continues to have impressive credentials from the most prestigious universities and the elaborate models, reports, and research groups it has sponsored over the years were widely influential among the "development experts" in the field. This expertise, coupled with its claim to "neutrality" and its "apolitical" technocratic decision-making style, have given the World Bank an authoritative voice with which it has successfully dictated the content, direction, and scope of global development over the past fifty years. Similarly, official standing and long experience with relief efforts have endowed the UNHCR with "expert" status and consequent authority in refugee matters. This expertise, coupled with its role in implementing international refugee conventions and law ("the rules" regarding refugees), has allowed the UNHCR to make life and death decisions about refugees without consulting the refugees, themselves, and to compromise the authority of states in various ways in setting up refugee camps. Note that, as these examples show, technical knowledge and expertise need not be "scientific" in nature to create autonomy and power for IOs.

The power of IOs

If IOs have autonomy and authority in the world, what do they do with it? A growing body of research in sociology and anthropology has examined ways in which IOs exercise power by virtue of their culturally constructed status as sites of authority; we distill from this research three broad types of IO power. We examine how IOs (1) classify the world, creating categories of actors and action; (2) fix meanings in the social world; and (3) articulate and diffuse new norms, principles, and actors around the globe. All of these sources of power flow from the ability of IOs to structure knowledge.

Classification

An elementary feature of bureaucracies is that they classify and organize information and knowledge. This classification process is bound up with power. "Bureaucracies," writes Don Handelman, "are ways of making, ordering, and knowing social worlds." They do this by "moving persons among social categories or by inventing and applying such categories."[4] The ability to classify objects, to shift their very definition and identity, is one of bureaucracy's greatest sources of power. This power is frequently treated by the objects of that power as accomplished through caprice and without regard to their circumstances but is legitimated and justified by bureaucrats with reference to the rules and regulations of the bureaucracy. Consequences of this bureaucratic exercise of power may be identity defining, or even life threatening.

Consider the evolving definition of "refugee." The category "refugee" is not at all straightforward and must be distinguished from other categories of individuals who are "temporarily" and "involuntarily" living outside their country of origin – displaced persons, exiles, economic migrants, guest workers, diaspora communities, and those seeking political asylum. The debate over the meaning of "refugee" has been waged in and around the UNHCR. The UNHCR's legal and operational definition of the category strongly influences decisions about who is a refugee and shapes UNHCR staff decisions in the field – decisions that have a tremendous effect on the life circumstance of thousands of people. These categories are not only political and legal but also discursive, shaping a view among UNHCR officials that refugees must, by definition, be powerless, and that as powerless actors they do not have to be consulted in decisions such as asylum and repatriation that will directly and dramatically affect them. Guy Gran similarly describes how the World Bank sets up criteria to define someone as a peasant in order to distinguish them from a farmer, day laborer, and other categories. The classification matters because only certain classes of people are recognized by the World Bank's development machinery as having knowledge that is relevant in solving development problems.[5] Categorization and classification are a ubiquitous feature of bureaucratization that has potentially important implications for those being classified. To classify is to engage in an act of power.

The fixing of meanings

IOs exercise power by virtue of their ability to fix meanings, which is related to classification. Naming or labeling the social context establishes the parameters, the very boundaries, of acceptable action. Because actors are oriented toward objects and objectives on the basis of the meaning that they have for them, being able to invest situations with a particular meaning constitutes an important source of power. IOs do not act alone in this regard, but their organizational resources contribute mightily to this end.

There is strong evidence of this power from development studies. Arturo Escobar explores how the institutionalization of the concept of "development" after World War II spawned a huge international apparatus and how this apparatus has now spread its tentacles in domestic and international politics through the discourse of development. The discourse of development, created and arbitrated in large part by IOs, determines not only what constitutes the activity (what development is) but also who (or what) is considered powerful and privileged, that is, who gets to do the developing (usually the state or IOs) and who is the object of development (local groups).

Similarly, the end of the Cold War encouraged a reexamination of the definition of security. IOs have been at the forefront of this debate, arguing that security pertains not only to states but also to individuals and that the threats to security may be economic, environmental, and political as well as military. In forwarding these alternative definitions of security, officials from various IOs are empowering a different set of actors and legitimating an alternative set of practices. Specifically, when security meant safety from invading national armies, it privileged state officials and invested power in military establishments. These alternative definitions of security shift attention away from states and toward the individuals who are frequently threatened by their own government, away from military practices and toward other features of social life that might represent a more immediate and daily danger to the lives of individuals.

One consequence of these redefined meanings of development and security is that they legitimate, and even require, increased levels of IO intervention in the domestic affairs of states – particularly Third World states. This is fairly obvious in the realm of development. The World Bank, the International Monetary Fund (IMF), and other development institutions have established a web of interventions that affect nearly every phase of the economy and polity in many Third World states. As "rural development," "basic human needs," and "structural adjustment" became incorporated into the meaning of development, IOs were permitted, even required, to become intimately involved in the domestic workings of developing polities by posting in-house "advisors" to run monetary policy, reorganizing the political economy of entire rural regions, regulating family and reproductive practices, and mediating between governments and their citizens in a variety of ways.

The consequences of redefining security may be similar. Democratization, human rights, and the environment have all now become tied to international peace and security, and IOs justify their interventions in member states on these grounds, particularly in developing states. For example, during the anti-apartheid struggle in South Africa, human rights abuses came to be classified as security threats by the UN Security Council and provided grounds for UN involvement there. Now, that linkage between human rights and security has become a staple of the post-Cold War environment. Widespread human rights abuses anywhere are now cause for UN intervention, and, conversely, the UN cannot carry out peacekeeping missions without promoting human rights. Similarly, environmental disasters in Eastern Europe and the newly independent states of the former Soviet Union and water rights allocations in the Middle East have also come to be discussed under the rubric of "environmental security" and are thus grounds for IO intervention. The United Nations Development Program argues that there is an important link between human security and sustainable development and implicitly argues for greater intervention in the management of environment as a means to promote human security.

Diffusion of norms

Having established rules and norms, IOs are eager to spread the benefits of their expertise and often act as conveyor belts for the transmission of norms and models of "good" political behavior. There is nothing accidental or unintended about this role. Officials in IOs often insist that part of their mission is to spread, inculcate, and enforce global values and norms. They are the "missionaries" of our time. Armed with a notion of progress, an idea of how to create the better life, and some understanding of the conversion process, many IO elites have as their stated purpose a desire to shape state practices by establishing, articulating, and transmitting norms that define what constitutes acceptable and legitimate state behavior. To be sure, their success depends on more than their persuasive capacities, for their rhetoric must be supported by power, sometimes (but not always) state power. But to overlook how state power and organizational missionaries work in tandem and the ways in which IO officials channel and shape states' exercise of power is to disregard a fundamental feature of value diffusion.

Consider decolonization as an example. The UN Charter announced an intent to universalize sovereignty as a constitutive principle of the society of states at a time when over half the globe was under some kind of colonial rule; it also established an institutional apparatus to achieve that end (most prominently the Trusteeship Council and the Special Committee on Colonialism). These actions had several consequences. One was to eliminate certain categories of acceptable action for powerful states. Those states that attempted to retain their colonial privileges were increasingly viewed as illegitimate by other states. Another consequence was to empower international bureaucrats (at the Trusteeship Council) to set norms and standards for "stateness." Finally, the UN helped to ensure that throughout decolonization the sovereignty of these new states was coupled with territorial inviolability. Colonial boundaries often divided ethnic and tribal groups, and the UN was quite concerned that in the process of "self-determination," these governments containing "multiple" or "partial" selves might attempt to create a whole personality through territorial adjustment – a fear shared by many of these newly decolonized states. The UN encouraged the acceptance of the norm of sovereignty-as-territorial-integrity through resolutions, monitoring devices, commissions, and one famous peacekeeping episode in Congo in the 1960s.

Note that, as with other IO powers, norm diffusion, too, has an expansionary dynamic. Developing states continue to be popular targets for norm diffusion by IOs, even after they are independent. The UN and the European Union are now actively involved in police training in non-Western states because they believe Western policing practices will be more conducive to democratization processes and the establishment of civil society. But having a professional police establishment assumes that there is a professional judiciary and penal system where criminals can be tried and jailed; and a professional judiciary, in turn, presupposes that there are lawyers that can come before the court. Trained lawyers presuppose a code of law. The result is a package of reforms sponsored by IOs aimed at transforming non-Western societies into Western societies. Again, while Western states are involved in these activities and therefore their values and interests are part of the reasons for this process, international bureaucrats involved in these activities may not see themselves as doing the bidding for these states but rather as expressing the interests and values of the bureaucracy.

Other examples of this kind of norm diffusion are not hard to find. The IMF and the World Bank are explicit about their role as transmitters of norms and principles from advanced market economies to less-developed economies. The IMF's Articles of Agreement specifically assign it this task of incorporating less-developed economies into the world economy, which turns out to mean teaching them how to "be" market economies. The World Bank, similarly, has a major role in arbitrating the meaning of development and norms of behavior appropriate to the task of developing oneself, as was discussed earlier. The end of the Cold War has opened up a whole new set of states to this kind of norm diffusion task for IOs. According to former Secretary of Defense William Perry, one of the functions of NATO expansion is to inculcate "modern" values and norms into the Eastern European countries and their militaries.[6] The European Bank for Reconstruction and Development has, as part of its mandate, the job of spreading democracy and private enterprise. The OSCE is striving to create a community based on shared values, among these respect for democracy and human rights. This linkage is also strong at the UN as evident in *The Agenda for Democratization* and *The Agenda for Peace*. Once democratization and human rights are tied to international peace and security, the distinctions between international and domestic governance become effectively erased and IOs have license to intervene almost anywhere in an authoritative and legitimate manner.

Realists and neoliberals may well look at these effects and argue that the classificatory schemes, meanings, and norms associated with IOs are mostly favored by strong states. Consequently, they would argue, the power we attribute to IOs is simply epiphenomenal of state power. This argument is certainly one theoretical possibility, but it is not the only one and must be tested against others. Our concern is that because these theories provide no ontological independence for IOs, they have no way to test for autonomy nor have they any theoretical cause or inclination to test for it since, by theoretical axiom, autonomy cannot exist. The one empirical domain in which the statist view has been explicitly challenged is the European Union, and empirical studies there have hardly produced obvious victory for the "intergovernmentalist" approach. Recent empirical studies in the areas of human rights, weapons taboos, and environmental practices also cast doubt on the statist approach by providing evidence about the ways in which nongovernmental and intergovernmental organizations successfully promote policies that are not (or not initially) supported by strong states. Certainly there are occasions when strong states do drive IO behavior, but there are also times when other forces are at work that eclipse or significantly dampen the effects of states on IOs. Which causal mechanisms produce which effects under which conditions is a set of relationships that can be understood only by intensive empirical study of how these organizations actually do their business – research that would trace the origins and evolution of IO policies, the processes by which they are implemented, discrepancies between implementation and policy, and overall effects of these policies.

Notes

1   H.H. Gerth and C. Wright Mills, *From Max Weber: Essays in Sociology* (Oxford University Press, New York, 1978), p. 299 (italics in original).
2   ibid., p. 199.
3   ibid., pp. 216, 250, 299.
4   Don Handelman, "Comment," *Current Anthropology*, vol. 36(2), pp. 280–81.
5   Guy Gran, "Beyond African Famines: Whose Knowledge Matters?," *Alternatives*, 11, pp. 275–96.
6   William Perry, "Defense in an Age of Hope," *Foreign Affairs*, vol. 75(6), 1996, pp. 64–79.

2.6 Transnational advocacy networks in international politics

Margaret E. Keck and Kathryn Sikkink

Source: *Activists beyond Borders: Transnational Advocacy Networks in International Politics* (Cornell University Press, Ithaca, NY, 1998), pp. 9–29.

Keck and Sikkink identify transnational advocacy networks, based on principled ideas and values, as a key feature of a world characterized by growing transnational relations. Such networks increase the access and the voice available to citizens in the international system, and can provide resources both in international and in domestic political processes. Because such networks blur the boundaries between domestic and international politics, they challenge practices of national sovereignty, and thus the centrality of state authorities in world politics.

[Keck and Sikkink begin by charting the growth of transnational advocacy networks, and their relationships to other social movements. They then move on to note their key features.]

What is a transnational advocacy network?

Networks are forms of organization characterized by voluntary, reciprocal, and horizontal patterns of communication and exchange. The organizational theorist Walter Powell calls them a third mode of economic organization, distinctly different from markets and hierarchy (the firm). "Networks are 'lighter on their feet' than hierarchy" and are "particularly apt for circumstances in which there is a need for efficient, reliable information," and "for the exchange of commodities whose value is not easily measured."[1] His insights about economic networks are extraordinarily suggestive for an understanding of political networks, which also form around issues where information plays a key role, and around issues where the value of the "commodity" is not easily measured.

In spite of the differences between domestic and international realms, the network concept travels well because it stresses fluid and open relations among committed and knowledgeable actors working in specialized issue areas. We call them advocacy networks because advocates plead the causes of others or defend a cause or proposition. Advocacy captures what is unique about these transnational networks: they are organized to promote causes, principled ideas, and norms, and they often involve individuals advocating policy changes that cannot be easily linked to a rationalist understanding of their "interests."

Some issue areas reproduce transnationally the webs of personal relationships that are crucial in the formation of domestic networks. Advocacy networks have been particularly important in value-laden debates over human rights, the environment, women, infant health, and indigenous peoples, where large numbers of differently situated individuals have become acquainted over a considerable period and developed similar world views. When the more visionary among them have proposed strategies for political action around apparently intractable problems, this potential has been transformed into an action network.

Major actors in advocacy networks may include the following: (1) international and domestic nongovernmental research and advocacy organizations; (2) local social movements; (3) foundations; (4) the media; (5) churches, trade unions, consumer organizations, and intellectuals; (6) parts of regional and international intergovernmental organizations; and (7) parts of the executive and/or parliamentary branches of governments. Not all these will be present in each advocacy network. Initial research suggests, however, that international and domestic NGOs play a central role in all advocacy networks, usually initiating actions and pressuring more powerful actors to take positions. NGOs introduce new ideas, provide information, and lobby for policy changes.

Groups in a network share values and frequently exchange information and services. The flow of information among actors in the network reveals a dense web of connections among these groups, both formal and informal. The movement of funds and services is especially notable between foundations and NGOs, and some NGOs provide services such as training for other NGOs in the same and sometimes other advocacy networks. Personnel also circulate within and among networks, as relevant players move from one to another in a version of the "revolving door."

Relationships among networks, both within and between issue areas, are similar to what scholars of social movements have found for domestic activism. Individuals and foundation funding have moved back and forth among them. Environmentalists and women's groups have looked at the history of human rights campaigns for models of effective international institution building. Refugee resettlement and indigenous people's rights are increasingly central components of international environmental activity, and vice versa; mainstream human rights organizations have joined the campaign for women's rights. Some activists consider themselves part of an "NGO community."

Besides sharing information, groups in networks create categories or frames within which to generate and organize information on which to base their campaigns. Their ability to generate information quickly and accurately, and deploy it effectively, is their most valuable currency; it is also central to their identity. Core campaign organizers must ensure that individuals and organizations with access to necessary information are incorporated into the network; different ways of framing an issue may require quite different kinds of information. Thus frame disputes can be a significant source of change within networks.

Why and how have transnational advocacy networks emerged?

Advocacy networks are not new. We can find examples as far back as the nineteenth-century campaign for the abolition of slavery. But their number, size, and professionalism, and the speed, density, and complexity of international linkages among them has grown dramatically in the last three decades. As Hugh Heclo remarks about domestic issue networks, "if the current situation is a mere outgrowth of old tendencies, it is so in the same sense that a 16-lane spaghetti interchange is the mere elaboration of a country crossroads."[2]

We cannot accurately count transnational advocacy networks to measure their growth over time, but one proxy is the increase in the number of international NGOs committed to social change. Because international NGOs are key components of any advocacy network, this increase suggests broader trends in the number, size, and density of advocacy networks generally. Table 1 suggests that the number of international nongovernmental social change groups has increased across all issues, though to varying degrees in different issue areas. There are five times as many organizations working primarily on human rights as there were in 1950, but proportionally human rights groups have remained roughly a quarter of all such groups. Similarly, groups working on women's rights accounted for 9 percent of all groups in 1953 and in 1993. Transnational environmental organizations have grown most dramatically in absolute and relative terms, increasing from two groups in 1953 to ninety in 1993, and from 1.8 percent of total groups in 1953 to 14.3 percent in 1993. [. . .]

International networking is costly. Geographic distance, the influence of nationalism, the multiplicity of languages and cultures, and the costs of fax, phone, mail, and air travel make the proliferation of international networks a puzzle that needs explanation. Under what conditions are networks possible and likely, and what triggers their emergence?

Transnational advocacy networks appear most likely to emerge around those issues where (1) channels between domestic groups and their governments are blocked or hampered or where such channels are ineffective for resolving a conflict, setting into motion the "boomerang" pattern of influence characteristic of these networks (see Figure 1); (2) activists or "political entrepreneurs" believe that networking will further their missions and campaigns, and actively promote networks; and (3) conferences and other forms of international contact create arenas for forming and strengthening networks. Where channels of participation are blocked, the international arena may be the only means that domestic activists have to gain attention to their issues. Boomerang strategies are most common in campaigns where the

Table 1 International nongovernmental social change organizations (categorized by the major issue focus of their work)

Issue area (N)	1953 (N=110)	1963 (N=141)	1973 (N=183)	1983 (N=348)	1993 (N=631)
Human rights	33	38	41	79	168
	30.0%	27.0%	22.4%	22.7%	26.6%
World order	8	4	12	31	48
	7.3	2.8	6.6	8.9	7.6
International law	14	19	25	26	26
	12.7	13.4	13.7	7.4	4.1
Peace	11	20	14	22	59
	10.0	14.2	7.7	6.3	9.4
Women's rights	10	14	16	25	61
	9.1	9.9	8.7	7.2	9.7
Environment	2	5	10	26	90
	1.8	3.5	5.5	7.5	14.3
Development	3	3	7	13	34
	2.7	2.1	3.8	3.7	5.4
Ethnic unity/Group rts.	10	12	18	37	29
	9.1	8.5	9.8	10.6	4.6
Esperanto	11	18	28	41	54
	10.0	12.8	15.3	11.8	8.6

Source: Union of International Associations, *Yearbook of International Organizations* (1953, 1963, 1973, 1983, 1993). We are indebted to Jackie Smith, University of Notre Dame, for the use of her data from 1983 and 1993, and the use of her coding form and codebook for our data collection for the period 1953–73.

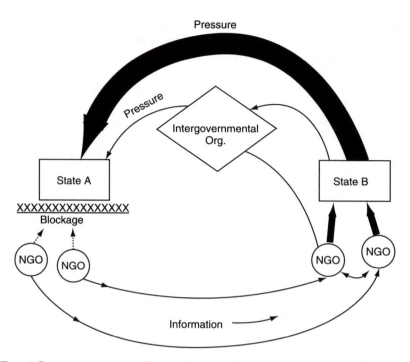

Figure 1 Boomerang pattern. State A blocks redress to organizations within it; they activate
network, whose members pressure their own states and (if relevant) a third-party
organization, which in turn pressure State A.

target is a state's domestic policies or behavior; where a campaign seeks broad procedural
change involving dispersed actors, strategies are more diffuse.

The boomerang pattern

It is no accident that so many advocacy networks address claims about rights in their
campaigns. Governments are the primary "guarantors" of rights, but also their primary
violators. When a government violates or refuses to recognize rights, individuals and domestic
groups often have no recourse within domestic political or judicial areanas. They may seek
international connections finally to express their concerns and even to protect their lives.

When channels between the state and its domestic actors are blocked, the boomerang
pattern of influence characteristic of transnational networks may occur: domestic NGOs
bypass their state and directly search out international allies to try to bring pressure on their
states from outside. This is most obviously the case in human rights campaigns. Similarly,
indigenous rights campaigns and environmental campaigns that support the demands of
local peoples for participation in development projects that would affect them frequently
involve this kind of triangulation. Linkages are important for both sides: for the less powerful
third world actors, networks provide access, leverage, and information (and often money)
they could not expect to have on their own; for northern groups, they make credible the
assertion that they are struggling with, and not only for, their southern partners. Not
surprisingly, such relationships can produce considerable tensions.

On other issues where governments are inaccessible or deaf to groups whose claims may nonetheless resonate elsewhere, international contacts can amplify the demands of domestic groups, pry open space for new issues, and then echo back these demands into the domestic arena. The cases of rubber tappers trying to stop encroachment by cattle ranchers in Brazil's western Amazon and of tribal populations threatened by the damming of the Narmada River in India are good examples of this.

Political entrepreneurs

Just as oppression and injustice do not themselves produce movements or revolutions, claims around issues amenable to international action do not produce transnational networks. Activists – "people who care enough about some issue that they are prepared to incur significant costs and act to achieve their goals"[3] – do. They create them when they believe that transnational networking will further their organizational missions – by sharing information, attaining greater visibility, gaining access to wider publics, multiplying channels of institutional access, and so forth. For example, in the campaign to stop the promotion of infant formula to poor women in developing countries, organizers settled on a boycott of Nestlé, the largest producer, as its main tactic. Because Nestlé was a transnational actor, activists believed a transnational network was necessary to bring pressure on corporations and governments. Over time, in such issue areas, participation in transnational networks has become an essential component of the collective identities of the activists involved, and networking a part of their common repertoire. The political entrepreneurs who become the core networkers for a new campaign have often gained experience in earlier ones.

The growth of international contact

Opportunities for network activities have increased over the last two decades. In addition to the efforts of pioneers, a proliferation of international organizations and conferences has provided foci for connections. Cheaper air travel and new electronic communication technologies speed information flows and simplify personal contact among activists.

Underlying these trends is a broader cultural shift. The new networks have depended on the creation of a new kind of global public (or civil society), which grew as a cultural legacy of the 1960s. Both the activism that swept Western Europe, the United States, and many parts of the third world during that decade, and the vastly increased opportunities for international contact, contributed to this shift. With a significant decline in air fares, foreign travel ceased to be the exclusive privilege of the wealthy. Students participated in exchange programs. The Peace Corps and lay missionary programs sent thousands of young people to live and work in the developing world. Political exiles from Latin America taught in U.S. and European universities. Churches opened their doors to refugees, and to new ideas and commitments.

Obviously, internationalism was not invented in the sixties. Religious and political traditions including missionary outreach, the solidarity traditions of labor and the left, and liberal internationalism have long stirred action by individuals or groups beyond the borders of their own state. While many activists working in advocacy networks come out of these traditions, they tend no longer to define themselves in terms of these traditions or the organizations that carried them. This is most true for activists on the left who suffered disillusionment from their groups' refusal to address seriously the concerns of women, the environment, or human rights violations in eastern bloc countries. Absent a range of options that in earlier decades would have competed for their commitments, advocacy and activism through either NGOs or grassroots movements became the most likely alternative for those seeking to "make a difference."

Although numerous solidarity committees and human rights groups campaigned against torture and disappearances under Latin American military regimes, even on behalf of the same individuals they employed different styles, strategies, and discourses, and understood their goals in the light of different principles. Solidarity organizations based their appeals on common ideological commitments – the notion that those being tortured or killed were defending a cause shared with the activists. Rights organizations, in principle, were committed to defending the rights of individuals regardless of their ideological affinity with the ideas of the victim. One exception to this ideal involved the use of violence. Amnesty International, for example, defended all prisoners against torture, summary execution, or the death penalty, but it would adopt as its more visible and symbolic "prisoners of conscience" only those individuals who had not advocated violence.

Although labor internationalism has survived the decline of the left, it is based mainly on large membership organizations representing (however imperfectly) bounded constituencies. Where advocacy networks have formed around labor issues, they have been transitory, responding to repression of domestic labor movements (as in labor support networks formed around Brazil, South Africa, and Central America in the early 1980s).

Advocacy networks in the north function in a cultural milieu of internationalism that is generally optimistic about the promise and possibilities of international networking. For network members in developing countries, however, justifying external intervention or pressure in domestic affairs is a much trickier business, except when lives are at stake. Linkages with northern networks require high levels of trust, as arguments justifying intervention on ethical grounds confront the ingrained nationalism common to many political groups in the developing world, as well as memories of colonial and neocolonial relations.

How do transnational advocacy networks work?

Transnational advocacy networks seek influence in many of the same ways that other political groups or social movements do. Since they are not powerful in a traditional sense of the word, they must use the power of their information, ideas, and strategies to alter the information and value contexts within which states make policies. The bulk of what networks do might be termed persuasion or socialization, but neither process is devoid of conflict. Persuasion and socialization often involve not just reasoning with opponents, but also bringing pressure, arm-twisting, encouraging sanctions, and shaming. [. . .]

Our typology of tactics that networks use in their efforts at persuasion, socialization, and pressure includes (1) *information politics*, or the ability to quickly and credibly generate politically usable information and move it to where it will have the most impact; (2) *symbolic politics*, or the ability to call upon symbols, actions, or stories that make sense of a situation for an audience that is frequently far away; (3) *leverage politics*, or the ability to call upon powerful actors to affect a situation where weaker members of a network are unlikely to have influence; and (4) *accountability politics*, or the effort to hold powerful actors to their previously stated policies or principles.

A single campaign may contain many of these elements simultaneously. For example, the human rights network disseminated information about human rights abuses in Argentina in the period 1976–83. The Mothers of the Plaza de Mayo marched in circles in the central square in Buenos Aires wearing white handkerchiefs to draw symbolic attention to the plight of their missing children. The network also tried to use both material and moral leverage against the Argentine regime, by pressuring the United States and other governments to cut off military and economic aid, and by efforts to get the UN and the Inter-American Commission on Human Rights to condemn Argentina's human rights practices. Monitoring is a variation on information politics, in which activists use information strategically to ensure accountability with public statements, existing legislation and international standards.

The construction of cognitive frames is an essential component of networks' political strategies. David Snow has called this strategic activity "frame alignment": "by rendering events or occurrences meaningful, frames function to organize experience and guide action, whether individual or collective."[4] "Frame resonance" concerns the relationship between a movement organization's interpretive work and its ability to influence broader public understandings. The latter involve both the frame's internal coherence and its experiential fit with a broader political culture.[5] In recent work, Snow and his colleagues and Sidney Tarrow, in turn, have given frame resonance a historical dimension by joining it to Tarrow's notion of protest cycles.[6] Struggles over meaning and the creation of new frames of meaning occur early in a protest cycle, but over time "a given collective action frame becomes part of the political culture – which is to say, part of the reservoir of symbols from which future movement entrepreneurs can choose."[7]

Network members actively seek ways to bring issues to the public agenda by framing them in innovative ways and by seeking hospitable venues. Sometimes they create issues by framing old problems in new ways; occasionally they help transform other actors' understandings of their identities and their interests. Land use rights in the Amazon, for example, took on an entirely different character and gained quite different allies viewed in a deforestation frame than they did in either social justice or regional development frames. In the 1970s and 1980s many states decided for the first time that promotion of human rights in other countries was a legitimate foreign policy goal and an authentic expression of national interest. This decision came in part from interaction with an emerging global human rights network. We argue that this represents not the victory of morality over self-interest, but a transformed understanding of national interest, possible in part because of structured interactions between state components and networks. This changed understanding cannot be derived solely from changing global and economic conditions, although these are relevant.

Transnational networks normally involve a small number of activists from the organizations and institutions involved in a given campaign or advocacy role. The kinds of pressure and agenda politics in which advocacy networks engage rarely involve mass mobilization, except at key moments, although the peoples whose cause they espouse may engage in mass protest (for example, those ousted from their land in the Narmada dam case). Boycott strategies are a partial exception. Instead of mass mobilization, network activists engage in what Baumgartner and Jones, borrowing from law, call "venue shopping," which relies "more on the dual strategy of the presentation of an image and the search for a more receptive political venue."[8] The recent coupling of indigenous rights and environmental issues is a good example of a strategic venue shift by indigenous activists, who found the environmental arena more receptive to their claims than human rights venues had been.

Information politics

Information binds network members together and is essential for network effectiveness. Many information exchanges are informal – telephone calls, E-mail and fax communications, and the circulation of newsletters, pamphlets and bulletins. They provide information that would not otherwise be available, from sources that might not otherwise be heard, and they must make this information comprehensible and useful to activists and publics who may be geographically and/or socially distant.

Nonstate actors gain influence by serving as alternate sources of information. Information flows in advocacy networks provide not only facts but testimony – stories told by people whose lives have been affected. Moreover, activists interpret facts and testimony, usually framing issues simply, in terms of right and wrong, because their purpose is to persuade people and stimulate them to act. How does this process of persuasion occur? An effective frame must show that a given state of affairs is neither natural nor accidental, identify the responsible party or parties, and propose credible solutions. These aims require clear, powerful messages that appeal to shared principles, which often have more impact on state policy than advice of technical experts. An important part of the political struggle over information is precisely whether an issue is defined primarily as technical – and thus subject to consideration by "qualified" experts – or as something that concerns a broader global constituency.

Even as we highlight the importance of testimony, however, we have to recognize the mediations involved. The process by which testimony is discovered and presented normally involves several layers of prior translation. Transnational actors may identify what kinds of testimony would be valuable, then ask an NGO in the area to seek out people who could tell those stories. They may filter the testimony through expatriates, through traveling scholars like ourselves, or through the media. There is frequently a huge gap between the story's original telling and the retellings – in its sociocultural context, its instrumental meaning, and even in its language. Local people, in other words, sometimes lose control over their stories in a transnational campaign. How this process of mediation/translation occurs is a particularly interesting facet of network politics.

Networks strive to uncover and investigate problems, and alert the press and policymakers. [. . .] To be credible, the information produced by networks must be reliable and well documented. To gain attention, the information must be timely and dramatic. Sometimes these multiple goals of information politics conflict, but both credibility and drama seem to be essential components of a strategy aimed at persuading publics and policymakers to change their minds.

The notion of "reporting facts" does not fully express the way networks strategically use information to frame issues. Networks call attention to issues, or even create issues by using language that dramatizes and draws attention to their concerns. A good example is the recent campaign against the practice of female genital mutilation. Before 1976 the widespread practice of female circumcision in many African and a few Asian and Middle Eastern countries was known outside these regions mainly among medical experts and anthropologists. A controversial campaign, initiated in 1974 by a network of women's and human rights organizations, began to draw wider attention to the issues by renaming the problem. Previously the practice was referred to by technically "neutral" terms such as female circumcision, clitoridectomy, or infibulation. The campaign around female genital "mutilation" raised its salience, literally creating the issue as a matter of public international concern. By renaming the practice the network broke the linkage with male circumcision (seen as a personal medical or cultural decision), implied a linkage with the more feared procedure of castration, and reframed the issue as one of violence against women. It thus resituated the practice as a human rights violation. The campaign generated action in many countries, including France and the United Kingdom, and the UN studied the problem and made a series of recommendations for eradicating certain traditional practices.

Uncertainty is one of the most frequently cited dimensions of environmental issues. Not only is hard information scarce (although this is changing), but any given data may be open to a variety of interpretations. The tropical forest issue is fraught with scientific uncertainty about the role of forests in climate regulation, their regenerative capacity, and the value of undiscovered or untapped biological resources. Environmentalists are unlikely to resolve these questions, and what they have done in some recent campaigns is reframe the issue, calling attention to the impact of deforestation on particular human populations. By doing so, they called for action independent of the scientific data. Human rights activists, baby food campaigners, and women's groups play similar roles, dramatizing the situations of the victims and turning the cold facts into human stories, intended to move people to action. [. . .]

Nongovernmental networks have helped legitimize the use of testimonial information along with technical and statistical information. Linkage of the two is crucial, for without the individual cases activists cannot motivate people to seek changed policies. Increasingly, international campaigns by networks take this two-level approach to information. In the 1980s even Greenpeace, which initially had eschewed rigorous research in favor of splashy media events, began to pay more attention to getting the facts right. Both technical information and dramatic testimony help to make the need for action more real for ordinary citizens.

A dense web of north–south exchange, aided by computer and fax communication, means that governments can no longer monopolize information flows as they could a mere half-decade ago. These technologies have had an enormous impact on moving information to and from third world countries, where mail service has often been slow and precarious; they also give special advantages of course, to organizations that have access to them. A good example of the new informational role of networks occurred when U.S. environmentalists pressured President George Bush to raise the issue of gold miners' ongoing invasions of the Yanomami indigenous reserve when Brazilian president Fernando Collor de Mello was in Washington in 1991. Collor believed that he had squelched protest over the Yanomami question by creating major media events out of the dynamiting of airstrips used by gold miners, but networks members had current information faxed from Brazil, and they countered his claims with evidence that miners had rebuilt the airstrips and were still invading the Yanomami area.

The central role of information in these issues helps explain the drive to create networks. Information in these issue areas is both essential and dispersed. Nongovernmental actors depend on their access to information to help make them legitimate players. Contact with like-minded groups at home and abroad provides access to information necessary to their work, broadens their legitimacy, and helps to mobilize information around particular policy targets. Most nongovernmental organizations cannot afford to maintain staff people in a variety of countries. In exceptional cases they send staff members on investigation missions, but this is not practical for keeping informed on routine developments. Forging links with local organizations allows groups to receive and monitor information from many countries at a low cost. Local groups, in turn, depend on international contacts to get their information out and to help protect them in their work.

The media is an essential partner in network information politics. To reach a broader audience, networks strive to attract press attention. Sympathetic journalists may become part of the network, but more often network activists cultivate a reputation for credibility with the press, and package their information in a timely and dramatic way to draw press attention.

Symbolic politics

Activists frame issues by identifying and providing convincing explanations for powerful symbolic events, which in turn become catalysts for the growth of networks. Symbolic interpretation is part of the process of persuasion by which networks create awareness and expand their constituencies. Awarding the 1992 Nobel Peace Prize to Maya activist Rigoberta Menchú and the UN's designation of 1993 as the Year of Indigenous Peoples heightened public awareness of the situation of indigenous peoples in the Americas. Indigenous people's use of 1992, the 500th anniversary of the voyage of Columbus to the Americas, to raise a host of issues well illustrates the use of symbolic events to reshape understandings.

The 1973 coup in Chile played this kind of catalytic role for the human rights community. Because Chile was the symbol of democracy in Latin America, the fact that such a brutal coup could happen there suggested that it could happen anywhere. For activists in the United States, the role of their government in undermining the Allende government intensified the need to take action. Often it is not one event but the juxtaposition of disparate events that makes people change their minds and act. For many people in the United States it was the juxtaposition of the coup in Chile, the war in Vietnam, Watergate, and the Civil Rights Movement that gave birth to the human rights movement. Likewise, dramatic footage of the Brazilian rainforest burning during the hot summer of 1988 in the United States may have convinced many people that global warming and tropical deforestation were serious and linked issues. The assassination of Brazilian rubber tapper leader Chico Mendes at the end of that year crystallized the belief that something was profoundly wrong in the Amazon.

Leverage politics

Activists in advocacy networks are concerned with political effectiveness. Their definition of effectiveness often includes some policy change by "target actors" such as governments, international financial institutions like the World Bank, or private actors like transnational corporations. In order to bring about policy change, networks need to pressure and persuade more powerful actors. To gain influence the networks seek leverage (the word appears often in the discourse of advocacy organizations) over more powerful actors. By leveraging more powerful institutions, weak groups gain influence far beyond their ability to influence state practices directly. The identification of material or moral leverage is a crucial strategic step in network campaigns.

Material leverage usually links the issue to money or goods (but potentially also to votes in international organizations, prestigious offices, or other benefits). The human rights issue became negotiable because governments or financial institutions connected human rights practices to military and economic aid, or to bilateral diplomatic relations. In the United States, human rights groups got leverage by providing policy-makers with informa-tion that convinced them to cut off military and economic aid. To make the issue negotiable, NGOs first had to raise its profile or salience, using information and symbolic politics. Then more powerful members of the network had to link cooperation to something else of value: money, trade, or prestige. Similarly, in the environmentalists' multilateral development bank campaign, linkage of environmental protection with access to loans was very powerful.

Although NGO influence often depends on securing powerful allies, their credibility still depends in part on their ability to mobilize their own members and affect public opinion via the media. In democracies the potential to influence votes gives large membership organizations an advantage over nonmembership organizations in lobbying for policy change; environmental organizations, several of whose memberships number in the millions, are more likely to have this added clout than are human rights organizations.

Moral leverage involves what some commentators have called the "mobilization of shame," where the behavior of target actors is held up to the light of international scrutiny. Network activists exert moral leverage on the assumption that governments value the good opinion of others; insofar as networks can demonstrate that a state is violating international obligations or is not living up to its own claims, they hope to jeopardize its credit enough to motivate a change in policy or behavior. The degree to which states are vulnerable to this kind of pressure varies, and will be discussed further below.

Accountability politics

Networks devote considerable energy to convincing governments and other actors to publicly change their positions on issues. This is often dismissed as inconsequential change, since talk is cheap and governments sometimes change discursive positions hoping to divert network and public attention. Network activists, however, try to make such statements into opportunities for accountability politics. Once a government has publicly committed itself to a principle – for example, in favor of human rights or democracy – networks can use those positions, and their command of information, to expose the distance between discourse and practice. This is embarrassing to many governments, which may try to save face by closing that distance.

Perhaps the best example of network accountability politics was the ability of the human rights network to use the human rights provisions of the 1975 Helsinki Accords to pressure the Soviet Union and the governments of Eastern Europe for change. The Helsinki Accords helped revive the human rights movement in the Soviet Union, spawned new organizations like the Moscow Helsinki Group and the Helsinki Watch Committee in the United States, and helped protect activists from repression. [. . .]

Domestic structures through which states and private actors can be held accountable to their pronouncements, to the law, or to contracts vary considerably from one nation to another, even among democracies. The centrality of the courts in U.S. politics creates a venue for the representation of diffuse interests that is not available in most European democracies. It also explains the large number of U.S. advocacy organizations that specialize in litigation. The existence of legal mechanisms does not necessarily make them feasible instruments, however; Brazil has had a diffuse interests law granting standing to environmental and consumer advocacy organizations since 1985, but the sluggishness of Brazil's judiciary makes it largely ineffective.

Under what conditions do advocacy networks have influence?

To assess the influence of advocacy networks we must look at goal achievement at several different levels. We identify the following types or stages of network influence: (1) issue creation and agenda setting; (2) influence on discursive positions of states and international organizations; (3) influence on institutional procedures; (4) influence on policy change in "target actors" which may be states, international organizations like the World Bank, or private actors like the Nestlé Corporation; and (5) influence on state behavior.

Networks generate attention to new issues and help set agendas when they provoke media attention, debates, hearings, and meetings on issues that previously had not been a matter of public debate. Because values are the essence of advocacy networks, this stage of influence may require a modification of the "value context" in which policy debates takes place. The UN's theme years and decades, such as International Women's Decade and the Year of Indigenous Peoples, were international events promoted by networks that heightened awareness of issues.

Networks influence discursive positions when they help persuade states and international organizations to support international declarations or to change stated domestic policy positions. The role environmental networks played in shaping state positions and conference declarations at the 1992 "Earth Summit" in Rio de Janeiro is an example of this kind of impact. They may also pressure states to make more binding commitments by signing conventions and codes of conduct.

The targets of network campaigns frequently respond to demands for policy change with changes in procedures (which may affect policies in the future). [. . .]

Procedural changes can greatly increase the opportunity for advocacy organizations to develop regular contact with other key players on an issue, and they sometimes offer the opportunity to move from outside to inside pressure strategies.

A network's activities may produce changes in policies, not only of the target states, but also of other states and/or international institutions. Explicit policy shifts seem to denote success, but even here both their causes and meanings may be elusive. We can point with some confidence to network impact where human rights network pressures have achieved cutoffs of military aid to repressive regimes, or a curtailment of repressive practices. Sometimes human rights activity even affects regime stability. But we must take care to distinguish between policy change and change in behavior; official policies regarding timber extraction in Sarawak, Malaysia, for example, may say little about how timber companies behave on the ground in the absence of enforcement.

We speak of stages of impact, and not merely types of impact, because we believe that increased attention, followed by changes in discursive positions, make governments more vulnerable to the claims that networks raise. (Discursive changes can also have a powerfully divisive effect on networks themselves, splitting insiders from outsiders, reformers from radicals. A government that claims to be protecting indigenous areas or ecological reserves is potentially more vulnerable to charges that such areas are endangered than one that makes no such claim. At that point the effort is not to make governments change their position but to hold them to their word. Meaningful policy change is thus more likely when the first three types or stages of impact have occurred.

Both issue characteristics and actor characteristics are important parts of our explanation of how networks affect political outcomes and the conditions under which networks can be effective. Issue characteristics such as salience and resonance within existing national or institutional agendas can tell us something about where networks are likely to be able to insert new ideas and discourses into policy debates. Success in influencing policy also depends on the strength and density of the network and its ability to achieve leverage. Although many issue and actor characteristics are relevant here, we stress issue resonance, network density, and target vulnerability.

Issue characteristics

Issues that involve ideas about right and wrong are amenable to advocacy networking because they arouse strong feelings, allow networks to recruit volunteers and activists, and infuse meaning into these volunteer activities. However, not all principled ideas lead to network formation, and some issues can be framed more easily than others so as to resonate with policymakers and publics. In particular, problems whose causes can be assigned to the deliberate (intentional) actions of identifiable individuals are amenable to advocacy network strategies in ways that problems whose causes are irredeemably structural are not. The real creativity of advocacy networks has been in finding intentionalist frames within which to address some elements of structural problems. Though the frame of violence against women does not exhaust the structural issue of patriarchy, it may transform some of patriarchy's effects into problems amenable to solution. Reframing land use and tenure conflict as environmental issues does not exhaust the problems of poverty and inequality, but it may improve the odds against solving part of them. Network actors argue that in such reframing they are weakening the structural apparatus of patriarchy, poverty, and inequality and empowering new actors to address these problems better in the future. Whether or not they are right, with the decline almost everywhere of mass parties of the left, few alternative agendas remain on the table within which these issues can be addressed.

As we look at the issues around which transnational advocacy networks have organized most effectively, we find two issue characteristics that appear most frequently: (1) issues involving bodily harm to vulnerable individuals, especially when there is a short and clear causal chain (or story) assigning responsibility; and (2) issues involving legal equality of opportunity. The first respond to a normative logic, and the second to a juridical and institutional one.

Issues involving physical harm to vulnerable or innocent individuals appear particularly compelling. Of course, what constitutes bodily harm and who is vulnerable or innocent may be highly contested. As the early failed campaign against female circumcision shows, one person's harm is another's rite of passage. Still, campaigns against practices involving bodily harm to populations perceived as vulnerable or innocent are most likely to be effective transnationally. Torture and disappearance have been more tractable than some other human rights issues, and protesting torture of political prisoners more effective than protesting torture of common criminals or capital punishment. Environmental campaigns that have had the greatest transnational effect have stressed the connection between protecting environments and protecting the often vulnerable people who live in them.

We also argue that in order to campaign on an issue it must be converted into a "causal story" that establishes who bears responsibility or guilt. But the causal chain needs to be sufficiently short and clear to make the case convincing. The responsibility of a torturer who places an electric prod to a prisoner's genitals is quite clear. Assigning blame to state leaders for the actions of soldiers or prison guards involves a longer causal chain, but accords with common notions of the principle of strict chain of command in military regimes.

Activists have been able to convince people that the World Bank bears responsibility for the human and environmental impact of projects it directly funds, but have had a harder time convincingly making the International Monetary Fund (IMF) responsible for hunger or food riots in the developing world. In the latter case the causal chain is longer, more complex, and much less visible, since neither the IMF nor governments reveal the exact content of negotiations.

An example from the Nestlé Boycott helps to illustrate the point about causal chains. The boycott was successful in ending direct advertising and promotion of infant formula to mothers because activists could establish that the corporation directly influenced decisions about infant feeding, with negative effects on infant health. But the boycott failed to prevent corporations from donating infant formula supplies to hospitals. Although this was the single most successful marketing tool of the corporation, the campaign's longer and more complex story about responsibility failed here because publics believe that doctors and hospitals buffer patients from corporate influence.

The second issue around which transnational campaigns appear to be effective is increased legal equality of opportunity (as distinguished from outcome). Our discussions of slavery and woman suffrage in Chapter 2 address this issue characteristic, as does one of the most successful transnational campaigns we don't discuss – the antiapartheid campaign. What made apartheid such a clear target was the legal denial of the most basic aspects of equality of opportunity. Places where racial stratification is almost as severe as it is in South Africa, but where such stratification is not legally mandated, such as Brazil and some U.S. cities, have not generated the same concern.

Actor characteristics

However amenable particular issues may be to strong transnational and transcultural messages, there must be actors capable of transmitting those messages and targets who are vulnerable to persuasion or leverage. Networks operate best when they are dense, with many actors, strong connections among groups in the network, and reliable information flows. (Density refers both to regularity and diffusion of information exchange within networks and to coverage of key areas.) Effective networks must involve reciprocal information exchanges, and include activists from target countries as well as those able to get institutional leverage. Measuring network density is problematic; sufficient densities are likely to be campaign-specific, and not only numbers of "nodes" in the network but also their quality – access to and ability to disseminate information, credibility with targets, ability to speak to and for other social networks – are all important aspects of density as well.

Target actors must be vulnerable either to material incentives or to sanctions from outside actors, or they must be sensitive to pressure because of gaps between stated commitments and practice. Vulnerability arises both from the availability of leverage and the target's sensitivity to leverage; if either is missing, a campaign may fail. Countries that are most susceptible to network pressures are those that aspire to belong to a normative community of nations. This desire implies a view of state preferences that recognizes states' interactions as a social – and socializing – process. Thus moral leverage may be especially relevant where states are actively trying to raise their status in the international system. Brazilian governments since 1988, for example, have been very concerned about the impact of the Amazon issue on Brazil's international image. President José Sarney's invitation to hold the 1992 United Nations Conference on Environment and Development in Brazil was an attempt to improve that image. Similarly, the concern of recent Mexican administrations with Mexico's international prestige has made it more vulnerable to pressure from the human rights network. In the baby food campaign, network activists used moral leverage to convince states to vote in favor of the WHO/UNICEF codes of conduct. As a result, even the Netherlands and Switzerland, both major exporters of infant formula, voted in favor of the code.

[Keck and Sikkink go on to relate transnational advocacy networks to the growth of debates about globalization and 'global civil society', and to the generation of transnational norms and principles.]

Notes

1 Walter W. Powell, "Neither Market Nor Hierarchy: Network Forms of Organization," *Research in Organizational Behavior* 12, 1990, pp. 295–96, 303–4.
2 Hugh Heclo, "Issue Networks and the Executive Establishment," in Anthony King (ed.), *The New American Political System* (American Enterprise Institute, Washington, DC, 1978), p. 97.
3 Pamela E. Oliver and Gerald Maxwell, "Mobilizing Technologies for Collective Action," in Aldon D. Morris and Carol McClurg Mueller (eds.), *Frontiers in Social Movement Theory* (Yale University Press, New Haven, 1992), p. 252.
4 David A. Snow et al., "Frame Alignment Processes, Micromobilization, and Movement Participation," *American Sociological Review* 51, 1986, p. 464.
5 David A. Snow and Robert D. Benford, "Ideology, Frame Resonance, and Participant Mobilization," in Bert Klandemans, Hanspeter Kriesi, and Sidney Tarrow (eds), *From Structure to Action: Comparing Social Movement Research Across Cultures* (JAI Press, Greenwich, CT, 1998), pp. 197–217.
6 David A. Snow and Robert D. Benford, "Master Frames and Cycles of Protest," in *Frontiers in Social Movement Theory* (Note 3), pp. 133–55.
7 Sidney Tarrow, 'Mentalities, Political Cultures, and Collective Action Frames: Constructing Meanings Through Action', in *Frontiers in Social Movement Theory* (Note 3), p. 184.
8 Frank Baumgartner and Bryan Jones, "Agenda Dynamics and Policy Subsystems," *Journal of Politics* vol. 53(4), 1991, p. 1050.

2.7 Power, interdependence and the information age

Robert O. Keohane and Joseph S. Nye, Jr

Source: *Power and Interdependence*, 3rd ed. (Little, Brown, Boston, 2001), pp. 215–27.

Keohane and Nye focus on key dimensions of change in world politics, especially the impact of new technologies. In particular, they note the effects of the 'information revolution' and the ways in which they change the roles of states in a world of 'complex interdependence'. The argue that the 'information revolution' has changed the nature of interdependence and the roles of states, and that it has created a new 'politics of credibility' based on the capacity of international actors to get their message(s) across in the global arena.

[Keohane and Nye begin by considering past predictions about the impact of new technologies on world politics, and point to the inherently global nature of the new information technologies.]

The information revolution and complex interdependence

By "information revolution," we refer to the rapid technological advances in computers, communications, and software that have led to dramatic decreases in the cost of processing and transmitting information. The price of a new computer has dropped by 19 percent per year since 1954, and information technologies have risen from 7 to about 50 percent of new investment. "Moore's Law," which has held for three decades, describes a doubling in the capacity of chips every eighteen months. Similarly, growth of the Internet and the World Wide Web has been exponential. The Internet was only opened to the public in 1990. Communications bandwidths are expanding rapidly, and communications costs continue to fall. As with steam at the end of the eighteenth century and electricity at the end of the nineteenth, there have been lags in productivity growth as society learns to utilize the new technologies. Although many industries and firms have been undergoing rapid structural changes since the 1980s, the economic transformation is far from complete. It is generally agreed that we are still in the early stages of the information revolution.

For our purposes, the distinguishing mark of the information revolution is the enormous reduction in the cost of transmitting information. For all practical purposes, the actual transmission costs have become negligible; hence the amount of information that can be transmitted is effectively infinite – as the proliferation of "spam" on the Internet suggests. Furthermore, neither costs nor the time taken to transmit messages are significantly related to distance. An Internet message to a colleague a few miles away may be routed through thousands of miles of computer networks; but neither the sender nor the recipient knows nor cares.

However, the information revolution has not transformed world politics to a new politics of complete complex interdependence. One reason is that information does not flow in a vacuum, but in political space that is already occupied. States have for the last four centuries established the political structure within which information flows across borders and other transactions take place.

The information revolution itself can only be understood within the context of the globalization of the world economy. [. . .] Globalization was deliberately fostered by United States policy, and by international institutions, for half a century after the end of World War II. In the late 1940s the United States sought to create an open international economy to forestall another depression and contain communism. The resulting international institutions, formed on the basis of multilateral principles, fostered an environment that put a premium on information and were themselves affected by developments in the technologies of transportation and communications. It became increasingly costly for states to turn away from the patterns of interdependence that had been created.

The information revolution occurred not merely within a preexisting political context, but within one characterized by continuing military tensions and conflicts. Although the end of the Cold War removed one set of military-related tensions, it left some in place (as in the Middle East), and created situations of state-breaking and state-making in which violence was used ruthlessly to attain political ends – notably in Africa, the Caucasus, central Asia, and southeastern Europe. Even in East Asia, the scene until recently of rapid economic growth, political-military rivalries persist. At the same time, the military presence of the United States plays a clearly stabilizing role in East Asia, Central Europe, and – tenuously – the Balkans. Contrary to some early predictions after the end of the Cold War, NATO remained popular in Western and Central Europe. Markets thrive only with secure property rights, which depend on a political framework – which in turn requires military security.

Outside the democratic zone of peace, the world of states is not a world of complex interdependence: in many areas, realist assumptions about the role of military force and the hierarchy of issues remain valid. However, where the information revolution has had the most pronounced impact relates to the third assumption, about multiple channels of contact among societies. Here is the real change. We see an order of magnitude shift as a result of the information revolution. Now anyone with a computer is a desktop publisher, and anyone with a modem can communicate with distant parts of the globe at trivial costs. Barriers to entry into the world "information market" have been dramatically lowered.

Earlier transnational flows were heavily controlled by large bureaucratic organizations like multinational corporations or the Catholic Church, with the resources to establish a communication infrastructure. Such organizations remain important, but the vast cheapening of information transmission has now opened the field to loosely structured network organizations, and even individuals. These nongovernmental organizations and networks are particularly effective in penetrating states without regard to borders and using domestic constituencies for agenda setting. By vastly increasing the number of channels of contact among societies, the information revolution is changing the extent to which politics is approximating our model of complex interdependence.

However, information is not like goods or pollution, for which quantities flowing across borders are meaningful. The quantity of information available in cyber-space means little by itself. Philosophers could debate whether a Web page that no one ever looks at really exists; political scientists know that it would not be meaningful. As many observers have pointed out, the information revolution has made attention the scarce resource. We used to ask: who has the capacity to transmit information? That question has become trivial, since the answer is: everyone with an Internet hookup. We now must ask: who has the capacity to attract others' attention to the information that he or she transmits? Getting others' attention is a necessary condition for using information as a political resource.

To focus only on the quantity of information, and on attention, would be to overlook the issue of information quality and distinctions among types of information. Information does not just exist; it is created. We therefore need to pay attention, as economists do, to incentives to create information. When we do so, we discover that each of three different types of information tends to generate a different type of politics:

1   *Free information.* This is information that actors are willing to acquire and send without financial compensation. The sender gets advantages from the receiver believing the information, and hence has incentives to produce it. Scientific information falls into this category. So do persuasive messages, such as those in which politicians specialize.

2   *Commercial information.* This is information that actors are willing to acquire and send at a price. Actors neither gain nor lose by others' believing in the information, apart from the compensation they receive. For such information to be available on the Internet, issues of property rights must be resolved, so that producers of information can be compensated for it by users. Creating commercial information before one's competitors can – if there is an effective system to protect intellectual property rights – creates first-mover advantages and enormous profits, as the history of Microsoft demonstrates.

3   *Strategic information.* This is information that confers the greatest advantage on actors only if their competitors do not possess it. One way to think of strategic information is that it constitutes asymmetrical knowledge of a competitor's strategy so that the outcome of a game is altered. There is nothing new about strategic information: it is as old as espionage. One of the enormous advantages possessed by the United States in World War II was that the United States had broken the Japanese codes, but the Japanese were not aware of this fact. The capacity to transmit large quantities of strategic information may not be particularly important. For example, the strategic information available to the United States about the weapons programs of North Korea, Pakistan, or Iraq may depend more on having reliable spies (even if their messages had to be sent concealed in a traveler's shoe) than on the existence of the Internet.

With respect to free information, creators of information benefit from others believing in the information they possess. With respect to commercial information, information-creators benefit if compensated. But with respect to strategic information, information-creators only benefit if their possession of the information is not known to others.

The information revolution alters patterns of complex interdependence by exponentially increasing the number of channels of communication in world politics – among individuals in networks, not just among individuals within bureaucracies. But it appears within the context of an existing political structure, and its effects on the flows of different types of information are highly variable. Free information will flow in the absence of regulation. Strategic information will be protected as much as possible – for example, by encryption technologies. The flow of commercial information will depend on whether effective rules are established for cyberspace – by governments, business, or nongovernmental organizations – which protect property rights. Politics will affect the direction of the information revolution as much as vice versa.

Information and power

Knowledge is power: but what is power? A basic distinction can be made between behavioral power – the ability to obtain outcomes you want – and resource power – the possession of the resources that are usually associated with the ability to get the outcomes you want. Behavioral power, in turn, can be divided into hard and soft power. Hard power is the ability to get others to do what they otherwise would not do through threat of punishment or promise of reward. Whether by economic carrots or military sticks, the ability to coax or coerce has long been the central element of power. [. . .] asymmetrical interdependence is an important source of hard power. The ability of the less vulnerable to manipulate or escape the constraints of an interdependent relationship at low cost is an important source of power. In the context of hard power, asymmetries of information can greatly strengthen the hand of the less vulnerable party.

Soft power, on the other hand, is the ability to get desired outcomes because others want what you want; it is the ability to achieve desired outcomes through attraction rather than coercion. It works by convincing others to follow or getting them to agree to norms and institutions that produce the desired behavior. Soft power can rest on the appeal of one's ideas or culture or the ability to set the agenda through standards and institutions that shape the preferences of others. It depends largely on the persuasiveness of the free information that an actor seeks to transmit. If a state can make its power legitimate in the eyes of others and establish international institutions that encourage others to define their interests in compatible ways, it may not need to expend as many of its costly traditional economic or military resources.

Hard and soft power are related, but they are not the same. Samuel P. Huntington is correct when he says that material success makes a culture and ideology attractive, and decreases in economic and military success lead to self-doubt and crises of identity.[1] He is wrong when he argues that soft power is power only when it rests on a foundation of hard power. The soft power of the Vatican did not wane as the size of the papal states diminished. Canada, Sweden, and the Netherlands tend to have more influence than some other states with equivalent economic or military capability. The Soviet Union had considerable soft power in Europe after World War II but squandered it with the invasions of Hungary and Czechoslovakia even at a time when Soviet economic and military power were continuing to grow. Soft power varies over time and different domains. America's popular culture, with its libertarian and egalitarian currents, dominates film, television, and electronic communications in the world today. However, not all aspects of that culture are attractive to all others, for example conservative Moslems. In that domain, American soft power is limited. Nonetheless, the spread of information and American popular culture has generally increased global awareness of and openness to American ideas and values. To some extent this reflects deliberate policies, but more often soft power is an inadvertent by-product. For example, companies all over the world voluntarily subject themselves to the financial disclosure standards of the U.S. Securities and Exchange Commission because of the importance of American capital markets.

The information revolution is also affecting power measured in terms of resources rather than behavior. In the eighteenth century European balance of power, territory, population, and agriculture provided the basis for infantry, which was a crucial power resource, and France was a principal beneficiary. In the nineteenth century, industrial capacity provided the crucial resources that enabled Britain and, later, Germany to gain dominance. By the mid-twentieth century, science and particularly nuclear physics contributed crucial power resources to the United States and the Soviet Union. In this century, information capability broadly defined is likely to be the most crucial power resource. [. . .]

The new conventional wisdom is that the information revolution has a decentralizing and leveling effect. As it reduces costs, economies of scale, and barriers of entry to markets, it should reduce the power of large states and enhance the power of small states and nonstate actors. In practice, however, international relations are more complex than the technological determinism of the new conventional wisdom suggests. Some aspects of the information revolution help the small, but some help the already large and powerful. There are several reasons why. First, important barriers to entry and economies of scale remain in some aspects of power that are related to information. For example, soft power is strongly affected by the cultural content of what is broadcast or appears in movies and television programs. Large, established entertainment industries often enjoy considerable economies of scale in content production and distribution. The dominant American market share in films and television programs in world markets is a case in point.

Second, even where it is now cheap to disseminate existing information, the collection and production of new information often requires major costly investments. In many competitive situations, it is the newness of information at the margin that counts more than the average cost of all information. Intelligence collection is a good example. States like America, Britain, and France have capabilities for collection and production that dwarf those of other nations. In some commercial situations, a fast follower can do better than a first mover, but in terms of power among states, it is usually better to be a first mover than a fast follower.

Third, first movers are often the creators of the standards and architecture of information systems. The path dependent development of such systems reflects the advantage of the first mover. The use of the English language and the pattern of top-level domain names on the Internet provide relevant examples. Partly because of the transformation of the American economy in the 1980s (which was missed or misunderstood by the prophets of decline) and partly because of large investments driven by the Cold War military competition, the United States was often the first mover and still enjoys a lead in the application of a wide variety of information technologies.

Fourth, military power remains important in some critical domains of international relations. Information technology has some effects on the use of force that benefit the small and some that favor the already powerful. The off-the-shelf commercial availability of what used to be costly military technologies benefits small states and nonstate actors and contributes to the vulnerability of large states. Information systems add lucrative targets for terrorist (including state-sponsored) groups. Other trends, however, strengthen the already powerful. Many military analysts refer to a "revolution in military affairs" that has been produced by the application of information technology. Space-based sensors, direct broadcasting, high-speed computers, and complex software provide the ability to gather, sort, process, transfer, and disseminate information about highly complex events that occur in wide geographic areas. [. . .]

Contrary to the expectations of some theorists, the information revolution has not greatly decentralized or equalized power among states. If anything, thus far it has had the opposite effect. Table 1 summarizes the effects of the information revolution on power.

The paradox of plenty and the politics of credibility

A plenitude of information leads to a poverty of attention. Attention becomes the scarce resource, and those who can distinguish valuable signals from white noise gain power. Editors,

Table 1 Effects of information technology on power

	Hard power	Soft power

Benefit to large actors	Revolution in military affairs
	First mover and architecture
	Technical intelligence collection
		Economies of scale in content
		   production
		Attention scarcity and
		   marketing power

Benefit to small actors	Commercial availability
	Infrastructure vulnerability
	Markets and economic intelligence
		NGOs and cheap interactive
		   communication
		Narrowcasting and new virtual
		   communities

filters, and cue-givers become more in demand, and this is a source of power. There will be an imperfect market for evaluators. Brand names and the ability to bestow an international seal of approval will become more important.

But power does not necessarily flow to those who can withhold information. As George Akerlof has argued, under some circumstances private information can cripple the credibility of those who have it.[2] For instance, sellers of used cars have more knowledge about their defects than potential buyers. But an awareness of this situation and the fact that owners of bad cars are more likely to sell than owners of good ones lead potential buyers to discount the price they are willing to pay in order to adjust for unknown defects. Hence the result of the superior information of sellers is not to improve the mean price they receive, but instead to make them unable to sell good used cars for their real value. Unlike asymmetrical interdependence in trade, where power goes to those who can afford to hold back or break trade ties, information power flows to those who can edit and credibly validate information to sort out what is both correct and important.

Hence among editors and cue-givers, credibility is the crucial resource, and asymmetrical credibility is a key source of power. Reputation has always mattered in world politics, and it becomes even more important because of the "paradox of plenty." The low cost of transmitting data means that the ability to transmit it is much less important as a power resource than it used to be, but the ability to filter information is more so. Political struggles focus less on control over the ability to transmit information than over the creation and destruction of credibility.

One implication of the abundance of information sources, and the role of credibility, is that soft power is likely to become less a function simply of material resources than in the past. When ability to produce and disseminate information is the scarce resource, limiting factors include the control of printing presses, radio stations, and newsprint. Hard power, for instance using force to take over a radio station, can generate soft power. In the case of worldwide television, wealth can also lead to soft power. For instance, CNN was based in Atlanta rather than Amman or Cairo because of America's leading position in the industry. When Iraq invaded Kuwait in 1990, the fact that CNN was basically an American company helped to frame the issue, worldwide, as aggression (analogous to Hitler's actions in the 1930s) rather than as a justified attempt to reverse colonial humiliation (analogous to India's capture of Goa). [. . .]

Broadcasting has long had an impact on public opinion. By focusing on some conflicts and human rights problems, broadcasters have pressed politicians to respond to some foreign conflicts rather than others – e.g., Somalia rather than Southern Sudan. Not surprisingly, governments have sought to influence, manipulate, and control television and radio stations and have been able to do so with considerable success, since a relatively small number of physically located broadcasting sites were used to reach many people with the same message. However, the shift from broadcasting to narrowcasting has major political implications. Cable and the Internet enable senders to segment and target audiences. Even more important for politics is the interactive role of the Internet; it not only focuses attention but facilitates coordination of action across borders. Interactivity at low cost allows for the development of new virtual communities: people who imagine themselves as part of a single group regardless of how far apart they are physically from one another.

These new technologies create opportunities for nongovernmental actors. Advocacy networks find their potential impact vastly expanded by the information revolution, since the fax machine and the Internet enable them to send messages from the most obscure corners of the world: from the oil platforms of the North Sea to the forests of Chiapas. The 1997 Landmine Conference was a coalition of network organizations working with middle power governments like Canada and some individual politicians and celebrities to capture attention and set the agenda. The role of NGOs was also important as a channel of communication across delegations in the global warming discussions. Environmental groups and industry competed in Kyoto in 1997 for the attention of the media from major countries, basing their arguments in part on the findings of nongovernmental scientists. Many observers have heralded a new era for NGOs as a result of the information revolution, and there seems little doubt that substantial opportunities exist for a flowering of issue advocacy networks and virtual communities.

Yet the credibility of these networks is fragile. Greenpeace, for instance, imposed large costs on Royal Dutch Shell by criticizing Shell's planned disposal of its Brentspar drilling rig. Greenpeace, however, itself lost credibility and membership when it later had to admit the inaccuracy of some of its factual claims. The findings of atmospheric scientists about climate change have gained credibility, not just from the prestige of science but from the procedures developed in the Intergovernmental Panel on Climate Change (IPCC) for extensive and careful peer review of scientific papers and intergovernmental review of executive summaries. The IPCC is an example of an intergovernmental information-legitimating institution, whose major function is to give coherence and credibility to masses of scientific information about climate change.

As the IPCC example shows, the importance of credibility is giving increasing importance to what Peter Haas has called "epistemic communities": transnational networks of like-minded experts.[3] By framing issues where knowledge is important, epistemic communities become important actors in forming coalitions and in bargaining processes. By creating knowledge, they can provide the basis for effective cooperation. But to be effective, the procedures by which this information is produced have to appear unbiased. It is increasingly recognized that scientific information is socially constructed; to be credible, the information has to be produced through a process that is dominated by professional norms and that appears transparent and procedurally fair. Even if their information is credible, professional communities will not resolve contentious issues that involve major distributional costs. But they will become more significant actors in the politics of decision.

The politics of soft power do not depend only on the "information shapers," who seek to persuade others to adopt their practices and values. They also depend on the characteristics of their targets: the "information takers," or the targets of information flows. Of course, the shapers and takers are often the same people, organizations, or countries, in different capacities. Information shapers, as we have seen, require credibility. The takers, on the other hand, will be differentially receptive depending on the character, and internal legitimacy, of their own institutions. Self-confident information takers with internal legitimacy can absorb flows of information more readily, with less disturbance, than can institutions (governmental or nongovernmental) lacking such legitimacy and self-confidence.

Not all democracies are leaders in the information revolution, but, as far as countries are concerned, all information shapers are democracies. This is not accidental. Their societies are familiar with free exchange of information and their institutions of governance are not threatened by it. They can shape information because they can also take it. Authoritarian states, typically among the laggards, have more trouble. At this point, governments such as China's can control the access of their citizens to the Internet by controlling Internet service providers. It is possible, but costly, to route around such restrictions, and control does not have to be complete to be effective for political purposes. But as societies like Singapore reach levels of development where their knowledge workers want free access to the Net, they run the risk of losing their scarcest resource for competing in the information economy. Thus Singapore is wrestling with the dilemma of reshaping its educational system to encourage the individual creativity that the information economy will demand, and at the same time maintain existing social controls over the flow of information. Singapore's leaders realize they cannot hope to control the Internet in the long run. Closed systems become more costly.

One reason that closed systems become more costly is that it is risky for foreigners to invest funds in a country where the key decisions are made in an opaque fashion. Transparency is becoming a key asset for countries seeking investments. The ability to keep information from leaving, which once seemed valuable to authoritarian states, undermines the credibility and transparency necessary to attract investment on globally competitive terms. This point is illustrated by the 1997 Asian financial crisis. Governments that are not transparent are not credible, since the information they offer is seen as biased and selective. Moreover, as economic development progresses and middle-class societies develop, repressive measures become more expensive not merely at home, but also in terms of international reputation. Both Taiwan and South Korea discovered in the late 1980s that repression of rising demands for democracy would be expensive in terms of their reputation and soft power. By having begun to democratize earlier, they have strengthened their capacity – as compared with, for instance, Indonesia – to cope with economic crisis.

Whatever the future effects of interactivity and virtual communities, one political effect of increased free information flows through multiple channels is already clear: states have lost much of their control over information about their own societies. States that seek to develop (with the exception of some energy suppliers) need foreign capital and the technology and organization that go with it. Geographical communities still matter most, but governments that want to see rapid development will find that they will have to give up some of the barriers to information flows that protected officials from outside scrutiny. No longer will governments that want high levels of development be able to afford the comfort of keeping their financial and political situations inside a black box. The motto of the global information society might become, "If you can't take it, you can't shape it."

From a business standpoint, the information revolution has vastly increased the marketability and value of commercial information, by reducing costs of transmission and the transaction costs of charging information users. Politically, however, the most important shift concerns free information. The ability to disseminate free information increases the potential for persuasion in world politics – as long as credibility can be attained and maintained. NGOs and other states can more readily influence the beliefs of people within other jurisdictions. If one actor can persuade others to adopt similar values and policies, whether it possesses hard power and strategic information may become relatively less important. Soft power and free information can, if sufficiently persuasive, change perceptions of self-interest, and therefore how hard power and strategic information are used. If governments or NGOs are to take advantage of the information revolution, they will have to establish reputations for credibility in the world of white noise that constitutes the information revolution.

In conclusion, the new conventional wisdom is wrong in its predictions of an equalizing effect of the information and communications revolutions in the distributions of power among states. In part, this is because economies of scale and barriers to entry persist in regard to strategic information, and in part because with respect to free information, the larger states will often be well-placed in the competition for credibility. On the other hand, the information revolution is altering the degree of control that all states can exert in today's world. Cheap flows of information have created an order-of-magnitude change in channels of information. Nongovernmental actors operating transnationally have much greater opportunities to organize and to propagate their views. States are more easily penetrated and less like black boxes. The coherence and elite maintenance of hierarchical ordering of foreign policy issues is diminished.

The net effect of the information revolution is to change political processes in a way where soft power becomes more important in relation to hard power than it was in the past. Credibility becomes a key power resource both for governments and NGOs, giving more open, transparent organizations an advantage with respect to free information. Although the coherence of government policies may diminish in more pluralistic and penetrated states, those same countries may be better placed in terms of credibility and soft power. And among many states, political processes will come to more closely approximate the ideal type of complex inter-dependence. Geographically based states will continue to structure politics in an information age, but they will rely less on material resources than in the past, and more on their ability to remain credible in a world awash with information.

Notes

1   S. Huntington, *The Clash of Civilizations and the Remaking of World Order* (Simon and Schuster, New York, 1996).
2   G. Akerlof, "The Market for Lemons," *Quarterly Journal of Economics*, August 1970, pp. 488–500.
3   P. Haas, "Epistemic Communities and International Policy Coordination," *International Organization*, Winter 1992, pp. 1–36.

2.8 Globalization and the evolution of rules

Wayne Sandholtz

Source: Aseem Prakash and Jeffrey A. Hart (eds), *Globalization and Governance* (Routledge, London, 1999), pp. 77–102.

Sandholtz argues that international relations constitute a social system, defined by rules and institutions. Processes of globalization create a demand for new rules to govern new relationships of communication and exchange. These new rules are typically developments of existing rules, and they function to shape not only material exchanges but also normative discourses. This extract focuses on the ways in which such rules emerge and are sustained in a variety of contexts.

[Sandholtz begins by outlining his approach to international institutions and rules, contrasting it with purely materialistic approaches based on transaction costs and state-to-state bargaining. He then goes on to develop his arguments about the emergence of rules and institutions.]

Rules, interests, and choice

As a point of departure, I broadly accept the basic constructivist premise that social structures and agents constitute each other, and Onuf's proposition that rules are what link social structures and individual actors.[1] Any kind of sustained interaction leads to the development of rules that define roles and assign rights and responsibilities to them. I define rules as statements that identify standards of conduct for given sets of actors in given situations. As such, rules are the substance of institutions, and institutions are at the heart of governance.

Rules cause behaviors both directly and indirectly. They produce behavior directly by constraining actor choices. Rules prescribe who can act, how, and when. In formal organizations, the rules are usually supported by penalties or coercive authorities. Rules cause behavior indirectly in two ways. First, they define roles and identities – the "self" in "self-interest." Second, they provide reasons for acting in one way rather than another. That is, when confronted with alternative courses of action, an actor weighs the various rules that are implicated by the situation and chooses according to which rules provide the most persuasive reasons.

The argument so far does not banish self-interested behavior from the social universe. Actors have goals, and prefer to be better off. But what it means to be "better off" depends crucially on one's roles, which are rooted in social contexts, defined by rules. Rules, in other words, are logically prior to self-interest. Rules thus establish the horizons for what people can imagine as their interests and objectives; rules also delineate the range of legitimate means for achieving those ends. People with genuinely autonomous utility functions and those who ignore shared notions of acceptable means are either hermits or psychopaths.

Finally, rules vary in numerous ways, but two key axes of variation for my purposes are along the formal-informal dimension and the specific-general dimension. Formal rules are codified in writing according to institutionalized procedures. Treaties, charters, and constitutions all contain formal rules. Informal rules are shared understandings, nowhere codified, about what constitutes warranted conduct. Informal rules include the non-use of mercenaries and, for a long period of time, the norm that treaties should be observed (which was informal until codified in the Vienna Convention). On the specific-general dimension, the most general rules are those that constitute the actors, that is, that define roles (what is a state) or membership (who can join the United Nations). General rules can embrace broad categories of behavior ("States should promote free trade"). In contrast, the most specific rules concern particular, narrowly defined acts (as proscriptions, prescriptions, or permissions), like: "Do not conduct nuclear tests in the open atmosphere."

Rules and institutions

Rules do not stand alone; they are linked in clusters, or in other words, institutions. In fact, I define institutions as rule structures. Ronald Jepperson similarly defines institutions as socially constructed "program or rule systems."[2] Organizations are a subset of institutions. Organizations comprise clusters of rules, but they are also composed of people. An organization has members, an institution does not (despite common usage). Though some international organizations (IOs) may serve largely as passive bargaining forums, others are purposive, problem-solving entities. For instance, international organizations like the World Health Organization and the International Whaling Commission exist to solve jointly identified problems. They may, by the way, be the sites of extensive interstate bargaining and they may even enhance the efficiency of that bargaining. But the organizations exist to solve common problems, and bargaining is simply part of the process by which IOs work (not necessarily their *raison d'être*).

Some international organizations provide what Onuf calls "institutional supports" for their rules (I will use the term "organizational supports" but the idea is the same)[3] At the heart of organizational supports are specific kinds of rules. First, organizational supports generally include secondary rules that specify how legitimate behavioral rules are to be produced and applied. Second, organizational supports include formally constituted roles whose inhabitants are authorized (the rules assign rights and duties) to monitor compliance, interpret the rules in specific cases, resolve disputes, impose sanctions on violators, and carry out the penalties. [. . .] In domestic society, these roles are familiar: police officers, district attorneys, judges, prison wardens (among others). Some IOs similarly (though not identically) constitute actors whose role is to foster compliance with the behavioral rules. Some IOs designate officials whose duties are to monitor conduct, interpret and apply the rules in specific cases, reach determinations as to actors' conformity with the rules, signal violations (or certify compliance), and sometimes even impose penalties.

The European Union is probably the most dramatic example of an international institution with well-developed organizational supports. The Commission of the EC has substantial independent powers, including authority to review and overrule state subsidies to industry, to investigate companies suspected of anti-competitive practices (price-fixing, cartels), to impose fines on firms found to have violated the competition rules, to vet proposed company mergers and impose conditions or disallow them, to take countries to the

European Court of Justice for failure to implement Community law, and more. The Commission can in addition act as a policy entrepreneur, offering proposals and mobilizing coalitions. Equally significant, the European Court of Justice (ECJ) has created for itself powers of judicial review. In addition to adjudicating disputes between EU organizations or between them and member states, the ECJ has broad power to interpret and apply EU law in cases referred from national courts. It can hold national governments liable for their failure to implement properly EU legislation, and its decisions are enforced by national courts. These formal organizational supports for its rules distinguish the EU from almost all other international institutions, leading some analysts to conclude that the EU is not an international institution but rather a decentralized or "multi-level" polity. The difficulty in classifying the EU disappears if we think of all political systems as rule clusters (or sets of linked rule clusters).

In this perspective, international society and national states are not different in kind, but only in degree (of formalization and specificity of the rules, and of organizational supports for them). States are highly formalized (codified) rule systems with a high degree of behavioral specificity and full-fledged organizational supports. International institutions tend to have low levels of formalization, specificity, and organizational supports, though there is considerable variation. Since rules vary along two dimensions (formal-informal, specific-general), we can also classify international institutions according to the character of the rules that define them. We can place a cluster of rules (an institution) governing a set of behaviors with respect to both dimensions, yielding the two-by-two matrix shown in Figure 1. The figure illustrates a typology of international institutions. Though it shows discrete boxes for clarity of exposition, the dimensions are actually continuous ranges capable of situating institutions at various points between the poles.

Institutions that are general but formalized – in treaties, charters, and conventions – I call *orders*, since they concern primarily broad frameworks for regulating relations. In other words, orders are primarily rules about rules, governing membership, franchise and decision-making procedures. Examples include the Concert of Europe and the United Nations system. Note that orders can include subordinate clusters of rules that are more specific; the UN, for example, establishes a general order but also includes specific agencies like the UN Environmental Program or the Food and Agriculture Organization (FAO). Specific and informal institutions have rules for specific sets of behaviors, but the rules are uncodified. I call them *tacit regimes*. Tacit rules generate weaker commitments than formal rules and are more contested, yet they are recognized as rules (albeit with lesser weight or legitimacy) by

	Informal	Formal
General	**International society:** constitutive rules for international society.	**Orders:** consensus on broad objectives and on the need for an explicit ordering framework; rules of membership, franchise, and decision-making.
Specific	**Tacit regimes:** regularized patterns of interaction in particular domains, with implicit rules but few concrete commitments.	**Problem-solving organizations:** substantial consensus on well-defined ends and means; state claims and actions justified on legal or technical grounds.

Figure 1 A typology of international institutions, with examples

those participating in the institutions. Decolonization, spheres of influence, and nuclear deterrence are examples.

Specific and formal institutions are *problem-solving organizations* established to address quite narrowly defined sets of problems. Specific, formal institutions will also include more finely-grained behavioral prescriptions, proscriptions, and permissions. The specificity and formality dimensions also generate expectations as to the extent of organizational supports in institutions. General, informal institutions would likely have minimal or no organizational supports for compliance. Specific, formal institutions could vary considerably in the degree to which they possess them, but institutions with highly developed organizational supports will cluster in the southeast corner of the specificity/formality plane.

Rule structures and international politics

I have suggested that international relations – like all social life – are pervasively rule-guided. Since rules are linked to each other in institutions, and institutions are linked to broader institutions, there are complex structures of rules that shape international politics. In principle, then, one could map the rule structures that shape international politics. Scholars have in recent years undertaken a number of useful studies of the historical development of specific international rules (usually called "norms"); what remains is the larger task of linking rules into clusters and to larger rule structures. In this section I outline one way of approaching that task.

I suggest that there are four basic rule complexes that constitute international society: technical rules, system rules, state rules, and liberal rules. The logic supporting the selection of these four rule structures is that they cover four essential levels of analysis in the international social realm: the natural world, the international system, states, and individuals.

Technical rules guide how people (individually and in groups) relate to the natural world, the broadest or most inclusive level of analysis. The complex of technical rules is a system for validating knowledge and action, based on positivism and scientific methods. It grew out of Western rationalism and the scientific revolutions that began in the fifteenth century and continues to unfold in the twentieth. Technical rules demystify nature and social relations. That is, the material and social realms are no longer seen as expressions of the supernatural or divine. Instead, the universe works according to impersonal, material laws that are, in principle, discoverable through the methods of science. Scientifically generated knowledge thus holds privileged status. This is not to say that technical rules, or scientific knowledge, displace politics, only that they establish norms for how protagonists must frame their arguments and claims.

Scientific epistemology in turn legitimates a "technical" approach to solving problems. In the face of misfortune (floods, epidemics, recessions, gang violence), we seek not to placate the gods but to discover the causes. As it has been constructed, science allows people to uncover causal relations and general laws; solving material or social problems means intervening at the proper point in the causal chain. The basic rules of technical rationality have become so universal that they shape everyday thinking as well as specific collective enterprises (fixing a refrigerator, saving the ozone layer, promoting Third World development). Given the impressive successes of scientific-technical rationality in a number of domains (medicine, agriculture, information technologies, and so on), and the dominance of Western education, it is no surprise that the technical rule complex has covered essentially the entire world; there are no substantial alternatives to scientific rules of knowledge and technical problem solving (even confessional regimes want scientific-technical industries and militaries).

International system rules cover relations among the actors in international relations. The basic principle anchoring this complex of rules is the equality of sovereign states. The system rules thus recognize states as the basic units and provide standards of conduct for their dealings with each other and with other (non-state) actors. The system rules developed gradually, from before the Peace of Westphalia (which represented a formal and collective recognition of a rule of exclusive internal jurisdiction) through the Vienna Convention on the Law of Treaties, and beyond. This complex includes the basic rule that treaties should be obeyed, as well as the rules that govern diplomatic practices.

State rules constitute the internal institutions and structures of states, the dominant political units of the modern era. State rules are not the only normative structures within any given territorial space; there are diverse and overlapping political and cultural rule systems in every state. Nevertheless, states possess the most elaborate and formal of rule structures, as well as the most thoroughly developed organizational supports (in the form of educational, regulatory, investigative, policing, judicial, and penal agencies). The Weberian conception of states as possessing a legitimate monopoly of coercive force within their borders is reasonable as an ideal type, one that also allows us to recognize divergent cases where the supremacy of the state's rules is diminished by internal fragmentation (ex-Yugoslavia, Afghanistan) or supra-national authority (the European Union). International system rules create space for states as rule structures, by recognizing states as the dominant actors in international society. Indeed, to be recognized in the international arena, an entity must in fact be a rule structure that resembles the ideal-typical state – having effective "rule" within a given territory. [. . .] States in turn support the international system rules by sustaining the larger rule complexes (treaties, organizations, diplomatic practices) that validate states. The interaction between international system rules and state rules is a perfect instance of co-constitution.

Liberal rules enshrine the individual as the basic unit of, and ultimate value in, the social world. Liberal rules, growing out of Enlightenment thought, posit the inherent worth, dignity, and freedom of the individual. They define a panoply of individual political and civil rights. Economic freedoms (the rights associated with ownership and control of private property) similarly derive from fundamental liberal values (Locke). Markets are founded on the notion of freely exchanging, autonomous individuals who have exclusive control over their own property. The massive rule systems that have developed to guarantee property rights, market competition, and free trade, all trace back to basic notions of individual freedom and rights (with economic theories attaching a supplementary, pseudo-scientific justification on the grounds of "efficiency"). Later formulations of basic rights include additional economic rights (the right to a basic standard of living, for instance). Group rights (assembly, collective bargaining, and self-determination, for examples) derive from individual rights and in fact exist to protect individuals in the exercise of their fundamental rights. The development of liberal ideals and rules was driven in large part by the desire to fix boundaries to the extraordinary degree of agency accorded to states as rule structures. In theory, if not usually in practice, the prerogatives of monarchs had been absolute; the liberal revolutions delimited state powers by grounding them not in the divine right of kings but in the natural, inalienable rights of people.

Whereas state-system rules cover the entire globe, in that all states participate in international relations on terms established by the rules of sovereignty and diplomatic practice, the liberal rule structure has more uneven coverage. Liberal ideals emerged in Europe and have taken root most deeply in European societies and in countries culturally and historically closely linked to them (North America, Oceania). Colonialism carried European liberal ideas to most of the rest of the world, but the degree to which they became embedded and institutionalized in colonial possessions varies somewhat. Liberal rules have thus become established in Asia, Africa, and Latin America only partially and unevenly. Consequently, the meaning of liberal categories and rules can vary across regions, as evidenced by recurring assertions that "human rights" and "democracy" mean something different in Singapore or Malaysia than they do in "the West."

The gradual encroachment of liberal rules upon international system rules has, in a sense, charted the evolution of international relations. For instance, state sovereignty rules initially granted almost unlimited latitude to rulers in the initiation and conduct of war. Liberal rules have slowly eroded and delimited the war prerogatives, restricting the conditions under which states could legitimately turn to war as well as the methods by which they could conduct the fighting. Norms of intervention in cases of extreme human rights violations or genocide have begun to erode the rule of exclusive internal sovereignty. And some of the thorniest issues for the near future in international politics deal precisely with the tension between international system rules and liberal rules: China's integration into international economic institutions will likely continue to run up against the question of domestic human rights. Ethnic violence within states will provoke calls for international intervention, again pitting liberal rules against sovereignty rules. More generally, the evolution of normative structures, and the resulting tensions between different rule complexes, may be one of the fundamental forces driving international change.

The four basic rule structures thus define the fundamental elements of modern international society. They govern its basic categories of relationships (state-state, state-individual, individual-individual, and relations between people and the natural world). Other elements of these rule structures have emerged or accreted over time, linked by a justifying discourse to the basic rules. The four basic rule structures are general and informal (at least initially, the UN Charter having formalized some of the basic rules of state society as well as some liberal rules relating to human rights).

Dynamism and change

The notion of rule structures might create an impression of fixity. But, in fact, rule change is constant. Change occurs through a ceaseless interaction between rules and practice. What connects rules to practice, and ensures that they evolve together, is the dialogue among actors concerning both the meaning of the rules and the meaning of behaviors. My approach emphatically does not argue that only "texts" exist. Rather, I hold that there are observable behaviors (including speech), but that their significance depends on the principled discussions that occur among actors. Those discussions (or "discourses" or "dialogues") begin with existing rules, but inevitably produce change in the rules. That is, normative and institutional innovations cannot be conjured up out of thin air; they always refer to pre-existing rules and emerge out of the dialogues that actions engender.

I argued earlier that social behavior is rule-guided. This does not mean that the process of linking rules to situations yields unambiguous behavioral directions. Consequently, it is pointless to think of behaviors as falling neatly into the dichotomous categories of "compliance" and "non-compliance." Instead, what matters is the social process by which actors attempt to persuade others that the actions in question did (or did not) constitute warranted behavior. A consensus that a specific act violated rules, instead of establishing the inefficacy of the rules, reaffirms their relevance. Failure to achieve consensus regarding the justifiability of a specific act implies that the meaning of the rules is ambiguous or contested. One actor explains and rationalizes its conduct, perhaps casting it as a justifiable exception to the rules; others respond, criticize, exculpate, or condemn.

Of course, international society is not a debating society, in which those actors with the best arguments and the greatest persuasive skills prevail. Indeed, actors bring to bear both persuasive reasons and material resources. Those with the resources can bribe or compel others to assent to their arguments and interpretations. Thus powerful actors win more arguments than weak ones, as when the British Navy enforced the abolition of the slave trade. But that is not to say that capabilities (or power, or resources) explain everything, for not even the most powerful actors can remove themselves from the webs of rules that define "actorhood" and establish the bounds of the thinkable. Rather, the purposes on behalf of which actors exercise power are shaped by the rules that define roles, interests, and even how to count gains and losses. In other words, power cannot be separated from purpose, and purpose is dependent on socially constructed roles and values. Furthermore, even powerful actors seek to justify their actions. In doing so they can only deploy the categories and normative principles that are available in the existing structures of rules.

What makes the process dynamic is that in the process of dialogue, actors interpret, apply, clarify, and thus modify the rules. The meaning of the rules, and sometimes new rules, emerge from the dialogue. The modified rules then provide reasons for subsequent behaviors; the interpretations from an early discourse shape the terms of later ones. Actors acquire from the dialogues a sense of what range of behaviors can be justified. The new round of action and dialogue again modifies the rules, and the process continues as a cycle. In a sense, then, rules come from rules. Figure 2 is a schematic representation of this dynamic process. Behaviors generate dialogues about the rules, which modify the rules, which in turn provide reasons for subsequent behaviors and discourses, and so on.

Globalization and the evolution of rules

I have argued that rule structures, or institutions, are a fundamental and pervasive feature of international relations. Rules provide the context in which actors conceive of their interests and delineate ranges of justifiable action in pursuit of those interests. Rules, then, must be central to any notion of governance. Indeed, I would propose the following as a workable

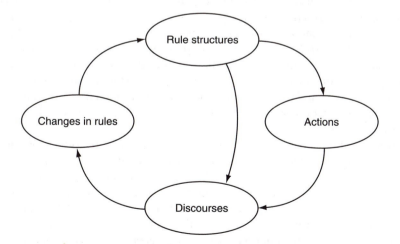

Figure 2 Dynamic relations among rules, actions, and discourses

definition: *governance is the process by which rules are generated*. Governance thus defined can include both formal organizations that authoritatively establish and enforce rules, as well as patterned social interactions that produce shared rules without the formal structures of government. The emergence of rule structures, or institutions, is the manifestation of governance.

One powerful question is how economic globalization affects international governance. Building on contemporary integration theory, I derive specific propositions concerning the relationship between globalization and governance. The key insight was developed with reference to the European Union, but it is easily generalizable. Globalization, defined as a set of processes leading to the integration of intermediate, factor, and product markets across geographical boundaries, implies rising levels of communication and exchange across national borders. Those involved in these increasingly dense cross-border interactions experience a need for new, and more specific, rules to govern relationships that are outside the familiar and highly structured context of domestic law. For those involved in cross-border interactions (trade, finance, investment, multinational production, distribution, and so on), separate national legal regimes can cast up a variety of obstacles to potentially profitable transnational exchange. In the absence of a transnational or supra-national framework of rules, cross-border transactions are disadvantaged relative to domestic exchange (of course, this is precisely the objective of many national rules). As national markets integrate, cross-border transactions and communications increase, and so therefore does the societal demand for trans- or supra-national rules. Governments can respond to this demand by creating or extending international organizations and rules, or private actors can agree on common standards and procedures without governmental involvement. Of course, governments can resist or obstruct market integration and the associated demand for transnational rules, but only at a cost to cross-border transactors and possibly to the national economy as a whole.

My first proposition is therefore that globalization leads to the expansion of transnational rules. Rule structures will develop where actors need them to guide their relations. This is, to be clear, *not* a prediction that globalization will lead to the expansion of formal international regimes and international law.

A second proposition is that the rules that emerge in response to globalization will be elaborations of, or modeled after, existing rules. New rules cannot be created out of nothing. Indeed, as I have argued above, rule structures provide the necessary social context in which interactions, normative discourses, and rule making can occur. In one sense, rule structures continuously generate new rules: behavior triggers discourses that inevitably reinterpret or modify the rules. Even when groups of actors consciously set out to create formal organizations or rules (treaties, conventions, charters), they work with the materials at hand, namely, existing organizations and rules. A powerful actor can sometimes impose its own forms as models for international institutions. But institutional design can also be a process whereby collectivities pattern new institutions on those most widely seen to be successful or appropriate.

As rule structures become increasingly articulated, they begin to sustain normative discourses that define and redefine the meaning of the rules, and thus the bounds of warranted behavior. The most articulated rule systems have formal, written rules (law), along with specific organizations charged with maintaining the rule system itself (legislatures, courts, police). As rule systems become more elaborate they start to resemble legal systems, with an accompanying tendency toward formalization. A third proposition is therefore that if globalization continues, some transnational rule systems will become increasingly formalized and will gradually develop specific organizations for managing the rules and resolving disputes.

A caveat is in order regarding these propositions. The term "globalization" sometimes, and misleadingly, suggests worldwide uniformity in the expansion of cross-border exchange. In practice, "globalization" means increasing exchange among certain actors, or among some countries, or within some regions. As a result, emerging rule structures will *not* be global in their coverage. On the contrary: transnational rules will develop where the growth of transnational interactions is most pronounced. Transnational rule making (governance) will shadow rising levels of exchange, producing highly variegated, overlapping rule structures of different kinds and at different levels. Some rule structures will develop within geographic regions (the EU), or among non-contiguous sets of countries (e.g., the OECD). Others will emerge among sub-state units (along the Rhine river, for example, or among the US and Mexican border states) or private actors (international commercial arbitration). Some rule structures will be oriented toward a set of actors and their relations, but others will be defined with respect to specific issues or problems.

[Sandholtz goes on to explore a number of empirical examples, including the European Union, the World Trade Organization, transnational business contracts and international commercial arbitration processes.]

Notes

1   See Nicholas Onuf, *World of Our Making* (University of South Carolina Press, Columbia, 1989) and Nicholas Onuf, "Rules, Agents, Institutions: A Constructivist Account," Working Papers on International Society and Institutions, No. 96–2 (Global Peace and Conflict Studies, University of California, Irvine).
2   Ronald Jepperson, "Institutions, Institutional Effects and Institutionalism," in Paul J. DiMaggio and Walter W. Powell (eds.), *The New Institutionalism in Organizational Analysis* (Chicago University Press, Chicago, 1991), pp. 149, 157.
3   Onuf, *World of Our Making*, pp. 136–40.

2.9 A framework for the study of security communities

Emanuel Adler and Michael Barnett

Source: Emanuel Adler and Michael Barnett (eds), *Security Communities* (Cambridge University Press, Cambridge, 1998), pp. 37–48.

Adler and Barnett set out to identify the key qualities of security communities and their roles in expressing 'dependable expectations of peaceful change' among states and societies. They begin by examining the conceptual foundations of security communities, and discern three stages or 'tiers' in the formation of such communities. First, there are a number of precipitating conditions; second, there are interactions between the structure of a region and its social processes; finally, there is the formation of mutual trust and collective identity formation.

States can become embedded in a set of social relations that can be properly understood as a community. Sometimes a community of states will establish pacific relations, sometimes a community will not. But those that do have formed a security community. Security communities are relatively rare developments, though their very existence has been made conceptually invisible because of the dominance of realist theories of international security. The obvious challenge is to isolate the conditions under which the development of a community produces dependable expectations of peaceful change.

The conceptual foundations of security communities

To answer this challenge we proceed in a highly stylized manner, building deductively from past research and inductively on recent empirical studies that attempt to delineate the factors contributing to peaceful change. Specifically, our framework is organized around three tiers. The first tier concerns the precipitating conditions. The second tier examines the positive, dynamic, and reciprocal relationship between the structure of the region, defined by material power and knowledge, and social processes, defined by organizations, transactions, and social learning. These dynamics create the conditions for the third tier: mutual trust and collective identity formation. This model can be diagrammed as in figure 1.

Tier one

Because of exogenous or endogenous factors states begin to orient themselves in each other's direction and desire to coordinate their relations. Technological developments, an external threat that causes states to form alliances, the desire to reduce mutual fear through security coordination, new interpretations of social reality, transformations in economic, demographic and migration patterns, changes in the natural environment, these and other

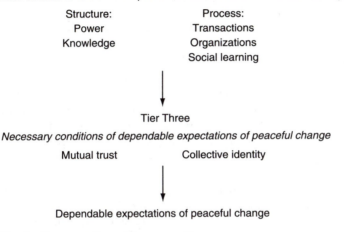

Tier One

Precipitating conditions

- Change in technology, demography, economics, the environment
- Development of new interpretations of social reality
- External threats

Tier Two

Factors conducive to the development of mutual trust and collective identity

Structure:	Process:
Power	Transactions
Knowledge	Organizations
	Social learning

Tier Three

Necessary conditions of dependable expectations of peaceful change

Mutual trust	Collective identity

Dependable expectations of peaceful change

Figure 1 The development of security communities

developments can propel states to look in each other's direction and attempt to coordinate their policies to their mutual advantage. There is no expectation that these initial encounters and acts of cooperation produce trust or mutual identification; but because they are premised on the promise of more pleasant and more numerous interactions, they provide the necessary conditions for these very possibilities. In general, states have an incentive to promote face-to-face interactions, dialogue, and policy coordination for any number of reasons; such developments can, at the least, allow states to achieve pareto superior outcomes, and, at the most, provide the context for the development of new social bonds. The more general implication is that security communities are likely to exhibit equafinality: common endpoints can have very disparate beginnings.

Tier two

Perhaps the defining feature of this tier is that states and their peoples have become involved in a series of social interactions that have begun to transform the environment in which they are embedded. The task, then, is to isolate the structural context in which states are embedded and that shape their interactions, and how these interactions begin to transform their "possible roles and possible worlds." To simplify matters and to present the materials in ways that are consistent with past international relations scholarship, we divide this tier into the "structural" categories of power and knowledge and the "process" categories of transactions, international organizations and institutions, and social learning. The dynamic, positive, and reciprocal relationship between these variables provides the conditions under which a collective identity and mutual trust can form, without which there could not be dependable expectations of peaceful change.

Structure

Power and knowledge are the structural girders for the development of a security community. Past theoretical work and empirical studies suggest that power is central for understanding their development. According to Deutsch, "larger, stronger, more politically, administratively, economically, and educationally advanced political units were found to form the cores of strength around which in most cases the integrative process developed."[1] We also hypothesize that power plays a major role in the development and maintenance of security communities. Power conventionally understood can be an important factor in the development of a security community by virtue of a core state's ability to nudge and occasionally coerce others to maintain a collective stance. Yet power can be alternatively understood as the authority to determine shared meaning that constitutes the "we-feeling" and practices of states and the conditions which confer, defer, or deny access to the community and the benefits it bestows on its members. In other words, power can be a magnet; a community formed around a group of strong powers creates the expectations that weaker states that join the community will be able to enjoy the security and potentially other benefits that are associated with that community. Thus, those powerful states who belong to the core of strength do not create security *per se*; rather, because of the positive images of security or material progress that are associated with powerful and successful states, security communities develop around them. For instance, the former Eastern bloc states have not waited for the "Club of Europe" to extend invitations, they have invited themselves.

Knowledge also constitutes part of the international structure, and in this instance we are interested in cognitive structures, that is, shared meanings and understandings. In other words, part of what constitutes and constrains state action is the knowledge that represents categories of practical action and legitimate activity. In recent years international relations theorists have become interested in how such shared meanings are created out of practice and social interactions, but to simplify matters here we are interested in those cognitive structures that facilitate practices that are tied to the development of mutual trust and identity, and analytically tied to conflict and conflict resolution. Deutsch offered little guidance on this issue because he descriptively established the connection between liberal democracy and market values and the formation of the North Atlantic community, and failed to consider whether there might be other ideas that are compatible with the development of peaceful change. In other words, part of the structural backdrop of Deutsch's study concerns the fact that these North Atlantic states shared certain ideas concerning the meaning of markets and democracy that were implicitly tied to a system of practices that facilitated transactions and, eventually, trust.

At the present moment if scholars of international politics are likely to identify one set of political ideas and meanings that are related to a security community it is liberalism and democracy. To demonstrate that liberalism is a necessary condition for the formation of security communities, however, requires demonstrating how liberal ideas are more prone than are other ideas for the promotion of a collective identity, mutual trust, and peaceful change. More simply, what is it about the quality of the ideas themselves – rather than the mere fact that they are shared – that leads people who reside in different territorial spaces to feel secure from organized violence in a liberal security community?

Two related hypotheses might account for connection between liberalism and security communities. First, liberal ideas are more prone to create a shared transnational civic culture, whose concepts of the role of government, tolerance, the duty of citizens, and the rule of law may shape the transnational identity of individuals of the community. Secondly, liberal ideas may be better able to promote strong civil societies – and the networks of organized processes between them – through the interpenetration of societies and the exchange of people, goods, and ideas. Yet other intersubjective ideas may also account for the formation of security communities. For example, a shared developmentalist ideology, perhaps similar to that pursued by Southeast Asian states, may promote not only transnational exchanges and policy coordination, but, more fundamentally, a shared project – characterized by increasing amount of transactions and the development of common institutions; in doing so, such exchange and this shared project might conceivably promote collective purposes around which emerge a shared identity and, thereafter, dependable expectations of peaceful change. In general, the causal connection between a particular set of ideas and the development of security communities must be theoretically and empirically demonstrated rather than simply asserted.

Process

The process categories involve transactions, international organizations and institutions, and social learning. A transaction can be defined as a "bounded communication between one actor and another."[2] A transaction, therefore, admits various types of exchanges, including symbolic, economic, material, political, technological, and so on. The more intensive and extensive transactions are related to the concept of "dynamic density," "the quantity, velocity, and diversity of transactions that go on within society."[3] According to Emile Durkheim, dynamic density is able to create and transform social facts. In this respect, social facts do not depend on material resources alone, but also on collective experience and human consensus. Thus, a qualitative and quantitative growth of transactions reshapes collective experience and alters social facts.

International organizations and institutions contribute directly and indirectly to the development of security communities. Following Oran Young, we differentiate between social institutions and formal organizations by defining social institutions as "social practices consisting of easily recognized roles coupled with clusters of rules or conventions governing the relations among the occupants of these roles," and organizations as "material entities possessing physical locations, offices, personnel, equipment, and budgets."[4] Although social institutions might have a concrete organizational expression, it is important not to conflate the two.

Institutions and organizations can be categorized as part of process. At first blush this move may seem puzzling. After all, a key constructivist point is that norms, rules and institutional contexts constitute actors and constrain choices; and international relations theory conventionally treats international institutions as constraints on state actions. But institutions and organizations may be depicted either as structures or as processes. As Alexander Wendt observes,

> Although theories of structure explain how structures regulate and/or constitute practices and interactions, and as such are essentially static even if they reveal transformative possibilities within a structure, [t]heories of process explain how practices and interactions reproduce and/or transform structures, and as such are essentially dynamic even if what they explain is reproduction rather than transformation.[5]

Because we are interested in the development of security community, which involves a consideration of the conditions under which and the media that makes possible the transformation of social relations, we are attentive to and attempt to isolate the actors that are not only constituted by that structure but also might transform it.

The interest in examining how international organizations and institutions indirectly promote other factors that contribute to, and directly promote, mutual trust, shared identity elevates four issues, First, security and non-security organizations can contribute to the development of trust. At the most intuitive level, they facilitate and encourage transactions and trust by: establishing norms of behavior, monitoring mechanisms, and sanctions to enforce those norms. But to the the extent that economic institutions contribute to an overall development of trust, they can have a security-related function and be instrumental to the development of a security community. The role of economic organizations and institutions as furthering this pacific propensity is one of the enduring principles of neofunctionalism and a hallmark of Deutsch's framework. In general, a key concern here is with how organizations and institutions encourage transactions and the development of trust.

Secondly, international organizations make possible state action by virtue of their trust-building properties. But their trust-building properties extend beyond their monitoring capacities, for they also can encourage actors to discover their preferences, to reconceptualize who they are, and to reimagine their social bonds. Organizations, in this important respect, are sites of socialization and learning, places where political actors learn and perhaps even "teach" others what their interpretations of the situation and normative understandings are. Because identities are created and reproduced on the basis of knowledge that people have of themselves and others, learning processes that occur within and are promoted by institutions can lead actors to develop positive reciprocal expectations and thus identify with each other.

Thirdly, international organizations may be conducive to the formation of mutual trust and collective identities, because of their often understimated capacity to "engineer" the very conditions – for example, cultural homogeneity, a belief in a common fate, and norms of unilateral self-restraint – that assist in their development. International organizations, for instance, may be able to foster the creation of a regional "culture" around commonly held attributes, such as, for example, democracy, developmentalism, and human rights. And they may be able to promote regional projects that instill belief in a common fate, such as, for example, a common currency; and/or generate and enhance norms and practices of self-restraint, such as, for example, mediation.

Behind every innovative institution stand creative and farsighted political elites. Political elites that are connected to international organizations use them to promote new possibilities. Deutsch's relative lack of attention to institutional agents, and, indeed, to political elites and even charismatic individuals, was a crucial short-coming that we wish to correct. As John Hall argues, while "the creation of new social identities by intellectuals – that is, their capacity to link people across space so as to form a new community – is necessarily a rare historical phenomenon," it is one that scholars of international relations need to take seriously.[6] While communication between peoples, learning processes, and the thickening of the social environment plays a crucial role in the evolution of political communities, these are but propensities until agents transform them into political reality through institutional and political power.

Such matters highlight the critical role of social learning, which can be described as an active process of redefinition or reinterpretation of reality – what people consider real, possible and desirable – or the basis of new causal and normative knowledge. In this respect, social learning is more than "adaptation" or "simple learning," that is, when political actors choose more effective means of achieving ends as a response to changes in the international environment. Social learning represents the capacity and motivation of social actors to manage and even transform reality by changing their beliefs of the material and social world and their identities. In this critical respect, it explains why norms and other cognitive and cultural categories that are tied to a collective identity, interests, and practices, are transmitted from individual to individual and nation to nation, are internalized by individuals and are institutionalized in the halls of governments and in society. While social learning can occur at the mass level, and such changes are critical when discussing collective identities, our bias is to look to policymakers and other political, economic, and intellectual elites that are most critical for the development of new forms of social and political organization that are tied to the development of a security community.

Social learning plays a critical role in the emergence of security communities, and is facilitated by transactions that typically occur in organizational settings, and core powers. First, during their transactions and social exchanges, people communicate to each other their self-understandings, perceptions of reality, and their normative expectations. As a result, there can occur changes in individual and collective understandings and values. To the extent that they promote shared normative and epistemic criteria and provide a fertile ground for the transmission of practices, transactions are essential features for the development of collective learning and collective identities.

Secondly, learning often occurs within institutionalized settings. Institutions promote the diffusion of meanings from country to country, may play an active role in the cultural and political selection of similar normative and epistemic understandings in different countries, and may help to transmit shared understanding from generation to generation.

Thirdly, social learning may not be sufficient for the development of a security community unless this learning is connected to functional processes that are traceable to a general improvement in the state's overall condition. This is why core powers are so important to the process. States that possess superior material power, international legitimacy, and have adopted norms and practices that are conducive to peaceful change tend to confer increased material and moral authority to the norms and practices they diffuse and, thus, may also induce their political adoption and institutionalization. Indeed, while this process entails power projection and even hegemony, it cannot come to fruition without active socialization and social learning. Said otherwise, social learning frequently occurs through a communicative exchange in the context of power asymmetries. That said, even those asymmetrical relationships can involve a situation where "teachers" and "students" negotiate a new regional collective identity around consensual norms and mutual understandings.

In general, social learning explains why transactions and institutional actions can encourage the development of mutual trust and collective identity. By promoting the development of shared definitions of security, proper domestic and international action, and regional boundaries, social learning encourages political actors to see each other as trustworthy. And it also leads people to identify with those who were once on the other side of cognitive divides.

The structural and process conditions are necessary for the development of mutual trust and collective transnational identities. Understanding how these variables effect the development of mutual trust and the creation, transformation, and reproduction of collective identities, requires, however, that we take full cognisance of their dynamic and reciprocal interactions. Trust, for instance, may be promoted by institutions that significantly increase the number and quality of transactions, which, in turn, further the diffusion of norms. And the emergence of collective identities may be prompted by learning processes that occur within institutionalized settings, and subsequently lead to changes in cognitive structures. In any event, the processes that develop are critical for the development of a security community.

Tier three

The dynamic and positive relationships among the variables we described above are the wellsprings of both mutual trust and collective identity, which, in turn, are the proximate necessary conditions for the development of dependable expectations of peaceful change. Trust and identity are reciprocal and reinforcing: the development of trust can strengthen mutual identification, and there is a general tendency to trust on the basis of mutual identification. That said, because a minimal measure of mutual trust is needed for a collective identity to develop, trust logically comes prior to identity. Once some measure of trust develops, however, a collective identity is likely to reinforce and increase the depth of trust.

Trust can best be understood as believing despite uncertainty. Barbara Mistzal nicely captures this essential feature of trust in the following way:

> Trust always involves an element of risk resulting from our inability to monitor others' behavior, from our inability to have complete knowledge about other peoples' motivations and, generally, from the contingency of social reality. Consequently one's behavior is influenced by one's beliefs about the likelihood of others behaving or not behaving in a certain way rather than solely by a cognitive understanding or by a firm and certain calculation.[7]

Trust is a social phenomenon and dependent on the assessment that another actor will behave in ways that are consistent with normative expectations. Often times trust is facilitated by third-party mechanisms, as discussed in the previous section, but the social construction of trust shifts our attention to the beliefs that we have about others, beliefs that, in turn, are based on years of experiences and encounters.

When international relations theorists turn their attention to trust they generally elevate how anarchy makes trust highly elusive if not impossible. This is one reason why states establish international organizations and other means to monitor the behavior of others – "trust, but verify" as Ronald Reagan famously quipped. But the development of a security community – the very existence of dependable expectations of peaceful change – suggests that states no longer rely on concrete international organizations to maintain trust but do so through knowledge and beliefs about the other. For instance, democratic nuclear powers do not feel threatened by each other's nuclear weapons; even when in 1965 France withdrew from the NATO integrated command and insisted on maintaining an independent nuclear force, other NATO allies did not interpret this as a military threat against their physical survival. But these same countries are quite concerned when Iraq or Iran are feared as developing a nuclear weapons program. Identification of friend or foe, the social basis of trust, is a judgement based on years of experiences and encounters that shapes the cultural definition of the threat. Uncertainty, in such matters, is generated not by technological capabilities or its absence but by knowledge founded on mutual identification and trust.

Although there are many definitions of identity, most begin with the understanding of oneself in relationship to others. Identities, in short, are not only personal or psychological, but are social, defined by the actor's interaction with and relationship to others; therefore, all political identities are contingent, dependent on the actor's interaction with others and place within an institutional context. This relational perspective informs the view that national and state identities are formed in relationship to other nations and states – that the identities of political actors are tied to their relationship to those outside the boundaries of the community and the territory, respectively. To be sure, not all transactions will produce a collective identity; after all, interactions are also responsible for creating an "other" and defining threats. Therefore, we must consider not only the quantity but also the quality of the transactions in order to gauge the conditions and prospects for collective identity.

We have already described the critical factors leading to the creation of transnational collective identities. Keep in mind that collective identities entail that people not only identify (positively) with other people's fate but, also, identify themselves, and those other people, as a group in relation to other groups. Such identities are likely to be reinforced by symbols and myths that serve to define the group and its boundaries. The distinction between loosely coupled and tightly coupled security communities acquires special significance. In the former case, it is mainly a social identity that generates a positive identification between peoples of members states. For instance, the category of democrat defines the group "by systematically including them with some, and excluding them from other related categories. They state at the same time what a person is and is not."[8] It follows, then, that when members of a loosely coupled security community assume a particular social category they are able to answer, in part, the question "who am I?" (and who I am not) and have a fairly proximate understanding of "what makes them tick." [. . .]

The closer we get to tightly coupled security communities, however, the shorter is the collective cognitive distance between its members, and the more the community acquires a corporate identity. In these communities, the identities of the people who exist within them no longer derives from the international environment (if they ever did) or from the self-contained nation (if it ever existed) but rather from the community's identity and norms as well. Indeed, even the meaning, purpose, and role of the state derives from the community. The state's interests, and the identity of its people, can be exchangeable with those of the community, and the foreign policy of the state takes on a whole new meaning and purpose. The discourse of the state and the language of legitimation, moreover, also should reflect that the relevant community is no longer coterminous with the state's territorial boundaries but rather with the region. With the emergence of tightly coupled security communities, therefore, state officials will increasingly refer to the boundaries of an expanded definition of community.

In sum, we envision a dynamic and positive relationship between core powers and cognitive structures on the one hand, and transactions, institutions and organizations, and social learning on the other. The positive and dynamic interaction between these variables undergirds the development of trust and the process of collective identity formation, which, in turn, drives dependable expectation of peaceful change.

Notes

1   Karl W. Deutsch et al., *Political Community and the North Atlantic Area* (Princeton University Press, Princeton, 1957), p. 38.
2   Charles Tilly, "Durable Inequality," Center for Studies of Social Change, Working Paper Series, No. 224, (New School For Social Research, New York), p. 20.
3   John G. Ruggie, 'Continuity and Transformation in the World Polity: Toward a Neorealist Synthesis', *World Politics* 35, January 1983, p. 148. The concept derives from Emile Durkheim, *The Division of Labor in Society* (Free Press, New York, 1984).
4   Oran Young, *International Cooperation* (Cornell University Press, Ithaca, 1989), p. 32.

5   Alexander Wendt, *Social Theory of International Politics* (Cambridge University Press, Cambridge, 1999), p. 328.
6   John Hall, "Ideas and the Social Sciences," in Judith Goldstein and Robert Keohane (eds), *Ideas and Foreign Policy* (Cornell University Press, Ithaca, 1993), p. 51.
7   Barbara Mistzal, *Trust in Modern Societies* (Polity Press, Cambridge, 1996), p. 19.
8   John C. Turner, "Towards a Cognitive Redefinition of the Social Group," in Henry Tajfel (ed.), *Social Identity and Intergroup Relations* (Cambridge University Press, Cambridge, 1982), p. 18.

2.10 Global civil society

Jan Aart Scholte

Source: Ngaire Woods (ed.), *The Political Economy of Globalization* (Macmillan, London, 2000), pp. 178–90.

Scholte explores the key features of a global civil society: that is to say, the growing range of groups and associations that set out to influence policies, norms and social structures in the global arena. He is particularly concerned to identify the growth (but also the limitations) of a specifically global civil society, reflecting processes of globalization but also the persistence of national political and economic authorities. This extract sets out the features and some of the implications of this process.

[Scholte begins by identifying the features of civil societies in general, and then moves on to the global level.]

What is *global* civil society?

While notions of 'civil society' go back to the sixteenth century, specific reference to 'global civil society' has emerged only in the 1990s. Commentators have spoken in a related vein of 'international non-governmental organizations', 'transnational advocacy networks', 'global social movements', a 'new multilateralism', and so on. Such discussions are part of a wider concern with globality (the condition of being global) and globalization (the trend of increasing globality). Our conception of global civil society is thus inseparable from our notion of 'global-ness' more generally. [. . .]

Five broad kinds of ideas about globalization can be distinguished. First, many people equate the term 'globalization' with 'internationalization'. From this perspective, a 'global' situation is one marked by intense interaction and interdependence between country units. Second, many commentators take the word 'globalization' to mean 'liberalization'. In this usage, globality refers to an 'open' world where resources can move anywhere, unencumbered by state-imposed restrictions like trade barriers, capital controls and travel visas. Third, many analysts understand 'globalization' to entail 'universalization'. In this case, a 'global' phenomenon is one that is found at all corners of the earth. Fourth, some observers invoke the term 'globalization' as a synonym for 'Westernization' or 'Americanization'. In this context, globality involves the imposition of modern structures, especially in an 'American' consumerist variant. Fifth, some researchers identify 'globalization' as 'deterritorialization'. Here 'global' relations are seen to occupy a social space that transcends territorial geography.

Only the last of these five conceptions captures a distinctive trend that sets the world political economy of the late twentieth century apart from earlier periods. The other four notions merely apply a new word to pre-existent circumstances. Internationalization, liberalization, universalization and Westernization have all figured significantly at previous junctures a hundred or even a thousand and more years in the past. No vocabulary of 'globalization' was required on those earlier occasions, and it seems unnecessary now to invent new words for old phenomena. In contrast, contemporary large-scale deterritorialization is unprecedented, and 'globalization' offers a suitable new terminology to describe these new circumstances.

In the present discussion, then, 'global' relations are social connections in which territorial location, territorial distance and territorial borders do not have a determining influence. In global space, 'place' is not territorially fixed, territorial distance is covered in effectively no time, and territorial frontiers present no particular impediment. Thus global relations have what could be called a 'supraterritorial', 'transborder' or 'transworld' character. (The latter three terms will be used as synonyms for 'global' in the rest of this chapter.)

Examples of global phenomena abound in today's world. For instance, faxes and McDonald's are global in that they can extend anywhere on the planet at the same time and can unite spots anywhere on earth in effectively no time. Ozone depletion, CNN broadcasts and Visa credit cards are little restricted by territorial places, distances or borders. Global conditions can and do surface simultaneously at any point on earth that is equipped to host them (for example, a Toshiba plant or an internet connection). Global phenomena can and do move almost instantaneously across any distance on the planet (as evidenced by telephone calls or changes in foreign exchange rates).

This is by no means to say that territorial geography has lost all relevance in the late twentieth century. We inhabit a global*izing* rather than a completely global*ized* world. Social relations have undergone relative rather than total deterritorialization. Indeed, territorial places, distances and borders still figure crucially in many situations as we enter the twenty-first century. Among other things, territoriality often continues to exert a strong influence on migration, our sense of identity and community, and markets for certain goods. Yet while territoriality may continue to be important, globalization has brought an end to territorial*ism* (that is, a condition where social space is reducible to territorial coordinates alone). Alongside longitude, latitude and altitude, globalization has introduced a fourth, supraterritorial dimension to social geography.

If we identify globality as supraterritoriality, then what does global civil society involve? In a word, global civil society encompasses civic activity that: (a) addresses transworld issues; (b) involves transborder communication; (c) has a global organization; (d) works on a premise of supraterritorial solidarity. Often these four attributes go hand-in-hand, but civic associations can also have a global character in only one or several of these four respects. For example, a localized group that campaigns on a supraterritorial problem like climate change could be considered part of global civil society even though the association lacks a transborder organization and indeed might only rarely communicate with civic groups elsewhere in the world. Conversely, global civic networks might mobilize in respect of a local development like the 1994 genocide in Rwanda.

To elaborate these four points in turn, global civil society exists in one sense when civic associations concern themselves with issues that transcend territorial geography. For example, as well as addressing climate change, various civic associations have campaigned on ecological problems like the loss of biological diversity and the depletion of stratospheric ozone that similarly have a supraterritorial quality. Transworld diseases like AIDS have also stimulated notable civic activity. Many civic organizations have raised questions concerning the contemporary globalizing economy, in relation to transborder production, trade, investment, money and finance. Considerable civic activism has been directed at global governance agencies like the United Nations (UN), the Bretton Woods institutions, the Organization for Economic Cooperation and Development (OECD), and the World Trade Organization (WTO). Human rights groups have promoted standards that are meant to apply to people everywhere on earth, regardless of the distances and borders that might lie between them. Some civil society bodies have also treated armament questions like bans on chemical weapons and landmines as global issues.

A second way that civic associations can be global lies in their use of supraterritorial modes of communication. Air travel, telecommunications, computer networks and electronic mass media allow civic groups to collect and disseminate information related to their causes more or less instantaneously between any locations on earth. Jet aircraft can bring civil society representatives from all corners of the planet together in a global congress. In this way, for example, an NGO Forum has accompanied the various UN issue conferences of the 1990s as well as the Annual Meetings of the International Monetary Fund (IMF) and the World Bank since 1986. Telephone, fax and telex permit civic groups to share information and coordinate activities across the world as intensely as across town. As noted earlier, much civic activism has also become global through the internet.

Civil society is global in a third sense when campaigns adopt a transborder organization. According to the Union of International Associations, there were in 1998 some 16500 active civic bodies whose members are spread across several countries. As noted earlier, the mode of organization can vary. Some supraterritorial bodies are unitary and centralized: for instance, the World Economic Forum (WEF), which assembles some 900 transborder companies under the motto of 'entrepreneurship in the global public interest'. Alternatively, the transworld association may take a federal form, as in the case of the International Confederation of Free Trade Unions (ICFTU). Meanwhile some transborder organizations take the shape of networks without a coordinating secretariat. Illustrative cases in this regard are the Latin America Association of Advocacy Organizations (ALOP), which links 50 groups in 20 countries, and Peoples' Global Action against 'Free' Trade and the World Trade Organization (PGA), which mainly networks through a website. Other global organizations are ephemeral coalitions that pursue a campaign around a particular policy. For example, on various occasions grassroots groups have combined forces with development and/or environmental NGOs to lobby the World Bank on one or the other of its projects.

Finally, civil society can be global insofar as voluntary associations are motivated by sentiments of transworld solidarity. For example, civic groups may build on a sense of collective identity and destiny that transcends territoriality – on lines of age, class, gender, profession, race, religious faith or sexual orientation. In addition, some global civic activity (for example, in respect of human rights, humanitarian assistance and development) has grown largely out of a cosmopolitan inspiration to provide security, equity and democracy for all persons, regardless of their territorial position on the planet.

Taking these four manifestations of supraterritoriality in sum, global civil society has acquired substantial proportions in the late twentieth century. To be sure, by no means has all civic association acquired a global character. Nor has the global aspect of civic campaigns been equally pronounced and sustained in all cases. Nevertheless, owing to the contemporary growth of global issues, global communications, global organization and global solidarities, civic activity can today no longer be understood with a territorialist conception of state–society relations.

Why has global civil society developed?

Global civil society, like globalization in general, is not completely new to the late twentieth century. For example, abolitionists pursued a transatlantic campaign (albeit without global communications) beginning in the eighteenth century. Pacifists, anarchists, the first and second workers' internationals, Pan-Africanists, advocates of women's suffrage and Zionists all held prototypical global meetings during the nineteenth century. In the area of humanitarian relief, the International Red Cross and Red Crescent Movement dates back to 1863.

However, civil society has mainly acquired supraterritorial attributes since the 1960s. To cite but one indicator that the chief increase has occurred recently, less than 10 per cent of the transborder civic associations active in 1998 were more than 40 years old. In this light Lester Salamon has spoken of: 'a global "associational revolution" that may prove to be as significant to the latter twentieth century as the rise of the nation-state was to the latter nineteenth'.[1] While it seems premature to draw quite such dramatic conclusions, Salamon is right to date the principal growth of global civil society to recent history.

What has prompted this rapid expansion? Insofar as the spread of global civil society has been part of a wider process of globalization, some of the forces behind growing transborder civic activity are the same as those that have propelled globalization in general. I have argued at greater length elsewhere that the rise of supraterritoriality has resulted mainly from the mutually reinforcing impulses of global thinking, certain turns in capitalist development, technological innovations, and enabling regulations.[2]

All four of these conditions have been vital to globalization. Global thinking is crucial since people must be able to imagine the world as a single place in order for concrete global relations to be constructed. Without a global mindset, civic activists cannot 'see' global issues of the kind named earlier. Capitalist development is crucial since globalization has largely been spurred by the strivings of entrepreneurs to maximize sales and minimize costs. In addition, global spaces have offered new opportunities for surplus accumulation through sectors like electronic finance and the internet. Technology is crucial since developments in communications and information processing have supplied the infrastructure for global connections. Finally, regulation is crucial since measures like standardization and liberalization have provided a legal framework that encourages globalization.

Another legal trend has had more specific relevance for the contemporary growth of civil society, both global and otherwise: that is, in the 1990s many governments have rewritten laws in ways that facilitate civic organization. Countries in transition from state socialism provide an obvious example, though some, like Romania and Russia, have made slower and more limited reforms than others. Elsewhere, a new constitution enacted in Thailand in 1997 has explicitly promoted the growth of civil society in various respects. In Japan, too, legislators have recently replaced a highly restrictive code on civic associations with a much more permissive regime.

Further stimulus to civic activity has arisen in the 1980s and 1990s with certain reductions in direct state provision of social security. The finances of many public-sector welfare programmes have come under strain in the late twentieth century. Among the reasons for these difficulties, governments have faced pressures to reduce taxes and labour costs in the name of enhancing 'global competitiveness'. In these circumstances states (and also multilateral agencies like the World Bank and the UN High Commission for Refugees) have often contracted transborder civic associations as more cost-effective suppliers of, for example, development aid and humanitarian relief. In other cases NGOs and grassroots groups have stepped into the breach with private donations and voluntary assistance when public-sector provision of social security has become inadequate. This scenario has arisen, for example, in some countries undergoing neoliberal structural adjustment programmes.

Finally, the contemporary expansion of global civil society can also be ascribed in part to a more general altered position of the state in the face of globalization. To be sure, the rise of supraterritoriality has by no means heralded the demise of the state, but the new geography has ended the state's effective monopoly on governance that developed under conditions of territorialism. Large numbers of people have understandably concluded that, in these changed (one might term them 'post-sovereign') circumstances, elections centred on the state are not by themselves an adequate expression of citizenship and democracy. After all, substantial regulation now also occurs through public multilateral agencies like the IMF and the Bank for International Settlements (BIS) where elected legislators have little direct influence. In addition, some governance of global markets occurs through so-called 'self-regulatory' agencies of the private sector, like the International Accounting Standards Committee. Such bodies are even further removed from party politics. Global civil society has therefore also grown in part as citizens have attempted to acquire a greater voice in post-sovereign governance, for example, by directly lobbying global governance institutions.

In sum, then, global civil society first surfaced in earlier centuries and has greatly expanded since the 1960s owing to several forces. Some of the causes of this growth have at the same time been causes for the spread of supraterritoriality more generally. Other causes have related more specifically to civil society. Taken together, these impulses have created momentum on a considerable scale behind increased transborder civic activism. Hence it seems most unlikely that global civil society will shrink in the foreseeable future and all the more probable that it will further expand.

How has global civil society affected politics?

Having assessed causes, what of the consequences? In what ways and to what extent has the growth of global civil society changed the workings of politics? Several broad repercussions can be highlighted: multilayered governance; some privatization of governance; and moves to reconstruct collective identities, citizenship and democracy. Together, these five developments have contributed to the end of sovereign statehood. That said, the extent of these changes should not be overstated. For example, the rise of global civil society has on no count brought an end to the territorial state, national loyalties and party politics. The following paragraphs elaborate these various matters in turn.

Taking the first point first, global civic activism has often contributed to the contemporary turn toward multilayered governance. Prior to accelerated globalization – and particularly during the late nineteenth and early twentieth centuries – regulation was focused almost exclusively on national-level laws and institutions. Governance effectively meant government: the centralized territorial state. However, recent decades have brought a general retreat from 'nationalized' governance with concurrent trends of devolution, regionalization and globalization. As a result, agencies at substate and suprastate levels have obtained greater initiative and impact in politics. Governance has shifted from a unidimensionality of statism to a multidimensionality of local, national, regional and global layers of regulation.

The growth of global civil society has not been the sole force behind this development, of course, but civic groups have frequently furthered the trend. Global business associations, grassroots organizations, NGOs, trade unions and so on have directed their lobbying at whatever layer of governance seems relevant to their cause. Thus, for example, transborder development cooperation groups have often engaged with provincial and local authorities in the South. Various women's organizations have engaged at a regional level with European Union bodies. Several trade union federations have engaged with transworld economic institutions like the IMF and the WTO. Almost all of the major regional and global governance agencies have by now established institutional mechanisms for liaison with civil society, both at their head offices and in their member countries. Indeed, it could be argued that, through this engagement, civic associations have – whether intentionally or inadvertently – lent increased legitimacy to suprastate governance.

Regarding the second general consequence, that of privatized governance, global civil society has often become directly involved in the formulation and implementation of regulations. Not only has contemporary governance become dispersed across different geographical levels, but it has also extended beyond the public sector. Various non-official bodies have thereby acquired regulatory functions. This trend, too, has reduced state-centrism in politics.

Global civil society has contributed to this development on several counts. For one thing, as already mentioned in the preceding section, many official agencies have turned to civic associations to help execute policies, especially social welfare programmes. For example, the share of official development assistance from the OECD countries that is channelled through NGOs rose from 4.5 per cent in 1989 to 14 per cent in 1993. Likewise, much humanitarian relief has come to flow through transborder organizations like CARE (with an income of $586 million in 1995) and the aptly named Médecins sans frontières ('doctors without borders', with an income of $252 million in 1996).

Civil society associations have also on a number of occasions entered official channels of policy-making, thereby further blurring the public/private divide in governance. For example, some civic organizations have accepted invitations from states like Australia and the Netherlands to occupy places on government delegations to UN-sponsored conferences. The African National Congress, the International Committee of the Red Cross, and the Palestine Liberation Organization have held (non-voting) seats in the UN General Assembly. Several proposals in the 1990s have called for a 'People's Assembly' of civil society representatives to be created in the United Nations alongside the General Assembly of states. Certain environmental groups have held observer status in the body that oversees implementation of the 1987 Montreal Protocol on Substances that Deplete the Ozone Layer. The International Council of Scientific Unions played an important advisory role in setting up the Inter-governmental Panel on Climate Change in 1988. Some critics worry that such incorporation into official governance may limit the critical and creative potentials of civil society.

On further occasions global civil society has promoted a full-scale privatization of governance, in which official agencies have little or no involvement. For example, the Ford Foundation has insisted that its grants should not be subject to scrutiny or approval by state authorities. In global finance, business organizations like the International Federation of Stock Exchanges, the International Primary Market Association, the International Securities Market Association, and the International Council of Securities Associations have between them loosely filled the role of a transworld securities and exchange commission. The International Accounting Standards Committee and the International Federation of Accountants have developed the main global accountancy and auditing norms currently in use. Such activities take what others have termed 'governance without government' to an extreme.

A third general way that the growth of global civil society has altered the contours of politics relates to collective identities – that is, the ways that people form group affiliations and communal solidarity. The period of state-centrism in governance (at its height during the late nineteenth and first half of the twentieth centuries) was paralleled by a period of nation-centrism in collective identities. Indeed, the two conditions strongly reinforced each other. Although recent decades of large-scale globalization have not dissolved state-nations (that is, national communities that correspond to territorial states), this form of collective identity has lost its previous position of overwhelming primacy. In the late twentieth century world politics is also deeply shaped by substate solidarities like ethno-nations and by nonterritorial, transborder communities based on class, gender, race, religion, sexual orientation and other aspects of identity.

Global civic activity has clearly contributed to this trend toward pluralism. Many transborder associations have united people on the basis of nonterritorial identity: for example, as workers, people of colour, Muslims or gay men. To take but one specific illustration of this altered identity politics, over 30 000 women in civic groups attended the NGO Forum and Fourth United Nations Conference on Women, held at Beijing in 1995. Meanwhile bodies like the World Economic Forum and the Institute of International Finance (IIF, which links over 300 financial service providers headquartered in 56 countries) have helped to forge something of a global managerial class.

Transborder associations have also in various cases promoted the development of ethnic identities. For example, a number of environmental NGOs have supported indigenous peoples' movements in Africa, the Americas and the Indian Subcontinent. Transborder networks have also helped diasporas of Armenians, Irish, Kurds, Palestinians, Sikhs and Timorese to gain political force. Both across and within states, then, global civil society has promoted increased diversity in the identities that stimulate and shape political action.

Shifts in the shape of collective identities under the influence of globalization have been closely connected with shifts in the construction of citizenship, that is, the set of rights and duties that constitute persons as members of a sociopolitical community. In the statist and nationalist world that prevailed prior to the 1960s, citizenship was a question of legal nationality and the various entitlements and obligations that are associated with that status. Although this national-state framework of citizenship remains important, it has become insufficient by itself in a world of large-scale globalization. For example, the growth of the global human rights regime since the 1940s has institutionlized numerous supraterritorial entitlements. Concurrently, global communications and global ecological changes have heightened senses of duties beyond borders for 'world citizens'. Millions of people have, where possible, resorted to dual or multiple national citizenships to accommodate their post-territorialist lives. Meanwhile some environmentalists, feminists and other radical critics have attacked the very institution of territorial nation-state citizenship, regarding it as antithetical to ecological integrity, gender equality or other vital nonterritorial concerns.

Global civil society has also figured significantly in this reconfiguration of politics. Indeed, many transborder civic activists regard themselves as world citizens in addition to (or even more than) national-state citizens. Such a self-concept has helped, for example, to spur human rights advocates in their promotion of global conventions of children's, women's and worker's rights. More recently, civic groups have spearheaded a campaign to establish a permanent International Criminal Court. Humanitarian relief organizations, development cooperation groups, environmentalists and various other civil society associations have, both implicitly and explicitly, advanced the notion that people have global civic duties.

The various developments described above all raise questions about – and point to changes in – concepts and practices of democracy. Prior to contemporary large-scale globalization, 'rule by and for the people' meant rule of the *state* by and for the *nation*. Yet today governance involves more than the state, community involves more than the nation, and citizenship involves more than national entitlements and obligations. Thus issues of democracy like participation, consultation, open debate, representativeness, transparency and accountability are not adequately addressed in terms of territorial institutions and communities alone.

Global civil society has broadened the scope of democratic practice. Transborder civic associations have created additional channels of popular participation, additional modes of popular consultation, additional forums for popular debate, new sites of popular representation alongside elected councils and legislatures, and new popular pressures for open and responsible governance. These innovations have been especially important in bringing citizens into closer touch with regional and transworld regulatory agencies. That said, global civil society has by no means fully countered the many democratic deficits that exist in contemporary politics, as the next section of this chapter will elaborate.

In sum, the growth of global civil society has, in tandem with the spread of supraterritoriality more generally, shifted the framework of politics away from its previous core principle of sovereign statehood. Multilayered and partially privatised governance, pluralistic identity politics, and new forms of citizenship and democracy all contradict traditional practices of sovereignty. No longer does – or can – one site of authority exercise supreme, comprehensive, absolute and exclusive rule over a discrete jurisdiction. The territorial state has lost the attribute of sovereignty (as it was traditionally understood), and no other institution of governance looks likely to take over this mantle. Hence the expansion of global civil society has – together with parallel developments like the growth of global communications, global markets and so on – figured significantly in the shift from sovereign to post-sovereign governance.

Of course, the end of sovereignty has to be distinguished from the end of the territorial state: a world without sovereignty does not imply a world without states. Indeed, on the whole the post-sovereign state is as robust as its sovereign predecessor. States can no longer exercise sole and total jurisdiction over an assigned territory and population, but they have retained many other capacities and have also gained some new ones like computerised surveillance. Most people and most prevailing laws still define citizenship first of all in terms of state affiliation. Thus states continue to exert major influence over civil society, global and otherwise. (Of course, some governments – such as those in the OECD countries – have considerably greater leverage *vis-à-vis* civil society than others – such as those in much of Africa.) Also, given their persistent significance, states continue to be a prime target of civic activism, both territorial and global.

Similarly, in respect of collective identities, the end of nation-centrism in the face of globalization has on no count heralded the end of nations. On the contrary, state-nations persist across the world, and they have been joined by scores of ethno-nations at a substate level and several region-nations (Arab, European, etc.) at a suprastate level. Indeed, as indicated earlier, global civic associations have often promoted the national projects of indigenous peoples and diasporas. More subtly, many transborder networks have also reproduced the nationality principle by organising themselves in terms of national branches.

Finally, the new forms of collective identity, citizenship and democracy advanced by global civil society have by no means signalled the demise of party politics. True, party memberships and election turnouts have declined during recent years in most liberal democracies. Some global civic associations have followings and funds that dwarf those of most political parties. Many citizens have turned to civic activism at least partly out of disillusionment with traditional party politics. Nevertheless, control of the state still confers substantial power in the contemporary globalizing world, and competition within and between political parties remains a key way to gain governmental office in most countries.

In short, the contemporary growth of global civil society has encouraged several important shifts in political institutions and processes, but the extent of those changes must not be exaggerated. In particular, the post-sovereign world includes ample space for states, nations and parties. Global civil society has not replaced older channels of politics so much as opened up additional dimensions.

[Scholte goes on to examine the opportunities and risks – or as he puts it, the 'promises and perils' of global civil society, noting that the benefits of an emergent world of transnational associations are not automatic or automatically positive for all concerned.]

Notes

1 Lester Salamon, "The Rise of the Nonprofit Sector," *Foreign Affairs*, 73, 1994, p. 109. See also Salamon et al., *The Emerging Sector Revisited: A Summary* (Institute for Policy Studies, Johns Hopkins University, Baltimore, 1998).
2 Jan Aart Scholte, *Globalization: A Critical Introduction* (Macmillan, Basingstoke, 2000), chapter 5.

2.11 Cosmopolitanism: globalization tamed?

David Held

Source: *Review of International Studies*, vol. 29, 2003, pp. 465–80.

Held focuses on the challenges posed by processes of globalization, especially those that create new problems of governance. Nationalism and statism are seen as providing inadequate political resources to meet the challenges of globalization, and cosmopolitanism is proposed as a new and more appropriate way of framing politics in a global age, including the shaping of institutions for global governance. Held's argument contains both a materialist element – focused on the nature of appropriate institutions – and a moral component based upon respect for the individual in a global society.

[Held begins by pointing out that there is nothing new about processes of globalization, nor about the challenges of governance they pose. He then goes on to explore the specific character of contemporary globalization.]

Contemporary globalisation embodies elements in common with past phases, but is distinguished by some unique organisational features, creating a world in which the extensive reach of human relations and networks is matched by its relative high intensity, high velocity and high impact propensity across many facets of social life. The result is the emergence of a global economy, 24 hour trading in financial markets, multinational corporations which command economic resources in excess of those enjoyed by many countries, new forms of international regulation, the development of regional and global governance structures and the creation of global systemic problems – global warming, ozone depletion, AIDS, mass terrorism, market volatility, money laundering, the international drugs trade, among other phenomena. A number of striking challenges to the nature and form of governance are posed by these developments.

Globalisation: the challenges to governance

First, contemporary processes of globalisation and regionalisation create overlapping networks of power and interaction. These cut across territorial boundaries, putting pressure on, and straining, a world order designed in accordance with the Westphalian principle of exclusive sovereign rule over a delimited territory. One consequence of this is that the locus of effective political power is no longer simply that of national governments; effective power is shared, contested and bartered by diverse forces and agencies, public and private, crossing national, regional and international domains.

A distinctive element of this shift is the emergence of 'global politics'. Political actions in one part of the world can rapidly acquire worldwide effects. Sites of political action can become linked through rapid communications into complex networks of political inter-action. Associated with this 'stretching' of politics is a frequent intensification of global processes such that 'action at a distance' permeates the social conditions and cognitive worlds of specific communities. As a result, developments at the global level – whether economic, social or environmental – can acquire almost instantaneous local consequences and *vice versa*.

The idea of global politics challenges the traditional distinctions between the domestic and the foreign, and between the territorial and the non-territorial, as embedded in modern conceptions of 'the political'. These distinctions not only shaped modern political theory, but also institution-building, as a clear division of labour was established between great ministries of state founded to focus on domestic matters, and those created to pursue geo-political questions. Global politics highlights the richness and complexity of the interconnec-tions which now transcend states and societies in the global order. Moreover, global politics is anchored today not just in traditional geopolitical concerns (power, security, trade), but in a large diversity of social and ecological questions. Pollution, drugs, human rights and terrorism are amongst an increasing number of transnational policy issues which cut across territorial jurisdictions and existing political boundaries, and which require international cooperation for their satisfactory resolution.

Against the background of dense networks of global interaction, the power of even the greatest states comes to depend on cooperation with others for its effective execution. Nothing highlights this better than the current war on terrorism led by the US. For the fight against terrorism will depend ultimately not just on the sharing of military intelli-gence, hardware and personnel around the world, but also upon the capacity of the US to win the fight 'for the hearts and minds' of people in many regions, people who currently see the US as a self-interested bastion of privilege and arrogance. Without addressing this latter battle, the US will in all likelihood achieve, at best, only partial victories in this conflict.

We are 'unavoidably side by side', as Kant most eloquently put it over two hundred years ago. Nonetheless, in a world where powerful actors and forces cut across the boundaries of national communities in diverse ways, and where the decisions and actions of leading states can ramify across the world, the questions of who should be accountable to whom, and on what basis, do not easily resolve themselves.

The second challenge to governance concerns the development of three regulatory and political gaps which weaken political institutions, national and international. These are:

- A jurisdictional gap – the discrepancy between national, separate units of policy-making and a regionalised and globalised world, giving rise to the problem of external-ities such as the degradation of the global commons, who is responsible for them, and how these agents can be held to account;
- An incentive gap – the challenge posed by the fact that, in the absence of any supra-national entity to regulate the supply of global public goods, many states will seek to free ride and/or fail to find durable collective solutions to pressing transnational problems; and
- A participation gap – the failure of the existing international system to give adequate voice to many leading global actors, state and non-state.

While governance in the global order involves multilayered, multidimensional and multi-actor processes in which institutions and politics matter a great deal to the determination of policy outcomes, these are distorted in favour of leading states and vested interests. Hence, for example, despite the vociferous dissent of many protest groups in recent years, the promotion of the global market has taken clear priority over many pressing social and environmental issues.

It is a troubling fact that while nearly 4,000 people died on 9/11, almost 30,000 children under five die each day in the developing world from preventable diseases, which have all been practically eradicated in the West. Such overwhelming disparities in life chances are not just found in the area of health, but are reproduced across almost every single indicator of global development. The third challenge to governance emerges from a reflection on this and involves what might be called a 'moral gap'; that is, a gap defined by:

1   A world in which over 1.2 bn people live on less than a dollar a day; 46 per cent of the world's population live on less than $2 a day; and 20 per cent of the world's population enjoy over 80 per cent of its income; and
2   Commitments and values of, at best, 'passive indifference' to this, marked by UN expenditure per annum of $1.25 bn (plus peace-keeping); US *per annum* confectionery expenditure of $27 bn; US *per annum* alcohol expenditure of $70 bn, and US *per annum* expenditure on cars of $550 bn.

This is not an anti-America statement, of course. Equivalent EU figures could have been highlighted. [. . .]

That global systems of rules and inequalities spark conflict and contestation can hardly be a surprise, especially given the visibility of the world's life-styles in an age of mass media. How others live is now generally known to us, and how we live is generally known to them.

Fourth, there has been a shift from relatively distinct national communication and economic systems to their more complex and diverse enmeshment at regional and global levels, and from government to multilevel governance. Yet, there are few grounds for thinking that a parallel 'globalisation' of political identities has taken place. One exception to this is to be found among the elites of the global order – the networks of experts and specialists, senior administrative personnel and transnational business executives – and those who track and contest their activities, the loose constellation of social movements (including the anti-globalisation movement), trade unionists and (a few) politicians and intellectuals. But these groups are not typical. Thus, we live with a challenging paradox – that governance is becoming increasingly a multilevel, intricately institutionalised and spatially dispersed activity, while representation, loyalty and identity remain stubbornly rooted in traditional ethnic, regional and national communities. One important qualification can usefully be added to this point; while those who have a commitment to the global order as a whole and to international institutions are a distinct minority, a generational divide is evident. Those born after the Second World War are more likely to see themselves as cosmopolitans, to support the UN system and lend their support to the free trade system and the free movement of migrants. [. . .]

Hence, the shift from government to multilayered governance, from national economies to economic globalisation, is a potentially unstable shift, capable of reversal in some respects and certainly capable of engendering a fierce reaction – a reaction drawing on nostalgia, romanticised conceptions of political community, hostility to outsiders (refugees) and a search for a pure national state (for example, in the politics of Le Pen in France). But this reaction itself is likely to be highly unstable, and perhaps a relatively short- or medium-term phenomenon. To understand why this is so, nationalism has to be disaggregated.

As 'cultural nationalism' it is, and in all probability will remain, central to people's identity; however, as political nationalism – the assertion of the exclusive political priority of national identity and the national interest – it may not remain as significant; for political nationalism cannot deliver many sought-after public goods without seeking accommodation with others, in and through regional and global collaboration. In this respect, only an international or, better still, a cosmopolitan outlook can, ultimately, accommodate itself to the political challenges of a more global era, marked by overlapping communities of fate and multilevel/multilayered politics.

What is cosmopolitanism?

Cosmopolitanism is concerned to disclose the cultural, ethical and legal basis of political order in a world where political communities and states matter, but not only and exclusively. It dates at least to the Stoics' description of themselves as cosmopolitans – 'human beings living in a world of human beings and only incidentally members of polities'.[1] The Stoic emphasis on the morally contingent nature of membership of a political community might seem anachronistic after over three hundred years of state development. But what is neither anachronistic nor misplaced is the recognition of the partiality, one-sidedness and limitedness of 'reasons of state' when judged from the perspective of a world of 'overlapping communities of fate' – where the trajectories of each and every country are tightly entwined. States can be conceived as vehicles to aid the delivery of effective public regulation, equal liberty and social justice, but they should not be thought of as ontologically privileged. They can be judged by how far they deliver these public goods and how far they fail; for the history of states is, of course, marked not just by phases of corruption and bad management but also by the most brutal episodes. Cosmopolitanism today must take this as a starting point, and build an ethically sound and politically robust conception of the proper basis of political community, and of the relations among communities. This requires recognition of at least four fundamental principles.

The first is that the ultimate units of moral concern are individual people, not states or other particular forms of human association. Humankind belongs to a single moral realm in which each person is equally worthy of respect and consideration. This notion can be referred to as the principle of individualist moral egalitarianism or, simply, egalitarian individualism. To think of people as having equal moral value is to make a general claim about the basic units of the world comprising persons as free and equal beings. This broad position runs counter to the view of moral particularists that belonging to a given community limits and determines the moral worth of individuals and the nature of their autonomy. It does so not to deny cultural diversity and difference, but to affirm that there are limits to the moral validity of particular communities – limits which recognise, and demand, that we must treat with equal respect the dignity of reason and moral choice in every human being.

The second principle emphasises that the status of equal worth should be acknowledged by everyone. It is an attribute of every living person, and the basis on which each person ought to constitute their relations with others. Each person has an equal stake in this universal ethical realm and is, accordingly, required to respect all other people's status as a basic unit of moral interest. This second element of contemporary cosmopolitanism can be called the principle of reciprocal recognition.

The third principle, the principle of consent, recognises that a commitment to equal worth and equal moral value requires a non-coercive political process in and through which people can negotiate and pursue their interconnections, interdependence and differences. Interlocking lives, projects and communities require forms of decision-making which take account of each person's equal status in such processes. The principle of consent constitutes the basis of non-coercive collective agreement and governance.

The fourth principle, which I call the principle of inclusiveness and subsidiarity, seeks to clarify the fundamental criterion of drawing proper boundaries around units of collective decision-making, and on what grounds. At its simplest, it connotes that those significantly (that is, non-trivially) affected by public decisions, issues or processes should, *ceteris paribus*, have an equal opportunity, directly or indirectly through elected representatives, to influence and shape them. Those affected by public decisions ought to have a say in their making. Accordingly, collective decision-making is best located when it is closest to, and involves, those whose opportunities and life chances are determined by significant social processes and forces.

Principle four points to the necessity of both the decentralisation and centralisation of political power. If decision-making is decentralised as much as possible, it maximises the opportunity of each person to influence the social conditions that shape his or her life. But if the decisions at issue are translocal, transnational or transregional, then political institutions need not only be locally based but must also have a wider scope and framework of operation. In this context, the creation of diverse sites and levels of democratic fora may be unavoidable. It may be unavoidable, paradoxically, for the very same reasons as decentralisation is desirable: it creates the possibility of including people who are significantly affected by a political issue in the public (in this case, transcommunity public) sphere. The principle of inclusiveness and subsidiarity yields the possibility of multilevel democratic governance; it may require diverse and multiple democratic public fora for its suitable enactment. Accordingly, the ideal type of appropriate democratic jurisdictions cannot be assumed to take just one form – as it does in the theory of the liberal democratic nation-state. [. . .]

I take cosmopolitanism to connote, in the last instance, the ethical and political space which sets out the terms of reference for the recognition of people's equal moral worth, their active agency and what is essential for their autonomy and development; it seeks to recognise, affirm and nurture human agency, and to build on principles that all could reasonably assent to. On the other hand, this cosmopolitan point of view must also recognise that the meaning of ideas such as equal dignity, equal respect and equal consideration cannot be specified once and for all. [. . .]

The principles of egalitarian individualism, reciprocal recognition, consent, and inclusiveness and subsidiarity find direct expression in significant post-Second World War legal and institutional initiatives. To begin with, the 1948 UN Declaration of Human Rights and subsequent 1966 Covenants of Rights raised the principle of egalitarian individualism to a universal reference point: the requirements that each person be treated with equal concern and respect, irrespective of the state in which they were born or brought up, is the central plank of the human rights world-view. In addition, the formal recognition in the preamble to the UN Declaration of all people as persons with 'equal and inalienable rights', and as 'the foundation of freedom, justice and peace in the world', marked a turning point in the development of cosmopolitan legal thinking. Single persons are recognised as subjects of international law and, in principle, the ultimate source of political authority. The principle of consent is crucial to this development.

The tentative acceptance of the equal worth and equal political status of all human beings finds reinforcement in a host of post-Second World War legal and institutional developments – in the acknowledgment of the necessity of a minimum of civilised conduct found in the laws of war and weapons diffusion; in the commitment to the principles of the Nuremberg and Tokyo war crimes tribunals (1945–46, 1946–48), the Torture Convention (1984) and the statute of the International Criminal Court (1998) which outlaws genocide, war crimes and crimes against humanity; in the growing recognition of democracy as the fundamental standard of political legitimacy which finds entrenchment in the International Bill of Human Rights and in a number of regional treaties; and in the unprecedented flurry of regional and global initiatives, regimes, institutions and networks seeking to tackle global warming, ozone depletion, the pollution of oceans and rivers, and nuclear risks, among many other factors.

Nonetheless, while there may be cosmopolitan elements to existing international law and regulation, these have not, it hardly needs emphasising, generated a new deep-rooted structure of cosmopolitan regulation and accountability. The principle of egalitarian individualism may be widely recognised, but it scarcely structures much political and economic policy, north or south. The principle of universal recognition informs the notion of human rights and other legal initiatives such as the 'common heritage of humankind' (embedded in the Law of the Sea, 1982), but it is not at the heart of the politics of sovereign states or corporate colossi. The principle of consent might be appealed to in order to justify limits on the actions of particular states and IGOs, but it is, at best, only an incidental part of the institutional dynamics that have created such chronic political problems as the externalities generated by many national economic and energy policies. The principle of inclusiveness and subsidiarity might be invoked to ensure that states, rich or poor, can block direct interference in their sovereign affairs, but it is generally bypassed in a world of overlapping communities of fate in areas as diverse as health, the environment and the global distribution of wealth and income. This should not come as a surprise.

The susceptibility of the UN to the agendas of the most powerful states, the weaknesses of many of its enforcement operations (or lack of them altogether), the underfunding of its organisations, the continued dependency of its programmes on the financial support of a few major states, the inadequacies of the policing of many environmental regimes (regional and global) – are all indicative of the disjuncture between cosmopolitan aspirations and their partial and one-sided application. Cosmopolitan theory, with its emphasis on illegitimate structures of power and interest, has to be reconnected to cosmopolitan institution-building. We require a shift from a club-driven and executive-led multilateralism – which is typically secretive and exclusionary – to a more transparent, accountable and just form of governance – a socially backed, cosmopolitan multilateralism.

Cosmopolitan multilateralism

Cosmopolitan multilateralism takes as its starting point a world of 'overlapping communities of fate'. Recognising the complex structures of an interconnected world, it views certain issues – such as housing, sanitation and policing – as appropriate for spatially delimited political spheres (the city, region or state), while it sees others – such as the environment, world health and economic regulation – as requiring new, more extensive institutions to address them. Deliberative and decision-making centres beyond national territories are appropriately situated when cosmopolitan principles can only be upheld properly in a transnational context; when those significantly affected by a public matter constitute a transnational grouping; and when 'lower' levels of decision-making cannot satisfactorily manage transnational or international policy questions. Of course, the boundaries demarcating different levels of governance will always be contested, as they are, for example, in many existing local, sub-national regional and national polities. Disputes about the appropriate jurisdiction for handling particular public issues will be complex and intensive; but better complex and intensive in a clear public framework than left simply to powerful geopolitical interests (dominant states) or market-based organisations to resolve them alone.

The possibility of a cosmopolitan polity must be linked to an expanding framework of states and agencies bound by cosmopolitan principles and rules. How should this be understood from an institutional point of view? Initially, the possibility of cosmopolitan politics would be enhanced if the UN system actually lived up to its Charter. Among other things, this would mean pursuing measures to implement key elements of the rights Conventions, and enforcing the prohibition on the discretionary right to use force. However, while each move in this direction would be helpful, it would still represent, at best, a move towards a very incomplete form of accountability and justice in global politics. For the dynamics and logic of the current hierarchical interstate system (with the US in pole position) would still represent an immensely powerful force in global affairs; the massive disparities of power and asymmetries of resource in the global political economy would be left virtually unaddressed; *ad hoc* responses to pressing international and transnational issues would remain typical; and the 'gaps' emphasised earlier would remain unbridged.

Thus, a cosmopolitan polity would need to establish an overarching network of public fora, covering cities, nation-states, regions and the wider global order. It is possible to conceive of different types of political engagement on a continuum from the local to the global, with the local marked by direct and participatory processes while larger domains with significant populations are progressively mediated by representative mechanisms. The possibilities of direct involvement in the public affairs of small communities are clearly more extensive compared to those which exist in highly differentiated social, economic and political circumstances. However, the simple juxtaposition of participatory with representative democracy is now in flux, given developments in information technology which put simultaneous two-way communication within reach of larger populations; stakeholder innovations in democratic representation, which emphasise the significance of the direct involvement of representatives of all major groupings affected by a public process, instead of all the possible individuals involved; and new approaches in deliberative democracy which do not take citizens' preferences as simply given or pre-set and, instead, seek to create accessible, diverse fora for the examination of opinion. The aim would be to establish a deliberative process whose structure grounds 'an expectation of rationally acceptable results'.[2] Such a process can be conceived of in terms of diverse public spheres in which collective views and decisions are arrived at through deliberation, deliberation which is guided by the test of impartiality, as opposed to that of simple self-interest, in the formation of political will and judgement.

[Held goes on to explore the desirable features of such a cosmopolitan political process, and to counter the claim that this is utopian; he asserts the need to articulate and promote the arguments in the face of the prevailing pessimism.]

Notes

1   Brian Barry, 'Statism and Nationalism: A Cosmopolitan Critique', in I. Shapiro and L. Brilmayer (eds), *Global Justice* (New York University Press, New York, 1999), p. 35.
2   See Jürgen Habermas, *Between Facts and Norms* (Polity, Cambridge, 1996).

Part III

The politics of dominance and resistance

Introduction

The extracts in this part draw on a radical perspective, which is critical of the prevailing structure of the world arena, and which advocates resistance to processes such as globalization. Dominance and resistance are evaluative as well as descriptive terms and they are designed to draw attention to the mechanisms which advocates of this perspective see as creating and perpetuating inequality within the world community. The roots of this perspective can be traced back to Marx who believed that is possible to develop a scientific understanding of the exploitation which takes place in capitalist systems and to identify the forces of changes which can transform such systems and bring an end to exploitation. Marx was later seen to have taken insufficient account of the international system in his theory, a deficiency remedied at least in part by Lenin, whose theory of imperialism explained how the acquisition of colonies was related to the development of capitalism. Lenin also tried to show that conflict among the imperialist states was an inevitable feature of capitalism, but this view was contested by Kautsky who identified the potential for 'ultra-imperialism' with capitalists cooperating in order to ensure the continuation of a system from which they all benefited.

Although the appropriateness of Marx's analysis has been disputed and was thought by some to have been fatally undermined by the collapse of Soviet Communism at the end of the Cold War, there is a sense in which it is as relevant as ever. There is no doubt that the world contains dominant capitalist systems – arguably even more dominant after the Cold War than in earlier periods – and that it manifests fundamental inequalities arising from differences of wealth, of access to resources and of cultural cleavages. Not only this, but in the contemporary era the processes of globalization can be seen to have sharpened these inequalities and created new dimensions of economic, political and cultural subordination. Alongside this, it can also be argued that the excesses of the dominant (Western) global powers place in jeopardy a number of global assets that should be safeguarded in the interests of all rather than exploited for the benefit of the wealthy few. It is in this context that there has arisen not only a set of theories and perspectives arguing for resistance to globalization and to the inequalities and risks it entails but also a set of political practices by the anti-globalization movement or by national and regional authorities who wish to stem the tide of 'hyper-globalization'. The extracts gathered together here deal both with some of the longer standing interpretations of capitalism and imperialism and with some of the more recent interpretations of global harm, insecurities and the need for strategies of resistance.

The first three extracts are chosen to show some of the ways in which dominance and exploitation were interpreted before the age of globalization. Galtung (3.1), writing in the 1960s, was concerned to provide an account of the essential processes of imperialism and subordination. His model takes account of the conflict and inequalities both within and between states, and contends that domination and subordination are structural and systematic outcomes of the nature of capitalism. Galtung's model shows how the ruling class of an imperial state can use the ruling class of a penetrated state as a bridgehead in the process of establishing imperialism, and how this can be used to transmit dominant economic, political and cultural ideas and institutions. Class conflict – a central feature of classical Marxism – is thus related to the explanation of imperialism in the contemporary world. Wallerstein (3.2) offers a broader framework for thinking about dominance and dependency in the world arena. He argues that in the course of world history there have been two types of world systems: first, world empires, where the structure of the centralized political system coincides with the structure of the centralized economic system, and second, world economies, where the integrated structure of the world economy is contrasted with the fragmented political structure provided by a system of independent states. Both types of system are characterized by inequality, but the remarkable fact about the contemporary world economy is that it can be traced back to the sixteenth century. Wallerstein attributes the survival of this system to the existence of semi-peripheral states which have acted as a cushion between the exploiting centre states and the exploited periphery. Hymer (3.3) represents a different strand in the development of thinking about dominance and dependence, focusing on the growing potential for conflict between polarization and conflict between institutions representing the transnational interests of international capital and the nation states where transnational corporations are physically located. Hymer sees multinational corporations as the major agent of transnationalization; by using information technology, MNCs have been able to impose increasing centralization on the world economy. But he argues that this process will be threatened in the Third World of poor countries if there is a failure to ensure that sufficient benefits 'trickle down' to national communities. Without these benefits, the MNCs will come to rely increasingly on repression. By making this argument, Hymer sets a central part of the scene for later treatments of dominance and resistance in a globalizing world.

The two following selections take forward analysis of the ways in which globalization has reflected continuity and change in the nature of dominance and dependence. Robinson (3.4) takes a historical materialist view on the development of capitalism, emphasising as Marx did the material relations between classes and groups. He starts from the position that globalization is a new phase in the development of capitalism, characterized by the transnational expansion of capital and the 'marketization' of social life on a global scale. He goes on to highlight the development of a 'transnational state' reflecting the interests of the transnational capitalist class, and expressed in a range of institutions, not only national states but also international organizations, that transmit and apply the disciplines of global capitalism. Amongst other effects, this creates a new insecurity and danger of exclusion for the working class world wide, not simply at the national level. Peter Gowan (3.5) takes a different angle on the issue by exploring the nature of what he terms 'neo-liberal cosmopolitanism': the set of ideas and strategies associated with the dominant transnational class, which also governs political and economic aspects of the behaviour of states. The neo-liberal world order entails the imposition of limits on the sovereignty of subordinate states, along with active intervention either by states or by global organizations; it promotes the interests of what Gowan calls the 'Pacific Union' of rich Western states, led by the United States.

This vision of dominant world capitalist classes, associated with dominant states, especially the United States, has fundamental implications for the analysis of key global issues. The next three extracts by Fox Piven, Kaldor and Duffield focus sharply on a number of these issues. Fox Piven (3.6) explores the ways in which capitalist globalization intersects with 'identity politics', creating new and often intractable political cleavages. The undermining of nationally-based political organizations creates a fluid constellation of culturally or ethnically based movements; rather than creating new avenues of influence and access (as would be argued by authors in Part II of this book) this new set of divisions perpetuates insecurity and provides new channels for exploitation of vulnerable and excluded groups. Kaldor (3.7) focuses on the 'global war economy', arguing that there is a strong link between the globalized capitalist economy, the changing character of war and violence, and the spread of 'new wars' in the post-Cold War era. By taking this position, she challenges the traditional (national and state-centric) view of the 'war economy' and proposes an uncomfortable alternative to Western views of the 'new world order'. Duffield (3.8) accepts Kaldor's basic argument about 'new wars' and relates it specifically to issues of development; his core argument is that the emerging 'liberal' world system privileges a core of highly developed capitalist states, thereby marginalizing, excluding and subordinating the 'global south' of less developed countries. This situation redefines ideas such as 'peace', 'development' and 'security' and contributes to the interventionism also discerned by Kaldor.

The final three extracts in this part deal with the ways in which globalization can be 'imagined' and the ways in which strategies of resistance to the forces of globalization might be developed and applied. Angus Cameron and Ronen Palan (3.9) focus on the ways in which narratives and 'imagined economies' have developed around the apparent 'loss' of the national economy and the emergence of diverse expressions of globalization and 'globality'. In particular, they identify a 'trifurcation' of the state: this is expressed in overlapping narratives about both the role of the state and 'social exclusion' or poverty in the globalizing world, and it has important implications for notions of resistance to globalization. Using ideas from a range of thinkers, Chin and Mittelman (3.10) conceptualize resistance in three ways: 'counter-hegemony', 'counter-movements' and 'infrapolitics'. The first of these implies strategies of resistance designed to modify or overthrow hegemonic state institutions, the second implies opposition to market forces, and the third implies the generation of new 'counter-discourses' of ideas among individuals and social groups. It can readily be seen that this set of ideas emphasizes subversive or 'bottom-up' strategies aimed at transforming the dominant social and ideational structures. The final selection, by Petras and Veltmayer, begins by reiterating a number of ideas about globalization, but then goes on to relate this to the development of a 'new imperialism' centred on the United States and to the characteristics and strategies of the anti-globalization movement. By taking this perspective, they are able to point out the complexities and divisions that exist within the anti-globalization movement itself.

It can be seen from this summary that the extracts in this part of the book reflect the diversity of views within the range of authors dealing with dominance and resistance. A number of themes emerge very strongly, however. First, all of the authors stress the importance of historical and cultural processes, which reveal both the continuities of exploitation and inequality and the novelty of the problems produced by globalization. Second, all of them are critical of the current world order, believing that it perpetuates inequality, insecurity and the risk of global crises (although some, such as Cameron and Palan, are more concerned to identify competing conceptions of that global order). Equally, all of the extracts see the current situation as unacceptable or as subject to competing definitions, and this leads them to debate not only the mechanisms that create this situation but also (more explicitly in some cases than in others) the strategies that might be used to resist, modify or even overthrow the current capitalist world order. There is not a great deal of optimism that this can be achieved, at least in the near future, but there is an awareness of opportunities that might be used to gain some leverage against the dominant forces, or of ways in which the grounds for political action might be effectively re-defined.

3.1 A structural theory of imperialism

Johan Galtung

Source: *Journal of Peace Research*, vol. 13, no. 2 (1971), pp. 81–94.

Galtung develops a theory of imperialism to account for inequality within and between nations and the resistance of this inequality to change. He distinguishes between centre and periphery countries and argues that those in power in the former have a community of interest with those in power in the latter. The result is a relationship which operates at the expense of the majority of the people in peripheral countries, but which is largely in the interest of the majority of the people in centre countries.

Introduction

This theory takes as its point of departure two of the most glaring facts about this world: the tremendous inequality, within and between nations, in almost all aspects of human living conditions, including the power to decide over those living conditions; *and* the resistance of this inequality to change. The world consists of Center and Periphery nations; and each nation, in turn, has its centers and periphery. Hence, our concern is with the mechanism underlying this discrepancy.

[Galtung goes on to discuss this discrepancy in terms of imperialism.]

Briefly stated, imperialism is a system that splits up collectivities and relates some of the parts to each other in relations of *harmony of interest*, and other parts in relations of *disharmony of interest*, or *conflict of interest*.

Defining 'conflict of interest'

'Conflict of interest' is a special case of conflict in general, defined as a situation where parties are pursuing incompatible goals. In our special case, these goals are stipulated by an outsider as the 'true' interests of the parties, disregarding wholly or completely what the parties themselves say explicitly are the values they pursue. One reason for this is the rejection of the dogma of unlimited rationality: actors do *not* necessarily know, or they are unable to express, what their interest is. Another, more important, reason is that rationality is unevenly distributed, that some may dominate the minds of others, and that this may lead to 'false consciousness'. Thus, learning to suppress one's own true interests may be a major part of socialization in general and education in particular.

Let us refer to this true interest as LC, *living condition*. It may perhaps be measured by using such indicators as income, standard of living in the usual materialistic sense – but notions of *quality of life* would certainly also enter, not to mention notions of *autonomy*. But the precise content of LC is less important for our purpose than the definition of conflict of interest:

> There is *conflict*, or *disharmony of interest*, if the two parties are coupled together in such a way that the LC *gap* between them is *increasing*.
>
> There is *no conflict*, or *harmony of interest*, if the two parties are coupled together in such a way that the LC *gap* between them is *decreasing down to zero*.

[. . .] It is clear that the concept of interest used here is based on an ideology, or a *value premise of equality*. An interaction relation and interaction structure set up such that inequality is the result is seen as a coupling not in the interest of the weaker party. This is a value premise like so many other value premises in social science explorations, such as 'direct violence is bad', 'economic growth is good', 'conflict should be resolved', etc. As in all other types of social science, the goal should not be an 'objective' social science freed from all such value premises, but a more honest social science where the value premises are made explicit.

Defining 'imperialism'

We shall now define imperialism by using the building blocks presented in the preceding two sections. In our two-nation world, imperialism can be defined as one way in which the Center nation has power over the Periphery nation, so as to bring about a condition of disharmony of interest between them. Concretely, *imperialism* is a relation between a Center and a Periphery nation so that

1   there is *harmony of interest* between the *center in the Center* nation and the *center in the Periphery* nation,
2   there is more *disharmony of interest* within the Periphery nation than within the Center nations,
3   there is *disharmony of interest* between the *periphery in the Center* nation and the *periphery in the Periphery* nation.

Diagrammatically it looks something like Figure 1. This complex definition, borrowing largely from Lenin, needs spelling out. The basic idea is, as mentioned, that the center in the Center nation has a bridgehead in the Periphery nation, and a well-chosen one: the center in the Periphery nation. This is established such that the Periphery center is tied to the Center center with the best possible tie: the tie of harmony of interest. They are linked so that they go up together and down, even under, together.

Inside the two nations there is disharmony of interest. They are both in one way or another vertical societies with LC gaps – otherwise there is no possibility of locating a center and a periphery. Moreover, the gap is not decreasing, but is at best constant. But the basic idea, absolutely fundamental for the whole theory to be developed, is that *there is more disharmony in the Periphery nation than in the Center nation*. At the simplest static level of description this means there is more inequality in the Periphery than in the Center. At the more complex level we might talk in terms of the gap opening more quickly in the Periphery than in the Center, where it might even remain constant. Through welfare state activities, redistribution takes

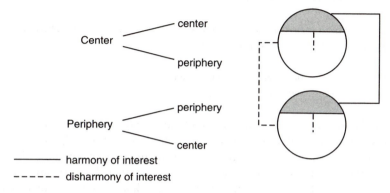

center

Center

periphery

periphery

Periphery

center

——————— harmony of interest

– – – – – – disharmony of interest

Figure 1 The structure of imperialism

place and disharmony is reduced for at least some LC dimensions, including income, but usually excluding power.

If we now would capture in a few sentences what imperialism is about, we might perhaps say something like this:

In the Periphery nation, the center grows more than the periphery, due partly to how interaction between center and periphery is organized. Without necessarily thinking of economic interaction, the center is more enriched than the periphery. However, for part of this enrichment, the center in the Periphery only serves as a transmission belt (e.g. as commercial firms, trading companies) for value (e.g. raw materials) forwarded to the Center nation. This value enters the Center in the center, with some of it drizzling down to the periphery in the Center. Importantly, there is less disharmony of interest in the Center than in the Periphery, so that *the total arrangement is largely in the interest of the periphery in the Center.* Within the Center the two parties may be opposed to each other. But in the total game, the periphery see themselves more as the partners of the center in the Center than as the partners of the periphery in the Periphery – and this is the essential trick of the game. Alliance formation between the two peripheries is avoided, while the Center nation becomes more and the Periphery nation less cohesive – and hence less able to develop long-term strategies. [. . .]

The mechanisms of imperialism

The two basic mechanisms of imperialism both concern the *relation* between the parties concerned, particularly between the nations. The first mechanism concerns the *interaction relation* itself, the second how these relations are put together in a larger interaction structure:

1   the principle of *vertical interaction relation*
2   the principle of *feudal interaction structure.*

The basic point about interaction is, of course, that people and nations have different values that complement each other, and then engage in exchange. Some nations produce oil, other nations produce tractors, and they then carry out an exchange according to the principles of comparative advantages. Imagine that our two-nation system has a prehistory of no interaction at all, and then starts with this type of interaction. Obviously both will be changed by it, and more particularly: a gap between them is likely to open and widen if the interaction is cumulatively asymmetric in terms of what the two parties get out of it.

To study whether the interaction is symmetric or asymmetric, on equal or unequal terms, *two* factors arising from the interaction have to be examined:

1   *the value-exchange between the actors – inter-actor effects*
2   *the effects inside the actors – intra-actor effects.*

In *economic* relations the first is most commonly analyzed, not only by liberal but also by Marxist economists. The inter-actor flow can be observed as flows of goods and services in either direction, and can literally be measured at the main points of entry: the customs houses and the national banks. The flow both ways can then be compared in various ways. Most important is the comparison in terms of *who benefits most*, and for this purpose intra-actor effects also have to be taken into consideration. [. . .]

It is certainly meaningful and important to talk in terms of unequal exchange or asymmetric interaction, but not quite unproblematic what its precise meaning should be. For that reason, it may be helpful to think in terms of three stages or types of exploitation, partly reflecting historical *processes* in chronological order, and partly reflecting types of *thinking* about exploitation.

In the first stage of exploitation, A simply engages in looting and takes away the raw materials without offering anything in return. If he steals out of pure nature there is no human interaction involved, but we assume that he forces 'natives' to work for him and do the extraction work. It is like the slave-owner who lives on the work produced by slaves – which is quantitatively not too different from the landowner who has land-workers working for him five out of seven days a week.

In the second stage, A starts offering something 'in return'. Oil, pitch, land, etc. is 'bought' for a couple of beads – it is no longer simply taken away without asking any questions about ownership. The price paid is ridiculous. However, as power relations in the international systems change, perhaps mainly by bringing the power level of the weaker party up from zero to some low positive value, A has to contribute more: for instance, pay more for the oil. The question is now whether there is a cut-off point after which the exchange becomes equal, and what the criterion for that cut-off point would be. Absence of subjective dissatisfaction – B says that he is now content? Objective market values or the number of man-hours that have gone into the production on either side?

There are difficulties with all these conceptions. But instead of elaborating on this, we shall rather direct our attention to the shared failure of all these attempts to look at *intra-actor effects*. Does the interaction have enriching or impoverishing effects *inside* the actor, or does it just lead to a stand-still? This type of question leads us to the third stage of exploitation, where there may be some balance in the flow between the actors, but great differences in the effect the interaction has within them.

As an example let us use nations exchanging oil for tractors. The basic point is that this involves different levels of processing, where we define 'processing' as an activity imposing Culture on Nature. In the case of crude oil the product is (almost) pure Nature; in the case of tractors it would be wrong to say that it is a case of pure Culture, pure *form* (like mathematics, music). A transistor radio, an integrated circuit, these would be better examples because Nature has been brought down to a minimum. The tractor is still too much iron and rubber to be a pure case.

The major point now is the *gap in processing level* between oil and tractors and the differential effect this gap will have on the two nations. In one nation the oil deposit may be at the water-front, and all that is needed is a derrick and some simple mooring facilities to pump the oil straight into a ship – e.g. a Norwegian tanker – that can bring the oil to the country where it will provide energy to run, among other things, the tractor factories. In the other nation the effects may be extremely far-reaching due to the complexity of the product and the connectedness of the society. [. . .]

If the first mechanism, the *vertical interaction relation*, is the major factor behind inequality, then the second mechanism, the *feudal interaction structure*, is the factor that maintains and reinforces this inequality by protecting it. There are four rules defining this particular interaction structure:

1   interaction between Center and Periphery is *vertical*;
2   interaction between Periphery and Periphery is *missing*;
3   multilateral interaction involving all three is *missing*;
4   interaction with the outside world is *monopolized* by the Center with two implications:
     a   Periphery interaction with other Center nations is *missing*;
     b   Center as well as Periphery interaction with Periphery nations belonging to other Center nations is *missing*.

This relation can be depicted as in Figure 2. As indicated in the figure the number of Periphery nations attached to any given Center nation can, of course, vary. In this figure we have also depicted the rule 'if you stay off my satellites, I will stay off yours'.

Some important *economic* consequences of this structure should be spelled out.

First and most obvious: the *concentration on trade partners*. A Periphery nation should, as a result of these two mechanisms, have most of its trade with 'its' Center nation. In other words, empirically we would expect high levels of *import concentration* as well as *export concentration* in the Periphery, as opposed to the Center, which is more free to extend its trade relations in almost any direction – except in the pure case, with the Periphery of other Center nations.

Second, and not so obvious, is the *commodity concentration*: the tendency for Periphery nations to have only one or very few primary products to export. This would be a trivial matter if it could be explained entirely in terms of geography, if e.g. oil countries were systematically poor as to ore, ore countries poor as to bananas and coffee, etc. But this can hardly be assumed to be the general case: Nature does not distribute its riches that way.

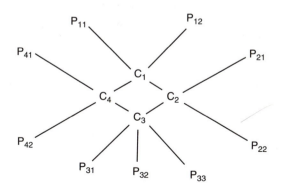

Figure 2 A feudal Center–Periphery structure

There is a historical rather than a geographical explanation to this. A territory may have been exploited for the raw materials most easily available and/or most needed in the Center, and this, in turn, leads to a certain social structure, to communication lines to the deposits, to trade structures, to the emergence of certain center groups (often based on ownership of that particular raw material), and so on. To start exploiting a new kind of raw material in the same territory might upset carefully designed local balances; hence, it might be easier to have a fresh start for that new raw material in virgin territory with no bridge-head already prepared for imperialist exploits. In order to substantiate this hypothesis we would have to demonstrate that there are particularly underutilized and systematically underexplored deposits precisely in countries where one type of raw materials has already been exploited.

The combined effect of these two consequences is a *dependency* of the Periphery on the Center. Since the Periphery usually has a much smaller GNP, the trade between them is a much higher percentage of the GNP for the Periphery, and with both partner and commodity concentration, the Periphery becomes particularly vulnerable to fluctuations in demands and prices. At the same time the center in the Periphery depends on the Center for its supply of consumer goods. Import substitution industries will usually lead to consumer goods that look homespun and unchic, particularly if there is planned obsolescence in the production of these goods in the Center, plus a demand for equality between the two centers maintained by demonstration effects and frequent visits to the Center.

However, the most important consequence is political and has to do with the systematic utilization of feudal interaction structures as a way of protecting the Center against the Periphery. The feudal interaction structure is in social science language nothing but an expression of the old political maxim *divide et impera*, divide and rule, as a strategy used systematically by the Center relative to the Periphery nations. How could – for example – a small foggy island in the North Sea rule over one quarter of the world? By isolating the Periphery parts from each other, by having them geographically at sufficient distance from each other to impede any real alliance formation, by having separate deals with them so as to tie them to the Center in particularistic ways, by reducing multilateralism to a minimum with all kinds of graded membership, *and* by having the Mother country assume the role of window to the world.

However, this point can be much more clearly seen if we combine the two mechanisms and extend what has been said so far for relations between Center and Periphery *nations* to relations between center and periphery *groups* within nations. Under an imperialist structure the two mechanisms are used not only between nations but also within nations, but less so in the Center nation than in the Periphery nation. In other words, there is vertical division of labor within as well as between nations. And these two levels of organization are intimately linked to each other (as A.G. Frank always has emphasized) in the sense that the center in the Periphery interaction structure is also that group with which the Center nation has its harmony of interest, the group used as a bridgehead.

Thus, the combined operation of the two mechanisms at the two levels builds into the structure a subtle grid of protection measures against the major potential source of 'trouble', the periphery in the Periphery. [. . .]

Obviously, the more perfectly the mechanisms of imperialism within and between nations are put to work, the less overt machinery of oppression is needed and the smaller can the center groups be, relative to the total population involved. *Only imperfect, amateurish imperialism needs weapons; professional imperialism is based on structural rather than direct violence.*

The types of imperialism

We shall now make this more concrete by distinguishing between five types of imperialism depending on the *type* of exchange between Center and Periphery nations:

1   *economic*
2   *political*
3   *military*
4   *communication*
5   *cultural.*

The order of presentation is rather random: we have no theory that one is more basic than the others, or precedes the others. Rather, this is like a Pentagon or a Soviet Star: imperialism can start from any corner. They should all be examined regarding the extent to which they generate interaction patterns that utilize the two *mechanisms* of imperialism so as to fulfill the three *criteria* of imperialism, or at least the first of them.

The most basic of the two mechanisms is *vertical* interaction, which in its modern form is conceived of as interaction across a gap in processing level. In other words, what is exchanged between the two nations is not only not the same things (which would have been stupid) but things of a quite different kind, the difference being in terms of where the most complex and stimulating operations take place. One tentative list, expanding what has been said in the previous section about economic interaction, might look like Table 1. [. . .]

The vertical nature of this type of *economic* interaction has been spelled out in detail above since we have used that type of imperialism to exemplify definition and mechanisms. Let us look more at the other types of vertical interaction.

The *political* one is clear: the concept of a 'mother' country, the Center nation, is also an indication of how the decision-making center is dislocated, away from the nation itself and towards the Center nation. These decisions may then affect economic, military, communication, and cultural patterns. Important here is the division of labor involved: some nations produce decisions, others supply obedience. The decisions may be made upon application, as in 'bilateral technical assistance', or in consultation – or they may simply emerge by virtue of the model-imitator distinction. Nothing serves that distinction quite so well as unilinear concepts of 'development' and 'modernization', according to which Center nations possess some superior kind of structure for others to imitate (as long as the Center's central position is not seriously challenged), and which gives a special aura of legitimacy to any idea emanating from the Center. Thus, structures and decisions developed in the 'motherland of liberalism' or in the 'fatherland of socialism' serve as models by virtue of their place of origin, not by virtue of their substance.

Table 1 The five types of imperialism

Type	Center nation provides	Periphery nation provides
Economic	Processing, means of production	Raw materials, markets
Political	Decisions, models	Obedience, imitators
Military	Protection, means of destruction	Discipline, traditional hardware
Communication	News, means of communication	Events, passengers, goods
Cultural	Teaching, means of creation – autonomy	Learning, validation – dependence

The *military* implications or parallels are also rather obvious. It cannot be emphasized enough that the economic division of labor is also one which ensures that the Center nations economically speaking also become the Center nations in a military sense: only they have the industrial capacity to develop the technological hardware – and also are often the only ones with the social structure compatible with a modern army. He who produces tractors can easily produce tanks, but he who delivers oil cannot defend himself by throwing it in the face of the aggressors. He has to depend on the tank-producer, either for protection or for acquisition (on terms dictated by the Center). And just as there is a division of labor with the Center nation producing manufactured goods on the basis of raw materials extracted in the Periphery nation, there is also a division of labor with the *Center nations processing the obedience provided by the Periphery nations into decisions that can be implemented.* Moreover, there is also a division of labor with the Center providing the protection (and often also the officers or at least the instructors in 'counter-insurgency') and the Periphery the discipline and the soldiers needed – not to mention the apprentices of 'military advisors' from the Center.

As to the fourth type, *communication* imperialism, the emphasis in the analysis is usually turned toward the second mechanism of imperialism: the feudal interaction structure. That this largely holds for most world communication and transportation patterns has been amply demonstrated. But perhaps more important is the vertical nature of the division of labor in the field of communication/transportation. It is trivial that a high level of industrial capacity is necessary to develop the latest in transportation and communication technology. The preceding generation of *means of communication/transportation* can always be sold, sometimes secondhand, to the Periphery as part of the general vertical trade/aid structure, alongside the *means of production* (economic sector), the *means of destruction* (military sector), and the *means of creation* (cultural sector). The Center's planes and ships are faster, more direct, look more reliable, attract more passengers, more goods. And when the Periphery finally catches up, the Center will already for a long time have dominated the field of communication satellites.

One special version of this principle is a combination of cultural and communication exchange: *news communication*. We all know that the major agencies are in the hands of the Center countries, relying on Center-dominated, feudal networks of communication. What is not so well analyzed is how Center news takes up a much larger proportion of Periphery news media than vice versa, just as trade with the Center is a larger proportion of Periphery total trade than vice versa. In other words, the pattern of partner concentration as something found more in the Periphery than in the Center is very pronounced. The Periphery nations do not write or read much about each other, especially not across bloc borders, and they read more about 'their' Center than about other Centers – because the press is written and read by the center in the Periphery, who want to know more about that most 'relevant' part of the world – for them.

Another aspect of vertical division of labor in the news business should also be pointed out. Just as the Periphery produces raw material that the Center turns into processed goods, *the Periphery also produces events that the Center turns into news.* This is done by training journalists to see events with Center eyes, and by setting up a chain of communication that filters and processes events so that they fit the general pattern.

The latter concept brings us straight into *cultural* imperialism, a subtype of which is scientific imperialism. The division of labor between teachers and learners is clear: it is not the division of labor as such (found in most situations of transmission of knowledge) that constitutes imperialism, but the location of the teachers, and of the learners, in a broader setting. If the Center always provides the teachers and the definition of that worthy of being taught (from the gospels of Christianity to the gospels of Technology), and the Periphery always provides the learners, then there is a pattern which smacks of imperialism. The satellite nation in the Periphery will also know that nothing flatters the Center quite so much as being encouraged to teach, and being seen as a model, and that the Periphery can get much in return from a humble, culture-seeking strategy (just as it will get little but aggression if it starts teaching the Center anything – like Czechoslovakia, who started lecturing the Soviet Union on socialism). For in accepting cultural transmission the Periphery also, implicitly, validates for the Center the culture developed in the center, whether that center is intra- or international. This serves to reinforce the Center as a center, for it will then continue to develop culture along with transmitting it, thus creating lasting demand for the latest innovations. Theories, like cars and fashions, have their life-cycle, and whether the obsolescence is planned or not there will always be a time-lag in a structure with a pronounced difference between center and periphery. Thus, the tram workers in Rio de Janeiro may carry banners supporting Auguste Comte one hundred years after the center of the Center forgot who he was. [. . .]

In science we find a particular version of vertical division of labor, very similar to economic division of labor: the pattern of scientific teams from the Center who go to Periphery nations to collect data (raw material) in the form of deposits, sediments, flora, fauna, archeological findings, attitudes, behavioral patterns, and so on for data processing, data analysis and theory formation (processing, in general) in the Center universities (factories), so as to be able to send the finished product, a journal, a book (manufactured goods) back for consumption in the center of the Periphery – after first having created a demand for it through demonstration effect, training in the Center country, and some degree of low level participation in the data collection team. This parallel is not a joke, it is a *structure*. If in addition the precise nature of the research is to provide the Center with information that can be used economically, politically, or militarily to maintain an imperialist structure, the cultural imperialism becomes even more clear. And if to this we add the *brain drain* (and body drain) whereby 'raw' brains (students) and 'raw' bodies (unskilled workers) are moved from the Periphery to the Center and 'processed' (trained) with ample benefits to the Center, the picture becomes complete.

3.2 The rise and future demise of the world capitalist system: concepts for comparative analysis

Immanuel Wallerstein

Source: *Comparative Studies in Society and History*, vol. 16, no. 4 (1974), pp. 387–415.

Wallerstein examines the functions of states within the capitalist world economy. He identifies three structural positions – core, peripheral and semi-peripheral – the last of which is essential to the smooth running of the world-economy since it acts as a bridge between core and periphery and a channel for development. He goes on to review historical evidence for this pattern and to project it into the future.

The structural differences of core and periphery are not comprehensible unless we realize that there is a third structural position: that of the semi-periphery. This is not the result merely of establishing arbitrary cutting-points on a continuum of characteristics. Our logic is not merely inductive, sensing the presence of a third category from a comparison of indicator curves. It is also deductive. The semi-periphery is needed to make a capitalist world-economy run smoothly. Both kinds of world-system, the world-empire with a redistributive economy and the world-economy with a capitalist market economy, involve markedly unequal distribution of rewards. Thus, logically, there is immediately posed the question of how it is possible politically for such a system to persist. Why do not the majority who are exploited simply overwhelm the minority who draw disproportionate benefits? The most rapid glance at the historic record shows that these world-systems have been faced rather rarely by fundamental system-wide insurrection. While internal discontent has been eternal, it has usually taken quite long before the accumulation of the erosion of power has led to the decline of a world-system, and as often as not, an external force has been a major factor in this decline.

There have been three major mechanisms that have enabled world-systems to retain relative political stability (not in terms of the particular groups who will play the leading roles in the system, but in terms of systemic survival itself). One obviously is the concentration of military strength in the hands of the dominant forces. The modalities of this obviously vary with the technology, and there are to be sure political prerequisites for such a concentration, but nonetheless sheer force is no doubt a central consideration.

A second mechanism is the pervasiveness of an ideological commitment to the system as a whole. I do not mean what has often been termed the 'legitimation' of a system, because that term has been used to imply that the lower strata of a system feel some affinity with or loyalty towards the rulers, and I doubt that this has ever been a significant factor in the survival of world-systems. I mean rather the degree to which the staff or cadres of the system (and I leave this term deliberately vague) feel that their own well-being is wrapped up in the survival of the system as such and the competence of its leaders. It is this staff which not only propagates the myths; it is they who believe them.

But neither force nor the ideological commitment of the staff would suffice were it not for the division of the majority into a larger lower stratum and a smaller middle stratum. Both the revolutionary call for polarization as a strategy of change and the liberal economium to consensus as the basis of the liberal polity reflect this proposition. The import is far wider than its use in the analysis of contemporary political problems suggests. It is the normal condition of either kind of world-system to have a three-layered structure. When and if this ceases to be the case, the world-system disintegrates.

In a world-empire, the middle stratum is in fact accorded the role of maintaining the marginally-desirable long-distance luxury trade, while the upper stratum concentrates its resources on controlling the military machinery which can collect the tribute, the crucial mode of redistributing surplus. By providing, however, for an access to a limited portion of the surplus to urbanized elements who alone, in pre-modern societies, could contribute political cohesiveness to isolated clusters of primary producers, the upper stratum effectively buys off the potential leadership of coordinated revolt. And by denying access to political rights for this commercial-urban middle stratum, it makes them constantly vulnerable to confiscatory measures whenever their economic profits become sufficiently swollen so that they might begin to create for themselves military strength.

In a world-economy, such 'cultural' stratification is not so simple, because the absence of a single political system means the concentration of economic roles vertically rather than horizontally throughout the system. The solution then is to have three *kinds* of states, with pressures for cultural homogenization within each of them – thus, besides the upper stratum of core states and the lower stratum of peripheral states, there is a middle stratum of semi-peripheral ones.

The semi-periphery is then assigned as it were a specific economic role, but the reason is less economic than political. That is to say, one might make a good case that the world-economy as an economy would function every bit as well without a semi-periphery. But it would be far less *politically* stable, for it would mean a polarized world-system. The existence of the third category means precisely that the upper stratum is not faced with the *unified* opposition of all the others because the *middle* stratum is both exploited and exploiter. It follows that the specific economic role is not all that important, and has thus changed through the various historical stages of the modern world-system. We shall discuss these changes shortly.

Where then does class analysis fit in all of this? And what in such a formulation are nations, nationalities, peoples, ethnic groups? First of all, without arguing the point now, I would contend that all these latter terms denote variants of a single phenomenon which I will term 'ethno-nations'.

Both classes and ethnic groups, or status groups, or ethno-nations are phenomena of world-economies and much of the enormous confusion that has surrounded the concrete analysis of their functioning can be attributed quite simply to the fact that they have been analyzed as though they existed within the nation-states of this world-economy, instead of within the world-economy as a whole. This has been a Procrustean bed indeed.

The range of economic activities being far wider in the core than in the periphery, the range of syndical interest groups is far wider there. Thus, it has been widely observed that there does not exist in many parts of the world today a proletariat of the kind which exists in, say, Europe or North America. But this is a confusing way to state the observation. Industrial activity being disproportionately concentrated in certain parts of the world-economy, industrial wage-workers are to be found principally in certain geographic regions. Their interests as a syndical group are determined by their collective relationship to the world-economy. Their ability to influence the political functioning of this world-economy is shaped by the fact that they command larger percentages of the population in one sovereign entity than another. The form their organizations take has, in large part, been governed too by these political boundaries. The same might be said about industrial capitalists. Class analysis is perfectly capable of accounting for the political position of, let us say, French skilled workers if we look at their structural position and interests in the world-economy. Similarly with ethno-nations. The meaning of ethnic consciousness in a core area is considerably different from that of ethnic consciousness in a peripheral area precisely because of the different class position such ethnic groups have in the world-economy.

Political struggles of ethno-nations or segments of classes within national boundaries of course are the daily bread and butter of local politics. But their significance or consequences can only be fruitfully analyzed if one spells out the implications of their organizational activity or political demands for the functioning of the world-economy. This also incidentally makes possible more rational assessments of these politics in terms of some set of evaluative criteria such as 'left' and 'right'.

The functioning then of a capitalist world-economy requires that groups pursue their economic interests within a single world-market while seeking to distort this market for their benefit by organizing to exert influence on states, some of which are far more powerful than others but none of which controls the world-market in its entirety. Of course, we shall find on closer inspection that there are periods where one state is relatively quite powerful and other periods where power is more diffuse and contested, permitting weaker states broader ranges of action. We can talk then of the relative tightness or looseness of the world-system as an important variable and seek to analyze why this dimension tends to be cyclical in nature, as it seems to have been for several hundred years.

We are now in a position to look at the historical evolution of this capitalist world-economy itself and analyze the degree to which it is fruitful to talk of distinct stages in its evolution as a system. The emergence of the European world-economy in the 'long' sixteenth century (1450–1640) was made possible by an historical conjuncture: on those long-term trends which were the culmination of what has been sometimes described as the 'crisis of feudalism' was superimposed a more immediate cyclical crisis plus climatic changes, all of which created a dilemma that could only be resolved by a geographic expansion of the division of labor. Furthermore, the balance of inter-system forces was such as to make this realizable. Thus a geographic expansion did take place in conjunction with a demographic expansion and an upward price rise.

The remarkable thing was not that a European world-economy was thereby created, but that it survived the Hapsburg attempt to transform it into a world-empire, an attempt seriously pursued by Charles V. The Spanish attempt to absorb the whole failed because the rapid economic–demographic–technological burst forward of the preceding century made the whole enterprise too expensive for the imperial base to sustain, especially given many structural insufficiencies in Castilian economic development. Spain could afford neither the bureaucracy nor the army that was necessary to the enterprise, and in the event went bankrupt, as did the French monarchs making a similar, albeit even less plausible, attempt.

Once the Hapsburg dream of world-empire was over – and in 1557 it was over forever – the capitalist world-economy was an established system that became almost impossible to unbalance. It quickly reached an equilibrium point in its relations with other world-systems: the Ottoman and Russian world-empires, the Indian Ocean proto-world-economy. Each of the states or potential states within the European world-economy was quickly in the race to bureaucratize, to raise a standing army, to homogenize its culture, to diversify its economic activities. By 1640, those in northwest Europe had succeeded in establishing themselves as the core states; Spain and the northern Italian city-states declined into being semi-peripheral; northeastern Europe and Iberian America had become the periphery. At this point, those in semi-peripheral status had reached it by virtue of decline from a former more pre-eminent status.

It was the system-wide recession of 1650–1730 that consolidated the European world-economy and opened stage two of the modern world-economy. For the recession forced retrenchment, and the decline in relative surplus allowed room for only one core state to survive. The mode of struggle was mercantilism, which was a device of partial insulation and withdrawal from the world-market of *large* areas themselves hierarchically constructed – that is, empires within the world-economy (which is quite different from world-empires). In this struggle England first ousted the Netherlands from its commercial primacy and then resisted successfully France's attempt to catch up. As England began to speed up the process of industrialization after 1760, there was one last attempt of those capitalist forces located in France to break the imminent British hegemony. This attempt was expressed first in the French Revolution's replacement of the cadres of the regime and then in Napoleon's continental blockade. But it failed.

Stage three of the capitalist world-economy begins then, a stage of industrial rather than of agricultural capitalism. Henceforth, industrial production is no longer a minor aspect of the world market but comprises an ever large percentage of world gross production – and even more important, of world gross surplus. This involves a whole series of consequences for the world-system.

First of all, it led to the further geographic expansion of the European world-economy to include now the whole of the globe. This was in part the result of its technological feasibility both in terms of improved military firepower and improved shipping facilities which made regular trade sufficiently inexpensive to be viable. But, in addition, industrial production *required* access to raw materials of a nature and in a quantity such that the needs could not be supplied within the former boundaries. At first, however, the search for new markets was not a primary consideration in the geographic expansion since the new markets were more readily available within the old boundaries, as we shall see.

The geographic expansion of the European world-economy meant the elimination of other world-systems as well as the absorption of the remaining mini-systems. The most important world-system up to then outside of the European world-economy, Russia, entered in semi-peripheral status, the consequence of the strength of its state-machinery (including its army) and the degree of industrialization already achieved in the eighteenth century. The independences in the Latin American countries did nothing to change their peripheral status. They merely eliminated the last vestiges of Spain's semi-peripheral role and ended pockets of non-involvement in the world-economy in the interior of Latin America. Asia and Africa were absorbed into the periphery in the nineteenth century, although Japan, because of the combination of the strength of its state-machinery, the poverty of its resource base (which led to a certain disinterest on the part of world capitalist forces), and its geographic remoteness from the core areas, was able quickly to graduate into semi-peripheral status.

The absorption of Africa as part of the periphery meant the end of slavery world-wide for two reasons. First of all, the manpower that was used as slaves was now needed for cash-crop production in Africa itself, whereas in the eighteenth century Europeans had sought to *discourage* just such cash-crop production. In the second place, once Africa was part of the periphery and not the external arena, slavery was no longer economic. To understand this, we must appreciate the economics of slavery. Slaves receiving the lowest conceivable reward for their labor are the least productive form of labor and have the shortest life span, both because of undernourishment and maltreatment and because of lowered psychic resistance to death. Furthermore, if recruited from areas surrounding their work-place the escape rate is too high. Hence, there must be a high transport cost for a product of low productivity. This makes economic sense only if the purchase price is virtually nil. In capitalist market trade, purchase always has a real cost. It is only in long-distance trade, the exchange of preciosities, that the purchase price can be in the social system of the purchaser virtually nil. Such was the slave trade. Slaves were bought at low immediate cost (the production cost of the items actually exchanged) and none of the usual invisible costs. That is to say, the fact that removing a man from West Africa lowered the productive potential of the region was of *zero* cost to the European world-economy since these areas were not part of the division of labor. Of course, had the slave trade totally denuded Africa of all possibilities of furnishing further slaves, then a real cost to Europe would have commenced. But that point was never historically reached. Once, however, Africa was part of the periphery, then the real cost of a slave in terms of the production of surplus in the world-economy went up to such a point that it became far more economical to use wage-labor, even on sugar or cotton plantations, which is precisely what transpired in the nineteenth-century Caribbean and other slave-labor regions.

The creation of vast new areas as the periphery of the expanded world-economy made possible a shift in the role of some other areas. Specifically, both the United States and Germany (as it came into being) combined formerly peripheral and semi-peripheral regions. The manufacturing sector in each was able to gain political ascendancy, as the peripheral subregions became less economically crucial to the world-economy. Mercantilism now became the major tool of semi-peripheral countries seeking to become core countries, thus still performing a function analogous to that of the mercantilist drives of the late seventeenth and eighteenth centuries in England and France. To be sure, the struggle of semi-peripheral countries to 'industrialize' varied in the degree to which it succeeded in the period before the First World War: all the way in the United States, only partially in Germany, not at all in Russia.

The internal structure of core states also changed fundamentally under industrial capitalism. For a core area, industrialism involved divesting itself of substantially all agricultural activities (except that in the twentieth century further mechanization was to create a new form of working the land that was so highly mechanized as to warrant the appellation industrial). Thus whereas, in the period 1700–40, England not only was Europe's leading industrial exporter but was also Europe's leading agricultural exporter – this was at a high point in the economy-wide recession – by 1900, less than 10 per cent of England's population were engaged in agricultural pursuits.

At first under industrial capitalism, the core exchanged manufactured products against the periphery's agricultural products – hence, Britain from 1815 to 1873 was the 'workshop of the world'. Even to those semi-peripheral countries that had some manufacture (France, Germany, Belgium, the US), Britain in this period supplied about half their needs in manufactured goods. As, however, the mercantilist practices of this latter group both cut Britain off from outlets and even created competition for Britain in sales to peripheral areas, a competition which led to the late nineteenth-century 'scramble for Africa', the world division of labor was reallocated to ensure a new special role for the core: less the provision of the manufactures, more the provision of the machines to make the manufactures as well as the provision of infra-structure (especially, in this period, railroads).

The rise of manufacturing created for the first time under capitalism a large-scale urban proletariat. And in consequence for the first time there arose what Michels has called the 'anti-capitalist mass spirit',[1] which was translated into concrete organizational forms (trade-unions, socialist parties). This development intruded a new factor as threatening to the stability of states and of the capitalist forces now so securely in control of them as the earlier centrifugal thrusts of regional anti-capitalist landed elements had been in the seventeenth century.

At the same time that the bourgeoisies of the core countries were faced by this threat to the internal stability of their state structures, they were simultaneously faced with the economic crisis of the latter third of the nineteenth century resulting from the more rapid increase of agricultural production (and indeed of light manufactures) than the expansion of a potential market for these goods. Some of the surplus would have to be redistributed to someone to allow these goods to be bought and the economic machinery to return to smooth operation. By expanding the purchasing power of the industrial proletariat of the core countries, the world-economy was unburdened simultaneously of two problems: the bottle-neck of demand, and the unsettling 'class conflict' of the core states – hence, the social liberalism of welfare-state ideology that arose just at that point in time.

The First World War was, as men of the time observed, the end of an era; and the Russian Revolution of October 1917 the beginning of a new one – our stage four. This stage was to be sure a stage of revolutionary turmoil but it also was, in a seeming paradox, the stage of the *consolidation* of the industrial capitalist world-economy. The Russian Revolution was essentially that of a semi-peripheral country whose internal balance of forces had been such that as of the late nineteenth century it began on a decline towards a peripheral status. This was the result of the marked penetration of foreign capital into the industrial sector which was on its way to eliminating all indigenous capitalist forces, the resistance to the mechanization of the agricultural sector, the decline of relative military power (as evidenced by the defeat by the Japanese in 1905). The Revolution brought to power a group of state-managers who reversed each one of these trends by using the classic technique of mercantilist semi-withdrawal from the world-economy. In the process of doing this, the now USSR mobilized considerable popular support, especially in the urban sector. At the end of the Second World War, Russia was reinstated as a very strong member of the semi-periphery and could begin to seek full core status.

Meanwhile, the decline of Britain which dates from 1873 was confirmed and its hegemonic role was assumed by the United States. While the US thus rose, Germany fell further behind as a result of its military defeat. Various German attempts in the 1920s to find new industrial outlets in the Middle East and South America were unsuccessful in the face of the US thrust combined with Britain's continuing relative strength. Germany's thrust of desperation to recoup lost ground took the noxious and unsuccessful form of Nazism.

It was the Second World War that enabled the United States for a brief period (1945–65) to attain the same level of primacy as Britain had in the first part of the nineteenth century. United States growth in this period was spectacular and created a great need for expanded market outlets. The Cold War closure denied not only the USSR but Eastern Europe to US exports. And the Chinese Revolution meant that this region, which had been destined for much exploitative activity, was also cut off. Three alternative areas were available and each was pursued with assiduity. First, Western Europe had to be rapidly 'reconstructed', and it was the Marshall Plan which thus allowed this area to play a primary role in the expansion of world productivity. Secondly, Latin America became the reserve of US investment from which now Britain and Germany were completely cut off. Thirdly, Southern Asia, the Middle East and Africa had to be decolonized. On the one hand, this was necessary in order to reduce the share of the surplus taken by the Western European inter-mediaries, as Canning covertly supported the Latin American revolutionaries against Spain in the 1820s. But also, these countries had to be decolonized in order to mobilize productive potential in a way that had never been achieved in the colonial era. Colonial rule after all had been an *inferior* mode of relationship of core and periphery, one occasioned by the strenuous late-nineteenth-century conflict among industrial states but one no longer desirable from the point of view of the new hegemonic power.

But a world capitalist economy does not permit true imperium. Charles V could not succeed in his dream of world-empire. The Pax Britannica stimulated its own demise. So too did the Pax Americana. In each case, the cost of *political* imperium was too high economic-ally, and in a capitalist system, over the middle run when profits decline, new *political* formu-lae are sought. In this case the costs mounted along several fronts. The efforts of the USSR to further its own industrialization, protect a privileged market area (Eastern Europe), and force entry into other market areas led to an immense spiralling of military expenditure, which on the Soviet side promised long-run returns, whereas for the US it was merely a question of running very fast to stand still. The economic resurgence of Western Europe, made necessary both to provide markets for US sales and investments and to counter the USSR military thrust, meant over time that the Western European state structures collect-ively became as strong as that of the US, which led in the late 1960s to the 'dollar and gold crisis' and the retreat of Nixon from the free-trade stance which is the definitive mark of the self-confident leader in a capitalist market system. When the cumulated Third World pressures, most notably Vietnam, were added on, a restructuring of the world division of labor was inevitable, involving probably in the 1970s a quadripartite division of the larger part of the world surplus by the US, the European Common Market, Japan, and the USSR.

Such a decline in US state hegemony has actually *increased* the freedom of action of capitalist enterprises, the larger of which have now taken the form of multinational corpor-ations which are able to maneuver against state bureaucracies whenever the national politi-cians become too responsive to internal worker pressures. Whether some effective links can be established between multinational corporations, presently limited to operating in certain areas, and the USSR remains to be seen, but it is by no means impossible.

This brings us to the seemingly esoteric debate between Liu Shao-Chi and Mao Tse-Tung as to whether China was, as Liu argued, a socialist state, or whether, as Mao argued, socialism was a *process* involving continued and continual class struggle. No doubt to those to whom the terminology is foreign the discussion seems abstrusely theological. The issue, however, is real. If the Russian Revolution emerged as a reaction to the threatened further decline of Russia's structural position in the world-economy, and if fifty years later one can talk of the USSR as entering the status of a core power in a *capitalist* world-economy, what then is the meaning of the various so-called socialist revolutions that have occurred in a third of the world's surface? First let us notice that it has been neither Thailand nor Liberia nor Paraguay that has had a 'socialist revolution' but Russia, China and Cuba. That is to say, these revolutions have occurred in countries that, in terms of their internal economic struc-tures in the pre-revolutionary period, had a certain minimum strength in terms of skilled personnel, some manufacturing, and other factors which made it plausible that, within the framework of a capitalist world-economy, such a country could alter its role in the world division of labor within a reasonable period (say 30–50 years) by the use of the technique of mercantilist semi-withdrawal. (This may not be all that plausible for Cuba, but we shall see.) Of course, other countries in the geographic regions and military orbit of these revolutionary forces had changes of regime without in any way having these characteristics (for example, Mongolia or Albania). It is also to be noted that many of the countries where similar forces are strong or where considerable counterforce is required to keep them from emerging also share this status of minimum strength. I think of Chile or Brazil or Egypt – or indeed Italy.

Are we not seeing the emergence of a political structure for *semi-peripheral* nations adapted to stage four of the capitalist world-system? The fact that all enterprises are nationalized in these countries does not make the participation of these enterprises in the world-economy one that does not conform to the mode of operation of a capitalist market-system: seeking increased efficiency of production in order to realize a maximum price on sales, thus achieving a more favorable allocation of the surplus of the world-economy. If tomorrow US Steel became a worker's collective in which all employees without exception received an identical share of the profits and all stockholders were expropriated without compensation, would US Steel thereby cease to be a capitalist enterprise operating in a capitalist world-economy?

What then have been the consequences for the world-system of the emergence of many states in which there is no private ownership of the basic means of production? To some extent, this has meant an internal reallocation of consumption. It has certainly undermined the ideological justifications in world capitalism, both by showing the political vulnerability of capitalist entrepreneurs and by demonstrating that private ownership is irrelevant to the rapid expansion of industrial productivity. But to the extent that it has raised the ability of the new semi-peripheral areas to enjoy a larger share of the world surplus, it has once again depolarized the world, recreating the triad of strata that has been a fundamental element in the survival of the world-system.

Finally, in the peripheral areas of the world-economy, both the continued economic expansion of the core (even though the core is seeing some reallocation of surplus internal to it) and the new strength of the semi-periphery have led to a further weakening of the political and hence economic position of the peripheral areas. The pundits note that 'the gap is getting wider', but thus far no one has succeeded in doing much about it, and it is not clear that there are very many in whose interests it would be to do so. Far from a strengthening of state authority, in many parts of the world we are witnessing the same kind of deterioration Poland knew in the sixteenth century, a deterioration of which the frequency of military coups is only one of many signposts. And all of this leads us to conclude that stage four has been the stage of the *consolidation* of the capitalist world-economy.

Consolidation, however, does not mean the absence of contradictions and does not mean the likelihood of long-term survival. We thus come to projections about the future, which has always been man's great game, his true *hybris*, the most convincing argument for the dogma of original sin. Having read Dante, I will therefore be brief.

There are two fundamental contradictions, it seems to me, involved in the workings of the capitalist world-system. In the first place, there is the contradiction to which the nineteenth-century Marxian corpus pointed, which I would phrase as follows: whereas in the short-run the maximization of profit requires maximizing the withdrawal of surplus from immediate consumption of the majority, in the long-run the continued production of surplus requires a mass demand which can only be created by redistributing the surplus withdrawn. Since these two considerations move in opposite directions (a 'contradiction'), the system has constant crises which in the long-run both weaken it and make the game for those with privilege less worth playing.

The second fundamental contradiction, to which Mao's concept of socialism as process points, is the following: whenever the tenants of privilege seek to co-opt an oppositional movement by including them in a minor share of the privilege, they may no doubt eliminate opponents in the short-run; but they also up the ante for the next oppositional movement created in the next crisis of the world-economy. Thus the cost of 'co-option' rises ever higher and the advantages of co-option seem ever less worthwhile.

There are today no socialist systems in the world-economy any more than there are feudal systems because there is only *one* world-system. It is a world-economy and it is by definition capitalist in form. Socialism involves the creation of a new kind of *world*-system, neither a redistributive world-empire nor a capitalist world-economy but a socialist world-government. I don't see this projection as being in the least utopian but I also don't feel its institution is imminent. It will be the outcome of a long struggle in forms that may be familiar and perhaps in very new forms, that will take place in *all* the areas of the world-economy (Mao's continual 'class struggle'). Governments may be in the hands of persons, groups or movements sympathetic to this transformation but *states* as such are neither progressive nor reactionary. It is movements and forces that deserve such evaluative judgments.

Note

1   Robert Michels. 'The Origins of the Anti-Capitalist Mass Spirit', in *Man in Contemporary Society* (Columbia University Press, New York, 1955), vol. 1, pp. 740–65.

3.3 The multinational corporation and the law of uneven development

Stephen Hymer

Source: J.N. Bhagwati (ed.), *Economics and World Order* (Collier-Macmillan, London, 1972), pp. 113–40.

Hymer describes the process by which multinational corporations contribute to the development of an international hierarchy and thus restrict the possibilities for national development in peripheral areas. He then examines the possibilities for the continued viability of a global economy based on MNCs, given the problems created by the exclusion of many areas from the benefits of their activities, the need to maintain a modernized 'centre' to the world economy, and the rather ambivalent role of state authorities.

[Hymer begins the article by outlining the historical evolution of the multinational corporation and then turns to the implications for the future of the pattern of industrial organization implicit in that evolution.]

Uneven development

Suppose giant multinational corporations (say 300 from the US and 200 from Europe and Japan) succeed in establishing themselves as the dominant form of international enterprise and come to control a significant share of industry (especially modern industry) in each country. The world economy will resemble more and more the United States economy, where each of the large corporations tends to spread over the entire continent, and to penetrate almost every nook and cranny. What would be the effect of a world industrial organization of this type on international specialization, exchange and income distribution? The purpose of this section is to analyse the spatial dimension of the corporate hierarchy.

A useful starting point is Chandler and Redlich's scheme for analysing the evolution of corporate structure. They distinguish 'three levels of business administration, three horizons, three levels of task, and three levels of decision making [. . .] and three levels of policies'.[1] Level III, the lowest level, is concerned with managing the day-to-day operations of the enterprise, that is with keeping it going within the established framework. Level II, which first made its appearance with the separation of head office from field office, is responsible for coordinating the managers at Level III. The functions of Level I – top management – are goal-determination and planning. This level sets the framework in which the lower levels operate. In the Marshallian firm, all three levels are embodied in the single entrepreneur or undertaker. In the national corporation, a partial differentiation is made in which the top two levels are separated from the bottom one. In the multidivisional corporation, the differentiation is far more complete. Level I is completely split off from Level II and concentrated in a general office whose specific function is to plan strategy rather than tactics.

The development of business enterprise can therefore be viewed as a process of centralizing and perfecting the process of capital accumulation. The Marshallian entrepreneur was a jack-of-all-trades. In the modern multidivisional corporation, a powerful general office consciously plans and organizes the growth of corporate capital. It is here that the key men who actually allocate the corporation's available resources (rather than act within the means allocated to them, as is true for the managers at lower levels) are located. Their power comes from their ultimate control over *men* and *money* and although one should not overestimate the ability to control a far-flung empire, neither should one underestimate it. [. . .]

What is the relationship between the structure of the microcosm and the structure of the macrocosm? The application of location theory to the Chandler-Redlich scheme suggests a *correspondence principle* relating centralization of control within the corporation to centralization of control within the international economy.

Location theory suggests that Level III activities would spread themselves over the globe according to the pull of manpower, markets, and raw materials. The multinational corporation, because of its power to command capital and technology and its ability to rationalize their use on a global scale, will probably spread production more evenly over the world's surface than is now the case. Thus, in the first instance, it may well be a force for diffusing industrialization to the less developed countries and creating new centres of production. (We postpone for a moment a discussion of the fact that location depends upon transportation, which in turn depends upon the government which in turn is influenced by the structure of business enterprise.)

Level II activities, because of their need for white-collar workers, communications systems, and information, tend to concentrate in large cities. Since their demands are similar, corporations from different industries tend to place their coordinating offices in the same city, and Level II activities are consequently far more geographically concentrated than Level III activities.

Level I activities, the general offices, tend to be even more concentrated than Level II activities, for they must be located close to the capital market, the media, and the government. Nearly every major corporation in the United States, for example, must have its general office (or a large proportion of its high-level personnel) in or near the city of New York, because of the need for face-to-face contact at higher levels of decision making.

Applying this scheme to the world economy, one would expect to find the highest offices of the multinational corporations concentrated in the world's major cities – New York, London, Paris, Bonn, Tokyo. These, along with Moscow and perhaps Peking, will be the major centres of high-level strategic planning. Lesser cities throughout the world will deal with the day-to-day operations of specific local problems. These in turn will be arranged in a hierarchical fashion: the larger and more important ones will contain regional corporate headquarters, while the smaller ones will be confined to lower-level activities. Since business is usually the core of the city, geographical specialization will come to reflect the hierarchy of corporate decision making, and the occupational distribution of labour in a city or region will depend upon its function in the international economic system. The 'best' and most highly paid administrators, doctors, lawyers, scientists, educators, government officials, actors, servants and hair-dressers, will tend to concentrate in or near the major centres.

The structure of income and consumption will tend to parallel the structure of status and authority. The citizens of capital cities will have the best jobs – allocating men and money at the highest level and planning growth and development – and will receive the highest rates of remuneration. (Executives' salaries tend to be a function of the wage bill of people under them. The larger the empire of the multinational corporation, the greater the earnings of top executives, to a large extent independent of their performance. Thus, growth in the hinterland subsidiaries implies growth in the income of capital cities, but not vice versa.)

The citizens of capital cities will also be the first to innovate new products in the cycle which is known in the marketing literature as trickle-down or two-stage marketing. A new product is usually first introduced to a select group of people who have 'discretionary' income and are willing to experiment in their consumption patterns. Once it is accepted by this group, it spreads, or trickles down to other groups via the demonstration effect. In this process, the rich and the powerful get more votes than everyone else; first, because they have more money to spend, second, because they have more ability to experiment, and third, because they have high status and are likely to be copied. This special group may have something approaching a choice in consumption patterns; the rest have only the choice between conforming or being isolated.

The trickle-down system also has the advantage – from the centre's point of view – of reinforcing patterns of authority and control. According to Fallers,[2] it helps keep workers on the treadmill by creating an illusion of upward mobility even though relative status remains unchanged. In each period subordinates achieve (in part) the consumption standards of their superiors in a previous period and are thus torn in two directions: if they look backward and compare their standards of living through time, things seem to be getting better; if they look upward they see that their relative position has not changed. They receive a consolation prize, as it were, which may serve to keep them going by softening the reality that in a competitive system, few succeed and many fail. It is little wonder, then, that those at the top stress growth rather than equality as the welfare criterion for human relations.

In the international economy trickle-down marketing takes the form of an international demonstration effect spreading outward from the metropolis to the hinterland. Multinational corporations help speed up this process, often the key motive for direct investment, through their control of marketing channels and communications media.

The development of a new product is a fixed cost; once the expenditure needed for invention or innovation has been made, it is forever a bygone. The actual cost of production is thus typically well below selling price and the limit on output is not rising costs but falling demand due to saturated markets. The marginal profit on new foreign markets is thus high, and corporations have a strong interest in maintaining a system which spreads their products widely. Thus, the interest of multinational corporations in underdeveloped countries is larger than the size of the market would suggest.

It must be stressed that the dependency relationship between major and minor cities should not be attributed to technology. The new technology, because it increases interaction, implies greater interdependence but not necessarily a hierarchical structure. Communications linkages could be arranged in the form of a grid in which each point was directly connected to many other points, permitting lateral as well as vertical communication. This system would be polycentric since messages from one point to another would go directly rather than through the centre; each point would become a centre on its own; and the distinction between centre and periphery would disappear.

Such a grid is made *more* feasible by aeronautical and electronic revolutions which greatly reduce costs of communications. It is not technology which creates inequality; rather, it is *organization* that imposes a ritual judicial asymmetry on the use of intrinsically symmetrical means of communications and arbitrarily creates unequal capacities to initiate and terminate exchange, to store and retrieve information, and to determine the extent of the exchange and terms of the discussion. Just as colonial powers in the past linked each point in the hinterland to the metropolis and inhibited lateral communications, preventing the growth of independent centres of decision making and creativity, multinational corporations (backed by state powers) centralize control by imposing a hierarchical system.

This suggests the possibility of an alternative system of organization in the form of national planning. Multinational corporations are private institutions which organize one or a few industries across many countries. Their polar opposite (the antimultinational corporation, perhaps) is a public institution which organizes many industries across one region. This would permit the centralization of capital, i.e. the coordination of many enterprises by one decision-making centre, but would substitute regionalization for internationalization. The span of control would be confined to the boundaries of a single polity and society and not spread over many countries. The advantage of national planning is its ability to remove the wastes of oligopolistic anarchy, i.e. meaningless product differentiation and an imbalance between different industries within a geographical area. It concentrates *all* levels of decision making in one locale and thus provides each region with a full complement of skills and occupations. This opens up new horizons for local development by making possible the social and political control of economic decision making. Multinational corporations, in contrast, weaken political control because they span many countries and can escape national regulation.

A few examples might help to illustrate how multinational corporations reduce options for development. Consider an underdeveloped country wishing to invest heavily in education in order to increase its stock of human capital and raise standards of living. In a market system it would be able to find gainful employment for its citizens within its *national boundaries* by specializing in education-intensive activities and selling its surplus production to foreigners. In the multinational corporate system, however, the demand for high-level education in low-ranking areas is limited, and a country does not become a world centre simply by having a better educational system. An outward shift in the supply of educated people in a country, therefore, will not create its own demand but will create an excess supply and lead to emigration. Even then, the employment opportunities for citizens of low-ranking countries are restricted by discriminatory practices in the centre. It is well known that ethnic homogeneity increases as one goes up the corporate hierarchy; the lower levels contain a wide variety of nationalities, the higher levels become successively purer and purer. In part this stems from the skill differences of different nationalities, but more important is the fact that the higher up one goes in the decision-making process, the more important mutual understanding and ease of communications become; a common background becomes all-important.

A similar type of specialization by nationality can be expected within the multinational corporation hierarchy. Multinational corporations are torn in two directions. On the one hand, they must adapt to local circumstances in each country. This calls for decentralized decision making. On the other hand, they must coordinate their activities in various parts of the world and stimulate the flow of ideas from one part of their empire to another. This calls for centralized control. They must, therefore, develop an organizational structure to balance the need for coordination with the need for adaptation to a patch-work quilt of languages, laws and customs. One solution to this problem is a division of labour based on nationality. Day-to-day management in each country is left to the nationals of that country who, because they are intimately familiar with local conditions and practices, are able to deal with local problems and local government. These nationals remain rooted in one spot, while above them is a layer of people who move around from country to country, as bees among flowers, transmitting information from one subsidiary to another and from the lower levels to the general office at the apex of the corporate structure. In the nature of things, these people (reticulators) for the most part will be citizens of the country of the parent corporation (and will be drawn from a small, culturally homogeneous group within the advanced world), since they will need to have the confidence of their superiors and to be able to move easily in the higher management circles. Latin Americans, Asians and Africans will at best be able to aspire to a management position in the intermediate coordinating centres at the continental level. Very few will be able to get much higher than this, for the closer one gets to the top, the more important is 'a common cultural heritage'.

Another way in which the multinational corporations inhibit economic development in the hinterland is through their effect on tax capacity. An important government instrument for promoting growth is expenditure on infrastructure and support services. By providing transportation and communications, education and health, a government can create a productive labour force and increase the growth potential of its economy. The extent to which it can afford to finance these intermediate outlays depends upon its tax revenue.

However, a government's ability to tax multinational corporations is limited by the ability of these corporations to manipulate transfer prices and to move their productive facilities to another country. This means that they will only be attracted to countries where superior infrastructure offsets higher taxes. The government of an underdeveloped country will find it difficult to extract a surplus (revenue from the multinational corporations, less cost of services provided to them) from multinational corporations to use for long-run development programmes and for stimulating growth in other industries. In contrast, governments of the advanced countries, where the home office and financial centre of the multinational corporation are located, can tax the profits of the corporation as a whole as well as the high incomes of its management. Government in the metropolis can, therefore, capture some of the surplus generated by the multinational corporations and use it to further improve their infrastructure and growth.

In other words, the relationship between multinational corporations and underdeveloped countries will be somewhat like the relationship between the national corporations in the United States and state and municipal governments. These lower-level governments tend always to be short of funds compared to the federal government which can tax a corporation as a whole. Their competition to attract corporate investment eats up their surplus, and they find it difficult to finance extensive investments in human and physical capital even where such investment would be productive. This has a crucial effect on the pattern of government expenditure. For example, suppose taxes were first paid to state government and then passed on to the federal government. What chance is there that these lower-level legislatures would approve the phenomenal expenditure on space research that now goes on? A similar discrepancy can be expected in the international economy with overspending and waste by metropolitan governments and a shortage of public funds in the less advanced countries.

The tendency of the multinational corporations to erode the power of the nation state works in a variety of ways, in addition to its effect on taxation powers. In general, most governmental policy instruments (monetary policy, fiscal policy, wage policy, etc.) diminish in effectiveness the more open the economy and the greater the extent of foreign investments. This tendency applies to political instruments as well as economic, for the multinational corporation is a medium by which laws, politics, foreign policy and culture of one country intrude into another. This acts to reduce the sovereignty of all nation states, but again the relationship is asymmetrical, for the flow tends to be from the parent to the subsidiary, not vice versa. The United States can apply its anti-trust laws to foreign subsidiaries to stop them from 'trading with the enemy' even though such trade is not against the laws of the country in which the branch plant is located. However, it would be illegal for an underdeveloped country which disagreed with American foreign policy to hold a US firm hostage for acts of the parent. This is because legal rights are defined in terms of property-ownership, and the various subsidiaries of a multinational corporation are not 'partners in a multinational endeavour' but the property of the general office.

In conclusion, it seems that a regime of multinational corporations would offer under-developed countries neither national independence nor equality. It would tend instead to inhibit the attainment of these goals. It would turn the underdeveloped countries into branch-plant countries, not only with reference to their economic functions but throughout the whole gamut of social, political and cultural roles. The subsidiaries of multinational corporations are typically amongst the largest corporations in the country of operations, and their top executives play an influential role in the political, social and cultural life of the host country. Yet these people, whatever their title, occupy at best a medium position in the corporate structure and are restricted in authority and horizons to a lower level of decision making. The governments with whom they deal tend to take on the same middle manage-ment outlook, since this is the only range of information and ideas to which they are exposed. In this sense, one can hardly expect such a country to bring forth the creative imagination needed to apply science and technology to the problems of degrading poverty. [. . .]

The political economy of the multinational corporation

The viability of the multinational corporate system depends upon the degree to which people will tolerate the unevenness it creates. It is well to remember that the 'New Imperial-ism' which began after 1870 in a spirit of Capitalism Triumphant, soon became seriously troubled and after 1914 was characterized by war, depression, breakdown of the inter-national economic system and war again, rather than Free Trade, Pax Britannica and Material Improvement.

A major, if not the major, reason was Great Britain's inability to cope with the byproducts of its own rapid accumulation of capital; i.e. a class-conscious labour force at home; a middle class in the hinterland; and rival centres of capital on the Continent and in America. Britain's policy tended to be atavistic and defensive rather than progressive, more concerned with warding off new threats than creating new areas of expansion. Ironically, Edwardian England revived the paraphernalia of the landed aristocracy it had just destroyed. Instead of embarking on a 'big push' to develop the vast hinterland of the Empire, colonial adminis-trators often adopted policies to slow down rates of growth and arrest the development of either a native capitalist class or a native proletariat which could overthrow them.

As time went on, the centre had to devote an increasing share of government activity to military and other unproductive expenditures; they had to rely on alliances with an inefficient class of landlords, officials and soldiers in the hinterland to maintain stability at the cost of development. A great part of the surplus extracted from the population was thus wasted locally.

The new Mercantilism (as the Multinational Corporate System of special alliances and privileges, aid and tariff concessions is sometimes called) faces similar problems of internal and external division. The centre is troubled: excluded groups revolt and even some of the affluent are dissatisfied with the roles. (The much talked about 'generation gap' may indicate the failure of the system to reproduce itself.) Nationalistic rivalry between major capitalist countries (especially the challenge of Japan and Germany) remains an important divisive factor, while the economic challenge from the socialist bloc may prove to be of the utmost significance in the next thirty years. Russia has its own form of large-scale economic organizations, also in command of modern technology, and its own conception of how the world should develop. So does China to an increasing degree. Finally, there is the threat presented by the middle classes and the excluded groups of the underdeveloped countries.

The national middle classes in the underdeveloped countries came to power when the centre weakened but could not, through their policy of import substitution manufacturing, establish a viable basis for sustained growth. They now face a foreign exchange crisis and an unemployment (or population) crisis – the first indicating their inability to function in the international economy, and the second indicating their alienation from the people they are supposed to lead. In the immediate future, these national middle classes will gain a new lease on life as they take advantage of the spaces created by the rivalry between American and non-American oligopolists striving to establish global market positions. The native capitalists will again become the champions of national independence as they bargain with multinational corporations. But the conflict at this level is more apparent than real, for in the end the fervent nationalism of the middle class asks only for promotion within the corporate structure and not for a break with that structure. In the last analysis their power derives from the metropolis and they cannot easily afford to challenge the international system. They do not command the loyalty of their own population and cannot really compete with the large, powerful, aggregate capitals from the centre. They are prisoners of the taste patterns and consumption standards set at the centre, and depend on outsiders for technical advice, capital and, when necessary, for military support of their position.

The main threat comes from the excluded groups. It is not unusual in underdeveloped countries for the top 5 per cent to obtain between 30 and 40 per cent of the total national income, and for the top one-third to obtain anywhere from 60 to 70 per cent. At most, one-third of the population can be said to benefit in some sense from the dualistic growth that characterizes development in the hinterland. The remaining two-thirds, who together get only one-third of the income, are outsiders, not because they do not contribute to the economy, but because they do not share in the benefits. They provide a source of cheap labour which helps keep exports to the developed world at a low price and which has financed the urban-biased growth of recent years. Because their wages are low, they spend a moderate amount of time in menial services and are sometimes referred to as under-employed as if to imply they were not needed. In fact, it is difficult to see how the system of most underdeveloped countries could survive without cheap labour since removing it (e.g. diverting it to public works projects as is done in socialist countries) would raise consumption costs to capitalists and professional elites. Economic development under the multinational corporation does not offer much promise for this large segment of society and their antagonism continuously threatens the system.

The survival of the multinational corporate system depends on how fast it can grow and how much trickles down. Plans now being formulated in government offices, corporate headquarters and international organizations sometimes suggest that a growth rate of about 6 per cent per year in national income (3 per cent *per capita*) is needed. (Such a target is, of course, far below what would be possible if a serious effort were made to solve basic problems of health, education and clothing.) To what extent is it possible?

The multinational corporation must solve four critical problems for the underdeveloped countries, if it is to foster the continued growth and survival of a 'modern' sector. First, it must break the foreign-exchange constraint and provide the underdeveloped countries with imported goods for capital formation and modernization. Second, it must finance an expanded programme of government expenditure to train labour and provide support services for urbanization and industrialization. Third, it must solve the urban food problem created by growth. Finally, it must keep the excluded two-thirds of the population under control.

The solution now being suggested for the first is to restructure the world economy allowing the periphery to export certain manufactured goods to the centre. Part of this programme involves regional common markets to rationalize the existing structure of industry. These plans typically do not involve the rationalization and restructuring of the entire economy of the underdeveloped countries but mainly serve the small manufacturing sector which caters to higher-income groups and which, therefore, faces a very limited market in any particular country. The solution suggested for the second problem is an expanded aid programme and a reformed government bureaucracy (perhaps along the lines of the Alliance for Progress). The solution for the third is agribusiness and the green revolution, a programme with only limited benefits to the rural poor. Finally, the solution offered for the fourth problem is population control, either through family planning or counter-insurgency.

It is doubtful whether the centre has sufficient political stability to finance and organize the programme outlined above. It is not clear, for example, that the West has the technology to rationalize manufacturing abroad or modernize agriculture, or the willingness to open up marketing channels for the underdeveloped world. Nor is it evident that the centre has the political power to embark on a large aid programme or to readjust its own structure of production and allow for the importation of manufactured goods from the periphery. It is difficult to imagine labour accepting such a re-allocation (a new repeal of the Corn Laws as it were), and it is equally hard to see how the advanced countries could create a system of planning to make these extra hardships unnecessary.

The present crisis may well be more profound than most of us imagine, and the West may find it impossible to restructure the international economy on a workable basis. One could easily argue that the age of the multinational corporation is at its end rather than at its beginning. For all we know, books on the global partnership may be the epitaph of the American attempt to take over the old international economy, and not the herald of a new era of international cooperation.

Conclusion

The multinational corporation, because of its great power to plan economic activity, represents an important step forward over previous methods of organizing international exchange. It demonstrates the social nature of production on a global scale. As it eliminates the anarchy of international markets and brings about a more extensive and productive international division of labour, it releases great sources of latent energy.

However, as it crosses international boundaries, it pulls and tears at the social and political fabric and erodes the cohesiveness of national states. Whether one likes this or not, it is probably a tendency that cannot be stopped.

Through its propensity to nestle everywhere, settle everywhere, and establish connections everywhere, the multinational corporation destroys the possibility of national seclusion and self-sufficiency and creates a universal interdependence. But the multinational corporation is still a private institution with a partial outlook and represents only an imperfect solution to the problem of international cooperation. It creates hierarchy rather than equality, and it spreads its benefits unequally.

In proportion to its success, it creates tensions and difficulties. It will lead other institutions, particularly labour organizations and government, to take an international outlook and thus unwittingly create an environment less favourable to its own survival. It will demonstrate the possibilities of material progress at a faster rate than it can realize them, and will create a world-wide demand for change that it cannot satisfy.

The next round may be marked by great crises due to the conflict between national planning by governments and international planning by corporations. For example, if each country loses its power over fiscal and monetary policy due to the growth of multinational corporations (as some observers believe Canada has), how will aggregate demand be stabilized? Will it be possible to construct super-states? Or does multinationalism do away with Keynesian problems? Similarly, will it be possible to fulfil a host of other government functions at the supranational level in the near future? During the past twenty-five years many political problems were put aside as the West recovered from the depression and the war. By the late 1960s the bloom of this long upswing had begun to fade. In the 1970s, power conflicts are likely to come to the fore.

Whether underdeveloped countries will use the opportunities arising from this crisis to build viable local decision-making institutions is difficult to predict. The national middle class failed when it had the opportunity and instead merely reproduced internally the economic dualism of the international economy as it squeezed agriculture to finance urban industry. What is needed is a complete change of direction. The starting point must be the needs of the bottom two-thirds, and not the demands of the top third. The primary goal of such a strategy would be to provide minimum standards of health, education, food and clothing to the entire population, removing the most obvious forms of human suffering. This requires a system which can mobilize the entire population and which can search the local environment for information, resources and needs. It must be able to absorb modern technology, but it cannot be mesmerized by the form it takes in the advanced countries; it must go to the roots. This is not the path the upper one-third chooses when it has control.

The wealth of a nation, wrote Adam Smith two hundred years ago, is determined by 'first, the skill, dexterity and judgement with which labour is generally applied; and, secondly by the proportion between the number of those who are employed in useful labour, and that of those who are not so employed'.[3] Capitalist enterprise has come a long way from this day, but it has never been able to bring more than a small fraction of the world's population into useful or highly productive employment. The latest stage reveals once more the power of social cooperation and division of labour which so fascinated Adam Smith in his description of pin-manufacturing. It also shows the shortcomings of concentrating this power in private hands.

Notes

1   A.D. Chandler and F. Redlich, 'Recent Developments in American Business Administration and their Conceptualization', *Business History Review* (Spring 1961).
2   L.A. Fallers, 'A Note on the Trickle Effect', in P. Bliss (ed.), *Marketing and the Behavioral Sciences* (Allyn and Bacon, 1963).
3   A. Smith, *The Wealth of Nations* (The Modern Library, New York, 1937 edn).

3.4 Capitalist globalization and the transnationalization of the state

William I. Robinson

Source: M. Rupert and H. Smith (eds), *Historical Materialism and Globalization* (London, Routledge, 2002), pp. 211–21.

Robinson takes a historical materialist view of globalization, seeing it as a stage in the development of world capitalism characterized by the rise of transnational capital and the supersession of the nation-state system. He goes on to develop a view of the 'transnational state' that contrasts strongly with the views of realists and liberals, and then relates this to a new phase in the global relations between capital and labour.

[Robinson begins by arguing that the nation-state is in the process of being transcended by the 'transnational state' and the rise of a global ruling class. He then goes on to explore the nature of capitalist globalization.]

Globalization: the latest stage of capitalism

Periodization of capitalism is an analytical tool that allows us to grasp changes in the system over time. In my view, globalization represents an epochal shift, the fourth in the history of world capitalism. The first, mercantilism and primitive accumulation, was ushered in with the birth of capitalism out of its feudal cocoon in Europe and outward expansion. The second, competitive, or classical capitalism, marked the industrial revolution, the rise of the bourgeoisie, and the forging of the nation-state. The third was the rise of corporate (monopoly) capitalism, the consolidation of a single world market and the nation-state system into which world capitalism became organized. The first epoch ran from the symbolic dates of 1492 through to 1789, the second to the late nineteenth century, and the third into the early 1970s. Globalization as the fourth (the *current*) epoch began with the world economic crisis of the 1970s and the profound restructuring of the system that has been taking place since. It features the rise of transnational capital and the supersession of the nation-state system as the organizing principle of capitalist development. As an epochal period globalization constitutes not a new process but the near culmination of the centuries-long process of the spread of capitalist production relations around the world and its displacement of all pre-capitalist relations. The system is undergoing a dramatic intensive expansion. The era of the primitive accumulation of capital is coming to an end. In this process, those cultural and political institutions that fettered capitalism are swept aside, paving the way for the total commodification or 'marketization' of social life world-wide.

Economic globalization has been well researched. Capital has achieved a newfound global mobility and is reorganizing production world-wide in accordance with the whole gamut of political and factor cost considerations. This involves the worldwide decentralization of production together with the centralization of command and control of the global economy in transnational capital. In this process, national productive apparatuses become fragmented and integrated externally into new globalized circuits of accumulation. Here we can distinguish between a *world economy* and a *global economy*. In the earlier epochs each country developed national circuits of accumulation that were linked to each other through commodity exchange and capital flows in an integrated international market (a world economy). In the emerging global economy, the globalization of the production process itself breaks down and functionally integrates these national circuits into *global* circuits of accumulation. Globalization, therefore, is unifying the world into a single mode of production and bringing about the organic integration of different countries and regions into a global economy and society. The increasing dissolution of space barriers and the subordination of the logic of geography to that of production, what some have called 'time-space compression', is without historic precedence. It compels us to reconsider the geography and the politics of the nation-state. As we shall see, the TNS embodies new social practices and class relations bound up with this global economy.

The political reorganization of world capitalism has lagged behind its economic reorganization, with the result that there is a disjuncture between economic globalization and the political institutionalization of new social relations unfolding under globalization. Nevertheless, as the material basis of human society changes so too does its institutional organization. From the seventeenth-century treaties of Westphalia into the 1960s, capitalism unfolded through a system of nation-states that generated concomitant national structures, institutions, and agents. Globalization has increasingly eroded these national boundaries, and made it structurally impossible for individual nations to sustain independent, or even autonomous, economies, polities, and social structures. A key feature of the current epoch is the supersession of the nation-state as the organizing principle of capitalism, and with it, of the inter-state system as the institutional framework of capitalist development. In the emerging global capitalist configuration, transnational or global space is coming to supplant national spaces. There is no longer anything external to the system, not in the sense that this is a 'closed' system but in that there are no longer any countries or regions that remain outside of world capitalism, any pre-capitalist zones for colonization, or autonomous accumulation outside of the sphere of global capital. The internal social nexus therefore is now a global one. Such organic social relations are always institutionalized, which makes them 'fixed' and makes their reproduction possible. As the organic and internal linkage between peoples become truly global, the whole set of nation-state institutions is becoming superseded by transnational institutions.

Globalization has posed serious difficulties for theories of all sorts. The embedded nation-state centrism of many extant paradigms, in my view, impedes our understanding of the dynamics of change under globalization. My propositions regarding the integration of the entire superstructure of world society is a conception of the current epoch that differs from that of world system analysis, which posits a world system of separate political and cultural superstructures linked by a geographic division of labour, and from many Marxist analyses, which see the nation-state as immanent to capitalist development. The notion that the continued internationalization of capital and the growth of an international civil society has involved as well the internationalization of the state has been recognized by a number of traditions in the social sciences. And the interdisciplinary literature on globalization is full of discussion on the increasing significance of supra- or transnational institutions. However, what these diverse accounts share is a nation-state centrism that entraps them in a global-national dualism. They assume phenomena associated with a TNS to be international extensions of the nation-state system. The conception is one of *inter*national institutions created by nation-states individually or collectively as mechanisms to regulate the flow of goods and capital across their borders and to mediate inter-state relations. Here I distinguish between *inter*national and *trans*national (or global). The former is a conception of world dynamics founded on an existing system of nation-states while the latter identifies processes and social relations that tend towards superseding that system.

Conceptualizing a transnational state apparatus: from Weber to Marx

The question of the state is at the heart of the globalization debate. But this debate has been misinformed by the persistent conflation of the nation-state and the state. The two are not coterminous. Here we need to distinguish analytically between a number of related terms: nation, country, nation-state, state, national state, and transnational state. Nation-states are geographical and juridical units and sometimes cultural units, and the term is interchangeable as used here with country or nation. States are power relations embodied in particular sets of political institutions. The conflation of these two related but analytically distinct concepts is grounded in a Weberian conception of the state that informs much analysis of this subject, even analyses by many Marxists. For Weber, the state is a set of cadre and institutions that exercise authority, a 'legitimate monopoly of coercion', over a given territory. In the Weberian construct, the economic and the political (in Weberian terms, 'markets and states') are externally related, separate and even oppositional, spheres, each with its own independent logic. Nation-states interact externally with markets.[1] Consequently, globalization is seen to involve the economic sphere while the political sphere may remain constant, an immutable nation-state system. State managers confront the implications of economic globalization and footloose transnational capital as an external logic. This state-market dualism has become the dominant framework for analysis of globalization and the state, and is closely related to the global-national dualism. Globalization is said to be overstated or even imaginary since nation-states 'have more power' than is claimed, or because there are 'national' explanations that explain phenomena better than globalization explanations. In this construct, what takes place 'within' a nation-state becomes counterposed to what takes place in the global system. In these recurrent dualisms, economic globalization is increasingly recognized but is analysed as if it is independent of the institutions that structure these social relations, in particular, states and the nation-state. Separate logics are posited for a globalizing economy and a nation-state based political system.

The way out of these antinomies is to move beyond Weber and return to a historical materialist conception of the state. In the Marxist conception, the state is the institutionalization of class relations around a particular configuration of social production. The separation of the economic from the political for the first time under capitalism accords each an autonomy – and implies a complex relationship that must be problematized – but also generates the illusion of independent externally related spheres. In the historical materialist conception, the economic and the political are distinct moments of the same totality. The relation between the economy, or social production relations under capitalism, and states as sets of institutionalized class relations that adhere to those production relations, is an *internal* one. It is not possible here to revisit the theoretical debates that have raged since the revival of interest in the state in the 1960s – which have remained inconclusive and open-ended. Note, however, that (1) Marxist theories on the relative autonomy of the state, whether emphasizing a 'structuralist' or 'instrumental' subordination of the state to economically dominant classes, do not posit an *independent* state as a separate sphere with its own logic [. . .]. The task of analysis is to uncover the complex of social processes and relations that embed states in the configuration of civil society and political economy; (2) there is nothing in the historical materialist conception of the state that *necessarily* ties it to territory or to nation-states. That capitalism has historically assumed a geographic expression is something that must be problematized.

States as coercive systems of authority are class relations and social practices congealed and operationalized through institutions. In Marx's view, the state gives a political form to economic institutions and production relations. Markets are the site of material life while states spring from economic (production) relations and represent the institutionalization of social relations of domination. Consequently, the economic globalization of capital cannot be a phenomenon isolated from the transformation of class relations and of states. In the Weberian conception, states are by definition territorially bound institutions and therefore a TNS cannot be conceived as long as the nation-state system persists. Weberian state theory reduces the state to the state's apparatus and its cadre and thereby reifies the state. States are not actors as such. Social classes and groups are historical actors. States do not 'do' anything *per se*. Social classes and groups acting in and out of states (and other institutions) 'do' things as collective historical agents. State apparatuses are those instruments that enforce and reproduce the class relations and practices embedded in states. The institutional structures of nation-states may persist in the epoch of globalization, but globalization requires that we modify our conception of these structures. A TNS apparatus is emerging under globalization *from within* the system of nation-states. The material circumstances that gave rise to the nation-state are presently being superseded by globalization. What is required is a return to an historical materialist theoretical conceptualization of the state, not as a 'thing' but as a specific social relation inserted into larger social structures that may take different, and historically determined, institutional forms, only one of which is the nation-state.

To summarize and recapitulate: a state is the congealment of a particular and historically determined constellation of class forces and relations, and states are always embodied in sets of political institutions. Hence states are: (a) a moment of class power relations; (b) a set of political institutions (an 'apparatus'). The state is not one or the other; it is both in their unity. The separation of these two dimensions is purely methodological (Weber's mistake is to reduce the state to 'b'). National states arose as particular embodiments of the constellations of social groups and classes that developed within the system of nation-states in the earlier epochs of capitalism and became grounded in particular geographies. What then is a transnational state? Concretely, what is the 'a' and the 'b' of a TNS? It is a particular constellation of class forces and relations bound up with capitalist globalization and the rise of a transnational capitalist class, embodied in a diverse set of political institutions. These institutions are transformed national states plus diverse international institutions that serve to institutionalize the domination of this class as the hegemonic fraction of capital world-wide.

Hence, the state as a class relation is becoming transnationalized. The class practices of a new global ruling class are becoming 'condensed', to use Poulantzas' imagery, in an emergent TNS. In the process of the globalization of capital, class fractions from different countries have fused together into new capitalist groups within transnational space. This new transnational bourgeoisie or capitalist class is that segment of the world bourgeoisie that represents transnational capital. It is comprised of the owners of the leading world-wide means of production as embodied principally in the transnational corporations and private financial institutions. What distinguishes the transnational capitalist class from national or local capitalist fractions is that it is involved in globalized production and manages global circuits of accumulation that give it an objective class existence and identity spatially and politically in the global system above any local territories and polities.

The TNS comprises those institutions and practices in global society that maintain, defend, and advance the emergent hegemony of a global bourgeoisie and its project of constructing a new global capitalist historical bloc. This TNS apparatus is an emerging network that comprises transformed and externally integrated national states, *together with* the supranational economic and political forums and that has not yet acquired any centralized institutional form. The rise of a TNS entails the reorganization of the state in each nation – I will henceforth refer to these states of each country as *national states* – and it involves simultaneously the rise of truly supranational economic and political institutions. These two processes – the transformation of nation-states and the rise of supranational institutions – are not separate or mutually exclusive. In fact, they are twin dimensions of the process of the transnationalization of the state.

The TNS apparatus is multi-layered and multi-centred, linking together functionally institutions that exhibit distinct gradations of 'state-ness' and which have different histories and trajectories. The supranational organizations are both economic and political, formal and informal. The economic forums include the International Monetary Fund (IMF), the World Bank (WB), the World Trade Organization (WTO), the regional banks, and so on. Supranational political forums include the Group of 7 and the recently formed Group of 22, as well as more formal forums such as the United Nations (UN), the European Union (EU), and so on. They also include regional groupings such as the Association of South East Asian Nations (ASEAN), and the juridical administrative and regulatory structures established through regional agreements such as the North American Free Trade Agreement (NAFTA) and the Asia-Pacific Economic Cooperation (APEC) forum. These supranational planning institutes are gradually supplanting national institutions in policy development and global management and administration of the global economy. The function of the nation-state is shifting from the formulation of national policies to the administration of policies formulated through supranational institutions. However, it is essential to avoid the national-global duality: national states are not external to the TNS but are becoming incorporated into it as component parts. The supranational organizations function in consonance with transformed national states. They are staffed by transnational functionaries that find their counterparts in transnational functionaries who staff transformed national states. These *transnational state cadres* act as midwives of capitalist globalization.

The TNS is attempting to fulfil the functions for world capitalism that in earlier periods were fulfilled by what world-system and international relations scholars refer to as a 'hegemon', or a dominant capitalist power that has the resources and the structural position that allows it to organize world capitalism as a whole and impose the rules, regulatory environment, etc., that allows the system to function. We are witnessing the decline of US supremacy and the early stages of the creation of a transnational hegemony through supranational structures that are not yet capable of providing the economic regulation and political conditions for the reproduction of global capitalism. Just as the national state played this role in the earlier period, the TNS seeks to create and maintain the preconditions for the valorization and accumulation of capital in the global economy, which is not simply the sum of national economies and national class structures and requires a centralized authority to represent the whole of competing capitals, the major combinations of which are no longer 'national' capitals. The nature of state practices in the emergent global system resides in the exercise of transnational economic and political authority through the TNS apparatus to reproduce the class relations embedded in the global valorization and accumulation of capital.

The power of national states and the power of transnational capital

As class formation proceeded through the nation-state in earlier epochs, class struggle world-wide unfolded through the institutional and organizational logic of the nation-state system. During the nation-state phase of capitalism, national states enjoyed a varying but significant degree of autonomy to intervene in the phase of distribution and surpluses could be diverted through nation-state institutions. Dominant and subordinate classes struggled against each other over the social surplus through such institutions and fought to utilize national states to capture shares of the surplus. As a result, to evoke Karl Polanyi's classical analysis, a 'double movement' took place late last century,[2] made possible because capital, facing territorial, institutional and other limits bound up with the nation-state system, faced a series of constraints that forced it to reach an historic compromise with working and popular classes. These classes could place redistributive demands on national states and set some constraints on the power of capital (these possibilities also contributed to the split in the world socialist movement and the rise of social democracy). Popular classes could achieve this because national states had the ability to capture and redirect surpluses through interventionist mechanisms. The outcome of world class struggles in this period were Keynesian or 'New Deal' states and Fordist production in the cores of the world economy and diverse multiclass developmentalist states and populist projects in the periphery ('peripheral Fordism'), what Lipietz and others have called the 'Fordist class compromise'.[3]

In each of these cases, subordinate classes mediated their relation to capital through the nation-state. Capitalist classes developed within the protective cocoon of nation-states and developed interests in opposition to rival national capitals. These states expressed the coalitions of classes and groups that were incorporated into the historic blocs of nation-states. There was nothing transhistoric, or predetermined, about this process of class formation world-wide. It is now being superseded by globalization. What is occurring is a process of transnational class formation, in which the mediating element of national states has been modified. As national productive structures become transnationally integrated, world classes whose organic development took place through the nation-state are experiencing supra-national integration with 'national' classes of other countries. Global class formation has involved the accelerated division of the world into a global bourgeoisie and a global proletariat and has brought changes in the relationship between dominant and subordinate classes. Specifically, by redefining the phase of distribution in the accumulation of capital in relation to nation-states the global economy fragments national cohesion around processes of social reproduction and shifts the site of reproduction from the nation-state to transnational space. The consequent liberation of transnational capital from the constraints and commitments placed on it by the social forces in the nation-state phase of capitalism has dramatically altered the balance of forces among classes and social groups in each nation of the world and at a global level towards the transnational capitalist class and its agents. (Indeed, the restraints on accumulation imposed by popular classes world-wide in the nation-state phase of capitalism was what drove capital to transnationalization in the first instance.)

The declining ability of the nation-state to intervene in the process of capital accumulation and to determine economic policies reflects the newfound power that transnational capital acquired over popular classes. Different classes and groups contest (national) state power but real power in the global system is shifting to a transnational space that is not subject to 'national' control. This structural power of transnational capital over the direct power of national states has been utilized to instil discipline or to undermine policies that may emanate from these states when they are captured by popular classes or by national fractions of local dominant groups, as popular forces that won state power in Haiti, Nicaragua, South Africa, and elsewhere in the 1970s–1990s discovered. This appears as an institutional contradiction between the structural power of transnational capital and the direct power of states. But this is a structural contradiction internal to an evolving capitalist system, at whose core are class relations, as the inner essence of a condition whose outward manifestation is an institutional contradiction. One set of social relations reflects a more fundamental set of social relations. On the surface, the structural power of capital over the direct power of states is enhanced many times over by globalization. In its essence, the relative power of exploiting classes over the exploited classes has been enhanced many times over, at least in this momentary historic juncture.

The newfound relative power of global capital over global labour is becoming fixed in a new global capital–labour relation, what some have called the global casualization or informalization of labour, or diverse contingent categories, involving alternative systems of labour control associated with post-Fordist 'flexible accumulation'. Central to this new capital–labour relation is the concept of a restructuring crisis. The crisis of the long post-war boom in the 1970s ushered in a radical shift in the methods and sites of global capitalist accumulation, resulting, in Hoogvelt's analysis, in a transformation in the mechanisms of surplus value extraction.[4] These new systems of labour control include subcontracting and contract labour, outsourcing, part-time and temporary work, informal work, home-work, the revival of patriarchal, 'sweatshop', and other oppressive production relations. Well-known trends associated with the restructuring of the labour-capital relation taking place under globalization include 'downward levelling', deunionization, 'ad hoc' and 'just-in-time' labour supply, the superexploitation of immigrant communities as a counterpart to capital export, the lengthening of the working day, the rise of a new global 'underclass' of supernumeraries or 'redundants' subject to new forms of social control and even to genocide, and new gendered and racialized hierarchies among labour.

These new relations have been broadly discussed in the globalization literature. What interests us here is the larger social and political context in which they are embedded, and the extent to which states and nation-states continue to mediate these contexts. State practices and the very structure of states are negotiated and renegotiated in specific historic periods through changes in the balance of social forces as capitalism develops and classes struggle. Capital began to abandon earlier reciprocities with labour from the 1970s onwards, precisely because the process of globalization has allowed it to break free of nation-state constraints. These new labour patterns are facilitated by globalization in a dual sense: first, capital has exercised its power over labour through new patterns of flexible accumulation made possible by enabling 'third wave' technologies, the elimination of spatial barriers to accumulation, and the control over space these changes bring; second, globalization itself involves the culmination of the primitive accumulation of capital world-wide, a process in which millions have been wrenched from the means of production, proletarianized, and thrown into a global labour market that transnational capital has been able to shape. In this new capital–labour relation, labour is increasingly only a naked commodity, no longer embedded in relations of reciprocity rooted in social and political communities that have historically been institutionalized in nation-states.

The dissolution of the 'welfarist' or Keynesian 'class compromise' rests on the power acquired by transnational capital over labour, which is objectively transnational but whose power is constrained and whose subjective consciousness is distorted by the continued existence of the system of nation-states. Here we see how the continued existence of the nation-state serves numerous interests of the transnational capitalist class. For instance, central to capitalism is securing a politically and economically suitable labour supply, and at the core of all class societies is the control over labour and disposal of the products of labour. Under capitalist globalization, the linkage between securing labour and territoriality is changing, and national labour pools are merging into a single global labour pool that services global capitalism. The global labour supply is, in the main, no longer coerced (subject to extra-economic compulsion) due to the ability of the universalized market to exercise strictly economic discipline, but its movement is juridically controlled. Here, national borders play a vital function. Nation-states are about the configuration of space, what sociologist Philip McMichael has called 'population containment zones'.[5] But their containment function applies to labour and not to capital. Globally mobile capital is not regulated by centralized national political authorities but labour is. The inter-state system thus acts as a condition for the structural power of globally mobile transnational capital over labour which is transnational in its actual content and character, but is subjected to different institutional arrangements and to the direct control of national states.

How then is the newfound relative power of global capital over global labour related to our analysis of the transnationalization of the state? Out of the emerging transnational institutionality the new class relations of global capitalism and the social practices specific to it are becoming congealed and institutionalized. For instance, when the IMF or the WB condition financing on enactment of new labour codes to make workers more 'flexible', or on the roll-back of a state-sponsored 'social wage' through austerity programmes, they are producing this new class relation. Similarly, the types of practices of national states that became generalized in the late twentieth century – deregulation, fiscal conservatism, monetarism, tax regressivity, austerity, etc. – produce this relation, resulting in an increase in state services to, and subsidization of, capital, and underscoring the increased role of the state in facilitating private capital accumulation. With this comes a shift in income and in power from labour to capital. These outcomes generate the broader social and political conditions under which the new capital–labour relation is forged.

But now we need to specify further the relationship of national states to the TNS. Capital acquires its newfound power *vis-à-vis* (*as expressed within*) national states, which are transformed into transmission belts and filtering devices. But national states are also transformed into proactive instruments for advancing the agenda of global capitalism. This assertion that transnational social forces impose their structural power over nations and the simultaneous assertion that states, captured by transnational fractions, are proactive agents of the globalization process, only appear as contradictory if one abandons dialectics for the Weberian dualist construct of states and markets and the national–global dualism. Governments are undertaking restructuring and serve the needs of transnational capital not simply because they are 'powerless' in the face of globalization, but because a particular historical constellation of social forces now exists that presents an organic social base for this global restructuring of capitalism. Hence it is not that nation-states become irrelevant or powerless *vis-à-vis* transnational capital and its global institutions. Rather, power as the ability to issue commands and have them obeyed, or more precisely, the ability to shape social structures, shifts from social groups and classes with interests in national accumulation to those whose interests lie in new global circuits of accumulation.

The contradictory logics of national and global accumulation are at work in this process.

Class fractionation is occurring along a new national/transnational axis with the rise of transnational corporate and political elites. The interests of one group lie in national accumulation, including the whole set of traditional national regulatory and protectionist mechanisms, and the other in an expanding global economy based on world-wide market liberalization. The struggle between descendant national fractions of dominant groups and ascendant transnational fractions was often the backdrop to surface political dynamics and ideological processes in the late twentieth century. These two fractions have been vying for control of local state apparatuses since the 1970s. Transnational fractions of local elites have ascended politically in countries around the world, clashing in their bid for hegemony with nationally based class fractions. In the 1970s and the 1980s incipient transnationalized fractions set out to eclipse national fractions in the core capitalist countries of the North and to capture the 'commanding heights' of state policy-making. From the 1980s into the 1990s, these fractions became ascendant in the South and began to vie for, and in many countries to capture, national state apparatuses. National states, captured by transnational social forces, internalize the authority structures of global capitalism. The global is incarnated in local social structures and processes. The disciplinary power of the global capitalism shifts actual policy-making power within national states to the global capitalist bloc, which is represented by local social forces tied to the global economy. Gradually, transnational blocs became hegemonic in the 1980s and 1990s within the vast majority of countries in the world and began to transform their countries. They utilized national state apparatuses to advance globalization and established formal and informal liaison mechanisms between the national state structures and TNS apparatuses.

By the 1990s the transnational capitalist class had become the hegemonic class fraction globally. This denationalized bourgeoisie is class conscious, and conscious of its transnationality. Its interests are administered by a managerial elite that controls the levers of global policy-making and exercises transnational state power through the multilayered configuration of the TNS. But this transnational bourgeoisie is not a unified group. 'The same conditions, the same contradiction, the same interests necessarily called forth on the whole similar customs everywhere', noted Marx and Engels in discussing the formation of new class groups. 'But separate individuals form a class only insofar as they have to carry on a common battle against another class; otherwise they are on hostile terms with each other as competitors.' Fierce competition among oligopolist clusters, conflicting pressures, and differences over the tactics and strategy of maintaining class domination and addressing the crises and contradictions of global capitalism make any real internal unity in global ruling class impossible. In sum, the capturing of local states by agents of global capitalism resolves the institutional contradiction discussed above between transnational capital and national states, that is, local state practices are increasingly harmonized with global capitalism. But this only intensifies the underlying class and social contradictions. Before discussing these contradictions, let us reconstruct in brief the emergence of a TNS in the latter decades of the twentieth century, tracing *how* the transnational capitalist class sought to institutionalize its interests within a TNS.

[Robinson goes on to examine empirical evidence for these tendencies and to argue that popular classes need to 'transnationalize' their struggles against transnational capital.]

Notes

1   M. Weber, *Economy and Society*, 2 vols, G. Roth and C. Wittich (eds) (University of California Press, Berkeley, 1978), pp. 353–4.
2   K. Polanyi, *The Great Transformation* (Beacon Press, Boston, 1944).
3   A. Lipietz, *Towards a New Economic Order: Postfordism, Ecology and Democracy* (Oxford University Press, New York, 1992).
4   A. Hoogvelt, *Globalization and the Postcolonial World* (Johns Hopkins University Press, Baltimore, 1997).
5   P. McMichael, *Development and Social Change* (Pine Forge Press, Thousand Oaks, CA, 1996).

3.5 Neoliberal cosmopolitanism

Peter Gowan

Source: *New Left Review*, vol. 11, September–October 2001, pp. 79–93.

Gowan argues that neo-liberal cosmopolitanism encapsulates a vision of global order that will govern political and economic aspects of the internal and external behaviour of states. This order entails the imposition of conditions on sovereignty by the 'international community', either through active intervention or through 'global governance' and international institutions. A key vehicle for this is the post-Cold War 'Pacific Union' of rich peaceful Western states, led by the United States.

[Gowan begins by setting out the basis of the 'new liberal cosmopolitanism' (NLC) in the triumph of liberal democracy after the Cold War and the dominance of of the United States and its allies.]

Mapping global dominance

Crucial to the NLC version of today's world is the claim, not just that the 'Pacific Union' has remained united, but that its members have broken with power politics as their governing impulse. What this, of course, represses is the central fact of contemporary international relations: one single member of the Pacific Union – the United States – has acquired absolute military dominance over every other state or combination of states on the entire planet, a development without precedent in world history. The US government, moreover, has shown no sign whatever that it is ready to relinquish its global dominance. American defence spending, as high today as it was in the early 1980s, is increasing, and a consensus across the Clinton and Bush administrations has developed in favour of scrapping the Anti-Ballistic Missile Treaty. The underlying reality of the Pacific Union is a set of bilateral, hub-and-spokes military alliances under US leadership. In the past liberal theorists usually explained the forging of these alliances as responses to powerful Communist and Soviet threats to democratic values and regimes. Yet, though liberalism and democracy are now widely held to be a prevailing norm, and the Warsaw Pact has vanished, these 'defensive' alliances have not quit the stage. On the contrary, Washington has worked vigorously to reorganize and expand them during the 1990s.

NLC theorists protest that the United States has, nevertheless, abandoned egoistic national interest as its strategic guideline. After all, are not liberal democratic values tirelessly lauded and expounded in the speeches of US leaders – most imperishably, by the late President Clinton? Such declarations are no novelty – ringing proclamations of disinterested liberal principle go back to the days of classical nineteenth-century power politics and Lord

Palmerston. If, on the other hand, we turn to actual policy guidelines for US diplomacy in the 1990s, we find them wholly dedicated to the calculations of power politics. Where such documents refer to the icons of free trade and liberal democracy, they are presented as conditions for the advancement of US power and prosperity.

Do these power-political instruments and orientations at least exempt other members of the Pacific Union from the calculus of domination? By no means. Hegemonic military alliances have two faces – one external and one internal: the first directed against potential enemies, the second serving to keep auxiliaries in line. Lord Ismay, the first Secretary-General of NATO, expressed this duality with crystal clarity when he famously remarked in the 1950s that the purpose of NATO was keep the Russians out and the Germans down. The same dual objective has remained at the centre of American Grand Strategy for the post-Cold War epoch – witness the Pentagon's forthright injunction, in a document leaked to the *New York Times* early in 1992, that the US 'discourage the advanced industrialized nations from even aspiring to a larger global or regional role'.[1] Conventional apologias for the American-led war against Yugoslavia as a disinterested rescue mission for human rights, free of any power-political consideration, ignore the regimenting function of the Balkan intervention within NATO itself – the demonstration effect on European allies of overwhelming US military might in their own borderlands, consolidating the unequal structure of the Atlantic Pact internally.

In these respects, realist accounts of the nineties are clearly superior to the prospectuses of the new liberal cosmopolitans. Zbigniew Brzezinski has summed up the actual nature of [the] Pacific Union with characteristic bluntness, remarking that compared to the British Empire of the nineteenth century,

> the scope and pervasiveness of American global power today are unique [. . .] Its military legions are firmly perched on the western and eastern extremities of Eurasia, and they also control the Persian Gulf. American vassals and tributaries, some yearning to be embraced by even more formalties to Washington, dot the entire Eurasian continent.[2]

Brzezinski offers us a map of 'US geopolitical preponderance and other areas of US political influence'. The whole of Western Europe, Japan, South Korea, Australia and New Zealand, as well as some parts of the Middle East and Canada fall into the category of US 'preponderance' – not just influence. The main zones with the resource capacities to challenge US hegemony are precisely those where the US has most firmly established its political sway.

Brzezinski's map also indicates the large parts of the planet which are of little strategic interest to the US. There can, of course, be objections to Brzezinski's selection of areas of vital concern and areas of relative neglect, marked as it is by his own geopolitical preoccupations – others might wish to emphasize a more 'geo-economic' pattern of power-projection, with greater priority accorded to the most important centres of capital accumulation or natural resources (above all petroleum). Yet such a stress would also reveal a highly selective focus (and one that scarcely differed from Brzezinski's). Although the United States and other Pacific Union governments publicly stress the need for the global spread of liberal rights and regimes, their policies actually obey a double derogation. In 'strategic back-waters', such as most of sub-Saharan Africa today, even real genocide can be casually covered or countenanced, as the experience of Rwanda has shown. Where delinquent states are pivotal to American strategic interests, on the other hand, they are vigilantly shielded from human rights pressures, as the cases of Saudi Arabia, Israel, Turkey or Indonesia, to name only the most flagrant examples, have long made clear.

World institutions

Any form of liberal cosmopolitan project for a new world order requires the subordination of all states to some form of supra-state planetary authority. NLC occlusion of the role of the US in the Pacific Union is compounded by a misrepresentation of the relationship between the US and the various institutions of 'global governance' that are either in place or being canvassed. There is no evidence that these institutions have strengthened their jurisdiction over the dominant power in the international system. If anything, the evidence of the 1990s suggests a trend in the opposite direction, as most of these organizations are able to function effectively only insofar as they correspond to the perceived policy priorities of the United States, or at least do not contradict them; indeed, in many instances they should rather be viewed as lightly disguised instruments of US policy.

The United Nations is a striking case in point. With the end of the Cold War, the US has been able to utilize the UN for its ends in a style not seen even in the days of the Korean War. The expedition of Desert Storm in 1991, followed by a decade of sanctions against Iraq, in which UN 'inspection missions' have been openly colonized by the CIA, and the Balkan War, whose violation of the UN Charter was rewarded with the promotion of NATO to UN subcontractor, have only been the most prominent examples of the submission of the Security Council to American dictates. The Secretary-General holds office only at US pleasure. When Boutros-Ghali proved insufficiently malleable – 'unable to understand the importance of cooperation with the world's first power' in the words of White House factotum James Rubin – he was summarily removed in favour of an American placeman, Kofi Annan, who regularly makes public assertions of the need for the UN to cater to the pre-eminence of Washington at which Trygve Lie himself would have blushed. None of this, of course, has meant that the US feels it necessary even to pay its dues to the UN. In similar spirit, the United States has set up a War Crimes Tribunal under the UN label to punish those it views as its enemies in the Balkans, and protect those it deems its friends, while at the same time declining to sign up to an international court of Human Rights, on the grounds that members of its own armed services might unseasonably be charged before it, or too visibly given special exemption from legal sanction under the escape clause carefully crafted for the US in the treaty.

If we turn to international financial institutions, the pattern is even starker. The IMF is so completely an agency of American will that when the Mexican debt crisis struck in 1995, the Treasury in Washington did not even bother to consult European or Japanese members of the Fund, but – in brazen contravention of its Charter – simply instructed the IMF overnight to bail out American bond-holders, while appropriating additional funds, not even tenuously at its disposal, from the Bank of International Settlements in Basle for the same purpose. The East Asian crisis of 1997–8 offers further evidence, if it were needed, of the ability of the US Treasury to use the IMF as an instrument of its unilateralism, most flagrantly and coercively in the South Korean case. The latest arrival in the panoply of 'global governance', the World Trade Organization, repeats the pattern.

Ratification of the WTO Treaty was explicitly made conditional upon the WTO proving 'fair' to US interests, which since the late 1980s has always meant an unabashed rejection of any rule deemed 'unfair' to those interests – an approach the impeccably orthodox economist Jagdish Bhagwati has called 'aggressive unilateralism'. Bhagwati highlights the creation and use of so-called Super 301 and Special 301 laws, but to these could be added 'anti-dumping' provisions and countervailing duties. Such measures have been far from marginal in US international economic policy: as Miles Kahler points out, 'the number of actions brought against "unfair" trading practices increased dramatically' during the 1990s.[3] According to another authority, 'no other economic regulatory programme took on such an increase in case-loads'.[4] Alongside this refusal to be bound by cosmopolitan economic law, meanwhile, there have been vigorous attempts to extend the jurisdictional reach of US domestic law internationally, applying it to non-American corporations operating outside the United States, in the notorious Helms–Burton pursuit of foreign firms trading with Cuba.

In short, the reality is an asymmetrical pattern of change in the field of state sovereignty: a marked tendency towards its erosion in the bulk of states in the international system, accompanied by an accumulation of exceptional prerogatives on the part of one state. We must, in other words, make a sharp distinction between the members of the Pacific Union: the United States has not exhibited any discernible tendency either to abandon power politics or to subordinate itself to supra-state global authorities. Expressions of official enthusiasm for norm-based cosmopolitanism as an institutionalized order, although by no means wanting in Washington (the majority of NLC theorists are, after all, American), have been more profuse on the other side of the Atlantic. During the 1990s, as the European Union committed itself to developing a Common Foreign and Security Policy, and prepared for enlargement to the East in the wake of NATO expansion, it started to lay ever greater emphasis on applying its ideological and legal regimes to external partner states. Today, the EU regularly outdoes the US itself in lecturing other states on the inseparability of the free market from the rule of law and democratic government, and in posing as guardian of universal liberal principles. In practice, however, it has consistently acted as a regional subordinate of the US, save where narrow trade, investment and production interests are concerned – still liable to spark contention at a lower level.

The various West European states would all prefer the US to proceed with less unilateralism. But their conception of what passes for 'multilateral' – essentially a matter of style rather than substance – remains sufficiently minimal not to present any threat to American hegemony. At no period since the end of the Second World War has Western Europe been so closely aligned, ideologically and politically, with the United States as today. The anxiety with which the incoming Bush administration was greeted in European capitals was a sign of dependence rather than distance. The days of Adenauer and De Gaulle, or even Edward Heath and Helmut Schmidt, are long past.

Trade regimes

Let us counter-factually suppose, however, that the allies of the United States could inveigle it into a more collegial form of Pacific Union dominance. Is there any evidence that such a configuration would usher in a liberal cosmopolitan order subordinating the sovereignty of national states to universalist liberal norms and institutions, applied equally to all? To answer this question, we need to ask: what are the social and economic transformations that are now jointly promoted by the Pacific Union, and how do these affect the international system of states? The theorists of NLC present the fundamental changes under way as, firstly, steady progress towards a global free market, subject to negotiated regulation, and secondly, the spread of liberal democracy across the earth, unifying the peoples of the world in representative government, monitored by global institutions protecting human rights. These are large claims. Let us begin by looking at the economic prospectus held out by NLC.

The common notion, taken more or less for granted by NLC theorists, that the companies of Pacific Union states inaugurated economic globalization by escaping the control of their own states ignores the fact that the patterns of international economic exchange have continued to be shaped in large measure by state diplomacy, establishing the legal and institutional framework for the operation of markets. NLC doctrine tends to assume that the regulatory and market-shaping impulses of states have been and are geared towards liberal free-trade regimes. Contemporary evidence suggests that this is misleading: the drift of the international economic policy of core countries in the 1990s has been marked by resistance to free-trade principles in sectors of critical importance to economies outside the core – agricultural products, steel, textiles and apparel – and by moves towards managed trade and 'reciprocity' in a number of others. Examples include various key aspects of US–Japanese trade, where the total range of imports or exports to be achieved in various sectors is specified in advance; the use of Voluntary Export Restraints, pricing agreements and other non-tariff barriers by the EU to control the level of imports from Eastern Europe; and so-called 'rules of origin' designed to exclude from free entry into a given market goods produced with varying amounts of inputs from third countries. The effect of such protectionist and mercantilist methods is, typically, to generate chronic trade and current account deficits on the part of less developed countries – a near universal problem facing East European states – exacerbating already huge debts, and making peripheral governments increasingly desperate to gain supposedly compensating inflows of capital from the core states. This is a pattern that all too often renders them vulnerable and unstable, hence incapable of generating sustained improvement in the well-being of their populations.

Furthermore, the bulk of the economic changes made in the 1990s did not concern international trade at all. Although described in the Western media as 'trade regimes' or 'trade negotiations', they have been overwhelmingly about the property rights of foreign capitals in other states: that is, the ability of foreign operators to gain ownership of domestic assets, or establish businesses within states on the same terms as domestic companies, to move money in and out of the country freely, and to enforce monopoly rents on intellectual property. The public-policy issues raised in these areas concern such matters as the costs and benefits of allowing global oligopolies to gain ownership of domestic assets and integrate them into their profit streams; of ending controls on the free movement of private finance; of privatizing (mainly into foreign ownership) domestic social-service provisions and utilities; and last, but by no means least, the costs and benefits of making domestic financial systems – and thereby entire national economies – highly vulnerable to sudden and massive gyrations in global monetary relations and in international financial markets.

Current trends in international trade and in the internal transformations of non-core political economies are thus very far from guaranteeing virtuous circles of cosmopolitan economic and social gains for the world's populations. There is overwhelming evidence of a huge and growing polarization of wealth between the immiserated bulk of humanity and extremely wealthy social groups within the core countries. Neither is there the slightest indication that, were its allies within the Pacific Union to subordinate the US to a more collegial system, this pattern of economic relations would alter in any way. Indeed, one of the main bases for perceptions of common cause between the US and its allies is precisely their joint interest in perpetuating this drive for control of new profit streams from non-core economies.

Permeable sovereignty

NLC theorists confuse juridical forms with social substance. They depict the world as a fragmented system of state sovereignties on one side, and a proliferating number of regional, international and global regimes and institutions on the other. In the midst of these institutional patterns they perceive a swelling mass of individuals, increasingly free to maximize their welfare in markets. This juridical perspective provides the basis for hoping that global regimes can encase state sovereignties in a legally egalitarian, cosmopolitan rule of law in which citizens of the world can unite in free exchange. If, however, we view this same international order from the angle of social power, it looks more like a highly centralized pyramid of capitalist market forces dominated by the Pacific Union states and strongly supported by their state officials. This reality is captured by Justin Rosenberg's notion of an 'empire of civil society.'[5] In this empire, we find substantial unity between the states and market forces of the core countries, rather than the antagonism suggested by theorists of globalization and liberal cosmopolitanism. We also find substantial unity across the societies of the Pacific Union, whose empire is guarded not by any supra-state authority, but by a single hegemon.

We do not have ready to hand a language for describing this pattern of global social power. We are used to thinking of both state sovereignty and international markets as the opposites of imperialism. This could be said to have been true of the various European colonialisms of the nineteenth and first half of the twentieth centuries, for these were largely juridical empires claiming sovereign legal power over conquered territories and peoples. But the distinctive feature of the Pax Americana has been the enlargement of US social control within the framework of an international order of juridically sovereign states. Samuel Huntington has provided the classic statement of how US imperial expansion has worked:

> Western Europe, Latin America, East Asia, and much of South Asia, the Middle East and Africa fell within what was euphemistically referred to as 'the Free World', and what was, in fact, a security zone. The governments within this zone found it in their interest: a) to accept an explicit or implicit guarantee by Washington of the independence of their country and, in some cases, the authority of the government; b) to permit access to their country to a variety of US governmental and non-governmental organizations pursuing goals which those organizations considered important [. . .] The great bulk of the countries of Europe and the Third World found the advantages of transnational access to outweigh the costs of attempting to stop it.[6]

During most of the Cold War, as Huntington notes, the principal lever of US expansion was the security pact. Since the beginning of the 1980s a second instrument has supplemented it: financial and market-access pacts for states facing financial crisis. These pacts not only allow entry of Atlantic capitals into lesser sovereign states; they also allow national and international market structures to be redesigned so as to favour systematically the market dominance of Atlantic multinational corporations. In liberal thought, the rejection by the dominant core states of formalized legal authority over territory can seem to suggest a far weaker form of political power than the European juridical empires of old. This is because liberal approaches often tend to conceive power as 'command'. But he who takes legal command over a territory assumes responsibility for everything that happens on it – frequently a heavy burden and potentially a dangerous one. On the other hand, he who shapes the relevant environment of a given state authority can ensure that it acts in ways conducive to his interests. The emergent global system is geared to shaping the environments of sovereign states so that developments within them broadly match the interests of the Pacific Union – while responsibility for tackling these developments falls squarely on the governments of the sovereign states concerned. This new type of international order, then, does not make the system of penetrated sovereign states a legal fiction. They remain crucial cornerstones of the world order, but their role becomes above all that of maintaining political control over the populations within their jurisdiction.

Domestic liberalization

The second principal basis for NLC optimism lies in the spread of liberal democratic forms of polity across the globe. Yet, paradoxically, severe pressures on the foundations of many newly liberal-democratic states have come from the very Pacific Union seen by liberal cosmopolitans as the fount of international harmony. States are forced to open their economies to monetary and financial movements to which the employment conditions of their citizens become extremely vulnerable. Their elites are encouraged to impose policies which widen the gap between rich and poor. Economically weak countries are driven to compete for the entry of foreign capital by reducing taxes on the business classes – thereby undermining their capacity to maintain social and educational services. All these pressures have been taking their toll: as Geoffrey Hawthorn has noted, states under strain or in disintegration, the emergence of shadow states or outright state collapse are becoming common sights in the contemporary world. In such conditions liberal girders burst, and groups will often increasingly turn to organized crime or break with the homogenizing national political values of the state, demanding exit as national minorities.

These trends are not confined to polities outside the Pacific Union. They are also reflected in a general malaise within the 'consolidated' liberal democracies of the core, well captured by Philippe Schmitter:

> Privatization of public enterprises; removal of state regulations; liberalization of financial flows; conversion of political demands into claims based on rights; replacement of collective entitlements by individual contributions; sacralization of property rights; downsizing of public bureaucracies and emoluments; discrediting of 'politicians' in favour of 'entrepreneurs'; enhancement of the power of 'neutral technical' institutions, like central banks, at the expense of 'biased political' ones – all these modifications have two features in common: 1) they diminish popular expectations from public choices, and 2) they make it harder to assemble majorities to overcome the resistance of minorities, especially well-entrenched and privileged ones.

Schmitter goes on to note the decline in democratic participation in those advanced liberal democracies 'most exposed to the "more liberalism" strategy', commenting:

> whether this process of 'dedemocratization' can continue is, of course, the all-important question. Its justification rests almost exclusively on the superior economic performance that is supposed to accrue to a liberalized system of production and distribution – along with the deliberate effort to foster a strong normative rejection of politics as such.[7]

Finally, of course, NLC theorists welcome military intervention at large by the Pacific Union in the name of human rights – or even 'civilization' – as an inspiring step forward towards the realization of a world ruled by liberal principles rather than power. On closer inspection, however, these expeditions offer a model of power-projection that virtually inverts this description. When constitutional polities descend into civil war, liberal procedures collapse – as liberal theory acknowledges, allowing for emergency situations when liberal norms are suspended. Typically, in such crisis conditions, both sides to a political conflict will accuse the other of violating provisions of the law, which becomes a largely rhetorical token in a struggle over other issues, such as separatism, irredentism, or confessional division. During the 1990s, states of the Pacific Union intervened in several such conflicts, proclaiming the need to uphold liberal norms, while taking no political position on the issues that have caused them. The NATO attack on Yugoslavia in 1999, lauded by NLC theorists as a triumph of humanitarian principle, should rather be seen as an example of politically unprincipled, arbitrary imperial government. The conflict between the Yugoslav government and the Kosovar Albanians concerned the right of the latter to secede from Yugoslavia. The Pacific Union states in effect declared this political issue irrelevant and themselves incapable of laying down any general principle to resolve it, resorting instead to an arbitrary 'pragmatism' that seems set to repeat itself in any such future operations. The revenge attacks being planned in the wake of the destruction of the World Trade Centre seem unlikely to be aimed at mitigating the tensions racking Saudi Arabian society – home to the majority of the hijackers – whose extraordinarily repressive confessional regime has, as noted, long been smiled upon by the Pacific Union.

For even if the Pacific Union states were to overcome all tensions amongst themselves and merge into a minority condominium over the planet, there is every reason to suppose that they would continue to place contradictory demands upon the system over which they currently preside. On the one hand, they demand internal arrangements within those states which suit the interests of the 'empire of civil society'. But on the other they rely upon those states to preserve domestic order and control their local populations. These incompatible policy requirements stem from an essentially arbitrary attitude towards enforcing universalist liberal norms of individual rights. The evidence mustered by the supporters of the new liberal cosmopolitanism to claim that humanity is finally on the verge of being united in a single, just world order is not convincing. The liberal-individualist analytical corset does not fit the world as it is: it fails to strap American power into its prognosis of a supra-state order. The cosmopolitan project for unifying humanity through the agency of the dominant capitalist states – on the normative basis that we are all individual global citizens with liberal rights – will not work: it is more likely to plunge the planet into increasingly divisive turmoil.

Notes

1   This was the 1992 draft of the Pentagon Defense Planning Guidance.
2   Z. Brzezinski, *The Grand Chessboard: American Primacy and its Geostrategic Imperatives* (New York, 1997), p. 23.
3   M. Kahler, *Regional Futures and Transatlantic Economic Relations* (New York, 1995), p. 46.
4   P. Nivola, *Regulating Unfair Trade* (Washington DC: 1993), p. 21.
5   J. Rosenberg, *The Empire of Civil Society* (Verso, London and New York, 1995).
6   S. Huntington, 'Transnational Organizations in World Politics', *World Politics*, vol. 25(3), 1973, p. 344.
7   P. Schmitter, 'Democracy's Future: More Liberal, Preliberal or Postliberal?', *Journal of Democracy*, vol. 6(1), January 1995.

3.6 Globalizing capitalism and the rise of identity politics

Frances Fox Piven

Source: *Socialist Register*, 1995, pp. 102–16.

Fox Piven focuses on the ways in which the globalization of capitalism intersects with 'identity politics', creating new and often intractable political divisions. One of the effects of global capitalism is to penetrate and subordinate nationally based political organizations, especially those based in the working class, and to create a fluid constellation of culturally or ethnically based movements. Fox Piven argues that this creates new forms of insecurity and exploitation of vulnerable groups, and that the result is subordination of working-class movements globally to supranational institutions created by capitalism. The result is increasing fragmentation and insecurity, exacerbated by large-scale dislocations and processes such as migration.

[Fox Piven begins by noting that hopes for the universalization of working class politics have been dashed because of the new cleavages promoted by globalization.]

A good deal of the recent discussion of identity politics takes the form of arguments about whether to be for it, or against it. The dispute is in one sense pointless. Identity politics is almost surely inevitable, because it is a way of thinking that reflects something very elemental about human experience. Identity politics seems to be rooted quite simply in attachments to the group, attachments that are common to humankind, and that probably reflect primordial needs that are satisfied by the group, for material survival in a predatory world, as well as for recognition, community, security, and perhaps also a yearning for immortality. Hence people construct the 'collective identities' which define the common traits and common interests of the group, and inherit and invent shared traditions and rituals which bind them together. The mirror image of this collective identity is the invention of the Other, whoever that may be, and however many they may be. And as is often pointed out, it is partly through the construction of the Other, the naming of its traits, the demarcation of its locality, and the construction of a myth-like history of struggle between the group and the Other, that the group recognizes itself. All of this seems natural enough.

If identification with the group is ubiquitous, it is also typically the case that groupness and Otherness are understood as the result of biological nature. Perhaps this is simply because nature provides the most obvious explanation of groupness that is available to people. Even when groups are demarcated by their religion or culture, these mentalities are often regarded as traits so deeply rooted as to be virtually biological, inevitably passed on to future generations. Moreover, the pernicious traits attributed to the Other can easily be woven into explanations of the travails that people experience, into theories of why the rains don't come, or why children sicken and die, or why jobs are scarce and wages fall. This sort of racial theorizing makes the world as people experience it more comprehensible. Even labour politics, ideas about a universalistic proletarian class notwithstanding, was riddled with identity politics. Thus Hobsbawm makes the sensible point that the very fact that 20th century political movements proferred religious, nationalist, socialist and confessional credos suggests that their potential followers were responsive to all these appeals.[1] Politicized workers were bonded together not only and perhaps not mainly by common class position, but by the particularisms of maleness, of whiteness, and of diverse European ethnic and religious identities. In short, features of the human condition seem to drive people to identity politics and, if it is not an inevitable way of thinking, it is surely widespread.

But if identity politics is ubiquitous because of what it offers people in protection, comfort and pride, it has also been a bane upon humankind, the source of unending tragedy. The fatal flaw in identity politics is easily recognized. Class politics, at least in principle, promotes vertical cleavages, mobilizing people around axes which broadly correspond to hierarchies of power, and which promote challenges to these hierarchies. By contrast, identity politics fosters lateral cleavages which are unlikely to reflect fundamental conflicts over societal power and resources and, indeed, may seal popular allegiance to the ruling classes that exploit them. This fatal flaw at the very heart of a popular politics based on identity is in turn regularly exploited by elites. We can see it dramatically, for example, in the unfolding of the genocidal tribal massacres in Rwanda, fomented by a Hutu governing class which found itself losing a war with Tutsi rebels. And of course the vulnerability to manipulation resulting from identity politics is as characteristic of modern societies as tribal societies.

Thus identity politics makes people susceptible to the appeals of modern nationalism, to the bloody idea of loyalty to state and flag, which is surely one of the more murderous ideas to beset humankind. State builders cultivate a sort of race pride to build allegiance to an abstract state, drawing on the ordinary and human attachments that people form to their group and their locality, and drawing also on the animosity to the Other that is typically the complement of these attachments. The actual group that people experience, the local territory that they actually know, comes to be joined with the remote state and its flag, just as the external enemy of the state comes to be seen as the menacing Other, now depicted as a threat not only to the group and its locale, but as a threat to the nation state. I hardly need add that this melding of identity politics with state patriotism can stir people to extraordinary acts of destruction and self-destruction in the name of mystical abstractions, and the identity politics that energizes them. Napoleon was able to waste his own men easily in his murderous march across Europe because they were quickly replaced with waves of recruits drawn from a French population enthused by their new attachment to the French nation. And World War I showed that modern states could extract even more extraordinary contributions of life and material well-being from their citizenry, as Europeans seized by nationalist passions joined in a frenzy of destruction and death in the name of state patriotism.

In the United States, popular politics has always been primarily about race, ethnicity and religion. Perhaps a population of slaves and immigrants of diverse origins, captive and free, provided some objective basis for the cultivation of identity politics, constructed by ordinary people themselves, and of course by political and economic elites who have never been slow to see that division ensured domination. From the colonial era, public policy engraved distinctions among whites, blacks and native Americans by enshrining elaborate racial hierarchies by law, by prohibiting sexual liaisons across racial lines, and by punishing with particular ferocity the insurrections in which humble people of different races joined together.

The institutions of the American South, especially the post reconstruction South, are illustrative, for they can be understood as a vast complex of social arrangements which, by strictly segregating Afro-Americans, and specifying their obligations of deference, made factitious racial differences real. Similar practices by industrialists had similar if less total consequences in inscribing difference. Employers deliberately drew from diverse ethnic groups for their workforce, and then artfully arranged job assignments, wage scales and residential quarters in company towns so as to maintain and underline those differences. Or note the strident emphasis on ethnic, religious, and later racial identities in the organizations, the mobilizing strategies and the policy outcomes of big city politics. The labour movement was riddled by these influences and, if it was sometimes strengthened by the gender, racial and ethnic solidarities that flourished within it, particularistic identities also blinded workers to their commonalities, making them vulnerable to employers who pitted one group against another, and leading them also to engage in terrible episodes of labour fratricide. Needless perhaps to add, this history still marks American politics today.

All this notwithstanding, identity politics can also be a potentially liberating and even equalizing development, especially among subordinate groups, and the more so in a political culture already dominated by identity politics. This possibility has sometimes been difficult for liberals honed on ideals of universalism to appreciate. Certainly it has been difficult for a Left preoccupied with class to appreciate.

Contemporary complaints about identity politics would be more understandable if they were aimed at elites who help foment and manipulate divisions. Instead, however, they are often directed at the subordinate groups who assert fractious identities. It may well be, however, that identity politics is especially necessary to lower status peoples, to those who are more insecure, and who are more likely to be deprived of recognition and respect by wider currents of culture and social interaction. Subordinate groups try to construct distinctive and sometimes defiant group identities, perhaps to defend themselves against dominant definitions, at least when they are allowed the cultural space to do so. Moreover, the construction of distinctive identities may be a necessary prelude to self-organization and political assertion, and particularly so in a political culture organized by identity politics. Indeed, in the cauldron of an American politics based on difference, immigrants who had previously recognized only a village or a locale as their homeland invented new national identities the better to survive and do battle in contests among nationalities. For them, the construction of new identities was a vehicle of at least psychic emancipation, and sometimes of political empowerment as well.

The black movement of the post World War II era, which is often (unreasonably) blamed for heightened identity politics, is a good example of the emancipatory construction and assertion of group identity. The celebration of Blackness was in the first instance reactive to the racism of American society: to the experience of racial subordination and terror in the South, to the extreme subordination imposed by the North whose cultural imagery at its most benign featured minstrels in blackface, Sambos, and so on. Blacks reconstructed their identity in the face of these imposed identities, and this was almost surely essential to the rise of a movement demanding racial liberation – and to the substantial achievements of that movement in dismantling the caste arrangements which had engraved racial identity politics.

However, these achievements set in motion a train of repercussions that were not simple. The new assertions of Black pride and the political demands that pride fuelled provoked alarmed and angry reactions from other groups whose own identities depended on the subordination of blacks. And of course political elites, especially but not only Republican party operatives, who stood to benefit from the politics of backlash, worked to sharpen these reactions, making such code words of race hatred as 'quotas,' or 'law and order,' or 'welfare dependency,' focal to their popular appeals. Still, the very emergence of far-reaching race conflict reflected the fact that subordination had come to be contested. Blacks were no longer allowing others to define their identity, repress their interests, and stamp out their aspirations. That was an achievement.

The rise of gender politics followed a similar course. While women do not have what is recognized as a distinctive language or turf, the understanding of gender has in other ways been prototypical of the understanding of group identity. Gender identities are closely similar to racial identities, because the traits which were thought to be feminine or masculine, and the social roles to which women and men were consigned, were always understood as the natural consequence of biological difference. Necessarily, therefore, the emergence of a liberatory movement among women was preceded and accompanied by an effort to cast off this inherited identity and construct new identities that disavowed biological fatalism or, in some variants, celebrated biological difference. Indeed, Zaretsky writes of 'the profundity and the intensity of the identity impulse among women that emerged in the early seventies.'[2] The most salient issues of the women's movement – the struggle for the Equal Rights Amendment, for reproductive rights, and the campaigns against rape and sexual harassment – are closely reflective of this effort to reconstruct the meaning of gender by challenging the biological underpinnings of traditional meanings. The mounting of such a challenge to the most ancient of subordinations, and a subordination rooted in understandings of nature itself, is surely a stunning accomplishment.

As with Blacks, the consequences were not simple. Liberatory reconstructions of gender struck at deeply imprinted understandings, threatening and arousing people still embedded in more traditional relationships, including many women embedded in traditional relationships. And as had been the case with conflict over racial identities, the contest over understandings of gender became the focus of elite manipulations in electoral politics. By 1980, the Republicans had taken notice, and in an effort to turn the widening anxieties provoked by gender conflict to electoral advantage, struck support for ERA from their platform, and initiated a campaign that culminated in the odd spectacle of American Presidents – leaders of the richest and most technologically advanced nation in the world – casting themselves as leaders of a holy war against abortion.

While identity politics may always be with us, the contemporary world appears to be engulfed by particularistic conflicts of rising intensity and destructiveness, in a pattern reminiscent of the rising tide of nationalist furies of the late 19th century. The main reasons for this, then and now, can be traced to the transformation of world capitalism. First, in the contemporary period, capitalist expansion is at least partly responsible for the weakening or collapse of nation states, with horrific consequences for ethnic and religious conflict. Second, economic restructuring is enfeebling existing forms of working class political organization which in the past sometimes restrained particularistic conflicts in the interests of class solidarity. Finally, even while the restraining capacities of governments and working class organizations are diminishing, capitalist restructuring is aggravating group conflict, by accelerating the migration of peoples, by intensifying competition for scarce resources, and by creating the widespread economic and social insecurity which always accompanies large-scale change, and particularly so when the changes for many people are for the worse.

Of course, not every instance of the weakening or collapse of central governments that had previously restrained group conflict can be traced to the current global capitalist transformation. Ancient animosities can erupt whenever central governments no longer hold them in check. The withdrawal of the British Raj unleashed bloody conflicts in India which persist to this day, and the withdrawal of the colonial powers from Africa also spurred tribal conflicts. But other instances of central government collapse cannot easily be disentangled from the changes wrought by world capitalism. Waves of anarchic warfare in the developing world are at least partly the result of saddling third world governments with debt through the imposition of neo-liberal credit policies. The fall of the Yugoslavian government, and the ethnic wars that resulted, was similarly at least partly the result of the shock therapy administered by the IMF. And other Eastern European governments were undermined by the spread of a consumer culture which fuelled popular discontent with state provision. (The Eastern European revolutions, says Benjamin R. Barber, were less over the right to vote than the right to shop.)[3]

Other consequences of capitalist tranformation for the intensification of identity politics are more direct. In a sense, the old prediction has proved true; the bourgeoisie is on the move with a series of universalizing projects which promise utterly to transform the world, penetrating and homogenizing social life across the globe. But instead of nourishing a growing proletariat, a missionary capitalism is destroying the working class formations of the older industrial order, at least in the rich countries of the West.

I do not want to overstate the unifying influence of the labour movement at its peak. I have already pointed out that worker mobilizations were riven by the particularistic divisions of race and ethnicity, and sometimes gender. Nevertheless, the promise of the labour movement was that class solidarity would override particularisms, and even that proletarian internationalism would override state patriotism. And in instance after instance, where the successful use of the strike power demanded it, labour did indeed override the divisions of identity politics, even in the United States. Now that moderating influence has weakened.

The basic lines of capitalist restructuring and the impact on organized labour are familiar. First, the expansion of global trade, itself promoted by the internationalizing of markets in finance and production, as well as by improvements in transportation and communications, has lead to the intensified exploitation of labour and resources across the globe. From Indonesia to China to Haiti, previously peripheral peoples and places are being incorporated into capitalist markets, with the consequence that organized workers in the mother countries find themselves competing with products made by low wage workers across the globe, including workers made docile by coercive authoritarian governments.

Second, the power constellations patterning the policies of national governments have shifted. Organized labour has lost ground dramatically to new supra-national institutions created by capital. It is true, as Panitch says, that the nation states are major authors of these institutions, and also continue to serve important functions for internationalizing capital.[4] Nevertheless, once in existence, international organizations and networks, including multinational corporations and international banking organizations, together with their domestic corporate and financial allies who freely use the threat of disinvestment as leverage in their dealings with governments, become major constraints on the policy options of the state. Constraints on the state are also constraints on the ability of democratic publics, including the organized working class, to exert influence through electoral-representative arrangements. The trade unions and political parties constructed by organized workers in the mother countries gained what influence they had through their leverage on governments, where strike power, trade union organization and working class voting numbers made them a force with which to be reckoned. If capitalist internationalism circumscribes what national governments can do, it inevitably also circumscribes working class political power.

Third, as a consequence of both internationalism and the shifting power constellations within nations, the economies and polities of the mother-counties of industrial capitalism are being restructured, with dire consequences for the old working class. This process is most advanced in England and the United States where unions are weaker and welfare state protections less adequate. The old mass production industries which created the industrial working class are being dismantled or reorganized and decentralized, with the consequence that the numbers of blue collar workers are shrinking. And as communities disperse and the mass media supplants the local pub, the old working class culture also crumbles. Those who remain have become excruciatingly vulnerable to the threat power of a mobile capital, unable to resist shrinking wages and benefits, and the worsening terms of work, including speedup, and forced overtime for some, and involuntary part-time or temporary work for others, all of which undermines union organization. At the same time, capitalists have launched a specifically political project to dismantle the institutional supports created by working class politics, by attacking unions, and slashing welfare state income and service protections which shielded workers from the market, and by discrediting Keynesian macro-economic political regulation.

Finally, a capitalist class on the move has launched an ideological campaign to justify and promote its expansionary mission. International markets exist, but they have also been cast as a superordinate order, operating according to a kind of natural law, penetrating national economies more deeply than they actually do, and beyond the reach of politics. In fact, this neo-laissez faire doctrine cloaks the capitalist class with the mantle once claimed by the proletariat. Capital is forging the way to the future, it is the great force for progress, the hope of humankind. And as with 19th century laissez faire notions to which this doctrine owes its main tenets, the ideology is touched with fanaticism, with a zealous utopianism that ignores the actual needs of the human subjects of any world order. Of course, this ideological campaign is as persuasive as it is because international markets are also real, and the palpable evidence of capital and goods mobility lends the sweeping doctrine of neo-laissez faire a certain material reality.

In all of these ways a universalizing capitalism has weakened the old industrial working class as a political force. No wonder unions and labour parties that were the instrument of this class have also lost their ideological footing. The imagery which gave working-class politics its élan, the idea that the future belonged to the workers, and that workers acted for all humankind, has collapsed. That universalizing myth now belongs to a capitalist class on the move.

The surge of identity politics is not just the result of a collapsing central government or a receding class politics. It is also the result of the massive dislocations of people set in motion by capitalist restructuring. More and more people are being drawn into the orbit of capitalism. Considered abstractly, that process is universalizing. In the actual experience of people, it has had the effect of heightening particularistic identities and conflicts. Gellner, writing of an earlier phase of capitalist transformation and the nationalist furies it helped to set loose, showed how an 'explosive blend of early industrialism (dislocation, mobility, acute inequality *not* hallowed by time and custom) seeks out, as it were, all the available nooks and crannies of cultural differentiation, wherever they be.'[5] The pattern is being repeated in the contemporary era. In other words, instead of wiping out the 'train of ancient and venerable prejudices,' the advance of global capitalism is whipping ancient prejudices to fever pitch.

Identity politics is pervasive, and probably inevitable. But group conflict is likely to rise under some conditions, and subside under others. One important source of disturbance has to do with the large-scale migration of people spurred by capitalist penetration of subsistence agricultural economies, with the consequence that conflicts over land escalate, and people no longer able to survive in agriculture migrate to urban centres. At the same time, the spread of consumer culture also attracts people from the periphery, while the development of globe-spanning circuits of communication and transportation facilitates the recruitment of cheap labour to the metropole. 'Every migration,' says Enzensberger, 'no matter what triggered it, what motive underlies it, whether it is voluntary or involuntary, and what scale it assumes, leads to conflicts.'[6] Or as Jean Daniel, editor of *Le Nouvel Observateur*, warns about population movements and the 'unprecedented' mingling of peoples, we should remember that 'Babel [. . .] was a curse.'[7]

If unfamiliar proximity is likely to intensify group consciousness and fractionalism, this is especially so when outsider groups are seen as competitors for limited jobs, neighbourhood space, honour and influence. In his last book, Ralph Miliband wrote that intra-class conflicts among wage-earners involving race or gender or ethnicity or religion can reasonably be understood as the effort to find scapegoats to explain insecurity and alienation.[8] If he was not entirely right, he was surely at least significantly right. Group conflict is far more likely when people feel growing uncertainty about their own future and as is true in many instances, are experiencing real declines in living standards. When times get harder, and competition for scarce resources intensifies, theories about the Other, and how the Other is to blame for these turns in events, being ubiquitous, are readily available. And, of course, such interpretations are more likely to be seized upon when alternative and perhaps more systemic explanations of the troubles people face are not available, or when such explanations yield no practicable line of action. No wonder there has been a spread of an identity politics, often a hate-filled identity politics, in the metropole. As Vaclav Havel says, 'The world of our experiences seems chaotic, confusing [. . .] And the fewer answers the era of rational knowledge provides [. . .] the more deeply it would seem that people behind its back as it were, cling to the ancient certainties of their tribe.'[9]

Finally, as so many times before, the group divisions of identity politics are being worsened by political elites who seize the opportunity for gaining advantage from popular division. In particular, politicians on the Right – Le Pen's Front National in France, the Christian Right in the United States, the Freedom Party in Austria, the Falangists in Spain, the Lombard League in Italy, or the Republicans in Germany where half a million immigrants arrived in 1992 alone – work to stoke the anger against outsiders. They draw popular attention away from the economic transformations underway, and try to hold or win anxious voters by directing resentment against outsiders. Or, as a retired Russian officer commented to a *New York Times* reporter about the conflict between the Tatars and ethnic Russians, 'Half the population is building mosques, the other half is building churches. And the bosses are building big brick houses for themselves.'

Notes

1   On the overlap and tension between the appeals of national identity and class in working class political mobilization, see Eric Hobsbawm, *Nations and Nationalism Since 1789* (Cambridge University Press, Cambridge, 1990).
2   E. Zaretsky, 'Responses', *Socialist Review*, vol. 23(3), 1994.
3   B. Barber, 'Jihad vs. McWorld', *Atlantic Monthly*, March 1992.
4   L. Panitch, 'Globalization and the State', *The Socialist Register*, 1994.
5   E. Gellner, cited in Hobsbawm, *Nations and Nationalism*, p. 112.

6   Hans Enzensberger, *Civil Wars from L.A. to Bosnia* (The New Press, 1994).
7   See J. Daniel, 'God is Not a Head of State', *New Perspectives Quarterly*, vol. 11(2), Spring 1994.
8   R. Miliband, *Socialism for a Sceptical Age* (Polity Press, Cambridge, 1994), pp. 22, 192–3.
9   V. Havel, 'The New Measure of Man', *New York Times*, July 8, 1994.

3.7 The globalized war economy

Mary Kaldor

Source: *New and Old Wars: Organized Violence in a Global Era* (Polity Press, Cambridge, 2001), pp. 90–111.

Kaldor draws a sharp distinction between the traditional (national state-centric) view of the 'war economy' and the new type of globalized war economy, which challenges conventional views of the role of states and the possibility of conflict resolution. One of the key effects of this change is that the nature of participants in war and violence has become much more diverse and unpredictable. Kaldor goes on to describe the changing character of war and violence, to assess the ways in which 'new wars' are resourced and to explore the reasons for the spread of new forms of war.

The term 'war economy' usually refers to a system which is centralized, totalizing and autarchic, as was the case in the total wars of the twentieth century. Administration is centralized to increase the efficiency of the war and to maximize revenue to pay for the war. As many people as possible are mobolized to participate in the war effort either as soldiers or in the production of arms and necessities. By and large, the war effort is self-sufficient, although in World War II, Britain and the Soviet Union received lend-lease assistance from the United States. The main aim of the war effort is to maximize the use of force so as to engage and defeat the enemy in battle.

The new type of war economy is almost totally the opposite. The new wars are 'globalized' wars. They involve the fragmentation and decentralization of the state. Participation is low relative to the population both because of lack of pay and because of lack of legitimacy on the part of the warring parties. There is very little domestic production, so the war effort is heavily dependent on local predation and external support. Battles are rare, most violence is directed against civilians, and cooperation between warring factions is common.

Those who conceive of war in traditional Clausewitzean terms, based on definable geopolitical goals, fail to understand the underlying vested interests, both political and economic, in the continuation of war. They tend to assume that political solutions can be found without any need to address the underlying economic logic. At the same time, however, those who recognize the irrelevance of traditional perceptions of war and observe the complexity of the political, social and economic relationships expressed in these wars tend to conclude that this type of violence can be equated with anarchy. In these circumstances, the most that can be done is to treat the symptoms through, for example, humanitarian assistance.

[. . .] I argue that it is possible to analyse the typical political economy of new wars so as to draw conclusions about possible alternative approaches. Indeed, the implication of such an analysis is that many of the well-meaning efforts of various international actors, based on inherited assumptions about the character of war, may turn out to be counterproductive. Conflict resolution from above may merely enhance the legitimacy of the warring parties and allow time for replenishment; humanitarian assistance may contribute to the functioning of the war economy; peacekeeping troops may lose legitimacy either by standing aside when terrible crimes are committed or by siding with groups who commit terrible crimes. [. . .]

The privatization of military forces

Madeleine Albright, the US Secretary of State, has used the term 'failed states' to describe countries with weak or non-existent central authority – the classic examples are Somalia or Afghanistan. Jeffrey Herbst argues that many African states never enjoyed state sovereignty in the modern sense – that is, 'unquestioned physical control over the defined territory, but also an administrative presence throughout the country and the allegiance of the population to the idea of the state'.[1] One of the key characteristics of failing states is the loss of control over and fragmentation of the instruments of physical coercion. A disintegrative cycle sets in which is almost the exact opposite of the integrative cycle through which modern states were established. The failure to sustain physical control over the territory and to command popular allegiance reduces the ability to collect taxes and greatly weakens the revenue base of the state. In addition, corruption and personalistic rule represents an added drain on state revenue. Often, the government can no longer afford reliable forms of tax collection; private agencies are sometimes employed who keep part of the takings, much as happened in Europe in the eighteenth century. Tax evasion is widespread both because of the loss of state legitimacy and because of the emergence of new forces who claim 'protection money'. This leads to outside pressure to cut government spending, which further reduces the capacity to maintain control and encourages the fragmentation of military units. Moreover, outside assistance is predicated on economic and political reforms which many of these states are constitutionally incapable of implementing. A downward spiral of loss of revenue and legitimacy, growing disorder and military fragmentation creates the context in which the new wars take place. Effectively, the 'failure' of the state is accompanied by a growing privatization of violence.

Typically, the new wars are characterized by a multiplicity of types of fighting units both public and private, state and non-state, or some kind of mixture. For the purpose of simplicity, I identify five main types: regular armed forces or remnants thereof; paramilitary groups; self-defence units; foreign mercenaries; and, finally, regular foreign troops generally under international auspices. [. . .]

While the small-scale character of the fighting units has much in common with guerrilla warfare, they lack the hierarchy, order and vertical command systems that have been typical of guerrilla forces and that were borrowed from modern warfare as well as the structure of Leninist or Maoist political parties. These various groups operate both independently and in cooperation. What appear to be armies are actually horizontal coalitions of breakaway units from the regular armed forces, local militia or self-defence units, criminal gangs, groups of fanatics, and hangers-on, who have negotiated partnerships, common projects, divisions of labour or spoils. Robert Reich's concept of the 'spider's web' to characterize the new global corporate structure [. . .] is probably also applicable to the new warfare. [. . .]

The end of the Cold War and of related conflicts like Afghanistan or South Africa greatly increased the availability of surplus weapons. In some cases, wars are fought with weapons raided from Cold War stockpiles; such is largely the case in Bosnia–Herzegovina. In other cases, redundant soldiers sell their weapons on the black market, or small-scale producers (as in Pakistan) copy their designs. In addition, arms enterprises which have lost state markets seek new sources of demand. Certain conflicts, for example Kashmir, took on a new character as a result of the influx of arms, in this case a spill over from the conflict in Afghanistan. The new wars could be viewed as a form of military waste-disposal – a way of using up unwanted surplus arms generated by the Cold War, the biggest military build-up in history.

Patterns of violence

The techniques of the new fighting units owe much to the types of warfare that developed during and after the Second World War as a reaction to modern war. Revolutionary warfare, as articulated by Mao Tse-tung and Che Guevara, developed tactics that were designed to find a way round large-scale concentrations of conventional forces and that were almost quite counter to conventional strategic theory.

The central objective of revolutionary warfare is the control of territory through gaining support of the local population rather than through capturing territory from enemy forces. The zones under revolutionary control are usually in remote parts of the country which cannot be easily reached by the central administration. They provide bases from which the military forces can engage in tactics which sap the morale and efficiency of enemy forces. Revolutionary warfare has some similarities with manoeuvre theory. It involves decentralized dispersed military activity, with a great emphasis on surprise and mobility. But a key feature of revolutionary warfare is the avoidance of head-on collisions which guerrilla units are likely to lose because of inferior numbers and equipment. Strategic retreats are frequent. According to Mao Tse-tung: 'The ability to run away is precisely one of the characteristics of guerrillas. Running away is the chief means of getting out of passivity and regaining the initiative.'[2]

Great stress is placed by all revolutionary writers on winning 'hearts and minds' not just in the territory under revolutionary control, but in enemy territory as well so that the guerrilla can operate, according to Mao's well-known dictum, 'like a fish in the sea', although, of course, terroristic methods were also used. Counterinsurgency, which has been an almost universal failure, was designed to counter this type of warfare using conventional military forces. The main strategy has been to destroy the environment in which the revolutionaries operate, to poison the sea for the fish. Techniques like forcible resettlement developed by the French in Algeria, or area destruction through scattering mines or herbicides or napalm developed by the Americans in Vietnam, have also been used by, for example, the Indonesians in East Timor or the Turkish government against the Kurds.

The new warfare borrows from both revolutionary warfare and counterinsurgency. It borrows from revolutionary warfare the strategy of controlling territory through political control rather than through capturing territory from enemy forces. This is somewhat easier than it was for revolutionary forces, since in most cases the central authority is very weak and the main contenders for the control of territory are not governments with conventional modern forces but rather similar types of fighting units, even if they bear the name of regular armies. Nevertheless, as in the case of revolutionary warfare, the various factions continue to avoid battle mainly in order to conserve men and equipment. Strategic retreats are typical and ground is conceded to what appears to be the stronger party. Often, the various factions cooperate in dividing up territory between them.

An important difference between revolutionaries and the new warriors, however, is the method of political control. For the revolutionaries, ideology was very important; even though fear was a significant element, popular support and allegiance to the revolutionary idea was the central aim. Hence, the revolutionaries tried to build model societies in the areas under their control. In contrast, the new warriors establish political control through allegiance to a label rather than an idea. In the brave new democratized world, where political mobilization is based on labels and where elections and referenda are often forms of census-taking, this means that the majority of people living in the territory under control must admit to the right label. Anyone else has to be eliminated. Indeed, even in non-democratized areas, fear of opposition, dissidence or insurgency reinforces this demand for homogeneity of population based on identity.

This is why the main method of territorial control is not popular support, as in the case of revolutionary warfare, but population displacement – getting rid of all possible opponents. To achieve this, the new warfare borrows from counterinsurgency techniques for poisoning the sea – techniques which were refined by guerrilla movements created or promoted by Western governments with experience of counterinsurgency to topple left-wing governments in the 'low-intensity' conflicts of the 1980s such as RENAMO in Mozambique, the *Mujahidiin* in Afghanistan, or the Contras in Nicaragua. Indeed, this approach was a reaction to the failure of counterinsurgency in Vietnam and Southern Africa and the implicit realization that a conventional modern war is no longer a viable option.

Instead of creating a favourable environment for the guerrilla, the new warfare aims to create an unfavourable environment for all those people it cannot control. Control of one's own side depends not on positive benefits, since in the impoverished, disorderly conditions of the new warfare, there is not much that can be offered. Rather, it depends on continuing fear and insecurity and on the perpetuation of hatred of the other. Hence the importance of extreme and conspicuous atrocity and of involving as many people as possible in these crimes so as to establish a shared complicity, to sanction violence against a hated 'other' and to deepen divisions. [. . .] Essentially, what were considered to be undesirable and illegitimate side-effects of old war have become central to the mode of fighting in the new wars. It is sometimes said that the new wars are a reversion to primitivism. But primitive wars were highly ritualistic and hedged in by social constraints. These wars are rational in the sense that they apply rational thinking to the aims of war and refuse normative constraints.

The pattern of violence in the new type of warfare is confirmed by the statistics of the new wars. The tendency to avoid battle and to direct most violence against civilians is evidenced by the dramatic increase in the ratio of civilian to military casualties. At the beginning of the twentieth century, 85–90 per cent of casualties in war were military. In World War II, approximately half of all war deaths were civilian. By the late 1990s, the proportions of a hundred years ago have been almost exactly reversed, so that nowadays approximately 80 per cent of all casualties in wars are civilian.[3]

The importance of population displacement is evidenced by the figures on refugees and displaced persons. According to UNHCR, the global refugee population has risen from 2.4 million people in 1975 to 10.5 million people in 1985 and 14.4 million people in 1995 (a decline from 18.2 million in 1992 due to the repatriation of some 9 million people). This figure only includes refugees who cross international boundaries. According to the same figures, another 5.4 million people are internally displaced.[4] Figures provided by the US Committee on Refugees are much higher, increasing from 22 million in 1980 to 38 million in 1995, of whom approximately half were internally displaced persons.[5] Using the latter figures, Myron Weiner has calculated that the number of refugees per conflict has roughly doubled since 1969, increasing from 287,000 per conflict to 459,000 per conflict in 1992. But the increase in internally displaced persons has shown an even more dramatic increase, from 40,000 per conflict in 1969 to 857,000 per conflict in 1992.[6]

Financing the war effort

The new wars take place in a context which could be represented as an extreme version of globalization. Territorially-based production more or less collapses either as a result of liberalization and the withdrawal of state support, or through physical destruction (pillage, shelling, etc.), or because markets are cut off as a result of the disintegration of states, fighting, or deliberate blockades imposed by outside powers, or more likely, by fighting units on the ground, or because spare parts, raw material and fuel are impossible to acquire. In some cases, a few valuable commodities continue to be produced – e.g. diamonds in Angola and Sierra Leone, lapis lazuli and emeralds in Afghanistan, drugs in Colombia and Tadjikistan – and they provide a source of income for whoever can provide 'protection'. Unemployment is very high and, as long as governments continue to spend, inflation is rampant. In extreme cases, the currency collapses to be replaced by barter, the use of valuable commodities as currency or the circulation of foreign currencies, dollars or deutschmarks.

Given the erosion of the tax base both because of the collapse of production and because of the difficulties of collection, governments, like privatized military groups, need to seek alternative sources of funding in order to sustain their violent activities. Given the collapse of productive activity, the main sources of funding are either what Mark Duffield calls 'asset transfer',[7] i.e. the redistribution of existing assets so as to favour the fighting units, or external assistance. The simplest form of asset transfer is loot, robbery, extortion, pillage and hostage-taking. This is widespread in all contemporary wars. Rich people are killed and their gold and valuables stolen; property is transferred in the aftermath of ethnic cleansing; cattle and livestock are raided by militiamen; shops and factories are looted when towns are taken. Hostages are captured and exchanged for food, weapons or other hostages, prisoners of war or dead bodies.

A second form of asset transfer is market pressure. A typical characteristic of the new wars are the numerous checkpoints which control the supply of food and necessities. Sieges and blockades, the division of territory between different paramilitary groups, allow the fighting units to control market prices. Thus a typical pattern, observed in Sudan, former Yugoslavia and other places, is that urban dwellers or even farmers will be forced to sell their assets – cars, fridges, televisions or cows – at ridiculously low prices in exchange for highly priced necessities simply in order to survive.

More sophisticated income-generating activities include 'war taxes' or 'protection' money from the production of primary commodities and various forms of illegal trading. The production and sale of drugs is a key source of income in Colombia, Peru and Tadjikistan. It is estimated that income from drugs accounts for 70 per cent of the opposition revenue in Tadjikistan, while the income of the Colombian guerrillas is said to amount to some $US800 million a year, which compares with government defence expenditure of $US1.4 billion.[8] Trading in drugs, arms or laundered money, and sanctions busting are all examples of revenue-raising criminal activities in which the various military groups are engaged.

However, given the collapse of domestic production, external assistance is crucial, since arms, ammunition, food, not to mention Mercedes cars or Rayban sunglasses, have to be imported. [. . .]

Essentially, the fragmentation and informalization of war is paralleled by the informaliza-tion of the economy. In place of the national formal economy with its emphasis on industrial production and state regulation, a new type of globalized informal economy is established in which external flows, especially humanitarian assistance and remittances from abroad are integrated into a local and regional economy based on asset transfer and extra-legal trading. Figure 1 illustrates the typical resource flows of a new war. It is assumed that there is no production and no taxation. Instead, external support to ordinary people, in the form of remittances and humanitarian assistance, is recycled via various forms of asset transfer and black-market trading into military resources. Direct assistance from foreign governments, protection money from producers of commodities and assistance from the diaspora enhance the capacity of the various fighting units to extract further resources from ordinary people and thus sustain their military efforts. [. . .]

Some writers argue that economic motivation explains the new type of warfare. David Keen suggests that a 'war where one avoids battles but picks on unarmed civilians and perhaps eventually acquires a Mercedes may make more sense [. . .] [than] risking death in the name of the nation-state with little or no prospect of significant financial gain'.[9] But economic motivation alone is insufficient to explain the scale, brutality and sheer viciousness of new wars. No doubt some join the fighting as a way of legitimizing criminal activities, providing a political justification for what they do and socially sanctioning otherwise illegal methods of financial gain. No doubt there are others – rational power-seekers, extreme fanatics or victims intent on revenge – who engage in criminal activities to sustain their political military goals. Yet others are press-ganged into the fighting, propelled by fear and hunger.

The point is rather that the modern distinctions between the political and the economic, the public and the private, the military and the civil are breaking down. Political control is required to embed the new coercive forms of economic exchange, which in turn are required to provide a viable financial basis for the new gangsters/powerholders in the context of state disintegration and economic marginalization. A new retrograde set of social relationships is being established in which economics and violence are deeply intertwined within the shared framework of identity politics.

The spread of violence

The new type of warfare is a predatory social condition. While it may be possible to contain particular groups or individuals, it is very difficult to contain the social condition either in space or in time. Neighbouring countries are the most immediately affected. The cost of the war in terms of lost trade, especially where sanctions or communications blockades are introduced or where borders are closed, either deliberately or because of fighting; the burden of refugees, since generally it is the neighbouring states who accept the largest numbers; the spread of illegal circuits of trade; and the spill-over of identity politics – all these factors reproduce the conditions that nurture the new forms of violence. [. . .]

Conclusion

The new wars have political goals. The aim is political mobilization on the basis of identity. The military strategy for achieving this aim is population displacement and destabilization so as to get rid of those whose identity is different and to foment hatred and fear. Nevertheless, this divisive and exclusive form of politics cannot be disentangled from its economic basis. The various political/military factions plunder the assets of ordinary people as well as the remnants of the state and cream off external assistance destined for the victims, in a way that is only possible in conditions of war or near war. In other words, war provides a legitimation for various criminal forms of private aggrandizement while at the same time

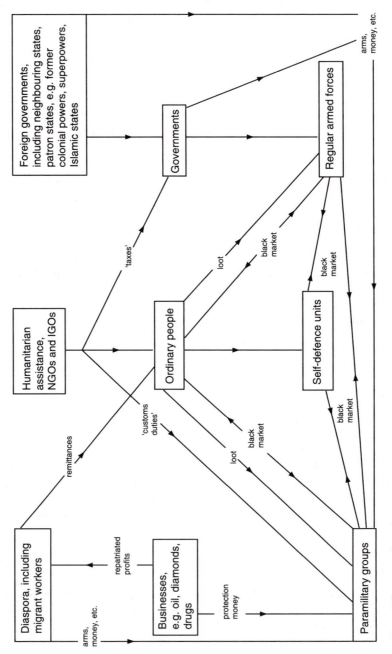

Figure 1 Resource flows in new wars

these are necessary sources of revenue in order to sustain the war. The warring parties need more or less permanent conflict both to reproduce their positions of power and for access to resources.

While this predatory set of social relationships is most prevalent in the war zones, it also characterizes the surrounding regions. Because participation in the war is relatively low (in Bosnia, only 6.5 per cent of the population took part directly in the prosecution of the war) the differences between zones of war and apparent zones of peace are not nearly as marked as in earlier periods. Just as it is difficult to distinguish between the political and the economic, public and private, military and civil, so it is increasingly difficult to distinguish between war and peace. The new war economy could be represented as a continuum, starting with the combination of criminality and racism to be found in the inner cities of Europe and North America and reaching its most acute manifestation in the areas where the scale of violence is greatest.

If violence and predation are to be found in what are considered zones of peace, so it is possible to find islands of civility in nearly all the war zones. They are much less known about than the war zones, because it is violence and criminality and not normality that is generally reported. But there are regions where local state apparatuses continue to function, where taxes are raised, services are provided and some production is maintained. There are groups who defend humanistic values and refuse the politics of particularism. The town of Tuzla in Bosnia–Herzegovina represents one celebrated example. The self-defence units created in Southern Rwanda are another example. In isolation, these islands of civility are difficult to preserve, squeezed by the polarization of violence, but the very fragmentary and decentralized character of the new type of warfare makes such examples possible.

Precisely because the new wars are a social condition that arises as the formal political economy withers, they are very difficult to end. Diplomatic negotiations from above fail to take into account the underlying social relations; they treat the various factions as though they were proto-states. Temporary ceasefires or truces may merely legitimize new agreements or partnerships that, for the moment, suit the various factions. Peacekeeping troops sent in to monitor ceasefires which reflect the status quo may help to maintain a division of territory and to prevent the return of refugees. Economic reconstruction channelled through existing 'political authorities' may merely provide new sources of revenue as local assets dry up. As long as the power relations remain the same, sooner or later the violence will start again.

Notes

1   J. Herbst, 'Responding to State Failure in Africa', *International Security* vol. 21(3), Winter 1996/7, pp. 121–2.
2   Quoted in Simkin, *Race to the Swift: Thoughts on Twenty-First Century Warfare* (Brassey's, London, 1985), p. 311.
3   For the earlier figures, see Dan Smith, *The State of War and Peace Atlas* (Penguin Books, London, 1997). The figure for the 1990s is my own calculation: see M. Kaldor, 'Introduction', in M. Kaldor and B. Vashee (eds), *Restructuring the Global Military Sector Volume I: New Wars* (Cassell/Pinter, London, 1997).
4   UNHCR, *The State of the World's Refugees: In Search of Solutions* (Oxford University Press, Oxford, 1995).
5   These figures can be found in the regular *World Refugee Survey* published by the U.S. Committee on Refugees, Washington DC.
6   M. Weiner, 'Bad Neighbours, Bad Neighbourhood: An Inquiry into the Causes of Refugee Flows', *International Security* vol. 21(1), Summer 1996.

7   M. Duffield, 'The Political Economy of Internal War: Asset Transfer, Complex Emergencies and International Aid' in J. Macrae and A. Zwi (eds), *War and Hunger: Rethinking International Responses* (Zed Press, London, 1994).
8   'Central Asia's Narcotics Industry', *Strategic Comments* vol. 3(5), June 1997; 'Colombia's Escalating Violence: Crime, Conflict and Politics', *Strategic Comments* vol. 3(4), May 1997.
9   D. Keen, 'When War Itself is Privatized', *Times Literary Supplement*, December 1995.

3.8 The new development-security terrain

Mark Duffield

Source: *Global Governance and the New Wars: The Merging of Development and Security* (Zed Books, London, 2001), pp. 1–17.

Duffield situates the relationship between war and development in the characteristics of the emerging 'liberal' world system, which privileges a core of highly developed capitalist states. This has the effect of marginalizing or excluding the 'global South' of less developed countries and regions, and thus of subordinating them. Duffield goes on to argue that this situation leads to a redefinition of notions of peace, development and security, and to a tendency towards intervention in the cause of development and democracy.

The optimism of the early post-Cold War years that the world was entering a new era of peace and stability has long since evaporated. It has been swept aside by a troubled decade of internal and regionalised forms of conflict, large-scale humanitarian interventions and social reconstruction programmes that have raised new challenges and questioned old assumptions. During the mid-1990s the need to address the issue of conflict became a central concern within mainstream development policy. Once a specialised discipline within international and security studies, war and its effects are now an important part of development discourse. At the same time, development concerns have become increasingly important in relation to how security is understood. It is now generally accepted that international organisations should be aware of conflict and its effects and, where possible, gear their work towards conflict resolution and helping to rebuild war-torn societies in a way that will avert future violence. Such engagement is regarded as essential if development and stability are to prevail. [. . .]

Today, security concerns are no longer encompassed solely by the danger of conventional interstate war. The threat of an excluded South fomenting international instability through conflict, criminal activity and terrorism is now part of a new security framework. Within this framework, underdevelopment has become dangerous. This reinterpretation is closely associated with a radicalisation of development. Indeed, the incorporation of conflict resolution and societal reconstruction within aid policy – amounting to a commitment to transform societies as a whole – embodies this radicalisation. Such a project, however, is beyond the capabilities or legitimacy of individual Northern governments. In this respect, the changing nature of North–South relations is synonymous with a shift from hierarchical and territorial relations of government to polyarchical, non-territorial and networked relations of governance. The radical agenda of social transformation is embodied within Northern strategic networks and complexes that are bringing together governments, NGOs, military establishments and private companies in new ways. Such complexes are themselves part of an emerging system of global liberal governance.

[Duffield goes on to explore the development of the 'liberal world system' based on globalization and the predominance of the 'North'; at the same time, the 'South' is excluded from key dominant networks in the globalized world economy and the 'global informational economy', whilst it has also experienced increasing integration with the 'North' through various types of informal transborder activity. The result is a breakdown of normative order accompanied by increasing interventions in the form of new governance networks and global institutions. Duffield goes on to relate this to 'liberal peace'.]

Liberal peace

The new development–security terrain remains underresearched and its study has yet to establish its own conceptual language. One can, however, make a few preliminary remarks. In terms of methodology, a useful distinction is that between mechanical and complex forms of analysis. This difference sets apart Newtonian physics from the emerging complexity sciences such as quantum theory, non-linear mathematics, biotechnology and cybernetics. It can be summarised as the difference between seeing the world as a machine and seeing it as a living system or organism. The Newtonian view of the cosmos is that of a vast and perfect clockwork machine governed by exact mathematical laws. Within this giant cosmic machine everything can be determined and reduced to a scientific cause and effect. The material particles that make it up, and the laws of motion and forces that hold or repel them, are fixed and immutable. Set in motion at the birth of the cosmos, this huge mechanism has been running ever since. While having earlier origins, by the mid-twentieth century the Newtonian world view had been superseded. From quantum theory, for example, a new physics has emerged. Rather than mechanical precepts, this is based on organic, holistic and ecological principles. What is suggested is not a mechanism made up of different basic parts but a unified and determining whole created from the relations between its separate units. The new physics represents a shift from the study of objects to that of interconnections.

A concern with interconnections defines a systems approach. Systems are integrated wholes that cannot be reduced to their separate parts. Instead of concentrating on basic elements, systems analysis places emphasis on the principles of organisation. From this perspective, a number of distinctions can be made between machines and systems. Machines are controlled and determined by their structure and characterised by linear chains of cause and effect. They are constructed from well-defined parts that have specific functions and tasks. Systems, on the other hand, are analogous to organisms. They grow and are process-oriented. Their structures are shaped by this orientation and they can exhibit a high degree of internal flexibility. Systems are characterised by cyclical patterns of information flow, non-linear interconnections and self-organisation within defined limits of autonomy. Moreover, using the analogy of an organism, a system is concerned with self-renewal. This is important, since while a machine carries out specific and predictable tasks, a system is primarily engaged in a process of renewal and, if necessary, self-transformation. It is a central contention in this book that aid policy, both generally and in relation to the new wars, continues to exhibit a Newtonian or mechanical view of the world. In developing a critique of aid policy as embodying emergent forms of liberal governance, and in analysing the new wars themselves, a systems orientation has been adopted: one that emphasises complex holistic systems in, which interconnection, mutation and self-transformation are key characteristics.

Examining aid policy as an expression of global governance – as a political project in its own right – demands attention to its particular forms of mobilisation, justification and reward. The idea of *liberal peace*, for example, combines and conflates 'liberal' (as in contemporary liberal economic and political tenets) with 'peace' (the present policy predilection towards conflict resolution and societal reconstruction). It reflects the existing consensus that conflict in the South is best approached through a number of connected, ameliorative, harmonising and, especially, transformational measures. While this can include the provision of immediate relief and rehabilitation assistance, liberal peace embodies a new or political humanitarianism that lays emphasis on such things as conflict resolution and prevention, reconstructing social networks, strengthening civil and representative institutions, promoting the rule of law, and security sector reform in the context of a functioning market economy. In many respects, while contested and far from assured, liberal peace reflects a radical developmental agenda of social transformation. In this case however, this is an international responsibility and not that of an independent or single juridical state.

During the first half of the 1990s the main concern of the international community regarding conflict was that of humanitarian intervention: developing new institutional arrangements that allowed aid agencies to work in situations of ongoing conflict and to support civilians in war zones. Partly due to the limited success of these interventions and the difficulties encountered, since the mid-1990s the policy focus has shifted towards conflict resolution and post-war reconstruction. This change of emphasis does not mean that conflicts have necessarily reduced in number or lessened in terms of their seriousness. Rather, it is policy that has changed. Instead of revolving around humanitarian assistance *per se*, the new humanitarianism has invested developmental tools and initiatives with ameliorative, harmonising and transformational powers that, it is hoped, will reduce violent conflict and prevent its recurrence. While the initiatives that make up liberal peace are usually understood as being a response to specific needs and requirements, liberal peace is a political project in its own right. The aim of liberal peace is to transform the dysfunctional and war-affected societies that it encounters on its borders into cooperative, representative and, especially, stable entities.

While states remain important, since the 1970s, under the influence of what is commonly known as globalisation, they have been drawn into multi-level and increasingly non-territorial decision-making networks that bring together governments, international agencies, non-governmental organisations, and so on, in new and complex ways. Consequently, there has been a noticeable move from the hierarchical, territorial and bureaucratic relations of government to more polyarchical, non-territorial and networked relations of governance. While clearly they have deeper historical roots, relations of governance have come to shape and dominate political life over the past several decades. In this respect, liberal peace is not manifest within a single institution of global government; such a body does not exist and probably never will. It is part of the complex, mutating and stratified networks that make up global liberal governance. More specifically, liberal peace is embodied in a number of flows and nodes of authority within liberal governance that bring together different *strategic complexes* of state–non-state, military–civilian and public–private actors in pursuit of its aims. Such complexes now variously enmesh international NGOs, governments, military establishments, IFIs, private security companies, IGOs, the business sector, and so on. They are strategic in the sense of pursuing a radical agenda of social transformation in the interests of global stability. In the past, one might have referred to these complexes as representing the development or aid industry; now, however, they have expanded to constitute a network of strategic governance relations that are increasingly privatised and militarised.

The networks of liberal peace achieve their greatest definition on the borders of global governance, where its strategic actors confront systems and normative structures that are violently different from its own. In mainstream policy terms, these shifting border areas are usually described as constituting a complex emergency or, since the mid-1990s, a complex political emergency. Among UN agencies, a complex emergency is understood as denoting a conflict-related humanitarian disaster involving a high degree of breakdown and social dislocation and, reflecting this condition, requiring a system-wide aid response from the international community. The widespread upheaval and social displacement associated with Somalia and Bosnia during the early part of the 1990s, for example, typifies this condition. In requiring a system-wide response, these emergencies have made it necessary for UN agencies, donor governments, NGOs and military establishments to develop new roles, mechanisms of coordination and ways of working together. While the transformational aim of liberal peace now describes the political content of such system-wide operations, attempts to establish a liberal peace have been subject to controversy, marked unevenness and increasing patterns of regional differentiation and hierarchies of concern. Where complex emergencies are encountered, however, some form of strategic complex involving thicker or thinner networks of state–non-state actors is usually involved. This can range from what amounts to global governance's best efforts at social reconstruction, as presently found in the Balkans, to what Boutros-Ghali once referred to as Africa's orphan wars.

The new wars

In relation to the new post-Cold War conflicts, the conventional approach is to look for causes and motives and, rather like Victorian butterfly collectors, to construct lists and typologies of the different species identified. Ideas based on poverty, communication breakdown, resource competition, social exclusion, criminality and so on are widely accepted among strategic actors as providing an explanation. At the same time, various forms of collapse, chaos and regression are seen as the outcome. While such causes and outcomes may well exist, in terms of advancing our understanding of the new wars the search for causes is of limited use. The approach adopted here is to regard war as a given: an everpresent axis around which opposing societies and complexes continually measure themselves and reorder social, economic, scientific and political life. Apart from being a site of innovation, this process of restructuring is also one of imitation and replication. If opposing societies or complexes are not to suffer compromise or defeat, they must match or counter the innovations that each is liable to make. Not only is war an axis of social reordering, historically it has been a powerful mechanism for the globalisation of economic, political and scientific relations. In this respect, the development of the modern and centralised nation state has been closely associated with the restructuring and globalising effects of war.

When the competence of nation states begins to change and they become qualified and enmeshed within non-territorial and networked relations of governance, one can assume that the nature of war has also changed. This relates not only to the way the new wars are fought, in this case beyond the regulatory regimes formally associated with nation states, but also to the manner in which societies are mobilised, structured and rewarded in order to address them. [. . .] the strategic complexes of liberal peace, that is, the emerging relations between governments, NGOs, militaries and the business sector, are not just a mechanical response to conflict. In fact, they have a good deal in common, in structural and organisational terms, with the new wars. For example, strategic complexes and the new wars are both based on increasingly privatised networks of state–non-state actors working beyond the conventional competence of territorially defined governments. Through such flows and networks each is learning how to project power in new non-territorial ways. With contrasting results, liberal peace and the new wars have blurred and dissolved conventional distinctions between peoples, armies and governments. At the same time, new systems of reward and mobilisation, especially associated with privatisation, have emerged in the wake of the out-moding of such divisions. Liberal peace and the new wars are also both forms of adaptation to the effects of market deregulation and the qualification and attenuation of nation-state competence. In many respects, the networks and complexes that compose liberal peace also reflect an emerging liberal way of war.

In the case of the new wars, market deregulation has deepened all forms of parallel and transborder trade and allowed warring parties to forge local–global networks and shadow economies as a means of asset realisation and self-provisioning. The use of illicit alluvial diamonds to fund conflicts in West and Southern Africa is a well-known example of a system that has a far wider application. Rather than expressions of breakdown or chaos, the new wars can be understood as a form of non-territorial *network war* that works through and around states. Instead of conventional armies, the new wars typically oppose and ally the transborder resource networks of state incumbents, social groups, diasporas, strongmen, and so on. These are refracted through legitimate and illegitimate forms of state–non-state, national–international and local–global flows and commodity chains. Far from being a peripheral aberration, network war reflects the contested integration of stratified markets and populations into the global economy. Not only can the forms of innovation and state–non-state networking involved be compared to those of liberal peace; more generally, they stand comparison with the manner in which Northern political and economic actors have similarly adapted to the pressures and opportunities of globalisation. In this respect, as far as it is successful, network war is synonymous with the emergence of new forms of protection, legitimacy and rights to wealth. Rather than regression, the new wars are organically associ-ated with a process of social transformation: the emergence of new forms of authority and zones of alternative regulation.

Instead of complex political emergencies, global governance is encountering *emerging polit-ical complexes* on its borders. Such complexes are essentially non-liberal. That is, they follow forms of economic logic that are usually antagonistic towards free-market prescriptions and formal regional integration. At the same time, politically, the new forms of protection and legitimacy involved tend to be socially exclusive rather than inclusive. However, for those that are included, such political complexes nonetheless represent new frameworks of social representation and regulation. In other words, political complexes themselves are part of a process of social transformation and system innovation, a characteristic that embodies the ambiguity of such formations. While their economic and political logic can find violent and disruptive expression, in many cases such complexes are the only forms of existing or actual authority that have the powers to police stability. This ambiguity, however, pervades the general encounter of the new wars with the strategic complexes of liberal peace. The aid agencies, donors and NGOs involved also reflect and embody ideals of protection, legitimacy and rights. They also have transformational aims – in this case, however, liberal ones.

Global governance and the emerging political complexes are in competition in relation to the forms of authority and regulation they wish to establish. This competition establishes a fluctuating border area that is as much social as territorial across which a range of transac-tions, confrontations and interventions are possible. At its most general, it is the site of numerous discursive exchanges and narratives. The symbolic role of privatisation is a good example. Among many of the strategic actors of liberal governance, privatisation denotes a move towards a sound economy and the prospects of development. Among state actors and local strongmen, however, it can represent an innovative way to further the non-liberal political logic of the complex concerned. At the same time, at various points along this border, competition turns into antagonism and the site of more direct forms of intervention. If the Cold War represented a Third World War, then the contested, uneven and differential confrontation between the strategic complexes of liberal peace and the political complexes of the new wars is the site of the Fourth.

The merging of development and security

That liberal peace contains within it the emerging structures of liberal war is suggested in the blurring and convergence during the 1990s of development and security. The transformational aims of liberal peace and the new humanitarianism embody this convergence. The commitment to conflict resolution and the reconstruction of societies in such a way as to avoid future wars represents a marked radicalisation of the politics of development. Societies must be changed so that past problems do not arise, as happened with development in the past; moreover, this process of transformation cannot be left to chance but requires direct and concerted action (Stiglitz 1998). Development resources must now be used to shift the balance of power between groups and even to change attitudes and beliefs. The radicalisation of development in this way is closely associated with the reproblematisation of security. Conventional views on the causes of the new wars usually hinge upon their arising from a developmental malaise of poverty, resource competition and weak or predatory institutions. The links between these wars and international crime and terrorism are also increasingly drawn. Not only have the politics of development been radicalised to address this situation but, importantly, it reflects a new security framework within which the modalities of underdevelopment have become dangerous. This framework is different from that of the Cold War when the threat of massive interstate conflict prevailed. The question of security has almost gone full circle: from being concerned with the biggest economies and war machines in the world to an interest in some of its smallest.

In many policy statements there is a noticeable convergence between the notions of development and security. Through a circular form of reinforcement and mutuality, achieving one is now regarded as essential for securing the other. Development is ultimately impossible without stability and, at the same time, security is not sustainable without development. This convergence is not simply a policy matter. It has profound political and structural implications. In relation to the strategic complexes of liberal governance it embodies the increasing interaction between military and security actors on the one hand, and civilian and non-governmental organisations on the other. It reflects the thickening networks that now link UN agencies, military establishments, NGOs and private security companies. Regarding NGOs, the convergence of development and security has meant that it has become difficult to separate their own development and humanitarian activities from the pervasive logic of the North's new security regime. The increasingly overt and accepted politicisation of aid is but one outcome.

The encounter of the strategic complexes of liberal peace with the political complexes of the new wars has established a new development–security terrain. It is developmental in that liberal values and institutions have been vested with ameliorative and harmonising powers. At the same time, it represents a new security framework since these powers are being deployed in a context in which the modalities of underdevelopment have become dangerous and destabilising. This contested terrain, which looks set to deepen and shape our perceptions over the coming decades, remains underresearched and is not captured in conventional and increasingly prescriptive and policy-oriented development and international studies. It is comprised of complex relations of structural similarity, complicity and, at the same time, new asymmetries of power and authority.

In terms of similarity, both liberal peace and the new wars have blurred traditional distinctions between people, army and government and, at the same time, forged new ways of projecting power through non-territorial public-private networks and systems. Along the social border between these two complexes, relations of accommodation and complicity are common and find many forms of expression. Rather than eliminating famine, for example, aid agencies have been charged with obstructing this aim. The international hierarchy of concern that exists also denotes a susceptibility within global liberal governance to normalise violence and accept high levels of instability as an enduring if unfortunate characteristic of certain regions. This new development–security terrain also contains marked asymmetries of power. Indeed, it tends to reverse and upset traditional notions of what power is and where it lies. It is a terrain where, in confronting new challenges, the authority of the major states is in a process of reconfiguration. While the growth of increasingly privatised and non-territorial strategic complexes reflect new ways of projecting liberal power, the effectiveness of these forms of authority is still an open question – especially when they confront political actors who have a strong sense of right and history, despite being part of economically weaker systems. Whether donor governments, militaries, aid agencies and the private sector can secure a liberal peace remains an open question. One thing, however, is perhaps more clear. It is difficult to imagine that the increasingly privatised and regionally stratified strategic complexes of liberal governance will be able to deliver the geographically and socially more extensive patterns of *relative* security that characterised the Cold War years. Understanding this new terrain should therefore be a priority for us all.

3.9 The imagined economies of globalization

Angus Cameron and Ronen Palan

Source: *The Imagined Economies of Globalization* (Sage, London, 2004), Introduction, pp. 11–22.

Cameron and Palan argue that globalization should be approached through exploration of the different narratives surrounding it. These narratives entail complex processes of 'remembering' and 'forgetting' that constitute powerful influences on the practices of global society. In this extract, they focus first on the ways in which the national economy was traditionally conceptualized and on the ways in which the 'loss' of national economic control has thus been imagined. They move on to identify a process of 'trifurcation' through which statehood has been redefined or re-imagined, and to focus particularly on what this means for the conceptualization of 'social exclusion' at the global scale. This leads finally to an exploration of the ways in which poverty has been recast within world politics, and to a questioning of existing approaches to political engagement in the era of 'globalization'.

The 'lost' national economy

But why should the redrawing of *conceptual* boundaries be so significant? Why place the emphasis on rhetoric and perception? Surely the 'real' legal and physical boundaries between societies and economies continue to function much as they always have – irrespective of any conceptualization? The meaning of an alleged change in the concept of the spatiality of the nation-state can be interpreted only within an interpretation of the meaning of the nation-state itself. What discursive baggage does the concept of the nation-state carry? What kinds of practice does the concept legitimize? The answer to these questions, of course, cannot be simple – there never was just one fiction of the state but rather a set of normative expectations interpreted and applied in local contexts and according to local conditions. The national state of the industrialized north is manifestly very different from the post-imperial state of the south, and the east Asian state of the early twenty-first century is not the same as the European state of the nineteenth century, however much conventional state theory may seek to establish them as equivalents. [. . .]

Despite the many empirical differences between states, there has been nevertheless what the French sociologist Dominique Schnapper calls 'the idea of the state' – a pervasive and idealized, if not as universal as we tend to think, notion of the nature of society and its relationship to the state. This ideal-typical conception of the state has long provided simultaneously both a 'normal' format of state-society relationship, and a legitimizing ideology of this same format called the nation-state. So long as this idea of the state is generally accepted – is plausible – the world can be seen as 'naturally' divided into 'nations' or 'peoples'. These nations and people construct institutional structures that advance their unique notion of the 'good life'. The state serves (or at least should serve) as the political expression and the institutional arm of the nation. The state, therefore, should advance the economic, cultural and political goals of the nation as a whole. The nature of the 'national economy' has conventionally been understood in similar terms, as a servant to the nation. The 'world economy' has, therefore, traditionally been conceived of as aggregate discrete 'national' economies separated along political boundaries.

It is because of this traditional conception of state, nation and economy as territorially and normatively co-extensive that Zygmunt Bauman maintains that the development of the modern nation-state accompanied the rise of calculative rationality. The specific category of the nation-state is founded on the notion of society as an organized and mechanical organization of people. In a similar vein, Nicos Poulantzas saw the nation-state as an historically specific matrix of spatial and temporal forms, the precise combination of which would alter over time as the nature of economy and society altered. In both cases, this need to self-consciously design, monitor and adapt 'society' reveals that it has always been a fundamentally reflexive form of social organization. In that sense it may be argued that from its earliest formal manifestations, the state has been constantly (re-)created in pursuit of changing needs and conceptions of the nation. The material reality of the 'nation', of course, was represented in the state – hence these are mutually constitutive concepts.

There were certain logical imperatives embedded in the concept of the nation which also pervade political discourse. They served as 'intuitive' truths and, therefore, as common narratives. An immanent and discrete collectivity represents the nation-state, as Bauman notes, as a self-organizing historical entity sharing in the formation and execution of collective goals. The matter of collective goals is simultaneously a question about ethics, i.e., which of these goals are honourable, and a question about technique: how a self-organizing community is best to achieve such goals. The representation of economic closure, of an homogenized 'national economy', was central to the idea of the subordination of market forces to the goals of the state. It may be debated at length whether there was indeed ever a 'nation', let alone a 'national economy', that corresponded to the ideal of closure (we would argue that there was not), however, the imperative of the logic of the nation legitimized a particular political economy centred on the closure of the state. The idea that the state was the political arm of the nation or the community was translated into the practice that the community had a responsibility to educate its population, to provide them with work, healthcare and so on. The state, as the collective arm of the nation, had the right to control and subordinate market forces for the benefit of the nation.

The identification of the 'nation' as constitutive of the social body generates a series of logical propositions, which the state must then enact. The 'nation' was predicated upon the presupposition that its members share in some epic spiritual journey. The agglomerations of people who happen to reside within a given political boundary and/or share linguistic or other attributes were viewed as having a common destiny. In this context patriotic feelings were translated into various forms of nationalist ideology which ascribed meaning to the collectivity and to the role of the individual within it.

Consequently, nationalist theory is strongly prescriptive in that it suggests that the 'spiritual unity' of the nation must be translated into both a responsibility on the part of each individual towards the whole and, in turn, a responsibility on the part of the nation towards the individual. The lofty goals of the nation necessitated that the individual, legally and morally constituted as a 'member' (citizen), subordinate him or herself to the 'common good'. Each member of the nation was charged with responsibility towards maintaining the physical and spiritual continuity of the 'father/motherland' and with providing future generations with the right conditions to continue the journey. Throughout its history, therefore, the nation has performed a central constitutive role with regard to the state, informing and legitimizing new forms of social organizations and new forms of surveillance.

This is equally true with regard to specific formation of the national economy. The strongly territorial idea of the nation-state was from the outset closely bound up with the extension of regulatory control over the assets and transactions of the national population and the emergent institutions of the private and public sectors. From the late Middle Ages to the mid-nineteenth century a gradual but very deliberate process of carving out and consolidating the 'fiscal state' took place throughout Europe – a process that subsequently informed processes of 'nation-building' throughout the world. At the same time as delineating demographic, political and juridical spaces, the state border also serves to separate and *create* the 'domestic' and the 'international' economies as discrete spaces. Some conception of a bounded political economy is, for example, a prerequisite for the regulation of all forms of inter-*national* trade, a concept that has no meaning except in a world economy divided by national borders. The image is of an inter-national economy with the emphasis on the reflexively mediated goals of mutually recognized state economic and political sovereignty. John Maynard Keynes, for example, argued that in order that 'free' trade achieves its intended goals, capital markets should be strictly controlled by national governments. Even neo-liberal economists argue enthusiastically for a goal of global free trade as an instrument of 'national' economic growth and welfare maximization.

Whereas the national economy was understood in the nineteenth century as the material base for the spiritual pursuits of the nation, a power base from the strategic and spiritual goals of the nation, the same 'national economy' in the twenty-first century implies something very different: the primacy of a national form of regulation in support of capitalist accumulation. An imaginary vision of a national economy was set to legitimize the shared goal of the new interventionist state. The Bretton Woods agreement, for instance, imposed strict limitations on international movements of capital in order to protect the new national macroeconomic planning measures of the 1930s.

Notwithstanding its contradictions, the assumed relationship of spatial correlation between economy and society contains an assumption of subordination that remains commonplace throughout the social sciences. Among sociologists it is represented most clearly in the work of the structural functionalists. Talcott Parsons, for instance, viewed the economy and politics as two functional sub-systems of the 'social system'. Similarly David Easton followed the Marginalists in defining the political system as an alternative mode of 'resource allocation' analogous to that of the economy. These ideas were then echoed in the first wave of development theory, namely 'modernization', which was predicated on the necessity of the creation of 'proper' (economically, politically and morally) conditions for the economic success of the nation-state in a world economy.

But in advocating a particular political system, modernization theorists and liberal economists, together with the rest of the literature predicated on the concept of a 'national economy', were already acknowledging the centrality of *political choice*. The notion of the national 'system' – which is in practice the discrete 'political' and 'economic' systems of the state working in combination as the 'national economy' – implied not only a discrete separation from external environments (the world market, other 'sovereign' states), but also a self-organizing and self-producing capacity on the part of the nation-state itself. National economic policy is, after all, a matter of choice, a choice which is, ostensibly at least, open to 'the nation'. The nation may choose to adopt open borders and a free trade policy, or it may choose instead a varying degree of protectionist policies. Economists have on the whole argued in favour of the former and against the latter, but the issue of choice, and hence the ideological debate surrounding national choices, was central to the political debate. During the golden years of the sovereign national economy, therefore, the period between roughly 1930 and 1980, we saw impassioned debates as to which national economic policy was to be taken. It was a period characterized throughout the world by a battle between 'isolationists' and 'universalists', between advocates of protectionist, nationalist and socialist policies, and advocates of free trade and open borders. Under this ideological guise, governments of all political persuasions and degrees of democracy presented their constituencies with a stark choice between 'going it alone' or submerging the national economy in an increasingly transnationalized economy.

These sorts of political debates were predicated on a single central assumption, namely that the state was the sole and proper intermediary between the demands of the international market and the demands of its citizens for social and economic equality and other social goals. The 'myth' of the nation-state can be seen broadly as a guide for action. The problem that globalization poses, so the argument goes, is precisely that by 'eroding', and 'undermining' not only the state, but also the 'idea' of the state, the entire format of political life that dominated the past two centuries is also under threat.

The trifurcation of the state

What then, is this new narrative of state and society that has emerged to replace the old one? How do the new imagined economies of globalization differ from the imagined community of the nation-state? The dominant, if paradoxically hidden, imagery of globalization, the imagery that is at the base of policy-making, we argue, is not the conventional cartography of two-dimensional lines delineating spaces of territory, a shift from the national to the global, but a tri-partite 'cognitive map' distinguishing between distinct socio-economic *spaces* characterized in part by different socio-economic *velocities*. As this suggests, globalization does not create a global system that is little more than the 'state-writ-large' – by which we mean, having essentially similar attributes to the familiar system of nation-states as described above, albeit now operating on a vastly larger scale. Rather, in the emerging imagined economies of the state the various systems of authority and sovereignty can no longer be seen to occupy the same spaces as they did in the territorial state and nor are their boundaries coextensive. They are posited instead in an array of different normative and cognitive spaces whereby the boundaries of the state (which have never been depicted as so secure and so 'real' as they are in the context of debates on globalization) are rendered multiple, complex and dynamic. For the purposes of our argument, we have labelled these emergent spatialities as the *offshore*, *private* and *anti*-economies.

This trifurcation of socio-economic space does not mean that the emergent spatialities are equivalent. Rather, there is a distinct hierarchy between them and an unavoidable historical dynamic. This hierarchy can be expressed in two ways. First, the status of placeless globality (the so-called 'borderless world'), exemplified here by the offshore economy, has a strongly normative content in relation to the other two. Globality, whether understood as a consequence of inexorable and concrete historical processes or as part of general social theory, is presented as an ideal socio-economic destination for the other two, which must adapt themselves – or, rather, those people, places and institutions that they contain – to become more global. Second, a distinction is drawn between a space of globality and 'near globality' – characterized by competitiveness, fluidity, flexibility and 'social inclusion' – and a space of non-globality and/or anti-globality – characterized by boundedness, stasis, redundancy and a specific form of archaic 'localness', that of 'social exclusion'.

Private sector		Third sector/ Public sector social economy
Offshore	**Private**	**Anti-**
Institutions:	*Institutions:*	*Institutions:*
World/global economy	National economy	Local/peripheral
Global markets	National state bodies	economy
Global firms	Formal labour market	Community
Merchant banking	Local state bodies	Family
Global cities	Domestic firms	Neighbourhood
Media corporations	Borders	Welfare state
Global governance	Domestic market	Informal labour market
(WTO, UN, OECD, World Bank, etc.)	Retail banking	
TNCs		
Alliance capitalism		
Processes:	*Processes:*	*Processes:*
Globalization	Privatization	Dependency
Technicization	Liberalization	Stagnation
Securitization	Deregulation	Decline
Virtualization	Modernization	Exclusion
Growth	Globalization	Marginalization
	Growth	Obsolescence
Normative characteristics:	*Normative characteristics:*	*Normative characteristics:*
Economic	Political	Static
Dynamic	Dynamic	Uncompetitive
Site of competition	Competitive	Inflexible
Impersonal	Entrepreneurial	Pre-global
Apolitical	Flexible	Residual
Fluid	Globalizing	Dependent
Future-oriented	Privatizing	(aid or welfare)
Developing	Enabling (business)	Un- or de-skilled
Expanding	Modernizing	Outmoded
Technological	Market-led	Third world
'Real'	Employed	Unemployed
	Onshore	Underclass

'Mainstream' Economy ('Social inclusion')	**'Welfare' and/or 'informal' economy ('social exclusion')**

Change in status only available through: Flexibilization,
Retraining, Reskilling, Insertion, Integration,
Modernization, Development, Formalization, etc.

Figure 1 Cognitive map of the imagined economies of globalization and social exclusion

Despite the hype, people still inhabit – as the anti-globalizers are correct to point out – the world of states, and these states, if anything, are playing an ever bigger role in the control, organization and surveillance of daily life. But what the anti-globalizers (that is, those who deny that globalization is taking place) appear to ignore is the fact that these are very different sorts of states from the ideals of the nation-state to which they appeal. To begin with, a good portion of 'national' economic activity, particularly finance, has increasingly shifted towards a de-territorialized 'space of flows'. This 'offshore' economy consists of largely unregulated legal spaces, external to but nevertheless supported by the state system and which appear to be perfectly suited for capitalist accumulation. This space of the offshore economy has long been confused by the hyperglobalizers (whether proponents or opponents) with globalization itself. When such commentators talk about a global market, global trade or global finance, what they have in mind is essentially the offshore financial market. But however significant it might be, the offshore economy is far from encompassing the entire range of human activities in the modern world. On the contrary, for the greater proportion of humanity that is touched by globalization, the experience of global finance and offshore is mediated in one of two formats. These we describe as the private economy – or competition state – and the anti-economy – a space of 'exclusion' lying beyond the norms and practices of the emergent global order.

The private economy or the competition state is the increasingly dominant discourse of statehood in the context of globalization. This in itself shows the folly of the hyperglobalizers. No longer content to organize national life within its boundaries, the modern state seeks to legitimize itself as a competitive entity operating in a globalized world – which means, as we will see, a world that acknowledges the centrality of offshore. This conception of the private economy has been expressed in a number of ways by several different authors and in many policy programmes, but in all instances refers to the need for the state, real or perceived, to 'adapt' to globalization. This adaptation, in all cases, involves a gradual withdrawal from the direct ownership of the means of production (usually through a process of privatization), coupled with various measures to increase the competitiveness of domestic workforces (for example, through (re-)training programmes, wage and productivity deals and/or the curtailment of union power), lower regulatory barriers to both domestic and international investment (for example, through the creation of export processing zones) and so on. Both ways of describing the adaptive moves of the state combine to transform the 'public' space of the nation-state into a realm that is essentially private and economic in terms of its normative character. This does not, of course, mean that the public character of the state has disappeared, but rather that with the fragmentation and dislocation of the spatial unity of the nation-state, the public realm has ceased to be the definitive one. This is, for example, clearly expressed in the discourse of 'governance', as differentiated from 'government' in many globalization debates. Rather than the primary role of the state being the reproduction of the 'nation', therefore, it is increasingly geared far more towards the reproduction of the private national economy against normative standards set by an ideal-typical economic 'globality'. In its role as a normative space, however, the private economy of the contemporary state also plays another, significant function – that of policing the boundaries of the 'real' state. As such, the private economy of the state, however much it may be separate (at least theoretically) from offshore, in fact combines with it to form a single, if differentiated, space of 'inclusion'. The private economy, therefore, also serves as the *central axis* upon which the mapping of the spaces of globalization is currently configured and in response to which a wide series of policy measures are enacted by states, firms and other international actors.

The creation of this normative space of inclusion reveals a third aspect of globalization – one that has gained least attention and which has tended to be kept separate in the public and academic imagination; that of 'social exclusion'. How and why have the poor come to be understood as the socially excluded? How, indeed, is it possible to conceive of a notion of social exclusion at all? Where is the space beyond the social to which the poor have been consigned? Where, for that matter, is the space of social *inclusion*? We want to argue that the emergence of both the concepts of globalization and social exclusion (both first appear in the 1970s) is not coincidental. Rather, globalization and social exclusion both represent attempts to capture something essential taking place in the nature of social spatiality and specifically the spatiality of the nation-state. The concept of social exclusion entails a subtle (and occasionally not so subtle) respatialization of social relations and, quite specifically, an elision of social and economic identities. [. . .]

It appears to us, therefore, that the discourse of social exclusion opens up a third imagined economy within the contemporary state – a space of *anti*-economy where the rules of globalism and privatism do not, or do not yet, apply. By calling this the 'anti' economy we are not suggesting that spaces and places of poverty and exclusion are in any sense 'uneconomic'. Rather, we are suggesting that in the emergent normative spatial hierarchy, certain modes of existence that were once accommodated within 'the idea of the state' have effectively been written out of 'normal' society – normality being defined in terms of proximity to ideals of 'global' economic participation and consumption.

The power of the discourse of globalization is the underlying but always implicit assumption concerning the immanent and mutually constitutive nature of these three spatialities. These three overlapping elements simultaneously delineate the content of the 'global' and generate a spatial and temporal hierarchy for the state in relation to it. Each is distinguished by different normative characteristics, types and levels of institution, dynamic historical processes, degrees of territorial embeddedness, and levels of access to reflexivity as an instrumental resource.

The tripartite scheme above summarizes our attempts to map together the elements of the configured imaginary of contemporary techno-economic globalization. The offshore, private and anti-economies presented here are constituted within and constitutive of the narrative configurations of globalization. The three categories are not intended as fixed or wholly separate spatial categories, but rather combine to form an overlapping hierarchy of normative economic domains which are located within and across states to varying degrees, are subject to varying degrees of political and legal influence, and are constituted through differing institutional structures. Whilst each of these concepts, offshore, private and anti-economy, contain a strong implication of spatiality, these 'spaces' do not, and indeed are not intended in our narrative to conform to a conventional territorial geography, nor are they wholly separate from it. Their relationship to conventional territorial spatialities is best envisaged as becoming less place bound, and therefore increasingly 'placeless', with increasing globality. The relative degree of access to and mobility between these three domains by individuals and firms has significant consequences for their respective degrees of access to the fruits of the world economy. Each element of this scheme has both a discursive and a concrete institutional form already, though they are understood to be in a process of active evolution.

These cognitive spaces, it should be stressed, are only partly descriptive of tangible spatialities. Although each can be associated with particular spaces, places and institutions, their importance lies less in what they *describe* than in what they *narrate*. In representing a dynamic respatialization of social and economic relations, the discourses of globalization and exclusion posit the immanent development of new spatial forms to which policy-makers, industrialists, jurists and ordinary people must adapt. The evidence for the existence of these cognitive spaces lies, therefore, as much in the pronouncements and futurologies of politicians and business leaders – which will lead to concrete institutional changes – as it does in tangible phenomena.

The global politics of poverty and the poverty of 'global politics'

In the course of its growing plausibility and acceptance, a concept with the power of globalization entails the recasting and, in some cases, the forgetting of older stories. Nowhere is this more true than in the case of poverty. As the basic metaphors of social life have changed, so specific sets of social relationships, which relied on older forms of social solidarity, have also changed. In the case of the poor, who have, for centuries, 'always been with us' – in other words constituted as part of a social whole to which 'us', the non-poor, have a responsibility – they have been renamed as the 'socially excluded', placed somehow 'outside' of society.

The effects of this recasting of poverty as exclusion are, as a number of commentators have argued, profound indeed. In a world where identity is forged through consumption and is itself consumed, the poor have achieved, in Bauman's terms, the status of 'flawed consumers'. As such they are 'cast out of the realm of moral obligations', in a society where mutual obligation on the basis of belonging has been replaced by mutual obligation to consume. However, and just as alarming, the respatialization of social relations which both of these concepts represent has far-reaching consequences for the possibilities of what 'we' can do about poverty. As the basic metaphors of social life are being transformed, as we are passing from the imagined community and into a world of disjointed and fluid imagined economies, so the possibilities of politics also change. This is not just because existing political institutions might be simply rescaled (for example, through the creation of 'global' institutions of governance such as the WTO or the International Criminal Court in place of/additional to national institutions), but because the meaning of the political itself must change.

How can we resolve the increasing dislocation of geographies of economies from geographies of societies and polities? For some, the solution to the respatialization of the political engendered by globalization is straightforward; political engagement itself must 'go global'. And some forms of political action have indeed 'gone global' on the streets of Seattle, Milan, London, Johannesburg and anywhere else the travelling circus of 'global governance' comes briefly to earth. Calls are also heard, often as part of the same strategy, to 'go local', to resist the inexorable rise of faceless global institutions by reinvesting in community and place. Colin Hines, for example, has gone so far as to propose 'localization' as the most appropriate and salient manner of resistance to globalization as though somehow simply going in the opposite spatial direction will serve to reinvent older forms of political and social solidarity. For all that we may share some of the concerns of the various anti-globalization movements that have developed in recent years, this is not what we mean here by the political. The anti-globalization movement is one aspect of a *politics of globalization* (that is, a politics that is reactive to globalization taken as fact) but does not represent, in our view, a particularly coherent response to the changes outlined above – the vertical and normative fragmentation of the very idea of society and, by extension, the possibility of an effective polity. In short, until we understand the complex respatialization of social life of which globalization and social exclusion are two important narrative components, the nature of the political will remain elusive. Of one thing we can be sure, however: the politics of the imagined community of the nation-state cannot pass easily into a viable politics for the imagined economies of globalization.

[. . .] the fundamental purpose of developing this argument represents an attempt to investigate and discover the boundaries of the domain of the political that emerge from our understanding of the emergent spatiality of the contemporary world. It is our contention that the political (either in the general sense or in the form of specific political responses) cannot simply or easily be read off from contemporary debates about globalization and/or exclusion, because to do so takes them too literally as descriptors of concrete phenomena. Rather, the spatialization of the political must necessarily be linked directly to the complex spatialities of the social that are being produced through the transformation of the fundamental imaginaries of the state. If this politics has, for the time being at least, a small 'p', this is because it is to be found less in the actions and pronouncements of the 'official' political debate – the public globalizers and their public opponents and the formal debate on exclusion – than in the ways the various narratives of globalization and exclusion have come to be incorporated and institutionalized in everyday life. If this suggests a much more mundane account of globalization and social exclusion than that provided by the passions of high politics, then this, we argue, is precisely because both globalization and social exclusion have become mundane. It is their utter *normality* – a normality that has been achieved with a quite extraordinary speed – wherein lies their power.

3.10 Conceptualizing resistance to globalization

Christine B.N. Chin and
James H. Mittelman

Source: Barry K. Gills (ed.), *Globalization and the Politics of Resistance* (Macmillan, Basingstoke, 2000), pp. 30–44.

Chin and Mittelman explore the works of a range of political and social thinkers to identify three conceptualizations of resistance: counter-hegemony (based in the writings of Antonio Gramsci), counter-movements (based on work by Karl Polanyi) and 'infrapolitics' (an idea coined by James C. Scott). They examine the implications of these ideas and then relate them to forms of resistance in the face of the shifting challenges presented by globalization. In particular they focus on the idea that resistance movements shape and are constitutive of cultural processes which relate to the whole of social life, rather than simply to material processes such as production or exchange.

For us, and in brief, culture may be regarded as interest-constituted social processes that create specific and different whole ways of life, of which material social life is an inextricable part. There is no dearth of culturally laden manifestations of resistance to globalization. Culminating in the election of a Government of National Unity, led by the African National Congress, in South Africa in 1994, the worldwide anti-apartheid movement against a racial monopoly of the means of production, buttressed by substantial flows of foreign capital, may be the foremost example of a movement against globalization from above. There are numerous illustrations of more localized resistance, such as the Zapatista armed uprising among the Maya Indians against the Mexican government's neoliberal reforms, symbolically launched on 1 January 1994, the day of the inauguration of the North American Free Trade Agreement. But it would be facile to conceptualize resistance only as declared organized opposition to institutionalized economic and military power. One must dig deep to excavate the everyday individual and collective activities that fall short of open opposition. To grasp resistance to globalization, one must also examine the subtexts of political and cultural life, the possibilities and potential for structural transformation.

We begin to delve the constitutive role of power in shaping cultural critiques of economic globalization as well as patterns of struggle by revisiting the works of three master theorists of resistance, even if their writing was not explicitly directed at the contemporary phase of globalization: Antonio Gramsci's concept of counterhegemony, Karl Polanyi's notion of countermovements, and James C. Scott's idea of infrapolitics. For the sake of brevity, our compass is limited to these authors; other conceptualizations and systematic empirical referents cannot be provided within the space allotted to us. We hold that the trialectic of Gramsci-Polanyi-Scott [. . .] offers a sound basis for reconceptualizing resistance. The conclusion then probes the convergence and contrasting emphases within the triad, and also suggests directions for further study and exploratory research.

Resistance as counterhegemony

Ostensibly, Gramsci's analysis of social change as explicated in *Selections from the Prison Notebooks* neither could have anticipated nor accounted for globalization. The notes were written between 1929 and 1935 while Gramsci, a member of parliament and the general secretary of the Communist Party, was imprisoned by the fascist regime in Italy. In his discussions of state-society relations, Gramsci was concerned particularly with orthodox Marxist and bourgeois liberal theoretical frameworks that privileged 'economism' by reducing transformations in all aspects of social life to economic determinants.

Gramsci's theoretical efforts to transcend economism are applicable to conceptualizing resistance at the turn of the millennium. In place of economism, he developed the concept of hegemony. Hegemony encompasses whole ways of life: it is a dynamic lived process in which social identities, relations, organizations, and structures based on asymmetrical distributions of power and influence are constituted by the dominant classes. Hegemony, then, is as much economic as it is 'ethico-political' in shaping relations of domination and subordination.

The institutions of civil society such as the church, family, schools, media, and trade associations give meaning and organize everyday life so that the need for the application of force is reduced. Hegemony is established when power and control over social life are perceived as emanating from 'self-government' (i.e., self-government of individuals embedded in communities) as opposed to an external source(s) such as the state or the dominant strata. Since hegemony is a lived process, different historical contexts will produce different forms of hegemony with different sets of actors, such as the nineteenth-century 'passive revolution' of the Risorgimento, in which the bourgeoisie in Italy attained power without fundamental restructuring from below, and the early twentieth-century proletarian revolutionary leadership in Russia.

The processes of establishing hegemony, however, can never be complete because the hegemonic project presumes and requires the participation of subordinate groups. While hegemony is being implemented, maintained, and/or defended, it can be challenged and resisted in the interlocking realms of civil society, political society, and the state.

Different forms and dimensions of resistance to hegemony are subsumed under the rubric of counterhegemony. Implicit in the counterhegemonic project are 'wars of movement' and 'wars of position', in which people engage in openly declared collective action against the state. Wars of movement are frontal assaults against the state (e.g., labour strikes or even military action), whereas wars of position can be read as nonviolent resistance, e.g. boycotts, that are designed to impede everyday functions of the state. The objective of both types of war is to seize control of the state.

Wars of movement and position are expressions of counterhegemonic consciousness at the collective level. They represent moments in history when individuals come together in violent and nonviolent confrontations with the state. The question remains, how and why does counterhegemonic consciousness emerge in everyday life, leading to openly declared collective action?

Gramsci's discussion of common sense in the development of counterhegemonic consciousness is crucial to explaining historical and/or contemporary forms of resistance. Common sense that is held and practised in everyday life is neither linear nor unitary; it is the product of an individual's relationship to and position in a variety of social groups. Importantly, the coexistence of conformity and resistance in common sense can give rise to inconsistencies between thought and action, which help explain contradictory behaviour on the part of a subaltern group which may embrace its 'own conception of the world' while still adopting conceptions borrowed from dominant classes. By arguing that individuals and groups possess critical consciousness – albeit 'in flashes' – of their subordinate positions in society, Gramsci acknowledged the ambiguity of resistance and dismissed the overly deterministic and unidimensional explanation of false consciousness.

Nevertheless, in the discussion of thought and action, Gramsci was careful not to suggest that submission in the face of domination is the simple product of the subaltern's rational calculation of costs and benefits (in the sense that resistance would be futile at best, or would elicit retaliatory action, at worst). The fragmentation of social identity which characterizes and is characterized by simultaneous membership in different groups means that it is possible, if not probable, that the subaltern can be progressive on certain issues and reactionary on others in the same instance.

A Gramscian reading of resistance would have to explicate the development of counter-hegemonic consciousness that informs wars of movement and position, as well as national-popular actions led by organic intellectuals from all walks of life who can meld theory and praxis to construct and embed a new common sense that binds disparate voices and consciousness into a coherent program of change. In his time, Gramsci called for organic intellectuals to infuse common sense with a philosophy of praxis that encourages subaltern groups' critical understanding of their subordination in society. The objective is a 'national-popular' movement constituted by alliances between the leaders (in league with their organic intellectuals) and the led (subaltern). Whereas wars of movement and position capture the state, the national-popular movement provides the new basis for whole ways of life.

Gramsci did not offer programmatic ways that a philosophy of praxis could transcend the fragmentation of identity and interests. With contemporary globalization, the interpenetration of forces at the local, national, regional, and world levels implies that different peoples enter into alliances that can be and are ever more contradictory: e.g. low-wage female factory workers in Free Trade Zones who also are members or supporters of Islamist movements in Southeast Asia. A new common sense has to address effectively or make coherent women's critical understanding of the tensions, limitations, and opportunities inherent in their identities as daughters or wives in the household, as low wage workers on the factory floor, as citizens, and as Muslims in the local, national, and transnational Islamic communities.

Moreover, globalization begets openly declared forms of resistance that may or may not have the state as a target. In a context in which liberal, authoritarian, and ex-communist states-in-transition alike are becoming facilitators for transnational capital, if and when it occurs the driving force(s) of openly declared resistance against the state must be analysed within a larger framework. At issue are the contradictory ways in which state structures and policies assume 'educative' functions that nurture a new kind of citizenry and civilization commensurate with the requirements of transnational capital, while trying to maintain the legitimacy with which to govern. In this connection, one can profitably invoke Gramsci's insights into civil society and resistance, about which he offered many pointers, although they were not always congruent with one another.

Although wars of movement and position may still be discerned, sometimes in nascent form, the compression of time and space has created new venues of and for collective resistance transcending national borders. Contemporary social movements simultaneously occupy local, national, transnational and/or global space as a result of innovations in, and applications of, technologies that produce instantaneous communication across borders (e.g. the Internet, facsimile machines, cellular mobile phones, and globalized media). The Gramscian framework of resistance must be stretched to encompass new actors and spaces from which counterhegemonic consciousness is expressed. In the following section, we discuss the possibility of further considering social movements as a form of resistance.

Resistance as countermovements

In *The Great Transformation: The Political and Economic Origins of Our Time*, Karl Polanyi argued that the causes of global political, economic and social crises of the 1930s leading to World War Two may be traced to state-supported implementation of the 'self-regulating' market system during the eighteenth and nineteenth centuries. The movement to install and expand the self-regulating market sparked protective measures or countermovements to re-exert social control over the market – hence, the notion of a double movement.

Polanyi understood resistance in the form of countermovements as having arisen from, and affecting, different and whole ways of life. Protecting workers from the commodification process implies defending the social relations and institutions of which they are a part:

> In disposing of a man's labor power the system would, incidentally, dispose of the physical, psycho-logical, and moral entity 'man' attached to that tag. Robbed of the protective covering of cultural institutions, human beings would perish from the effects of social exposure [emphasis added]; they would die as victims of acute social dislocation through vice, perversion [. . .] No society could stand the effects of such a system of crude fiction even for the shortest stretch of time unless its human and natural substance as well as its business organization was protected against the ravages of this satanic mill.[1]

The movement-countermovement framework thus allows one to conceptualize contempor-ary social movements as a form of resistance since the latter are, in the main, defined as 'a form of collective action (a) based on solidarity, (b) carrying on a conflict, (c) breaking the limits of the system in which action occurs.' The level of analysis would have to be extended from the national to the transnational and/or global levels since some contemporary social movements, e.g. those that concern environmental destruction, women's rights, and indigenous peoples' rights, appear to bypass the state in search of transnational or global solutions.

There are two implicit problems in the counter/social movement framework. Collectivity is assumed in the notion 'movement' and this has the effect of constructing counter/social movements as united fronts in and of themselves. In the past decade or so, the fragmented nature of the feminist movement is evidenced in the internal conflict and domination gener-ated from differences of race, religion, class, and nationality, in spite of, and because of, attempts to address national and global patriarchy.

Also imputed in counter/social movements is the presence of organizational structure. This may be the case with some social movements (e.g. Greenpeace and Friends of the Earth in the environmental movement), but 'submerged networks' with no clearly defined organizational structure too have formed in an era of globalization. Participants in sub-merged networks live their everyday lives mostly without engaging in openly declared contestations:

They question definition of codes, nomination of reality. They don't ask, they offer. They offer by their own existence other ways of defining the meaning of individual and collective action. They act as new media: they enlighten what every system doesn't say of itself, the amount of silence, violence, irrationality which is always hidden in dominant codes.[2]

The presence of submerged networks gives new meaning to resistance. Even though participants can mobilize to protest state policies, open engagement or confrontation with the state or even transnational corporations is not the immediate or even ultimate objective. In the absence of openly declared collective action, resistance has to be read as the ways in which peoples live their everyday lives. Submerged networks affirm that even though resistance can be manifestly political and/or economic, it is shaped by and shapes whole ways of life. In advanced industrialized societies, examples of submerged networks are those in which families and their friends make it a point – in their consumption habits – to refuse to buy tuna fish caught using methods that destroy entire dolphin populations, or to purchase only consumer products from companies that actively practice environmental conservationism. Such acts have economic consequences in the corporate world, and political consequences for policy-makers. Significantly, submerged networks are sites of emerging alternative values and lifestyles.

In Egypt, for example, submerged networks exist in the popular quarters and among the common people, known as the *sha'b*. Networks radiate from the family – the basic unit of social organization in the *sha'b* – to include ties that transcend class, occupation, and kin. The 'familial ethos' governs the allocation and distribution of material and symbolic resources in the *sha'b*. In the present unspoken pact between the Egyptian state and the *sha'b*, state legitimacy is maintained by the distribution of basic goods and services to the *sha'b* in return for political acquiescence. Participants of the *sha'b* acquiesce to, as much as they engage in, resistance against the state. Members of the Islamist movement, who also are members of the *sha'b*, have been known to and can draw on submerged network ties to smuggle arms, and on occasion, to mobilize and organize mass protests against the state.

The notion of the Polanyian double movement thus has a distinct advantage of neatly encapsulating openly declared demands on the national, transnational, and/or global levels, for protective measures against various dimensions in the implementation and expansion of the self-regulating market. As discussed, however, the movement-countermovement framework neither advances analysis of differences within countermovements nor anticipates undeclared forms of resistance, both of which have emerged and must be addressed in conceptualizing collective resistance to globalization.

Resistance as infrapolitics

In 1990, James C. Scott introduced the idea of 'infrapolitics' as everyday forms of resistance conducted singularly and/or collectively, but which fall short of openly declared contestations. What began as his attempt to understand the conditions for peasant rebellions in Southeast Asia and the absence of openly declared resistance in a village in rapidly industrializing Malaysia gradually led to the conceptualization of 'infrapolitics' to explain the changing meaning of politics and resistance in most forms of day-to-day dominant-subordinate relations.

Scott warned that in the context of increasingly complex societies, the absence of openly declared contestations should not be mistaken for acquiescence. It is in the realm of informal assemblages such as the parallel market, workplace, household, and local community, when people negotiate resources and values on an everyday basis, that 'counterhegemonic consciousness is elaborated.'[3] These are the sites of infrapolitical activities that range from footdragging, squatting, and gossip to the development of dissident subcultures.

Taken at face value, such activities cannot tell us anything about counterhegemonic discourse until we account for the conditions from which they emerge. Infrapolitics is identified by juxtaposing what Scott calls the 'public' and 'hidden transcripts'. Public transcripts are verbal and nonverbal acts carried out by the dominant party or, 'to put it crudely, the *self-portrait of dominant elites as they would have themselves seen'.*[4] They are the public record of superior–subordinate relations in which the latter appears to willingly acquiesce in the stated and unstated expectations of the former. Hidden transcripts, on the other hand, consist of what subordinate parties say and do beyond the realm of the public transcript or the observation of the dominant. In the context of surveillance structures set up by the dominant class(es) or the state, hidden transcripts record infrapolitical activities that surreptitiously challenge practices of economic, status, and ideological domination.

The study of infrapolitics, we believe, is premised on what sociologists call ontological narratives. Ontological narrativity does not refer to the mode of representation or the traditional 'story-telling' method of historians (i.e. a method of presenting historical knowledge) considered nonexplanatory and atheoretical by mainstream social scientists. Rather, ontological narratives are the stories that social actors tell, and in the process come to define themselves or to construct their identities and perceive conditions that promote and/or mitigate the possibility for change.

Even though hidden transcripts record contestations over material and symbolic resources and values in everyday life, they do not occur in a localized vacuum. Infrapolitical activities are the product of interactions between structure and agency: the ways that real and perceived constraints and opportunities affect the behaviour of subordinate groups. Scott's analysis of infrapolitical activities thus falls short of capturing the complexities inherent in undeclared forms of everyday resistance. In his study of landlord–peasant relations in a rural Malay village, Scott asserted that analysis of state structures and policies were important *only* to the extent that they impinged on local class relations. Especially during the 1980s and in the context of national agricultural development policies and fluctuating global prices of commodities, landlord–peasant relations were shaped by impingements on, and interactions among, the rural community, state structures and policies, as well as the transformations marking a globalizing economic system.

Superior-subordinate relations, such as those of the landlord–peasant, manager–worker, husband–wife, and state official–squatter, are embedded in the whole ways of life, of which state structures and policies play an important part. Take for instance, policies designed to normalize the patriarchal nuclear family form as most natural in and for the expansion and maintenance of capitalist free markets, and/or that privilege scientific/technical education at the expense of the humanities. Such policies enframe worldviews insofar as they directly and indirectly affect all aspects of social life from the rate of urbanization, housing development, and employment opportunities, to the control and distribution of resources in the household.

In increasingly complex social contexts, subalterns do not have an unproblematic unitary identity. Nor can their behaviour be explained by implicit reference to the economic model of the self-interested utility-maximizer. Put simply, infrapolitical activities are not the mere product of subaltern decisions to conduct undeclared resistance in the face of surveillance structures set up by the dominant strata.

Class is but one (albeit important) modality of identity in landlord–peasant or other forms of dominant–subordinate relations. The different and possibly conflicting modalities of sub-altern identity can be as real, and under certain conditions, as constraining on behaviour as the actual or perceived futility and fear of openly declared resistance in the face of domin-ation. By putting a unidimensional face on resistance, Scott inadvertently assigns a similar unidimensional face to domination, even though he analytically distinguishes economic, status, and ideological domination.

In this connection, Gramsci reminded us that subaltern identities are embedded in com-plex overlapping social networks in which individuals simultaneously assume positions of domination and subordination (perhaps as a husband or wife, an elder or junior, a manager or office clerk, and a donor or recipient of aid). Analysis of the manner in which particular combinations of identity are expressed in the context of structural constraints can help explain why, given systems of surveillance (in which rewards and punishments inhere), some conform while others engage in infrapolitical activities of different types. Conversely, this approach also deepens analysis of the changing nature of domination.

Hidden transcripts have the potential to facilitate understanding of the *internal politics* of subaltern groups. The phenomenon of 'domination within domination' occurs in cases in which contradictory alliances are formed between the dominant and the subordinate that, in turn, dominate others. Although Scott acknowledges this point, his emphasis on class with-out sufficient attention to the interactions between class and non-class forces undermines the efficacy of the infrapolitical framework. The immediate focus on class presumes that the development of class consciousness stands apart exclusively from other modalities of identity.

It is, indeed, possible to argue that class contests in the context of surveillance can and do lead to infrapolitical activities that are grounded in material life. This argument is made possible *only* after having considered how and why the class dimension comes to be privileged and expressed over other modalities of identity. To do otherwise would reaffirm what Gramsci called 'economism', and subsequently relegate non-economic considerations to the ambit of superstructure.

Infrapolitics is embedded in whole ways of life, part of which is the material dimension. They embody contestations over the processes of grounded identity construction, maintenance, and transformation, of which the symbolic and material dimensions of class are intertwined with other modalities of identity, such as age, gender, race-ethnicity, religion, nationality, and/or sexuality. The identification, juxtaposition, and analyses of public and hidden transcripts can highlight the conditions in which certain dimen-sions of counterhegemonic consciousness develop, and how different or even conflicting perspectives within hidden transcripts are negotiated and/or (not) resolved in everyday life.

Resistance conceptualized as infrapolitical activities offers a viable avenue for generating theoretically grounded studies of everyday responses to globalizing structures and processes. If conducted with sensitivity to the complex interplay between or among multiple identities in the context of structural constraints, the study of public and hidden transcripts may reveal changing notions and practices of work, family, and politics, for example, as peoples seek to negotiate a semblance of social control over the expansion of market forces in diverse spheres of their lives. At the same time, one should not overwork the broad category of infrapolitics by imagining that every sort of response to globalizing structures is resistance. Whereas Scott carefully argues that diverse modes of resistance may or may not coalesce to oppose authority structures, it is important to avoid treating resistance as an omnibus category.

An emerging framework

The conduct and meaning of resistance are culturally embedded. This foundational proposition is no less applicable or relevant in conceptualizing contemporary resistance to globalization, as it was to Gramsci, Polanyi, and Scott's analyses of social change in different historical periods. The three master theorists acknowledged, implicitly and explicitly, that resistance arises from and is constitutive of specific and whole ways of life.

From this elemental proposition, however, the theorists diverged in their respective discussions of the forms and dimensions of resistance. Gramsci and Polanyi focused on the collective level, whereas Scott drew attention more to the level of the individual, as well as class, in everyday life. As delineated by the grid below, the main targets and modes of resistance differ from one theorist to another: Gramscian wars of movement and position against the state (though not to the neglect of change within civil society short of toppling the state), Polanyian counter-movements against market forces, and Scott's infrapolitical activities in the face of everyday domination.

	Main target	*Mode of resistance*
Gramsci	state apparatuses (understood as an instrument of education)	wars of movement and position
Polanyi	market forces (and their legitimation)	countermovements aimed at self-protection
Scott	ideologies (public transcripts)	counterdiscourses

Differences in levels of analysis, main targets and modes of resistance should not be reasoned only by way of the intellectual proclivities of each theorist per se. Rather, the conceptual tensions among the theorists correspond to, and reflect, the changing conditions of social life: from Gramsci to Polanyi to Scott, as societies became more complex, so too did the targets and modes of resistance. Contemporary transformations in social life in general, and state–society relations in particular, imply that all three major targets and modes of resistance coexist and are modified in the globalizing process.

The important conversation and debate among theorists forms a framework that may be profitably fastened to neoliberal globalization. The emerging framework points to possibilities of identifying and contesting forms of domination, expanding political space, and opening new venues – hence redefinitions of politics. Seen from the observation points of this triad, a conceptualization of contemporary resistance to globalization sensitizes one to the following shift in ontology, suggested below.

Forms of resistance

As political and economic power becomes more diffuse and less institutionalized, so too will forms of resistance. Undeclared forms of resistance conducted individually and collectively in submerged networks parallel openly declared forms of resistance embodied in wars of movement and position, and countermovements. Depending on the context, everyday activities such as what one wears (e.g. the veil in Muslim societies or the 'dashiki' in the African-American community), buys, or consumes may qualify as resistance – as much as that of organized strikes, boycotts, and even armed insurgencies against states and transnational corporations throughout the world. One of the key challenges here is to problematize the absence of openly declared forms of resistance. Doing so can explicate the changing meaning of politics as a result of interactions between forces of change on the local, national, regional, and global levels.

Agents of resistance

In the past, agents of resistance were synonymous mostly with union workers, armed rebel/peasants, and political dissidents, including students and certain intellectuals, as class contestations assumed overt political and, in some cases, military dimensions. At present, agents of resistance are not restricted to such actors. They range from blue collar and white collar workers, and to clerics, home-makers, and middle managers. It is important to note that even state functionaries can resist the wholesale implementation of neoliberal development paths, e.g. those who insist on 'Asian-style democracy' in the midst of establishing open markets and free trade. It is the complex ways in which symbolic resources and values articulate with the material conditions of life in different societies that produce a variety of organic intellectuals, a more encompassing group in the current phase of globalization. Class contest only partly forms the basis of resistance. Instead, agents of resistance emerge from interactions between structure and agency that lead to the contextual privileging of particular intersections of different modalities of identity, i.e. class–nationality–gender–race/ethnicity–religion–sexuality. Implicit in the designation of different peoples as agents of resistance is an expansion of the boundaries associated with the traditional sites of political life.

Sites of resistance

Resistance is localized, regionalized, and globalized at the same time that economic globalization slices across geopolitical borders. What this means, in part, is that the 'public–private' dichotomy no longer holds, for most (albeit not all) dimensions of social life are affected, in varying and interconnected ways by globalizing forces. Everyday life in the household and the informal market can facilitate, as well as resist, such forces in distinctly material and symbolic ways. Another closely related phenomenon is the development of cyber-space, a site in which resistance finds its instantaneous audience via the Internet or World Wide Web. Counterdiscourse is a mode of globalized resistance in cyberspace. One has to bear in mind, however, that although states in general are incapable of effectively monitoring and censoring cyberspatial counterdiscourse, this particular mode of resistance is open mainly to those who have access to computers, modems, and the Internet.

Strategies of resistance

By strategies, we refer to the actual ways that people, whose modes of existence are threatened by globalization (e.g. through job loss, encroachment on community lands, or undermining of cultural integrity) respond in a sustained manner toward achieving certain objectives. While forms of struggle differ, groups may adopt varied means to contest, scale up or down, and link objectively and subjectively to their counterparts in other countries or regions. Local movements become transnational or global with sustained access to communication technologies that construct and maintain communities of like-minded individuals. For example, community activists and scholars meet at different forums for the exchange of information and plans. An emerging strategy of 'borderless solidarity' is to link single issues such as environmental degradation, women's rights, and racism, and to highlight the interconnectedness of varied dimensions of social life. Analyses of this may bring to bear the conditions and methods by which commonality can be achieved in spite of, and because of, the fragmentation of identities and interests as political life is being globalized. Nonetheless, evolving global strategies of resistance do not necessarily sidetrack the state. Under certain circumstances, strategies of resistance can and do pit state agencies against one another (e.g. in the case of shipping toxic waste to the developing world, state agencies in charge of environmental protection may join in protests, while their counterparts responsible for industrial development continue to encourage the kind and methods of industrialization that cause environmental destruction). Studies of global, transnational, and local resistance must then take into account transformations in state structures, whether or not strategies of resistance manifestly engage the state.

Quite clearly, an ontology of resistance to globalization requires grounding. When contextualized, the elements of *forms, agents, sites, and strategies* may be viewed in terms of their interactions so as to delimit durable patterns and the potential for structural transformation. The Gramsci–Polanyi–Scott triad calls for conceptual frameworks that link different levels of analysis. Integration of the local with the global can bring to the fore the conditions in which different *forms, agents, sites, and strategies* of resistance emerge from the conjunctures and disjunctures in the global political economy.

Notes

1   K. Polanyi, *The Great Transformation: The Political and Economic Origins of Our Time* (Beacon Press, Boston, 1944), p. 73.
2   A. Melucci, 'The Symbolic Challenge of Contemporary Social Movements', *Social Research*, vol. 52, 1985, p. 812.
3   J. Scott, *Domination and the Arts of Resistance: Hidden Transcripts* (Yale University Press, New Haven, 1990), p. 200 (emphasis in the original).
4   Scott, *Domination and the Arts of Resistance*, p. 18.

3.11 The dynamics of anti-globalization

James Petras and Henry Veltmeyer

Source: *System in Crisis: The Dynamics of Free Market Capitalism* (Fernwood Publishing/Zed Books, London, 2003), pp. 219–28.

Petras and Veltmeyer point to the various phases and trends in the evolution of globalization, especially as it concerns the relationship between ideas of development and globalization. They then identify a further transition in the post-Cold War era towards 'new imperialism' centred on the United States, and go on in this context to examine the evolution and characteristics of the anti-globalization movement. In particular, they note the complexities and tensions within the anti-globalization movement itself.

From development to globalization

Within the confines of the world order set up after the Second World War, several strategic geopolitical and geo-economic projects were launched: "development" (or "modernization," "industrialization"), "revolutionary transformation and socialism," "globalization" and "imperialism."

This world order included a system for promoting free trade, currency-exchange mechanisms, financial architecture to regulate the movement of capital, means to resolve temporary imbalances in international payments, and a funding mechanism for the economic reconstruction and development of Europe first, and then the new nations liberated from colonial rule and vulnerable to the lure of communism. At the national political level, the "system" included social contracts between capital and labour whereby the latter might participate in productivity gains, and the state was committed to ensuring employment, social welfare and health and education. At the international level, the United Nations, with its General Assembly, Security Council and agencies, and NATO, a military alliance of nations committed to "freedom, democracy and free enterprise" (to cite the national security report presented by George W. Bush to the US Congress in September 2002), were set up to ensure that no nation would dream of world domination or act unilaterally to bend the world to its political will and national interests. This was in the early 1950s, in the context of an emerging east–west ideological and military divide, when the US was not as secure in its own power and did not have hegemony over the system.

Within this institutional framework and historic context, the first major project to strategically control and direct the productive resources of the world system was based on the idea of "development." This project was launched in 1946 by Harry Truman in his "four-point program" to provide assistance to backward nations so they might defend themselves against the siren of communism. For some twenty-five years, this project directed the government policies of the rich industrialized states, each of which established an agency for international development and a program of overseas development assistance (ODA) to supplement the resources made available by multilateral agencies such as the World Bank. This ODA, or "foreign aid," became the largest stream of resource flow between the "developed" societies of the North and the "developing" societies of the South. In the 1970s, however, other forms of resource transfers came on stream – bank loans extended by US, and then European and Japanese commercial and investment banks; foreign direct investments by TNCs and investments made by a host of financial institutions in government bonds and other portfolio funds. [. . .] By the mid-1970s the crisis of the world capitalist system, already apparent in the late 1960s when labour launched what turned out to be its last great offensive, led to a serious rethinking of the entire development project and to a major counteroffensive of the capitalist class against the incursions of the state into "private property."

A small group of countries in the South was in the process of successful transition from "economic backwardness" or "underdevelopment" to "economic development," transforming themselves into "newly industrializing countries" (NICs). More generally, however, the North–South gap had grown and there was a divergence rather than convergence in the fortunes and prospects of the industrialized and the non-industrialized countries still caught up in the exploitative international division of labour that political economists in the radical stream of development thought termed "the old imperialism."

In the context of an emerging crisis the "development project" fragmented, leading to its involution within the mainstream of development thought and practice, and, on both the Right and the Left, to its abandonment. In the mainstream there was, first of all, a strong push towards reform, orienting development away from an economic growth-first policy towards meeting the basic needs of the world's population, one-quarter of which were discovered to be "poor".

A second response within the mainstream was to search for "another development," initiated *from below* and *within* (rather than *from above* and *outside*), and based on "appropriate technology," that is participatory, human in scale and form, equitable, socially inclusive and sustainable in terms of both the environment and livelihoods. In the 1980s this search led to a paradigmatic shift and a global movement for "alternative development."

A third response was to abandon the development project altogether or, rather, to replace it with another: "globalization." Pioneered by the "Chicago Boys" of Chile in the 1970s, who engineered what was described by McKinnon (quoted in *El Mercurio*, 18 October 1983: C14), one of the architects of the "new economic model" (or "neoliberalism"), as "the most sweeping reforms in history," the globalization project was widely implemented in the 1980s in the form of what became known as "structural adjustment programs," series of measures to reorient the domestic economic and social policies of nation-states in the direction of a global economy based on free trade and a free flow of capital. By the end of the decade, based on this move to create an integrated global economy driven by the principles of "freedom, democracy and private enterprise" (to use George W. Bush's terminology), a majority of countries in the developing world had been economically restructured, having introduced bold reforms and epoch-defining changes in their internal organizational structures and external relations. By the end of the 1990s and the beginning of the new millennium, "holdout" countries such as Brazil completed the "transition" and were brought into the fold with a new set of macroeconomic policies and emerging forms of governance. The "globalization project" had successfully integrated most countries, North and South – and Russia and other "countries in transition" – into the new world order. Globalization, as a template of prescribed policies and unavoidable changes, had become an irresistible reality.

However, neither the "transition" nor the path towards globalization has been smooth and easy. In fact, like "development," "globalization" has been, and remains, heavily contested, generating widespread discontent with the outcome (prosperity for the few, poverty for the many) among diverse groups and organizations all over the world, discontent that has been mobilized into forces of opposition and resistance. In the case of "development," these forces of opposition have led to a widespread search for a "new paradigm," alternative forms of development ranging from proposals for reform ("structural adjustment with a human face," "productive transformation with equity," a "New Social Policy") and more radical, if somewhat involuted, proposals for "societal transformation" (community-based or local forms of participatory development) to a rejection of the whole development project as a misbegotten enterprise.

In practice, many organizations in the popular sector have rejected the "development option," whether initiated "from above and outside" or "from within and below." Social movements have opted instead for direct and collective action oriented against government policies in the immediate context and towards "social transformation" (or socialist forms of organization) in the longer term. This is the case, for example, for each of the "new peasant social movements" that now dominate Latin America's political landscape – the MST, CONAIE, FARC and the EZLN, among others.

From globalization to the new imperialism

Both "development" and "globalization" can be viewed not only as geopolitical class projects but as theoretical models used to direct the forces of change in a broader class struggle waged by capital against labour. One of the first campaigns in this war was launched in the context of the 1973–74 crisis, as part of a broader counteroffensive against the advances of labour in its struggle for higher wages and better working conditions. Both "development" and "globalization" can be viewed as means of advancing the agendas of the "transnational capitalist class." In a similar way, it is possible to view the emergence of what could be termed "the new imperialism" as a project led by forces initially under the command of US President George W. Bush to advance the economic, geopolitical and security interests of the United States and re-establish hegemony over the system, if not world rule. Unlike development and globalization, this project relies not so much on economic institutions and agents such as multinational corporations, the IMF and the World Bank as on the projection of naked military power. In this form, imperialism has had a long history and inglorious pedigree, but since the latter half of the twentieth century has for the most part served as an adjunct to other favoured institutions and mechanisms. However, in the context of the 1980s and 1990s – economic crisis at home within the United States itself and serious losses of influence at the centre as well as the margins of empire – the imperialist project has emerged as the principal institutional approach towards renovating and securing a new world order – and US hegemony. In fact the emergence of international terrorism and the persistence of "rogue states" unwilling to bend to the will of the US administration have been very functional for the imperialist project. With the collapse of the USSR-led socialist bloc and the vaunted victory of the forces of "freedom, democracy and free enterprise" (i.e., capitalism), the US was in desperate need of an enemy to engage and justify its adventures and interventions.

The "Cold War" against "international communism" had served this purpose for more than thirty years. But al-Qaeda and the purported new threat to the United States posed by international terrorism provided a pretext needed for unilateral action, first against Afghanistan and then Iraq, although in the case of this latter member of the "axis of evil," the pretext could not be sustained and had to be changed to the production and presumed willingness to use "weapons of mass destruction" (nuclear, chemical and biological weapons). Only a few years earlier, no US president could have engaged in such unilateral military action geared to curb the threat of international terrorism, even under a pre-emptive strike policy. But the events of 9/11 have radically changed the context for launching the imperialist project, and George W. Bush and his cronies were not disposed to let the opportunity slip.

The changed political climate has been tested with a series of trial balloons and probing declarations that in earlier contexts would have been viewed as irrational right-wing craziness, if not suicidal. Voices in support of a "new imperialism" have risen on both sides of the Atlantic. While the political Left is caught up in the anti-globalization struggle and nurses fanciful notions of an emerging "empire without imperialism," that is, without a single state seeking world rule, the political Right openly and stridently argues the need to revert to rougher methods of an earlier era: the use of force, pre-emptive attacks, deception, whatever is necessary to deal with those in the premodern world of developing countries who still live in the nineteenth-century world of every state for itself. [. . .]

In this connection, the writings of *Financial Times* economic columnist Martin Wolf (10 October 2001: 13) have been used to point towards the need for a new, more direct form of imperialism that does not hesitate to use force whenever and wherever necessary. In Wolf's words, "To tackle the challenge of the failed state [in the impoverished third world], what is needed is not pious aspirations but an honest and organized coercive force." This is precisely the view that George W. Bush and his regime incorporate into their national security doctrine, which includes a right to take unilateral military action and make pre-emptive first strikes against the threat of "international terrorism" and "weapons of mass destruction."

The dynamics of anti-globalization and anti-capital

Just as the development project generated a search for alternatives, as well as forces of opposition and resistance, the idea – and project and thus process – of globalization and the new imperialism have given rise to movements of resistance and forces of opposition. These proposals for alternative forms of globalization, and associated forces of opposition and resistance, are part of what has become known as the "anti-globalization movement" (AGM).

The dynamics of this movement, part of an effort to construct a "global civil society," are not that well understood despite the multiplicity of recent efforts to document and analyze them. Is the AGM the juggernaut that it is frequently made out to be, able to mobilize, if not unite, the forces of resistance into an effective movement to derail the agenda of corporate capital? Or should it be viewed as a "jalopy," susceptible to breakdown and not likely to run the course? This question [. . .] is not yet settled. Despite the broad range of studies that have emerged to describe developments within the AGM, its dynamics require a closer look. Nevertheless, we can make several theoretical points.

The first is that the neoliberal model of capitalist development and globalization, in reality, is simply a dummy target, advanced in the contested terrain of world development as if in a game of "go," to force the opposition to waste energy in attacking a position that has already been abandoned. Hardly any of the many apparent apologists and defenders of the new world order are prepared to defend neoliberalism. Indeed, one and all have acknowledged the need for fundamental reform, for an alternative form of development/globalization sustained by new forms of international governance. For example, key members of the Council on Foreign Relations, one of several nodes in the global network set up by the self-appointed guardians of the new world order, have argued that the North-South gap is too deep to sustain no matter what system of governance is put into place. They argue that the resulting poverty will generate a social discontent that will be inherently destabilizing and too easily mobilized into movements of opposition. Others have pointed towards the need for a new financial architecture to regulate volatile movements of productive and speculative capital. Carlos Slim, the richest man in Mexico, a multibillionaire who has benefited immensely from his country's insertion into the new world order, goes so far as to say that the neoliberal agenda that drives "globalization" is nothing more than a form of "neocolonialism" that generates excessive social inequalities, non-functioning markets and political instability. The system, he says, simply does not work.

A second point that can be made about the AGM is that to a considerable extent its member organizations and leading activists have been in practice manipulated by the self-appointed guardians of the new world order, who have tried to limit opposition and direct proposals for alternative design and action, to keep them within acceptable limits, as a form of controlled dissent. To analyze the ways in which this is done is beyond the scope of this book, but the point can be illustrated by an analogy. The parasitic wasp of the genus *Hymenoepimecis*, unknown to the spider it targets, lays its eggs in the abdomen of the spider, which then goes to work spinning a pupal cocoon that it does not need but is necessary for the larvae, unwittingly serving the interests of the parasite. Similarly, the World Bank, as an agency of the "development" and "globalization" projects, has turned to non-governmental organizations, of what used to be viewed as "the third sector" but in current discourse is known as "civil society," as a partner institution, thus making the NGOs unwitting agents of a project they are in fact opposed to in principle. Together with other institutions at the disposal of the "transnational capitalist class," the World Bank seeks to ensure that the forces of opposition and resistance are contained within acceptable limits or channelled towards reform of the existing system, reform to which it is itself committed. Funding is one way to control dissent. Indeed, it seems that a good part of the organizational efforts and protest activities orchestrated by the AGM is in fact made possible by funding from governments and international organizations that espouse the activities to which they are opposed. In this and other ways the AGM in fact helps the guardians of the new world order to realize their agenda. For one thing, the AGM serves as a repository of ideas for improving and reforming the system, to secure its sustainability and "good governance."

A third critical issue in the political dynamics of anti-globalization is the split within the movement between the mass oriented towards reforming the system – changing the form taken by globalization, accepting its positive features as well as its inevitability but rejecting its current neoliberal form and its negative effects – and the number of groups and organizations that are against capitalism in all of its forms. The differences between these two streams of thought within the AGM are not only strategic (with regard to the ends of the struggle) but tactical (with regard to its proposed actions). The two sides differ over whether to favour direct action to the point of violent confrontation or a more pacific and controlled form of action and dialogue. However, the way this internal division plays out in the context of actual struggle is not clear. This too needs a closer look, and further study. But for the most part the institutional mechanisms of controlled dissent have appeared to be working, even at, for example, the greatest mobilizations of the AGM to date, at the Anti-G-8 Summit in Genoa in summer 2001 and at the World Social Summit in Porto Alegre in February 2002.

However, at a number of more recent protest actions, including the European Social Forum (ESF), which brought together close to forty thousand protesters from five hundred organizations in 105 countries, the two streams of the AGM have tended to converge, allowing for, if not leading to, a concertation of diverse strategies and tactics, as well as a more radical vision of the road ahead. This development was captured very well in the following assessment by Ramón Montovani, a Communist Renewal deputy, of the debate within and outside the anti-globalization movement. [. . .]

> There are those who think that neoliberal globalization can be reformed and those, that we believe to be in the majority, who think that there is no negotiation with neoliberalism, that something new has to be created. Any attempt to reform [the system] and humanize it is useless; it just serves to legitimize it. Today neoliberalism is war and destruction [. . .] this is the capitalism we have today. For this reason the forces of the Left have to understand that globalization is an attack on humanity and life itself, and that therefore the game has to be abandoned, and to create something new from below. The parties of the Left have to approach the [anti-globalization/anti-capital] movement with humility and learn from it, not pretend to direct it.
>
> (*La Jornada*, 11 November 2002: 24)

This appears to be a fairly accurate assessment of where the majority of the Left finds itself: caught between diverse political positions that have served to advance, on the one hand, the struggle for state power and, on the other, the construction of a new, all-encompassing socio-political movement capable of bringing the system down and creating something new.

These and other such reflections on the anti-globalization, i.e., anti-corporate, movement have opened up a debate on the political dynamics of the struggle involved. For one thing, the diverse theatres, forms and conditions (objective or structural, and subjective or political) of this struggle reach beyond the parameters of the elections, streets and factories. [. . .] These parameters undoubtedly involve some, if not most, of the major forms of this struggle, but, as we have argued, the major dynamics of anti-systemic struggle today need to be analyzed in the broader context of the economies and societies that are in crisis on the "periphery" of the system, on the south of a growing divide within the neoliberal world order. In this context, we have drawn attention to assemblies held by indigenous peasant communities in Ecuador and Chiapas; *cocaleros* (coca-producing peasants) in Bolivia; and unemployed workers – the *piqueteros* – in Argentina. These assemblies are also found in and around factories and industrial plants as well as in open and closed spaces in working-class neighbourhoods in Argentina, Brazil and elsewhere. They are the source of some of the most innovative and effective forms of anti-systemic struggle exhibited by the AGM today. Many of these struggles take place in the streets but are not just limited to street protests at meetings or forums of the WTO, the G-8 and other institutions of the capitalist world order. The forms of struggle are diverse and often combined, including negotiations with government officials and private sector representatives, street marches and protest actions, popular assemblies and occupations of public buildings and factories, hunger strikes, blockades and *cortas de ruta*, strikes and pitched battles behind barricades.

Towards a conclusion

June 2002 marked a critical turning point in the movement against corporate globalization. On the long road from Seattle to Genoa and Quebec City the AGM had been divided both as to its ultimate goals and its tactics of struggle. On the one side were diverse voices and a complex of non-governmental organizations, including significant elements of the labour movement, pushing for pacific or non-violent forms of confrontation, dialogue and cooperation that are directed towards moderate reform of the system. On the other side were the anti-capitalist proponents of direct action, pushing for confrontationalist politics and radical changes in social and economic forms of organization, not towards reform but rather a dismantling of the new world order.

This division is not new. It was evident from the beginning, in the confrontation with the WTO in Seattle in 1989 and in the successful derailing of its agenda to impose the Multilateral Agreement on Investment (MAI), a new set of globally applicable rules for securing the property rights of investors. However, in the aftermath of 9/11 this division seriously deepened, creating a fundamental rift within the AGM, with an increasing intolerance for radical change and confrontationalist politics. Events from September 2001 to June 2002 within the movement provided increasing evidence of this rift. But at the same time there was some evidence of efforts to mend fences within the movement and to heal the rift between the two wings.

This last point is illustrated by developments within the Canadian AGM. In Canada, demonstrations were organized in two cities to express opposition to the G-8 meetings in remote Kananaskis. The demonstrations evidenced a push for cooperation and concerted action against an admittedly distant common enemy. In this context, the more radical, direct-action wing of the Canadian AGM, led by Montreal's Anti-Capitalist Convergence (CLAC) and the Toronto-based Ontario Coalition Against Poverty (OCAP), organized two days of marches in Ottawa. Meanwhile, the labour movement and more moderate forces of anti-globalization such as the Council of Canadians joined local Alberta activists in organizing a week of events (including a People's Summit) in Calgary, the nearest city to Kananaskis.

Taken together, these various actions provide a moderately successful challenge to the G-8, especially considering the efforts of the governments involved to not only "control" dissent and protest but to prevent it altogether by locating meetings in remoter places, such as Qatar or Kananaskis. In Canada, not only did the government host the G-8 in a remote location where five separate checkpoints prevented anyone getting anywhere near the assembled dignitaries and leaders, but it paid off an Alberta farmer who had rented out land to protesters near the summit site, convincing him to withdraw this invitation (Judy Rebick, "All we are saying is give protests a chance," *Globe and Mail*, 3 July 2002: A11).

The particular forms taken by the protests reflected several months of deep discussion among individuals in the two wings of the AGM about the most appropriate tactics of struggle. Anarchist groups, opposed to any form of hierarchy and committed to notions of individual autonomy, insisted that an agreement to use only non-violent tactics at demonstrations was "authoritarian" and divisive. Echoing previous irruptions of the protest movement in the 1960s, 1970s and even earlier, they argued that only the principle of "diversity of tactics" would allow everyone to participate and ensure the growth and unity of the movement – "diversity within unity." At the same time, the refusal of the "anarchists" and other groups to exclude tactics of direct action and violence, to limit action to pacific forms of protest, deepened their split from the labour movement and the NGOs, exacerbating the cultural and political differences between the two. Marxist-oriented political groups within the labour movement, perhaps more accustomed to top-down decision-making and internal discipline, were only too happy to organize their own actions without having to deal with the unruly anarchists. Most "anti-corporate globalization" protesters could be found somewhere in between.

After the end of June 2001, the Canadian and European wings of the movement seemed to reach a critical turning point. In Canada, for example, although proponents of direct action were unwilling to compromise with more moderate elements in the labour movement for the sake of unity, they agreed to the principle of non-violence to ensure the involvement of immigrant and refugee communities. For whatever reason, demonstrations in both Ottawa and Calgary were surprisingly free of violence, in part the result of this agreement and in part the result of a new strategy by the forces of law and order. In Calgary, police on bicycles even distributed water to protesters, a far cry from the tactics adopted by these forces in Seattle, Paris, Melbourne, Barcelona and Genoa.

The question is: What, if anything, does this development within the AGM mean? What conclusions, if any, can be drawn from it? On the one hand, anti-capitalist organizers claimed victory for their ability to successfully mobilize and broaden the movement from university youth, non-governmental organizations and unionists to include immigrant communities and people of colour. On the other hand, the demonstrations and protests, albeit peaceful, were decidedly smaller than previous protests. While Calgary had probably never seen 2,500 anti-corporate protesters on its streets before, the march was modest by movement standards elsewhere in the world. But even the much larger meetings of the AGM in Porto Alegre managed to confine actions to public lectures, workshop discussion and peaceful marches, containing the dispositions of more radical elements of the movement towards direct action and violent confrontation.

Because the threat of violence at demonstrations has been at the root of divisions within the AGM, the peaceful nature of protest actions in both Calgary and Ottawa has led some to see a basis for movement convergence. As Judy Rebick (*Globe and Mail*, 3 July 2002: A11), for example, mused: "Imagine what could be accomplished if both wings came back together, respecting their differences but working in concert to build the kind of mass challenge to corporate globalization and war as their colleagues in Europe and Latin America." However, Rebick, publisher of *rabble.ca*, an interactive independent news magazine, here begs a question she has clearly not examined: What is behind the mass challenge represented by the AGM in Europe and Latin America? Is it convergence or is it a commitment to employ a diversity of tactics within a broader movement? Does the latter imply the former? Even if it does, what are its likely ramifications? What is the impact on the capacity of the AGM to mobilize forces of opposition and resistance and bring about substantive change? Is change in this context oriented towards, and limited to, reform of the system, creating a more humane form of capitalist development and globalization ("another world")? Or can the anti-capital forces of opposition and resistance thereby secure the conditions of revolutionary transformation, an alternate or new "system"?

These questions remain unanswered. One thing is clear, however. Any successful transformation of the system of capitalist development and globalization will necessarily entail a combination, and "concertation" of the diverse forms of struggle exhibited by the AGM with the broader class struggle of indigenous peasants in Bolivia, Ecuador, Mexico and elsewhere; of unemployed workers in Argentina and elsewhere; of the labour movement in its diverse forms, particularly in the streets and factories of countries in the "developing world" or "in transition." All of these and other forms of struggle have to be combined, if not concerted and led, in a massive mobilization of diverse oppositional forces, particularly those in a strategic position vis-à-vis the system (being able to close down or cut access to the production apparatus), taking advantage of the objective conditions generated by the contradictions of a system in crisis. The system has many diverse points of vulnerability and its crisis is generating both objective (structural) and subjective (political) conditions for anti-systemic action. This is to say, as Marx said in an earlier and very different context, capitalism in its current global projection is "creating its own gravediggers." The Left has the responsibility and historic mission to understand and actively support this process.

Part IV

Perspectives and world politics

Introduction

We have retained all the items that were included in the previous edition of this book, which we see as distinctive and important statements on perspectives, but we have also doubled the number of items in this section. The new items are intended to highlight that the contemporary study of world politics has become much more self-consciously aware of its philosophical underpinnings. One of the important effects of this development, perhaps not sufficiently acknowledged in the readings, is the huge upsurge of interest in the ethical implications of international relations. A second and related effect, absolutely central to this book, has been to raise significant questions about the nature of the field and how it should be studied and taught. Although we remain convinced that the format of this book is a valid and very useful way of approaching world politics, others see the approach as anachronistic. The new items suggest, at the very least, that questions about perspectives continue to lie at the heart of some of the key debates in the field. But we would go further and argue that although epistemological and methodological issues about how world politics should be studied began to be privileged in the 1990s, as we move into the twenty-first century, the pendulum has swung back again and the central focus is, once again, on ontological debates about the kind of world we are living in and the potential that exists for changing this world. Methodological and epistemological questions are still of crucial importance, however, and they now self-evidently underpin the more politically oriented architecture that structures this book.

Rothstein (4.1) starts from the presumption that theorists and practitioners have been overwhelmingly influenced by the realist perspective – elaborated in the first section of this reader. The perspective does not prescribe specific policies according to Rothstein but he does insist that it predisposes its adherents to think about international politics in a very circumscribed and ethnocentric fashion. Rothstein goes on to argue that the influence of realism is becoming increasingly dangerous and deceptive because of the revolution taking place in world politics which is invalidating basic realist assumptions. It becomes clear during the course of the argument, therefore, that Rothstein is evaluating realism from the perspective of interdependence and globalization. It also becomes apparent that Rothstein is not simply attacking realism because it is presenting an erroneous view of reality but because advocates of realism are endeavouring to maintain a world which Rothstein characterizes as elitist and undemocratic. The article reveals, therefore, that the differences between perspectives can be ethical as well as empirical.

Gilpin (4.2) adopts a much more eclectic approach to perspectives. He identifies three perspectives on the international political economy which to a very large extent overlap with the perspectives identified in this reader. It is central to his argument, however, that these perspectives are not amenable to empirical verification because they are based on assumptions about individuals and society which are not susceptible to any conclusive empirical test. Adherents of any specific perspective must, therefore, engage in an act of faith. Gilpin, himself, however, believes that he can stand apart from the three perspectives and assess their strengths and weaknesses. On this basis, he is able to draw on all three perspectives in his quest to understand the international political economy. There is, on the face of it, something rather attractive about this eclecticism but in fact it raises a number of difficult philosophical problems which it is not possible to enter into here.

Strange (4.3) who, like Gilpin, believes that it is necessary to adopt a position which transcends the interpretations of competing ideological perspectives argues that academic debates can have profound political significance. She insists that the outcome of the dispute about whether or not we are in the process of observing the demise of the American Empire will affect future events. She further asserts, however, that whatever the outcome, the debate has, in the past, been couched in terms of an outmoded perspective which prevents both sides from identifying the nature and amount of power possessed by the United States in the contemporary world.

The position adopted by Cox (4.4) provides an interesting contrast to Strange. The original item is extremely long and only a small portion of it is reproduced here. Nevertheless, the extract is sufficient to make clear that Cox has a very distinctive position on the role of perspectives. He draws a very sharp distinction between a problem-solving and a critical perspective. He argues that the problem-solving perspective takes the world as the theorist finds it. The perspective is designed to reveal how the status quo can be reproduced. By contrast, a critical perspective is designed to transcend the established order and to understand the nature of change. It calls into question institutions associated with the existing order and it makes provision for an ethical position which favours a transformed political and social order. The line of analysis developed by Cox makes it clear that he is unhappy with the established world order and that he wishes to adopt a posture on perspectives which opens up the possibility of radical change. Ironically, the argument has much in common with the one developed by Strange, except that she wishes to develop a critical posture which will ensure that the status quo is maintained.

Elshtain (4.5) throws fresh light on all the items. She is interested in using a feminist perspective as an alternative to the dominant perspectives on world politics and, in particular, realism. But before she can do this, she has to acknowledge the pervasive influence of realism, and she notes how an important strain of feminist thought has been cast in realist terms. She insists, though, that there is an alternative line of feminist ideas which provides the language necessary to engage in a very different form of discourse about international relations. Elshtain does not ascribe an autonomous role for language and discourse but she does insist that the language associated with one particular perspective may preclude consideration of unrealized possibilities which exist in the real world. The language provided by a new perspective may make these possibilities manifest.

Hooper (4.6) undoubtedly accepts the main thrust of Elstain's thesis, but she puts another twist on the argument. In particular, she wants to move away from the empiricist view that feminism does no more than provide another variable that can be incorporated into the analysis of a complex reality. She argues that it is not simply the case that women have been ignored in the theory and practice of world politics but that by failing to recognize the significance of gender not only has the essential masculinity of world politics remained unmasked, but also, and just as important, there has been insufficient recognition of the impact of international relations on the way that masculinity is defined. It follows that fundamental changes in world politics would necessarily involve a transformation in how we think about masculinity.

All the remaining items in this section help to shed light on how thinking about perspectives has moved on since the second edition of this book was published. Walt (4.7) provides a useful overview, endorsing the presupposition of this book that world politics can be examined from three distinct perspectives. However, he notes that by the 1980s, before the demise of the Soviet Union, Marxism was already on the wane and the radical position was being occupied by postmodern thinkers who focused on the importance of language and discourse. He acknowledges, however, that all three perspectives were profoundly affected by their collective failure to anticipate the end of the Cold War and the collapse of the Soviet Union. Since that time, Walt argues that all three perspectives have been endeavouring to make sense of the resulting changes in world politics. But whereas we see strong lines of continuity across all three perspectives, Walt suggests that the changes he identified in the radical perspective in the 1980s have been further accentuated over the last decade and he links these changes with the growing importance of the constructivist thesis that the world we live in is not dictated by material forces as realists and liberals tend to assume, but to prevailing discourses that shape our beliefs and interests.

Walt's position, however, is challenged by Wæver (4.8) who insists that the inter-paradigm debate engaged in by realists, liberals, and radicals is a product of the 1970s. By the 1980s, it was being overtaken by a much more philosophical debate that was being conducted along an axis with rationalism at one end and reflectivism at the other. Rationalists assume, for example, that international institutions are established on the basis of rational cost-benefit calculations. These institutions form because they reduce the transaction costs that inhibit international cooperation. In an attempt to establish their scientific credentials, during the 1980s, neo-realists and neo-liberals both adopted this rationalist mode of analysis, thereby effectively eliminating the key differences that separated the classical realists and liberals who had participated in the inter-paradigm debate. The dominance of this approach, however, was increasingly challenged by reflectivists who adopted a very different philosophical stance. They denied that we can understand world politics on the basis of rationally calculating actors and they operated on the basis of a much more sociological, historically sensitive, and postmodern approach to the discipline. Wæver concludes that postmodern reflectivists not only embrace a radical critique of mainstream social science, that includes Marxism, but also enables them to occupy ground that has been vacated by the neo-realists and the neo-liberals. More controversially, he suggests that we are moving into a new phase where it is accepted that there is a useful division of labour between the rationalists and the reflectivists.

The assumption made by Wæver that the study of world politics can now be mapped most effectively in terms of philosophical debates is taken further by Wendt (4.9). From Wendt's perspective, the rationalist/reflectivist axis conflates two interrelated philosophical debates. One focuses on the dispute about the impact of structures. Individualists insist that explanations must be formulated in terms of how individuals repond to the world. By contrast, holists insist that the interests and identities of individuals are shaped by social forces and structures of which individuals may well be unaware. There is, however, a second debate that centres on the importance of ideas. On the one hand, idealists argue that human beings are primarily motivated by the beliefs and ideas that they adhere to. On the other hand, materialists argue that human beings primarily respond to changes in their material circumstances. Wendt suggests that there is now a substantial raft of approaches to world politics, from feminism to postmodernism, that can be gathered under the heading of constructivism. These various constructivist approaches are clustered in the quadrant where holism and idealism intersect. Rationalists, for their part, occupy the quadrant where individualism and materialism intersect.

In the final item of this section, Barkin (4.10) problematizes the positions adopted by Walt, Wæver and Wendt. From his perspective, all three theorists fail to distinguish adequately between the nature of politics and ways of studying politics. Barkin insists that realism, liberalism and Marxism offer opposing views about the nature of politics. Constructivists and rationalists, by contrast, provide different tools for studying politics. For Barkin, it is important to make this distinction and he illustrates his argument by focusing on classical realists who, it is presupposed, could develop a more effective understanding of world politics by taking the constructivist approach on board. Barkin demonstrates that it is a mistake to assume that realists are locked into a materialist straitjacket. The potential exists for realists to draw on the tools provided by both idealists and holists. But the same argument can be extended to liberals and Marxists. Overall, what the items in this section suggest, therefore, is that attempts to comprehend world politics have become more complex and sophisticated over the past 30 years.

4.1 On the costs of realism

Robert L. Rothstein

Source: *Political Science Quarterly*, vol. LXXXVII, no. 3 (1972), pp. 347–62.

After identifying the chief characteristics of the realist view of world politics, Rothstein considers what the effect of this view has been upon politicians and diplomats since the Second World War and points to the dangers inherent in its continuing to dominate the thinking of foreign policy makers.

[The article begins by pointing to the contrast between the declining satisfaction with realism in academic circles and its continuing attraction for policy makers. It suggests that this contrast can be understood only by recognizing the nature of the realist vision.]

Realism involved commitment to a set of propositions about international politics which were essentially extrapolations from the diplomatic history of nineteenth-century Europe. They were propositions which the generation of statesmen in Europe after 1919 either had lost or misunderstood: re-education in the 'perennials' was clearly necessary. The catechism was simple. All states sought, or would seek, power, given the opportunity. It was an essential prerequisite for the achievement of any other goals. Today's enemy could be tomorrow's ally (n.b., not 'friend', for, as Salisbury put it, 'Great Britain has no permanent friends, only permanent interests'). The use of any means was acceptable (atomic weapons created a dilemma, resolved by silence or metaphysical despair), or at least possible, though only one or two might be appropriate at any single moment. The best operator was the man who possessed 'traditional wisdom'; and the man who possessed 'traditional wisdom' was the best operator.

The scenario and the stage directions are very familiar. The metaphor is deliberate, for many Realists considered international politics a great drama in which wise statesmen made 'hard choices' in a bitter but limited struggle for dominance. They were constrained by their own power and their own fallibility, but at the very least they never fell victim to illusions about the 'true' nature of the world. It was a world in which states were involved in an unending struggle with each other (because that was the nature of states in an anarchic world); power was necessary to survive in it or to continue to fight; all states were potential enemies (Realism requires enemies more than it needs friends), but the worst might be avoided by clever diplomacy and by virtue of the fact that all alike shared a similar conception of rational behavior. It was indeed a dramatic picture, and an especially exciting one, for it was a drama of war in which the wartime mind predominated. This made it particularly attractive to an emerging generation of statesmen whose views had been formed as a response to the failure to stop Hitler before it was too late and who were thus predisposed toward a doctrine which would guarantee that the same errors would not be committed against Stalin.

The Realist model of world politics was simple and elegant. An image of states as billiard balls, interacting within a specific arena and according to established rules, became increasingly prevalent. Once the implication of the metaphor was grasped, that there are only a few immutable patterns of behavior in politics – billiard balls, after all, are not very complex phenomena – the principal preoccupation of statesmen became clear. They were to judge, by experience and intuition, the requisite amount of force necessary to move one or another ball in a preferred direction. Purposes, as in wartime where the need for survival and victory dominated everything, could be taken for granted. Individual idiosyncrasies, which might influence choice of purpose, or domestic politics, which might destroy the elegance of the game, could be safely ignored, for they were hardly significant in comparison to the external imperatives imposed by life in the international arena. All states would respond to the same drummer, irrespective of internal differences, because they had no choice if they wished to survive (at any rate, as a Great Power).

Is there something beyond its elegance and simplicity which has made this doctrine so popular, so to speak so 'natural', to the practitioner? The power of fascination of a doctrine ultimately must rest on its apparent ability to provide answers to practical questions. The answers must be attributable to the doctrine, at least in the sense that some connection may safely be posited between successful practitioners and doctrinal commitment. In the case at hand, the ability to make that connection would imply that a substantive distinction exists between a Realist and a non-Realist.

Is it really that easy to distinguish a Realist from a non-Realist? The difficulty is that commitment to the Realists' image of world politics – a world scarred by a permanent quest for power by potentially wicked men – hardly guarantees realistic decisions about the practical world. Realists and non-Realists may disagree about the permanence of power as the decisive factor in international politics, but they can still reach similar judgments about specific cases. On the other hand, two confessed Realists may reach totally dissimilar conclusions about the same case – in fact, at times, it is difficult to relate an individual Realist's position on policy to his philosophical convictions. Correlating Morgenthau and Kennan on policy with Morgenthau and Kennan on 'Realism' requires a Talmudist's skill and patience, not to say a willingness to suspend disbelief. The difficulty is that reality is so complex and ambiguous that the policies which we choose to call 'realistic' at any particular moment depend to a significant degree on personal predispositions and perspectives.

What this suggests is that Realism involves something more than a temporal perspective on power and the nature of man. It also suggests that lists of characteristics presumably shared by all Realists are irrelevant: statesmen or analysts possessing all the characteristics can act very 'unrealistically' (which we know only after the fact), while others possessing none of the characteristics may act 'realistically' (which we also know only after the fact). The more subtle contention that Realists share an awareness that full security is beyond attainment and that compromise and adjustment of interests are necessary, is more helpful. It implies that Realism involves a state of mind with which to approach problems, rather than the possession of a few characteristics or attachment to the permanent significance of a single operating principle. Nevertheless, some groups have the same sense of the nature of politics and are not considered Realists (for example, some liberals). Moreover, the difficulty of discovering exactly why one policy position is more realistic than another persists.

Various efforts to give Realism an acceptable programmatic content have been inadequate, for the task itself is probably impossible. We can define a Realist arbitrarily as someone who possesses certain characteristics or who believes in certain doctrinal propositions, but there is no way in which we can convincingly relate those characteristics or beliefs to specific choices in the world of action. Realism simply constitutes belief in the wisdom of certain 'eternal verities' about politics, conveniently collected in a few texts and conveniently 'confirmed' by a series of all too recent blunders by non-Realists. The point surely is not that Realism is unimportant or irrelevant. But its real significance has not been in providing a (non-existent) direct connection between theory and action. Its power and influence over the choice of specific actions has been – and perhaps remains – pervasive, but indirect. It has conditioned the political climate so that some actions seem 'to stand to reason' and others seem naive – by definition. And it has furnished an authentic body of scripture to rationalize 'hard choices', to justify the notion that a democratic foreign policy is inconceivable, and to provide psychic support for the acolyte compelled to lie in defense of his own interpretation of the national interest.

The great hero in the Realist canon has always been the successful diplomat – many of the founders and followers of Realism were frustrated Castlereaghs, or better yet, Metternichs – and the great danger the bumbling amateur. Professionals, after all, could always 'work something out'. The very ambiguity and uncertainty of the relationship between the theory and the choice of specific actions guarantee the supremacy of the diplomat's role. What else but experience and intuition allow the necessary connections to be made? And who but the diplomat is trained (rather, one should say, 'experienced') to make the necessary judgments? It is peculiarly true, then, that the lack of an obvious connection between the theory and a practical action, and the ensuing necessity of relying on a corps of skilled intermediaries, has made Realism singularly attractive to professional diplomats. [. . .]

Realism presumes a world of similar states: it is a doctrine based upon, and beholden to, the behavioral styles of the traditional Great Power. Totalitarian, revolutionary, underdeveloped, and unstable states – as well as Small Powers, international organizations, and nongovernmental organizations, like the multinational corporation or the Ford Foundation – are all unwelcome anomalies. Such states violate and perhaps destroy the notion of a shared, if tacit, sense of a range of permissible behavior for states. It is not altogether inexplicable that many of the events which have surprised us – both theorists and practitioners – in the last twenty-five or so years have been perpetrated by these new kinds of states: the Nazi–Soviet pact in 1939, Pearl Harbor, the German blitz, Soviet acquisition of a nuclear capability, the Berlin blockade, North Korean aggression and Chinese intervention, Nasser's reaction to US Aswan Dam 'diplomacy', the sputniks, the Berlin wall, the installation of missiles in Cuba, and the more recent internal turmoil in both Indonesia and China. It is not that we failed to predict the exact moment or event; it is that we were neither politically nor psychologically prepared for them to happen at all.

It is important to note that many of these failures resulted from the inability of men trained to deal with concrete contingencies as they arise to understand the actions of men or states committed to an ideological interpretation of world affairs – or at least to an interpretation not derived from the history of the European state system. In addition, a congenital bias against planning made it difficult to deal with those who did have a plan. At any rate, both Realists and practitioners shared a bias toward analyzing and evaluating the world according to habits and precepts drawn from European history.

One other aspect of Realism has made it especially attractive to diplomats and practitioners. Concentrating on interaction between states perceived as billiard balls tends to turn attention away from structural alterations in the international system itself. The systemic environment, in the large, is taken as a constant – that is, as a field fluctuating around a metaphorical balance of power. The result has been a static theory concerned only with creating or preserving an equilibrium. As such, only tactical questions – operator's questions about means, not ends – appear truly interesting. The central preoccupation is never why or where the system is going (it is going no place, by definition), but rather how to preserve the existing order of things. It has meant that the Realists have been very poor guides through the thickets of bipolarity, multipolarity, polycentrism, and the like.

Practitioners generally object strenuously to the notion that they all believe in any single doctrine. They point to the indisputable fact that there are sharp disagreements within the government over major issues like Vietnam and the ABM. This mistakes disagreements about specifics for disagreement about general attitudes and approaches. Anyone who reads the memoirs of former practitioners, or who spends any substantial amount of time talking with them, can attest to the existence of widely shared beliefs and very similar perceptions of what can be taken for granted about the conduct of foreign affairs. These shared beliefs and convictions are not held or expounded with anything like the formal elegance or coherence which one finds in a Morgenthau or Kennan text. Nonetheless, they exist and they reinforce – or repeat – the Realist canon. It may be violently unsettling to the political practitioner, but he does indeed 'speak' theory – of a sort. It would be better for all of us if he were aware of it and understood what it implied.

The practical effects of realism

The extent to which Realism has been elitist and antidemocratic was masked – or ignored – for many years, for the policies which dominated American foreign policy rested on a substantial domestic consensus about the proper way to deal with the Soviet and Chinese threats. Not only the mass public but anyone who disagreed with the conventional wisdom could be disregarded, be they reporters, professors, or 'bleeding hearts' in general. What Realism passed on was a kind of romanticism about both policy – for the 'responsibilities of power' meant that we had a stake as policeman or judge in anything happening anywhere – and the policy-maker – who had to make 'hard choices' in spite of domestic stupidity or indifference. The 'professionals' would give Americans a good and prudent foreign policy even if they had to be tricked into it or misinformed or lied to. In effect, Realism has provided the high tone of necessity for a rather low range of behavior. In this sense, the revelation in the *Pentagon Papers* of a persistent disregard for the democratic process and a persistent fascination with fooling the press and obscuring the truth was entirely predictable.

Realism is also implicitly a conservative doctrine attractive to men concerned with protecting the status quo. It hardly predisposes its followers to look favorably at revolutionary change, for that kind of change threatens all the fences which Realism has erected: it means one might have to deal with some very untraditional states – and 'diplomats' – about some very untraditional issues. It means that disagreement about ends and values might begin to creep into the system, surely an unfortunate development from the point of view of men committed to the notion that only the proper choice of means is ever really at issue.

From one point of view, Realism has always been an eminently sensible doctrine: its emphasis on the virtues of moderation, flexibility, and compromise was an intelligent response to the difficulties and dangers of living in an anarchic world. But from another point of view, Realism has emphasized the necessity for Great Powers to maintain their prestige, status, and credibility. Great Powers, by definition, are compelled to play 'prestige politics', that is to say, a form of politics particularly difficult to compromise or control.

Turning the other cheek could be disastrous, or at least imprudent, in a world dominated by the quest for power. In fact, it has always been necessary to use, or to appear to be willing to use, limited amounts of force quickly in order to avoid having to use larger amounts belatedly. This seemingly sensible proposition, so fundamental to a generation who remembered the follies of Chamberlain and Daladier, was very dangerous for men who could remember – or learn – nothing else. Flexibility, moderation, and compromise would have to take a back seat to the necessity of teaching the aggressors a lesson and enhancing the credibility of one's word. An awful lot of 'brinkmanship' and waiting to see if 'the other guy would blink first' could result.

Realism asserts – and it can be neither proved nor disproved – that nothing much can be changed, that the only guide to the future is the past, and that the best interpreter of the way to get there safely is the operator skilled at negotiating limited compromises. It thus gives the 'generalist', the operator armed only with traditional procedural skills, a central role in the conduct of foreign policy. But it is also a conservative and anti-innovative role; as a result, the doctrine has provided a kind of metaphysical justification for the passivity and procedural inertia of the Foreign Service and the State Department, characteristics already built into the policy-making system by incrementalism and the play of bureaucratic politics.

The nature of the role which the practitioner is expected to play also has had a crucial effect on the nature of the training he is expected to undergo. The only unanswered questions are tactical questions about applications. And there is no way to train someone to make correct tactical decisions except 'on the job'. Thus the proper training for the practitioner is never analytical or intellectual; presumably, his proper role is simply to apply known principles to individual cases. That task, which rests on a combination of experience, intuition, and familiarity with the latest details, can be learned only by doing – or, more accurately, by imitating. It is one of the few illustrations of a profession which takes anti-intellectualism as a virtue. In any case, it sharply circumscribes the ability of the practitioner to deal with untraditional events.

The fact that Realism has operated with a strikingly narrow definition of politics also has had a major effect on the behavior of its practitioners. Diplomatic maneuvering to achieve or maintain the gains of 'high politics' became the norm – the analogy with the chessboard, an elegant and intricate arena of play, always seemed appropriate. New developments which undermine the utility of the analogy have to be either ignored or dismissed as irrelevant. Thus the State Department and its denizens have had little influence on a whole range of issues which have dominated foreign policy since World War II: for example, political and economic development in the underdeveloped countries, the relationship between nuclear weapons and political behavior, the control of the arms race, limited and sublimited war, and the erosion of the distinction between foreign and domestic policy. It is misleading to assert, as some critics have done, that these are issues which have been *taken* from the State Department: it is more accurate to say that they have been given away in the apparent hope that they would disappear, or at least not intrude upon the ordered universe of diplomacy.

Realism has the ring of truth to it for men compelled to work in an environment which they can not always understand and can never adequately control. It provides a few simple keys which facilitate understanding (if only, inevitably, by oversimplification) and an intellectual justification for the failure to control (for all is unpredictable – although hardly unexpectable). None of this means that Realism has been responsible for, or 'caused', any particular policy choice: it could just as well have been used, for example, to defend going into Vietnam as staying out. What it has done has been to foster a set of attitudes that predisposed its followers to think about international politics in a particularly narrow and ethno-centric fashion, and to set very clear bounds around the kinds of policies which it seemed reasonable to contemplate. And once decisions have been made, it has provided the necessary psychological and intellectual support to resist criticism, to persevere in the face of doubt, and to use any means to outwit or to dupe domestic dissenters.

The future of realism

The appeal of Realism is deceptive and dangerous, for it rests on assumptions about state behavior which have become increasingly irrelevant. It treats one time-bound set of propositions as if they were universally applicable, and thus turns everyone's attention to problems of application – to issues of 'how' not 'why'. It is always a doctrine which takes for granted the primacy of foreign policy and the dominance of the security issue defined in terms of simple notions of power. It is, in sum, not only the classic version of a state-centric doctrine but also an affirmation of the rightful dominance of the Great Powers and the autonomy of their foreign policies.

We could treat this discussion as being of only historical interest but for one fact: despite Realism's increasing irrelevance as an interpretation of the external world, its hold over the mind of the practitioner is still formidable. Why this should be so can only be explained by the dominant – and thus exceedingly attractive – role which Realism assigns to the 'generalist' practitioner (who gets a hunting license on all issues in spite of an absence of substantive expertise); and by the more general consideration that all doctrines persist at the practical level much beyond the point they begin to be assailed at the theoretical level. After all, for the practitioner to abandon or question what he considers to be his own particular expertise is to abandon or question the only thing which separates him from outsiders, and that is very threatening.

The greatest danger in this situation is that Realism is becoming even more irrelevant to the international system in the process of emerging. What we may be witnessing is the first systemic revolution occurring without the intervention of general war or the development of a wholly new kind of military technology. The central point is that the traditional security issue is no longer likely to be the dominant consideration in world politics. I am *very* far from asserting that security will no longer be an issue or that it will somehow disappear from the calculations of states – some analysts of the emerging system seem to take this position, at least implicitly, thus acting as if the realm of security and the realm of inter-dependence were in fact completely autonomous. It is clear, however, that security will be only one of the issues of world politics, albeit a crucial one, for it will have to share prominence with a range of issues heretofore left to technicians or to the play of domestic politics.

The growing interdependence of economic, social, and cultural matters within the state system obviously implies a system in which the autonomy and sovereignty of all the members – great and small – is being eroded. Rational decision-making on such issues requires a degree of international cooperation well beyond anything which has occurred in the field of security. (Even in NATO, for example, the United States always determined strategic questions by itself even though they affected all the allies.) This is particularly true because there is no guarantee that these issues will reduce the degree of conflict in the international system *unless* they are handled in a manner which is minimally satisfactory to all concerned. Inter-dependence clearly could just as well lead to trade wars and an insane effort to achieve autarchy as it could to increased prosperity and welfare; only a new style of decision-making and a change in basic thought patterns could turn these developments into an opportunity to enhance the degree of cooperation in the system. Finally, it deserves some mention that the security issue itself is becoming (or perhaps one should say, is finally being recognized as) increasingly one involving interdependence, as the recent agreements on the hot line and nuclear accidents attest. It will become even more so if nuclear weapons proliferate and arms technology itself continues to grow in complexity. Even a more mundane, but very critical, security issue like the control of conventional arms cannot be handled by any traditional formula – if it can be handled at all.

The attitudes and predispositions which Realism fosters constitute a classically inappropriate response to these developments. With its overly narrow conception of politics, and with its antiquated notions of sovereignty, Great Power dominance and the autonomy of foreign policy, the Realist response is bound to create conflict and destroy the possibility of working out new forms of cooperation. The potential which these issues have for creating either cooperation or conflict means that they must be deliberately manipulated to encourage cooperation; it may even be necessary to adopt a decision-making style borrowed from domestic politics, or to begin to take functions like planning seriously. We may also be compelled to contemplate other heresies. The Realist mentality would find it virtually impossible to even think about these matters in their proper dimension; worse yet, since Realism presupposes conflict, it is likely to turn the politics of interdependence into another exercise in the politics of security.

4.2 Three ideologies of political economy

Robert Gilpin

Source: *The Political Economy of International Relations* (Princeton University Press, Princeton, 1987), pp. 25–64.

In the book from which this section is drawn, Gilpin uses three ideologies or perspectives – liberalism, economic nationalism and Marxism – to examine a range of specific issues such as trade, investment and development, related to the international political economy. In this section he provides an overview and critique of each ideology and elaborates on what he means by an ideology. Although a liberal by persuasion, Gilpin concludes that Marxism identifies problems which liberalism may not be able to overcome.

Over the past century and a half, the ideologies of liberalism, nationalism, and Marxism have divided humanity. This book uses 'ideology' to refer to 'systems of thought and belief by which [individuals and groups] explain [. . .] how their social system operates and what principles it exemplifies' (Heilbroner, 1985, p. 107). The conflict among these three moral and intellectual positions has revolved around the role and significance of the market in the organization of society and economic affairs.

Through an evaluation of the strengths and weaknesses of these three ideologies it is possible to illuminate the study of the field of international political economy. Although my values are those of liberalism, the world in which we live is one best described by the ideas of economic nationalism and occasionally by those of Marxism as well. Eclecticism may not be the route to theoretical precision, but sometimes it is the only route available.

The three ideologies differ on a broad range of questions such as: What is the significance of the market for economic growth and the distribution of wealth among groups and societies? What ought to be the role of markets in the organization of domestic and international society? What is the effect of the market system on issues of war or peace? These and similar questions are central to discussions of international political economy.

These three ideologies are fundamentally different in their conceptions of the relationships among society, state, and market, and it may not be an exaggeration to say that every controversy in the field of international political economy is ultimately reducible to differing conceptions of these relationships. The intellectual clash is not merely of historical interest. Economic liberalism, Marxism, and economic nationalism are all very much alive at the end of the twentieth century; they define the conflicting perspectives that individuals have with regard to the implications of the market system for domestic and international society. Many of the issues that were controversial in the eighteenth and nineteenth centuries are once again being intensely debated.

It is important to understand the nature and content of these contrasting 'ideologies' of political economy. The term 'ideology' is used rather than 'theory' because each position entails a total belief system concerning the nature of human beings and society and is thus akin to what Thomas Kuhn has called a paradigm (Kuhn, 1962). As Kuhn demonstrates, intellectual commitments are held tenaciously and can seldom be dislodged by logic or by contrary evidence. This is due to the fact that these commitments or ideologies allege to provide scientific descriptions of how the world *does* work while they also constitute normative positions regarding how the world *should* work.

Although scholars have produced a number of 'theories' to explain the relationship of economics and politics, these three stand out and have had a profound influence on scholarship and political affairs. In highly oversimplified terms, economic nationalism (or, as it was originally called, mercantilism), which developed from the practice of statesmen in the early modern period, assumes and advocates the primacy of politics over economics. It is essentially a doctrine of state-building and asserts that the market should be subordinate to the pursuit of state interests. It argues that political factors do, or at least should, determine economic relations. Liberalism, which emerged from the Enlightenment in the writings of Adam Smith and others, was a reaction to mercantilism and has become embodied in orthodox economics. It assumes that politics and economics exist, at least ideally, in separate spheres; it argues that markets – in the interest of efficiency, growth, and consumer choice – should be free from political interference. Marxism, which appeared in the mid-nineteenth century as a reaction against liberalism and classical economics, holds that economics drives politics. Political conflict arises from struggle among classes over the distribution of wealth. Hence, political conflict will cease with the elimination of the market and of a society of classes.

[Gilpin then provides a more detailed discussion of the three ideologies. He concludes that they represent 'intellectual commitments' or 'acts of faith' because they cannot be disproved by logical argument or empirical evidence. He goes on to present several reasons why ideologies are resistant to empirical testing.]

In the first place, they are based on assumptions about people or society that cannot be subjected to empirical tests. For example, the liberal concept of rational individuals cannot be verified or falsified; individuals who appear to be acting in conflict with their own interest may actually be acting on incorrect information or be seeking to maximize a goal unknown to the observer and thus be fulfilling the basic assumption of liberalism. Moreover, liberals would argue that although a particular individual in a particular case might be shown to have behaved irrationally, in the aggregate the assumption of rationality is a valid one.

Second, predictive failure of a perspective can always be argued away through the introduction into the analysis of ad hoc hypotheses. Marxism is replete with attempts to explain the predictive failures of Marxist theory. Lenin, for example, developed the concept of 'false consciousness' to account for the fact that workers became trade unionists rather than members of a revolutionary proletariat. Lenin's theory of capitalist imperialism may also be viewed as an effort to explain the failure of Marx's predictions regarding the collapse of capitalism. More recently, as will be discussed below, Marxists have been compelled to formulate elaborate theories of the state to explain the emergence of the welfare state and its acceptance by capitalists, a development that Lenin said was impossible.

Third, and most important, the three perspectives have different purposes and to some extent exist at different levels of analysis. Both nationalists and Marxists, for example, can accept most of liberal economics as a tool of analysis while rejecting many of its assumptions and normative foundations. Thus Marx used classical economics with great skill, but his purpose was to embody it in a grand theory of the origins, dynamics, and end of capitalism. The fundamental difference, in fact, between liberalism and Marxism involves the questions asked and their sociological assumptions rather than the economic methodology that they employ.

As reformulated by Lenin, Marxism has become nearly indistinguishable from the doctrine of political realism. Political realism, like economic nationalism, stresses the primacy of the state and national security. Although the two are very close, realism is essentially a political position whereas economic nationalism is an economic one. Or, put another way, economic nationalism is based on the realist doctrine of international relations.

Both in Lenin's theory and in political realism, states struggle for wealth and power, and the differential growth of power is the key to international conflict and political change. However, the assumptions of the two theories regarding the basis of human motivation, the theory of the state, and the nature of the international system are fundamentally different. Marxists regard human nature as malleable and as easily corrupted by capitalism and correctable by socialism; realists believe that political conflict results from an unchanging human nature.

Whereas Marxists believe that the state is ultimately the servant of the dominant economic class, realists see the state as a relative autonomous entity pursuing national interests that cannot be reduced to the particularistic interests of any class. For Marxists, the international system and foreign policy are determined by the structure of the domestic economy; for realists, the nature of the international system is the fundamental determinant of foreign policy. In short, Marxists regard war, imperialism, and the state as evil manifestations of a capitalism that will disappear with the communist revolution; realists hold them to be inevitable features of an anarchical international political system.

The difference between the two perspectives, therefore, is considerable. For the Marxist, though the state and the struggles among states are a consequence of the capitalist mode of production, the future will bring a realm of true harmony and peace following the inevitable revolution that the evil capitalist mode of production will spawn. The realist, on the other hand, believes there will be no such nirvana because of the inherently self-centered nature of human beings and the anarchy of the international system itself. The struggle among groups and states is virtually ceaseless, although there is occasionally a temporary respite. It seems unlikely that either prediction will ever receive scientific verification.

Each of the three perspectives has strengths and weaknesses, to be further explored below. Although no perspective provides a complete and satisfactory understanding of the nature and dynamism of the international political economy, together they provide useful insights.

Critique of economic liberalism

Liberalism embodies a set of analytical tools and policy prescriptions that enable a society to maximize its return from scarce resources; its commitment to efficiency and the maximization of total wealth provides much of its strength. The market constitutes the most effective means for organizing economic relations, and the price mechanism operates to ensure that mutual gain and hence aggregate social benefit tend to result from economic exchange. In effect, liberal economics says to a society, whether domestic or international, 'if you wish to be wealthy, this is what you must do'.

From Adam Smith to the present, liberals have tried to discover the laws governing the wealth of nations. Although most liberals consider the laws of economics to be inviolable laws of nature, these laws may best be viewed as prescriptive guides for decision makers. If the laws are violated, there will be costs; the pursuit of objectives other than efficiency will necessarily involve an opportunity cost in terms of lost efficiency. Liberalism emphasizes the fact that such tradeoffs always exist in national policy. An emphasis on equity and redistribution, for example, is doomed to failure in the long run if it neglects considerations of efficiency. For a society to be efficient, as socialist economies have discovered, it cannot totally disregard the pertinent economic 'laws'.

The foremost defense of liberalism is perhaps a negative one. Although it may be true, as Marxists and some nationalists argue, that the alternative to a liberal system could be one in which all gain equally, it is also possible that the alternative could be one in which all *lose* in absolute terms. Much can be said for the liberal harmony of interest doctrine; yet, as E.H. Carr has pointed out, evidence to support this doctrine has generally been drawn from historical periods in which there was 'unparalleled expansion of production, population and prosperity' (Carr, 1951 [1939], p. 44). When sustaining conditions break down (as happened in the 1930s and threatens to occur again in the closing decades of the century), disharmony displaces harmony and, I shall argue, the consequent breakdown of liberal regimes tends to lead to economic conflict wherein everyone loses.

The major criticism leveled against economic liberalism is that its basic assumptions, such as the existence of rational economic actors, a competitive market, and the like, are unrealistic. In part, this attack is unfair in that liberals knowingly make these simplifying assumptions in order to facilitate scientific research; no science is possible without them. What is more important, as defenders correctly point out, is that they should be judged by their results and ability to predict rather than by their alleged reality. From this perspective and within its own sphere, economics has proven to be a powerful analytical tool. [. . .]

Critique of economic nationalism

The foremost strength of economic nationalism is its focus on the state as the predominant actor in international relations and as an instrument of economic development. Although many have argued that modern economic and technological developments have made the nation-state an anachronism, at the end of the twentieth century the system of nation-states is actually expanding; societies throughout the world are seeking to create strong states capable of organizing and managing national economies, and the number of states in the world is increasing. Even in older states, the spirit of nationalist sentiments can easily be inflamed, as happened in the Falklands War of 1982. Although other actors such as transnational and international organizations do exist and do influence international relations, the economic and military efficiency of the state makes it preeminent over all these other actors.

The second strength of nationalism is its stress on the importance of security and political interests in the organization and conduct of international economic relations. One need not accept the nationalist emphasis on the primary of security considerations to appreciate that the security of the state is a necessary precondition for its economic and political well-being in an anarchic and competitive state system. A state that fails to provide for its own security ceases to be independent. Whatever the objectives of the society, the effects of economic activities upon political independence and domestic welfare always rank high among its concerns.

The third strength of nationalism is its emphasis on the political framework of economic activities, its recognition that markets must function in a world of competitive groups and states. The political relations among these political actors affect the operation of markets just as markets affect the political relations. In fact, the international political system constitutes one of the most important constraints on and determinants of markets. Since states seek to influence markets to their own individual advantage, the role of power is crucial in the creation and sustaining of market relations; even Ricardo's classic example of the exchange of British woolens for Portuguese wine was not free from the exercise of state power. Indeed, as Carr has argued, every economic system must rest on a secure political base (Carr, 1951 [1939]).

One weakness of nationalism is its tendency to believe that international economic relations constitute solely and at all times a zero-sum game, that is, that one state's gain must of necessity be another's loss. Trade, investment, and all other economic relations are viewed by the nationalist primarily in conflictual and distributive terms. Yet, if cooperation occurs, markets *can* bring mutual (albeit not necessarily equal) gain, as the liberal insists. The possibility of benefit for all is the basis of the international market economy. Another weakness of nationalism is due to the fact that the pursuit of power and the pursuit of wealth usually do conflict, at least in the short run. The amassing and exercising of military and other forms of power entail costs to the society, costs that can undercut its economic efficiency. Thus, as Adam Smith argued, the mercantilist policies of eighteenth-century states that identified money with wealth were detrimental to the growth of the real wealth created by productivity increases; he demonstrated that the wealth of nations would have been better served by policies of free trade. Similarly, the tendency today to identify industry with power can weaken the economy of a state. Development of industries without regard to market considerations or comparative advantage can weaken a society economically. Although states in a situation of conflict must on occasion pursue mercantilistic goals and policies, over the long term, pursuit of these policies can be self-defeating.

In addition, nationalism lacks a satisfactory theory of domestic society, the state, and foreign policy. It tends to assume that society and state form a unitary entity and that foreign policy is determined by an objective national interest. Yet, as liberals correctly stress, society is pluralistic and consists of individuals and groups (coalitions of individuals) that try to capture the apparatus of the state and make it serve their own political and economic interests. Although states possess varying degrees of social autonomy and independence in the making of policy, foreign policy (including foreign economic policy) is in large measure the outcome of the conflicts among dominant groups within each society. Trade protectionism and most other nationalist policies result from attempts by one factor of production or another (capital, labor, or land) to acquire a monopoly position and thereby to increase its share of the economic rents. Nationalist policies are most frequently designed to redistribute income from consumers and society as a whole to producer interests. [. . .]

Critique of Marxist theory

Marxism correctly places the economic problem – the production and distribution of material wealth – where it belongs, at or near the center of political life. Whereas liberals tend to ignore the issue of distribution and nationalists are concerned primarily with the *international* distribution of wealth, Marxists focus on both the domestic and the international effects of a market economy on the distribution of wealth. They call attention to the ways in which the rules or regimes governing trade, investment, and other international economic relations affect the distribution of wealth among groups and states. However, it is not necessary to subscribe to the materialist interpretation of history or the primacy of class struggle in order to appreciate that the ways in which individuals earn their living and distribute wealth are a critical determinant of social structure and political behavior.

Another contribution of Marxism is its emphasis on the nature and structure of the division of labor at both the domestic and international levels. As Marx and Engels correctly pointed out in *The German Ideology*, every division of labor implies dependence and therefore a political relationship. In a market economy the economic nexus among groups and states becomes of critical importance in determining their welfare and their political relations. The Marxist analysis, however, is too limited, because economic interdependence is not the only or even the most important set of interstate relations. The political and strategic relations among political actors are of equal or greater significance and cannot be reduced to merely economic considerations, at least not as Marxists define economics.

The Marxist theory of international political economy is also valuable in its focus on international political change. Whereas neither liberalism nor nationalism has a comprehensive theory of social change, Marxism emphasizes the role of economic and technological developments in explaining the dynamics of the international system. As embodied in Lenin's law of uneven development, the differential growth of power among states constitutes an underlying cause of international political change. Lenin was at least partially correct in attributing the First World War to the uneven economic growth of power among industrial states and to conflict over the division of territory. There can be little doubt that the uneven growth of the several European powers and the consequent effects on the balance of power contributed to their collective insecurity. Competition for markets and empires did aggravate interstate relations. Furthermore, the average person's growing awareness of the effects on personal welfare and security of the vicissitudes of the world market and the economic behavior of other states also became a significant element in the arousal of nationalistic antagonisms. For nations and citizens alike, the growth of economic interdependence brought with it a new sense of insecurity, vulnerability, and resentment against foreign political and economic rivals.

Marxists are no doubt also correct in attributing to capitalist economies, at least as we have known them historically, a powerful impulse to expand through trade and especially through the export of capital. The classical liberal economists themselves observed that economic growth and the accumulation of capital create a tendency for the rate of return (profit) on capital to decline. These economists, however, also noted that the decline could be arrested through international trade, foreign investment, and other means. Whereas trade absorbs surplus capital in the manufacture of exports, foreign investment siphons off capital. Thus, classical liberals join Marxists in asserting that capitalist economies have an inherent tendency to export goods and surplus capital.

This tendency has led to the conclusion that the nature of capitalism is international and that its internal dynamics encourage outward expansionism. In a closed capitalist economy and in the absence of technological advance, underconsumption, surplus capital, and the resulting decline in the rate of profit would eventually lead to what John Stuart Mill called 'the stationary state'. Yet, in an open world economy characterized by expanding capitalism, population growth, and continuing improvement in productivity through technological advance, there is no inherent economic reason for economic stagnation to take place. [. . .]

The principal weakness of Marxism as a theory of international political economy results from its failure to appreciate the role of political and strategic factors in international relations. Although one can appreciate the insights of Marxism, it is not necessary to accept the Marxist theory that the dynamic of modern international relations is caused by the needs of capitalist economies to export goods and surplus capital. For example, to the extent that the uneven growth of national economies leads to war, this is due to national rivalries, which can occur regardless of the nature of domestic economies – witness the conflict between China and the Soviet Union. Although competition for markets and for capital outlets can certainly be a cause of tension and one factor causing imperialism and war, this does not provide an adequate explanation for the foreign policy behavior of capitalist states.

The historical evidence, for example, does not support Lenin's attribution of the First World War to the logic of capitalism and the market system. The most important territorial disputes among the European powers, which precipitated the war, were not those about overseas colonies, as Lenin argued, but lay within Europe itself. The principal conflict leading to the war involved redistribution of the Balkan territories of the decaying Ottoman Empire. And insofar as the source of this conflict was economic, it lay in the desire of the Russian state for access to the Mediterranean. Marxism cannot explain the fact that the three major imperial rivals – Great Britain, France, and Russia – were in fact on the same side in the ensuing conflict and that they fought against a Germany that had few foreign policy interests outside Europe itself.

In addition, Lenin was wrong in tracing the basic motive force of imperialism to the internal workings of the capitalist system. As Benjamin J. Cohen has pointed out in his analysis of the Marxist theory of imperialism, the political and strategic conflicts of the European powers were more important; it was at least in part the stalemate on the Continent among the Great Powers that forced their interstate competition into the colonial world. Every one of these colonial conflicts (if one excludes the Boer War) was in fact settled through diplomatic means. And, finally, the overseas colonies of the European powers were simply of little economic consequence. As Lenin's own data show, almost all European overseas investment was directed to the 'lands of recent settlement' (the United States, Canada, Australia, South Africa, Argentina, etc.) rather than to the dependent colonies in what today we call the Third World. In fact, contrary to Lenin's view that politics follows investment, international finance during this period was largely a servant of foreign policy, as was also the case with French loans to Czarist Russia. Thus, despite its proper focus on political change, Marxism is seriously flawed as a theory of political economy.

[Despite its serious limitations as a theory of the capitalist world economy, Gilpin insists that Marxists have drawn attention to three important issues in the contemporary world: (1) the economic and political implications of uneven economic growth; (2) the impact of the market economy on foreign policy; and (3) the capacity of a market economy to reform its less desirable features. Gilpin disagrees with the Marxist analyses of these issues and argues that the development of the welfare state has alleviated some of the problems identified by the Marxists. But he acknowledges that the future of capitalism remains problematic. He concludes by looking at the capacity of capitalism to survive.]

Welfare capitalism in a non-welfare internationalist capitalist world

[. . .] It is possible that, with the advent of the welfare state, the inherent contradictions of capitalism have simply been transferred from the domestic level of the nation-state to the international level. At this level there is no welfare state; there is no world government to apply Keynesian policies of demand management, to coordinate conflicting national policies, or to counter tendencies toward economic disequilibrium. In contrast to domestic society, there is no state to compensate the losers, as is exemplified in the dismissal by wealthy countries of the demands of the less developed countries for a New International Economic Order (NIEO); nor is there an effective international government response to cheating and market failures.

In the anarchy of international relations, the law of uneven development and the possibility of intracapitalist clashes still applies. One could even argue that the advent of national welfare states has accentuated the economic conflicts among capitalist societies. The new commitment of the capitalist welfare state to full employment and domestic economic well-being causes it to substitute interventionist policies for the free play of market forces and thereby brings it into conflict with the policies of other states pursuing a similar set of economic goals.

Welfare states are potentially highly nationalistic because governments have become accountable to their citizenry for the elimination of economic suffering; sometimes the best way to achieve this goal is to pass on economic difficulties to other societies. In times of economic crisis public pressures encourage national governments to shift the burdens of unemployment and economic adjustment to other societies; thus, economic and interstate competition through the market mechanism subtly shifts to interstate conflict for economic and political advantage. This nationalistic struggle to gain economic advantage and to shift the costs of economic distress to others again threatens the future of international capitalism.

The issue of the future of capitalist society in the era of the welfare state is central to the question of the applicability of the core of Marx's general theory of historical development to the world of the late twentieth century. One proposition of Marx's theory was that 'no social order ever perishes before all the productive forces for which there is room in it have developed; and new, higher relations of production never appear before the material conditions of their existence have matured in the womb of the old society itself' (Marx, 1977 [1859], p. 390), that is, one mode of production is not transcended by the next until it has exhausted its inherent productive potential. Each phase of human experience, according to Marxism, has its own historical mission to fulfill in elevating human productive capacities and thereby setting the stage for the phase to follow. Each mode advances until further progress is no longer possible; then historical necessity dictates that the fetters holding back society are removed by the class chosen to carry it to the next level of material achievement and human liberation.

The implications of this formulation are intriguing for the future of capitalism envisioned by Marxist theory. According to Marx, the historical function of capitalism was to develop the world and its productive potential and then to bequeath to its heir, socialism, a fully developed and industrialized world economy. Although Marx provided no timetable for this cataclysmic event to take place, he lived out his life in the expectation that the revolution was imminent.

As Albert Hirschman has shown, Marx failed to recognize (or more likely suppressed) the significance of these ideas for his analysis of the eventual demise of capitalism, that is, if no mode of production comes to an end until it plays out its historical role and if the assigned task of capitalism is to develop the world, then the capitalist mode of production has many decades, perhaps centuries or even millennia, yet to run (Hirschman, 1981, ch. 7). If one further discounts, as Marxists do, the 'limits to growth' argument, capitalism's assigned task of the economic development of the planet, including its oceans and nearby space, will require a very long time indeed.

Hirschman suggests that this must have been an uncomfortable thought for Marx, who until his dying day was so frequently disappointed in his longing to see the coming of the revolution. In Hirschman's view, this explains why Marx focused on European capitalism as a closed rather than an open economy and why he failed to develop a theory of imperialism even though one would have expected this of him as an assiduous student of Hegel. As Hirschman points out, Hegel anticipated all subsequent theories of capitalist imperialism.

Hirschman concludes that Marx, in his own writings, suppressed Hegel's theory of capitalist imperialism because of its disturbing implications for Marx's predictions concerning the survivability of capitalism. If no social system is displaced by another until it exhausts the productive potential inherent in it, then an imperialistic capitalism as it expands beyond Europe into Asia, Africa, and elsewhere will add new life to the capitalist mode of production. Through the mechanisms of overseas trade and foreign investment, the inevitable collapse of capitalism may thus be postponed for centuries. Indeed, if such a collapse must await the elevation of the developing world to the economic and technological levels of the most advanced economy, then in a world of continuing technological advance, the requisite full development of the productive capacities of capitalism may never be reached.

Rosa Luxemburg appears to have been the first major Marxist theorist to appreciate the historic significance of this reasoning; she argued that as long as capitalism remains an open system and there are underdeveloped lands into which the capitalist mode of production can expand, Marx's prediction of economic stagnation and political revolution will remain unfulfilled. In response to this troubling (at least for Marxists) prospect, Lenin's *Imperialism*, as noted earlier, transformed the Marxist critique of international capitalism. He argued that although capitalism does develop the world and is an economic success, the closing-in of political space through capitalist imperialism and the territorial division of the globe among rising and declining capitalist powers leads to international conflict. Thus, Lenin argued that the masses would revolt against capitalism as a war-prone political system rather than as a failed economic system.

Whether or not one accepts these several formulations and reformulations of Marxist thought, they do raise a fundamental issue. As Marx himself pointed out, the logic of the dynamics of a market or capitalist economy is expansive and international. The forces of the market reach out and bring the whole world within their confines, and they are destructive of traditional ways. The basic anarchy of the market mechanism produces instabilities in the lives of individuals and whole societies.

The modern welfare state and protectionism have developed to cushion these deleterious effects, and herein lies the most serious problem for the capitalist system and its survival. As Keynes appreciated, the logic of the welfare state is to close the economy, because the government must be able to isolate the economy from external restraints and disturbances in order to control and manage it. The international flow of trade, money, and finance undermines the Keynesian management of an economy by decreasing domestic policy autonomy. Goods, Keynes wrote at the height of the Great Depression, should be 'homespun', and capital should stay at home where it can benefit the nation and the nation's working class.

Thus, the logic of the market economy as an inherently expanding global system collides with the logic of the modern welfare state. While solving the problem of a closed economy, the welfare state has only transferred the fundamental problem of the market economy and its survivability to the international level. The problem of reconciling welfare capitalism at the domestic level with the nature of the international capitalist system has become of increasing importance.

The resolution of this basic dilemma between domestic autonomy and international norms is essential to the future viability of the market or capitalist economy. How can one reconcile these two opposed means of organizing economic affairs? Which will prevail – national economic interventionism or the rules of the international market economy? What are the conditions that promote peace and cooperation among market economies? Is a dominant or hegemonic power required to resolve the conflict? A look at the past successes and failures of international capitalism reveals that temporary resolutions of this dilemma or failures to resolve it have been crucial in recent history. In the 1980s the future of the world market economy and the continuing survival of the capitalist mode of production are dependent upon solutions developed or not developed by the United States and its major economic partners.

In another guise this was the problem posed by Richard Cooper in his influential book, *The Economics of Interdependence* (1968). An increasingly interdependent world economy requires either an international agreement to formulate and enforce the rules of an open world market economy and to facilitate the adjustment of differences or a high degree of policy coordination among capitalist states. Without one or the other, a market economy will tend to disintegrate into intense nationalist conflicts over trade, monetary arrangements, and domestic policies. With the relative decline of American power and its ability or willingness to manage the world economy, this issue has become preeminent in the world economy. If there is no increase in policy coordination or decrease in economic interdependence among the leading capitalist economies, the system could indeed break into warring states, just as Lenin predicted.

The long-term survivability of a capitalist or international market system, at least as we have known it since the end of the Second World War, continues to be problematic. Although the welfare state 'solved' the problem of domestic capitalism identified by Marx, continuing conflicts among capitalist societies over trade, foreign investment, and international monetary affairs in the contemporary world remind us that the debate between Lenin and Kautsky over the international nature of capitalism is still relevant. As American power and leadership decline due to the operation of the 'law of uneven development', will confrontation mount and the system collapse as one nation after another pursues 'beggar-my-neighbor' policies, as Lenin would expect? Or, will Kautsky prove to be correct that capitalists are too rational to permit this type of internecine economic slaughter to take place?

References

Carr, E.H. (1951/1939) *The Twenty Years' Crisis, 1919–1939*, 2nd edn (Macmillan, London).

Cooper, R. (1968) *The Economics of Interdependence: Economic Policy in the Atlantic Community* (McGraw-Hill, New York).

Heilbroner, R.L. (1985) *The Nature and Logic of Capitalism* (W.W. Norton, New York).

Hirschman, A.O. (1981) *Essays in Trespassing: Economics to Politics and Beyond* (Cambridge University Press, New York).

Kuhn, T.S. (1962) *The Structure of Scientific Revolutions* (University of Chicago Press, Chicago).

Marx, K. (1977/1950) *Karl Marx: Selected Writings*, edited by David McClellan (Oxford University Press, Oxford).

4.3 The future of the American Empire

Susan Strange

Source: *Journal of International Affairs*, vol. 42, no. 1 (1988), pp. 1–17.

Strange insists that arguments about the hegemonic decline of the United States have failed to take account of what she calls the structural power of the modern state. To do this, however, it is necessary to break away from the territorially based conception of power which has acted as a perspectival strait-jacket on attempts to understand the contemporary international system.

[Strange begins by arguing that the outcome of the debate about whether or not the US has lost its hegemonic status in the international system has practical consequences which will affect future policy choices by people in business, banking and government. The 'school of decline' is seen to make three claims: (1) the power of the US has declined; (2) Great Powers inevitably decline; (3) a likely consequence of the US decline will be political instability and economic disorder in the international system. Strange goes on to challenge each of these claims while accepting that we are approaching a fork in the road and that governments are facing 'momentous choices' ahead which may dwarf the outcome of the debate about US decline.]

American power

Paul Kennedy, in common with the rest of the decline school, starts from the age-old premise that 'to be a great power demands a flourishing economic base'.[1] Following Adam Smith the liberal, and Friedrich List the mercantilist, this is then interpreted to mean an economic base of manufacturing industry located within the territorial boundaries of the state. It is this interpretation of 'a flourishing economic base' that is obsolete and therefore open to doubt. Smith and List are both long dead. More recent changes, noted by Peter Drucker[2] among others, in the character of the world economy throw doubt on whether it is manufacturing that is now most important in developing the sinews of war; and, whether it is location within the boundaries of the territory that matters most.

My contention (which should surely be sustained by the champions of American service industries) is that it is the information-rich occupations, whether associated with manufacturing or not, that confer power, much more now than the physical capacity to roll goods off an assembly line. Secondly, I contend that the location of productive capacity is far less important than the location of the people who make the key decisions on what is to be produced, where and how, and who design, direct and manage to sell successfully on a world market. Is it more desirable that Americans should wear blue collars and mind the machines or that they should wear white collars and design, direct and finance the whole operation?

That is why all the figures so commonly trotted out about the US share of world manufacturing capacity, or the declining US share of world exports of manufactures are so misleading – *because they are territorially based*. Worse, they are irrelevant. What matters is the share of world output – of primary products, minerals and food and manufactured goods and services – that is under the direction of the executives of US companies. That share can be US-directed even if the enterprise directly responsible is only half owned by an American parent, and even, in some cases of technological dependence, where it is not owned at all but where the license to produce is granted or refused by people in the United States. The largest stock of foreign direct investments is still held by US corporations – even though the figures are neither precise, complete nor comprehensive. The fact that the current outflow from Japan is greater than that from the United States merely means that the gap is narrowing. But the Japanese still have a long way to go to rival the extent of US corporate operations in Europe, Latin America, Australasia, the Middle East and Africa, the assets of which are often valued at their historical prices not at their current values. [. . .]

At this point some people will object that when production moves away from the territory of the United States, the authority of the US government is diminished. At the same time, the same people sometimes complain against the 'invasion' of the United States by Japanese companies, as if 'selling off the farm' is diminishing the authority of the United States government. Clearly, both cannot be right. Rather, both perceptions seem to me to be wrong. What is happening is that the American Empire is spilling out beyond the frontier and that the very insubstantial nature of frontiers where production is concerned just shows the consolidation of an entirely new kind of nonterritorial empire.

It is that nonterritorial empire that is really the 'flourishing economic base' of US power, not the goods and services produced within the United States. One obvious indication of this fact is that foreign central banks last year spent roughly $140 billion supporting the exchange value of the dollar. Another is that Japanese and other foreign investors financed the lion's share of the US government's budget deficit by buying US government securities and investing in the United States. An empire that can command such resources hardly seems to be losing power. The fact that the United States is still the largest and richest (and mostly open) market for goods and services under one political authority means that all successful foreign companies will want to produce and sell there and will deem it prudent also to produce there, not simply to avoid protectionist barriers but in order to be close to the customers. And the worldwide reach of US-controlled enterprises also means that the capacity of the United States to exercise extraterritorial influence and authority is also greater than that of any other government. If only for security reasons, the ability of Washington to tell US companies in Japan what to do or not to do is immeasurably greater than the ability of Tokyo to tell Japanese companies in the United States what to do.

This points to another major fallacy in the decline school's logic – its inattention to matters of security. The US lead in the ability to make and deliver the means of nuclear destruction is the complement to its lead in influencing, through past investments overseas, the nature, modes and purposes of modern industrial production. Here, too, the gap may be narrowing as South Africa, Israel, India and others claim nuclear capability. Yet there is still no comparison between the military power of the United States to confer, deny or threaten the security of others with that of minor non-Communist states. That military power is now based far less on the capacity to manufacture nuclear weapons than on the capacity to recruit scientists, American or foreign, to keep ahead in design and invention, both offensive and defensive.

Historical parallels

The decline school so far has succeeded in promoting the idea that history teaches that it is 'normal' for great states and empires to decline, especially when they become militarily overextended, or else when they become socially and politically sclerotic, risk-averse and resistant to change or when they overindulge in foreign investment, and for any or all of these reasons when they lose preeminence in agricultural and industrial production, or in trade and military capability. In almost all this American literature on the rise and fall of empires, great attention and weight is characteristically (and for reasons of language and culture, perhaps understandably) given to the British experience. But the trouble with history, as the first great realist writer on international relations, E.H. Carr, rightly observed, is that it is necessarily selective – and that the historian selects facts as a fish shop selects fish, choosing some and discarding or overlooking others. In this debate, the historical analogy between Britain and America is particularly weak; and the other examples selected for consideration show a strong tendency to concentrate on the empires whose decline after the peaking of their power was more or less steady and never reversed.

First, it is not too difficult to show that what Britain and America have had in common – such as a tendency to invest heavily overseas – is much less important than all the differences that mark their experience. Britain's economic decline, beginning around the 1880s, was the result of a neglect of the then advanced technologies – notably in chemicals and engineering. This neglect reflected the weakness and low status of manufacturing industry in British politics and society – a social disdain such as American industry has never had to contend with. Even more important was the effect of two long debilitating wars on the British economy, by comparison with which the American experience of Vietnam was a flea bite. It is arguable that the British economy, dependent as it was on financial power, would not have suffered so great a setback if the whole international financial system on which it lived and prospered had not been twice destroyed – first in the Great War and then in the Second World War. The interwar period was too short – and policies were also ill-chosen – to allow a reversal of this British decline.

Finally, there is the great difference between a small offshore island running a large territorial empire and a great continental power managing (or sometimes mismanaging) a large nonterritorial empire. The island state made the fatal mistake after the Second World War of relying on sheltered colonial and sterling area markets – with disastrous effects on the competitiveness of its export industries and even some of its old, established multinationals. The continental power's confidence in its ability to dominate an open world economy, plus the strong commitment to antitrust policies at home, has created no such weakening crutches for its major transnational corporations.

Secondly, any historical study of empires of the past fails to reveal any standard or uniform pattern of rise and fall. They are like trees. Some grow fast and fall suddenly without warning. Others grow slowly and decay very gradually, even making astonishing recoveries from shock or injury. One author, Michael Doyle, who has shared less in the media attention perhaps because his work lent itself less readily to deterministic interpretations, drew an important conclusion from an analytical survey of empires that included those of the ancient world as well as the later European ones. It is worth quoting:

The historical alternatives had divided between persistence, which necessitated imperial development in both the metropole and the periphery, and decline and fall. Persistence in an extensive empire required that the metropole cross the Augustan threshold to imperial bureaucracy, and perhaps became in effect an equal political partner with the metropole.[3]

In plainer language, what I interpret this to mean is that the empires that lasted longest were those that managed to build a political system suited to the administration of the empire out of one suited to managing the core. In addition, those empires that survived managed to blur the distinction between the ruling groups of the core and the participating allies and associates of the periphery. This is a notion closely related to Gramscian concepts of hegemony and explanations of the persistent strength of capitalist political economies.

Michael Doyle's attention to the Roman Empire, which was much longer-lived than any of the nineteenth-century European empires, is important for the debate. This is so partly because there have been so many conflicting interpretations of its decline, from Edward Gibbon and Thomas Macaulay to Joseph Schumpeter and Max Weber, and partly because most historians seem to agree that it passed through periods of regeneration and reform before it finally broke up in disorder. Michael Mann, for instance, recently identified one such period of reform and regeneration in the twenty years after the accession of Septimus Severus in AD 193:

> Severus began withdrawing crack legions from the frontiers to mobile reserve positions, replacing them at the frontier with a settler militia. This was a more defensive, less confident posture. It also cost more, and so he attempted financial reform, abolishing tax farming and the tax exemption of Rome and Italy.[4]

This comment by a sociologist is interesting because it focuses on two important elements of power in imperial states: relations with key groups in the periphery, and the fiscal system by which unavoidable imperial expenditures are financed. When we consider the future of the American Empire, we find that these two issues are once again crucial to the outcome between Doyle's two alternatives – persistence or decline. Mann describes the Roman Empire as a 'legionary empire', indicating that the role and character of the legions were important in explaining Roman power.

I would argue that America's 'legions', in the integrated financial and production economy of today's world, are not military but economic. They are the corporate enterprises on which the military depends – as President Dwight Eisenhower foresaw in talking about the military-industrial complex. The American Empire in sociological terms therefore could be described as a 'corporation empire' in which the culture and interests of the corporations are sustained by an imperial bureaucracy. But this bureaucracy, largely set up after the Second World War, was not simply a national American one based in Washington, DC. A large and important part of it was and is multinational and works through the major international economic organizations such as the International Monetary Fund (IMF), the World Bank, the Organization for Economic Cooperation and Development (OECD) in Paris and the General Agreement on Tariffs and Trade (GATT) in Geneva.

The other feature of the Roman Empire that I believe is relevant to the current debate is that citizenship was not a matter of domicile, and that there were gradations of civil and political rights and responsibilities, ranging from slaves to senators, which did not depend on what we, today, understand by 'nationality', indicated by possession or nonpossession of a passport. If we can once escape the corset-like intellectual constraints of the conventional study of international relations and liberate our minds to ask new questions we begin to see new things about America's nonterritorial empire. Here, too, citizenship is becoming much more complex and graded than it used to be. The managers of US corporations, in Brazil, for example, may hold Brazilian and not US passports. But they are free to come and go with indefinite visas into the United States and they often exercise considerable delegated power in the running of US-directed enterprises vital to the Brazilian economy. Participation in the cultural empire depends not on passports but on competence in the American language and in many cases participation in US-based professional organizations – like the International Studies Association, for example. Similarly, participation in America's financial empire depends on the possession and use of US dollars and dollar-denominated assets and the ability to compete with US banks and in US financial markets.

Rather like a chrysalis in the metamorphosis from caterpillar to butterfly, the American Empire today combines features of a national-exclusive past with features of a transnational-extensive future. In military matters, it is still narrowly exclusive – though where advanced technology is concerned, even that is changing. Certainly, in financial and cultural matters, the distinction between first-class, passport-holding citizens and second-class, non-passport-holding participants is increasingly blurred. The peripheral allies have been unconsciously recruited into the American Empire. [. . .]

Power and systemic disorder

The third proposition of the decline school has been the one under longest discussion among scholars in international relations. Over most of the past decade, the lead in these discussions has been taken by specialists in the study of international organizations (for example, Joseph Nye, Robert Keohane, John Ruggie and Ernst Haas). It seems to me that they share a wishful reluctance to admit that international organizations, when they are not simply adaptive mechanisms through which states respond to technical change, are either the strategic instruments of national policies and interests, or else merely symbolic gestures toward a desired but unattainable world government. This reluctance to admit the inherent limitations of international organizations leads them subconsciously to the conclusion that it must be hegemonic decline that is the cause of economic instability and disorder and the coincident erosion of earlier international regimes.

This is a proposition that does not stand up well either to the record of recent international economic history or to structural analysis of power in the international political economy. I do not want to repeat myself, but *Casino Capitalism* was an attempt to show two things (among others): there were more ways than one of interpreting recent developments in the international monetary and financial system; and, these developments of the last fifteen years or so could be traced to a series of crucial (and mostly permissive) decisions by governments. Hence, the precarious and unstable state of the global financial structure – which has already been dramatically demonstrated once and probably will be so again – was no fortuitous accident of fate or history.[5]

Since that book was written, I find confirmation that it was not a decline of American power but rather a series of American managerial decisions of dubious wisdom that accounts quite adequately for financial and monetary disorder, without any need to adduce the decline of American hegemonic power. Not only is this the theme of David Calleo's *The Imperious Economy*,[6] it is also to be found buried in the text of Robert Gilpin's chapters on international money and finance:

Beginning with the Vietnam war and continuing into the Reagan Administration, the United States had become more of a 'predatory hegemon' to use John Conybeare's terms (1985), less willing to subordinate its own interests to those of its allies; instead it tended more and more to exploit its hegemonic status for its own narrowly defined purposes.[7]

Gilpin repeats the point twenty pages later, adding: 'Most of the troubles of the world economy in the 1980s have been caused by this shift in American policy.'

It will not escape careful students of this important text that Gilpin's historical analysis, and the use of the word 'mismanagement' with reference to American domestic and foreign financial policy, fundamentally contradicts his concluding thesis that a stable and prosperous world economy in the future calls for an American–Japanese condominium because of lost American hegemony.

Similarly, *States and Markets* extends the definition of international political economy beyond the conventional politics of international economic relations to ask more basic who-gets-what questions.[8] In that volume I find that a structural analysis of the basic issues in any political economy, when applied to the world system, strongly suggests that on balance American structural power may actually have increased in recent decades. It has done so through four interlocking structures. These structures concern the power conferred by the ability to offer, withhold or threaten security (the security structure); the ability to offer, withhold or demand credit (the financial structure); the ability to determine the locus, mode and content of wealth-creating activity (the production structure); and, not least, the ability to influence ideas and beliefs and therefore the kind of knowledge socially prized and sought after, and to control (and, through language, to influence) access to and communication of that knowledge (the knowledge structure).

Such a structural analysis suggests the existence under predominant American power and influence of an empire the likes of which the world has never seen before, a nonterritorial empire, whose only borders are the frontiers of the socialist great powers and their allies. It is not, in fact, such an eccentric idea. Two former US secretaries of state recently wrote:

> Far into the future, the United States will have the world's largest and most innovative economy, and will remain a nuclear super-power, a cultural and intellectual leader, a model democracy and a society that provides exceptionally well for its citizens.[9]

What, then, must be done?

[Strange concludes by warning that because the world is at a 'critical juncture' the US must use it enormous structural power and take the lead in future developments. This will involve forging a symbiotic relationship with Japan on the basis of an international 'new deal'. Other new deals will need to be struck with other areas of the world.]

New Deals, however, do not drop like manna from heaven. They do not come about without political vision and inspiration, or without hard intellectual effort to find the sustaining optimal bargain. Optimal bargains are those that last because they go some way to satisfy the needs and aspirations of the governed as well as those of the governors. Only then can the power of those in charge of empires (as of states, local party machines or labor unions) be sustained over the long run. The next four years will show not only Americans but the rest of us who live and work in the American Empire whether the defeatist gloom of the school of decline can be dissipated. They will show whether the necessary vision can still be found in the White House for a series of global New Deals and whether the necessary intellectual effort to design and negotiate them will be generated not only in the bureaucracies, national and international, but in the universities and research institutes of all our countries.

Notes

1   Paul Kennedy, *The Rise and Fall of the Great Powers: Economic Change and Military Conflict from 1500 to 2000* (New York, Random House, 1987).
2   Peter F. Drucker, 'The Changed World Economy', *Foreign Affairs*, 64: 4 (Spring 1986), pp. 768–91.
3   Michael Doyle, *Empires* (Cornell University Press, Ithaca, 1986), p. 353.
4   Michael Mann, *The Sources of Social Power*, vol. 1 (Cambridge University Press, New York, 1986).
5   Susan Strange, *Casino Capitalism* (Basil Blackwell, New York, 1986).
6   David P. Calleo, *The Imperious Economy* (Harvard University Press, Cambridge, Mass., 1962).
7   Robert Gilpin, *The Political Economy of International Relations* (Princeton University Press, Princeton, New Jersey, 1987), p. 345.
8   Susan Strange, *States and Markets* (Frances Pinter, London, 1988).
9   Henry Kissinger and Cyrus Vance, 'Bipartisan Objectives for American Foreign Policy', *Foreign Affairs*, 66: 5 (Summer 1988), pp. 899–921.

4.4 Social forces, states and world orders: beyond international relations theory

Robert W. Cox

Source: *Millennium: Journal of International Studies*, vol. 10, no. 2 (1981), pp. 126–55.

Cox is interested in the way that the structure of world order can change and he argues that to understand this process it is necessary to develop a methodology which can transcend the outlook of any specific perspective. The problem with the dominant perspective of realism is that it claims to have identified ahistorical truths. The claim, according to Cox, is ideological. He identifies realism as a problem-solving form of theory which works within and helps to sustain a state-dominated world order. Cox argues in favour of a critical form of theory which focuses not only on how a particular form of world order is maintained but also on how it can be transformed.

[Cox begins by arguing that theory must always be based upon changing practice and empirical historical study.]

On perspectives and purposes

Theory is always *for* someone and *for* some purpose. All theories have a perspective. Perspectives derive from a position in time and space, specifically social and political time and space. The world is seen from a standpoint definable in terms of nation or social class, of dominance or subordination, of rising or declining power, of a sense of immobility or of present crisis, of past experience, and of hopes and expectations for the future. Of course, sophisticated theory is never just the expression of a perspective. The more sophisticated a theory is, the more it reflects upon and transcends its own perspective; but the initial perspective is always contained within a theory and is relevant to its explication. There is, accordingly, no such thing as theory in itself, divorced from a standpoint in time and space. When any theory so represents itself, it is the more important to examine it as ideology, and to lay bare its concealed perspective.

To each such perspective the enveloping world raises a number of issues; the pressures of social reality present themselves to consciousness as problems. A primary task of theory is to become clearly aware of these problems, to enable the mind to come to grips with the reality it confronts. Thus, as reality changes, old concepts have to be adjusted or rejected and new concepts forged in an initial dialogue between the theorist and the particular world he tries to comprehend. This initial dialogue concerns the *problematic* proper to a particular perspective. Social and political theory is history-bound at its origin, since it is always traceable to a historically conditioned awareness of certain problems and issues, a problematic, while at the same time it attempts to transcend the particularity of its historical origins in order to place them within the framework of some general propositions or laws.

Beginning with its problematic, theory can serve two distinct purposes. One is a simple, direct response: to be a guide to help solve the problems posed within the terms of the particular perspective which was the point of departure. The other is more reflective upon the process of theorizing itself: to become clearly aware of the perspective which gives rise to theorizing, and its relation to other perspectives (to achieve a perspective on perspectives); and to open up the possibility of choosing a different valid perspective from which the problematic becomes one of creating an alternative world. Each of these purposes gives rise to a different kind of theory.

The first purpose gives rise to *problem-solving* theory. It takes the world as it finds it, with the prevailing social and power relationships and the institutions into which they are organized, as the given framework for action. The general aim of problem-solving is to make these relationships and institutions work smoothly by dealing effectively with particular sources of trouble. Since the general pattern of institutions and relationships is not called into question, particular problems can be considered in relation to the specialized areas of activity in which they arise. Problem-solving theories are thus fragmented among a multiplicity of spheres or aspects of action, each of which assumes a certain stability in the other spheres (which enables them in practice to be ignored) when confronting a problem arising within its own. The strength of the problem-solving approach lies in its ability to fix limits or parameters to a problem area and to reduce the statement of a particular problem to a limited number of variables which are amenable to relatively close and precise examination. The *ceteris paribus* assumption, upon which such theorizing is based, makes it possible to arrive at statements of laws or regularities which appear to have general validity but which imply, of course, the institutional and relational parameters assumed in the problem-solving approach.

The second purpose leads to *critical theory*. It is critical in the sense that it stands apart from the prevailing order of the world and asks how that order came about. Critical theory, unlike problem-solving theory, does not take institutions and social and power relations for granted but calls them into question by concerning itself with their origins and how and whether they might be in the process of changing. It is directed toward an appraisal of the very framework for action, or problematic, which problem-solving theory accepts as its parameters. Critical theory is directed to the social and political complex as a whole rather than to the separate parts. As a matter of practice, critical theory, like problem-solving theory, takes as its starting point some aspect or particular sphere of human activity. But whereas the problem-solving approach leads to further analytical subdivision and limitation of the issue to be dealt with, the critical approach leads toward the construction of a larger picture of the whole of which the initially contemplated part is just one component, and seeks to understand the processes of change in which both parts and whole are involved.

Critical theory is theory of history in the sense of being concerned not just with the past but with a continuing process of historical change. Problem-solving theory is nonhistorical or ahistorical, since it, in effect, posits a continuing present (the permanence of the institutions and power relations which constitute its parameters). The strength of the one is the weakness of the other. Because it deals with a changing reality, critical theory must continually adjust its concepts to the changing object it seeks to understand and explain. These concepts and the accompanying methods of inquiry seem to lack the precision that can be achieved by problem-solving theory, which posits a fixed order as its point of reference. This relative strength of problem-solving theory, however, rests upon a false premise, since the social and political order is not fixed but (at least in a long-range perspective) is changing. Moreover, the assumption of fixity is not merely a convenience of method, but also an ideological bias. Problem-solving theories can be represented, in the broader perspective of critical theory, as serving particular national, sectional, or class interests, which are comfortable within the given order. Indeed, the purpose served by problem-solving theory is conservative, since it aims to solve the problems arising in various parts of a complex whole in order to smooth the functioning of the whole. This aim rather belies the frequent claim of problem-solving theory to be value-free. It is methodologically value-free insofar as it treats the variables it considers as objects (as the chemist treats molecules or the physicist forces and motion); but it is value-bound by virtue of the fact that it implicitly accepts the prevailing order as its own framework. Critical theory contains problem-solving theories within itself, but contains them in the form of identifiable ideologies, thereby pointing to their conservative consequences, not to their usefulness as guides to action. Problem-solving theory stakes its claims on its greater precision and, to the extent that it recognizes critical theory at all, challenges the possibility of achieving any scientific knowledge of historical processes.

Critical theory is, of course, not unconcerned with the problems of the real world. Its aims are just as practical as those of problem-solving theory, but it approaches practice from a perspective which transcends that of the existing order, which problem-solving theory takes as its starting point. Critical theory allows for a normative choice in favor of a social and political order different from the prevailing order, but it limits the range of choice to alternative orders which are feasible transformations of the existing world. A principal objective of critical theory, therefore, is to clarify this range of possible alternatives. Critical theory thus contains an element of utopianism in the sense that it can represent a coherent picture of an alternative order, but its utopianism is constrained by its comprehension of historical processes. It must reject improbable alternatives just as it rejects the permanency of the existing order. In this way critical theory can be a guide to strategic action for bringing about an alternative order, whereas problem-solving theory is a guide to tactical actions which, intended or unintended, sustain the existing order.

The perspectives of different historical periods favor one or the other kind of theory. Periods of apparent stability or fixity in power relations favor the problem-solving approach. The Cold War was one such period. In international relations, it fostered a concentration upon the problems of how to manage an apparently enduring relationship between two superpowers. However, a condition of uncertainty in power relations beckons to critical theory as people seek to understand the opportunities and risks of change. Thus the events of the 1970s generated a sense of greater fluidity in power relationships, of a many-faceted crisis, crossing the threshold of uncertainty and opening the opportunity for a new development of critical theory directed to the problems of world order. To reason about possible future world orders now, however, requires a broadening of our inquiry beyond conventional international relations, so as to encompass basic processes at work in the development of social forces and forms of state, and in the structure of global political economy. Such, at least, is the central argument of this essay.

[Cox goes on to argue that there are two currents of thought – realism and Marxism – which have something important to say about international relations and world order. He suggests that while both draw on problem-solving and critical theory, realism is primarily informed by problem-solving theory whereas Marxism is informed by critical theory. He then restates the basic premises which underlie critical theory.]

1   An awareness that action is never absolutely free but takes place within a framework for action which constitutes its problematic. Critical theory would start with this

framework, which means starting with historical inquiry or an appreciation of the human experience that gives rise to the need for theory.

2   A realization that not only action but also theory is shaped by the problematic. Critical theory is conscious of its own relativity but through this consciousness can achieve a broader time-perspective and become less relative than problem-solving theory. It knows that the task of theorizing can never be finished in an enclosed system but must continually be begun anew.

3   The framework for action changes over time and a principal goal of critical theory is to understand these changes.

4   This framework has the form of a historical structure, a particular combination of thought patterns, material conditions and human institutions which has a certain coherence among its elements. These structures do not determine people's actions in any mechanical sense but constitute the context of habits, pressures, expectations and constraints within which action takes place.

5   The framework or structure within which action takes place is to be viewed, not from the top in terms of the requisites for its equilibrium or reproduction (which would quickly lead back to problem-solving), but rather from the bottom or from outside in terms of the conflicts which arise within it and open the possibility of its transformation.

Frameworks for action: historical structures

At its most abstract, the notion of a framework for action or historical structure is a picture of a particular configuration of forces. This configuration does not determine actions in any direct, mechanical way but imposes pressures and constraints. Individuals and groups may move with the pressures or resist and oppose them, but they cannot ignore them. To the extent that they do successfully resist a prevailing historical structure, they buttress their actions with an alternative, emerging configuration of forces, a rival structure.

Three categories of forces (expressed as potentials) interact in a structure: material capabilities, ideas and institutions (see Figure 1). No one-way determinism need be assumed among these three; the relationships can be assumed to be reciprocal. The question of which way the lines of force run is always a historical question to be answered by a study of the particular case.

Material capabilities are productive and destructive potentials. In their dynamic form these exist as technological and organizational capabilities, and in their accumulated forms as natural resources which technology can transform, stocks of equipment (for example, industries and armaments), and the wealth which can command these.

Ideas are broadly of two kinds. One kind consists of intersubjective meanings, or those shared notions of the nature of social relations which tend to perpetuate habits and expectations of behavior. Examples of intersubjective meanings in contemporary world politics are the notions that people are organized and commanded by states which have authority over

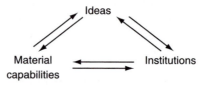

Figure 1

defined territories; that states relate to one another through diplomatic agents; that certain rules apply for the protection of diplomatic agents as being in the common interest of all states; and that certain kinds of behavior are to be expected when conflict arises between states, such as negotiation, confrontation, or war. These notions, though durable over long periods of time, are historically conditioned. The realities of world politics have not always been represented in precisely this way and may not be in the future. It is possible to trace the origins of such ideas and also to detect signs of a weakening of some of them.

The other kind of ideas relevant to a historical structure are collective images of social order held by different groups of people. These are differing views as to both the nature and the legitimacy of prevailing power relations, the meanings of justice and public good, and so forth. Whereas intersubjective meanings are broadly common throughout a particular historical structure and constitute the common ground of social discourse (including conflict), collective images may be several and opposed. The clash of rival collective images provides evidence of the potential for alternative paths of development and raises questions as to the possible material and institutional basis for the emergence of an alternative structure.

Institutionalization is a means of stabilizing and perpetuating a particular order. Institutions reflect the power relations prevailing at their point of origin and tend, at least initially, to encourage collective images consistent with these power relations. Eventually, institutions take on their own life; they can become a battleground of opposing tendencies, or rival institutions may reflect different tendencies. Institutions are particular amalgams of ideas and material power which in turn influence the development of ideas and material capabilities.

There is a close connection between institutionalization and what Gramsci called hegemony. Institutions provide ways of dealing with conflicts so as to minimize the use of force. There is an enforcement potential in the material power relations underlying any structure, in that the strong can clobber the weak if they think it necessary. But force will not have to be used in order to ensure the dominance of the strong to the extent that the weak accept the prevailing power relations as legitimate. This the weak may do if the strong see their mission as hegemonic and not merely dominant or dictatorial, that is, if they are willing to make concessions that will secure the weak's acquiescence in their leadership and if they can express this leadership in terms of universal or general interests, rather than just as serving their own particular interests. Institutions may become the anchor for such a hegemonic strategy since they lend themselves both to the representations of diverse interests and to the universalization of policy.

It is convenient to be able to distinguish between hegemonic and nonhegemonic structures, that is to say between those in which the power basis of the structure tends to recede into the background of consciousness, and those in which the management of power relations is always in the forefront. Hegemony cannot, however, be reduced to an institutional dimension. One must beware of allowing a focus upon institutions to obscure either changes in the relationship of material forces, or the emergence of ideological challenge to an erstwhile prevailing order. Institutions may be out of phase with these other aspects of reality and their efficacy as a means of regulating conflict (and thus their hegemonic function) thereby undermined. They may be an expression of hegemony but cannot be taken as identical to hegemony.

The method of historical structures is one of representing what can be called limited totalities. The historical structure does not represent the whole world but rather a particular sphere of human activity in its historically located totality. The *ceteris paribus* problem, which falsifies problem-solving theory by leading to an assumption of total stasis, is avoided by juxtaposing the connecting historical structures in related spheres of action. Dialectic is introduced, first, by deriving the definition of a particular structure, not from some abstract model of a social system or mode of production, but from a study of the historical situation to which it relates, and second, by looking for the emergence of rival structures expressing alternative possibilities of development. The three sets of forces indicated in Figure 1 are a heuristic device, not categories with a predetermined hierarchy of relationships. Historical structures are contrast models: like ideal types they provide, in a logically coherent form, a simplified representation of a complex reality and an expression of tendencies, limited in their applicability in time and space, rather than fully realized developments.

For the purpose of the present discussion, the method of historical structures is applied to the three levels, or spheres of activity: (1) organization of production, more particularly with regard to the *social forces* engendered by the production process; (2) *forms of state* as derived from a study of state/society complexes; and (3) *world orders*, that is, the particular configurations of forces which successively define the problematic of war or peace for the ensemble of states. Each of these levels can be studied as a succession of dominant and emergent rival structures.

The three levels are interrelated. Changes in the organization of production generate new social forces which, in turn, bring about changes in the structure of states; and the generalization of changes in the structure of states alters the problematic of world order. For instance, as E.H. Carr (1945) argued, the incorporation of the industrial workers (a new social force) as participants within western states from the late nineteenth century, accentuated the movement of these states toward economic nationalism and imperialism (a new form of state), which brought about a fragmentation of the world economy and a more conflictual phase of international relations (the new structure of world order).

The relationship among the three levels is not, however, simply unilinear. Transnational social forces have influenced states through the world structure, as evidenced by the effect of expansive nineteenth-century capitalism, *les bourgeois conquérants*, upon the development of state structures in both core and periphery. Particular structures of world order exert influence over the forms which states take: Stalinism was, at least in part, a response to a sense of threat to the existence of the Soviet state from a hostile world order; the military-industrial complex in core countries justifies its influence today by pointing to the conflictual condition of world order; and the prevalence of repressive militarism in periphery countries can be explained by the external support of imperialism as well as by a particular conjunction of internal forces. Forms of state also affect the development of social forces through the kinds of domination they exert, for example, by advancing one class interest and thwarting others.

Considered separately, social forces, forms of state, and world orders can be represented in a preliminary approximation as particular configurations of material capabilities, ideas and institutions (as indicated in Figure 1). Considered in relation to each other, and thus moving toward a fuller representation of historical process, each will be seen as containing, as well as bearing the impact of, the others (as in Figure 2).

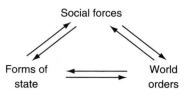

Figure 2

Hegemony and world orders

How are these reciprocal relationships to be read in the present historical conjuncture? Which of the several relationships will tell us the most? A sense of the historicity of concepts suggests that the critical relationships may not be the same in successive historical periods, even within the post-Westphalian era for which the term 'state system' has particular meaning. The approach to a critical theory of world order, adumbrated here, takes the form of an interconnected series of historical hypotheses.

Neo-realism puts the accent on states reduced to their dimension of material force and similarly reduces the structure of world order to the balance of power as a configuration of material forces. Neo-realism, which generally dismisses social forces as irrelevant, is not much concerned with differentiating forms of state (except insofar as 'strong societies' in liberal democratic polities may hamper the use of force by the state or advance particular interests over the national interest), and tends to place a low value on the normative and institutional aspects of world order.

One effort to broaden the realist perspective to include variations in the authority of international norms and institutions is the theory of 'hegemonic stability' which, as stated by Robert Keohane (1980), 'holds that hegemonic structures of power, dominated by a single country, are most conducive to the development of strong international regimes, whose rules are relatively precise and well-obeyed'. The classic illustrations of the theory discussed by Keohane are the *pax britannica* of the mid-nineteenth century and the *pax americana* of the years following the Second World War. The theory appears to be confirmed by the decline in observance of the norms of the nineteenth-century order which accompanied Britain's relative decline in state power from the late-nineteenth century. Exponents of the theory see a similar decline, since the early 1970s, in the observance of norms of the postwar order, relating it to a relative decline in US power. Robert Keohane has tested the theory in particular issue areas (energy, money and trade) on the grounds that power is not a fungible asset, but has to be differentiated according to the contexts in which a state tried to be influential. He finds that, particularly in the areas of trade and money, changes in US power are insufficient to explain the changes that have occurred and need to be supplemented by the introduction of domestic political, economic and cultural factors.

An alternative approach might start by redefining what it is that is to be explained, namely, the relative stability of successive world orders. This can be done by equating stability with a concept of hegemony that is based on a coherent conjunction or fit between a configuration of material power, the prevalent collective image of world order (including certain norms) and a set of institutions which administer the order with a certain semblance of universality (that is, not just as the overt instruments of a particular state's dominance). In this formulation, state power ceases to be the sole explanatory factor and becomes part of what is to be explained. This rephrasing of the question addresses a major difficulty in the neo-realist version signalled by Keohane and others, namely, how to explain the failure of the United States to establish a stable world order in the interwar period despite its preponderance of power. If the dominance of a single state coincides with a stable order on some occasions but not on others, then there may be some merit in looking more closely at what is meant by stability and more broadly at what may be its sufficient conditions. Dominance by a powerful state may be a necessary but not a sufficient condition of hegemony.

The two periods of the *pax britannica* and the *pax americana* also satisfy the reformulated definition of hegemony. In the mid-nineteenth century, Britain's world supremacy was founded on its sea power, which remained free from challenge by a continental state as a result of Britain's ability to play the role of balancer in a relatively fluid balance of power in Europe. The norms of liberal economics (free trade, the gold standard, free movement of capital and persons) gained widespread acceptance with the spread of British prestige, providing a universalistic ideology which represented these norms as the basis of a harmony of interests. While there were no formal international institutions, the ideological separation of economics from politics meant that the City could appear as administrator and regulator according to these universal rules, with British sea power remaining in the background as potential enforcer.

The historical structure was transformed in its three dimensions during the period running from the last quarter of the nineteenth century through the Second World War. During this period British power declined relatively, losing its undisputed supremacy at sea, first with the German challenge and then with the rise of US power; economic liberalism foundered with the rise of protectionism, the new imperialisms and ultimately the end of the gold standard; and the belated and abortive attempt at international institutionalization through the League of Nations, unsustained either by a dominant power or a widely accepted ideology, collapsed in a world increasingly organized into rival power blocs.

The power configuration of the *pax americana* was more rigid than that of the earlier hegemony, taking the form of alliances (all hinging on US power) created in order to contain the Soviet Union. The stabilization of this power configuration created the conditions for the unfolding of a global economy in which the United States played a role similar to that of Britain in the mid-nineteenth century. The United States rarely needed to intervene directly in support of specific national economic interests; by maintaining the rules of an international economic order according to the revised liberalism of Bretton Woods, the strength of US corporations engaged in the pursuit of profits was sufficient to ensure continuing national power. The *pax americana* produced a greater number of formal international institutions than the earlier hegemony. The nineteenth-century separation of politics and economics had been blurred by the experience of the Great Depression and the rise of Keynesian doctrines. Since states now had a legitimate and necessary overt role in national economic management, it became necessary both to multilateralize the administrative management of the international economy and to give it an intergovernmental quality.

The notion of hegemony as a fit between power, ideas and institutions makes it possible to deal with some of the problems in the theory of state dominance as the necessary condition for a stable international order; it allows for lags and leads in hegemony. For example, so appealing was the nostalgia for the nineteenth-century hegemony that the ideological dimension of the *pax britannica* flourished long after the power configuration that supported it had vanished. Sustained, and ultimately futile, efforts were made to revive a liberal world economy along with the gold standard in the interwar period. Even in the postwar period, British policy continued to give precedence to balance of payments problems over national industrial development and employment considerations. A 'lead' case is that of the United States, where the growth indicators of material power during the interwar period were insufficient predictors of a new hegemony. It was necessary that US leaders should come to see themselves in ideological terms as the necessary guarantors of a new world order. The Roosevelt era made this transition, including both the conscious rejection of the old hegemony (e.g. by torpedoing the world economic conference in 1933 and abandoning the gold standard) and the gradual incorporation of New-Deal principles into the ideological basis of the new world order. There followed US initiative to create the institutions to administer this order. Neo-mercantilists in the United States now warn against a danger of repeating the British error, urging US policymakers not to continue to operate according to doctrines appropriate to the *pax americana* when the United States can no longer afford to act as guarantor for a universalist world order. Their persuasive efforts underline the point that in these matters ideology is a determining sphere of action which has to be understood in its connections with material power relations.

[In the final section (not reproduced here) Cox goes on to argue that social forces now flow across state boundaries. As a consequence, states have started to play an intermediate, albeit autonomous, role between local and global structures. Using this insight, it becomes possible to understand how the nature of states and the configuration of power between them has changed over the last century.]

4.5 Reflections on war and political discourse: realism, just war, and feminism in a nuclear age

Jean Bethke Elshtain

Source: *Political Theory*, vol. 13, no. 1 (1985), pp. 39–57.

Elshtain accepts that the study of international relations and war has been dominated by a realist tradition, despite the existence of the long-standing rival just war tradition. She asserts, however, referring to the work of Hannah Arendt, that a feminist perspective not only makes it possible to deconstruct realist rhetoric and reveal its inconsistencies, but also can be used to open up a new and more hopeful line of discourse about war and international relations.

What makes realism run?

[. . .] Historic realism involves a way of thinking – a set of presumptions about the human condition that secretes images of men and women and the parts they play in the human drama; and, as well, a potent rhetoric. Whether in its uncompromising Hobbesian version or the less remorseless Machiavellian narrative, realism exaggerates certain features of the human condition and downgrades or ignores others. Interpreting foundational realist texts from a vantage point informed by feminist concerns, one is struck by the suppression and denial of female images and female-linked imperatives, hence alert to the restricted and oversimplifying terms through which realism constitutes symbolism and narrative roles more generally.

For example, Hobbes describes a world of hostile monads whose relations are dominated by fear, force, and instrumental calculation. Yet (and almost simple-mindedly) we know this to be anthropologically false. From the simplest tribal beginnings to the most complex social forms, women have had to tend to infants – no matter what the men were up to – if life was to go on in any sustained manner. That important features of the human condition are expunged from Hobbes's universe suggests that his realism is a dramatic distortion rather than a scientific depiction of the human condition at rock bottom. To acknowledge this by insisting that the state of nature is an analytic fiction fails to address the concerns I raise here. Fictions are also truths and what gets left out is often as important as what is put in and assumed.

To be sure, the contemporary realist is unlikely to endorse a full constellation of Hobbesian presumptions. He might reject Hobbes's vision of the state of nature, and his depiction of social relations, as dire and excessive. It is likely, however, that he would continue to affirm the wider conclusions Hobbes drew by analogy from the miserable condition of human beings in the state of nature to the unrelenting fears and suspicions of states in their relations to one another. Yet it seems plausible that if Hobbes omitted central features of human existence internal to civil societies and families, perhaps he is guilty of similar one-sidedness in his characterization of the world of states. To take up this latter possibility is to treat Hobbes's realism as problematic, not paradigmatic.

Machiavelli goes down more smoothly in large part because we have internalized so much of his legacy already. We all know the story. Human beings are inconstant and trustworthy only in their untrustworthiness. Political action cannot be judged by the standards of Christian morality. Civic virtue requires troops 'well disciplined and trained' in times of peace in order to prepare for war: this is a 'necessity', a law of history. *Si vis pacem, para bellum*, a lesson successive generations (or so the story goes) must learn, though some tragically learn it too late, others in the nick of time.

Machiavelli's narrative revolves around a public–private split in and through which women are constituted, variously, as mirrors to male war-making (a kind of civic cheerleader) or as a collective 'other', embodying the softer values and virtues out of place within, and subversive of, *realpolitik*. Immunized from political action, the realist female may honor the Penates but she cannot embark on a project to bring her values to bear on the civic life of her society. J.G.A. Pocock calls Machiavelli's 'militarization of citizenship' a potent legacy that subverts (even for some feminists, as I argue below) consideration of alternatives that do not bind civic and martial virtue together. Military preparedness, in this narrative, becomes the sine qua non of a viable polity. Although women cannot embody armed civic virtue, a task for the man, they are sometimes drawn into the realist picture more sharply as occasions for war (we must fight to protect her), as goads to action, as designated weepers over the tragedies war trails in its wake, or, in our own time, as male prototypes mobilized to meet dwindling 'manpower' needs for the armed forces.

Rethinking realism using feminist questions defamiliarizes its central categories: the male *homme de guerre* retains his preeminent role, to be sure, but we recognize explicitly the ways in which his soldierly virilization is linked to the realist woman's privatization, and so on. But matters are never quite so simple. There are variants of modern feminist argumentation indebted to realist discourse in its Hobbesian and Machiavellian modes respectively.

Hard-line feminist realists, for example, endorse a Hobbesian social ontology and construe politics as a battleground, the continuation of war by war-like means. They advise women to learn to 'fight dirty'. Making generous use of military metaphors (Who is the enemy? Where is he located?), Hobbesian feminists declare politics and political theory inevitably a 'paradigm case of the Oppressor and the Oppressed'.[1] There is tough talk about sex-war, shock troops, and the need for women to be integrated into the extant power structure construed as the aggregate of all those who defend law and order, wear uniforms, or carry guns for a living – 'the national guard [. . .] state troopers [. . .] sheriffs'. Women are enjoined to prepare for combat as the only way to end their 'colonization'.[2]

Such feminist realists share with their Hobbesian forefather a self-reproducing discourse of fear, suspicion, anticipated violence, and force to check-mate force. Their discussions are peppered with worst-case scenarios and proclamations of supreme emergency that reaffirm the bleakest images of 'the enemy' and pump up the will to power of combatants. Possibilities for reciprocity between men and women, or for a politics not reducible to who controls or coerces whom, are denied in much the same way Hobbes eliminates space for any noninstrumental human relations.

This hard-line position is less important, however, than the modified realism, more Machiavellian in its claims and categories, expressed in a 1981 legal brief filed by the National Organization for Women as part of a challenge to all-male military registration. Beginning with the claim that compulsory, universal military service is central to the concept of citizenship in a democracy, NOW buttresses an ideal of armed civic virtue. If women are to gain 'first-class citizenship' they, too, must have the right to fight. Laws excluding women from draft registration and combat duty perpetuate 'archaic notions' of women's capabilities; moreover, 'devastating long-term psychological and political repercussions' are visited upon women given their exclusion from the military of their country.

NOW's brand of equal opportunity or integrationist feminism here loses a critical edge, functioning instead to reinforce 'the military as an institution and militarism as an ideology' by perpetuating 'the notion that the military is so central to the entire social order that it is only when women gain access to its core that they can hope to fulfill their hopes and aspirations'.[3] In its deep structure, NOW's legal narrative is a leap out of the female/private side of the public/private divide basic to Machiavellian realism and straight into the arms of the hegemonic male whose sex-linked activities are valorized thereby. Paradoxically, NOW's repudiation of 'archaic notions of women's role' becomes a tribute to 'archaic notions of men's role'. Because of the indebtedness of their discourse to presumptions geared historically against women and the values to which they are symbolically if problematically linked, feminist realism, whether in its Hobbesian or less extreme 'armed civic virtue' forms, fails to provide a sustained challenge to the Western narrative of war and politics. Ironically, female-linked symbolism is once again suppressed or depreciated this time under a feminist imprimature as a male-dominant ideal – the 'dirty fighter' or the 'citizen-warrior' is urged on everyone.

Just wars as modified realism

In a world organized along the lines of the realist narrative, there are no easy ways out. There is, however, an alternative tradition to which we in the West have sometimes repaired either to challenge or to chasten the imperatives realism claims merely to describe and denies having in any sense wrought.

Just war theory grows out of a complex genealogy, beginning with the pacifism and withdrawal from the world of early Christian communities through later compromises with the world as Christianity took institutional form. The Christian saviour was a 'prince of peace' and the New Testament Jesus deconstructs the powerful metaphor of the warrior central to Old Testament narrative. He enjoins Peter to sheath his sword; he devirilizes the image of manhood; he tells his followers to go as sheep among wolves and to offer their lives, if need be, but never to take the life of another in violence. From the beginning, Christian narrative presents a pacific ontology, finding in the 'paths of peace' the most natural as well as the most desirable way of being. Violence must justify itself before the court of nonviolence.

Classic just war doctrine, however, is by no means a pacifist discourse. St Augustine's *The City of God*, for example, distinguishes between legitimate and illegitimate use of collective violence. Augustine denounces the *Pax Romana* as a false peace kept in place by evil means and indicts Roman imperialist wars as paradigmatic instances of unjust war. But he defends, with regret, the possibility that a war may be just if it is waged in defense of a common good and to protect the innocent for certain destruction. As elaborated over the centuries, noncombatant immunity gained a secure niche as the most important of *jus in bello* rules, responding to unjust aggression is the central *jus ad bellum*. Just war thinking requires that moral considerations enter into all determinations of collective violence, not as a post hoc gloss but as a serious ground for making political judgments.

In common with realism, just war argument secretes a broader world-view, including a vision of domestic politics. Augustine, for example sees human beings as innately social. It follows that all ways of life are laced through with moral rules and restrictions that provide a web of social order not wholly dependent on external force to keep itself intact. Augustine's household, unlike Machiavelli's private sphere, is 'the beginning or element of the city' and domestic peace bears a relation to 'civic peace'.[4] The sexes are viewed as playing complementary roles rather than as segregated into two separate normative systems governed by wholly different standards of judgment depending upon whether one is a public man or a private woman. [. . .]

My criticisms of just war are directed to two central concerns: one flows directly from just war teaching; the other involves less explicit filiations. I begin with the latter, with cultural images of males and females rooted, at least in part, in just war discourse. Over time, Augustine's moral householders (with husbands cast as just, meaning neither absolute nor arbitrary heads) gave way to a discourse that more sharply divided males and females, their honored activities, and their symbolic force. Men were constituted as just Christian warriors, fighters, and defenders of righteous causes. Women, unevenly and variously depending upon social location, got solidified into a culturally sanctioned vision of virtuous, nonviolent womanhood that I call the 'beautiful soul', drawing upon Hegel's *Phenomenology*.

The tale is by no means simple but, by the late eighteenth century, 'absolute distinctions between men and women in regard to violence' had come to prevail.[5] The female beautiful soul is pictured as frugal, self-sacrificing, and, at times, delicate. Although many women empowered themselves to think and to act on the basis of this ideal of female virtue, the symbol easily slides into sentimentalism. To 'preserve the purity of its heart', writes Hegel, the beautiful soul must flee 'from contact with the actual world'.[6] In matters of war and peace, the female beautiful soul cannot put a stop to suffering, cannot effectively fight the mortal wounding of sons, brothers, husbands, fathers. She continues the long tradition of women as weepers, occasions for war, and keepers of the flame of nonwarlike values.

The just warrior is a complex construction, an amalgam of Old Testament, chivalric, and civic republican traditions. He is a character we recognize in all the statues on all those commons and greens of small New England towns: the citizen-warrior who died to preserve the union and to free the slaves. Natalie Zemon Davis shows that the image of warlike manliness in the later Middle Ages and through the seventeenth century, was but one male ideal among many, having to compete, for example, with the priest and other religious who foreswore use of their 'sexual instrument' and were forbidden to shed blood. However, 'male physical force could sometimes be moralized' and 'thus could provide the foundation for an ideal of warlike manliness'.[7] This moralization of collective male violence held sway and continues to exert a powerful fascination and to inspire respect.

But the times have outstripped beautiful souls and just warriors alike; the beautiful soul can no longer be protected in her virtuous privacy. Her world, and her children, are vulnerable in the face of nuclear realities. Similarly, the just warrior, fighting fair and square by the rules of the game, is a vision enveloped in the heady mist of an earlier time. War is more and more a matter of remote control. The contemporary face of battle is anomic and impersonal, a technological nightmare, as weapons technology obliterates any distinction between night and day, between the 'front' and the 'rear'. [. . .]

Few feminist writers on war and peace take up just war discourse explicitly. There is, however, feminist theorizing that may aptly be situated inside the broader frames of beautiful souls and just warriors as features of inherited discourse. The strongest contemporary feminist statement of a beautiful soul position involves celebrations of a 'female principle' as ontologically given and superior to its dark opposite, masculinism. (The male 'other' in this vision is not a just warrior but a dangerous beast.) The evils of the social world are traced in a free-flowing conduit from masculinism to environmental destruction, nuclear energy, wars, militarism, and states. In utopian evocations of 'cultural feminism', women are enjoined to create separate communities to free themselves from the male surround and to create a 'space' based on the values they embrace. An essentially Manichean vision, the discourse of feminism's beautiful souls contrasts images of 'caring' and 'connected' females in opposition to 'callous' and 'disconnected' males. Deepening sex segregation, the separatist branch of cultural feminism draws upon, yet much exaggerates received understandings of the beautiful soul.

A second feminist vision indebted implicitly to the wider discursive universe of which just war thinking is a part features a down-to-earth female subject, a soul less beautiful than virtuous in ways that locate her as a social actor. She shares just war's insistence that politics must come under moral scrutiny. Rejecting the hard-line gendered epistemology and meta-physic of an absolute beautiful soul, she nonetheless insists that ways of knowing flow from ways of being in the world and that hers have vitality and validity in ways private and public. The professed ends of feminists in this loosely fitting frame locate the woman as a moral educator and a political actor. She is concerned with 'mothering', whether or not she is a biological mother, in the sense of protecting society's most vulnerable members without patronizing them. She thinks in terms of human dignity as well as social justice and fairness. She also forges links between 'maternal thinking' and pacifist or nonviolent theories of con-flict without presuming that it is possible to translate easily particular maternal imperatives into a public good.

The pitfalls of this feminism are linked to its intrinsic strengths. By insisting that women are in and of the social world, its framers draw explicit attention to the context within which their constituted subjects act. But this wider surround not only derogates maternal women, it bombards them with simplistic formulae that equate 'being nice' with 'doing good'. Even as stereotypic maternalisms exert pressure to sentimentalize, competing feminisms are often sharply repudiating, finding in any evocation of 'maternal thinking' a trap and a delusion. A more robust concept of the just (female) as citizen is needed to shore up this disclosure, a matter I take up below.

Rescuing politics from war: Hannah Arendt's hope

[Elshtain then raises a number of concerns about a dominant form of discourse, encouraged by living in a world which is characterized by 'armed' peace which draws on the belief that politics is an extension of war.]

Hannah Arendt's *On Violence* responds to these concerns by exposing our acceptance of politics as war by other means. Arendt asks what historic transformations and discursive practices made possible a consensus 'among political theorists from Left to Right [. . .] that violence is nothing more than the most flagrant manifestation of power?'[8] (The violence Arendt has in mind is that of groups or collectives, not individual outrage culminating in a single violent act; Melville's *Billy Budd* is her example.) Her answer is multiple: teleological constructions of historic inevitability (known to us as Progress); theories of absolute power tied to the emergence of the nation-state; the Old Testament tradition of God's Com-mandments that fed command-obedience conceptions of law in Judaeo-Christian discourse; the infusion of biologism into political discourse, particularly the notion that destruction is a law of nature and violence a 'life promoting force' through which men purge the old and rotten. All these 'time-honored opinions have become dangerous'. Locked into dangerously self-confirming ways of thinking, embracing 'progress' as a standard of evaluation, we manage to convince ourselves that good will come out of horrendous things; that somehow, in history, the end does justify the means. Both classical liberals and their Marxist adversaries share this discursive terrain, Arendt argues, though she is especially critical of 'great trust in the dialectical "power of negation" ' that soothes its adherents into believing that evil 'is but a temporary manifestation of a still-hidden good'.

By conflating the crude instrumentalism of violence with power, defined by Arendt as the human ability to act in concert and to begin anew, we guarantee further loss of space within which authentic empowerment is possible. In this way violence nullifies power and stymies political being. One important step away from the instrumentalism of violence and toward the possibility of politics is to resist the reduction of politics to domination. Arendt evokes no image of isolated heroism here; rather, she underscores the ways in which centralized orders dry up power and political possibility. If we recognize the terms through and means by which this happens, we are less susceptible to unreflective mobilization and more open to finding and creating public space in the current order. As citizens through their actions break repetitive cycles of behavior, power as the 'true opposite' of violence reveals itself.

Arendt's discourse constitutes its subjects as citizens: neither victims nor warriors. She paints no rosy picture of her rescue effort. Just as Grey argues that the will to war is deepened by the emptiness of a false peace, Arendt believes that the greater a society's bureaucratization, the greater will be secret fantasies of destruction. She repudiates grandiose aims and claims, refusing to dictate what politics should do or accomplish instrumentally, for that would undermine her exposé of the future oriented teleologies on which violence and progress feed. To the extent that we see what she is doing and let it work on us, her symbolic alternative for political being offers a plenary jolt to our reigning political metaphors and categories – state of nature, sovereignty, statism, bureaucratization, contractualism, nationalist triumphalism, and so on. If we remain entrapped in this cluster of potent typifications, each of them suffused with violent evocations or built on fears of violence, we will face only more, and deadlier, of what we've already got. Contrastingly, Arendt locates as central a powerful but pacific image that engenders hope, the human capacity that sustains political being.

Evidence of hopelessness is all around us. The majority of young people say they do not believe there will be a future of any sort. We shake our heads in dismay, failing to see that our social arrangements produce hopelessness and require it to hold themselves intact. But the ontological possibility for hope is always present, rooted, ultimately, in 'the fact of natality'. Arendt's metaphor, most fully elaborated in the following passage from *The Human Condition*, is worth quoting in full:

> The miracle that saves the world, the realm of human affairs, from its normal, 'natural' ruin is ultimately the fact of natality, in which the faculty of action is ontologically rooted. It is, in other words, the birth of new human beings and the new beginning, the action they are capable of by being born. *Only the full experience of this capacity can bestow upon human affairs faith and hope, those two essential characteristics of human existence* [. . .] that found perhaps their most glorious and most succinct expression in the new words with which the Gospels accounted their 'glad tiding': 'A Child has been born unto us.'[9]

The infant, like all beginnings is vulnerable. We must nurture that beginning, not knowing and not being able to control the 'end' of the story.

Arendt's evocation of natal imagery through its most dramatic ur-narrative is not offered as an abstraction to be endorsed abstractly. Rather, she invites us to restore long atrophied dispositions of commemoration and awe; birth, she declares, is a 'miracle', a beginning that renews and irreversibly alters the world. Hers is a fragile yet haunting figuration that stirs recognition of our own vulnerable beginnings and our necessary dependency on others. Placed alongside the reality of human beginnings, many accounts of political beginnings construed as the actions of male hordes of contractualists seem parodic in part because of the massive denial (of 'the female') on which they depend. A 'full experience' of the 'capacity' rooted in birth helps us to keep before our mind's eye the living reality of singularities, differences, and individualities rather than a human mass as objects of possible control or manipulation.[10]

By offering an alternative genealogy that problematizes collective violence and visions of triumph, Arendt devirilizes discourse, not in favor of feminization (for the feminized and masculinized emerged in tandem and both embody dangerous distortions), but politicalization, constituting her male and female objects as citizens who share alike the 'faculty of action'. At this juncture, Arendt's discourse makes contact with that feminism I characterized as a modified vision of the beautiful soul. Her bracing ideal of the citizen adds political robustness to a feminist picture of women drawn to action from their sense of being and their epistemic and social location. Arendt's citizen, for example, may act from her maternal thinking but not as a mother – an important distinction that could help to chasten sentimentalism or claims of moral superiority.

But war is the central concern of this essay. Does Arendt's discourse offer a specifiable orientation toward international relations? Her discourse shifts the ground on which we stand when we think about states and their relations. We become skeptical about the forms and the claims of the sovereign state; we deflate fantasies of control inspired by the reigning teleology of progress; we recognize the (phony) parity painted by a picture of equally 'sovereign states' and are thereby alert to the many forms hegemony can take. Additionally, Arendt grants 'forgiveness' a central political role as the only way human beings have to break remorseless cycles of vengeance. She embraces an 'ascesis', a refraining or withholding that allows refusal to bring one's force to bear to surface as a strength not a weakness.

Take the dilemma of the nuclear arms race that seems to have a life and dynamic of its own. From an Arendtian perspective, we see current arms control efforts for what they are – the arms race under another name negotiated by a bevy of experts with a vested interest in keeping the race alive so they can 'control' it. On the other hand, her recognition of the limiting conditions internal to the international political order precludes a leap into utopian fantasies of world order or total disarmament. For neither the arms control option (as currently defined) nor calls for immediate disarmament are bold – the first because it is a way of doing business as usual; the second because it covertly sustains business as usual by proclaiming 'solutions' that lie outside the reach of possibility.

Instead, Arendt's perspective invites us – as a strong and dominant nation of awesome potential force – to take unilateral initiatives in order to break symbolically the cycle of vengeance and fear signified by our nuclear arsenals. Just as action from an individual or group may disrupt the automisms of everyday life, action from a single state may send shock waves that reverberate throughout the system. Arendt cannot be pegged as either a 'systems dominance' nor 'sub-systems dominance' thinker – a form of argumentation with which she has no patience in any case. She recognizes systemic imperatives yet sees space for potentially effective change from 'individual (state) action'. The war system is so deeply rooted that to begin to dismantle it in its current and highly dangerous form requires bold strokes.

At this juncture, intimations of an alternative genealogy emerge. Freeman Dyson suggests the *Odyssey* or the theme of homecoming rather than the *Iliad* or the theme of remorseless force as a dominant ur-political myth if we break the deadlock of victims versus warriors. Socrates, Jesus of Nazareth, and Nietzsche, in some of his teachings, emerge as articulators of the prototypical virtues of restraint and refusal to bring all one's power to bear.[11] For it was Nietzsche, from his disillusionment, who proclaimed the only way out of 'armed peace' to be a people, distinguished by their wars and victories who, from strength, not weakness, 'break the sword' thereby giving peace a chance. 'Rather perish than hate and fear', he wrote, 'and twice rather perish than make oneself hated and feared.'[12] Historic feminist thinkers and movements who rejected politics as force take center stage rather than being relegated to the periphery in this alternative story.

To take up war-as-discourse compels us to recognize the powerful sway of received narratives and reminds us that the concepts through which we think about war, peace, and politics get repeated endlessly, shaping debates, constraining consideration of alternatives, often reassuring us that things cannot really be much different than they are. As we nod an automatic yes when we hear the truism (though we may despair of the truth it tells) that 'there have always been wars', we acknowledge tacitly that 'there have always been war stories', for wars are deeded to us as texts. We cannot identify 'war itself' as an entity apart from a powerful literary tradition that includes poems, epics, myths, official histories, first-person accounts, as well as the articulated theories I have discussed. War and the discourse of war are imbricated, part and parcel of political reality. Contesting the discursive terrain that identifies and gives meaning to what we take these realities to be does not mean one grants a self-subsisting, unwarranted autonomy to discourse; rather, it implies a recognition of the ways in which received doctrines, 'war stories', may lull our critical faculties to sleep, blinding us to possibilities that lie within our reach.

Notes

1 Ti-Grace Atkinson, 'Theories of Radical Feminism', Notes from the Second Year: *Women's Liberation*, edited by Shulamith Firestone (n.p., 1970), p. 37.

2 Susan Brownmiller, *Against Our Will: Men, Women and Rape* (Simon and Schuster, New York, 1975), p. 388.

3 Cynthia Enloe, *Does Khaki Become YOU? The Militarization of Women's Lives* (Pluto Press, London, 1983), pp. 16–17.

4 Henry Paolucci (ed.), *The Political Writings of St. Augustine* (Henry Regnery, Chicago, 1967), p. 151.

5 Natalie Zemon Davis, 'Men, Women and Violence: Some Reflections on Equality', *Smith Alumnae Quarterly* (April 1972), p. 15.

6 G. W. F. Hegel, *The Phenomenology of Spirit*, trans. A.V. Miller (Clarendon Press, Oxford, 1977), pp. 399–400.

7 Davis, 'Men, Women and Violence', p. 13.

8 Hannah Arendt, *On Violence* (Harcourt Brace, New York, 1969), p. 35.

9 Hannah Arendt, *The Human Condition* (University of Chicago Press, Chicago, 1958), p. 247.

10 Arendt, *On Violence*, p. 81.

11 Freeman Dyson, *Weapons and Hope* (Basic Books, New York, 1984).

12 Cited in J. Glenn Gray, *The Warriors: Reflections on Men in Battle* (Harper Colophon, New York, 1970), pp. 225–6.

4.6 Masculinities, IR and the 'gender variable'

Charlotte Hooper

Source: *Review of International Studies*, vol. 25, 1999, pp. 475–91.

Hooper demonstrates that gender is not simply a variable that can be added on to existing mainstream approaches to international relations. She does this by identifying practices in international relations that discipline men and help to produce masculine identities. Mainstream IR is seen to be oblivious to this relationship between its subject matter and the process of identity formation because it fails to acknowledge the integral links that exist between theory and practice.

One point feminist contributors to IR have made on numerous occasions, and which even sympathetic mainstream academics seem particularly resistant to, is the idea that gender cannot just be grafted onto existing explanatory approaches which are profoundly 'masculinist'. An adequate analysis of gender requires more radical changes, including an ontological and epistemological revolution. In arguing this, feminists have tried to counter the naive approach to gender which argues along the following lines: if international relations marginalises both women and the feminine, then why can't women and the feminine be brought in to mainstream approaches in the same way that other previously neglected variables have been incorporated? For that matter, in the interests of 'balance', why can't a gender focused analysis of men and masculinity also be incorporated into mainstream approaches? This article would like to argue that while in some limited way, it might be possible to add the 'gender variable' to the long list of variables which are variously deemed to inform the practices of international relations, to do so would be to exclude analysis of the most salient ingredients of the relationship between gender and international relations. Such ingredients should be of interest to mainstream IR scholars because they are bound up with power politics – albeit power politics of a different sort from the ones usually focused on in the discipline.

While, as indicated above, this is hardly a novel argument in feminist circles, it has not been readily understood or accepted by others, beyond a few post-positivist sympathisers. Mainstream critics of feminist approaches, who might consider themselves open to persuasion with regard to the 'gender variable', have been baffled by both the language and concerns of feminists, and have accused them – particularly post-structuralist feminists – of failing to produce a relevant research agenda. Feminist discussions of the epistemological limitations and inherent masculinism of mainstream IR have on the whole started from the premise that international relations *reflects* men and 'masculinity' and excludes women and 'femininity'. Their subsequent explanations that one cannot merely add women and the feminine because gender constructions are relationally defined, that they are linked to a whole series of gendered dichotomies in which masculine traits are valued and feminine ones devalued (forming a residual 'other'); and that scientific methodologies reflect valued masculine traits rather than devalued feminine ones, appear to fall on deaf, or at least sceptical ears.

But the argument that mainstream approaches are ontologically and epistemologically inadequate to deal with gender can also be approached from a different angle, one which would perhaps provide another opportunity for sceptics to reconsider their dismissal of the relevance of feminist claims, and to think through the possible range of consequences of acknowledging gender in their work. Rather than focusing on what is excluded from the discipline as conventionally defined, one can focus on what is included: that is the activities of men in the international arena. While it is commonplace to argue that international relations *reflects* a world of men and masculinity, it is also worth examining the possibility of a current of influence running in the other direction. One could ask whether international relations plays any role in the shaping, defining and legitimating of such masculinity or masculinities? Might causality, or at least the interplay of complex influences, run in both directions, in mutually reinforcing patterns? Might international relations discipline men as much as men shape international relations?

In order to investigate the intersections between gender identities and international relations, one cannot rely on approaches which would take gender identities as 'givens', or as independent, externally derived variables. Instead one would need to move towards those which could examine the (international) politics of identity construction. As this article will argue, such a move, even if it is primarily concerned with the generation of an empirical research agenda with regard to the production of masculine identities through practices which form the so-called 'core' of the discipline (such as war, foreign policy, and the globalisation of the world economy) will almost certainly reveal some of the ontological, methodological, and ultimately, the epistemological limitations of mainstream approaches. This is because such approaches attempt to restrict the relevant field to the 'public' if not the 'international' levels of analysis, and also treat theory as entirely separate from the subject matter being investigated – whether the purpose of such theory is scientific 'explanation' or more historically oriented 'interpretation'.

International relations and the production of masculinities

In asking whether international relations might influence masculinity or masculinities, there is an assumption that masculinity is not a fixed, biologically based set of personality characteristics, but is in some way malleable to social influences. While lack of space precludes a long discussion on the construction of gender identities, it is worth briefly noting that historical and anthropological research suggests that there is no single 'masculinity' or 'femininity' and that both are subject to numerous and fairly fast-changing historical and cultural variations. For example, dominant forms of Anglo-Saxon masculinity have drawn on an eclectic mix of competing and partially overlapping and historical archetypes. The main ones include, firstly, a Greek citizen/warrior model which combined militarism with rationalism and equated manliness with citizenship in a masculine arena of free speech and politics. This was joined by a patriarchal Judaeo/Christian model with a domesticated ideal of manly responsibility, ownership and the authority of the father of fathers. Later came an aristocratic honour/patronage model in which personal bonds between men, military heroism and taking risks were highly valued, with the duel as the ultimate test of masculinity.

Finally, there developed a Protestant bourgeois rationalist model which idealised competitive individualism, reason and self-control – and combined respectability as breadwinner and head of household with calculative rationality in public life. Elements from and combinations of all these models are still in cultural circulation today.

Gender also intersects with other social divisions such as class, race and sexuality to produce complex hierarchies of (gendered) identities in which the relevant ingredients of 'masculinity' and 'femininity' may vary considerably. For example, while 'rationality' has historically been associated with masculinity in European modernity, in racist hierarchies black men have been deemed incapable of this trait. Meanwhile the physical frailness of Victorian femininity was also apparently confined to white women.

What, one might ask, has any of this to do with international relations? Firstly, if there is no single 'masculinity' attributable to all men, but rather a range of historically and culturally specific masculinities, than perhaps it might be worth examining whether specific gender identities embodied by groups of actors produce patterns of predictable behaviour. If so, such patterns might act as explanatory variables which could be incorporated into strategic analysis in much the same way as other local 'cultural' or 'ethnic' variables. Particular processes of gender identification may inform other, more conventionally defined political and military struggles identified in IR literature. For example, US foreign policies in the latter part of the Vietnam War and its aftermath – up to and including the Gulf War, may have been inflected by a desire to rescue and bolster American manhood after its humiliation at the hands of the Vietcong (sometimes characterised as a bunch of women and children) as much as by rational foreign policy interests. However, the picture generated by an analysis of gender *motivations* would not be very illuminating, if it ignored the *effects* on gender identity produced through the practices of international relations. The model of gender identification put forward here does not confine its interest to developmental matters but rather implicates all areas and levels of social and political life in the production and maintenance of gender identities. International relations would be no exception. Indeed, as international relations, conventionally defined, is made up largely of the activities of men, then it may be an area of life that is particularly significant for the production and maintenance of masculinities. It is likely that political events and masculine identities are both *simultaneous* products of men's participation in the practices of international relations.

Considering the three dimensions of gender identity discussed above, all the possible links between men and the practices of international relations are illustrated by the arrows in Figure 1.

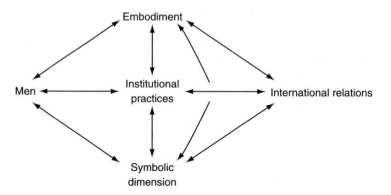

Figure 1 The relationship between men and international relations

The two way arrows indicate that not only do men make international relations but that international relations may discipline men and help produce and maintain masculine identities through the same channels in reverse. The separation of elements in this diagram is illustrative only. Of course there are complex relationships between the dimensions of embodiment, institutional practices and symbolic meanings – which are often all present in the same 'event'. Nevertheless for explanatory purposes the connections are separated here. To illustrate this diagram and explain these connections there follows a fairly arbitrary selection of examples drawn from existing research. Some illustrate the links through all three dimensions, while others operate most clearly through one or two dimensions. All have been chosen to highlight the influence of international relations on masculinities rather than *vice versa*, as this is the direction of influence under consideration.

Military combat in the pursuit of wars is a clear example of how international relations helps to shape men. War has been deemed central to the discipline itself, and has historically played a large part in defining what it means to be a man in the modern era, symbolically, institutionally and through the shaping of men's bodies. Firstly, the symbolic dimension: the argument that men take life while women give it is a cornerstone of one powerful ideology of gender differences. This ideology has been central to modern warfare and underpins the masculinity of soldiering and the historic exclusion of women from combat. In symbolic terms, engaging in war is often deemed to be the clearest expression of men's enduring natural 'aggression', as well as their manly urge to serve their country and 'protect' their female kin, with the one implying the other. The popular myth is that military service is the fullest expression of masculinity, and in 1976 there were about 20 million men under arms in about 130 standing armies world-wide.

However, as Barbara Ehrenreich argues, 'it is not only men that make wars, it is wars that make men'[1] – literally and physically. Military service has served as a rite of passage for boys to be made men throughout much of the modern era, while at the level of embodiment, military training explicitly involves the physical and social shaping of the male body. Indeed it can be argued that 'war and the military represent one of the major sites where direct links between hegemonic masculinities and men's bodies are forged'.[2] Joanna Bourke has examined the relationship between masculinities and embodiment in Britain in the First World War, when soldiering became intimately bound up with notions of masculinity.[3] Soldiering disciplined the male body, helping to shape its style of masculinity as well as its physical contours. This shaping was inflected by class. As one middle-class soldier, Ralph Scott, graphically noted in his diary:

> I looked at my great murderous maulers and wondered idly how they had evolved from the sensitive manicured fingers that used to pen theses on 'Colloidal Fuel' and 'The Theory of Heat Distribution in Cylinder Walls.' And I found the comparison good.[4]

If middle class men found themselves transformed from bourgeois rationalists to warrior-citizens, then for the working classes, the emphasis was much more on basic fitness. At the beginning of the war British authorities had been horrified at the quality of their raw material, as British manhood was by and large malnourished, disease ridden, stunted in their growth and poorly educated. Such men had to be 'converted' into soldiers, both physically and mentally. The increased surveillance and regulation of male bodies which this entailed was sustained through the inter-war years, when regular exercise through military type drills was widely adopted in schools and other institutions. Military drill therefore constituted an institutional practice which had been established through war and which had a widespread effect on men's bodies. Drill was also deemed to make men economically efficient, to promote emotional self control, and even to enhance brain development.

Men who did not fight were looked down on, while the 'real' men who fought carried a high risk of death or physical disablement. The return of thousands of youthful war-mutilated servicemen, who were hailed as masculine heroes, changed the medical and technological approach to disablement for good, and even modified public attitudes for a while. Initially, although the most disfigured were kept out of sight, the lightly maimed soldier was regarded as 'not less but more of a man'. These were 'active' rather than 'passive' sufferers, who deserved respect, not pity, and who were even deemed especially attractive to women. To be physically maimed was far more manly than to be a 'malingerer' or shell shock victim. The dead were also heroes. In the long term however, sympathy changed to disgust at the carnage involved, and disabled ex-servicemen who could not fulfil a role as breadwinners became increasingly marginalised and feminised. [. . .]

[Hooper goes on to provide further examples of how international practices have helped to shape prevailing conceptions of masculinity.]

David Campbell argues that in the American case, an explicit goal of foreign policy was the construction and maintenance of an American identity. A 'society of security' was created in which a vigorous loyalty/security program sought to define Americans by exclud-ing the communist 'other', both externally and internally.[5] Campbell notes the gendered nature of such exclusionary practices, so that, for example, communists and other 'undesirables' were linked through feminisation, as indicated by the abusive term 'pinko'. Although he doesn't emphasise the point, this American identity which was constructed through communist witch hunts and the associated tests of 'loyalty' was essentially a mascu-line identity. Indeed it was the very same form of masculinity which was also shaped by fear of 'latent homosexuality' as discussed by Barbara Ehrenreich.[6] The threat of effeminacy, or latent homosexuality, was used to coerce American men into forming a reliable work force who would voluntarily support wives and children in the 1950s. Masculinity was equated with adulthood, marriage and the bread winning role, and homosexuality was demonised as the ultimate escapism. This ideology was backed up by theories from a host of psychological, medical and sociological experts. Any man who failed to fully live up to the bread winning role by walking out on his wife or job (or worse still – remained unmarried or unemployed in the first place) might be diagnosed as suffering from 'latent' or 'pseudo' homosexuality. Every heterosexual man was on his guard against such possibilities. It was the equation of latent homosexuality with femininity rather than with sexual deviance which guaranteed its effectiveness as a threat.

Integrating Campbell's and Ehrenreich's work, it becomes clear that vigilance against the possibility that unsuspecting liberals might unwittingly help the communist cause, paralleled and intersected with the vigilance needed to ward off the threat of 'latent homosexuality'. While the institutional practices which supported this identity were eventually reduced in reach and scope, Ehrenreich suggests that the symbolic legacy lasted longer, so that 'com-munism kept masculine toughness in style long after it became obsolete in the corporate world and the consumer marketplace'.

Academic IR and the politics of identity

The above discussion indicates that there may be numerous ways in which international relations are implicated in the construction of masculinities and masculine identities: through the direct disciplining of male bodies, through political and institutional practices, and through broader cultural and ideological links. In contrast IR as a discipline has generally shown little interest in, and has been ill-equipped to deal with, issues related to the politics of identity construction. The consequence of this is not only that mainstream international relations remains blind to its own masculinist reflections, but also that the construction of gendered identities through the practices of international relations is rendered invisible to the discipline. Before the intervention of feminists, the closest mainstream IR got to acknowledging the relevance of gender identities was in the assumptions about (masculine) human nature which underpinned theory in the classical tradition, and which tended to mirror the prevailing naturalised discourses of gender. For example, Keohane quotes Morgenthau as describing the 'limitless character of the lust for power' which 'reveals a general quality of the human mind', and which accounted for war.[7] After the Second World War, much of IR theory was revolutionised by behaviourism, which sought to turn it into a science of quantifiable and measurable exactness. Such assumptions were questioned and criticised as being vague and unprovable, but rather than criticisms opening up a series of interesting political questions about the absence of foundational identities in politics, attempts were made to contain questions of identity in bureaucratic or psychological models of human behaviour; to mechanise them in the ubiquitous rational actor model, or to do away with them (along with many other relevant topics) by resorting to purely systemic explanations, all in the name of science. Given these moves to either codify, or, in Waltz's case, to remove 'human nature' from the discipline it is hardly surprising that the politics of identity construction has been neglected.

Leaving the epistemological questions raised by the behavioural revolution aside, one can see that one reason for the inability of IR to deal with questions of gender identity is ontological, and is connected to the way in which the discipline itself has historically been conceptualised in mainstream theory and analysis. International politics has been divorced from politics within states in disciplinary terms because of apparently distinct features which make international politics qualitatively different from other kinds of politics. In the 1950s and 60s, the dominant view was that while politics and 'the good life' could be pursued within the secure borders of states, survival, fragile laws, and uneasy alliances and balances were all that could be expected in an international arena which is above all characterised by anarchy. With anarchy (between states) and sovereignty (within states) as its principal guiding forces, IR theory found it easy to 'black box' the state, deeming all that goes on in it as irrelevant except where it is expressed as 'national interests'.

As the discipline of IR has developed since then, the domestic politics/international relations division has not been strictly adhered to. It has often been breached, for example in foreign policy analysis, when both the domestic determinants of foreign policy and the international determinants of domestic politics have been examined. Such breaches have led to debates over the 'levels of analysis' problem, which asks whether international relations should be explained by reference to properties of the system of states, to the behaviour of individual states, to pressures arising from domestic politics, or to the activities of individual people such as particular statesmen. Moreover, characterisations of international 'anarchy' have also become much more varied and sophisticated. It would be unfair and inaccurate to say that mainstream IR now 'black boxes' the state, except in one or two influential examples. However, anarchy of one kind or another is still the defining feature of inter-national relations for mainstream analysis, and the domestic politics/international relations divide retains a crucial symbolic importance, as it remains the principal justification for the existence of a separate discipline of IR in the first place.

Breaching the domestic politics/international relations division, however, will not in itself lead to a clearer understanding of the involvement of international relations in the politics of identity construction or the production of masculinities. This is because of a second boundary (or rather series of overlapping boundaries) which is rarely referred to in main-stream IR literature but which is also highly relevant to its conceptual space. This is the boundary between the public sphere of politics (and economics) and the private sphere of families, domestic labour and reproduction, which has been challenged by feminists. Domestic and family life has tended to fall outside both the state and civil society in liberal schemes. As for the newer distinction between the public realm and personal life, the right to privacy has merely tended to reinforce the idea that family relations should be exempt from questions of public and social justice.

Putting these private/public and domestic/international boundaries together, modern life has been conceptually divided into a number of separate spheres (a division which has only been strengthened by the disciplinary separation of IR from Politics and Government). These spheres can be categorised in a number of ways, but include the domestic/private (which can be divided into familial and personal); the non-domestic/public (which can be further divided into the public state and private civil society); and the international. Thus personal life, domestic and family life, and even much of civil society has been evacuated from IR. Where IR dips into the 'black box' of the state it is usually to deal with public political or economic issues and affairs of the state – and even liberal perspectives that emphasise trans-nationalism rarely transgress the public/private divides. The production of masculinities through the practices of international relations, as illustrated above, is ren-dered invisible by these divisions that discourage an examination of the interconnections between the international, and the private world of personhood. Questions of gender iden-tity are generally assumed to be private aspects of adult personality (invoking the right to privacy from public scrutiny), and are rooted in the domestic realm of childhood and family life (invoking the familial/non-familial or domestic/non-domestic divide), if not determined at birth – far from the reach of IR's focus of analysis.

One might argue that transcending the levels of analysis problem and widening the remit of international relations to include an analysis of domestic and personal subject areas previously excluded would solve the problem of how to analyse the connections between international relations and masculine identities more thoroughly. This would also bring into view women and their traditional supporting roles, as advocated by Cynthia Enloe, who coined the phrase 'the personal is international'.[8] Such a move would go a long way towards bringing gender into view, but only if accompanied by appropriate methodologies. In terms of scientific methodologies, while more profound and extensive criticisms could be and have been made in relation to gender, it should be immediately apparent from the discussion above that if gender identities are simultaneously *causes* and *effects* of international relations then there is no clear-cut unit of analysis on which to base explanations. Rational actor models and other such units of analysis are totally unsuited to the task of investigating how identities themselves are formed. They would have to bear yet another round of improbable modification and qualification or be dispensed with altogether. Assuming this could be done, the scientific language of cause and effect, with its emphasis on being able to isolate distinct and measurable phenomena, would also probably have to give way to one of mutually reinforcing influences. Nor, given the scientific interest in uncovering behavioural regularities, and making predictions on the basis of these, are scientific methods as generally applied in IR particularly suited to the analysis of phenomena that are undergoing rapid and multidimensional historical change.

If scientific or explanatory approaches are not particularly suited to this type of investigation then perhaps the traditional alternative of historical analysis would be more applicable. Drawing on the methods of the humanities this approach leans more towards understanding than explanation and involves a less constraining methodology. However, while such an approach may better capture the complexities of the two way influences between masculinities and international relations there would remain an epistemological problem that might block a full analysis of these interconnections. This problem is connected to the symbolic dimension of gender identities, and the problem is that both the discipline of IR and the perspectives and theories produced within it form part of the symbolic realm. Thus IR scholarship is itself implicated in the production of masculinities through the symbolic dimension of gender identification. No perspective that treats theory as distinct and separate from social reality can fully explore this aspect of the relationship between international relations and the gender identities of men. Therefore, when it comes to analysing IR's own contribution to the production of masculine identities, post-positivist or reflectivist epistemological positions which can examine the symbolic and discursive functions of IR scholarship itself would be the most effective. Such approaches need not be unduly abstract or ephemeral. For example, Campbell's analysis of the symbolic and discursive functions of US foreign policy, discussed above, is a good example of historically detailed post-structuralist scholarship.

Reflectivist methods can uncover or deconstruct the ways in which masculinities are inscribed into the discipline. Feminist critiques of IR's masculinism already provide a wealth of information on this point and make a good starting place for further investigation. Tickner, for example, finds 'three models of man' inscribed into different perspectives on IPE.[9] Building on Tickner's observations, one can see that the different archetypes of hegemonic masculinity mentioned above are variously incorporated into different IR perspectives. Neorealism embodies an eclectic and often contradictory combination of the warrior-citizen (Machiavelli), patriarchal (Hobbes) and bourgeois rational (scientific language and rational actor) models. Meanwhile neo-liberal institutionalism more clearly reflects bourgeois rational masculinity which is itself closely connected to liberalism. The often fierce inter-paradigm debates which have marked the development of the discipline may include a dimension of rivalry between these different masculinities. New forms of elite Anglo-American masculinity associated with technocracy and globalisation are also emerging, both within the discipline and on the ground.

Returning to the private/public/international divides discussed above, an important feature of such divides is their highly gendered nature. The conceptual relegation of women and the 'feminine' to the domestic and the private, in classical and liberal theory is well documented as is their almost total practical exclusion from the international and all but the lowliest of public spheres. International relations then symbolically forms a wholly masculine sphere of war and diplomacy, at the furthest conceptual extreme from the domestic sphere of families, women and reproduction in the private/public/international divides of modernity. Gender divisions and inequalities depend to a great extent on the segregation of social life into separate spheres for men and women, so that gender differences can be constructed and the lines of difference made visible. The cultural and social production of gender differences and gendered character traits segregates the sexes in various ways, in order to construct and make visible the lines of difference between them. Generating gendered constructions is an integral part of any such segregational practice.

As the private/public/international divisions inscribe international relations as a virtually all-male sphere, then it follows that the activities and qualities associated with this gender-segregated space cannot help but inform the definition and production of masculinities. The emphasis on power politics in both theory and practice then reinforces the associations between such masculinities and power itself, associations that are crucial to masculinism. Having inscribed an all-male sphere which serves as an arena for the production of masculinities, the private/public/international divisions simultaneously obscure this process. The structuring of IR theory to exclude questions of the politics of identity has some interesting effects. It both serves to uphold the existing gender order and also indirectly confirms the importance of international politics as one of the primary sites for the production and naturalisation of masculinities in the modern era.

Conclusions

This article challenges the disciplinary assumption that international relations and the politics of identities (including gender identities) are discrete areas of research that have no important interconnections. It has not been concerned to answer in any adequate way the question of how international relations helps produce masculine identities, but rather to demonstrate how merely asking the question and beginning to consider how it might be answered highlights some of the ontological, methodological and epistemological problems of mainstream approaches to IR with regard to gender. If breaching the domestic/international and private/public divides which help to define the discipline of IR in order to examine the production of masculine identities through international relations would profoundly alter the ontology of the discipline, then a full examination of the symbolic dimension of gender identification also raises epistemological issues about the role of theory and the discipline itself. This is a case where the attempt to create an applied, empirical research agenda might quickly lead to the post-positivist revolution in order to facilitate a more comprehensive analysis of the so-called 'gender variable'.

That an account of the relationship between masculine identities and international relations would be extremely difficult within conventional approaches should be clear. One cannot simply take mainstream IR and merely add 'men' or 'masculinities' to get a gendered analysis, any more than one can take mainstream approaches and add either 'women' or 'femininity'. Gender issues profoundly disturb conventional forms of analysis. Molly Cochran argues that even empirically oriented feminist IR scholarship may have implications too radical for its easy incorporation into mainstream analysis.[10] This echoes the feminist argument that even liberal feminism (often seen as the mildest form), if carried through to its conclusion, would have profoundly disturbing consequences for liberal politics. Therefore, because of its ultimately radical potential, empirical and historical analysis of the relationship between (masculine) gender identities and international relations would be helpful, even where overtly reflectivist approaches are rejected (after all, feminists themselves adopt a variety of epistemological positions).

In many ways this question of the 'gender variable' parallels the security debate and forms part of the question of identities and culture more generally. The salience of such questions for international relations has been highlighted recently, both in the post-Cold War resurgence of ethnic rivalry and of identity politics in domestic, international and transnational situations, and in the writings of post-positivist academics. As Yosef Lapid argues, 'a swing of the pendulum toward culture and identity is [. . .] strikingly evident in post-Cold War theorizing'. This is in response to an awareness amongst IR scholars' of their mounting theoretical difficulties with apparently 'exponential increases in global heterogeneity and diversity'.[11] As a consequence, constructivist approaches to identity and security have begun to influence mainstream IR academics, although not unproblematically. As Tickner argues, most feminist scholarship also takes a broadly constructivist (although not necessarily structuralist) approach to gender.[12]

If it is important at this juncture for IR scholarship to get a grip on both gender and the politics of identities, then at the minimum, sympathetic mainstream academics who are willing to look at constructivist arguments with regard to security and cultural identities, need to expand their horizons to include gender. At the same time, they could usefully draw on the insights of feminism with regard to the politics, social construction and embodiment of identities more generally. They would need to be willing to transcend the 'levels of analysis' problem and transgress the private/public/international divides. They would probably have to make fairly major methodological changes if they are used to working with scientific rather than historical methods. Hopefully, sooner or later, they might also find themselves willing to actively engage with the substance, if not the language, of post-positivist debates and positions with regard to the role of theory. What is completely inadequate to the task of dealing with the issue of gender identity however, even in empirical terms, is the straightforward grafting of a 'gender variable' on to mainstream analysis.

Notes

1 Barbara Ehrenreich 'Introduction' in Klaus Theweleit, ed., *Male Fantasies*, vol. 1 (Cambridge University Press, Cambridge, 1987) p. xvi.
2 Joanna Bourke, *Dismembering the Male: Men's Bodies and the Great War* (Reaktion, London, 1996).
3 David H.J. Morgan, 'Theatre of War: Combat, the Military and Maculinities', in Harry Brod and Michael Kaufman, eds, *Theorizing Masculinities* (Sage, London, 1994), p. 168.
4 Quoted in ibid. pp. 15–16.
5 David Campbell, *Writing Security: United States Foreign Policy and the Politics of Identity* (Manchester University Press, Manchester, 1992), p. 166.
6 Barbara Ehrenreich (see fn 1).
7 Robert O. Keohane, 'Realism, Neorealism and the Study of World Politics' in *Neorealism and Its Critics* (Columbia University Press, New York, 1986) pp. 11–12.
8 Cynthia Enloe, *Bananas, Beaches and Bases: Making Feminist Sense of International Relations* (Pandora, London, 1990), p. 195.
9 J. Ann Tickner, *Gender in International Relations* (Columbia University Press, New York, 1992).
10 Terrell Carver, Molly Cochran and Judith Squires, 'Gendering Jones: Feminisms, IRs, Masculinities', *Review of International Studies* vol. 24(2) (1998), pp. 283–97.
11 Yosef Lapid, 'Culture's Ship: Returns and Departures in International Relations Theory' in Yosef Lapid and Friedrich Kratochwil, eds., *The Return of Culture and Identity* (Lynne Rienner, Boulder, Co., 1996), p. 7.
12 J. Ann Tickner, 'Identity in International Relations Theory: Feminist Perspectives' in ibid.

4.7 International relations: one world, many theories

Stephen M. Walt

Source: *Foreign Policy*, no. 110, Special Edition: Frontiers of Knowledge, Spring 1998, 29–46.

Walt argues that there is an inescapable link between theory and practice. During the Cold War, he identifies three dominant theoretical approaches to international relations: realism, liberalism and radicalism. Although all three approaches were challenged by the end of the Cold War, realism and liberalism have proved to be extremely resilient, while more radical thinkers have moved away from a material perspective and now focus on the importance of ideas within a constructivist perspective.

Why should policymakers and practitioners care about the scholarly study of international affairs? Those who conduct foreign policy often dismiss academic theorists (frequently, one must admit, with good reason), but there is an inescapable link between the abstract world of theory and the real world of policy. We need theories to make sense of the blizzard of information that bombards us daily. Even policymakers who are contemptuous of "theory" must rely on their own (often unstated) ideas about how the world works in order to decide what to do. It is hard to make good policy if one's basic organizing principles are flawed, just as it is hard to construct good theories without knowing a lot about the real world. Everyone uses theories – whether he or she knows it or not – and disagreements about policy usually rest on more fundamental disagreements about the basic forces that shape international outcomes.

Take, for example, the current debate on how to respond to China. From one perspective, China's ascent is the latest example of the tendency for rising powers to alter the global balance of power in potentially dangerous ways, especially as their growing influence makes them more ambitious. From another perspective, the key to China's future conduct is whether its behavior will be modified by its integration into world markets and by the (inevitable?) spread of democratic principles. From yet another viewpoint, relations between China and the rest of the world will be shaped by issues of culture and identity: Will China see itself (and be seen by others) as a normal member of the world community or a singular society that deserves special treatment?

In the same way, the debate over NATO expansion looks different depending on which theory one employs. From a "realist" perspective, NATO expansion is an effort to extend Western influence – well beyond the traditional sphere of U.S. vital interests – during a period of Russian weakness and is likely to provoke a harsh response from Moscow. From a liberal perspective, however, expansion will reinforce the nascent democracies of Central Europe and extend NATO's conflict-management mechanisms to a potentially turbulent region. A third view might stress the value of incorporating the Czech Republic, Hungary, and Poland within the Western security community, whose members share a common identity that has made war largely unthinkable.

No single approach can capture all the complexity of contemporary world politics. Therefore, we are better off with a diverse array of competing ideas rather than a single theoretical orthodoxy. Competition between theories helps reveal their strengths and weaknesses and spurs subsequent refinements, while revealing flaws in conventional wisdom. Although we should take care to emphasize inventiveness over invective, we should welcome and encourage the heterogeneity of contemporary scholarship.

Where are we coming from?

The study of international affairs is best understood as a protracted competition between the realist, liberal, and radical traditions. Realism emphasizes the enduring propensity for conflict between states; liberalism identifies several ways to mitigate these conflictive tendencies; and the radical tradition describes how the entire system of state relations might be transformed. The boundaries between these traditions are somewhat fuzzy and a number of important works do not fit neatly into any of them, but debates within and among them have largely defined the discipline.

Realism

Realism was the dominant theoretical tradition throughout the Cold War. It depicts international affairs as a struggle for power among self-interested states and is generally pessimistic about the prospects for eliminating conflict and war. Realism dominated in the Cold War years because it provided simple but powerful explanations for war, alliances, imperialism, obstacles to cooperation, and other international phenomena, and because its emphasis on competition was consistent with the central features of the American-Soviet rivalry.

Realism is not a single theory, of course, and realist thought evolved considerably throughout the Cold War. "Classical" realists such as Hans Morgenthau and Reinhold Niebuhr believed that states, like human beings, had an innate desire to dominate others, which led them to fight wars. Morgenthau also stressed the virtues of the classical, multipolar, balance-of-power system and saw the bipolar rivalry between the United States and the Soviet Union as especially dangerous.

By contrast, the "neorealist" theory advanced by Kenneth Waltz ignored human nature and focused on the effects of the international system. For Waltz, the international system consisted of a number of great powers, each seeking to survive. Because the system is anarchic (i.e., there is no central authority to protect states from one another), each state has to survive on its own. Waltz argued that this condition would lead weaker states to balance against, rather than bandwagon with, more powerful rivals. And contrary to Morgenthau, he claimed that bipolarity was more stable than multipolarity.

An important refinement to realism was the addition of offense-defense theory, as laid out by Robert Jervis, George Quester, and Stephen Van Evera. These scholars argued that war was more likely when states could conquer each other easily. When defense was easier than offense, however, security was more plentiful, incentives to expand declined, and cooperation could blossom. And if defense had the advantage, and states could distinguish between offensive and defensive weapons, then states could acquire the means to defend themselves without threatening others, thereby dampening the effects of anarchy.

For these "defensive" realists, states merely sought to survive and great powers could guarantee their security by forming balancing alliances and choosing defensive military postures (such as retaliatory nuclear forces). Not surprisingly, Waltz and most other neorealists believed that the United States was extremely secure for most of the Cold War. Their principal fear was that it might squander its favorable position by adopting an overly aggressive foreign policy. Thus, by the end of the Cold War, realism had moved away from Morgenthau's dark brooding about human nature and taken on a slightly more optimistic tone.

Liberalism

The principal challenge to realism came from a broad family of liberal theories. One strand of liberal thought argued that economic interdependence would discourage states from using force against each other because warfare would threaten each side's prosperity. A second strand, often associated with President Woodrow Wilson, saw the spread of democracy as the key to world peace, based on the claim that democratic states were inherently more peaceful than authoritarian states. A third, more recent theory argued that international institutions such as the International Energy Agency and the International Monetary Fund could help overcome selfish state behavior, mainly by encouraging states to forego immediate gains for the greater benefits of enduring cooperation.

Although some liberals flirted with the idea that new transnational actors, especially the multinational corporation, were gradually encroaching on the power of states, liberalism generally saw states as the central players in international affairs. All liberal theories implied that cooperation was more pervasive than even the defensive version of realism allowed, but each view offered a different recipe for promoting it.

Radical approaches

Until the 1980s, marxism was the main alternative to the mainstream realist and liberal traditions. Where realism and liberalism took the state system for granted, marxism offered both a different explanation for international conflict and a blueprint for fundamentally transforming the existing international order.

Orthodox marxist theory saw capitalism as the central cause of international conflict. Capitalist states battled each other as a consequence of their incessant struggle for profits and battled socialist states because they saw in them the seeds of their own destruction. Neomarxist "dependency" theory, by contrast, focused on relations between advanced capitalist powers and less developed states and argued that the former – aided by an unholy alliance with the ruling classes of the developing world – had grown rich by exploiting the latter. The solution was to overthrow these parasitic élites and install a revolutionary government committed to autonomous development.

Both of these theories were largely discredited before the Cold War even ended. The extensive history of economic and military cooperation among the advanced industrial powers showed that capitalism did not inevitably lead to conflict. The bitter schisms that divided the communist world showed that socialism did not always promote harmony. Dependency theory suffered similar empirical setbacks as it became increasingly clear that, first, active participation in the world economy was a better route to prosperity than autonomous socialist development; and, second, many developing countries proved themselves quite capable of bargaining successfully with multinational corporations and other capitalist institutions.

As marxism succumbed to its various failings, its mantle was assumed by a group of theorists who borrowed heavily from the wave of postmodern writings in literary criticism and social theory. This "deconstructionist" approach was openly skeptical of the effort to devise general or universal theories such as realism or liberalism. Indeed, its proponents emphasized the importance of language and discourse in shaping social outcomes. However, because these scholars focused initially on criticizing the mainstream paradigms but did not offer positive alternatives to them, they remained a self-consciously dissident minority for most of the 1980s.

Domestic politics

Not all Cold War scholarship on international affairs fit neatly into the realist, liberal, or marxist paradigms. In particular, a number of important works focused on the characteristics of states, governmental organizations, or individual leaders. The democratic strand of liberal theory fits under this heading, as do the efforts of scholars such as Graham Allison and John Steinbruner to use organization theory and bureaucratic politics to explain foreign policy behavior, and those of Jervis, Irving Janis, and others, which applied social and cognitive psychology. For the most part, these efforts did not seek to provide a general theory of international behavior but to identify other factors that might lead states to behave contrary to the predictions of the realist or liberal approaches. Thus, much of this literature should be regarded as a complement to the three main paradigms rather than as a rival approach for analysis of the international system as a whole.

New wrinkles in old paradigms

Scholarship on international affairs has diversified significantly since the end of the Cold War. Non-American voices are more prominent, a wider range of methods and theories are seen as legitimate, and new issues such as ethnic conflict, the environment, and the future of the state have been placed on the agenda of scholars everywhere.

Yet the sense of déjà vu is equally striking. Instead of resolving the struggle between competing theoretical traditions, the end of the Cold War has merely launched a new series of debates. Ironically, even as many societies embrace similar ideals of democracy, free markets, and human rights, the scholars who study these developments are more divided than ever.

Realism redux

Although the end of the Cold War led a few writers to declare that realism was destined for the academic scrapheap, rumors of its demise have been largely exaggerated.

A recent contribution of realist theory is its attention to the problem of relative and absolute gains. Responding to the institutionalists' claim that international institutions would enable states to forego short-term advantages for the sake of greater long-term gains, realists such as Joseph Grieco and Stephen Krasner point out that anarchy forces states to worry about both the absolute gains from cooperation and the way that gains are distributed among participants. The logic is straightforward: If one state reaps larger gains than its partners, it will gradually become stronger, and its partners will eventually become more vulnerable.

Realists have also been quick to explore a variety of new issues. Barry Posen offers a realist explanation for ethnic conflict, noting that the breakup of multiethnic states could place rival ethnic groups in an anarchic setting, thereby triggering intense fears and tempting each group to use force to improve its relative position. This problem would be particularly severe when each group's territory contained enclaves inhabited by their ethnic rivals – as in the former Yugoslavia – because each side would be tempted to "cleanse" (preemptively) these alien minorities and expand to incorporate any others from their ethnic group that lay outside their borders. Realists have also cautioned that NATO, absent a clear enemy, would likely face increasing strains and that expanding its presence eastward would jeopardize relations with Russia. Finally, scholars such as Michael Mastanduno have argued that U.S. foreign policy is generally consistent with realist principles, insofar as its actions are still designed to preserve U.S. predominance and to shape a postwar order that advances American interests.

The most interesting conceptual development within the realist paradigm has been the emerging split between the "defensive" and "offensive" strands of thought. Defensive realists such as Waltz, Van Evera, and Jack Snyder assumed that states had little intrinsic interest in military conquest and argued that the costs of expansion generally out-weighed the benefits. Accordingly, they maintained that great power wars occurred largely because domestic groups fostered exaggerated perceptions of threat and an excessive faith in the efficacy of military force.

This view is now being challenged along several fronts. First, as Randall Schweller notes, the neorealist assumption that states merely seek to survive "stacked the deck" in favor of the status quo because it precluded the threat of predatory revisionist states – nations such as Adolf Hitler's Germany or Napoleon Bonaparte's France that "value what they covet far more than what they possess" and are willing to risk annihilation to achieve their aims. Second, Peter Liberman, in his book *Does Conquest Pay?*, uses a number of historical cases – such as the Nazi occupation of Western Europe and Soviet hegemony over Eastern Europe – to show that the benefits of conquest often exceed the costs, thereby casting doubt on the claim that military expansion is no longer cost-effective. Third, offensive realists such as Eric Labs, John Mearsheimer, and Fareed Zakaria argue that anarchy encourages all states to try to maximize their relative strength simply because no state can ever be sure when a truly revisionist power might emerge.

These differences help explain why realists disagree over issues such as the future of Europe. For defensive realists such as Van Evera, war is rarely profitable and usually results from militarism, hypernationalism, or some other distorting domestic factor. Because Van Evera believes such forces are largely absent in post-Cold War Europe, he concludes that the region is "primed for peace." By contrast, Mearsheimer and other offensive realists believe that anarchy forces great powers to compete irrespective of their internal characteristics and that security competition will return to Europe as soon as the U.S. pacifier is withdrawn.

New life for liberalism

The defeat of communism sparked a round of self-congratulation in the West, best exemplified by Francis Fukuyama's infamous claim that humankind had now reached the "end of history." History has paid little attention to this boast, but the triumph of the West did give a notable boost to all three strands of liberal thought.

By far the most interesting and important development has been the lively debate on the "democratic peace." Although the most recent phase of this debate had begun even before the Soviet Union collapsed, it became more influential as the number of democracies began to increase and as evidence of this relationship began to accumulate.

Democratic peace theory is a refinement of the earlier claim that democracies were inherently more peaceful than autocratic states. It rests on the belief that although democracies seem to fight wars as often as other states, they rarely, if ever, fight one another. Scholars such as Michael Doyle, James Lee Ray, and Bruce Russett have offered a number of explanations for this tendency, the most popular being that democracies embrace norms of compromise that bar the use of force against groups espousing similar principles. It is hard to think of a more influential, recent academic debate, insofar as the belief that "democracies don't fight each other" has been an important justification for the Clinton administration's efforts to enlarge the sphere of democratic rule.

It is therefore ironic that faith in the "democratic peace" became the basis for U.S. policy just as additional research was beginning to identify several qualifiers to this theory. First, Snyder and Edward Mansfield pointed out that states may be more prone to war when they are in the midst of a democratic transition, which implies that efforts to export democracy might actually make things worse. Second, critics such as Joanne Gowa and David Spiro have argued that the apparent absence of war between democracies is due to the way that democracy has been defined and to the relative dearth of democratic states (especially before 1945). In addition, Christopher Layne has pointed out that when democracies have come close to war in the past their decision to remain at peace ultimately had little do with their shared democratic character. Third, clearcut evidence that democracies do not fight each other is confined to the post-1945 era, and, as Gowa has emphasized, the absence of conflict in this period may be due more to their common interest in containing the Soviet Union than to shared democratic principles.

Liberal institutionalists likewise have continued to adapt their own theories. On the one hand, the core claims of institutionalist theory have become more modest over time. Institutions are now said to facilitate cooperation when it is in each state's interest to do so, but it is widely agreed that they cannot force states to behave in ways that are contrary to the states' own selfish interests. On the other hand, institutionalists such as John Duffield and Robert McCalla have extended the theory into new substantive areas, most notably the study of NATO. For these scholars, NATO's highly institutionalized character helps explain why it has been able to survive and adapt, despite the disappearance of its main adversary.

The economic strand of liberal theory is still influential as well. In particular, a number of scholars have recently suggested that the "globalization" of world markets, the rise of transnational networks and nongovernmental organizations, and the rapid spread of global communications technology are undermining the power of states and shifting attention away from military security toward economics and social welfare. The details are novel but the basic logic is familiar: As societies around the globe become enmeshed in a web of economic and social connections, the costs of disrupting these ties will effectively preclude unilateral state actions, especially the use of force.

This perspective implies that war will remain a remote possibility among the advanced industrial democracies. It also suggests that bringing China and Russia into the relentless embrace of world capitalism is the best way to promote both prosperity and peace, particularly if this process creates a strong middle class in these states and reinforces pressures to democratize. Get these societies hooked on prosperity and competition will be confined to the economic realm.

This view has been challenged by scholars who argue that the actual scope of "globalization" is modest and that these various transactions still take place in environments that are shaped and regulated by states. Nonetheless, the belief that economic forces are superseding traditional great power politics enjoys widespread acceptance among scholars, pundits, and policymakers, and the role of the state is likely to be an important topic for future academic inquiry.

Constructivist theories

Whereas realism and liberalism tend to focus on material factors such as power or trade, constructivist approaches emphasize the impact of ideas. Instead of taking the state for granted and assuming that it simply seeks to survive, constructivists regard the interests and identities of states as a highly malleable product of specific historical processes. They pay close attention to the prevailing discourse(s) in society because discourse reflects and shapes beliefs and interests, and establishes accepted norms of behavior. Consequently, constructivism is especially attentive to the sources of change, and this approach has largely replaced marxism as the preeminent radical perspective on international affairs.

The end of the Cold War played an important role in legitimating constructivist theories because realism and liberalism both failed to anticipate this event and had some trouble explaining it. Constructivists had an explanation: Specifically, former president Mikhail Gorbachev revolutionized Soviet foreign policy because he embraced new ideas such as "common security."

Moreover, given that we live in an era where old norms are being challenged, once clear boundaries are dissolving, and issues of identity are becoming more salient, it is hardly surprising that scholars have been drawn to approaches that place these issues front and center. From a constructivist perspective, in fact, the central issue in the post-Cold War world is how different groups conceive their identities and interests. Although power is not irrelevant, constructivism emphasizes how ideas and identities are created, how they evolve, and how they shape the way states understand and respond to their situation. Therefore, it matters whether Europeans define themselves primarily in national or continental terms; whether Germany and Japan redefine their pasts in ways that encourage their adopting more active international roles; and whether the United States embraces or rejects its identity as "global policeman."

Constructivist theories are quite diverse and do not offer a unified set of predictions on any of these issues. At a purely conceptual level, Alexander Wendt has argued that the realist conception of anarchy does not adequately explain why conflict occurs between states. The real issue is how anarchy is understood – in Wendt's words, "Anarchy is what states make of it." Another strand of constructivist theory has focused on the future of the territorial state, suggesting that transnational communication and shared civic values are undermining traditional national loyalties and creating radically new forms of political association. Other constructivists focus on the role of norms, arguing that international law and other normative principles have eroded earlier notions of sovereignty and altered the legitimate purposes for which state power may be employed. The common theme in each of these strands is the capacity of discourse to shape how political actors define themselves and their interests, and thus modify their behavior.

Domestic politics reconsidered

As in the Cold War, scholars continue to explore the impact of domestic politics on the behavior of states. Domestic politics are obviously central to the debate on the democratic peace, and scholars such as Snyder, Jeffrey Frieden, and Helen Milner have examined how domestic interest groups can distort the formation of state preferences and lead to suboptimal international behavior. George Downs, David Rocke, and others have also explored how domestic institutions can help states deal with the perennial problem of uncertainty, while students of psychology have applied prospect theory and other new tools to explain why decision makers fail to act in a rational fashion.

The past decade has also witnessed an explosion of interest in the concept of culture, a development that overlaps with the constructivist emphasis on the importance of ideas and norms. Thus, Thomas Berger and Peter Katzenstein have used cultural variables to explain why Germany and Japan have thus far eschewed more self-reliant military policies; Elizabeth Kier has offered a cultural interpretation of British and French military doctrines in the interwar period; and Iain Johnston has traced continuities in Chinese foreign policy to a deeply rooted form of "cultural realism." Samuel Huntington's dire warnings about an imminent "clash of civilizations" are symptomatic of this trend as well, insofar as his argument rests on the claim that broad cultural affinities are now supplanting national loyalties. Though these and other works define culture in widely varying ways and have yet to provide a full explanation of how it works or how enduring its effects might be, cultural perspectives have been very much in vogue during the past five years. This trend is partly a reflection of the broader interest in cultural issues in the academic world (and within the public debate as well) and partly a response to the upsurge in ethnic, nationalist, and cultural conflicts since the demise of the Soviet Union.

Tomorrow's conceptual toolbox

While these debates reflect the diversity of contemporary scholarship on international affairs, there are also obvious signs of convergence. Most realists recognize that nationalism, militarism, ethnicity, and other domestic factors are important; liberals acknowledge that power is central to international behavior; and some constructivists admit that ideas will have greater impact when backed by powerful states and reinforced by enduring material forces. The boundaries of each paradigm are somewhat permeable, and there is ample opportunity for intellectual arbitrage.

Which of these broad perspectives sheds the most light on contemporary international affairs, and which should policymakers keep most firmly in mind when charting our course into the next century? Although many academics (and more than a few policymakers) are loathe to admit it, realism remains the most compelling general framework for understanding international relations. States continue to pay close attention to the balance of power and to worry about the possibility of major conflict. Among other things, this enduring preoccupation with power and security explains why many Asians and Europeans are now eager to preserve – and possibly expand – the U.S. military presence in their regions. As Czech president Václav Havel has warned, if NATO fails to expand, "we might be heading for a new global catastrophe [. . .] [which] could cost us all much more than the two world wars." These are not the words of a man who believes that great power rivalry has been banished forever.

As for the United States, the past decade has shown how much it likes being "number one" and how determined it is to remain in a predominant position. The United States has taken advantage of its current superiority to impose its preferences wherever possible, even at the risk of irritating many of its long-standing allies. It has forced a series of one-sided arms control agreements on Russia, dominated the problematic peace effort in Bosnia, taken steps to expand NATO into Russia's backyard, and become increasingly concerned about the rising power of China. It has called repeatedly for greater reliance on multilateralism and a larger role for international institutions, but has treated agencies such as the United Nations and the World Trade Organization with disdain whenever their actions did not conform to U.S. interests. It refused to join the rest of the world in outlawing the production of land-mines and was politely uncooperative at the Kyoto environmental summit. Although U.S. leaders are adept at cloaking their actions in the lofty rhetoric of "world order," naked self-interest lies behind most of them. Thus, the end of the Cold War did not bring the end of power politics, and realism is likely to remain the single most useful instrument in our intellectual toolbox.

Yet realism does not explain everything, and a wise leader would also keep insights from the rival paradigms in mind. Liberal theories identify the instruments that states can use to achieve shared interests, highlight the powerful economic forces with which states and soci-eties must now contend, and help us understand why states may differ in their basic prefer-ences. Paradoxically, because U.S. protection reduces the danger of regional rivalries and reinforces the "liberal peace" that emerged after 1945, these factors may become relatively more important, as long as the United States continues to provide security and stability in many parts of the world.

Meanwhile, constructivist theories are best suited to the analysis of how identities and interests can change over time, thereby producing subtle shifts in the behavior of states and occasionally triggering far-reaching but unexpected shifts in international affairs. It matters if political identity in Europe continues to shift from the nation-state to more local regions or to a broader sense of European identity, just as it matters if nationalism is gradually sup-planted by the sort of "civilizational" affinities emphasized by Huntington. Realism has little to say about these prospects, and policymakers could be blind-sided by change if they ignore these possibilities entirely.

In short, each of these competing perspectives captures important aspects of world polit-ics. Our understanding would be impoverished were our thinking confined to only one of them. The "compleat diplomat" of the future should remain cognizant of realism's emphasis on the inescapable role of power, keep liberalism's awareness of domestic forces in mind, and occasionally reflect on constructivism's vision of change.

4.8 The rise and fall of the inter-paradigm debate

Ole Wæver

Source: Steve Smith, Ken Booth and Marysia Zalewski, (eds), *International Theory: Positivism and Beyond* (Cambridge University Press, Cambridge 1996), pp. 149–85.

Wæver argues that the image of International Relations as three incommensurable paradigms or schools of thought (realism, liberalism and radicalism) is a product of the 1970s and represented a third debate in the discipline's history. By the late 1980s, this tripartite division was giving way to a fourth more philosophical debate between rationalism and reflectivism, with liberalism and realism converging around rationalism and radicalism converging around reflectivism. By the 1990s, Wæver suggests that incommensurability began to give way to a division of labour and the signs of a fifth debate.

A standard textbook presentation of International Relations (IR) has it that there are three paradigms, three dominant schools. The first is realism, the second is alternately called pluralism, interdependence and world society but it is in some sense always the liberal approach, and the third is Marxism or more broadly radicalism, structuralism or globalism. Some writers claim that this is the timeless pattern of International Relations debate – even in the classics, we find these three types of thinking. [. . .]

But 'the debate' is a misleading map and a bad guide to introduce students to. This is not the pattern of debate today. The story about an 'inter-paradigm debate' does not give a grip on the ongoing controversies in the discipline. The debate has moved on; self-referential story-telling in the discipline ought to move with it. We need to construct new, more up-to-date stories and invent new images and metaphors to replace the triangle of the late 1970s. [. . .]

What was the inter-paradigm debate?

The first great debate in IR was that of idealism versus realism in the 1940s and the second was behaviouralism versus traditionalism in the 1950s–1960s. In the late 1960s and throughout the 1970s, there was increasing criticism of the dominant realist paradigm, not primarily its methodology, but its image of the world, its alleged state-centrism, preoccupation with power and its blindness to various kinds of processes domestically, transnationally and beyond the political-military sphere.

The challengers not only formulated a criticism of realism but tried to present alternative conceptions of the international system. These went in terms of regional integration, transnationalism, interdependence, and a pluralist system of numerous sub-state and trans-state actors who made up a much more complicated image than the usual state-to-state one. States did not exist as such – various actors in the state interacted to produce what looked like state policy and sometimes even went around it and had their own linkages across borders. Not only were there more actors than the state, the state was not the state but was to be decomposed into networks of bureaucracies, interest groups and individuals in a pluralist perspective.

Increasingly, it became clear that the new theories were to win no easy victory. The realist imagery had a solid hold on decision makers who kept to some extent operating in a world of states, and the new formulations had difficulty consolidating into *theory* and not just complications *of* the realist theory. [. . .]

Such an understanding was assisted by the contemporary criticism of positivism and especially Thomas Kuhn's theory of *paradigms*.[1] From here the idea was borrowed, that relations among competing general theories cannot be judged in any over-arching, neutral language. Each 'paradigm' constructs its own basic concepts/units and questions – and thereby its data, criteria and not least its stories about paradigmatic experiments or similar scientific events. Paradigms are incommensurable, because they each generate their criteria of judgement and their own 'language'. Realism and its pluralist challenger appeared to be such incommensurable paradigms.

Meanwhile, a third paradigm had arisen: Marxism. Marxism was not new as a theory making powerful statements on international relations. Actually, it had done so at least as long as the discipline of IR had existed. [. . .] Theories of imperialism had been discussed vigorously – probably more blood was spilled here than in the debates of IR. But very few saw this as international relations (despite the dual allegiances of one of the founding fathers, Carr). In the 1970s, however, Marxism was increasingly seen as an alternative theory of international relations. It was not really equally well established within IR, but it became fashionable to present the discipline as engaged in a triangular debate. Maybe it was triangular, but it was *de facto* mainly a debate along one side of the triangle (Figure 1).

How did it differ from the other two great debates?

The debate took place mainly in the 1970s but gained its self-reflection *as* 'the inter-paradigm debate' or 'the third debate' in the beginning of the 1980s.

In contrast to the two previous debates, it increasingly was seen as a debate not to be won, but a pluralism to live with. In the first two debates, it was expected that one side would eventually win and International Relations would evolve as a coherent discipline in the winning camp. In the third debate, one increasingly (mostly implicitly) got the self-conception that the discipline *was* the debate. 'International Relations' was this disagreement, not a truth held by one of the positions. Each saw a side of reality that was important but could only be told from its perspective, not translated into the other two, nor subsumed in some grand synthesis. The discipline was thus in some sense richer for having all three voices, but also potentially in danger of fragmenting.

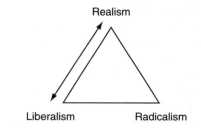

Figure 1 The inter-paradigm debate

The yellow jersey of the leader who was in a position to define the discipline has travelled a complicated route. The discipline was invented in the inter-war period by liberalist theoreticians, while the first debate carried over the jersey to the camp of the realists (where now also they wanted to develop a specific discipline, International Relations). Realism had its palmy days in the 1940s and 1950s, and in a sense one might say the discipline did too. There was a clear focus, a relatively widespread consensus both on what IR was and that one had relevant things to say. Then followed the second debate, where the challengers were even more sure that the study of international relations was worthwhile and could be put to use (but possibly at times more doubtful whether there was a separate discipline). The movement of the new techniques hardly established a fixed, successful programme, and produced instead a confused situation. An assortment of empirical studies came from this wing, but no new paradigm. (Instead the behaviouralist challenge had a long-term impact on realism; more on this in a moment.) The behaviouralist programme with its fixation on method was not ready to *replace* realism (this the empirical findings were supposed to do!). The crux of the discipline came – if we stay with the metaphor of the yellow jersey – to hang fluttering somewhere near realism but in strong wind from the methodological challenge. After a period of extensive but diffuse belief in the new scientificness of the discipline, we returned to realism but a less focused, less self-assured realism. IR research could be conducted in a multitude of ways, many of which were on arch-realist premises (e.g. with power political, egoistic states fitted into models of a game theoretical or system theoretical nature). Thus the discipline flapped towards the 1970s when it definitely became triangular. With incommensurability, one no longer strived for ending debate, for finding who was right, but acknowledged that each 'paradigm' contained its own truth, and that they were all valuable. The debate is the discipline. This was definitely different from the two previous debates (as well as the one to follow it).

The debates have also differed as to arena or object of contest. The arena for competition in the inter-paradigm debate was largely 'basic assumptions' and 'basic images': what is international relations made up of – states, individuals, bureaucracies, a global economy, or what? Each paradigm was assumed to be locked, psychologically in its self-reaffirming conception which it could not convince the other of. The main issue of contention was 'the nature of international relations' (with ensuing political consequences) and the secondary one 'methodology'. [. . .]

How did it start?

The specific parties to the inter-paradigm debate will not be explained here. What is important in this context is the *form* of the debate: incommensurability. The paradigms could not have a real, normal 'debate'. They could not be tested against each other, since they basically did not speak the same language.

This at first had the 'liberating' function to allow weaker contenders to appear on the scene without being immediately bulldozed. It served a kind of 'infant industry' function and the reason for this pluralism was probably to be found in the weakened mainstream: American IR was marked by self-doubt after the Vietnam war, the student revolt and the oil shock. Without a sense of direction and a self-assured centre to control developments, without a voice of authenticity, there was suddenly room for more diversity in IR. In the longer run, however, the inter-paradigm debate might have had a conservative function. 'It became a welcomed barrier against any critique and a good legitimation for scientific routine. "Don't criticise me, we speak different languages" '.[2]

Thus, the main explanation for this peculiar form for a discipline to take is to be found in a weakening of the centre. This can be explained by a combination of *discipline history* (the attacks on realism) and *discipline external* developments (as mentioned: student revolt, Vietnam war, etc.). In this situation, the discipline avoided complete disintegration through the holding operation of the interparadigm debate. [. . .] The metaphor of *paradigms* was useful for reconstructing a more decentralised but stabilised image of the discipline in a time of troubles.

I would further suggest that there was also a kind of sideways inspiration from within the discipline. Implicitly, one seemed to borrow from the 'perceptions' studies that proliferated in the same period: we are all caught by our view of the world, and this structures our way of importing new information and evaluating it. Ideas of perceptions, images, and cognitive psychology which found in those years their way into the discipline, were (implicitly) applied to the discipline itself. [. . .]

How did it end?

In the mid and late 1980s we were no longer in the inter-paradigm debate, even if it was still used as a teaching tool and as schematism when some idea was to be evaluated 'across the discipline'. The 1980s constellation was different. Different because there was a change of fronts, and different because it moved to a different level and, not least, it moved beyond incommensurability.

In the triangular third debate, the three sides probably were never equal. The Marxist/structuralist side did not achieve full equivalence, and at least for a while the initiative was with 'interdependence' (the liberalist brand of the day). As often noted, Waltz's *Theory of International Politics* and Gilpin's *War and Change in World Politics* were the revenge of realism, an attempt to relaunch more 'scientific' versions of realism.[3] Especially Waltz's version, which became known under the name Robert Cox and Richard Ashley gave to them: 'neo-realism'.[4] [. . .] The really new thing about neo-realism is its *concept of science*. General speculation and reflection is no longer sufficient, realism has to express itself in the form of *theory*, of a system of clearly specified sentences. In this sense the shift from realism to neo-realism can be seen as a delayed and displaced victory for the 'scientific' side of the second debate.

This change has important and interesting effects on the relationship among 'paradigms'. (Neo-)Realism is no longer an ethico-philosophical position. Sweeping statements on the nature of life and politics are replaced by precise statements. Compare the rhetoric of classical realists like Morgenthau, Kissinger and Liska who generalise about the nature of human life (not necessarily human nature, but wisdom about the human condition) and tell stories about the inherently tragic nature of politics and other lessons at a level close to philosophy of history. Neo-realism in contrast says only 'a small number of big and important things', a conscious self-limitation.[5] Becoming scientific implies a certain minimalism, and plenty of space is left for developing theory and empirical studies on a number of other factors.

Liberal theory underwent a parallel development. It moved away from being a general interpretation of the nature of international relations or an idea of overall developments, and concentrated instead on asking a few precise questions. Or maybe simply one: 'how institutions affect incentives facing states'.[6] And the principal thesis is that variations in the institutionalization of world politics exert significant impacts on the behaviour of governments. In particular, patterns of cooperation and discord can be understood only in the context of the institutions that help define the meaning and importance of state action.[7] [. . .]

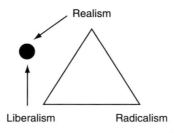

Figure 2 The neo-neo synthesis

During the 1980s, realism became neo-realism and liberalism neo-liberal institutionalism. Both underwent a self-limiting redefinition towards an anti-metaphysical, theoretical minimalism, and they became thereby increasingly compatible. A dominant *neo-neo synthesis* became the research programme of the 1980s (Figure 2). No longer were realism and liberalism 'incommensurable' – on the contrary they shared a 'rationalist' research programme, a conception of science, a shared willingness to operate on the premise of anarchy (Waltz) and investigate the evolution of co-operation and whether institutions matter (Keohane).

My term 'neo-neo' does not refer to an idea that this is newer than the new, a reformulation of neo-realism for instance. It refers to the synthesis between realism and liberalism that became possible, when realism was transformed into neo-realism and liberalism into neo-liberal institutionalism. [. . .]

In this environment, the main line of controversy shifted in the opposite direction to one between rationalists and reflectivists, the post-modernism debate. As the previous line of debate 'dried out', the radicals entered to fill the vacuum. Thus the two main poles became on the one hand a neo-realist, neo-liberal synthesis and on the other reflectivism (cf. Figure 3).

This constellation became authorised by Keohane's presidential address for ISA 1988 where he discussed 'two approaches to international institutions.'[8] The two approaches were on the one side the rationalist, clearly referring to the merged neo-realist neo-liberalist research programme of which he himself is one of the leaders, and the other side that Keohane united under the label 'reflectivists' which was to cover those inspired by French post-modernism, those with German hermeneutics as well as late-Wittgensteinian rules-perspectives and social constructivism. (Sometimes, the label reflectivist has – consciously or not – been changed to *reflexivists* in order to point to the self-reflective nature of the new critical approaches.)

Reflectivists, according to Keohane, are characterised by emphasising *interpretation*, the *reflections* of the actors as central to institutions. Norms and regimes cannot be studied positivistically but have to be seen as inter-subjective phenomena only researchable by non-positivist methods. Institutions are not something actors rationally construct following from their interests, since they act in meta-institutions (such as the principle of sovereignty) which create the actors rather than the other way round. Institutions and actors constitute each other mutually.

In the new set-up it could finally be noted how the reflectivists carry out a flanking operation (see Figure 3). In their work to reshape themselves in scientific form, realism as well as liberalism had to leave behind some of their traditional fields, political statesmen in the case of realism, and ethics in the case of liberalism. Reflectivists attempted to articulate these classical issues against the two neo-schools, who had become too scientific for such matters. Post-structuralists have argued that classical realism was in many ways superior to

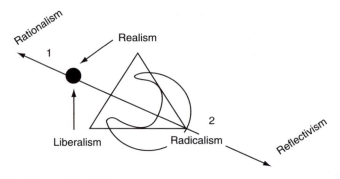

Figure 3 IR debate of the 1980s

neo-realism. Ethics, a traditionally liberalist theme, has in recent years been articulated more often from a reflectivist basis.

Why is reflectivism placed in the same corner as Marxism, why the vague covering term 'radicalism'? Reflectivists do not share many assumptions with the Marxists. Thus, if one wants to make an ahistorical model of different schools, they have to have clearly separate positions. But when the models are snapshots at a given time, they can be located in the same place – radicalism – since post-modernist approaches largely replaced Marxism as the 'extreme contender', the radical challenge. Some Marxists might claim that this is a plot of the establishment, because post-modernism is ultimately reactionary and thus it was a nice move for the establishment to get rid of the really dangerous challenge, Marxism, and be hospitable to an ultimately undangerous new challenger, post-modernism. Post-modernists will emphasise how their criticism of logo-centric, Western, essentialist theories punches Marxism at least as hard as it does the establishment, and therefore criticism has become more radical as they took over. Watching with the task of writing the history of the discipline, it can be noticed that the role of Marxism as contender in great debates clearly has waned. [. . .] There is still – maybe increasingly – important work from Marxists that contributes significantly in IPE, in foreign policy theory and not least in macro-historical reflection on the emergence and evolution of the modern state. In the debates which the discipline uses to orient itself, the position which used to be occupied by Marxists was in the mid and late 1980s taken over by post-modernists.

The rationalist–reflectivist axis was not the only but the biggest axis in the 1980s. [. . .] Table 1 sums up how on three dimentions, [the debate] has changed. Not only has this move taken us beyond the inter-paradigm debate; now we are probably beyond the fourth debate.

What's wrong with the inter-paradigm debate?

This implies actually two questions:

1   Is it true? Is the triangle of incommensurable paradigms the final, inevitable pattern? Can we rise above incommensurability, or is this 'relativist' argument actually impossible to deal with, because one's own argument will always remain one of the positions in this world of self-reaffirming positions who can't establish a joint language?
2   What's wrong with keeping this as an image of the discipline, using it as a handy way of introducing the discipline to students, and as a map when discussing broadly the

Table 1 Comparing the third and the fourth debates

	3rd debate (Inter-paradigm debate)	*4th debate (Reflectivist–rationalist)*
Form of relationship among debaters	Incommensurability	War
Theme (or substance) of disagreement	World view	Philosophy
Combatants	The three paradigms	Neo-neo synthesis against post-modernists

development of the discipline? Is it so important to argue over whether we are in the inter-paradigm debate or not?

A post-modern solution to the problem of incommensurability

It has often been assumed that post-structuralists should love the argument of incommensurability. [. . .] I will argue the opposite: the quandary of incommensurability – which most commonsensical Anglo-Saxon minded social scientists find unacceptable but difficult to rebut – can be dealt with most fundamentally from a post-structuralist perspective.

The first step is to notice that the concept of incommensurability is not the problem, the problem is the concept of commensurability. The *argument* about incommensurability rests on a dichotomy, between on the one hand radical incommensurability (and ultimate incommunicability) *among* paradigms and on the other hand radical commensurability and communicability *within* paradigms. A post-structuralist immediately reacts against the latter: total understanding *never* happens. No communication (in the phenomenological sense) is ever communication (in the ideal sense). But communication takes place all the time, so obviously human beings experience that it makes sufficient sense for us (or most of us) to go on. (Some even make a living of it, for instance as IR scholars and teachers.) [. . .] Post-structuralists argue that all meaning systems are open-ended systems of signs referring to signs referring to signs. No concept can therefore have an ultimate, unequivocal meaning. The image of closed paradigms or any other closed culture assumes that a closed sign system has been achieved which gives a stable and ultimate meaning to its participants. This would be possible within French *structuralism*, but exactly not in *post*-structuralism, the main difference between the two being that structuralism is a theory of signs, post-structuralism a critique of the sign; structuralism investigates how social phenomena can be explained by stable and pervasive meaning systems, post-structuralism shows how all meaning systems are precarious, self-defeating and only *strive* for closure without ever succeeding.

The image of paradigms internally communicating, externally only interacting, closely resembles late eighteenth–early nineteenth-century *romanticism*. Romanticism is a belief in closed cultures. Meaning rests with the community. Cultures are the carriers of meaning systems, and can only be understood from within, by the participants who share these cultures as complete persons, aesthetically, linguistically and sometimes even ethnically or historically. Especially in romantic nationalism it is clear how one assumes total understanding within (the complete, gratifying *understanding* in the warm embrace of the nation) and the total lack of understanding between cultures.

Incommensurability is only a meaningful term if combined with romanticising the warmth of community (as we see in its replay today in US multi-culturalism). Incommensurability as concept derives its meaning from a distinction, the distinction between incommensurability and commensurability – a deeply problematic distinction, as becomes most clear by investigating the concept of commensurability. Anglo-Saxon critics have attacked 'the myth of the framework' or 'the very idea of a conceptual scheme'. They focus on the exaggeration of *limits* to communication. A solution to the problem of incommensurability is to be found in an investigation of the exaggeration of *unlimited* communication. [. . .]

It is, however, not at all surprising that incommensurability arose out of Anglo-Saxon philosophy of science. Actually it is a logical question to arise out of their problematique – only to those who have believed in complete communication can walls of incommunicability and incommensurability appear.

When we have deconstructed this image of walls encircling crowds who are forced to communicate meaningfully only within their throng, and replaced it by a general image of difficult, incomplete, partial 'communication' which might exhibit variations in density and thus patterns or groupings, but no fixed, ultimate distinctions of an inside/outside nature, there is no reason to assume (radical) incommensurability (specifically) among paradigms. There is, however, one remaining argument which is often made for incommensurability: these paradigms are really political groupings. The three 'paradigms' are obviously the three classical political main orientations: conservative, liberal and radical. Therefore, they can never be brought to agree. Not because of cognitive filters or the closedness of sign systems, but because their world views are tied with different *normative* programmes. This argument, however, ought to lead to a *general* relativism or perspectivism. It can hardly sustain a picture of three paradigms. Even if there are these three grand ideologies, political struggles do not consistently form themselves in such triangles. Why does this discipline then? Paradigms have to be applied first of all as sociological concepts for discipline internal developments.

Do international relationists today still use 'incommensurability' as an implicit guide? No, we have seen the neo-neo synthesis which strives for a shared classical methodology, and even among the theories that do not vie for such close merger, there is a changed attitude. The trend of the last decade has exactly been for all the more dominant theories also to establish more self-knowledge and a better understanding of their limits, inner logic and their couplings to other kinds of theory. Thus, the mode of relating schools in the 1990s is not incommensurability but a kind of 'division of labour'. What the theory of science rationale of this attitude can be is a little less clear.

Based on scientific realist premises (i.e. that all theories are ultimately talking about the same reality out there), a division of labour can have evolved because the different explanatory sources are placed in different areas. Each theory carves out its own explanatory mechanisms and sources in ways that do not overlap. In the end they partly explain the same object, but they do not compete for this, and should not be tested against each other. They should be articulated, since they base themselves in separate parts of the system. Or as Ruggie has recently put it:

> Clearly, different bodies of contemporary international relations theory are better equipped to elucidate different domains of contemporary change and continuity. [. . .] Each, therefore, can become a 'grand theory' only by discounting or ignoring altogether the integrity of those domains of social life that its premises do not encompass. Nor are the various bodies of extant theory in any sense additive, so that we could arrive at a grand theory by steps.

There is no overarching logic *of* the different stories. They each have unfolded from their own inner logic, constructing a coherent story which has, however, in the last decade zoomed in on specific, partial levels, with the effect that the theories can be treated as complementary sources of negative predictions.

The theories do not modify each other – they have each their separate area: domestic, international political structure, systemic pressure, political action and interaction. They are each absolute demands. The theoretician has to accept the inner logic of Waltzianism when he enters an analysis in terms of international political structure. The same for the other places. They each have their inner logics, but they have managed to carve out complementary sections and they have made linkages that allow for a mutual serviceability.

This implicit emerging attitude, however well it functions as social ideal in the discipline, comes to rest on some heroic assumptions if it stays on realist ground (realist in theory of science sense). The different theories have moved in the direction of different fields/levels, but still they do have a lot of shared references (state, interest, politics, etc.) that are given different meaning in the different theories. To a realist, it then becomes problematic to combine the theories. This new attitude *could* then be reformulated as a more radical con-structivism in which the objects are seen as constructed by the separate theories.

Therefore these do not compete for explaining 'the same'. They each do different jobs. The theories can only be linked externally, when one theory reaches out on its own terms for another theory to exploit it, which it can then only do by grasping the inner logic of this other theory and its material. This self-referentiality of the theories in no way prevents researchers from entering several of these – the limitations are not in our heads but in the logic of the theories and their ensuing 'realities'. Grand 'synthesis' and (literal) co-operation (simultaneous running) of several theories (that might in some abstract sense be logically incompatible), thus becomes possible if the meta-theory is adjusted towards constructivism. This in a sense is to play *with* incommensurability, but against the cognitivist idea of different 'lenses' that create different pictures of 'the same'.

A strategic approach to 'IR debates'

The second question is the famous *and so what?* Does the inter-paradigm debate idea harm anyone? Yes, there is a tendency in it to produce straw men, not least of the realists. But more importantly these debates and the ideas about the debates are part of the self-reflection and thus self-management of the discipline. Thus, there are dangerous effects of counting wrongly.

My argument in terms of four debates is unconventional. According to established wisdom there is no fourth debate. We are still in or after the third, and now I even claim that we are leaving the fourth. The disagreement stems from the peculiar way of counting in International Relations: 1st debate, 2nd debate, 3rd debate, 3rd debate. Three is a magic number – three paradigms, three debates. In academic debates, there always have to be three positions, three options, three scenarios. I am convinced that there are (at least) four major debates. To ignore this enumeration error is problematic because it means to assimilate the fourth into the third. Hereby the third debate is prolonged. Self-reflection in International Relations of the 1980s and 1990s is blocked if presented with the choice of either using the triangle as scheme or abstaining from pictures of its own development. We need new meta-phors and depictions to foster self-reflection in the discipline.

This implies that a sub-theme of this article has been the uses and abuses of 'schools'. Danger arises especially when one model of schools gets fixed, such as the timeless triangle, and projected backwards as well as forwards, as the map of all possible positions. On the other hand, images of the internal battlelines do exist and they have effects. Thus, it is worth taking seriously how they function, what they are, and what could possibly be achieved by trying to reshape them. The 'debates' operate as a dialectic between implicit pictures and articulate self-representations of the discipline. The debates are partly constructed and artificially imposed on much more diverse activities, partly they are implicit operators in actual academic practice, they are distinctions involved in the work of the discipline. Academic work is always guided by a picture of the discipline itself as the immediate social context. Each of the debates first emerged as constellation, as implicit picture – the picture is not totally consistent from person to person, but since debate in a discipline is an inter-subjective and interactive phenomenon, there will be a certain convergence. Then in a second step, this constellation is *labelled*, which reinforces the constellation, but also guides the phase of moving beyond it, because the next phase will be defined in relation to this picture of the discipline.

Probably, 'the inter-paradigm debate' should be retained as a very informative metaphor for telling discipline history about the 1970s–early 1980s. To grasp the later 1980s and 1990s we need new images, possibly like the neo-neo merger and the pincer movement of the radicalists [. . .]. So again: even the 'after the fourth debate' of the 1990s will be mis-understood if read as a *rapprochement* among the positions of the third debate (the inter-paradigm debate) when actually it takes place among the contestants of the fourth debate (rationalists and reflectivists). There is a difference between being after the fourth debate and after the third debate. Especially if one wants to be prepared for the fifth debate, which will inevitably come. The discipline seems to organise itself through a constant oscillation between grand debates and periods in-between where the previous contestants meet. One of these debates was the inter-paradigm debate. None of these debates lasts forever. Even if they could all be constructed as nice typologies – exhaustive and exclusive – they would still become misleading at a point when the practitioners had organised themselves along different lines, arguing the next debate.

Notes

1   Thomas S. Kuhn, *The Structure of Scientific Revolutions* 2nd ed. (Chicago University Press, Chicago, 1970).
2   Stefano Guzzini, 'T.S. Kuhn and International Relations: International Political Economy and the Inter-Paradigm Debate' (London School of Economics and Political Science, Unpublished MSc Thesis, 1988), p. 13.
3   Kenneth N. Waltz, *Theory of International Politics* (Addison-Wesley Publishing Co, Reading, 1979) and Robert Gilpin, *War and Change in World Politics* (Cambridge University Press, Cambridge, 1981).
4   Robert Cox, 'Social Forces, States and World Orders: Beyond International Relations Theory', *Millennium* vol. 10(2), 1981, 126–155; Richard Ashley, 'The Poverty of Neorealism', *International Organization* 38(2) (1984), 225–286.
5   Kenneth N. Waltz, 'Reflections on *Theory of International Politics*: A Response to My Critics' (Columbia University Press, New York, 1986).
6   Robert O. Keohane, *International Institutions and State Power: Essays in International Relations Theory* (Westview Press, Boulder, CO, 1989), p. 11.
7   Ibid., p. 2.
8   Robert O. Keohane, 'International Institutions: Two Approaches', *International Studies Quarterly*, 32, 1988, 379–396.

4.9 Four sociologies of international politics

Alexander Wendt

Source: *Social Theory of International Politics* (Cambridge University Press, Cambridge, 1999) pp. 1–44.

Wendt argues that constructivism has become a central theoretical approach in the systemic study of international relations. He demonstrates that the divergent theories to international relations can all be located in one of four quadrants of a conceptual framework that embraces two key philosophical debates. One debate is over the relative importance of material forces and ideas and the other concerns the relationship between agents and structures. Constructivists are shown to privilege ideas and structures.

In recent academic scholarship it has become commonplace to see international politics described as "socially constructed." Drawing on a variety of social theories – critical theory, postmodernism, feminist theory, historical institutionalism, sociological institutionalism, symbolic interactionism, structuration theory, and the like – students of international politics have increasingly accepted two basic tenets of "constructivism": (1) that the structures of human association are determined primarily by shared ideas rather than material forces, and (2) that the identities and interests of purposive actors are constructed by these shared ideas rather than given by nature. The first represents an "idealist" approach to social life, and in its emphasis on the sharing of ideas it is also "social" in a way which the opposing "materialist" view's emphasis on biology, technology, or the environment, is not. The second is a "holist" or "structuralist" approach because of its emphasis on the emergent powers of social structures, which opposes the "individualist" view that social structures are reducible to individuals. Constructivism could therefore be seen as a kind of "structural idealism." [. . .]

The international system is a hard case for constructivism on both the social and construction counts. On the social side, while norms and law govern most domestic politics, self-interest and coercion seem to rule international politics. International law and institutions exist, but the ability of this superstructure to counter the material base of power and interest seems limited. This suggests that the international system is not a very "social" place, and so provides intuitive support for materialism in that domain. On the construction side, while the dependence of individuals on society makes the claim that their identities are constructed by society relatively uncontroversial, the primary actors in international politics, states, are much more autonomous from the social system in which they are embedded. Their foreign policy behavior is often determined primarily by domestic politics, the analogue to individual personality, rather than by the international system (society). Some states, like Albania or Burma, have interacted so little with others that they have been called "autistic." This suggests that the international system does not do much "constructing" of states, and so provides intuitive support for individualism in that domain (assuming states are "individuals"). The underlying problem here is that the social structure of the international system is not very thick or dense, which seems to reduce substantially the scope for constructivist arguments. [. . .]

The revival of constructivist thinking about international politics was accelerated by the end of the Cold War, which caught scholars on all sides off guard but left orthodoxies looking particularly exposed. Mainstream IR theory simply had difficulty explaining the end of the Cold War, or systemic change more generally. It seemed to many that these difficulties stemmed from IR's materialist and individualist orientation, such that a more ideational and holistic view of international politics might do better. The resulting wave of constructivist IR theorizing was initially slow to develop a program of empirical research, and epistemological and substantive variations within it continue to encourage a broad but thin pattern of empirical cumulation. But in recent years the quality and depth of empirical work has grown considerably, and this trend shows every sign of continuing. This is crucial for the success of constructivist thinking in IR, since the ability to shed interesting light on concrete problems of world politics must ultimately be the test of a method's worth. In addition, however, alongside and as a contribution to those empirical efforts it also seems important to clarify what constructivism is, how it differs from its materialist and individualist rivals, and what those differences might mean for theories of international politics.

Building on existing constructivist IR scholarship, I address these issues on two levels: at the level of foundational or second-order questions about what there is and how we can explain or understand it – ontology, epistemology and method; and at the level of substantive, domain-specific, or first-order questions.

Second-order questions are questions of social theory. Social theory is concerned with the fundamental assumptions of social inquiry: the nature of human agency and its relationship to social structures, the role of ideas and material forces in social life, the proper form of social explanations, and so on. Such questions of ontology and epistemology can be asked of any human association, not just international politics, and so our answers do not explain international politics in particular. Yet students of international politics must answer these questions, at least implicitly, since they cannot do their business without making powerful assumptions about what kinds of things are to be found in international life, how they are related, and how they can be known. These assumptions are particularly important because no one can "see" the state or international system. International politics does not present itself directly to the senses, and theories of international politics often are contested on the basis of ontology and epistemology, i.e., what the theorist "sees." Neorealists see the structure of the international system as a distribution of material capabilities because they approach their subject with a materialist lens; Neoliberals see it as capabilities plus institutions because they have added to the material base an institutional superstructure; and constructivists see it as a distribution of ideas because they have an idealist ontology. In the long run empirical work may help us decide which conceptualization is best, but the "observation" of unobservables is always theory-laden, involving an inherent gap between theory and reality (the "underdetermination of theory by data"). Under these conditions empirical questions will be tightly bound up with ontological and epistemological ones; how we answer "what causes what?" will depend in important part on how we first answer "what is there?" and "how should we study it?" Students of international politics could perhaps ignore these questions if they agreed on their answers, as economists often seem to, but they do not. I suggest below that there are at least four "sociologies" of international politics, each with many adherents. I believe many ostensibly substantive debates about the nature of international politics are in part philosophical debates about these sociologies. [. . .]

A map of structural theorizing

[. . .] Systemic theories of international politics conceptualize structure in different ways. In this section I interpret different forms of structural IR theory in light of two debates in social theory. One is about the extent to which structures are material or social, the other about the relationship of structure to agents. Each debate contains two basic positions, which yields four sociologies of structure (materialist, idealist, individualist, and holist) and a 2 × 2 "map" of combinations (materialist–individualist, materialist–holist, and so on). This map is applicable to any domain of social inquiry, from the family to the world system. It is important for me because it sets up the choices we have in thinking about the ontology of international structure. I sort out and identify types of structural theorizing and show the implications of these choices for the types of questions we ask and answers we can find.

Four sociologies

I'll begin by explaining each pair of sociologies of structure, making a continuum for each. The first pair is material–ideational. The debate over the relative importance of material forces and ideas in social life is an old one in IR scholarship. For purposes of creating a single continuum, let us define its central question as: "what difference do ideas make in social life?" or, alternatively, "to what extent are structures made of ideas?" It is possible to hold positions anywhere along this continuum, but in practice social theorists cluster into two views, *materialist* and *idealist*. Both acknowledge a role for ideas, but they disagree about how deep these effects go.

Materialists believe the most fundamental fact about society is the nature and organization of material forces. At least five material factors recur in materialist discourse: (1) human nature; (2) natural resources; (3) geography; (4) forces of production; and (5) forces of destruction. These can matter in various ways: by permitting the manipulation of the world, by empowering some actors over others, by disposing people toward aggression, by creating threats, and so on. These possibilities do not preclude ideas also having some effects (perhaps as an intervening variable), but the materialist claim is that effects of non-material forces are secondary. This is a strong claim, and in assessing it it is crucial that the hypothesized effects of material forces be strictly separated from the effects of ideas. Unfortunately this often is not done. In contemporary political science, for example, it has become commonplace to juxtapose "power and interest" to "ideas" as causes of outcomes, and to call the former "material" forces. I agree that power and interest are a distinct and important set of social causes, but this only supports materialism if their effects are not constituted by ideas. The materialist hypothesis must be that material forces *as such* – what might be called "brute" material forces – drive social forms.

Idealists believe the most fundamental fact about society is the nature and structure of social consciousness (what I later call the distribution of ideas or knowledge). Sometimes this structure is shared among actors in the form of norms, rules, or institutions; sometimes it is not. Either way, social structure can matter in various ways: by constituting identities and interests, by helping actors find common solutions to problems, by defining expectations for behavior, by constituting threats, and so on. These possibilities need not deny a role for material forces, but the idealist claim is that material forces are secondary, significant insofar as they are constituted with particular meanings for actors. The material polarity of the international system matters, for example, but *how* it matters depends on whether the poles are friends or enemies, which is a function of shared ideas. In contrast to the materialist tendency to treat ideas in strictly causal terms, therefore, idealists tend to emphasize what I call the constitutive effects of ideas. [. . .]

Materialists and idealists tend to understand the impact of ideas differently. Materialists privilege causal relationships, effects, and questions; idealists privilege constitutive relationships, effects, and questions. In a causal relationship an antecedent condition X generates an effect Y. This assumes that X is temporally prior to and thus exists independently of Y. In a constitutive relationship X is what it is in virtue of its relation to Y. X presupposes Y, and as such there is no temporal disjunction; their relationship is necessary rather than contingent. Causal and constitutive effects are different but not mutually exclusive. Water is caused by joining independently existing hydrogen and oxygen atoms; it is constituted by the molecular structure known as H_2O. H_2O does not "cause" water because without it something cannot *be* water, but this does not mean that that structure has no effects. Similarly, masters and slaves are caused by the contingent interactions of human beings; they are constituted by the social structure known as slavery. Masters do not "cause" slaves because without slaves they cannot *be* masters in the first place, but this does not mean the institution of slavery has no effects. The distinction is an old one, but poorly appreciated today. I think the blurring of causal and constitutive relationships has helped generate much of the current confusion in IR scholarship about the relationship between ideas and material forces. Resurrecting the distinction will probably not end these debates, but may help clarify what is at stake. [. . .]

The second debate concerns the relationship between agents and structures. The "agent–structure problem" has become a cottage industry in sociology, and increasingly in IR. For purposes of defining a continuum let me frame its central question as: "what difference does structure make in social life?" *Individualism* and *holism* (or "structuralism" in the Continental sense) are the two main answers. Both acknowledge an explanatory role for structure, but they disagree about its ontological status and about how deep its effects go. Individualism holds that social scientific explanations should be reducible to the properties or interactions of independently existing individuals. Holism holds that the effects of social structures cannot be reduced to independently existing agents and their interactions, and that these effects include the construction of agents in both causal and constitutive senses. People cannot be professors apart from students, nor can they become professors apart from the structures through which they are socialized. Holism implies a top–down conception of social life in contrast to individualism's bottom–up view. Whereas the latter aggregates upward from ontologically primitive agents, the former works downward from irreducible social structures.

The disagreement between individualists and holists turns in important part on the extent to which structures "construct" agents. In order to understand this idea we need two distinctions: the one made above between causal and constitutive effects, and a second one between the effects of structures on agents' *properties*, especially their identities and interests, and effects on agents' *behavior*. To say that a structure "constrains" actors is to say that it only has behavioral effects. To say that a structure "constructs" actors is to say that it has property effects. In systemic IR, theories that emphasize such effects have become known as "second image reversed" theories. Property effects are deeper because they usually have behavioral effects but not vice-versa. Both property and behavioral effects, in turn, can be either caused or constituted by structures. Since constitutive effects imply a greater dependence of agents on structures, I shall treat them as deeper as well.

Individualism tends to be associated with causal effects on behavior, but I shall argue that the individualist view is compatible in principle with more possibilities than its critics (or even proponents) typically acknowledge, most notably with structures having causal effects on agents' properties, for example through a socialization process. I say "in principle," however, because in *practice* it is holists and not individualists who have been most active in theorizing about the causal construction of agents. Most individualists treat identities and interests as exogenously given and address only behavioral effects. This is particularly true of the form of individualism that dominates mainstream IR scholarship, namely rationalism (rational choice and game theory), which studies the logic of choice under constraints. In a particularly clear statement of this view, George Stigler and Gary Becker argue that we should explain outcomes by reference to changing "prices" in the environment, not by changing "tastes" (identities and interests).[1]

Rationalist theory's restricted focus has been the object of much of the holist critique of individualism. Still, individualism in principle is compatible with a theory of how structures cause agents' properties. What it rules out is the possibility that social structures have constitutive effects on agents, since this would mean that structures cannot be reduced to the properties or interactions of ontologically primitive individuals. The constitutive possibility is the distinctively holist hypothesis.

As I indicated at the beginning of this chapter, the international system is a hard case for a holist argument, since its low density means that the identities and interests of states may be more dependent on domestic than systemic structures. The challenge for holists in IR becomes even more acute if we grant that individualism is compatible at least in principle with the *causal* construction of states by systemic structures. Perhaps under the influence of rationalism, however, in practice individualists in IR have neglected that possibility, and they do not acknowledge even in principle any *constitutive* effects that systemic structures might have on states. I believe the structure of the international system exerts both kinds of effects on state identities. These may be less than the effects of domestic structures, and certainly a complete theory of state identity would have a substantial domestic component. [. . .]

If we put the materialism–idealism debate on the *x*-axis, and individualism–holism on the *y*-, then we get the picture as shown in Figure 1. [. . .]

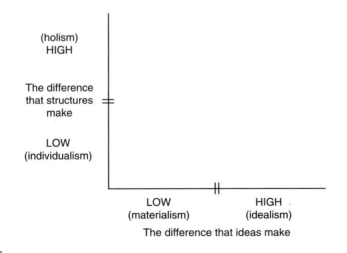

Figure 1

Locating international theories

Figure 1 provides a framework for thinking about the second-order differences among IR theories that are considered "structural." Each sociology constitutes the ontological core of a research program that exerts a centripetal force on substantive theorizing along the portion of the spectrum which it occupies, which undermines the continuous nature of each dimension in favour of a dichotomous one. What I mean is, research programs have specific ontological centers of gravity, so that even as they reach outward to incorporate the concerns of others – as materialists incorporate ideas, as holists incorporate agency – the resulting theories or arguments remain somewhat truncated.

In this section I suggest where different theories of international politics might fall on the map, including my own. My purpose is only illustrative; I will not make much further use of this classification. It should also be emphasized that the map, while applicable to any level of analysis, is applicable to only one level at a time. This will affect how we classify theories. If the designated level is the international system, then a theory which assumes states are constructed entirely by domestic structures will be classified as individualist. If we move to the domestic level of analysis, that same theory might be holist relative to a theory of the state which emphasizes individual people. The latter may itself be holist relative to one which emphasizes brain chemistry. And so on. What follows, therefore, is a map of *systemic* IR theory.

Theories in the lower-left quadrant have a materialist and individualist attitude toward social life. (1) *Classical Realism* holds that human nature is a crucial determinant of the national interest, which is an individualist argument because it implies state interests are not constructed by the international system. Classical Realists vary in the extent to which they are materialists, with some like E.H. Carr granting a significant role to "power over opinion,"[2] but their focus on human nature and material capabilities places them generally in this category. (2) *Neorealism* is more clearly materialist than Classical Realism, and attaches more explanatory weight to the structure of the international system. But insofar as it relies on micro-economic analogies it assumes this structure only regulates behavior, not constructs identities. (3) *Neoliberalism* shares with Neorealism an individualist approach to structure, and most Neoliberals have not challenged Waltz's view that power and interest are the material base of the system. But unlike Neorealists they see a relatively autonomous role for institutional superstructure.

Theories in the upper-left quadrant hypothesize that the properties of state agents are constructed in large part by material structures at the international level. At least three schools of thought can be found here. (1) *Neorealism* bleeds into this corner to the extent that it emphasizes the production of like units, although in practice most Neorealists take state identities as given, and the absence of constitutive effects from its conceptualization of structure in my view makes it ultimately compatible with individualism. (2) *World-Systems Theory* is more clearly holist, although its materialism must be qualified to the extent that it emphasizes the relations rather than forces of production. (3) *Neo-Gramscian Marxism* is more concerned than other Marxisms with the role of ideology, pushing it toward the eastern hemisphere, but it remains rooted in the material base.

Theories in the lower-right quadrant hold that state identities and interests are constructed largely by domestic politics (so individualism at the systemic level), but have a more social view of what the structure of the international system is made of. (1) *Liberalism* emphasizes the role of domestic factors in shaping state interests, the realization of which is then constrained at the systemic level by institutions. (2) And *Neoliberalism* moves into this corner insofar as it emphasizes the role of expectations rather than power and interest. But to my knowledge no Neoliberal has explicitly advocated an idealist view of structure, and I shall argue in chapter 3 that at the end of the day it is based on a Neorealist ontology.

The Neorealist–Neoliberal debate that has dominated mainstream IR theory in recent years has been basically a debate between the bottom-left and bottom-right quadrants: agreeing on an individualist approach to system structure, the two sides have focused instead on the relative importance of power and interest vs. ideas and institutions.

The principal challenge to this debate has come from scholars in the upper-right quadrant, who believe that international structure consists fundamentally in shared knowledge, and that this affects not only state behavior, but state identities and interests as well. I shall call any theory in this quadrant "constructivist." In addition to the work of John Ruggie and Friedrich Kratochwil, which has not become associated with a particular label, at least four schools might fit here. (1) The *English School* does not explicitly address state identity formation, but it does treat the international system as a society governed by shared norms, and Timothy Dunne has argued convincingly that it is a forerunner of contemporary constructivist IR theory.[3] (2) The *World Society* school focuses on the role of global culture in constructing states. (3) *Postmodernists* were the first to introduce contemporary constructivist social theory to IR, and continue to be the most thorough-going critics of materialism and rationalism. (4) And, finally, *Feminist* theory has recently made important inroads into IR, arguing that state identities are constructed by gendered structures at both the national and global levels. Summing up, then, we get something like Figure 2.

The argument of this book falls in the upper-right quadrant, and within that domain it is particularly indebted to the work of Ashley, Bull, and Ruggie. IR today being a discipline where theoretical allegiances are important, this raises a question about what the argument should be called. I do not know other than a "constructivist approach to the international system." [. . .]

Three interpretations

Now that I have positioned IR theories within my map of social theory assumptions, the question is: what is at stake with their second-order commitments? We can approach the answer from three perspectives, methodology, ontology, or empirics. Since these affect how

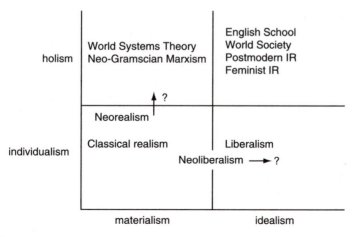

Figure 2

we subsequently think about the differences among systemic IR theories, each bears at least brief scrutiny. For purposes of illustration I will focus on the debate along the *y*-axis between those who take identities and interests as given (rationalists) and those who do not (constructivists). A similar illustration could be developed along the *x*-axis.

A methodological difference

On one level the difference between rationalism and constructivism is merely that they ask different questions, and different questions need not involve substantive conflict. All theories have to take something as given, and in so doing "bracket" issues that may be problematized by others. Rationalists are interested in how incentives in the environment affect the price of behavior. To answer this question they treat identities and interests as if they were given, but this is perfectly consistent with the constructivist question of where those identities and interests come from – and vice-versa. If the issue is no more than methodological, in other words, identities and interests can be seen as endogenous or exogenous to structure *with respect to theory only*, not reality. Neither approach is intrinsically "better" than the other, any more than it is "better" to inquire into the causes of malaria than smallpox; they are simply different. It is important to keep this in mind in view of the polemics that surround rational choice theory. On one level the theory is nothing more than a method for answering certain questions, and as such it makes no more sense to reject it than it did for early Marxist economists to reject mathematics because it was used by "bourgeois" economists. [. . .]

While questions and methods do not determine substantive theory, however, they are not always substantively innocent. There are at least two ways in which our questions and methods can affect the content of first-order theorizing, particularly if one set of questions comes to dominate a field.

First, whether we take identities and interests as given can affect the debate along the *x*-axis about the importance of ideas and material forces. Neorealists, for example, argue that state interests stem from the material structure of anarchy. If we start with this assumption, then ideas are reduced a priori to an intervening variable between material forces and outcomes. Ideas may still play a role in social life, for example by determining choices among multiple equilibria, but to take the Neorealist analysis of identity and interest as given is nevertheless implicitly to concede that the fundamental structure of international politics is material rather than social. [. . .]

A second danger, as noted by Ruggie, is that a methodology can turn into a tacit ontology. Rationalist methodology is not designed to explain identities and interests. It does not rule out explanations, but neither does it offer one itself. However, Neoliberals increasingly acknowledge that we need a theory of state interests. Where should we look for one? One place would be the international system; another, domestic politics. Neoliberals overwhelmingly favor the latter. This may be because state interests *really are* determined by domestic politics, but it may also be because Neoliberals have so internalized a rationalist view of the international system that they automatically assume that the causes of state interests must be exogenous to the system. By conditioning how rationalists think about the world, in other words, exogeneity in *theory* is tacitly transformed into an assumption of exogeneity in *reality*. The latter ultimately may be the right conclusion empirically, but that conclusion should be reached only after comparing the explanatory power of domestic and systemic theories of state identity formation. It should not be presumed as part of a method-driven social science. [. . .]

An ontological difference

Perhaps the most common interpretation of the dispute between rationalists and con-structivists is that it is about ontology, about what kind of "stuff" the international system is made of. [. . .] It also concerns how we should think about "what's going on" when actors interact, and in particular about what it means to take identities and interests as "given." Taking *something* as given is necessary in any explanatory endeavor by virtue of the simple fact that it is humanly impossible to problematize everything at once. Even postmodernists who want to problematize agents "all the way down" will end up taking certain things as given. This inescapable fact points back toward the methodological difference noted above. However, in taking identities and interests as methodologically given there is also an implicit ontological question of whether they are seen themselves as processes that need to be socially sustained (but which we just happen not to be interested in today), or as fixed objects that are in some sense outside of social space and time. In the latter view, the production and reproduction of identities and interests is not going on, not at stake, in social interaction. If that is true then how states treat each other in interaction does not matter for how they define who they are: by acting selfishly nothing more is going on than the attempt to realize selfish ends. In the constructivist view, in contrast, actions continually produce and repro-duce conceptions of Self and Other, and as such identities and interests are always in process, even if those processes are sometimes stable enough that – for certain purposes – we plausibly can take them as given. [. . .]

Despite their seeming intractability, ontological issues are crucial to how we do and should think about international life, and that IR scholarship today is insufficiently self-conscious about them. Having said this, however, I also want to inject this concern with ontology with an empirical sensibility. One might conclude from the ontological interpretation of their debate that rationalists and constructivists face a situation of radical incommensurability, such that we should simply pay our money and take our choice. This is unwarranted. Different ontologies often have different implications for what we should observe in the world. Empirical evidence telling against these ontologies might not be decisive, since defenders can argue that the problem lies with the particular theory being tested rather than the underlying ontology, but it may still be instructive. The possibility that different ontologies are incommensurable should not be treated as an excuse to avoid comparison. Ontology-talk is necessary, but we should also look for ways to translate it into propositions that might be adjudicated empirically.

An empirical difference

There are at least two empirical issues at stake in the debate between rationalists and constructivists. First, to what extent are state identities and interests constructed by domestic vs. systemic structures? To the extent that the answer is domestic, state interests will in fact be exogenous to the international system (not just "as if" exogenous), and systemic IR theorists would therefore be justified in being rationalists about the international system. This is basically the Neoliberal approach. To the extent that the answer is systemic, however, inter-ests will be endogenous to the international system. Rationalist theories are not well equipped to analyze endogenous preference formation, and thus a constructivist approach would be called for. Second, to what extent are state identities and interests constant? Rationalism typically assumes constancy, and if this is empirically warranted we would have an independent reason for being rationalists about the international system regardless of how the first question was answered. Even if states' identities and interests are constructed within the international system, if the results of that process are highly stable then we lose little by treating them as given.

Answering these questions would require an extensive program of theory building and empirical research, which is not the goal of this book. My point is that these questions are useful for IR because they are amenable to substantive inquiry in a way that ontological debates are not. Of course, I still maintain that IR scholars cannot escape ontological issues entirely, since what we observe in world politics is closely bound up with the concepts through which we observe it. In sum, then, my attitude toward these debates, to quote Hacking paraphrasing Popper, is that "it is not all that bad to be pre-scientifically metaphysical, for unfalsifiable metaphysics is often the speculative parent of falsifiable science."[4] [. . .]

Notes

1   George Stigler and Gary Becke, "De gustibus non est disputandum," *American Economic Review* 67 (1977) 76–90.
2   Edward Hallett Carr, *The Twenty Years' Crisis 1919–1939*, (Harper Torchbooks, New York, 1939/ 1964).
3   Timothy Dunne, "The Social Construction of International Society," *European Journal of International Relations* 1, (1995), 367–389.
4   Ian Hacking, *Representing and Intervening*, (Cambridge University Press, Cambridge), p. 3.

4.10 Realist constructivism

Samuel Barkin

Source: *International Studies Review*, no. 5, part 4, 2003, pp. 325–42.

Barkin contests the view that realism and constructivism are incompatible approaches. He distinguishes between paradigms, such as realism, liberalism, and Marxism, which build on competing assumptions about how politics work, and methodologies, such as constructivism and rationalism, which provide competing ways of studying politics. Once this distinction is clarified, it becomes possible to see how constructivism can enrich a realist approach to international politics.

Constructivism appears to have taken a place in the literature on international relations (IR) theory in direct opposition to realism. [. . .]

International relations pedagogy is also increasingly defining realism and constructivism as being categorically distinct, as witnessed by the increasing tendency in IR textbooks, even at the introductory level, to define realism and constructivism as two of three or more distinct paradigms in the field.

To claim that constructivism is an IR paradigm in the way that realism or liberalism are is misleading, and the tendency to do so in textbooks is rarely mirrored in the scholarly literature. In the latter, constructivism is usually identified as an ontology, epistemology, or methodology. As such, it is usually defined as being distinct from either materialism or rationalism. Recent state-of-the-field exercises, in fact, identified the rationalism–constructivism controversy as the central debate in contemporary IR theory. Constructivists who claim their methodology is incompatible with realism focus on the association between realism and both materialism and rationalism. Realists who claim their paradigm is incompatible with constructivism focus for the most part not on the methodology per se but on a perceived tendency for constructivists to be idealists or utopians.

Neither argument, however, holds up to careful scrutiny. Claims by constructivists that realist theory is incompatible with intersubjective epistemologies and methodologies are based on either caricatures or very narrow understandings of realism. And realist critics of constructivism are similarly guilty of inferring from the worldviews of some (perhaps many) practicing constructivists that the methodology is inherently biased toward liberalism. An examination of constructivist epistemology and classical realist theory suggests that they are, in fact, compatible; not, of course, that good constructivism is necessarily realist, but that constructivist research is as compatible with a realist worldview as with any other. [. . .]

Realism and constructivism

Many constructivists explicitly accept that power matters in international relations. Wendt, for example, notes that to the extent realism is about power, he too is a realist. He and other constructivist theorists often part company with realists because of the belief that, at its core, realist theory sees politics as having "a material rather than a social basis".[1] This charge has three parts: that realist theory (1) focuses on material capabilities, (2) views human nature as materialistic, and (3) emphasizes empiricism. These three charges are distinct from one another, and, if any of them were to hold, it would indicate an incompatibility between realism and constructivism. But, under scrutiny, none of them are sustainable.

The first of these charges, that the realist understanding of power favors a focus on material capabilities, has already been alluded to above. It is certainly true that many self-described realist researchers have attempted to reduce the idea of power to quantitative measures. But no reason exists to believe that such a procedure is inherent to realist theory. Indeed, the behavioral, and thus quantitative, turn in IR is generally considered to have happened decades after the realist turn, suggesting that the latter cannot be inherent to the former. Many seminal realist theorists, furthermore, have argued explicitly that nonmaterial factors are central to a complete understanding of power in international relations. Moreover, students of power analysis, some of them self-described realists, have pointed out how complex and multifaceted power analysis can be. [. . .] The fact that some realist researchers use quantitative measures of brute material capabilities should, therefore, not be interpreted to mean that this sort of materialism is inherent in realism.

The second charge is that realist logic requires certain materialist assumptions about human nature and human needs that govern the behavior of actors in international politics. The particular assumptions ascribed to realist understandings of human nature often include the presence of insecurity and fear. It is true that realists must begin with some theory of human nature. Indeed, as Wendt has observed, all social theory must begin with some theory of human nature, even if it is that human nature is infinitely malleable.[2] There exist theories of human nature that are incompatible with political realism, including those that argue that human nature is infinitely malleable or ultimately perfectible. But we can also identify a broad range of theories of human nature that are compatible with both realist and constructivist theory, including those that suggest that individuals differ. Realist logic does not require that all individuals be aggressive or self-interested, simply that some of them are. In other words, the theory requires that all individuals cannot be nonaggressive and other-oriented. As long as some people will try to accumulate power, and no countervailing power stops them, other people face insecurity. This logic is, for example, the heart of Randall Schweller's distinction between status quo and revisionist states.[3]

The third charge is that political realism is, variously, "positivist" or "empiricist" and, as a result, incompatible with constructivist methodology. This charge seems on its face to be methodological, but a number of constructivist theorists have recently taken to making it at the ontological level. This criticism is made via a reference to "scientific" or "critical" realism, a concept in the philosophy of science that bears no relationship to "political" realism. The essence of scientific realism as applied in the social sciences is the idea that real social structures exist out there, independent of our observation of them. In short, the view is that a "there" actually exists out there. This perspective contrasts with the logical positivist-empiricist notion that we can only know what we observe and the postmodern-deconstructivist notion that, because all social knowledge is discursively created, no social structures can exist out there independent of our discourses about them. Both the logical positivist and deconstructivist positions share the premise that there can be no knowledge of social phenomena separate from the observer, whereas the scientific realist position is that social phenomena can exist apart from the observer and can be adduced even when not directly observed. [. . .]

Heikki Patomäki and Colin Wight argue that political realism is too close to both the logical positivist position and the deconstructivist position, in that all share an anthropocentric view of knowledge that is incompatible with the scientific realism that they argue should underlie constructivism.[4] [. . .]

Morgenthau's writing on the "science" of political science can, indeed, seem confusing at first reading. In *Scientific Man versus Power Politics*, he argues that "scientific man," who would solve the problems of politics through the application of reason, is incapable of successfully addressing those problems.[5] In contrast, in *Politics among Nations*, Morgenthau speaks of political realism as "believing [. . .] in the objectivity of the laws of politics" and "the possibility of developing a rational theory that reflects" those laws.[6] Some constructivist critics of political realism posit that Morgenthau underwent a radical change of mind in the period between writing the two books. [. . .]

But to make this claim is to confuse predictive with prescriptive rationality, as was discussed above. What Morgenthau is arguing against in *Scientific Man* is the attempt to understand the world as a rational place rather than to rationally understand the world. What he is contending in *Politics among Nations* is that there is a problem in attempting to rationally understand the world, when the world is not, in fact, a rational place. In other words, both books are arguing the same point but coming at it from different directions. This interpretation does suggest an incompatibility between classical realism and rational choice theory. It also, however, suggests a compatibility between classical realism and neoclassical, or thin, constructivism. The antipathy to "scientific man," the acceptance of the importance of ideas, and the insistence that historical context matters found in the works of Morgenthau fit quite well into a statement of constructivist epistemology, whether neoclassical or postmodern. And the ontology of classical realism, accepting a reality separate from subjective opinion but not, as a result, denying the role of unobservables such as morality, is hardly the sort of brute materialism that constructivist critics sometimes associate with realism. [. . .]

Ideas, utopias, and liberals

"Ever since Carr's devastating critique, 'idealist' has functioned in IR primarily as an epithet for naivete".[7] Wendt makes this point after distinguishing between idealism as a theory of social politics and Idealism (which he capitalizes) as a theory of IR. The first idealism refers to social theory that looks at the importance of ideas, whereas the second refers to a theory of IR based on ideals rather than on realism. Wendt makes the claim that he is involved in doing the former, not the latter. This claim is disputed below. [. . .] Similarly Moravcsik tries explicitly to distance himself from "liberalism's historical role as an ideology" in his redefinition of a liberal theory in IR.[8]

Both these scholars are, in fact, trying to rehabilitate the terms idealism and liberalism (although in very different ways) from the charge that these concepts reflect a normative approach to social science: an ideology. The goal in this section is to rehabilitate the normative approach to IR from which both Moravcsik and Wendt are striving to distance themselves. As rhetorical foils to realism, Carr used "utopianism" and Morgenthau used "liberalism" and "scientific man."[9] Although the terms that Carr and Morgenthau employed seem quite different, both were, in fact, referring to the sort of liberal idealism and scientific humanism often associated with political scientists in the tradition of Woodrow Wilson. The essence of this school of thought is that people have consistent and reasonable (or at least predictable) preferences, which they pursue rationally. As a result, well-designed political institutions within which people can rationally pursue their preferences in a way that interferes as little as possible with the abilities of others to do so will appeal sufficiently to people's reasonableness as to obviate any necessity for power politics. In other words, for the liberal idealist the right political structure can, indeed, insure perpetual peace, to use Immanuel Kant's phrase.

The classical realist response is that no ultimate solutions are available. "Peace is subject to the conditions of time and space and must be established and maintained by different methods and under different conditions of urgency in the every-day relations of concrete nations. The problem of international peace as such exists only for the philosopher."[10] That is, the right institutions can deal successfully with particular political problems at a particular time and place, but this nexus of problem, time, and place is historically unique: there will inevitably be other problems in other times and places. To the extent that many, if not most, international political problems have at least some distributional ramifications, the relative gains or preferential distributions in the solutions to new problems, or problems in different times and places, will likely reflect the interests of the actors best able to stake their claim to those gains, that is, the actors with the greater power. As such, no matter how well designed the structure of political institutions, power will always be the ultimate arbiter of outcomes in international politics.

So, then, is there ultimately nothing other than power that matters in international relations? Quite the contrary, for Morgenthau, people are inherently moral as well as political animals; all political acts have ethical significance.[11] For Carr, "it is an unreal kind of realism which ignores the element of morality in any world order."[12] In classical realism, moral theory in the absence of a recognition of power is a futile exercise as the use of power in the absence of morality is an empty exercise. The latter is the case for two reasons, one practical and one philosophical. The practical reason is that, because humans are moral beings, they will not accept power without morality. Subjects of political domination will recognize the distinction we are trying to make here: between power used for good and power used for evil and will support the former and oppose the latter.

Classical realism, thus, views the art of international politics as the practical balancing of the demands of power on the one hand and morality on the other – as a dialectic between power and morality.

In short, from its inception realism has been viewed as a necessary corrective to idealism, but *not* as a replacement. Idealism, for the classical realist, is necessary to inform our actions and underlie our interests in the pursuit of international politics, but realism will always remain a necessary part of relations among states. Herein lies the difference between realists and "utopians" or "scientific men." Whereas the latter believe that we can ultimately build a world politics not based on power, the realist believes that we cannot. For realism, however well designed our international institutions, however well aligned our national interests, and however well intentioned our ideas, power will remain the ultimate arbiter (note, not the ultimate source) of outcomes. Because neither human nature nor human institutions are ultimately perfectible, we will always have to remain diligent both in identifying those who would subvert the system to their own ends and in dealing with them effectively.

Well and good, but does anyone actually disagree with the realist premise stated in this way? "The proposition that the nature of international politics is shaped by power relations invariably is listed as one of the defining characteristics of Realism. This cannot be a *uniquely*

Realist claim, however, since then every student of international politics would be a Realist."[13] With this statement, Wendt would seem to preempt the usefulness of the broad definition of realism being used in this essay. But it can be argued that many members of the groups that Wendt identifies as accepting the centrality of power, including both neoliberals and himself, in the end do not. Moravcsik, for example, includes in his list of scientific approaches to liberal theory proponents of the idea of a democratic peace.[14] The logical conclusion of the presence of a democratic peace is that if all countries were to become democratic, there would be no more war. Universalizing the right domestic political structures, in other words, would eliminate the threat posed by military power. This idealist conclusion is, as the terms are defined here, incompatible with realism. [. . .]

All of which is to say that there are still idealists; there are still liberals by the old normative or ideological definition. Not every student of international politics is a realist. But what of constructivists? Despite the quotation by Wendt in the previous paragraph, an argument can be made that most current constructivist theorists working in the United States are, in fact, liberal idealists. Support for this argument can be presented in two ways: through what might be called the macroperspective and through the microperspective. The former examines the way in which constructivism is, and has been, characterized as a general approach; the latter looks specifically at the work of leading constructivist theorists.

Using a macroperspective, reviews of constructivism by both practitioners and critics tend to characterize it, either explicitly or implicitly, as liberal-idealist. Moreover, such characterizations are rarely, if ever, disputed. A recent review of the study of norms in IR, for example, once again explicitly distances the contemporary study of norms from Carr's utopianism, but it argues that a fundamental part of the reintroduction of the study of norms is "aimed precisely at showing how the 'ought' becomes the 'is.' "[15] The claim of distance from Carr's utopianism is based on the improved standards of empirical research employed by today's scholars, making constructivist work an exercise in the systematic use of empirical evidence rather than an exercise in political theory. In essence, what Finnemore and Sikkink are contending is that Carr's utopians failed in methodology, not in worldview. They clearly imply that the study of norms and ideas in IR theory, the hallmarks of constructivism, involves examining the ways in which these two phenomena independently make the world better. Another recent review of constructivism by one of its originators, Nicholas Onuf, clearly identifies it politically with liberal institutionalism.[16]

Critics of constructivism, from both the neorealist and postmodernist directions, also associate constructivism with a liberal idealism that is not sufficiently cognizant of the role of power in international relations. For example, in a recent review of the relationship between postmodernism and feminism, Birgit Locher and Elisabeth Prügl compliment constructivism for its "transformational" characteristics, but criticize it for not accepting the central role of power in the construction of international politics.[17] This observation sounds very much like the classical realist critique of liberal idealism, that it puts too much stock in the ability of ideals alone, without power, to change the world.

Realist constructivism

This discussion leaves us with the observation that constructivism as a methodology in the study of international relations need not be idealist, but that in practice in the United States it tends to be liberal-idealist. Such a statement is in no way a derogation of either constructivism or liberal idealism. The classical realists argued quite explicitly that moral ideals are an integral and necessary part of the practice of international politics and that political realism in the absence of morality, in the absence of a vision of utopia, is both sterile and pointless. A realist constructivism would, thus, serve to help rehabilitate idealism by requiring as its corollary a self-consciously idealist constructivism and by contending that the study of ideals, as well as ideas, is integral to a full understanding of international politics. The original constructivist starting point was more a critique of the "structural" part of structural realism than of classical realism; the former allows much less scope for incorporating moral ideals than the latter. The classical realist argument is that to have an impact, any politics of moral ideals must be tempered by a politics of power.

A corollary of this argument is the observation that without addressing "the compromise between power and morality"[18] we cannot successfully address the phenomenon of political change.

Neither pure realism nor pure idealism can account for political change, only the interplay of the two, subject to the assumption that morality is contextual rather than universal.

Therefore, to the extent that constructivist methodology can illuminate the workings of international politics, both an idealist constructivism and a realist constructivism – distinct from, but in a dialectical relationship with, each other – are necessary to account for and explain change in the international system. The idealist constructivism would be freed from any perceived need to claim to study only ideas in an attempt to distance itself from the study of ideals. The realist constructivism would look at the way in which power structures affect patterns of normative change in international relations and, conversely, the way in which a particular set of norms affect power structures. Many of the theorists labeled above as idealist constructivists could respond that they already do one or the other of these things. Someone studying human rights networks in Latin America, for example, might respond that he or she is explicitly arguing that human rights norms are changing the power structure by empowering nongovernmental organizations at the expense of traditional governing elites. But underlying this research is inevitably a moral idealism that sees power in the hands of such organizations as better than power in the hands of the traditional elites. Therefore, the more power that flows from the latter to the former, the better.

We may well agree with this moral perspective. But the realist response is that power will ultimately be used by those who accrue it for a specific set of ends. Furthermore, not all ends toward which power can be invested, even if used in the interest of a moral ideal, will be compatible, because not all moral ideals are compatible. In other words, even once the human rights norms in question are generally accepted in the relations among countries, power will still matter. The specific groups that have been empowered by the norms will at some point find that their goals differ; at that time the relative power among them will begin to become important. Even if all actors in the international system at a given point in time accept the same basic set of normative structures, they will differ in their interpretations of those structures, whether for rationally self-interested reasons or for psychological reasons. When interpretations differ, the power of the interpreter continues to matter. The role of a realist constructivism, then, is to examine, skeptically from a moral perspective the interrelationships between power and international norms.

In this moral skepticism lies a key difference between idealism and realism. Idealism recognizes a single ideal, a universal political morality toward which we should strive. Realism argues that no universal political morality exists and, therefore, if we want ours to triumph, we must arrange to have it do so through the application of power. But the classical realists, particularly Carr, warn us that the relationship can be used both ways: morality can also be used as a tool of power. So that when we apply power to promote our preferred political morality, others might see it as a use of power simply to promote our interests.

Political psychology suggests, furthermore, that when we justify a use of power to ourselves as being for moral purposes, we may simply be fooling ourselves and rationalizing an action as moral that we want to take for other reasons. As such, even though power is hollow without political morality, the classical realist argument is that we must, nonetheless, apply to that morality, ours as well as others, a certain skepticism when it is used to justify power.

Stated as such, classical realism begins to sound much like certain kinds of critical theory as applied in IR. These sections include the argument that political actions in the international domain, even when motivated by the best of intentions, have ramifications on the distribution of power that can affect both the ultimate effectiveness of the actions and the way those actions are viewed by others. Thus, the League of Nations, even if it was created by the status quo powers to promote international peace, was viewed by others as an exercise in supporting the relative power of the states that created it. The tendency of US constructivism toward liberal idealism can similarly be viewed from outside the central status quo power as an exercise in maintaining that status quo – and clearly has been by some postmodern critics of IR theory.

A realist constructivism could specifically address these sorts of issues. It could study the relationship between normative structures, the carriers of political morality, and uses of power. And, as a result, realist constructivism could address issues of change in international relations in a way that neither idealist constructivism (with its ultimately static view of political morality) nor positivist-materialist realism (with its dismissive view of political morality) can manage. In doing so, a realist constructivism could fill a gap in theorizing in IR between mainstream theorizing and critical theory. It could do so by adopting the focus on power found in most critical theory without the negativity inherent in that theory's emancipatory project with its interest in emancipation "from" rather than "to." Realist constructivism could also do so by including in any exploration of power, not only postmodern theory's study of subjective text and positivist realism's study of objective phenomena, but also constructivism's study of intersubjectivity – of norms and social rules.

What, in the end, does this line of argument have to say about the conduct of research and discourse in the field of IR? To constructivists, it suggests that constructivism – whether understood as a methodology, epistemology, or ontology – should not be understood as a paradigm in the way that realism and liberalism and, for that matter, Marxism are. By paradigm is meant here a set of assumptions about how politics work. Constructivism is a set of assumptions about how to study politics. As such, it is compatible (as are other sets of assumptions about how to study politics, such as rationalism) with a variety of paradigms, including realism. To idealist constructivists (idealism here referring to ideals rather than ideas), this line of argument suggests that a realist constructivism should be seen as an opportunity. By distinguishing questions concerning the role of ideals from questions about the role of ideas, it allows idealists to focus on the ideals specifically and encourages them to be explicit about their idealism, to move beyond the stigma that has been associated with utopianism since *The Twenty Years' Crisis*.[19] In other words, it suggests that they not hide their ideals behind the claim of objective science. To realists, it says not only that constructivism can be a useful research methodology, but that addressing constructivist epistemological and ontological premises can provide a useful corrective to the assumptions of individual rationalism and materialism that have been confusing definitions of realism for the past few decades.

Notes

1 Alexander Wendt, *Social Theory of International Politics* (Cambridge University Press, Cambridge, 1999), pp. 13–14.
2 Ibid. p. 131.
3 Randall Schweller, *Deadly Imbalances: Tripolarity and Hitler's Strategy of Conquest* (Columbia University Press, New York, 1998).
4 Heikki Patomäki and Colin Wight, "After Postivism? The Promises of Critical Realism," *International Studies Quarterly* 44, 2000, pp. 213–237.
5 Hans J. Morgenthau, *Scientific Man Versus Power Politics* (University of Chicago Press, Chicago, 1946).
6 Hans J. Morgenthau, *Politics Among Nations: The Struggle for Power and Peace*, 6th ed. revised by Kenneth Thompson (McGraw Hill, New York, 1985 (1948)).
7 (Wendt (see footnote 1), p. 33.
8 Andrew Moravscik, "Taking Preferences Seriously: A Liberal Theory of International Politics," *International Organization* 51, 1997, 513–553, p. 514.
9 E.H. Carr, *The Twenty Years' Crisis: An Introduction to the Study of International Relations* (Harper and Row, New York, 1964) and Morgenthau (see footnote 5).
10 See Morgenthau (footnote 5), p. 217.
11 Ibid. pp. 177–8.
12 Carr (footnote 9), p. 235.
13 Wendt (footnote 1), pp. 96–7.
14 Moravscik (see footnote 8).
15 Martha Finnemore and Kathryn Sikkink, "International Norm Dynamics and Political Change", *International Organization* 52, 1998, pp. 887–917.
16 Nicholas Onuf, 'The Politics of Constructivism' in Karen Fierke and Knud Eric Jørgensen, eds. *Constructing International Relations: The Next Generation* (M.E. Sharpe, Armonk NY, 2001).
17 Birgit Loocher and Elizabeth Prügl, "Feminism and Constructivism: Worlds Apart or Sharing the Middle Ground," *International Studies Quarterly* 45, 2001, pp. 111–129.
18 Carr (see footnote 9), p. 210.
19 Carr (see footnote 9).

Index

absolutism 19, 20
Acheson, Dean 58
Achnacarry (As-Is) Agreement 87
Afghanistan 9–10, 40, 287, 289, 324
Africa 31, 42, 245–6, 282, 287
African National Congress (ANC) 218, 311
AIDS 214
Akerlof, George 191
Albania 405–6
Albright, Madeleine 287
Allende, Salvador 91, 180
alliances 68, 69, 88, 94, 104, 106–7, 235, 270
Allison, Graham 389
Amnesty International 176
anarchy 14–15, 56, 71, 82, 90, 381–2, 387, 392, 399; and sovereignty 33, 62
Anderson, Perry 19, 143, 145
Anglo-American Petroleum Agreement 87
Angola 22, 25, 40
Annan, Kofi 272
anti-apartheid movement 311
Anti-Capitalist Convergence of Montreal (CLAC) 327
anti-capitalist mass spirit 247
Anti-G-8 Summit (2001) 325
anti-globalization movement (AGM) 8, 229, 231, 309, 324–9; and division 325–6, 327–8
anti-trust laws 255–6
appeasement 70–1
Arendt, Hannah 372–5
Argentina 176–7, 326, 328
Armenians 30
arms races 55, 56–7, 374
Ashley, Richard 398
Asia: peripheral role 245
Asia-Pacific Economic Cooperation (APEC) 264
Asian financial crisis (1997–98) 52, 193, 272
asset transfer 290
Association of South East Asian Nations (ASEAN) 264
Augustine 370–1
Australia 31, 42

Austria 31
Austria-Hungary 32, 97, 127
Aztec empire 17

bait and bleed strategy 67
balance-of-power theory 15, 88, 104, 106, 133, 134, see also bipolarity; multipolarity; unipolarity
balancing strategy 68–9, 95–8, 106
Balfour, Arthur 57–8
Balkans 22, 43, 272
bandwagoning strategy 70, 98
Bangladesh 39, 41
Bank for International Settlements (BIS) 217, 272
Barbados 25
Barber, Benjamin R. 282
Basle Agreement (1988) 51
Bauman, Zygmunt 303, 309
Baumgartner, Frank 177
Belarus 23
Benelux states 131
Berger, Thomas 393
Bhagwati, Jagdish 272–3
Big Mac index 47
bipolarity 99, 102, 103, 104, 107, see also Cold War
Bismarck, Otto von 97, 104
blackmail strategy 66–7
Blacks: and identity politics 280–1
bloodletting strategy 67
Bodin, Jean 20
Bolivia 326, 328
Bosch, Juan 91
Bosnia 96, 112, 298, 393
Bosnia-Herzegovina 38, 41, 127–8, 287, 293
Boulding, K. 60
Bourke, Joanna 379
Boutros-Ghali, Boutros 272, 298
boycotts 177, 183–4
Bracken, Paul 118
Braun, R. 19

Brazil 175, 180, 181, 184, 322, 326; as modern nation-state 131
Bretton Woods system 95, 215, 304
Britain 30, 32, 33; decline 78, 256, 354; and democracy 91; and free trade 79; as hegemon 15, 77–8, 102–3, 247; and national security 55, 68–9; as postmodern nation-state 131; regional nationalism 33
Brodie, Bernard 115
Brzezinski, Zbigniew 271
buck-passing strategy 69–70
bureaucracy/bureaucratization 164–6, 167, 245
Burma 25, 405–6
Bush, George W. 179, 321, 322, 323, 324
Butterfield, Herbert 55, 57
Buzan, Barry 24
Byzantine Empire 17

Cable, Vincent 45
Calgary 327, 328
Calleo, David 356
Cambodia 40
Campbell, David 380, 383
Canada 32, 33, 41–2, 131; and anti-globalization movement 327, 328
Canning, George 248
capitalism 34, 84, 229, 242–50; and globalization 216, 229, 230, 260–9, 348–51; history of 260–1; and international conflict 388; power of capital 263–8, 283; survival of 348–51; and welfare states 348–51
capital–labour relations 266–7, 321, 323
CARE 218
Carr, E.H. 3, 345, 346, 354, 364, 410, 417–20
Carthage 66
Cassis de Dijon case (1979) 160
centre–periphery relationships 7, 234–5, 237–41; and multinational corporations (MNCs) 258, *see also* core states; periphery; semi-periphery
Chad 25, 39
Chandler, A.D. 251–2
Charles V of Spain 96, 244, 248
Charter of the Organization of American Society 92
Chiapas 326
Chicago Boys 322
Chile: 1973 coup 180
China 25, 30, 257, 391; and international institutions 200; and macroeconomic policy 49; as modern nation-state 131; relations with Russia 94, 97; rising power of 97, 108, 109, 386, 393; and socialism 248
Chinese Revolution 247
Chisholm, Donald 146
Christopher, Warren 91

citizenship 21, 219, 220, 355–6, 369–70
civil society *see* global civil society
civil wars 38, 40–1
class formation 265–8
clientelism 41–2; reverse suzereignty 41–2
CNN 191
Cochran, Molly 384
Cold War 40, 68, 247, 323, 361; Alliance victory 10, 97, 113; bipolarity 99, 103, 105; end of 10, 13, 25, 40, 46, 187, 229, 287, 392, 406; and realism 387–8
collective identities: and global civil society 218–19, 220; and Otherness 278–9; and security communities 209, 210–11
Collor de Mello, Fernando 179
Colombia 290
colonialism 55, 199–200, 229
Committee of the Regions 153
Commonwealth 41–2
Concert of Europe 197
Connally, Tom 58
conscription 22
constitutional bargain 135, 136–8, 140
constructivism 392, 393, 394, 405–6, 411, 412–14; and idealism 419–21; and institutions 135; and realism 415–17, 419–21
containment policy 9–10, 391
contemporary state 22–4
Contras 289
Cooper, Richard 130–1, 132, 351
cooperation 15, 81–9, 122, 223; defining 81–4; and institutional choice 142–50; international regimes 84–9
core states 243–4, 245, 246–7, 249
Corn Laws: repeal of 79
cosmopolitanism 123, 225–8; and multilateralism 227–8, *see also* new liberal cosmopolitanism (NLC)
Council on Foreign Relations 325
Council of Ministers 142, 145, 146, 151, 152, 155, 162
counterhegemony 231, 311, 312
countermovements 231, 311, 314–15, 318
Cox, Robert 398
Crimean war (1854–56) 102, 103, 105
critical theory 359, 360–2
Crowe, Eyre 56
crusades 91–2
Cuba 41, 248, 273; missile crisis 113
culture 34–5, 393
customs union 145, 160
Cyprus 23
Czechoslovakia 32, 59, 189

Daniel, Jean 284
Davis, Natalie Zemon 371
Dayton agreement 130

decolonization 3, 22, 24, 37, 169, 198, 248; and conflict 281–2
defence spending 68–9
Delors, Jacques 152, 157
democracy 24, 34; and global civil society 217, 219–20; and information revolution 193; and peace 90–2, 391, 392
Denmark 31
dependency 41–2, 230, 238, 388
deterrence 114–15, 116–17
deterritorialization 213–14
Deudney, Daniel 139
Deutsch, Karl W. 206, 208
development 168, 231, 322–3; and security 295–8, 300–1; uneven 251–6, 347–8, 349, 351
Dole, Robert 96
dominance and resistance perspective 3, 6–9, 10, 11, 229–32
Doyle, Michael 90, 91, 354–5, 391
Drucker, Peter 352
drug trade 26, 27, 290
Duffield, John 391
Duffield, Mark 290
Dulles, John Foster 56
Dunne, Timothy 411
Durkheim, Emile 207
Dyson, Freeman 375
Dyson, Kenneth 29

Earth Summit (Rio de Janeiro 1992) 182, 184
East Germany 23
Easton, David 304
Ecuador 326, 328
egalitarianism 225–7
Egypt 315
Ehrenreich, Barbara 379, 380
Eichengreen, Barry 52
Eisenhower, Dwight 355
El Salvador 40
Engels, Friedrich 267, 347
English Revolution (1688) 21
English School 411
Enloe, Cynthia 382
environmental campaigns 172, 174, 178–9, 180–1, 182, 183, 192
Enzenberger, Hans 284
Epstein, Klaus 58
Equal Rights Amendment (ERA) 281
Equatorial Guinea 25
Eritrea 25
Escobar, Arturo 168
Estonia 23, 39
Ethiopia 32, 39, 40, 41
ethnic groups: self-determination 38–9; wars 25, 40, 96, 282, 390
ethno-nations 38, 243, 244

Europe: and balance of power 109; and labour migration 47; new states 22–3; and regionalism 43–4
European Bank for Reconstruction and Development 170
European Commission 142–3, 145, 151, 196–7; and decision-making stage 155, 157–8; and ECJ 160, 161, 197; and expertise 146, 154, 157; and implemetation stage 158–9; as negotiator 157; and policy initiation 152–4, 162; Santer Commission 153
European Council 151, 152, 153, 154, 156–8, 162
European Court of Justice (ECJ) 142, 143, 146, 151, 155, 160–1, 162, 197
European Economic Monetary Union (EMU) 49, 160
European Energy Charter 154
European Parliament 142, 143, 145, 151; and decision-making stage 155, 156–7, 158; and expertise 146; and policy initiation 152, 153, 154
European Social Forum (ESF) 326
European Union 5, 14, 43–4, 97, 107, 129, 131, 151–63, 170, 264; and autonomous central bank 143; Common Foreign and Security Policy 273; decision-making 155–8, 161, 162; enlargement 273; and environmental policy 159; and evolution of rules 202; federalism v. nationalism 143–5; and global civil society 218; and inter-state cooperation 122, 142–50; multi-level governance model 122, 151, 154, 156–9, 161–2; and norm diffusion 169; and organizational supports 196–7; policy implementation 158–9; policy initiation 152–4, 162; and qualified majority voting (QMV) 142, 143, 148, 155, 161; relations with US 273; and state sovereignty 41, 142–5, 155–8, 161–3; and state-centric model 151, 152, 155, 158, 160, 161; technocratic governance 144, 145–7; and trade with Eastern Europe 274; and veto 155–6, 161–2
exclusion 230, 231, 305–6, 307–8, 309
exploitation 229–30, 231, 236–8, 242

failed states *see* weak and failed states
Falklands War (1982) 345
Fallers, L.A. 253
Federal Reserve (Fed) 48, 49, 50–1
female genital mutilation 178
feminism 411, 419; and masculinism of IR 376–7, 383, 384–5; and realism 332, 369–70; and war 371–2, 374–5, *see also* gender; women
Filmer, Robert 19
Ford Foundation 218
Fordism 265

foreign direct investment 47, 52, 322, 353
Fourth United Nations Conference on Women
 219
France 18, 19, 20, 21, 30, 32–3, 41, 103; and
 balancing strategy 68; and democracy 91; as
 postmodern nation-state 131; and security
 54, 56; and war strategies 66; withdrawal
 from NATO 94, 210; and world-economy
 245, 246
Francophonie 41
Frank, A.G. 238
French Revolution (1789) 21, 245
Frieden, Jeffrey 392
Fukuyama, Francis 90, 390

Gaulle, Charles de 32
Geertz, Clifford 85
Gellner, E. 283
gender 281, 332–3, 376–85, *see also* feminism;
 women
General Agreement on Tariffs and Trade
 (GATT) 86, 147, 148, 154, 156, 157, 355
genocide 96, 214, 271, 279
Germany 30, 31, 37, 39, 134; and democracy
 91; and expansionism 54; as future great
 power 97, 108; security 57–8; and
 world-economy 246, 247
Gibbon, Edward 355
Gilpin, Robert 133, 356–7, 398
global civil society 26, 123, 125, 213–21, 324,
 325; and collective identities 218–19, 220;
 and democracy 217, 219–20; development
 of 216–17; effect on politics 217–21; and
 multilayered governance 217–18, 220; and
 privatization of governance 218, 220; and
 social welfare 216, 218; and sovereignty 220
global governance 123, 130, 201–3, 222–8; and
 cosmopolitanism 123, 225–8; and emerging
 political complexes 299–300; and liberal
 peace 297–8, *see also* world order
global state 125–31; and centrality 128;
 inclusive and constitutive of other forms of
 state 129; and institutions 127–8; and rule
 making 129; and territorially demarcated
 area 128; Western-centred 129–30, *see also*
 Western state
global war economy 7, 231, 286–93, 299
globalization 121, 187; anti-economy 305, 306,
 307, 308; conditions for 216; consequences
 of 48; economic 45–53, 260–1; and
 evolution of rules 201–3; historical
 perspective 52–3; imagined economies of
 231, 305–10; as latest stage of capitalism 230,
 260–2; offshore economy 305, 306–7, 308;
 political 261; private economy 305, 306,
 307–8; and realism 340–1; resistance to 8,
 231, 309, 311–20; and state 14, 26, 121–2,

125–32, 261–2, 305; trifurcation of
 socio-economic space 305–8,
 see also cosmopolitanism
gold standard 46, 52
Gorbachev, Mikhail 13, 37, 38, 392
Gowa, Joanne 391
Gramsci, Antonio 311, 312–14, 317, 318, 320,
 363
Gran, Guy 167
Great Depression (1893–97) 79
Great Depression (1929–41) 53, 366
great power behaviour 14–15, 16, 55, 62–71;
 assumptions 62–3; operational state goals
 63–5; strategies 65–71
Great Powers: and decline 352, 354–6; and
 realism 338–9
Greek city-states 17
Greenland 23
Greenpeace 179, 192
Grey, Edward 57
Grey, J. Glenn 373
Grieco, Joseph 389
Group of 7 264
Group of 8 (G8) 327
Group of 22 264
Gulf War (1990–91) 39, 40, 43, 116, 118, 126

Haas, Ernst 145–6, 356
Haas, Peter 192
Hacking, Ian 414
Haiti 130, 266
Hall, John 208
Han Empire 17
Handelman, Don 167
Havel, Vaclav 284, 393
Hawthorn, Geoffrey 276
Heclo, Hugh 172
Hegel, G.W.F. 350, 371
hegemony: hegemonic theory 103–4, 133, 134,
 312; and international trading structure
 78–9; and power conservation 136–9;
 regional 14–15, 62, 63–4; and world orders
 365–7, *see also* power
Helms–Burton Act 273
Helsinki Accords (1975) 181
Henry VIII 20
Herbst, Jeffrey 287
Hines, Colin 309
Hirschman, Albert O. 73, 349–50
Hitler, Adolf 64, 96
Hobbes, Thomas 13, 21, 25, 368–70, 383
Hobsbawn, Eric 279
Hoogvelt, A. 266
Howard, Sir Michael 116
human rights campaigns 172, 174, 178, 183
Hume, David 90–1
Hungary 189

Huntington, Samuel P. 108, 189, 279, 393, 394
Hussein, Saddam 116
Hymer, Stephen 84

Iceland 23
idealism 417–21
identity politics 231, 278–85, 381–4; and
    Blackness 280–1; and capitalist
    transformation 281–4; and gender 281,
    376–85; and group conflict 283–4; and
    nationalism 279, 281, 284; and Otherness
    278–9, 284
Iklé, Fred 118
imperial state 32, 33
imperialism: and capitalism 229, 230, 348, 350;
    and conflict of interests 233–4; definition of
    234–5; and inequality 230, 233–41;
    mechanisms of 235–8; new 231, 323–4;
    types of 239–41
Inca empire 17
India 22, 30, 32, 281–2; as modern nation-state
    131
indigenous rights campaigns 174, 179, 180
Indonesia 272
industrial revolution 260
information revolution 123, 186–94;
    commercial information 188, 193; and
    complex interdependence 186–8; and
    credibility 190–4; free information 188,
    193–4; and power 189–90, 191; strategic
    information 188, 194
infrapolitics 231, 311, 315–17
insecurity spiral 14, 54–61, 121
Institute of International Finance (IIF) 219
institutional choice 142–50; credible
    commitments 144, 147–9; federalist ideology
    143–5; technocratic governance 144, 145–7
institutionalization 363, 366–7, 398
institutions: constructivist theory of 135;
    institutional agreement 136–7; liberal theory
    of 134–5, 391; rationalist theory of 135; and
    rules 195, 196–8, *see also* institutional choice;
    international institutions
Inter-American Commission on Human Rights
    177
Inter-governmental Panel on Climate Change
    (IPCC) 192, 218
inter-paradigm debate 333, 395–404; danger of
    403–4; end of 398–400; and
    incommensurability 397–8, 401–3; usefulness
    of 400–3
interdependence 92–4, *see also* cooperation
interdependence and globalization perspective
    3, 5–6, 8–9, 10, 11, 121–4
International Accounting Standards
    Committee 217, 218
International Bill of Human Rights 227

International Confederation of Free Trade
    Unions (ICFTU) 215
International Council of Scientific Unions 218
International Council of Securities Associations
    218
International Court of Justice 92
International Criminal Court 219, 227, 309
International Energy Agency 87, 388
International Federation of Accountants 218
International Federation of Stock Exchanges
    218
international institutions 28, 264; and
    development of security communities
    207–10; formal and informal 197–8; limited
    role of 94–5; and NLC 272–3; and pooling
    and delegation of sovereignty 148; and
    strategic restraint 138–9, 140, *see also*
    institutions; international organizations (IOs)
International Monetary Fund (IMF) 26, 41,
    183, 264, 355, 388; conditions 267; fixing
    meanings 168; and global civil society 215,
    217, 218; and norm diffusion 170; shock
    therapy 282; and US influence 272
international organizations (IOs) 4, 41, 45, 121,
    122, 356; and bureaucratization 164–6;
    classification of information 167, 170; and
    development of security communities
    207–10; and diffusion of norms 169–70;
    fixing meanings 168–9, 170; and governance
    125; and organized labour 282; power of
    26–7, 164–70; and rational-legal authority
    164, 165, 166; and rules 196, *see also*
    international institutions
International Primary Market Association 218
International Red Cross and Red Crescent
    Movement 216, 218
international regimes: and cooperation 84–9;
    defining and identifying 85–8; and self-help
    88–9
international relations (IR): conceptual
    framework 410–11; and constructivism 392,
    393, 394, 405–6, 411, 412–14, 415–17; and
    domestic politics 389, 392–3, 405; and
    gender 376–85; and identity politics 381–5;
    and individualism–holist debate 408–9;
    inter-paradigm debate 333, 395–404; and
    liberalism 388, 390–2, 393, 394, 398, 410,
    411; and Marxism 388–9, 396, 400, 410,
    411; and materialism–idealism debate 333,
    405, 407–8, 409, 412; and neorealist–
    neoliberal debate 410–11, 412; and
    rationalism 409, 412–14; and realism 387–8,
    389–90, 393, 394, 395–6, 410, 411, 415–17;
    reflectivist–rationalist debate 333, 395,
    399–400, 401; and social theory 405–14;
    theoretical approaches 386–94
International Securities Market Association 218

international trading structure 72–80; closure
73–4, 79, 80; and openness 72, 73, 74–7, 78,
79; and potential economic power 74, 75,
77–80; and state preferences 73–4
International Women's Decade 182
Internet 186, 190, 192, 193, 319
intervention 10, 37–8, 92, 96–7, 112, 130;
humanitarian 37, 126, 297, 298
Iran 34; as modern nation-state 131
Iran-Iraq war (First Gulf War) (1980–88) 40
Iraq 10, 37, 112, 191, 272, 324; as modern
nation-state 131
Ireland 30
Ismay, Lord 271
Israel 39, 40, 41, 272
Italian city-states 17, 19, 245

Jackson, Robert 24
Janis, Irving 389
Japan 30, 34, 41, 43, 47, 54; and democracy
91; and foreign investment 353; as future
great power 97, 108, 109; managed trade 93;
semi-peripheral role 245
Jepperson, Ronald 196
Jervis, Robert 387, 389
Jesus of Nazareth 375
Jews 30
Johnston, Iain 393
Jones, Bryan 177

Kahler, Miles 273
Kampuchea 25
Kananaskis 327
Kant, Immanuel 92, 223, 418
Kashmir 288
Katzenstein, Peter 393
Kautsky, Karl 229, 351
Keen, David 291
Kennan, George F. 55, 59, 336
Kennedy, Paul 352
Keohane, Robert 93, 95, 356, 365, 381
Keynes, John Maynard 53, 304, 350
Keynesianism 48, 265, 266, 366
Khrushchev, Nikita 56
Kier, Elizabeth 393
Kissinger, Henry 398
Königgrätz, Battle of (1866) 97
Korea 30, 31–2, 112, 193
Korean War 40, 113
Krasner, Stephen 389
Kratochwil, Friedrich 411
Kuhn, Thomas 343, 396
Kurds 30, 31, 39, 126
Kuwait 37, 116, 191
Kyoto Conference (1997) 192, 394

Labs, Eric 390

Landmine Conference (1997) 192
languages 22
Lapid, Yosef 384–5
Latin America 31, 248
Latin America Association of Advocacy
Organizations (ALOP) 215
Latvia 23, 39
law of one price 47
Layne, Christopher 391
Le Pen, Jean-Marie 284
Lebanon 25, 39
Leites, Nathan 55, 59
Lenin, V.I. 3, 229, 234, 343–4, 347, 348, 350,
351
Lewis, W. Arthur 52
liberal peace 296–8, 394; and new wars 298–9,
300–1
liberalism 10, 134–5, 199–200, 388; economic
342, 343, 344–5, 391
Liberman, Peter 390
Lindberg, Leon 146
Lindblom, Charles E. 81, 82
Lipietz, A. 265
Liska, George 398
List, Friedrich 352
Lithuania 23, 39
Liu Shao-Chi 248
Locher, Birgit 419
Lockhart, Bruce 57
Long War (1914–90) 15, 111, 117
Long-Term Agreement on Cotton Textiles 88
Louis XIV 18, 96
Luxembourg Compromise 155–6
Luxemburg, Rosa 350

Maastricht Treaty 143, 147, 155, 156, 160, 162
Macaulay, Thomas 355
McCalla, Robert 391
Machiavelli, Niccolo 13, 19, 369–70, 371, 383
McMichael, Philip 267
macroeconomic policy: effectiveness of 48–52;
fiscal policies 48–9, 51; government
borrowing 52; monetary policies 49, 50–2
Mahan, Alfred T. 55
Malaysia 25, 39
Malta 23
Mann, Michael 126, 127–9, 131, 355
Mansfield, Edward 391
Mao Tse-Tung 248, 250
market-state 119
Marshall Plan 247
Martin, Lisa L. 95
Marx, Karl 3, 229, 230, 262–3, 278, 329, 347,
350, 351
Marxism 84, 230, 249, 342, 343–4, 346–8,
349–50
Mauritius 25

Mearsheimer, John 390
Médecins sans frontières 218
Menchú, Rigoberta 180
Mendes, Chico 180
mercantilism 19, 245, 246–7, 260, 343, 346
Mexican financial crisis (1994–95) 52, 272
Mexico 328
Michels, Robert 247
migration 47, 284
Miliband, Ralph 284
Mill, John Stuart 347
Miller, J.D.B. 41
Milner, Helen 392
Milosevic, Slobodan 116
Mistzal, Barbara 210
Monnet, Jean 145
Montenegro 23
Montovani, Ramón 326
Montreal Protocol 218
Moravcsik, Andrew 417, 419
Morgenthau, Hans 55, 336, 381, 387, 388, 398, 417, 418
Mothers of the Plaza de Mayo 176–7
Mozambique 22, 25, 40, 289
Mueller, John 91
Mujahidiin 289
multi-level governance 122, 151, 154, 156–9, 161–2, 224
Multilateral Agreement on Investment (MAI) 327
multination-state 32–3
multinational corporations (MNCs) 5, 26, 27, 80, 180, 230, 251–9; evolution of corporate structure 251–2; and income and consumption structure 252–3; inhibiting development 254–6; and location theory 252; and national sovereignty 255; viability of 256–8
multipolarity 99, 102–3, 104, 108, 109, 110, *see also* Pax Britannica
Münster 21

Napoleon I 66, 96, 245, 279
Napoleonic Wars (1803–15) 102
Narmada River dam 175
nation-state 30, 118–19, 125, 126–7, 260, 261–2, 302–4; and economic globalization 45–53; and national economy 304–5
nation-states: modern 131–2; postmodern 131; and power of transnational capital 265–8; pre-modern 132
National Organization for Women (NOW) 369–70
national security 3, 4, 6, 14, 29–30, 33, 34–5, 121; and aggression 55, 63; and expansionism 54–5, *see also* insecurity spiral; security

nationalism 33, 34, 118, 143, 145, 224–5, 279, 303; economic 342, 344, 345–6
NATO (North Atlantic Treaty Organization) 58–9, 94–5, 128–9, 131, 134, 321, 391; expansion 386–7, 390, 393; and norm diffusion 170; and Yugoslavia 271, 272, 277
neoliberalism 322, 324–5, 383, 406, 410–11
neorealism 365, 383, 387–8, 390, 398–9, 406, 410–11; theories 133–4, 135
Nestlé 175, 181, 183, 184
Netherlands 31, 245
Neuman, Stephanie 97
New Deal 265
New International Economic Order (NIEO) 349
new liberal cosmopolitanism (NLC) 230, 270–7; and domestic liberalization 276–7; and international institutions 272–3; and Pacific Union 270–2, 276–7; and state sovereignty 275–6; and trade regimes 273–4
New Zealand 32
NGOs 172–3, 174, 176, 179, 215, 216, 218, *see also* global civil society
Nicaragua 40, 92, 266, 289
Niebuhr, Reinhold 55, 387
Nietzsche, Friedrich 375
Nigeria 25, 30
nineteenth-century state 21–2
Nixon, Richard 95, 248
Nobel Peace Prize 180
North American Free Trade Agreement (NAFTA) 43, 264, 311
North Korea 112
Norway 22
nuclear weapons: and compellance 116; mutual assured destruction (MAD) 13, 65; nonproliferation regime 86; nuclear superiority 64–5; and reassurance 116–17
Nuremburg war crimes tribunal 226–7
Nye, Joseph 93, 356

Ontario Coalition Against Poverty (OCAP) 327
Onuf, Nicholas 195, 196, 419
Operation Desert Storm 272
Organization for Economic Cooperation and Development (OECD) 215, 355
Organization of Petroleum Exporting Countries (OPEC) 87, 128
Organization for Security and Cooperation in Europe (OSCE) 170
organized labour 53, 282–3
Osnabrück 21
Otherness 278–9, 284

Pacific Union 270–1, 273–4
Pakistan 32, 39, 41
Palestine Liberation Organization (PLO) 218

Palestine/Palestinians 23, 30
Panama 92
Panitch, L. 282
Parkinson, Fred 38
Parsons, Talcott 304
part-nation-state 31–2
Patomäki, Heikki 417
Pax Americana 109, 248, 275, 365–7
Pax Britannica 94, 99, 103, 105, 248, 365–6
Payne, Anthony 41
Peace Corps 175
Peace of Westphalia (1648) 21, 118–19, 199, 261
Pentagon Papers 338
People's Global Action against Free Trade and WTO (PGA) 215
periphery 243–4, 245–6
Perry, William 170
Peru 290
Pocock, J.A. 369
Poland 64
Polanyi, Karl 265, 311, 314–15, 318, 320
policy coordination 81, 82–3
political economy: ideologies of 331–2, 342–51
polymorphous crystallization 126
Popper, Karl 414
Portugal 22
Posen, Barry 389–90
post-Cold War era: and conflict 295, 298; new states 23, 37; and realism 13, 15, 90–8, 394; and redundant strategic calculus 111–14; and return to anarchy 134; and Western order 133–41, *see also* unipolarity
postmodernism 411, 419
potato famine (1840s) 79
Poulantzas, Nicos 263, 303
Powell, Robert 135
Powell, Walter 171
power: asymmetrical 102, 103, 105, 134; and development of security communities 206; and flourishing economic base 352–4; and information revolution 189–90, 191; military 353–4; and systemic disorder 356–7, *see also* hegemony
power and security perspective 3, 4–5, 8–9, 10–11, 13–16
private property: right to 19
problem-solving theory 359, 360–2
protectionism 73, 79, 350
Prügl, Elisabeth 419

al-Qaeda 323–4
quasi-states 24
Quester, George 387

Rafoe Islands 23
rationalism 135, 395, 399

Ray, James Lee 391
Reagan, Ronald 210
realism 121, 331, 335–41, 344, 359, 368–72, 387–8, 410, 411; and constructivism 415–17; and feminism 332, 369–70; future of 90, 340–1; and idealism 417–21; and just war theory 370–2; and politics of power and security 9, 11, 13–14, 55; practical effects of 338–40, *see also* neorealism
Rebick, Judy 328
Red Line Agreement 87
Redlich, F. 251–2
reflectivism 395, 399–400
refugees 167, 289
regionalism 14, 43–4, 48
Reich, Robert 287
religion: freedom of 20
RENAMO 289
resistance: agents of 319; as counterhegemony 231, 311, 312–14; as countermovements 311, 314–15, 318; forms of 318–19; as infrapolitics 231, 311, 315–17; sites of 319; strategies of 319–20
Ricardo, David 346
Richardson, Lewis 56
Richelieu, Cardinal 18
Roman Empire 17, 355–6
Rosenau, James 26, 27
Rosenberg, Justin 275
Rousseau, Jean-Jacques 54, 82
Royal Dutch Shell 192
Rubin, James 272
Ruggie, John 85, 86, 356, 402, 411, 412
rules 123, 195–203; dynamism and change 200–1; evolution of 201–3; and institutions 195, 196–8; rule structures 198–200
Russett, Bruce 90, 391
Russia 23, 39, 391; arms control 393; and balancing strategy 68; collapse of ruble (1998) 52; as economic power 43, 246, 257; energy supply 154; and expansionism 54, 55; as modern nation-state 131; national security 57–9; and power 18, 32, 34, 97, 102–3, 109; relations with China 97; semi-peripheral role 245, 247
Russian Revolution (1917) 247, 248
Rwanda 25, 112, 214, 271, 279, 293

Salamon, Lester 216
Sarawak: timber extraction 182
Sarney, José 184
Saudi Arabia 74, 272, 277
Scandinavian states 131
Schattschneider, E.E. 80
Schelling, Thomas C. 116
Schmitter, Philippe 276
Schnapper, Dominique 302

Schumpeter, Joseph 355
Schweller, Randall 390, 416
Scott, James C. 311, 315–17, 318, 320
Scott, Ralph 379
Securities and Exchange Commission (US) 189
security: and development 295–8, 300–1; liberal peace 296–8; meaning of 168–9; new wars 298–300
security communities 123, 204–12; and collective identities 209, 210–11; development of 205–10; and mutual trust 209, 210–11; precipitating conditions 204–5; and social processes 204, 205, 207–10; and structure of region 204, 205, 206–7
security dilemma 14, 55–6, 60, *see also* insecurity spiral
self-determination 24, 33, 169
semi-periphery 242, 243, 245, 246, 249
separatism 32, 39, 41
Septimus Severus 355
Serbia 131
Seven Years' War (1756–63) 56
Singapore 25, 39, 193
Single European Act (SEA) 153, 155, 156, 160, 162
slavery 245–6
Slim, Carlos 325
Slovenia 39
Smith, Adam 81, 82, 259, 343, 346, 352
Smoot-Hawley Tariff (1935) 80
Snow, David 177
Snyder, Glenn 94
Snyder, Jack 390, 391, 392
socialism 248–9, 250
Socrates 375
Somalia 25, 37, 38, 39, 112, 130, 287, 298
Somaliland 23
South Africa 25, 34, 266, 311
South Korea 193
sovereignty 14, 17, 20–1, 28, 36, 41–2, 44; and anarchy 33, 62; and European Union 41, 142–5, 155–8, 161–3; and global civil society 220; and international economic relations 43; and multinational corporations (MNCs) 255; and new liberal cosmopolitanism (NLC) 275–6; pooling and delegation of in EC 142–5, 148; popular 21, 24; and rules 200; and self-help 88–9
Soviet Union 30, 32, 43, 64, 189; break-up of 13, 37, 38, 39, 40, 42; and clientelism 41; and containment 9–10, 391; as core state 248; and nationalism 34; and world-economy 248
Spain 18, 19, 20; semi-peripheral role 245
Spiro, David 391
Stalinism 364
state-centric approach 4, 14, 121, 124
state-nation 31

state-power theory 72–80, 78–9
state(s): concept of 29–35, 126–9, 262–3, 302–3; and control of economy 14, 48–53; and control of education 22; and globalization 14, 26, 121–2, 125–32, 261–2, 305; growing complexity of 14, 27–8, 127; and law 111; and monopoly of use of force 111, 118, 126–7; multifunctionality of 18, 23; and nation 14, 21–2, 29–33, 118–19, 125, 303–4; and national identity 21–2, 23–4; and national security 14, 29–30, 32, 33, 34–5; obsolesence of 5, 14, 25–7, 36; and organizing ideologies 33–4, 35; qualities of statehood 17–18; state collapse 24, 25, 39; strategies for survival 62–71; and transformation 25–7; transnationalization of 260–8; and use of force 111–16, 118, *see also* nation-state; sovereignty; states system
states system: and change 36, 42–4, 121; and dependency 41–2; equal statehood and unequal power 36–7, 38; new states 22–3, 37–8, 39; and rules of game 14, 38, 199; and state survival 37–9
Steinbruner, John 389
Strange, Susan 11, 26, 27, 52, 93
strategic calculus: compellance 114, 116; deterrence 114–15, 116–17; reassurance 114, 116–17; redundant 111–14
strategic restraint 136–9; binding 139; bonding 138–9; institutionalized voice opportunities 139
sub-Saharan Africa 42, 271
Sudan 25, 39, 40, 41
Sweden 21, 22
Switzerland 32

Tadjikistan 290
Taiwan 193
Tanzania 25
tariff levels 76–7
Tarrow, Sidney 177
taxation 18–19, 23, 49
Thucydides 13, 70
Tickner, J. Ann 383, 385
Tokyo war crimes tribunal 227
trade 46–7, 83; free trade 15, 73, 79–80, 81, 248, 304; illegal 26, 27, 290–1; managed 93; trade regimes 273–4; trading blocs 43, *see also* international trading structure
trade union federations 218
transnational advocacy networks 121, 123, 171–85; and accountability politics 176, 181; and actor characteristics 184; boomerang pattern of influence 173–5; definition of 171–2; emergence of 172–6; growth of international contact 175–6; influence of 181–4; and information politics 176, 177–9,

192, 194; and issue characteristics 182–4; and leverage politics 176, 180–1; major actors 172; and political entrepreneurs 175; and symbolic politics 176, 180; tactics 176–81

transnational corporations *see* multinational corporations (MNCs)

transnational state (TNS) 261, 262, 263–5, 267–8

Treaty of Prague 97

Treaty of Rome 155, 160, 161

Trinidad 25

Truman, Harry S. 321

trust 210

Turkey 272

Tuzla 293

Uganda 25, 39

Ukraine 23

ultra-imperialism 229

underdeveloped countries: and foreign direct investment 322; middle classes 257, 259; and multinational corporations (MNCs) 254–6, 257–8, 259

Union of International Associations 215

unipolarity 15, 96–7, 99–110; and alliances 106–7; comparison with previous systems 99–103; durability of 104, 105–9; and new regional unipolarities 107; and peace 103–5

United Nations 4, 41, 128, 129, 130, 131, 197, 264, 321; and Argentinian human rights abuses 177; authority 166; Charter 23, 200, 228, 272; and civil society groups 215, 216; Covenant of Rights (1966) 226; Declaration of Human Rights (1948) 226; Development Program (UNDP) 169; fixing meanings 168–9; High Commissioner for Refugees (UNHCR) 167, 289; and humanitarian intervention 298; and NATO 272; and new states 23, 169; and norm diffusion 169, 170; theme years and decades 180, 182; Torture Convention (1984) 227; and US interests 272, 394; weakness of 227

United States: alienating Russia and China 97–8; anti-trust laws 255–6; and balancing strategy 68; budget deficit 52, 353; centrality in global state 128, 130; and clientelism 41; and democracy 34, 91; and economic integration 47; and economic power 43, 77–8, 100–1, 230; and foreign investment 47, 52, 353; foreign policy 93, 96, 338, 383, 390; and free trade 79–80; geographical advantages 106–7; and global social power 275–6; hegemonic decline 248, 352–8, 365; hegemony 15, 43, 78–9, 139–41, 247, 248, 323; and identity politics 279–80; and information revolution 190, 191; and international institutions 92, 95, 272–3, 394;

and macroeconomic policy 49; and military interventions 10, 96–7, 112; and nation-building 30; and new imperialism 231, 323–4; and Pacific Union 270–2; as postmodern nation-state 131; and realism 338–40, 390; as state-nation 31; and strategic restraint 139–41; strategic thinking 114, 115; unilateralism 272–3, 340, 393–4; and unipolarity 10, 15, 96–7, 102, 108, 110; and world order 109, 117–18, 128; and world-economy 246, 248

US Committee for Refugees 289

US–Japan alliance 134

uti possidetis 38–9, 42

utopianism 417–19, 421

van Creveld, Martin 118

Van Evera, Stephen 387, 390

Vienna Convention on the Law of Treaties 199

Vietnam 31

Vietnam War 10, 40, 113, 248, 289, 339, 354, 357

Viner, Jacob 115

violence: control of 127

Voluntary Export Restraints 274

Waltz, Kenneth 82, 99, 104, 106, 110, 387–8, 390, 398, 410

war 40, 102, 112–14; bait and bleed strategy 67; bloodletting strategy 67; costs and benefits 66; democracies and 91–2; and development of public finance 18–19; economic motivation for 291–3; ethnic 25, 40, 96, 282, 390; financing 290–1, 292; global war economy 7, 231, 286–93, 299; as Great Power strategy 15, 65–6; just war theory 370–2; and masculinity 378, 379–80; new 298–301; patterns of violence 288–9; politics as extension of 372–5; and privatization of military forces 287–8; revolutionary warfare 288–9; and surplus weapons 287–8; and victory 97; and zones of peace 293

war crimes tribunals 226–7, 272

war on terrorism 223, 323–4

wars of movement and position 312, 313, 318

Warsaw Treaty Organization 94

weak and failed states 14, 24–5, 287; and dependency 41–2; and institutional agreement 136–7, 139; and non-intervention doctrine 37–8

wealth: maximization of 64

weapons of mass destruction (WMD) 6, 115, 117, 118, 324, *see also* nuclear weapons

Weber, Max 126, 164–6, 199, 262, 263, 267, 355

Weiner, Myron 289

welfare 22, 53, 348–51
Wendt, Alexander 207, 392, 416, 417, 419
Western state 122, 125, 129–30, 133–41
Westphalian state 18–21; and extraction and redistribution 19–20; and freedom of religion 20; income from colonies 19; and sovereignty 20–1; and taxation 18–19
Wight, Colin 417
Wilhelm II 96
Wilson, Woodrow 388, 418
Wolf, Martin 324
women: and citizenship 369–70; role of 382, 383; women's movement 172, 178, 218, 219, 281, *see also* feminism; gender
World Bank 26, 41, 264, 267, 355; advocacy networks and 180, 181, 183; and anti-globalization movement 325; and civil society groups 215, 216; and classification 167; expertise 166; fixing meanings 168; and norm diffusion 170
World Economic Forum (WEF) 215, 219
world order: and change 359–67; and development 321–3; historical structures 362–4; and institutionalization 363, 366–7, 398; and New Deal principles 366, *see also* global governance; hegemony; world-economy; world-empire
world politics: study of 1–3, 121
World Social Summit (2002) 325

world society school 411
World Trade Organization (WTO) 128, 215, 218, 264, 309; and US interests 272–3
World War I 58, 69, 77, 79, 247, 279, 347, 348, 354
World War II 53, 113, 247, 286, 314, 354
World Wide Web 186, 319
world-economy 242–50; contradictions 249–50; core states 243–4, 245, 246–7, 249; evolution of 244–9; and industrial production 243–4, 245, 246–7; peripheral states 243–4, 245–6; recession (1650–1730) 245; semi-periphery 242, 243, 245, 246, 249
world-empire 242, 243, 244, 248
world-systems theory 410, 411

Yanomami reserve 179
Year of Indigenous Peoples (1993) 180, 182
Yeltsin, Boris 38
Young, Oran 134, 207
Yugoslavia: break-up of 23, 39, 42, 92; ethnic wars 40, 96, 282, 390; as federative state 32, 33; NATO intervention 271, 277; US involvement 118

Zakaria, Fareed 390
Zapatistas 311
Zaretsky, E. 281